REGIMES, MOVEMENTS, and IDEOLOGIES

REGIMES, MOVEMENTS, and IDEOLOGIES

A COMPARATIVE INTRODUCTION TO POLITICAL SCIENCE

Mark N. Hagopian

LONGMAN
New York and London

In Memoriam: Robert P. Benedict/Herbert Schubert/
Richard Bolster/Edward Davis/Paul Anastasiou

Page 119, figure 3.2: From Leon Dion, "The Politics of
Consultation," *Government and Opposition* 8, no. 3
(1973): 335.

Page 131, figure 4.2: From Alan Wells, "The Coup d'Etat
in Theory and Practice: Independent Black Africa in the
1960's," *American Journal of Sociology* 79, no. 4 (1974):
885. Copyright © 1974 by the University of Chicago
Press. Reprinted by permission of the publisher.

REGIMES, MOVEMENTS, AND IDEOLOGIES
A Comparative Introduction to Political Science

Longman Inc., New York
Associated companies, branches and representatives
throughout the world.

Copyright © 1978 by Longman Inc.

Developmental Editor: Edward Artinian
Editorial and Design Supervisor: Linda Salmonson
Design: Pencils Portfolio, Inc.
Manufacturing and Production Supervisor: Louis Gaber
Composition: Fuller Typesetting of Lancaster
Printing and Binding: The Book Press

Library of Congress Cataloging in Publication Data

Hagopian, Mark N
    Regimes, movements, and ideologies.

    Includes index.
    1. Comparative government. 2. Ideology. I. Title.
JF51.H27   320.3   77–17718
ISBN 0–582–28044–3 pbk.

Manufactured in the United States of America

Preface

I would like to give many thanks to several people who were instrumental in the development of this text, noting that whatever virtues the book may have are a shared achievement, while its remaining defects are the author's sole responsibility. I had the enormous good fortune to have Virginia Hans once more as manuscript editor on a book. Professors Cynthia Enloe of Clark University and George Graham, Jr., of Vanderbilt read the entire manuscript, and their suggestions improved the final text considerably. My colleague, Professor Robert Markel of American International College, read several chapters and helped me clarify the basic approach in the text. Nicole Benevento and Linda Salmonson worked skillfully on the production of the text. Finally, Edward Artinian showed faith, patience, and enthusiasm through the whole project, for which I thank him.

Mark N. Hagopian

Introduction

This book is designed as a textbook in comparative political science at the introductory (freshman-sophomore) level. While in the past there was a tendency to separate the comparative politics approach from the more general introduction to political science, many political scientists have welcomed a convergence of outlook in recent years. At one time the field of comparative politics (or government) was largely descriptive of single foreign regimes, with very little explicit comparison and a rather limited conceptual framework. It was then considered the job of introductory political science to deal with the abstract conceptual framework.

The problem here was not only excessive abstractness—all science is abstract—but also neglect of systems outside the Western orbit. It was the post–World War II irruption of Third World countries into the world arena that increasingly spurred political scientists to make more truly comparative studies. This led to a more comparative thrust to the theories and concepts of political science in general. The present book reflects these two decades and more of reorientation. Depending on one's viewpoint, therefore, it is an introduction to political science or an introduction to comparative politics. The distinction nowadays is so hard to draw that we do not have to make it.

But to say that a comparative approach is the best introduction to political science does not give much of a handle on the specific problem of organizing information. A further step is to break down the realm of politics into three distinct, though interconnected, provinces. These are regimes, movements, and ideologies.

For the present we understand a *regime* as a particular institutional structure that characterizes a country's political system. It is thus broader than the mere government or group of officials who run the key political institutions. A *movement* is a more or less organized and mobilized segment of society, whose activities directly or indirectly influence the workings of political systems. An *ideology* can provisionally be understood as a systematic set of political ideas that determine and/or justify the structure of regimes, the policies of governments, or the antics of movements.

The grounds for this particular ordering are that political science from the times of the ancient Greeks has developed as an analysis of political institutions—the structure of regimes. To lose sight of this focus causes some approaches to political science to lose the true sense of the political. Movements, however, have to be brought in to show how institutions are used and abused by various social and political formations. Finally, ideologies enter the picture because of the principles and cultural values in the minds of the people who play roles in movements and regimes. The borders between these three provinces are fluid and, most assuredly, always in dispute. And yet they most certainly exist, as we can see by indulging in a sort of mental experiment.

Communism, fascism, nazism, liberalism, conservatism, socialism, nationalism, democracy, constitutionalism, traditionalism, parliamentarism—we encounter these and other "isms" in the mass media as well as in scholarly publications and discussions. Without considerable clarification, however, mention of nearly every one of these "isms" can lead us into a Tower of Babel. Take German National Socialism, or nazism, for example. What is an "analysis" or "explanation" of nazism really after? The existence of different answers to this question reveals that our ordinary political language *suggests* approaching politics through the triad of regimes, movements, and ideologies.

The three main parts of this book will serve to elaborate the trilogy of regime-movement-ideology in greater detail.* But for now let us explore this three-part approach by returning to our example of nazism. One student of nazism may see it mainly as a regime and be concerned with the institutions and policies that emerged after the Nazi takeover of January 30, 1933. What happened to the legislative, executive, and judicial institutions, the parties and interest groups during the dozen years of Hitler's Third Reich? Why did the constitutionalism and de-

---

* In literature a trilogy is a three-part work in which the three parts, though each is a self-contained work, constitute a larger unity. Each can stand on its own somewhat yet is part of a bigger picture.

mocracy of the Weimar Republic (1919–33) break down? Our regime specialist will not ignore ideology and movement, but will stress some special facts of recent German political history to account for the emergence of the Nazi regime. He may, for example, point out the tarnished legitimacy of the Weimar Republic as the product of German defeat and collapse in World War I. He will surely bring in the foot-dragging of the military and the bureaucracy in the effort to make Weimar institutions work effectively. And he will no doubt highlight the devastating impact of the Great Depression of 1929 on people and polity as well as the short-circuiting of parliamentary democracy through rule by "emergency decrees" in the last years of Weimar.

To someone trained in sociology or social psychology, however, the movement aspect of nazism may be foremost. While he will not neglect political institutions or ideology entirely, his preoccupation with nazism as a social movement leads him to ask different questions and proffer a different analysis or explanation for its rise. Our movement student will look either to psychological distress of certain types of individuals or to the social and economic problems of specific groups and strata to explain the growth of this radical right movement. Were the militant supporters of the Nazi movement drawn chiefly from authoritarian personalities or from the poignantly frustrated? Or was this movement fostered by the lower middle class of teachers, clerks, small farmers, and small businessmen who feared being pushed down into the ranks of the working class?

Still another student of nazism may see it mainly as an ideology. Accordingly, his account of it will probably take the form of a history of ideas or an analysis of the evolution of German culture. He will try to push the roots of Nazi ideology back to some point where German culture supposedly deviated from the mainstream of Western civilization. Maybe he will go back only so far as the early 1800s, when Napoleon's defeat of the Germans promoted an extreme form of nationalism. This nationalism then merged with romanticism in a common rejection of Western ideas of rationality and individual freedom. Perhaps a second student will trace things back to the 1500s with the German Reformation and Martin Luther. Still a third may see nazism's deepest roots in the fall of the Roman Empire in the West in the fifth century A.D. and thus see Nazi ideology as a recrudescence of the pre-Christian paganism of the old Germanic tribes.

Somewhat the same problem of focus pops up with communism and with the other "isms." Does communism stand for a class of once-revolutionary, dictatorial regimes ruled by a single-party as in the Soviet Union, China, North Korea, Vietnam, Albania, Cuba, or Czechoslovakia? Or should communism be viewed as a movement that sometimes involves a small sect of intellectuals, sometimes a medium-sized movement of urban industrial workers, and still other times a large nationalistic upheaval of peasant masses? Clearly analysis of the nature and origins of communism will take a different route according to whether the focus is on regime, movement, or ideology.

Who is right and who is wrong in the various foci of regimes, movements, and ideologies? The answer is that all are right, provided that we know beforehand what particular aspect a given student has in mind. Thus, with most of the "isms" we find a triangular relationship between the regime, the movement, and the ideology. For instance, every new regime is a disappointment to some members of the old movement. The exact shape of the regime and its policy cannot be deduced from the ideology or projected from the movement in the days before the attainment of power. Moreover, while the ideology is important, not every aspect or action of the relevant movement or regime is a simple or direct application of ideological principles.

Regime, movement, and ideology are intimately connected, in other words, but cannot be collapsed into each other. Our task is to explore these three aspects of politics on a comparative basis. Indeed, they are the basis of a truly comparative approach to political science. Part 1 of this book deals with regimes and includes five chapters. Part 2 covers movements in four chapters. Part 3 deals with ideologies and related themes, and embraces three chapters.

This division of subject matter has both advantages and disadvantages. It allows us to handle the formal political institutions or regimes, the dynamic movement aspects of politics, and the ideological and cultural framework of political life in three separate sections—our trilogy. As with any analytical distinction, there may seem to be times when complete discussion of all three aspects together would seem appropriate. Failure to do this would be most serious if our goal were full analysis of any given political system, such as that of the United States or China. But our goal in this book is both narrower and far broader than this: we seek to provide an understanding of politics both in modern and in some not-so-modern states.

To achieve this latter goal most effectively and economically, the three parts of the book on regimes, movements, and ideologies try to stick as closely as possible to their guiding themes. For example, the last chapter of part 3 surveys the ideological spectrum from left to right, covering ideologies such as communism, Christian democracy, and fascism. Many "isms" books not only expound the main ideas of such ideologies, but they try also to assess how regimes and movements espousing them have performed in achieving ideological goals. How faithful have the Soviets been to the principles of Karl Marx? How "Christian" have been the governments dominated by Christian Democratic parties, as in Italy and West Germany?

While such an assessment is an important topic, the accompanying historical description of the regimes and movements often gets in the way of a clear and distinct understanding of the ideas of the respective ideologies. This is one reason why we prefer maximum segregation of the three provinces of the realm of politics. But maximum segregation is not perfection, and we will violate strict separation whenever the topic covered requires background that "belongs" theoretically in other parts of the book.

Our tripartite approach also allows for flexibility in treatment. Although the sequence followed in this book is regimes-movements-ideologies, nonetheless, some political scientists might prefer to begin a comparative introduction to political science by treating the cultural-ideological framework first. Still others may feel that the social basis of politics—what we cover as movements—should come first. Thus there are, in all, six possible sequences in dealing with regimes, movements, and ideologies. Because of the tripartite approach, the book can be used with any of the five alternative sequences with minimal inconvenience.

Since our goal is general knowledge about politics and political science in a comparative perspective, our exposition involves frequent classifications or "typologies." These serve to arrange the often baffling complexity of political life into manageable categories. A strongly typological approach imposes order for us and steers a middle course between immersion in the unique facts of specific political systems (the "idiographic" approach) and concern with grandiose and universal "laws" of politics and political evolution (the "nomothetic" approach). The guiding principle in our choice of typologies will be to include those which are most serviceable to an introductory readership rather than necessarily the most recent ones. Students who go on in political science may eventually replace most of our typologies with more complex and esoteric ones.

Finally, several general characteristics of the book should be pointed out. As already indicated, the book has a dual goal. On the one hand it strives to cover most of the ground of traditional introductions to political science. On the other, it strives to equip students with concepts that will illuminate the comparative analysis of different political systems. Thus, it is intended both for one-semester introductory courses in political science and for the second semester of year courses that follow the traditional first-semester (American Government), second-semester (Foreign Governments) pattern.

Given these goals, two options exist. One would be to complement each topic throughout the book with fairly extensive "case studies" drawn from a set of four or more specific regimes (e.g., Great Britain, the Soviet Union, Tanzania, Mexico). There are several reasons for not following this course. Aside from the fact that a number of texts already have used this format, it is clear that an adequate employment of case studies would add a minimum of 150 pages to the text. Not only would this raise the cost of the book, there is also the distinct possibility that readers would get lost among the trees and fail to see the forest as a whole. That is, too many case studies in one text might be more of an obstacle than an aid to learning the main concepts and themes of comparative political science. The format followed in this book will allow the instructor to choose his own case studies, whether in lectures or supplementary readings.

Another option would be to forego bringing in the four or more governments in each chapter (or grouping them together in the second half of the book) and to give full ad hoc comparative examples for all the major concepts. But this too runs the risk of overinflating the bulk of the book and bogging down the readers in an excess of details. For these reasons both case studies and examples have been consciously limited. While this decision has its costs in the loss of some concreteness, the trade-off results in a somewhat more streamlined text. The resulting smaller book will allow instructors greater flexibility with possible supplementary texts. These might cover specific regimes in some depth, special "movement" topics (e.g., development, parties, or revolution), or general or specific treatments of ideology (e.g., anthologies of primary sources; monographs on socialism, communism).

Contents

PART I

Regimes

INTRODUCTION

The first five chapters of this book focus on regimes as one crucial aspect of a comparative political science. As indicated in the preface, we will treat regimes by abstracting them somewhat from the other two aspects of our trilogy, movements and ideologies, though naturally it is impossible to keep any of the three in wholly watertight compartments. Thus in part 1 of this book we make little of the salient fact that the institutions of political regimes are often created and molded by successful political movements. (This is most evident in the single-party dictatorships treated in chapters 4 and 5.) Since institutional analysis can stand on its own feet, part 1 is not primarily concerned with political movements in the "pre-takeover" period. Likewise, less than complete attention is devoted in part 1 to the other movement or dynamic aspects of politics, such as social classes and groups, political parties, and interest groups. The behavior of such groups—which animates the formal political institutions of legislatures, executives, bureaucracies, and judiciaries—is the concern of part 2. In effect part 2 constitutes a "sociology of politics," complementing the more static institutional approach of part 1.

Also missing from part 1 is a fullblown treatment of the various ideologies and ideological themes that recommend or justify the types of regimes discussed in chapters 2 through 5. Democratic liberalism and social democracy, for example, are the semiofficial ideological doctrines of the parliamentary (chapter 2) and presidential (chapter 3) varieties of modern constitutional government. Likewise, fascism, nationalism, communism, conservatism, racism, and other doctrines provide legitimation and some policy guidance for a broad array of military or single-party regimes discussed in chapters 4 and 5. Part 3 goes into the cultural and ideological backdrop of both regimes and movements.

Though intended mainly as a prelude to chapters 2 through 5, chapter 1 is also a kind of preliminary to parts 2 and 3. It sets forth a conception of how politics emerges in human societies and of how common human situations will inevitably bring forth some sort of political system (or polity). Considerable time is spent in this chapter in elaborating a typology of nonmodern polities that stand in contrast with the modern state, our focal point of discussion for the various regimes of chapters 2 through 5. Discussing these nonmodern polities is not done just to provide students with a historical perspective (a worthy enough goal), but also to show how the polities of many Third World countries work right now. Our point is that the modern state does not fully characterize such regimes. Instead there is a veneer of attitudes and institutions associated with the modern state superimposed on attitudes and institutions associated with premodern polities such as tribalism and patrimonialism. This fact will help us to understand why so-called moderate Third World regimes are so "corrupt" and often fall prey to military or revolutionary dictatorships.

The major portion of part 1, chapters 2 through 5, is concerned with regimes that assume the framework of the modern state, or with regimes that aim toward becoming modern states. Chapters 2 and 3 cover constitutional regimes of the parliamentary and presidential varieties. Chapters 4 and 5 deal with dictatorships of the authoritarian and totalitarian varieties. Chapters 2 and 3 on the one side and chapters 4 and 5 on the other reflect a basic dichotomy that is a modern version of a classic distinction. Aristotle (384–322 B.C.), the great political philosopher of the ancient Greek city-state, divided forms of government between those that were "natural" because they pursued the interest of the whole community and those that were "corrupt" because they pursued the narrow selfish interest of a part (large or small) of the community. Though our own dichotomy in part 1 between constitutionalism and dictatorship has a similar ring to Aristotle's, we use it more as an empirical benchmark than as a stark moral contrast.

While chapter 2 seeks an understanding of parliamentarism as a major type of modern constitutionalist regime, much of the discussion there, say, of legislatures is transferable to presidential-type regimes. Similarly chapter 3, which discusses presidentialism, also discusses topics of relevance to parliamentary systems or even sometimes to dictatorships. Although our principal goal in part 1 is general knowledge of types of regimes, the discussion of American presidentialism (chapter 3), the Mussolini and Franco dictatorships in Italy and Spain (chapter 4), as well as the Hitler, Stalin, and Mao dictatorships in Germany, Russia, and China (chapter 5) are partial concessions to a case-study approach. It is sometimes necessary to describe specific historical cases in some detail in order to show the concrete relevance of general comparative principles.

I
Politics and
the Modern State

A main object of comparative political science is the modern state in all its manifestations, transformations, and ramifications. Nowhere else in history has political power been so closely concentrated as in the modern state. But "political power" is a composite term, a juxtaposition of *political* and *power*. Some theorists would consider the term redundant, since every human situation that involves power is by definition political. Before accepting this view, we must examine the concept of power in general, for key concepts like power give rise to competing definitions.

POWER AND POLITICS

Most of the contesting definitions of "power" are found within two major schools of thought. The *structuralist view* holds that power is best understood as a relationship between two or more human entities or "actors." We must say entities or actors because power relationships are found among and between individuals, groups, factions, parties, states, alliances, etc. For the structuralist, power describes the situation wherein A (an individual, a group, etc.) is able to make B (an individual, a group, etc.) do something that B otherwise might fail to do or be disinclined to do. In this sense a robber has power over the victim when he forces him to hand over his money.

4

For structuralists, power is either *in use* or held *in reserve*. In the latter case it is employable whenever the powerful actor wishes to use it against the less powerful or powerless actor or actors. Structuralists call the whole system the "power structure" of societies; their favorite technique is graphically to depict the power structure of society X in the famous pyramid model dear to all social scientists. One influential version of the pyramid model was that of C. Wright Mills in the mid-1950s.[1]

Figure 1.1.   Mills' View of the American Power Structure

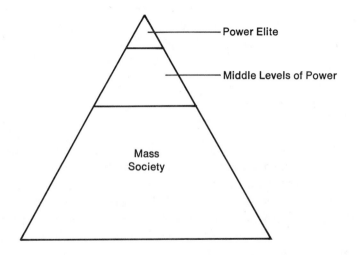

According to Mills, the "power elite" was a not fully integrated formation that virtually monopolized the vital decisions in American society. It consisted of three subgroups: the top military leaders or "warlords," the chief bureaucrats in Washington or "political directorate," and the economic leaders or "corporate rich." The "middle levels of power" embraced the great bulk of elected officials—senators, representatives, governors, mayors, and state legislators, plus the leaders of interest groups not contained in the power elite, such as trade unions. To these middle levels Mills assigned discretion over the details of major decisions, as well as over decisions too puny to warrant the power elite's

1. C. Wright Mills, *The Power Elite* (New York: Oxford University Press, 1956).

concern. The overwhelming majority of Americans were lumped in the wholly impotent, totally disorganized, and perpetually victimized "mass society."

Structuralist accounts of the power structure such as Mills' spur critics to offer strongly contrasting visions of the meaning of power. These critics deemphasize the winner-loser aspect of power and stress instead that power is better understood as the ability to get things done. Reflecting a *functionalist view* of power, Talcott Parsons suggests that although power "has to be divided or allocated," it must also be "produced and it has collective as well as distributive functions. It is the capacity to mobilize the resources of the society for the attainment of goals for which a general 'public' commitment has been made." [2] In other words Parsons warns us not to neglect what power does, that is, how it functions in behalf of an entire social system. Power, for example, would seem to answer his description when a government exerts power to mobilize a country's defenses in the face of a commonly perceived aggressive foreign threat.

Arriving at a Definition of "Political Power"

Before we can even hope to resolve the structuralist versus functionalist issue, we must return to our unresolved problem about where politics and political power begin and end. Common sense might suggest that since power permeates society (in the family, school, workplace, church, club, gang, etc.), political science should study all these arenas of power. Such a broad conception of the task of political science has supporters among political and other social scientists.

According to Harry Eckstein and Ted Robert Gurr, for example, the proper study of politics is "authority patterns," that is, sets of "asymmetric relations among hierarchically ordered members of a social unit that involve the direction of the unit." [3] Thus politics emerges whenever we find a human organization in which the members are "perceived and ranked in levels of superiority and inferiority." [4] "Direction of the unit" means defining its goals, regulating its members' conduct, and controlling the roles within it. Eckstein and Gurr clearly wish to extend the

2. Talcott Parsons, "The Distribution of Power in American Society," in *C. Wright Mills and the Power Elite,* ed. G. W. Domhoff and H. B. Ballard (Boston: Beacon Press, 1969), p. 83.
3. Harry Eckstein and Ted Robert Gurr, *Patterns of Authority: A Structural Basis for Political Inquiry* (New York: John Wiley, 1975), p. 22.
4. Ibid.

scope of politics and political power well beyond what they call the "state-organization." Thus the political scientist not only could, but should be perfectly at home sticking his nose into penal institutions, mental institutions, hospitals, businesses, churches, fraternal organizations, and the like.

If the dangers of such an omnibus conception of politics are not immediately evident when we think about the Eckstein-Gurr approach, a still broader view may bring the point home. In this perspective: "If a boy asks a girl for a date, . . . that is not politics (although it is an attempt to influence her). If he marries her, however, a dispute about where they are to live would be a political dispute."[5] Can we really accept a concept of the political that considers any domestic squabble as distinguishable only in scale from an American presidential campaign or the Russian Revolution?

Although our ordinary language frequently speaks of "union politics," "club politics," "university politics," and the like, these usages are clearly the product of analogies. Unions, clubs, and universities resemble political systems in that they often have "parties" or factions, deliberative bodies, elections, and so on. But similarity is not sameness; and though pursuing analogies is often fruitful, succumbing to them is always disastrous. Such a negative conclusion, however, still does not tell us what politics, the realm of the political, is all about.

What necessitates politics in the broadest and truest sense is a primordial fact about the human social condition—*relative scarcity*. Relative scarcity means that whatever the objects people desire in a society, there is not enough supply to meet all possible demand. Social psychologists, economists, philosophers, and others have tried to catalogue the needs that lead to demands for a share of socially valued objects. The needs run from the apparently simple and basic biological desires for food, clothing, shelter, and sexual gratification up to the more culturally conditioned desiderata such as power, safety, income, and deference.[6]

The Italian social theorist Vilfredo Pareto (1848–1923) found the roots of much of human behavior in six basic types of psychological instincts or "near-instincts." His theory of *residues* (basic needs that re-

5. R. Harrison Wagner, "The Concept of Power and the Study of Politics," in *Political Power*, ed. R. Bell, D. V. Edwards, and R. H. Wagner (New York: Free Press, 1969), p. 9.
6. Harold Lasswell, *Politics: Who Gets What, When, How* (New York: Meridian Books, 1965).

main behind after analysis) can serve as an example of the search for the psychological need patterns underlying social conflict.[7] Although Pareto acknowledges that material interests and social heterogeneity (natural human differences) also contribute to the social equilibrium, he lays great stress on the individual needs or residues seen in table 1.1.

TABLE 1.1. Pareto's Scheme of Residues

---

1. **Instinct for combinations:** a general need to manipulate ideas, men, and objects, which when dominant tends to produce a crafty, cunning, wheeling-and-dealing type of individual in economic and political life.
2. **Group-persistence:** produces a type of loyalty on the part of the individual to ideas, groups, and institutions that becomes blind devotion and self-sacrifice in extreme cases.
3. **Need for activity and self-expression:** a drive toward expressive, demonstrative conduct on the part of individuals, often manifested in ecstatic religious cults, etc.
4. **Sociality:** a broad category embracing needs to conform to the group, feelings of sympathy toward others, as well as sentiments of social hierarchy.
5. **Individual integrity:** the need to defend the self and what "belongs" to it, including vengeance against real or imagined offenders against the individual and his possessions.
6. **Sexuality:** the desire for sexual gratification, either in its pure or repressed form.

Even if we prefer some other analysis of human psychological need patterns to Pareto's, his theory suggests the staggering multiplicity of needs that emerge even in the simplest of societies.

With this in mind we can now offer this definition: *the political system (or polity) of a society is the set of processes and institutions that regulates the potentially explosive conflict arising from competition over gratification of human needs and wants.* To use the words of David Easton: "where a society exists, there will always be a kind of allocation of values that will be authoritative for all or most members of a society even though the allocation affects only on a few." [8] Without some sort of "authoritative allocation of values," the scarcity-induced conflict among groups and individuals would rend the fabric of society irreparably.

Easton also helps us grasp the scope of politics and political science

7. Pareto called these needs *residues* because they remain behind after analysis. When these were made manifest through rationalizations, ideologies, myths, religious doctrines, moral codes, etc., he called the derived entities *derivations*. See for all this, Vilfredo Pareto, *The Mind and Society*, vol. 2 (New York: Dover Publications, 1963).
8. David Easton, *The Political System* (New York: Alfred A. Knopf, 1963), p. 134.

by pointing out that "political science is not initially and centrally interested in all authoritative policies found in a society." [9] The political system is distinguished by the *general* scope of its decisions or policies. These are binding for *all* members of the community. Activity in purely private institutions becomes politically relevant only when it has an impact on the political process or when government regulates the rules of the game within social groups. This is clearest with laws about strikes, working conditions, hiring practices, treatment of children, etc. Political science, therefore, is not always interested in the family—that is a problem for specialist psychologists, sociologists, lawyers, and others. Rather, its interest lies in the impact of family organization and experience upon the formation of political attitudes and ideologies or what is called "political socialization." As we will see with respect to tribal and other polities, "kinship" can be of vital political importance, though the political scientist has no concern with it as an end in itself, so to speak.

Understanding the political system as dispenser of authoritative allocations of values allows us to pin down the term "political power." *Political power is the relationship whereby one actor can induce another actor to comply with his wishes at certain stages of the political process.* That process culminates when officials reach decisions or formulate policies about the authoritative allocation of values. This does not exclude the possibility that controversial issues may be headed off before they emerge in the official political institutions. This has been termed "nondecision-making" or the "practice of limiting the scope of actual decision-making to 'safe' issues by manipulating the dominant community values, myths, and political institutions and procedures." [10]

Power, Influence, and Authority

Political power thus understood must be related to and distinguished from two cognate terms: "political influence" and "political authority." In some views political power and political influence cannot be distinguished, since power is a form of influence and influence in turn is simply a manifestation of the universal cause-and-effect relationship.[11] Since this approach waters everything down to the nonpolitical, we prefer the traditional idea that what distinguishes power from mere

9. Ibid., p. 133.
10. Peter Bachrach and Morton S. Baratz, "Decisions and Nondecisions: An Analytical Framework," in *Political Power*, p. 100.
11. See the articles by March, Simon, and others in Bell, *Political Power*.

influence is the former's reliance on *sanctions*. In other words power involves the use or threat of physical or mental sanctions in cases of noncompliance with an original command. Influence, on the other hand, merely suggests that one actor may modify his conduct after learning that another actor's interests or beliefs lie in a certain direction. Influence thus is a more diffuse, more indirect component of the political process than is power.

Political authority is also frequently confused with political power. Some, if not all, of this confusion can be dispelled if we recall that our notion of political power leaves open the question of *why*, specifically, actor A can gain compliance from actor B. One simple answer is force, but it is not the only answer. Another answer is that B may consider A as having a "right" to issue such a command. Once we raise the question of the basis of such a conviction we run into the notion of political authority.

Gaetano Mosca (1858–1941), the great Italian political theorist and politician, was aware of this when he concluded that even though the organized minority or "ruling class" always dominates the disorganized majority, it is not by force alone. Every political regime requires justification or legitimation in terms of what Mosca called a "political formula," [12] or set of beliefs showing why the rulers are entitled to rule. While basically for mass consumption, the Moscan political formula could also serve as self-legitimation of the ruling class.

The German sociologist and political economist Max Weber (1864–1930), with his threefold analysis of "legitimate domination," delved more deeply and systematically into these issues. His typology of traditional domination, rational-legal domination, and charismatic domination demands sustained analysis, though it should be made clear beforehand that he considered the three types as *ideal types*, rarely encountered in pure form in actual experience.

Traditional domination involves a system of legitimacy or authority in which the subject obeys because the command is issued in a context that has the support of age-old custom. Things have "always" been this way. Moreover, in contrast to modern legislation, "obedience is owed not to enacted rules but to the person who occupies a position of authority by tradition or who has been chosen for it by the traditional master." [13] There are two patterns by which the commands of such persons are

12. Gaetano Mosca, *The Ruling Class* (New York: McGraw-Hill, 1939), p. 70.
13. Max Weber, *Economy and Society,* ed. G. Roth and C. Wittich (Totowa, N.J.: Bedminster Press, 1968), 1:227.

legitimized: (1) the specific context of the command is marked out by tradition, which also suggests that there are limits to the command; (2) the traditional legitimacy accrues to the *person* and allows him considerable latitude as to his specific command.

Rational-legal domination involves a drastically different motivational basis from traditional domination. Obedience in a rational-legal order involves a *calculation* to measure the appropriateness of a given command in terms of a rational commitment to a complex legal structure. A main characteristic of this type of domination is its abstract, "impersonal" quality. Someone obeys a superior not because of his personal qualities, but rather because he holds a position whose capability to issue commands "fits in" logically with the overall legal structure. It is not who he is but what he is that counts. The motivation to obey derives either from a rational commitment to a value system undergirding the legal order or from a rational calculation of self-interest.

Charismatic domination in its pure form is so highly personalistic that it seems to lie at the opposite pole to rational-legal domination. Weber borrowed the term "charisma" from the Christian religion, where it designates a unique relationship of one chosen man to God. In this sense Moses and other Old Testament leaders and prophets were charismatic because they were chosen by God for a special mission in communicating or implementing his will. Weber extended the term to apply to instances where a group of followers, religious or otherwise, believe that their leader is utterly unique and totally superior to the normal run of men. To a person of such dimensions the follower owed "blind" obedience and devotion. Certain twentieth-century dictators and political leaders have seemed to possess this kind of hold over certain members of their "movement" and over some parts of the general public.

Unfortunately, "charisma" has become a popular catchword applied by social scientists, journalists, and others to nearly every political leader with a demonstratively enthusiastic following. This tendency tends to rob the term of its analytic usefulness. To avoid this, James V. Downton has proposed that we discriminate between three fundamental types of *personal leadership,* only one of which is authentically charismatic. The first of these is "transactional leadership," wherein the followers endow the leader with legitimacy because of his ability to produce tangible benefits for them (positive transactions) or to inflict punishments or deprivations on them (negative transactions). Downton's second category is "inspirational leadership," which is easily mistaken for true charisma because the leader is able to articulate and (to some extent) personify the hopes and aspirations of the followership. Since the leader imparts meaning to the actions and sufferings of the mass, the latter reciprocates by endowing him with legitimacy. Finally we come to true "charismatic leadership," wherein the leader acquires legitimacy by satisfying certain highly individual psychological needs among his devotees. Contact with the leader seems to alleviate the symptoms of deep-seated mental disturbances found in the followers.[14]

This suggests that true charismatic authority is relatively unstable, and thus Weber developed his famous concept of the "routinization of charisma." When this occurs, "permanent structures and traditions replace the belief in the revelation and heroism of charismatic personalities." [15] As a religious movement or a political one becomes established or "takes power," there is a tendency for a formal organization to develop whose objectives, procedures, and leadership may be quite different from those of the original charismatic social movement. Mundane tasks of finance and administration tend to get the upper hand over the dynamic religious or political forces that were originally all-important. To the purist these changes must appear as corruption or betrayal of the original goals of the movement; to the social scientist they must also appear as inevitable concessions to traditional and rational-legal modes of domination.

We can sum up our conclusions about power and politics by maintaining that all societies possess a political system or polity, whose function is twofold: (1) to contain the possibilities of human conflict within certain tolerable limits by an authoritative allocation of values; (2) to do this in a way that favors some and disfavors others in the distribution of and competition for scarce values. Political power is exercised in the course of the political process in order to control or influence the decisions taken by the political system. The ambiguity of politics is reflected both in the dual function of political systems and in the dual basis of political power: force and authority.

NONMODERN POLITIES: A TYPOLOGY

A further step toward a comparative political science is a historical typology of nonmodern polities, embracing the major forms of political organization outside of the modern state. Not all historical political sys-

14. James V. Downton Jr., *Rebel Leadership* (New York: Free Press, 1972).
15. Weber, *Economy*, 3:1139.

tems can be called "states," since they lack certain key traits such as a high level of centralization, emergence of a full-time officialdom, a popular awareness of the central government, the issuance of rules that go beyond mere custom, and a reliable system of taxation. Our typology of nonmodern polities involves (1) the tribal polity, (2) the city-state, (3) feudalism, (4) the patrimonial polity, and (5) the semibureaucratic empire. A full typology of regimes would, of course, require the inclusion of the modern state.

These nonmodern political systems or regimes do not have a merely historical or antiquarian interest.[16] They are not just political museum specimens. They are in many cases living political forms in the midst of regimes that are trying with varying degrees of success to create the institutional basis for a truly modern state. Tribalism and patrimonialism, for example, are viable categories in the analysis of a host of Third World countries. Moreover, though feudalism in its pure form may be a thing of the past, the patron-client relationships so often discussed in the literature about Third World countries may resemble feudalism more than it does traditional kinship ties, to say nothing of the more modern citizen-official relationship. Finally, one suspects that politics in small countries dominated by a single city (e.g., Singapore, Luxembourg) may hearken back in important ways to the ancient Greek city-states.

The Tribal Polity

The tribal or "primitive" polity is the most basic form of political organization. Because tribal societies lack certain attributes of more complex political forms, they have often been described as "stateless societies." But this should not mean that such societies realize the ideal of anarchy. Quite clearly, they possess mechanisms for the resolution of conflict and the authoritative allocation of values. It is just that these mechanisms are less visible than the special officials, law codes, and "public buildings" found in modern states and elsewhere.

Expressed more technically, we can say that there is little differentia-

16. *Polity, political system,* and *regime* will be used more or less interchangeably throughout this book. These terms refer broadly to the fundamental organization of political life. They suggest the general structural features of the political order, rather than the particular officeholders or policies involved.

tion of social and political roles in a tribal polity.[17] Economic, political, religious, and family activities are jumbled together. Tribal leaders may be veritable jacks-of-all-trades and any given activity may be performing a variety of different functions, which are distinguishable only to outside observers. Furthermore, political activity (especially in the simpler societies) is intermittent so that "the diffused political life is revealed more by *situations* than by political institutions." [18] This means that only under certain circumstances does the political process emerge into full operation.

At the very heart of the tribal polity is the kinship system. Arrangements concerning marriage, residence, and child-rearing constitute a powerful influence on the structure of tribal polities. The basic kinship units involved are the *clan* and the *lineage*. The clan embraces "relatives" out to cousins very far removed as the term "extended family" suggests. The lineage is similar to the clan, but is actually a "descent group" whose members trace their ancestry back to a common founder, who may be real or mythical, human or animal or divine.

Tracing the elaborate schemes of taboos, marriage exchanges, matrilineal or patrilineal descent, age groups, clan hierarchies, etc., is not our concern here. It is sufficient to say that any picture of tribal life that sets off a dominant chief against a mass of more or less equal tribesmen is the grossest oversimplification. Part of the difficulty stems from our using the term "tribe" for rather different forms of social and political organization. Sensing this, modern anthropologists have discerned types of tribal systems that run the gamut from very simple "bands" up to tribes with complex "associations" and far-flung village subunits.[19]

For the sake of simplicity we can consider the ideal tribal polity as a system in which kinship is the predominant political influence (though it, of course, retains some importance in all political systems). Kinship and politics are closely intertwined with religion (and magic) in tribal polities, as all aspects of tribal life are permeated by mythical beliefs. According to the anthropologist Bronislaw Malinowski (1884–1942),

17. "Differentiation" means that various people perform distinct social roles. There is a complex division of social labor with separate individuals doing the specific jobs. An automobile assembly plant is the standard example of a highly differentiated division of labor.
18. Georges Balandier, *Political Anthropology* (New York: Vintage Books, 1972), pp. 64–65.
19. See, for example, S. N. Eisenstadt, "Primitive Political Systems: A Preliminary Comparative Analysis," *American Anthropologist* 61 (1959).

myth is a sort of "social charter that ensures the existing form of society with its system of distributing power, privilege, and property." [20] Many institutions and practices of a tribal polity possess a sacred meaning, which provides an inside track to political power for those who are adept in magic and religion. In fact, the autonomous play of politics can assert itself in covert manipulation of ritual practices and kinship organization for the sake of attaining and retaining political power.

The City-State

Our second basic form of political organization, the city-state, finds its best examples in the classical Greek polis and in medieval city-states in Italy and the Low Countries. In the Greek version, the polis embraced the urban center plus its immediate environs.[21] Furthermore, we find that by the peak period of the Greek polis (from about 600 B.C. to about 300 B.C.), kinship and tribal organization had lost much of their preeminence as a political factor. In their place emerged the ideal and practice of *citizenship*. Even in the most "democratic" of Greek city-states, however, the full citizen was the member of a rather exclusive club. Women were excluded, as were slaves, resident aliens, and others who lacked the requisite birth to enter the charmed circle. Such exclusiveness betrayed the lingering influence of tribal and kinship patterns.

The Greek citizen, as in Athens or Sparta, was someone who had full rights to participate in the religious-political activities of the polis. Gradations in the exercise of these rights existed according to whether the polis was organized in a "democratic" or "oligarchic" or some other manner. For our present purposes a more important consideration is development of political institutions that are relatively distinct from tribe and kingship. Though the exact institutional format differed from place to place, a closer look at the Spartan system will give us a fairly representative view of the basic city-state pattern.

The main political institutions of Sparta were the "dyarchy" or double kinship, the Ephorate, the Council of Elders, and the General Assem-

20. Bronislaw Malinowski, quoted in Balandier, *Political Anthropology*, p. 23.
21. "In fact, the territory of the Polis varied greatly in extent. Apart from Athens with rather more than 1000 square miles of territory, including Salamis and Oropus, and Sparta with about 3300 square miles, including Laconia and Messenia, there was hardly a Polis of the homeland or the islands with more than 400 square miles. Some, and some of importance, had less than 40." Victor Ehrenberg, *The Greek State* (New York: W. W. Norton, 1964), p. 29.

bly.[22] The dyarchy was an especially ancient institution with roots deep in the Dorian tribal past and perhaps represented a political compromise between tribal or clan factions. In recorded times the role of the Spartan kings had receded considerably and figured mostly in ceremonial-religious activities.

The Ephorate, with five members, had the greatest influence of all the main institutions on day-to-day politics and government in Sparta. All Spartan citizens were eligible for membership, and the choice was made by a joint session of the Council and the Assembly.

The Council of Elders, including the two kings ex officio, was a body of thirty members. The twenty-eight elected members were chosen by the Spartan citizenry from among male citizens aged sixty and over. Akin to similar procedures in Athens and elsewhere, the Council of Elders acted as a sort of proving ground for legislation before it was passed on for final approval to the assembly. In addition to its role in lawmaking, it had tasks of a judicial and administrative nature.

Figure 1.2.   The Spartan Regime

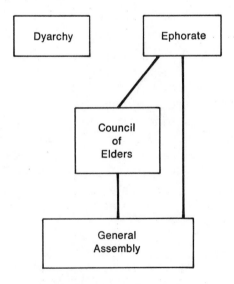

22. This account of Sparta is based on H. Michell, *Sparta* (Cambridge: Cambridge University Press, 1964).

The General Assembly was composed of all male citizens over the age of thirty who had not forfeited their rights by some unseemly act. As a large and unwieldy body it could exercise only a vague sort of control over the ephors. Nonetheless, many issues were brought before it for final disposition. It "decided on questions of peace or war and foreign policy. It appointed the generals and elected the *gerontes* [i.e., members of the Council of Elders], decided claims to the throne and voted on proposed laws." [23]

From this all too brief sketch one might conclude that the Greek polis did not differ all that much—save in size—from a modern representative regime. One vitally important ingredient was missing, however: a bureaucracy worthy of the name. In other words, "the official was just a citizen who, apart from his share in the popular assembly, the Council or the courts of law, temporarily discharged a task set him by the state." [24] The amateurishness and ad hoc quality of Greek public administration was accentuated by the common practice of appointing public officials by lot. There as elsewhere, however, we must recognize that the tasks of government were simpler and fewer than we find in the modern state.

Feudalism

The term "feudalism" has suffered considerably from overextension. For Marxists and others it stands for almost any "precapitalist" economy that stresses the landlord-peasant relationship as the paramount fact of social life. We prefer to call such societies "seigneurial societies" and to reserve the term "feudalism" for a political rather than an economic system. There is no better way to grasp the nature of this type of polity than to construct a syndrome [25] of European feudalism based upon the conclusions of the twentieth-century French historian Marc Bloch.[26]

To understand the emergence of Western European feudalism we must recall two essential facts of European history after the fall of Rome in A.D. 476. The first is that even after the receding of the first

23. Ibid., p. 144.
24. Ehrenberg, *Greek State*, p. 66.
25. The term "syndrome" has become very widespread in social science. It has been borrowed from medicine, where it refers to a set of symptoms that characterize a specific disease. Social scientists use it to designate the characteristics or traits of a social phenomenon that somehow hang together.
26. Marc Bloch, *Feudal Society* (Chicago: University of Chicago Press, 1966), 2:446.

TABLE 1.2. Syndrome of European Feudalism

1. A subject peasantry—serfdom
2. Use of the fief—i.e., an originally temporary grant of land instead of a salary
3. The supremacy of a class of specialized warriors—knighthood and nobility
4. Ties of obedience and protection between man and man—vassalage in the higher strata and serfdom in the lower
5. Fragmentation of authority, leading to extreme decentralization and disorder
6. Survival of other forms of association—family and state

waves of "barbarian" invasions in the fifth and sixth centuries, Western Europe was repeatedly invaded, especially in the tenth and eleventh centuries (Northmen from the north, Arabs from the south, Magyars and others from the east). For this and other reasons there occurred a partial demonetization of the Western European economy as currency was drained eastward and southward. These two factors help to explain why so many people high and low were willing to become dependent on "stronger" persons and why the ensuing obligations often took the form of personal service rather than cash payments.

To understand the distinctiveness of the resultant social order and polity based on serfdom and vassalage, some comparison with tribalism and the city-state is useful. While tribal political organization was largely determined by kinship, the feudal polity superimposed its bonds of lord and vassal, master and man, upon both kinship and residual tribal influences. This reflected a *relative* weakening of kinship ties in the face of challenges they could no longer meet. The failure of kinship to provide an adequate system of protection caused Marc Bloch to speak of "vassalage as a substitute for the kinship ties." [27]

Vassalage was an agreement between a superior and an inferior stipulating protection as the superior's duty and service as the inferior's. The bond was originally intended to be preeminently personal and was cemented by vows of homage and fealty. Accordingly, the relationship was supposed to terminate upon the death of one party, and the fief (usually a land grant) would revert to the original dispensing lord. In time, however, hereditary succession of fiefs and multiple vassalage undermined the original intimacy of the lord-vassal relationship. Serfdom, though originally a more or less free commitment, quickly became a hereditary status for the peasants. Generations were now bound to the

27. Ibid., 1:224.

same land or manor, subject to the general legal-political control of their lord.

In contrast to the city-state, which transcended kinship by means of the concepts of citizenship and the polis, feudalism produced a drastic curtailment of the power and authority of the central government. Max Weber called feudal monarchy "the most extreme type of systematically decentralized domination." [28] Though the king headed the feudal hierarchy, he often experienced the greatest difficulty in controlling his vassals, who in turn might have problems with their own, and so on down the scale. Furthermore, the Roman Catholic church was a powerful organization everywhere, which prompted the often quoted (though exaggerated) remark of J. N. Figgis that "the real State of the Middle Ages in the modern sense—if the words are not a paradox—is the Church." [29]

Essential public and welfare services that we nowadays assign to the central government were performed, when they were performed, either by local lords or by the towns. Likewise, formal legislation came close to disappearing, since "custom had become the sole living source of law, and princes even in their legislation, scarcely claimed to do more than interpret it." [30]

The Patrimonial Polity

Compared to feudalism, the patrimonial polity possesses more of the paraphernalia of a genuine state. In Western Europe it represents a sort of intermediate stage between feudalism and the modern state. But we should not assume a universal pattern of development (feudalism–patrimonialism–modern state), because in Europe feudalism was also *preceded* by the Carolingian patrimonial kingdoms.

Patrimonial monarchy differs from feudal monarchy chiefly in increased political centralization. The patrimonial monarchy is able to curtail the virtual sovereignty of the great feudal magnates. Officials appointed by the monarch and more or less loyal to him exercise considerable powers throughout the country. This officialdom, however,

28. Weber, *Economy*, 3:1079.
29. John Neville Figgis, *Political Thought from Gerson to Grotius* (New York: Harper Torchbooks, 1960), p. 19.
30. Bloch, *Feudal Society*, 1:111. Legislation proper means statute law that is conceived, proclaimed, and enforced by institutional subdivisions of a coherent government. Customary law, on the other hand, just "grows" in the sense that it began as a precedent and becomes legitimized over time.

does not as yet constitute a true modern bureaucracy. The reason for this lies mainly in the purchasability, ownership, and inheritance of many offices. Purchasers of offices were not necessarily moved by a sense of public duty, as many offices promised lucrative rewards. These rewards were often supplemented by what even by the different standards of that day must be judged "corrupt practices."

Moreover, these offices, as in seventeenth-century France, might also entitle the possessor or his heirs to aristocratic status. In this highly status-conscious society, the royal government would periodically create and sell status-bearing offices to provide needed monies for the treasury.

Administration effected by such aristocratic or quasi-aristocratic personnel made things much harder for ambitious monarchs than phrases like "absolute monarchy" or "divine right of kings" would suggest. The social standing of officials sometimes allowed them to subvert the application of royal decrees. Understandably, the impact of government activity declined rather sharply as it moved from the nucleus of the capital city (the center) to the outlying provinces (the periphery). Many provinces, towns, and corporate bodies (e.g., universities, guilds, monasteries) retained "rights" and privileges exempting them from direct controls by the royal government.

The main centralizing achievements of patrimonialism were in taxation and the military. Government expenditures were no longer completely defrayed by the monarch's personal wealth. Indirect taxes provided a substantial return, though the numerous revolts triggered by new taxes suggest that this was a dangerous game. One reason why the patrimonial monarch needed more money was the greater military power of the central government. Generally the forces involved were foreign mercenaries. On the other hand, this costly innovation did allow governments to extract more taxes from a reluctant populace.

Max Weber developed his analysis of patrimonialism in terms of a highly developed form of traditional domination. However, it has been suggested that by disassociating patrimonial rule from strict traditionalism, we can readily see that government in many Third World countries resembles the format of patrimonialism more than that of the modern state.[31] Such personal rulership, based as it is on material incentives and rewards, is obviously a particular form of the "positive transactional personal leadership" discussed above (see Downton's anal-

31. Guenther Roth, "Personal Leadership, Patrimonialism, and Empire-Building," in *Scholarship and Partisanship*, ed. R. Bendix and G. Roth (Berkeley: University of California Press, 1971).

ysis of *personal leadership*). With the weak bureaucratization in these polities, personal leadership is one way of getting things done.

The Semibureaucratic Empire

Of all the types of political organization contained in this typology, the most questionable inclusion is the semibureaucratic empire. Even the expression "semibureaucratic" suggests hesitation in labeling. Some theorists, however, have no doubts at all that ancient Egypt, the Chinese Empire, India at certain times, the Roman Empire, the Byzantine Empire, the empires of the Aztecs and the Incas, medieval Arab empires, the Ottoman Empire, and others constitute a separate category of regimes.

What impresses them is the vast territorial extent and the centralized administrations found in such empires. The word "bureaucratic" occurs so frequently in accounts of such regimes that there seems to be precious little difference between them and a genuinely modern state. One of the best known and most controversial treatments of empires is Karl Wittfogel's theory of *oriental despotism*.[32] Oriental despotism, according to this theory, is the result of the emergence of a "hydraulic state," so called because the political-administrative structure develops out of the need to control the effects and utilization of *water* over a large territory. Flood control and irrigation for agriculture under certain ecological conditions have led to highly centralized organization. A "bureaucracy" entrusted with far-reaching powers is required to administer the highly complex hydraulic system. In fact, Wittfogel considers these powers so "total" that they foreshadow those of modern totalitarian regimes.

The hydraulic state necessarily develops into a "despotism" because the bureaucracy uses its highly strategic power position to protect and promote its own selfish interests. It becomes a closed and exploitative clique, increasingly parasitical to the rest of society. In Wittfogel's view the hydraulic state is a "genuinely managerial state." What most resembles modern totalitarianism in this regime is that it "prevents the nongovernmental forces of society from crystallizing into independent bodies strong enough to counter-balance and control the political machine." [33]

A number of obstacles stand in the way of accepting these or even

32. Karl Wittfogel, *Oriental Despotism* (New Haven: Yale University Press, 1957), p. 19.
33. Ibid., p. 49.

milder claims about the historical distinctiveness of imperial political organization. In the first place many historic empires were rather motley conglomerations in which tribal, city-state, and even feudal political organization coexisted with the so-called central government. In fact, if we stick to our idea of a political system making decisions for a single, discernible society, there is a question about these regimes. One scholar has concluded that

> in the same geographical area several societies can exist side by side without functional social relations and without acculturation or assimilation. Political rule may in some way be superimposed upon all of them, upon some of them or only upon some parts of them. Political boundaries, even linguistic boundaries, do not delimit such societies.[34]

In other words, the lack of a single social system may *logically* mean the lack of a single political system in such a patchwork-quilt arrangement.

Even if we do not accept such an extreme conclusion, it raises at least two problems about empires. First, there appears to be a marked tendency to exaggerate the actual degree of political centralization and governmental effectiveness found in most empires. Second, the term "bureaucracy" may well be a misnomer when applied to some, if not all, historic empires. This conclusion is forced on us if we accept the Weberian model of bureaucracy to be discussed in the next section. It may well be that the concept of patrimonialism is flexible enough to encompass historic empires without our considering them a separate major category.

THE MODERN STATE

Bureaucracy and the Modern State

Since most treatments of the modern state hearken back sooner or later to the ideas of Max Weber, we must critically survey his teachings in order to grasp how Weber's concept of the modern state differs from the five nonmodern types of polity. Weber distinguished three major features of the modern state.[35] We can call these three features bureaucracy, territoriality, and the monopoly of legitimate violence. Their peculiar con-

34. Wolfram Eberhard, "Problems of Historical Sociology," in *State and Society,* ed. Reinhard Bendix (Boston: Little, Brown, 1968), p. 22.
35. Weber, *Economy,* 1:56.

TABLE 1.3.   Weber's Features of the Modern State

1. The administrative and legal order of the modern state can be changed by legislation. The organized activities of the administration are oriented by such legislation.
2. The order of the modern state has binding authority not only over native-born and other citizens, but also over nearly every action that takes place within its jurisdiction. It is a compulsory system based upon a given territory.
3. Force is considered legitimate only if permitted or exercised by the state.

figuration in the modern state is what distinguishes it from other political systems.

Bureaucracy, however, seems the most salient of these features. In fact, Weber comes close to identifying bureaucracy with modernity in general, and thus modernization with bureaucratization. He saw bureaucracy as the rational allocation of human resources (time, energy, skills, and motivation) for the attainment of clearly designated purposes. In terms of efficiency, bureaucratic administration and organization are as superior to alternatives such as feudal or patrimonial systems as a machine is to nonmachine technology. Weber saw this superiority reflected not only in the state but in education, business, the military, and the church as well. If other factors were equal, a more highly bureaucratized organization would always outdistance its competitors.

Though Weber was aware that bureaucratic overgrowth or "hypertrophy" could lead to inefficiency, he seems to have underestimated the constraints and rigidities inherent in bureaucratic organization. Red tape, delays, petty jurisdictional disputes, lack of initiative, hostility— these and other complaints have made many modern citizens surround the term "bureaucracy" with pejorative, even satirical connotations.[36] While Weber may have overestimated bureaucratic efficiency, his predictions about the spread of bureaucracy have certainly been confirmed. However, his further conclusion that bureaucratic organization once entrenched cannot be dislodged has been challenged by the antibureaucratic convulsions that racked China between 1966 and 1969 under the label of the Great Proletarian Cultural Revolution. And yet, the trend of the post-1970 period toward rebureaucratization has been accelerated by

36. The best-known example is "Parkinson's Law," which holds that "Work expands so as to fill the time available for its completion." C. Northcote Parkinson, *Parkinson's Law* (New York: Ballantine Books, 1964).

the passing of Chairman Mao in 1976. Weber may be right in the long run.

It is not merely the intrinsic superiority of bureaucratic organization that explains its spread in modern times. A variety of social, cultural, economic, and political factors have been involved. A certain "democratization" of social structure has broken the monopoly of high-status groups over administrative positions. Economic growth has developed a money economy that eases the funding of bureaucratic organization. It also stimulates new demands for services that bureaucratic organization alone can meet. The modern welfare state thus is a potent source of bureaucratization. Finally, technological advance has entailed a division of labor and increased specialization that lends itself to bureaucratic organization.

Even more challenging than his claims for bureaucratic effectiveness and growth is Weber's (exaggerated) conclusion that "in a modern state the actual ruler is necessarily and unavoidably the bureaucracy, since power is exercised neither through parliamentary speeches nor monarchical enunciations but through routines of administration." [37] We must now examine the structure of the Weberian bureaucratic model because, despite some possibly exaggerated claims about bureaucracy, this model sensitizes us to essential aspects about the modern state and its politics.

TABLE 1.4.   The Weberian Bureaucratic Model

---

1. Continuity of official business according to definite rules
2. A systematic division of labor
3. A definite administrative hierarchy
4. Technical training for officeholders
5. State funding of administration with public accountability of officials
6. No venality, private ownership, or inheritability of office
7. Written documentation of official business

Continuity of official business according to definite rules distinguishes bureaucratic organization from the more haphazard, intermittent type of public administration found in most nonmodern polities. Bureaucracy is a permanent, ongoing structure whose tasks are assigned and carried out within the framework of rational, discernible rules. The expression

37. Weber, *Economy*, 3:1393.

"standard operating procedures" suggests perfectly the stress on routinized practices found in bureaucracies.

A *systematic division of labor* is where the "bureaus" of bureaucracy come into the picture. Though the principle of the division of labor is no modern discovery, full exploitation of its possibilities for raw efficiency is a feature of the industrial revolution. Applied to human organizations, a systematic division of labor would ideally minimize duplication, forestall jurisdictional disputes, and allot the right tasks to the right groups and individuals. This sort of task distribution allows for the highly developed specialization that should speed up reaching organizational goals. The idea behind this conclusion is seen in the assembly line of large factories, where the total team of workers will produce many more units with each making a tiny addition than if each "made" the whole unit all by himself.

A *definite administrative hierarchy* means that bureaucratic structures involve a gradation of agencies, with agency heads on lower levels receiving orders and being responsible to the next higher level. In the typical administrative hierarchy, the higher agencies supervise the lower ones in the execution of their tasks. An order emanating from the top of the hierarchy simply filters down to ultimate execution in a clear "chain of command."

Technical training for officeholders is necessary for bureaucratic specialization. This idea contrasts sharply with "administration by notables," which is based on the notion that well-rounded, humanistically educated "amateurs" have enough versatility to absorb whatever "on-the-job" training is required for their current office. The assumption (or presumption) of modern bureaucracy is that public administration is more of a science than an art and that its "principles" can be formulated and put into manuals requiring considerable time for mastery. We might add that in bureaucracy "insiders" have a vested interest in inflating required "qualifications" so as to minimize outside competition.

State funding of administration with public accountability of officials counteracts the traditional practice whereby the official originally supplies funds expended in carrying out his office and then "bills" the government or deducts his share from public monies under his control. State funding enormously improves the control possibilities of the central authorities. On the other hand, Weber was not so naive as to think that public scrutiny and control over bureaucracies would ever be easy. Indeed he pointed out that extreme secretiveness was a kind of occupational disease of public officials in all societies.

Figure 1.3. A Typical Administrative Hierarchy

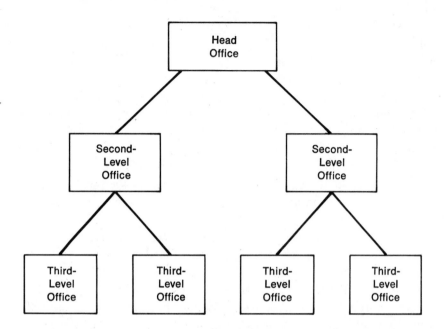

No venality, private ownership, or inheritability of office distinguishes a true bureaucracy from a patrimonial officialdom. Offices in modern public bureaucracies are ostensibly open to broad strata of the population and are to be filled according to standards of "merit" or "achievement." Offices therefore cannot be owned and are obtained and retained under the guidance of regularized and formalized procedures. Although tenure in bureaucratic offices is often for life or until retirement, rules exist for ousting incumbents under certain specified conditions.

Written documentation of official business is essential to the other aspects of bureaucracy such as rules, continuity, division of labor, and public accountability. Without accurate records, knowledge of who did what, when, and why would soon evaporate. The implications for the conduct of official business are obvious. On the other hand, we all know that a good thing can be carried too far. It was the French bureaucracy's practice of tying up their reams of records in red ribbon that has given us "red tape" as a symbol of bureaucratic hypercomplexity and sloth.

It does not take much knowledge of politics and administration to appreciate that both public and private bureaucracies often fail to work in the way Weber prescribed. And yet when they do not, we often imply that they should by talk of "corruption." A widespread notion of corruption sees it as a deviation from either general laws or bureaucratic rules and practices, for the sake of personal gain.[38] Corrupt practices can short-circuit all of the seven features of modern bureaucracy. If bureaucracy is premised upon objective, impersonal rules, bending or breaking those rules can become a lucrative activity. If employment and promotion require qualifications such as technical training, waiving these stipulations for a price or for family considerations (nepotism: literally, nephewism) undermines bureaucracy. Falsification or destruction of records can naturally "cover up" these and other corrupt practices.

Weber's account also stresses the "political neutrality" of bureaucracy. It is expected that political initiative would originate outside the bureaucracy and that the bureaucracy would faithfully execute decisions made by elected or other officials without interposing its own political preferences. Politics is supposedly one thing, administration another. There have even been cases where this somewhat optimistic expectation has been realized.

In Great Britain immediately after World War II it was feared (or hoped, as the case may be) that the mostly Conservative civil service would sabotage the sweeping social reforms initiated by the Labor Government of 1945–51. Little or no sabotage occurred. On the other hand, many consider the hostility of the German bureaucracy—Weber's firsthand example—to parliamentary government an important cause of the downfall of the Weimar Republic (1919–33).

Corruption and the Weberian Model

Obviously political considerations, as easily as outright corruption, can wreak havoc with expectations based upon the Weberian model. The question of hierarchical subordination is a good example. Hierarchical subordination suggests that an agency head can issue orders and demand accounting from a lower official in his department or from the head of a lower agency. But what if the two individuals concerned are members of the single ruling party and if the lower official outranks his chief in terms of *party offices*? The result may well be that the real power

38. Legal tradition has developed some distinctions on how corruption can operate to divert public servants from their duty. *Malfeasance* means doing something that is prohibited; *misfeasance* means doing something generally permissible but in an illicit way; *nonfeasance* means failure to perform a mandatory act.

relations between the two men is the reverse of the bureaucratically ordained one. Nazi Germany probably represents the ultimate in confusion on this score, but the problem emerges whenever strong parties have members in the bureaucracy.

No public bureaucracy is wholly immune from corruption or political pressures. In fact, perfect immunity might not even be ethically desirable. Not all commands should be faithfully executed. Another problem is that conceptions of probity and corruption derived from the Western experience lose much of their meaning when transposed to Third World countries, where tribal-kinship or patrimonial codes of behavior are still in force. In such cases an official's acceptance of gifts cannot so readily be called "bribery" since gift-giving has a ceremonial function in many cultures. Likewise, an official who neglected to fill positions with relatives and other dependents might be viewed as a moral freak rather than a model bureaucrat.

Impressed by these and other aspects of public administration in Third World countries, social scientists have launched an interesting debate on the costs and benefits of political corruption. Those stressing its possible benefits generally have an economic frame of reference, though sometimes political benefits such as strengthening loyalties to party or state figure in the calculations. In the first case corruption is considered beneficial because it allegedly contributes to economic growth. This argument presupposes that for whatever reasons (ideology, incompetence, etc.) existing government policies are not conducive to economic growth. A second assumption is that in the country studied economic growth is best fostered in the "private sector" (i.e., through the efforts of individual businessmen and firms).

What recommends corruption according to this theory is, quite frankly, its "subversion of the government's economic policy." [39] The government has declared a set of rules, a policy which, if faithfully implemented, would hamper the entrepreneurial activities of various businessmen. The only way that they can gain respite from the government's restrictions is by means of corruption. That is, they bribe officials not to enforce the government's policies in full rigor. Thus freed, they can "do their own thing" and contribute to general economic growth.

If the businessmen are of an alien or pariah ethnic group or sect, as is often true in Third World countries, corruption enables them to evade

39. See on all this, Arnold J. Heidenheimer, ed., *Political Corruption* (New York: Holt, Rinehart & Winston, 1970), pt. 4.

discriminatory laws and practices. Furthermore, this "positive" theory of corruption maintains that corruption increases efficiency by allowing only those firms to survive that can pay the added "overhead" of corrupt payments.

On the political side, corruption is believed to help create political bonds between people otherwise separated by ethnic, religious, kinship, and other differences. In countries where political integration is weak, a machine-type political system can promote cooperation between otherwise disparate elements. Bonds of material interests are not necessarily the weakest ones in political life.

Not surprisingly, other observers are convinced that the costs of corruption far outweigh its benefits. The simplest counterargument points out that corruption can subvert "good" just as easily as "bad" government policies. Ultimately the public foots the bill for the costs of corruption. First of all, services are more costly than they should be. "Kickbacks" raise public spending by awarding contracts contrary to the "lowest bid" principle. Perhaps even more damaging is the long-range political impact of widespread corruption. Though all regimes face problems of legitimacy and public support, this is nowhere more acute than in Third World countries. Corruption can lower a regime's legitimacy below a critical threshold.

Besides lowering the morale of civil servants, a strategically important group in many countries, corruption can create a narrow-minded interest politics that make courageous decision-making impossible. There is no doubt that the Communist victory in South Vietnam was eased by this type of political environment and that the Marcos coup in the Philippines was partially intended as an antidote to it.[40]

Structural Variants of the Modern State

The problem of the forms of the modern state differs from the traditional concern with "forms of government." Traditional classifications of governments generally assume one and the same type of political organization or polity. In classical Greece, for example, Plato, Aristotle, and others discussed the different forms of government, but always in terms of the polis. It is only by considering these traditional ideas somewhat apart from their original context that they have value for us.

40. James C. Scott stresses the negative aspects of corruption in his *Comparative Political Corruption* (Englewood Cliffs, N.J.: Prentice-Hall, 1972).

Our own ventures in forms of government found in the modern state provide much of the substance of the next four chapters. The present concern, however, is with the three structural variants of the modern state depicted in table 1.5.

TABLE 1.5. Confederation, Federation, Unitary State

Confederation	Federation	Unitary State
1. Weak centralization	1. Moderate centralization	1. High centralization
2. Sovereignty in the constituent units	2. Sovereignty divided between central government and constituent units	2. Undivided sovereignty
3. Acts directly on constituent units, not on individuals	3. Acts *both* on constituent units *and* individuals	3. Acts directly on individuals
4. Usually a formal right to secession	4. Generally no right to secession	4. No right to secession
5. Central government can be overruled by constituent unit governments— so-called nullification	5. National law supreme in its sphere; constituent units in theirs	5. National law supreme; local ordinances clearly subordinate
6. Central government funded by contributions from constituent units	6. Dual taxation system for both levels of government	6. Single taxation system; local variations must be approved by central authorities
7. Examples: United States before 1789, Switzerland before 1848, Germany before 1871	7. Examples: United States since 1789, Canada, West Germany, Australia, Switzerland, India, Brazil, Mexico	7. Examples: United Kingdom, France, Spain, Poland, Israel, Algeria

The main differences between confederations, federations, and unitary states are really derivable from points 1 and 3 in table 1.5. These three kinds of state differ most basically on the amount of political centralization and on the impact of governmental decisions on citizens and groups. The latter point can be portrayed graphically.

CONFEDERATION.   In a confederation the central government is reduced to making requests to the separate lower-unit governments for

Figure 1.4. Impact of Government on Citizens in the Three Forms of Modern State

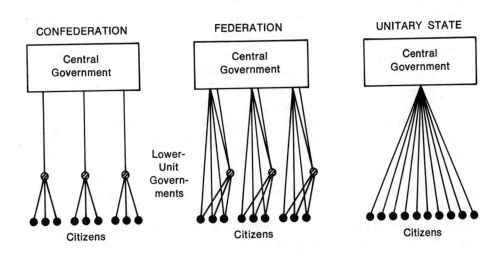

political action (see figure 1.4).[41] Then the lower units decide whether and how much to comply. Since the weak central government gets its operating expenses from more or less voluntary contributions from the lower-unit governments, the individual citizen feels the impact of the central government only indirectly and remotely. In fact, one is justified in wondering whether confederation is really a viable form of modern state at all. All the historical examples have changed into federations or separate unitary states. In fact the closest thing to a contemporary confederation is not a state at all—that is, the European Economic Community made up of France, Italy, West Germany, Belgium, The Netherlands, Luxemburg, Great Britain, Ireland, and Denmark. The EEC is now somewhere between a customs union and a low-grade confederation.

FEDERATION.   A federation is an inherently controversial, perhaps contradictory, form of polity. Jurisdictional disputes which are unthinkable either in a confederation or a unitary state are inherent to a

41. Among the terms used to designate lower governmental units in both federations and confederations are *states, provinces, Länder* (Germany), *cantons* (Switzerland), and *regions* (Italy).

federal system. Bickering punctuated by charges of usurpation of power at either end characterize the relationships between the central government and the government of the lower units. Nevertheless, advocates of federalism make claims for it that run from the "best possible form of modern state" to the "only solution for international anarchy" (world federalists). In the light of this, a survey of the "pros" and "cons" of federalism seems essential for better understanding of it.[42] We will first survey favorable and then unfavorable arguments about federalism.

According to the *responsiveness argument*, federalism reflects local needs and diversity better than the unitary state. It makes for a more intimate relationship between citizens and their government. Government is physically closer and local officials have wider areas of discretion than do their counterparts in unitary states. By strengthening such diversity federalism may provide a countervailing force to the trends of standardization and cultural homogenization inherent in modern mass society.

The *experimentation argument* maintains that by multiplying significant centers of government federalism encourages experimentation and innovation in public policy and administration. If successful on a small scale, the new procedure can be quickly adopted elsewhere. If it fails, the lesson is learned and the losses are minimized because the whole central apparatus was not committed in the abortive experiment.

The *participation argument* holds that federalism increases direct public participation in both selection of officials and general determination of public policy. This results because federalism maximizes the number of elected officials with real influence on policy.

The *size-of-territory argument* considers federalism as the best way to establish representative institutions in states of continental proportions. It is no accident that the most successful representative states of vast territory (the United States, Canada, India to 1975, and Australia) are also federal systems. Inability to strike a federal compromise or a bargain seems to condemn large states to dictatorship of some sort.

The *freedom argument* seems to reflect the nineteenth-century liberal fear of concentrated governmental power, as in Lord Acton's famous aphorism, "Power tends to corrupt, absolute power corrupts absolutely." Some advocates of federalism therefore suggest that by parceling out power between the two levels of government federalism forestalls a

42. This section relies heavily on the essays contained in A. W. MacMahon, ed., *Federalism: Mature and Emergent* (New York: Columbia University Press, 1955).

monopoly of power that would spell the end of individual freedom. Indeed a certain jealousy and tension between the two levels helps to preserve and enhance freedom. On the other hand, federalism is not anarchy: it allows both levels sufficient power to meet public needs.

Critics of federalism, of course, question the feasibility of most of these points. They point out that the truly successful federal systems were founded before the twentieth century and that India for a variety of reasons constitutes no real exception. Furthermore, the twentieth century is the century of the welfare state, and most public policies can be formulated and executed only at the national level. Ecology, unemployment, health, civil liberties, education, energy are problems that can be tackled only with the vast resources and central planning of a strong central government.

Likewise the political claims of federalism's supporters are tarnished, say the critics. The boundaries of the lower units are accidental and anachronistic, having no correspondence to contemporary political and administrative needs. In fact, the lower units can provide a refuge for vested interest groups, because they then can more easily dominate or influence their governments than they can the central government.

UNITARY STATE.   It is not our purpose to decide between favorable and unfavorable characterizations of federalism. Rather we should examine its main competitor, the unitary state. Here there is one basic level of government: all other governmental units are administrative subdivisions of the central government. Even though local government officials are often popularly elected, their powers are often curtailed and scrutinized by officials (such as the French or Italian prefects) who are bureaucratic appointees of the central government. The margin of local decision is often narrowly circumscribed, and local officials often complain about having to check with the ministry at the capital about minor decisions. Of course, differing political traditions can lead to different amounts of centralization in different countries. Great Britain and France are both unitary states, but British local government shows far greater autonomy and vitality than the French.

Nearly all dictatorships are de facto unitary states, though certain legal forms of federalism may be preserved for show. For example, the USSR (Union of Soviet Socialist Republics) "on paper" is a federal system made up of fifteen "union republics" as the lower units. In fact, reading the Soviet constitution we might be tempted to describe the Soviet Union as a confederation, because republics lying on the outer rim of the country are accorded a formal right to secession. Moreover, two of the republics, White Russia and the Ukraine, even have seats in the United Nations General Assembly! All of this, however, is mere appearance, and any attempt of republic officials to depart from Moscow's policies and directives would be quickly suppressed.

States and Nations

One of the most widespread and deeply rooted confusions in our political vocabulary concerns the terms "nation" and "state." A move toward clarification is to keep in mind that a state (either broadly understood as covering many types of polity or more narrowly understood as referring to the modern state) is a *form of political organization*. A nation, on the other hand, is a *group of people* who identify with each other. The resultant "we-feeling" separates them from others, who may or may not have a we-feeling of their own.

While ethnic groups and tribes have always exhibited strong feelings of internal solidarity and external hostility, a modern nation, even if ethnically based, is aware that there exist a number of other nations whose claims to recognition are also legitimate. Furthermore, in contrast to the situation in traditional tribes and ethnic groups, the member of a modern nation has a greater sense of his own individuality, which he chooses to merge in the collectivity, the nation. There is a factor of choice and will involved that goes beyond unconscious tribalism or ethnocentrism. This is why the nineteenth-century French historian Ernest Renan called a nation "a daily plebiscite." From this point of view a true national identity can be superimposed upon a myriad of loyalties to ethnic, tribal, religious, kinship, and regional groups. However, though these "primordial sentiments," to use Clifford Geertz's happy phrase, *can* be overcome, it is always difficult and often impossible to do so.

The psychological and subjective aspects of national identification warn us that the only truly foolproof definition of a nation is that of a group of people who consider themselves to be a nation. Understandably social scientists and historians have been reluctant to remain content with this near-tautology. Many have attempted to construct what can be called *an objective syndrome of nationhood*. Generally included are the following traits of nations: (1) language, (2) religion, (3) territoriality, (4) ethnicity, and (5) common culture.

To require the presence of all five traits as a test of nationhood goes too far. To suggest that any two or three or four will do is certainly more manageable, but still leaves us with a key problem. To illustrate this, let us say that we are willing to call a group a "nation" if it has any two of our traits; Group A, for instance, speaks a common language and embraces a common religion, while Group B shares territory and has common ethnic background. To call both groups nations is to do so on entirely different bases. This conclusion shows the inherent difficulty of the term "nation": *there is no single objective criterion that is always found in groups called nations.* To grasp the full meaning of this we must briefly survey the five traits mentioned above.

There is no doubt that in given cases *language* is the acid test that distinguishes members of a nation from nonmembers. Unfortunately, we find exceptions to this rule, which means that the rule is no rule at all. On the one hand, we find cases where people who speak a common language (more or less) are not members of the same nation. English-speakers are found in the American nation, the English nation, the Irish nation, and the Australian nation. Spanish and Arabic are the native languages of people identifying with a number of different nations. On the other hand, we have cases like that of Switzerland, where there is no "Swiss" language. Most Swiss have either French, German, Italian, or Romansch as their native language. While this situation causes many strains, it has not prevented the emergence of an authentic Swiss nation. Our first examples show that common language is not a *sufficient* condition for nationhood; the Swiss case, that it is not a *necessary* condition for it.[43]

Religion, like language (and often in conjunction with it), can be the decisive factor in determining the nation. But we can say here too that religion in general is neither a necessary nor sufficient condition for nationhood. Followers of the same religion identify with different nations, and many nations are composed of people of differing faiths. The most we can say is that historical circumstances will determine precisely the role played by religion in the emergence of nations.

With *territoriality* we would appear to have found a firm basis for nationhood. Grounds for such a conclusion can be found in the great modern student of nationalism, Hans Kohn:

> the most important outward factor in the formation of nationalities is a common territory, or rather, the state. Political frontiers tend to establish nationalities. . . . Generally we may say . . . that statehood or nationhood

---

43. A necessary condition is one that is indispensable if something is to exist or take place. A sufficient condition is not necessary, but if it is present it is enough to account for something existing or taking place.

(in the sense of common citizenship under one territorial government) is a constitutive element in the life of a nationality. The conditions of statehood need not be present when nationality originates; but in such a case . . . it is always the memory of a past state and the aspiration toward statehood that characterizes nationalities in the period of nationalism.[44]

Kohn's views, while still suggestive, were first written in the 1940s. The easy association of nationality and territoriality does not reflect the complexities presented by decolonization and the emergence of Third World countries. That "state-building" and "nation-building" were in a mutually reinforcing or symbiotic relationship in the history of certain Western countries does not mean that this is always the case. Cohabitation in the same territory has as often resulted in continued separation of groups as it has led to their amalgamation in a single nation. Resurgent ethnic nationalism in the Celtic "fringe" of Europe (e.g., in Scotland and Wales) should warn against hasty identification of nations with political units.

The belief, whether based on fact or fancy, that certain people share a common ethnic pedigree has been a potent unifying force with many nations. But here too, as with language and religion, *ethnicity* is neither necessary nor sufficient for common national identification. The American nation, the French nation, and others are composed of heterogeneous ethnic stock. Ethnic similarity, on the other hand, has not precluded the separate national identities of the Swedes and the Norwegians.

Common culture used as a criterion of nationhood has its own weaknesses. For one thing, the concept of culture is so broad and vague that attributing common culture to the members of a nation is a glorified way of saying they have things in common. But we know this already. Our demands for knowledge have to be much more specific: which artifacts of culture out of so many have been especially significant in generating, spreading, and reinforcing national sentiments. Myths, legends, and stories in both the written and oral traditions have been studied closely in this connection. Nonetheless, it has proven difficult to formulate a universal model of how the various aspects of culture contribute to the formation of nations.

Whatever the ultimate criteria and constituents of a nation, it is radically distinct from a state. This is why our talk of inter*national* politics, the United *Nations*, sovereign *nations* is misleading. There would be no

44. Hans Kohn, *The Idea of Nationalism* (New York: Macmillan, 1961), p. 15.

problem if all the states in the world were *nation-states* (i.e., states wherein the overwhelming majority considered themselves as part of one nation). However, the true nation-state situation is comparatively rare. A recent study by Walker Connor has concluded that out of 132 states analyzed: [45]

1. Only 12 (9.1%) can be described as nation-states.
2. Of these states 25 (18.9%) contain a nation or near-nation accounting for more than 90% of the population, but also contain an important minority.
3. Another 25 (18.9%) contain a nation or near-nation accounting for 75%– 89% of the population.
4. In 31 (23.5%) the largest ethnic element accounts for 50% to 74% of the population.
5. In 39 (29.5%) the largest nation or near-nation accounts for less than half of the population.

The main actors on the stage of world politics are thus nation-states, multinational states, and states without nations. Despite problems with minorities, both France and the United States qualify as nation-states. The Soviet Union, on the other hand, is a multinational state. While we often call that country "Russia" and its inhabitants "Russians," these terms are glaring mistakes. Russians, properly speaking, make up around half of the Soviet population. The rest comprises authentic nations such as the Lithuanians, Latvians, Estonians, Armenians, Georgians, and other groups. A state that as yet has not developed any nations is the former Congo, now known as Zaire.

Failure to recognize the rarity of true nation-states is not due merely to terminological confusions. Political aspirations and interests do play an important role because political elites in many Third World countries have in fact labeled their political activities "nation-building." If such is indeed their goal, we can use a modified version of the typology of different ethnic situations in the world first proposed by Clifford Geertz to grasp the enormous difficulties involved.[46]

Amalgamation of the groups depicted in these different situations into a single unified nation is a labor worthy of Hercules. The question that presents itself is the true meaning of the exertions and achievements

45. Walker Connor, "Nation-Building or Nation-Destroying," *World Politics* 24 (April 1972): 320.
46. Clifford Geertz, "The Integrative Revolution: Primordial Sentiments and Civic Politics in the New States," in *Old Societies and New States*, ed. Clifford Geertz (Glencoe, Ill.: Free Press, 1963).

TABLE 1.6.   A Typology of Ethnic Complexity in Contemporary States

1. **Dominance-dominated situation:** a politically and socially predominant group (usually also a numerical majority) confronts a single, troublesome minority—Greeks vs. Turks on Cyprus, Tamils vs. Sinhalese in Sri Lanka (Ceylon), English-speakers vs. French-speakers in Canada.
2. **Center-periphery situation:** a core ethnic group often concentrated in the geopolitical center of the country confronts several medium-sized, generally hostile minorities—Javanese vs. Balinese and Moluccans in Indonesia, Burmese vs. Karens and others in Burma, Castilians vs. Basques, Catalans in Spain.
3. **Bipolar situation:** two nearly balanced groups—Flemings and Walloons in Belgium, Chinese and Malays in former Malaysia.
4. **Descending scale situation:** several large groups shading off into a number of medium-sized ones—"ethnographic museums" such as India, Nigeria, and Kenya.
5. **Simple ethnic fragmentation situation:** a large number of variegated ethnic groups—Zaire.

of political centralization registered in many Third World countries. Is it really nation-building that is involved?

Walker Connor has suggested that rather than nation-building what we have is *state-building*. Ironically, this very process may actually result in *nation-destroying* in the sense that true nations become casualties in the struggle for political centralization. On the face of it, it seems much easier to establish a virtual monopoly of violence over a given territory (especially when the Americans, the Soviets, the Chinese, and others are willing to send lavish military aid and "technical advisers") than to overcome primordial ethnic feelings. It also seems easier to develop a rudimentary bureaucracy than to fashion a common identity among a plethora of ethnic, racial, cultural, regional, linguistic, and religious groups. In short, state-building seems easier than nation-building.

The relationship between states and nations in Western Europe has evolved through centuries. To think that the processes involved can be telescoped into years or decades, even in an age of rapid mass communications, is certainly naive. Faith in such possibilities explains the optical illusion whereby more or less successful state-building efforts in certain countries have been mistaken for successful nation-building. However, state-building success when it takes place at the expense of the ethnic nationalism of groups can be short-lived. Ethnic nationalism can be compared to a dormant volcano: when you least expect it, it can burst forth with shattering force. As Connor points out:

An individual (or an entire national group) can shed all of the overt cultural manifestations customarily attributed to his ethnic group and yet maintain his fundamental identity as a member of that nation. Cultural assimilation need not mean psychological assimilation.[47]

States are states and nations are nations and whether the twain shall meet in the nation-state is a matter of historical fact, not of a priori dogmatics.

Citizenship, Kinship, and Personalism

In this chapter we have established that the modern state is a distinctive form of polity differing markedly from earlier political structures. It is especially important to note the relevant differences between modern and nonmodern polities (especially regarding bureaucracy), as well as the survival of the earlier forms (tribalism, patrimonialism, and so on) as foreign bodies within modern or modernizing polities. This is helpful in understanding why experiments with modern constitutionalism and bureaucratic organization have resulted in political corruption and dictatorship in so many Third World countries.

The simple truth is that modern constitutionalism and bureaucracy presuppose a political culture in which citizenship prevails over kinship or personalism as a pattern of political association. Where kinship and personalism pose a strong challenge to citizenship (as in most Third World countries), the modern state and its bureaucratic apparatus cannot fully develop. These points require more analysis.

By "citizenship" we refer to an abstract form of political association in which the individuals in a community relate to each other (politically speaking) through common relationship to the overarching entity, the state. This phenomenon comes out most forcefully in the ancient Greek polis and the modern Western state. Kinship, we have seen, is a ubiquitous form of political association, but it predominates only in the tribal polity. The personalistic bond finds its epitome in feudal vassalage and serfdom.

However, a more moderate form of personalism is found in the patron-client relationship that many scholars see as a necessary stage between the decline of kinship and the rise of modern citizenship. The patron-client relationship involves an exchange between two individuals. According to Eric Wolf: "The two partners to the patron-client contract, however, no longer exchange equivalent goods and services. The offerings of the patron are more immediately tangible. He provides aid and

47. Connor, "Nation-Building," pp. 341–42.

protection against both the legal and illegal exactions of authority. The client, in turn, pays back in more intangible aspects." [48] The patron plays the role of the lord and the client that of the vassal, but in a looser, less mystical way than in true feudalism. The client owes his patron demonstrations of esteem, information on the machinations of others, and political support. When a powerful patron surrounds himself with many clients to form a clique, we can speak of a true and proper political machine. It should thus be evident that patron-client politics will be most prevalent in a patrimonial polity.

Thus, in a broad sense our brief analysis confirms Max Weber's view that the vicissitudes of bureaucracy and bureaucratization hold the key to understanding contemporary politics.[49] Much of the material in the next four chapters concerns how various sorts of constitutional and dictatorial regimes handle the problem of bureaucracy.

Another problem that will crop up throughout the book was also raised toward the end of this chapter: the relationship of nation and state. Our basic goal here is simply to emphasize that a nation is a group of people who identify with each other as a nation, while a state is a form of political organization. Even our brief discussion showed that nation-states were few and far between. And yet, this in no way lessens the zeal of a host of movements and regimes to achieve the goal of a nation-state. The problem of nationalism, therefore, will haunt us in later chapters.

STUDY QUESTIONS

1. Is it better to consider politics (a) as broadly concerned with power and authority in all human organizations or to view it more narrowly (b) as re-

48. Eric R. Wolf, "Kinship, Friendship, and Patron-Client Relations in Complex Societies," in *The Social Anthropology of Complex Societies* (London: Tavistock Publications, 1969), pp. 16–17. For a vast anthology on the subject of patron-client relationships, see Steffen W. Schmidt, James C. Scott, Carl Landé, and Laura Guasti, eds., *Friends, Followers, and Factions: A Reader in Political Clientelism* (Berkeley: University of California Press, 1977).

49. Some might challenge this conclusion on the grounds that it is the citizenship pattern which relates more to political participation and representative government. However, our position is close to J. Forward, who wrote that "it is effective bureaucracy which is the precondition for representative and stable government rather than *vice versa.*" "Toward an Empirical Framework for Ecological Studies in Comparative Public Administration," in *Readings in Comparative Public Administration,* ed. N. Raphaeli (Boston: Allyn & Bacon, 1967).

lating simply to the polity as the center of authoritative allocation of values in society?

2. What really distinguishes the modern state from previous or alternative forms of political organization?

3. How could political corruption short-circuit each of the main aspects of the Weberian model of modern bureaucracy?

4. In which ways would the ordinary citizen feel a different political impact according to whether he or she lived in a confederation, federation, or unitary state?

5. Distinguish the citizenship pattern of political association from the tribal-kinship and personalistic patterns.

6. What is a nation? What is a state? In the real political world, what are the main possible relationships between states and nations?

SUGGESTIONS FOR FURTHER READING

BALANDIER, GEORGES. *Political Anthropology*. New York: Vintage Books, 1972.

BELL, RODERICK; EDWARDS, D .V.; and WAGNER, R. H., eds. *Political Power*. New York: Free Press, 1969.

BENDIX, REINHARD, ed. *State and Society*. Boston: Little, Brown, 1968.

BLOCH, MARC. *Feudal Society*. 2 vols. Chicago: University of Chicago Press, 1966.

COHEN, RONALD, and MIDDLETON, JOHN, eds. *Comparative Political Systems*. Garden City, N.Y.: Natural History Press, 1967.

CONNOR, WALKER. "Nation-Building or Nation-Destroying." *World Politics* 24 (1972); 319–55.

EASTON, DAVID. *The Political System*. New York: Alfred A. Knopf, 1963.

ECKSTEIN, HARRY, and APTER, DAVID, eds. *Comparative Politics*. New York: Free Press, 1963.

EHRENBERG, VICTOR. *The Greek State*. New York: W. W. Norton, 1964.

HEIDENHEIMER, ARNOLD J., ed. *Political Corruption*. New York: Holt, Rinehart & Winston, 1970.

KOHN, HANS. *The Idea of Nationalism*. New York: Macmillan, 1961.

MACMAHON, A. W., ed. *Federalism: Mature and Emergent*. New York: Columbia University Press, 1955.

MACRIDIS, ROY C., and BROWN, BERNARD E., eds. *Comparative Politics: Notes and Readings*. 5th rev. ed. Homewood, Ill.: Dorsey Press, 1977.

MOSCA, GAETANO. *The Ruling Class*. New York: McGraw-Hill, 1939.

RIKER, WILLIAM H. *Federalism: Origin, Operation, Significance*. Boston: Little, Brown, 1964.

SCHMIDT, STEFFEN W.; SCOTT, JAMES C.; LANDÉ, CARL; and GUASTI, LAURA, eds. *Friends, Followers, and Factions: A Reader in Political Clientelism*. Berkeley: University of California Press, 1977.

SERVICE, ELMAN R. *Origins of the State and Civilization*. New York: W. W. Norton, 1975.

WEBER, MAX. *Economy and Society*. Edited by G. Roth. 3 vols. Totowa, N.J.: Bedminster Press, 1968.

WITTFOGEL, KARL. *Oriental Despotism*. New Haven: Yale University Press, 1957.

2

Constitutionalism and Parliamentarism

The concern of the next four chapters resembles the forms-of-government typologies of Plato (the ancient Greek philosopher of the fourth century B.C.) and his pupil Aristotle. While their frame of reference was chiefly the Greek polis, ours is mainly the modern state. Like theirs, our underlying contrast is dualistic. In fact, the distinction between constitutionalism and dictatorship elaborated in chapters 2 through 5 is similar to Plato's dichotomy of law-abiding and lawless governments.

In his dialogue *The Statesman*, Plato selects two main criteria with which to build his typology. The first is the number of rulers: one man, a few, or many. The second is whether or not government is respectful of law.[1] In using Plato's typology as a guide we will follow his second step only, disregarding the first step of subdividing governments according to the number of rulers (one, few, or many).

In rejecting this aspect of the classical teaching, we follow Gaetano Mosca. Mosca, whose views will concern us in later chapters, argued that

1. While Aristotle's distinction between the natural and corrupt forms of government is somewhat similar, let us recall that his emphasis was on whether or not the government pursues the interest of the whole community. To assume that this is the same problem as lawful versus lawless government or even constitutionalism versus dictatorship is to impose our own preferences upon a different culture.

TABLE 2.1.   Plato's Typology of Forms of Government

Who Rules	According to Law	Lawlessly
One	1. Kingship	4. Tyranny
Few	2. Aristocracy	5. Oligarchy
Many	3. Moderate democracy	6. Mob rule

both the rule of one man (monarchy) and the rule of the majority (democracy) are impossible of full realization. They represent trends and inclinations of government, rather than clear and distinct *forms* of government. Mosca's "political elitism" teaches that all regimes possess a relatively compact, more or less organized minority which dominates the disorganized majority. This dominant minority is called the "ruling" or "political" class. Our approach agrees with Mosca on the prevalence of elites, but stresses that institutional, cultural, and ideological factors (and most eminently, constitutionalism) profoundly influence the role of elites in different regimes.

In this context the job of the present chapter is twofold. First, we must get a clear idea of the nature of constitutional government. This involves not only distinguishing it from dictatorship, but also surveying some of the fine points of constitutional rule, such as written constitutions, separation of powers, constitutional dictatorship, and judicial review. Only thus will the somewhat abstract distinction of constitutionalism versus dictatorship begin to take on concreteness.

The second major task of this chapter is to examine parliamentarism as one mode of modern constitutional government. (The main alternative of presidentialism and some minor hybrids will be left for chapter 3.) A major concern is to contrast the classic or textbook model of parliamentarism with modern parliamentarism—the way things work generally nowadays. This involves finally a survey of the ways in which parliaments organize themselves and contribute to the political process.

CONSTITUTIONALISM

In the present context we employ "constitutionalism" to refer to a broad category of regimes (though in another context it might also refer to an ideology or even a political movement). A constitutional regime thus is one which has a "living" or operative constitution. The term "constitution" has an ancient, broad usage and a modern, narrow usage. According to the ancient Greeks a constitution (*politeia*) was simply any form of government or regime. All the six Platonic forms would thus be constitutions. The constitution was not merely the abstract skeletal structure of public offices and citizen rights. It included the "ethos" or spirit that animated the formal political institutions, what modern political science calls the "political culture." Each type of constitution required an appropriate set of public attitudes to make it work properly.

The modern, narrower idea of a constitution began its career by stipulating that a constitution must be a *written document.* Tom Paine once suggested that if you cannot fold it up and put it into your pocket, it was no constitution. There was the further implication that a constitution had to be adopted at a given point in time. While the ancient view stresses the *growth* of a constitution, the modern view sees its *enactment* as a conscious, rational, deliberate process. To this modern (liberal) viewpoint the conservative French political theorist Joseph de Maistre (1753–1821) advanced four objections: [2]

1. The fundamental principles of political constitutions exist prior to all written law.
2. Constitutional law is and can only be the development or sanction of a preexisting and unwritten law.
3. What is most essential, most inherently constitutional, and truly fundamental law is never written, and could not be, without endangering the State.
4. The weakness and fragility of a constitution are actually in direct proportion to the number of written constitutional articles.

Resolving the debate between the views represented by Paine and de Maistre runs into a major obstacle, namely, the British constitution. The British have no single document called "The British Constitution," yet their long reputation as a "free" people is closely associated with their veneration for, if not their obsession with, their constitution. In fact, a closer look at the British constitution might provide some ways out of the present dilemma.

In the first place the British constitution contains many written elements. Acts of Parliament such as the Reform Acts of 1832, 1867, and 1884, which extended the right to vote, are written statutes, as are "Orders-in-Council" issued by the Crown. But perhaps the most signifi-

2. Joseph de Maistre, *On God and Society* (Chicago: Henry Regnery, 1960), p. 14.

cant aspect of British constitutionalism lies in the *conventions*. These are long-established practices of the highest political significance, among which are included the appointment of the member of Parliament who enjoys majority support in the House of Commons as prime minister. Likewise his resignation (or the call for new elections) upon losing the support or "confidence" of that house is a matter of convention.

The major difference between conventions and statutes or laws is that only the latter are *justiciable* or capable of being decided by a court of justice. One can be tried and punished for violating a law, whereas the "punishment" for violating a convention is *political*. A British political leader who transgressed an important convention would arouse an uproar in the Parliament, the parties, and the general public.

With this in mind we can see that a constitution is a normative structure that guides government and whose gist may be embodied in a written document. The written core, however, is merely the broad framework of the operative constitution. The United States Constitution is a fully reliable guide to the structure of the American government only if we have in mind the many elaborations produced by the Supreme Court and other courts. Thus, the contrast between the British case and the American with its core document surrounded by interpretations and amplifications is considerably toned down.

A constitutional government is one in which governmental power is exercised and limited in certain legally prescribed and enforced ways. All governments (including dictatorships) encounter obstacles and limitations, political and otherwise, but a constitutional government has the additional set found in the constitution itself. We can roughly describe these limitations as *substantive* or *procedural*. Substantive limitations are prohibitions: they deny government the right to do certain things. For example, the United States Congress cannot establish an official religion nor can it levy a tax on exports. Procedural limitations mean that though the government can do something, it must be done according to a certain prescribed pattern or sequence. The government, so to speak, must touch all bases in the course of its legitimate action.

This double limitation of constitutional government involved a "price" sometimes obscured by the popularity of constitutionalism in Western countries. Inherent in all constitutional governments are both inaction and delay, though this aspect may be clearer to the ardent social reformer than to others. Inaction is merely the reverse side of the coin to substantive constitutional prohibitions. The government may be precluded from taking action in problem areas whose present condition (from somebody's standpoint) cries aloud for reform. Many early laws on child labor or minimum wages were struck down as beyond the scope of legitimate government activity. Procedural restraints on government also often take their toll in time and offer a golden opportunity for "vested interests" to slow the process of change down to a standstill. Many consider the cumbrous process of constitutional amendment as a hindrance to social change.

If a constitutional government did not automatically arouse considerable impatience and disappointment, it would not be constitutional. No doubt on some counts dictatorship is more "efficient" than constitutionalism. And in the broader context of state-building and nation-building, Carl J. Friedrich has raised doubts concerning "whether national unity can be achieved under a genuinely constitutional regime in which powers are divided and restrained and human rights effectively guaranteed." [3]

Friedrich's statement contains reference to the two major tasks of any constitution. The first such task is to prescribe some sort of division of labor among the political institutions of government. The American version of this problem is, of course, known as the "separation of powers" doctrine. Though the roots of this idea go back as far as political speculation itself, it was the version of the French political philosopher Montesquieu (1689–1755) that most influenced the founding fathers of the American Constitution. He articulated the tripartite division of powers into *legislative, executive,* and *judicial* as we understand these terms today. Furthermore, he defined political liberty in terms of the separation of these powers and political despotism in terms of their fusion. More broadly, political liberty would be maximized in a regime that satisfied two conditions: (1) three distinct institutions would basically exercise each of the three governmental powers; (2) the people filling the main offices in each of the three branches would be different.

Of course, neither Montesquieu nor the authors of *The Federalist Papers* imagined that separation would be or could be 100 percent complete. The executive had a role in legislation through the veto power, while the legislature could impeach both executive and judicial officials. Indeed, without some slight institutional overlap between the three basic "branches" of government, it is hard to imagine how one branch could ever exercise any real sort of check on the others. Three totally autonomous branches of government would be free to tyrannize, each

3. Carl J. Friedrich, *Constitutional Government and Democracy* (4th ed.; Waltham, Mass.: Ginn-Blaisdell, 1968), p. 166.

in its own bailiwick. This was as far from Montesquieu's wishes as the despotism of one man.[4]

Even with these qualifications, the separation of powers doctrine has evoked substantial criticism. Ironically, Montesquieu had based his theory on the British experience (1748), which perhaps then and certainly later did not exhibit the separation of powers in the way he described. The difficulties in his theory emerge because the chief functions of government nowhere maintain themselves in the three separate compartments.

Accordingly, contemporary political scientists such as Gabriel Almond have offered reformulations of the terminology of governmental action. Instead of legislative, executive, and judicial "powers" Almond prefers to talk of rule-making, rule-application, and rule-adjudication "functions." [5] This new terminology has three advantages. First, by speaking of "rules" we acknowledge that the term "law" may be misapplied in certain non-modern types of political system. Second, Almond's scheme reminds us that many important governmental decisions are politically binding but do not have the formal characteristics of law. Finally, it avoids the ethnocentric bias of some Americans that constitutional government has to have American-style separation of powers.

Almond's stress on functions shows us that much rule-making is done by administrative bodies technically within the executive, and that courts in the United States and elsewhere go rather beyond the existing legislation in setting up rigid policy guidelines and complex programs. Despite these and other departures from strict separation of powers, no government could be described as constitutional if it totally lacked some sort of division of labor between institutions. At the institutional level a certain measure of judicial independence, coupled with a representative assembly able to criticize the government, would meet the minimum requirements of constitutionalism.

The second major task of a constitution is to provide some description of the nature, rights, and duties of citizenship. The constitution spells out the political rights of voting and holding office, as well as the civil rights that provide for the basic freedoms of conscience, communication,

4. See on this whole problem M. J. C. Vile, *Constitutionalism and the Separation of Powers* (New York: Oxford University Press, 1969), chaps. 4 and 6.
5. In the present context "functions" are those types of activities necessary for a political system to run (i.e., to produce the "authoritative allocation of values" we mentioned in chapter 1). It is clear that the making, enforcing, and clarification of rules is essential to the overall functioning of political systems. Other functions will come up in later chapters.

and movement. Additionally, many constitutions adopted since World War II make reference to "social rights" concerning welfare, security, work, and so on. This last category of rights is often vague and can give rise to serious disputes and disappointments.

Constitutional Dictatorship

Though at first the term "constitutional dictatorship" seems to be glaringly self-contradictory, no other describes the political phenomenon involved with equal force and precision.[6] In fact, the term "dictatorship" itself did not originally evoke all the anticonstitutional connotations we see nowadays—quite the contrary. "Dictatorship" derives from the constitutional practice of the early and middle centuries of the Roman Republic. Etymologically the term "dictator" is related to the Latin verb *dicere* ("to speak or to say"). A dictator thus is one who speaks or says what shall be done. In times of peril to the Roman state one man, the dictator, was appointed with full powers to take all measures necessary to ward off the mortal danger posed by foreign war or civil strife.

The awesomeness of the Roman dictator's powers was limited in two key ways: (1) duration—six months maximum; and (2) scope—he could not permanently alter the constitutional structure of the Roman polity. Hopefully, the emergency would terminate before six months had passed, allowing the dictator to lay down his power and retire to private life. Moreover, afterward the ex-dictator was accountable for his conduct during his tenure. Thus the Roman dictatorship was not the permanent destruction of constitutional government (as with modern dictatorship) but was rather a kind of parenthesis in the course of normal constitutional practice.

Constitutional dictatorship along the lines of the Roman model is the way modern constitutional regimes confront the crises and emergencies of the present century. Four fundamental situations prompt constitutional regimes to resort to it: (1) foreign war, (2) internal rebellion, (3) economic depression, and (4) natural catastrophes. Thoughout history foreign wars have led to tightening controls over domestic life. However, the "total wars" of the present era, in contrast to the more limited belligerence of the past, call the very existence or independence of states

6. This section is largely based on Clinton Rossiter, *Constitutional Dictatorship* (New York: Harcourt, Brace & World, 1963).

into question. With the heightening of the stakes involved, it is no surprise that governmental efforts to preserve the state have reached the
unprecedented dimensions of the two world wars. One need only consult the war memoirs of Winston Churchill to see how the normal role
of the British Parliament was suspended. In certain areas Churchill's
powers were no less "dictatorial" than those of Hitler.

Containing and repressing rebellion is often a reason for resort to constitutional dictatorship. As it is also a frequent pretext for using constitutional dictatorship as a means to set up full-fledged dictatorship, we
must be able to distinguish real from trumped-up crises. Given the close
relationship between government and economy, the seriousness of modern economic crises such as the Great Depression of the 1930s has caused
governments to assume extraordinary powers of economic control. The
pivotal importance of the economy in modern industrial society means
that a threatened economic breakdown can be as disastrous as foreign
or internal war. Natural disasters such as floods, earthquakes, and
severe storms also have enormous disruptive potential, and modern
governments are likely to counter extraordinary devastation with extraordinary methods.

At the level of government, constitutional dictatorship means the fusion of powers in the executive. Both legislative and judicial bodies more
or less willingly give up their normal activities and either transfer them
to the executive or simply suspend their operation. When the executive
rules "by decree," for example, the parliamentary assembly either is disbanded or remains in session without conducting normal business.
Later on, the executive's decrees and action may have to be confirmed
by legislative action. Similarly, in situations of "martial law," normal
judicial procedures are superseded by arrest and trial according to military rules. The result of these altered circumstances is that the government has increased control over the lives and actions of citizens.

While fusion of powers and expanded governmental power are the
general traits of constitutional dictatorship, specific versions of it vary
enormously. One variable is the nature of the crisis itself. *Military rule*
with martial law is the usual response to internal war. Foreign war produces the formation of a *war government,* in which the chief executive
becomes not only active head of the military forces but also a sort of
"economic czar" directing economic production and planning. Civil
liberties are also considerably reduced. Economic depression generates
its own form of constitutional dictatorship, a *government of economic
concentration,* in which the executive intervenes far more deeply in the

economic life of the country. Finally, a great natural calamity generally produces martial rule, perhaps followed by a government of economic concentration.

Differences in constitutional and legal frameworks also cause variations in constitutional dictatorship. The contrast between the *common-law* and *code-law* approaches to law is relevant well beyond the present context. In the common-law framework, law is considered to have grown up over time immemorial. This is sometimes called "judge-made" law because the judge claims merely to have discovered and expressed legal precepts that have evolved through practice. In the common-law mentality, legal precedent is of decisive importance. Later decisions follow upon earlier ones so that the legal precept involved becomes firmly entrenched.

In the code-law framework, all law originates with some legislative body or executive council that has decree powers. All laws are statutes, which should be clearly spelled out in the books containing the "code" of laws. This cuts down the discretion of judges considerably since they could supposedly look up the explicit legal provisions that cover specific cases. Law does not grow or evolve through the practice of the community; it is enacted as statutes at specific moments by the "sovereign" or his agents.

In countries influenced by the British tradition of the common law, martial law and emergency measures are based upon legal precedent. Thus, there are explicit provisions for neither in the United States Constitution. This makes the situation of constitutional dictatorship highly anomalous from a constitutional point of view. The Supreme Court, however, has generally, but by no means always, been indulgent toward the federal executive.

In the code-law countries of continental Europe, there is often an "emergency clause" written into the constitution. This apparently clearer constitutional situation, however, has not led to more satisfactory results than the ambiguous practices of America. In fact, frequent invocation of Article 48 of the constitution of the German Republic in the early 1930s is considered by many a major political cause of the downfall of German constitutionalism and a prelude to the Nazi dictatorship. It should be pointed out, however, that the abuses connected with Article 48 were as much a symptom as a cause of the rapidly deteriorating economic and political situation of the day.

The justification of constitutional dictatorship lies in its being a temporary expedient to be followed as quickly as possible by a *return to con-*

stitutional normalcy. The executive should hand back rule-making power to the legislature; the courts should recover their autonomy and former jurisdiction; and citizens and groups should act as freely from political controls as in precrisis days.

Leaving aside cases where constitutional dictatorship was a disguised coup d'etat resulting in dictatorship, a full and unequivocal return to constitutional normalcy is never to be expected. This is so because the institutional balance has been bent and stretched out of shape for some time. Precedents have been created for the next bout of crisis and even normal government activities bear the impress of the recent past. Even the most resilient constitution and political system cannot return to earlier patterns, however desirable this may be. If constitutional dictatorship means in part a temporary fusion of powers, we are still left with the problem of how separation of powers can produce the checks and balances so prevalent in many theories of constitutionalism.

Judicial Review

The doctrine of checks and balances in constitutionalism requires that each "branch" of government has institutional "weapons" by which to counter the excesses of the other branches. Out of the reciprocal checks emerge the institutionalized limitations that characterize a truly constitutional regime. A mere separation-of-powers rule could be satisfied by *judicial independence,* meaning that judicial decisions are not unduly influenced by the executive or the legislature. But a checks-and-balances system requires in addition that the judiciary can apply the weapon of *judicial review* and overturn acts of the legislature or the executive on constitutional grounds. Thus, though checks and balances imply the presence of separation of powers, the reverse is not the case.

Modern judicial review finds its model in the experience of the American Supreme Court.[7] We must have a clear idea of that model to evaluate recent attempts to adopt the practice elsewhere. In America the Supreme Court and other courts have the capability to declare laws passed by legislative bodies (such as the Congress) and acts performed by execu-

---

7. A kind of judicial review, however, was exercised by courts in seventeenth-century France. See A. Lloyd Moote, *The Revolt of the Judges* (Princeton: Princeton University Press, 1971). Judicial review was not spelled out clearly in the American Constitution. Many scholars feel that it was read into the Constitution by Chief Justice John Marshall in *Marbury* v. *Madison* (1803).

tive officials (such as the president) "null and void" because they are repugnant to the Constitution. While the Supreme Court has so-called original jurisdiction in certain special cases (e.g., regarding ambassadors), it is with its *appellate jurisdiction* (i.e., with cases reaching the Supreme Court on appeals from lower courts) that we find those sometimes epoch-making cases in which legislation or executive action has been reversed.

Such appellate cases reach the Supreme Court on appeals from lower federal courts or state courts. This is so because the Supreme Court, officially speaking, can act only in the context of a given court case (i.e., during *litigation*). The reverse side of this situation is that the Supreme Court cannot issue *advisory opinions*. In other words, an executive official or member of Congress cannot ask the official opinion of the Supreme Court on the constitutionality of a bill or intended action before it is enacted or undertaken. Stated differently, this means that judicial *re*-view, but not judicial *pre*-view, is an attribute of the Supreme Court.[8]

Let us now examine how successful some recent European experiments with constitutional courts and councils have been in institutionalizing judicial review. Comparison between European and American high courts is hampered somewhat by the fact that the United States Supreme Court combines three different "highest court" functions into one organ, while in Europe these are separated into two or three distinct bodies. First, the Supreme Court is the "highest constitutional court" because through judicial review it interprets the current meaning of the United States Constitution. As one justice pithily put it, "The Constitution is what the Supreme Court says it is." Second, the Supreme Court is the "highest regular court" because there is no appeal beyond it in civil and criminal cases. It thus decides cases on points of law that involve no reinterpretation of basic constitutional principles. Third, the Supreme Court is the "highest administrative court" almost by default, since the American legal tradition does not distinguish administrative law so sharply from other law as do other legal traditions. Elsewhere special tribunals are set up to deal with disputes over administrative regulations and jurisdictions. Thus there is in other countries a special third track of litigation not found in the United States.

8. Two additional points need to be made here: (1) advisory opinions are allowed by some state constitutions; (2) it is doubtless true that individual Supreme Court justices advise presidents and other political leaders on certain issues, but they do so "off the record," so to speak.

These distinctions between court functions are partly observable in West Germany, where judicial review reminiscent of the American practice has grown in strength since the early 1950s.[9] The West German legal structure, however, follows a tripartite division of constitutional, civil-criminal, and administrative domains into distinct separate bodies. There is thus a Federal Supreme Court of about one hundred members (broken down into a number of panels), which is the highest regular court. However, there is no special highest administrative court. The highest constitutional court is called the Federal Constitutional Court, and its functions diverge in several ways from American-style judicial review. (1) With its *judicial review of legislation,* it can declare federal or land statutes unconstitutional, though its intervention (unlike that of the American Supreme Court) does not necessarily follow an appeals procedure. The federal or land authorities can ask for a direct ruling on a measure's constitutionality, as can lower courts or even private citizens. (2) It is *institutional arbiter* of federal-land relations and also resolves executive-legislative disputes, which the United States Supreme Court has generally tried to keep out of. (3) It is a sort of *citizen's protector* insofar as it hears individual complaints about loss of civil rights without previous litigation and without court costs to the plaintiff. (4) Somewhat in contrast to its role as citizen's protector, it can be called the *policeman of the constitution* in view of its powers to declare individuals and groups unconstitutional if these are deemed implacably hostile to the existing constitutional order.[10]

To advocates of judicial review it should be clear that the single-track American system is more conducive to strongly institutionalized judicial review than is the three-track European system. The American Supreme Court's supremacy in legal, constitutional, and administrative affairs gives it enormous prestige and leverage to sustain a claim to strong powers of judicial review. In the three-track European system, however, the final say in different types of cases may reside in three different highest courts. Such a division of labor results in a dispersal of prestige and political clout. With such weakened political resources, a European constitutional court must tread very carefully indeed.

Italy with its Constitutional Court has made some moves toward institutionalizing judicial review. But there too the tripartite structure

9. Arnold J. Heidenheimer, *The Governments of Germany* (3rd ed.; New York: Thomas Y. Crowell, 1971), pp. 232–39.
10. The Communist party was ruled unconstitutional in 1956 and the neo-Nazi Socialist Reich party was ruled so in 1952.

seems an obstacle to further development. The highest regular court is called the Court of Cassation,[11] and highest administrative jurisdiction is split between the Court of Accounts and the Council of State. The Constitutional Court itself is considerably less autonomous and influential than its German counterpart. Though it exercises judicial review and determines legislative-executive and national-regional disputes, it does not have the functions of citizen's protector or constitutional policeman. Access to it is also more restricted than in Germany. The French setup is similar to the Italian save that the Constitutional Court and the Council of State can give *nonbinding* advisory opinions to designated officials of the legislature and executive.

We can conclude provisionally that the tripartite legal structure of constitutional, regular, and administrative courts will retard the growth of judicial review. Another retarding influence is the strength in European political cultures of the idea of "parliamentary sovereignty." This means that the will of the people as expressed through its parliamentary representatives should override all obstacles. From this viewpoint judicial review might seem a curtailment of parliamentary and ultimately popular sovereignty.

PARLIAMENTARISM

Before we can discuss the basic forms of modern constitutional government, some basic distinctions must be firmly grasped. First, the role of *head of state* must be distinguished from that of the *head of government*. A head of state is the titular, ceremonial leader of a country, who symbolizes the sovereignty and majesty of the state. He ranks first in the ceremonial, honorific order and has a number of special tasks both in foreign and domestic matters. His official title can be king or queen, emperor or empress in a constitutional monarchy, or president in a presidential or parliamentary republic. Monarchs are heads of state in Sweden, Norway, Great Britain, Belgium, Denmark, the Netherlands, Spain, and elsewhere. Presidents have this job in the United States, France, West Germany, Italy, and other places.

While the head of state is the ceremonial chief, the head of government is the main active political leader of the country. He is called by

11. In French and Italian the word *cassation* refers to the ability to quash or overturn an earlier decision. Thus a Court of Cassation is simply a highest court of appeals, which has the ability to reverse the decisions of lower courts.

different names: prime minister, premier, chancellor, and (more officially) president of the council of ministers. He is the leading factor in policy-making and supervision of administration. The strength of this distinction of the two roles is illustrated in its presence even in outright dictatorships, which reject genuine constitutionalism. In Fascist Italy from 1922 to 1943 King Victor Emmanuel remained official head of state, while the dictator Benito Mussolini was head of government. In the contemporary Soviet Union the head of state is usually a political "lightweight" whose official title is chairman of the Presidium of the Supreme Soviet. The head of government is the chairman of the Council of Ministers. Ironically, the most powerful figure in Soviet politics is usually neither of these, but the secretary-general or head of the Communist party of the Soviet Union.

One of the many unique features of the American political system is that the president is both head of state and head of government. Furthermore, what Americans call "the Administration" is called "the Government" in parliamentary regimes. The Government does not include the head of state, but does include the prime minister, the members of the cabinet, and other "ministers" of less than cabinet rank.

The Classic Parliamentary Model

In order to gauge the real meaning and importance of these and related points, we must first survey the main facets of classic parliamentarism because contemporary parliamentary regimes depart significantly from the classic model. The closest historical approximations to the model are probably in nineteenth-century Great Britain, in nineteenth- and twentieth-century France (the Third French Republic from 1871 to 1940; the Fourth French Republic from 1946 to 1958), and to some extent in contemporary Italy. The essential features of classic parliamentarism are contained in table 2.2.

TABLE 2.2.   Main Features of the Classic Parliamentary Model

1. Government by assembly
2. The vote of confidence
3. The fusion of powers
4. The strong position of the individual member of parliament
5. The cabinet as a collegial body

---

1. *Government by assembly* suggests that the political center of gravity of classic parliamentarism lay in the elected national legislative assembly. Theories of representative and democratic government in the nineteenth century—the so-called Golden Age of Parliaments—taught that the legislature should be the dominant force in the political system because it was "closer" to the people than other government organs. Free elections would ensure that the legislative body would reflect the main contours of the "will of the people."

Accordingly, it was only right that the initiative for the main public policy decisions should be taken in the legislature. Executives and bureaucrats, who were suspect anyway because of the nineteenth-century liberal fear of concentrated power, were relegated to an essentially passive, instrumental role. Governments themselves were closely controlled, if not wholly dominated, by the legislative assembly.

Furthermore, since the "legal sovereignty" of the legislature was based ultimately upon the "political sovereignty" of the whole people, judicial review was unnecessary and even undemocratic. Why should a small appointive clique be able to frustrate the will of the people as expressed through their freely elected representatives? This mentality partly explains why the British, otherwise paragons of constitutionalism, have to this day not really incorporated judicial review into their system.[12]

2. *The vote of confidence* was the main instrument of legislative supremacy in classic parliamentarism. This means that a Government could remain in office only so long as it enjoyed the confidence (i.e., the majority support) of parliament. A Government was originally appointed by the head of state, who appointed the individual commanding majority support in parliament as the prime minister. The head of state usually confirmed the choices of the prime minister to fill all posts associated with the Government. In many cases, a newly formed Government had to expose itself to a test confidence vote to see if it really had a parliamentary majority behind it. Success in this vote was not automatic because of the lack of a majority party or the weakness of the pro-Government coalition.

Once in office a Government was under the perpetual threat of a vote of nonconfidence. It was not *any* chance defeat that absolutely re-

12. One might speculate that if some current proposals about federalizing Great Britain into England, Wales, and Scotland are realized, some sort of judicial review will have to emerge to adjudicate disputes between the federal government and the lower units.

quired the Government to resign. Rather, this occurred when a Government chose to (or was pressured to) gamble its existence on the successful passage of a particular bill. Defeat spelled resignation or in some cases new elections. While a vote of confidence was initiated or allowed by the Government itself, the members of parliament on their side could initiate a *vote of censure,* which, if successful, could bring down the Government.

Although the Government had no recourse against censure, it had one major weapon against the vote of nonconfidence. This was simply the threat or the reality of asking the head of state to dissolve parliament and call for new elections. The threat element operated to deter nonconfidence somewhat because of the understandable reluctance of politicians to run the risk (or face the expense) of fighting for their seats before it was absolutely necessary. More frequent use of the dissolution power in the Third (1871–1940) and Fourth (1946–58) French Republics would probably have cut down the number of government changeovers and "crises." [13]

3. *The fusion of powers* in classic parliamentarism does not violate our previous conclusion that some institutional division of labor is essential to constitutionalism. What fusion of powers means here is that most, if not all, members of the Government also had seats in one of the houses of parliament. In other words, in a fashion completely alien to the American system, the executive (the Government) emerged out of the legislative (parliament). In fact, governments sometimes included special members whose job was mainly to manage the Government's majority in parliament. In certain cases they had no specific departmental responsibilities and thus were called "ministers without portfolio." It was with this whole situation in mind that British political theorist Walter Bagehot in the last century described the British cabinet as a sort of "buckle" that joined the two major institutional aspects of modern government.

4. *The strong position of the individual member of parliament (M.P.)* is reflected in several important characteristics of classic parliamentarism. First of all, the individual lawmaker was much less under the control of party discipline and organization than is generally the case today. Parties were loose coalitions of like-minded people united more by

13. A "crisis" occurs in the parliamentary system when the old Government has resigned without a new one being formed. Very often, however, the old Government may remain in office in a "caretaker" capacity until its successor is named.

patronage and other interests than by profound ideological commitment. Parties and party leaders who tried to impose strict discipline upon their parliamentary contingents soon were faced with revolt or splintering. There were numerous members of parliament with no clear party affiliation. Without the weapon of strong party discipline to ensure a stable and docile majority, governments were left in an exposed position in relation to the legislature.

Another indicator of the importance of individuals was that "private members' legislation" bulked larger in the legislative timetable than government business. Only in Italy is this type of legislative individualism still preserved. Accordingly, earlier classic parliamentarism featured open and extensive debate, which often gave rise to oratorical contests of the highest quality. The reverse side of this expansive individual "freedom" is seen in the fact that procedures were more flexible, committees were less powerful, parties were less developed, and the Government was less powerful than we find in today's parliamentary regimes.

5. *The cabinet as a collegial body* means that in the classic parliamentary system cabinets were authentically collective decision-making groups. The prime minister was generally considered merely "the first among equals" rather than the unquestioned chief, although strong personalities such as the nineteenth-century British prime ministers Gladstone and Disraeli were no doubt powerful well beyond the average. Despite such exceptions as these, prime ministers were not so elevated above their colleagues as is the case today. Since policy areas were fewer and less esoteric and technical than nowadays, it was much easier to have meaningful general discussion involving the whole cabinet. This led to a more collective style of decision-making in cabinets than nowadays is the norm. As one scholar puts it regarding Great Britain, "While British government in the latter half of the nineteenth century can be described simply as Cabinet government, such a description would be misleading today. Now the country is governed by the Prime Minister who leads, co-ordinates and maintains a series of ministers all of whom are advised and backed by the Civil Service." [14]

In fact, the doctrine of "collective cabinet responsibility" expressed the collegial nature of cabinets perfectly. In this view every member of the cabinet was equally responsible for all the measures taken by it. The

14. John P. Mackintosh, *The British Cabinet* (Toronto: University of Toronto Press, 1962), p. 451.

individual minister either had to support his colleagues or resign. Particular mistakes of a given minister reflected upon the cabinet as a whole and might cause its wholesale resignation. In the language of the day a cabinet "rose and fell together."

The Transformation of Parliamentarism

While the classic parliamentary model provides some insight about contemporary parliamentary regimes, departures from it are perhaps more important and instructive. It is easy enough to describe the shift in general terms: *the executive—that is, the Government—has differentiated itself more and more from parliament and has forged a number of new weapons by which to stabilize itself and control policy and legislation.* Before surveying some specific institutional changes, we must look at several broad trends that help to account for the drastically altered balance of institutional power.

One trend is simply the growth of government. Government at all levels has increased steadily and comprehensively during the twentieth century. Greater management of the economy and multiplication of public services are the main areas of growth. The modern welfare state involves a vast expansion in the activities, expenditures, regulations, and personnel associated with government. Vast programs, projects, and policies, left before to the private sector or simply not done, require equally vast planning and administration. Much of this activity is long-term and requires constant supervision and readjustment. Technical expertise is at a premium.

These new or expanded government activities are inherently administrative and bureaucratic. Legislatures as now organized and staffed are not well suited to formulate and carry out elaborate programs. These tasks fall under the executive branch of government. The result is the enlargement of the executive's role and the curtailment of that of the parliamentary assembly. Thus, it is the growth of government per se that largely accounts for the changes included under the labels "the executive revolution" or the "decline of parliaments."

A second trend making for enhanced executive power and authority is the heightened importance of foreign policy in most countries. That the day-to-day conduct of foreign policy was inherently an executive function was admitted by the great British Liberal politician and advocate of legislative supremacy, John Locke (1632–1704). Large legislative bodies, while able to exercise a general supervision of foreign policy and to criticize specific aspects of it, are too unwieldy and inexpert to fashion the coherent overall foreign policy required by modern conditions. The head of government as chief diplomat receives whatever praise or blame results from foreign policy ventures.

A third trend in the exhaltation of the chief executive officer in modern constitutional regimes is the personalization of power. The important aspect here is the growth of the mass media, especially radio and television. Two considerations are uppermost in this situation. (1) The head of government can have almost automatic access to the radio and television to explain various problems or policies. (2) As political campaigning has resorted increasingly to the airwaves, the contest has become less and less one of parties and policies, and more and more one of the personality of the head of government and that of his main rivals. The style or "image" of one or a few men gains prominence in determining voter choice. This is easy to understand with the president of the United States, who is virtually elected by the people at large. But even in European countries, where a prospective prime minister himself runs only in a relatively small district, he is considered by many the real object of choice when they cast their vote for the party candidate (or party list) involved in their district. This duellike confrontation is especially clear in Great Britain, West Germany, and Austria.

These three broad trends and other factors have led to a transformation of classic parliamentarism into a significantly different type of regime. The extent of change, the rate of change, and the results of change vary considerably from country to country. One way to grasp the configuration of transformed parliamentarism would be to survey the institutional-political features of several countries. Here instead we will draw upon such information to illustrate the fate of the five features of classic parliamentarism discussed above.

1. *Government by assembly* is no longer an apt description of the institutional balance of transformed parliamentarism. Inroads on the "legal sovereignty" of parliaments have been many and far-reaching. One important change already mentioned is the growth of judicial review, which, however haltingly, has modified government by assembly in France, Italy, and West Germany. If a court can declare a law passed by parliament unconstitutional, then that parliament is no longer fully "sovereign" in the traditional sense.[15]

15. The concept of sovereignty has run into hard times in modern political science outside the study of international politics. The concept itself was developed by political philosophers such as Jean Bodin (1530–96) and

In France the scope of legislation is now somewhat limited, and some of parliament's former (Fourth Republic) powers have been transferred to the Government. The latter, for example, has the exclusive right to initiate money bills, and if parliament fails to act in seventy days the Government can simply decree them. The Government also dominates the legislative agenda and can predetermine how a bill will be handled regarding sections, amendments, and the like. Finally, the referendum, or direct appeal to the people, was used several times by President de Gaulle to gain support for policies over the head of parliament. Though France is an extreme case, similar institutional readjustments elsewhere reflect the change from the old to the new parliamentarism.

2. It is no surprise, then, that *the vote of confidence* is no longer what it used to be in most parliamentary regimes. In Great Britain we have to go back before World War I to find an instance where a Government that started out with a real majority behind it was forced out of office by a vote of nonconfidence. Cases of minority governments resigning after nonconfidence votes have not been registered since the early 1920s. Although this certainly means that the classic vote of nonconfidence is more of a reserve weapon than an active force, there are less direct ways in which parliamentary opinion affects the fate of governments. In fact, "erosion" of their majorities, if not nonconfidence votes, has contributed to the resignation of several recent British prime ministers. War defeats speeded the resignation of Neville Chamberlain in 1940; policy splits in his party led Clement Attlee to call for new elections in 1951; party troubles over the Suez fiasco of late 1956 led to Anthony Eden's resignation in 1957; and the Profumo sex-spy scandal forced Harold Macmillan's departure in 1963.

The Constitution of the Fifth French Republic (1958–   ) was written with the intent of making nonconfidence and censure votes much more difficult (and hence infrequent) than in the Fourth Republic. Rules such as those requiring absolute majorities instead of the majority

---

Thomas Hobbes (1588–1679) in order to raise the power of governments, especially monarchies, above other forces in the state. Their common underlying concern was to strengthen the state against divisive forces such as religious conflict, which had torn France and England apart. Sovereignty is supposed to refer to the highest legal power in the state, which is the source of law and which cannot be legally overruled. For a modern attempt to rehabilitate the idea of sovereignty, see W. J. Stankiewicz, ed., *In Defense of Sovereignty* (New York: Oxford University Press, 1969).

of those voting, a forty-eight-hour "cooling off" period, the limitation of the number of times a given deputy can sign a censure petition, and so on, were devised as hindrances to nonconfidence and censure. In fact, if a Government stakes its existence on a specific text or bill, and the National Assembly (lower house of parliament) fails to pass a censure vote, that text can become law without debate or vote. In West Germany the chief departure from the classic vote of confidence is the so-called constructive vote of nonconfidence. It requires that the Bundestag (lower house) in ousting the present chancellor must simultaneously nominate his successor.

3. A change from *the fusion of powers* to greater separation of powers has been less marked than other signs of the transformation of parliament. If this change should go too far, however, it would be doubtful whether the regime should still be called "parliamentary." This definitional problem comes out most clearly with France, where ministers hailing from parliament have to resign their seats within ninety days. Elsewhere the change has been more subtle and is mostly expressed in the fact that ministers tend to rate their role as executive assistants to the prime minister higher than their role as members of parliament.

4. *The strong position of the individual member of parliament* has suffered more than any other aspect of classic parliamentarism. The weakening stems from two causes. The first is the imposing development of party organization and discipline. Given the importance of parties in securing the election of members of parliament, it is understandable that the latter are reluctant to defy the directives of their party leadership. Resigning and joining another party may be going from the frying pan into the fire when it comes to discipline. Running as an independent is not usually crowned with success.

The second cause is the diminished role of the individual member in the work of parliament. When Government business occupies nine-tenths of the parliamentary agenda, as is the case in some countries, there simply is not time for much individual initiative. Debate procedures, in particular, have been modified so as to allow for speedy deliberation. The time for debate has been cut down drastically. Here, as in many realms of life, the individual has had to make way before the imperatives of organization.

5. *The cabinet in most countries today cannot be called a truly collegial body.* For reasons we have already discussed, there is a definite trend to exalt the prime minister above his cabinet colleagues. In Britain, for example, he has become so powerful and prestigious that some ob-

servers speak of a "quasi-presidential" system. Though the British cabinet retains more "collegiality" than its American counterpart, the prime minister nowadays tends to shape his policy in smaller groups through consultation with special advisers.

West German "chancellor democracy," perhaps reflecting the long and paternalistic leadership style of Konrad Adenauer in the formative years from 1949 to 1963, also falls short of the collegial approach. In other parliamentary countries similar trends exist but take a milder form.

Structural Aspects of Modern Parliaments

Structural aspects of modern parliaments include both the formal and informal organization of legislative bodies. "Formal organization" refers to the institutional features prescribed by the country's constitution and more importantly, by the standing orders of the parliament itself. "Informal organization" refers to the real power structure and operative rules of the body, which may differ considerably from the structure suggested by the formal organization. The questions of bicameralism, presiding officers, standing orders, and committee structure relate to formal organization, whereas party and group activity as well as the folkways of legislative bodies relate to informal organization.

Bicameralism

Most parliaments in constitutional regimes are bicameral: they have two houses or chambers, often distinguished as "upper" house and "lower" house. Notable exceptions are the *unicameral* legislatures in the northern European countries of Finland, Iceland, Denmark, Sweden, and Norway. Proponents of bicameralism argue that it makes for more deliberate, rational political decisions by avoiding the waves of passion that might overwhelm a single chamber. Critics maintain that in truly democratic polity one chamber directly reflecting the people's will is completely sufficient. They further emphasize the nondemocratic origins of many upper houses. Easy resolution of such issues is hampered by the wide diversity of the structures and functions of upper houses.

Before we survey some of the different political patterns of historic upper houses, a few features of lower houses should be stressed. Lower houses are intended to represent the people more directly and are thus nowadays chosen by some variant of the principle of "one man, one vote." In line with democratic theory, therefore, lower houses should have special powers denied to upper houses. In most parliamentary countries, for instance, it is only the lower house that can bring down a Government by a nonconfidence or a censure vote. Moreover, financial legislation (i.e., taxes and spending bills) is generally the prerogative of lower houses. Finally, as we will see, lower houses very often play a much more decisive role in the lawmaking process than do upper houses. With this in mind, the following discussion will develop our knowledge of both upper and lower houses.

HOUSES OF PEERS COMPOSED OF HEREDITARY NOBLEMEN.   The further we go back in history, the more the number and influence of houses of peers increases. Today the main example of such a body is the British House of Lords. Those eligible to sit number well over a thousand, but those actively participating are a small fraction of this. From a past position of legislative parity with the House of Commons, the contemporary House of Lords now takes a clearly subordinate political position. Legislation in 1911 and 1949 has reduced its legislative role to a "suspensive veto," whereby it can delay the enactment of legislation passed by the Commons by twelve months. Furthermore, the composition of the House of Lords has been altered somewhat by the addition of "life peers" appointed from the ranks of noted political, cultural, and economic leaders.[16]

FEDERAL UPPER HOUSES.   These reflect the two-tier governmental structure of any federal system. We can distinguish, however, between pure federalism and modified federalism. Under pure federalism each constituent unit (states, provinces, etc.) has an equal number of seats in the federal upper chamber regardless of population. Additionally, these chambers are more or less equal legislative partners with the lower, population-based chambers. The United States and Switzerland are the best examples of this pattern. Though the United States House of Representatives has special powers of initiating financial legislation, the Senate's special role in approving treaties and presidential appointees balances this advantage off somewhat.

Modified federalism is found in West Germany, where Land (state) membership in the upper house (Bundesrat) varies from three to five, according to population. Also the Bundesrat cannot be described as an equal partner to the popularly elected Bundestag. The Bundesrat is

16. The Italian Senate, while most of its members are elective, also has a few life appointees.

chosen by the various Land governments, and though its legislative competence is quite impressive in theory, in practice it is reduced to a suspensive veto overridable by the Bundestag.

SOCIOECONOMIC CHAMBERS.   Though these bodies evoke substantial discussion, their past association with Fascist and authoritarian regimes has limited recent experimentation with them. The idea behind them is known as "functional representation." Instead of trying to represent citizens living in specific geographical constituencies, functional representation claims to represent them through the activities or social functions in which they are involved. Thus, a socioeconomic chamber (or "functional parliament") would be made up of members stemming from labor, business, agricultural, professional, consumer, educational, and cultural organizations.

The Irish Seanad has some attributes of such chambers, but more significant is the French Economic and Social Council, which in the Fifth Republic has exercised some significant consultative-advisory, but not really lawmaking, powers. In fact, merger of the Economic and Social Council with the indirectly elected Senate was part of an abortive attempt by President de Gaulle in 1969 to transform the character of the French upper house.

INDIRECTLY ELECTED CHAMBERS.   These bodies illustrate a wide variety of electoral patterns. They are indirectly chosen or elected because they emerge from some group which itself was directly (or occasionally indirectly) elected by the people. Indirectly elected chambers are found in both federal and unitary states. As a federal example we can cite the selection of United States senators by the respective state legislatures before a constitutional amendment changed things in 1913. In the Netherlands, a unitary state, the members of the First (upper) Chamber are selected by provincial councils. The French Senate is chosen by departmental electoral colleges made up mostly of departmental and local officials.[17]

Despite the diverse origins, composition, and organization of upper chambers, several cautious generalizations can be offered about them. First, with notable exceptions, upper houses are rather less powerful than lower houses. In almost every case they are debarred from introducing financial-budgetary legislation. With nonfinancial legislation their role is generally restricted to a suspensive veto, which often

17. France is divided into some eighty-odd departments. These are administrative subdivisions of a unitary state and lack the real autonomy of federal units such as the American states or the German Länder.

amounts to a brief delay. In some cases they cannot themselves introduce any legislation and remain therefore mere "revising chambers."
The Dutch First Chamber has neither the power to initiate nor revise
legislation, but does retain an absolute right to reject legislation.

On the other hand, on certain points upper chambers are sometimes
stronger than lower ones. For example, though the Government is
usually given the right to dissolve lower houses, a number of upper
houses are not subject to dissolution. This is obviously true of the British
House of Lords through its essentially hereditary basis, but the German
Bundesrat and the French Senate are constitutionally exempted from
dissolution as well.

Another feature of some upper houses is their "staggered" election.
As examples, the United States Senate has elections for one-third of its
seats every two years; the Dutch First Chamber is replenished by one-
half every three years; the Swiss Council of States has variable terms
determined differently by each canton; the Swedish Upper Chamber
before its abolition in 1975 renewed one-eighth of its seats every year.
Implied in these and other examples is a further strength of upper
chambers: their terms of office run considerably longer than in the
lower houses.

The relatively small size of upper houses, plus their usually narrowed-
down lawmaking competence, provides them with a precious legislative resource—time. Upper houses can thus debate and investigate
issues in a manner quantitatively and qualitatively better than is possible in the more crowded and hectic conditions of a lower house.

Finally, upper houses because of their smaller size and past aristocratic associations are generally more prestigious than lower houses.
Related to this are the special advisory functions (to the Government)
that are reserved to upper houses. We have already mentioned the
United States Senate's "advise and consent" power regarding presidential appointees and treaties. In other countries, such as West Germany,
the Government has to consult with the upper house (Bundesrat) on
certain issues before introducing legislation to the lower house (Bundestag).

Procedures

Every large body that hopes to accomplish anything on an ongoing
basis requires rules and organization. Parliamentary bodies are no exception; in fact their accumulated practices, codified as in *Robert's Rules*

of Order, have become a norm and model for the formal proceedings of a vast number of social organizations and institutions. Three aspects of legislative procedure will be briefly treated here: the first is the standing orders of legislative bodies, the second involves the various officers selected to guide and aid the work of parliaments, and the third concerns legislative committees. These three aspects of formal parliamentary procedure have to be completed by reference to informal procedure and groups—namely, the "folkways" and parties of legislative assemblies.

STANDING ORDERS.   The standing orders of a parliamentary body are, in effect, its written constitution. They spell out the formal organization of the house and prescribe the general course of the legislative process. Reading the standing orders, for example, should tell us how a regime's legislative agenda is determined. (1) Does the Government do it? (2) Does the presiding officer do it? Or (3) does the whole house do it, on the advice of its leadership groups? [18] Also covered by standing orders are the number and composition of standing committees and their responsibilities, as well as (and equally important) the rules governing the time and terms of debate.

GUIDING OFFICERS.   With some idealization and oversimplification we can distinguish in formal parliamentary organization: (1) a presiding officer, (2) a bureau to help him, (3) a secretary-general, and (4) an administrative staff.[19] The *presiding officer* of a parliamentary organization has different powers and is differently selected in different countries. The officer's basic job, of course, is to guide debate and smooth out the path of the legislative process. He can have more or less powers in appointing members to various kinds of committees.

Perhaps the main difference among presiding officers is between political and neutral Speakers. The American Speaker of the House of Representatives is a good example of a political Speaker. Though he is expected to be fair, he is also the most powerful person in the majority party. In fact, should adverse elections transform the majority party into the minority, the former Speaker becomes minority leader. Thus, the American Speaker is not expected to be "above parties" and within limits is expected to further partisan causes. The Speaker of the British House

18. Interparliamentary Union, *Parliaments* (New York: Frederick A. Praeger, 1962), p. 155.
19. The publication of the Interparliamentary Union, *Parliaments*, suggested much of the structure of this section.

of Commons, on the other hand, though originally hailing from a major party, is expected to divest himself of all partisan connection after selection as Speaker. According to current British practice—there have been some deviations—the Speaker, who actually resigns from his party, is reelected to his post annually without contest. He is even unopposed in his district at the general election.

Many parliaments institute a special *bureau* to aid the presiding officer in his various tasks. Some of these bureaus are so strong that the actual leadership of the legislative body is collegial rather than individual. Others operate as an advisory board clearly subordinated to the presiding officer.

In West Germany this bureau in the Bundestag (lower house) is called the Council of Elders. The Council is composed of the Bundestag president and vice-president and twenty others according to party strength. As the views of the Council reflect a consensus of party leaders, they can reach procedural decisions that the Bundestag president will almost certainly abide by. Gerhard Loewenberg has summed up the work of the Council in the following terms:

> The Council is the place for negotiation and registration of interparty agreements on the agenda of the Bundestag, the order and the number of speakers in debate, and the designation of the committees to which bills are to be referred. It also informs the President of any disagreements among the parties on these points, prepares him for the procedural problems to be faced in the coming session, and prepares the Parliamentary whips for such procedural rulings as the President may intend to make.[20]

As with most complex organizations, a modern parliament involves a host of operations largely sheltered from the public eye. Supervision of the various administrative services supplied to the whole legislature or its individual members is entrusted to an official sometimes called the *secretary-general*. This official may also double as a parliamentarian, able to advise the presiding officer on ticklish points of parliamentary procedure.

Finally, there is an *administrative staff* that helps the legislature by research, drafting of legislation, aiding investigations, and the like. A common complaint points out the inadequacy of such legislative staffs in the face of the high-powered research capabilities of both government

20. Gerhard Loewenberg, *Parliament in the German Political System* (Ithaca: Cornell University Press, 1966), pp. 203–4.

bureaucracies and the better organized interest groups. This situation puts the legislature at a disadvantage because it has to rely on technical information of questionable objectivity.

On this score conditions vary enormously from country to country. While American congressmen and senators decry their weak resources, their situation is much better than that of British M.P.s. A good ratio is two to three staff members for each legislator; a bad ratio is one staff member or less for each legislator.

COMMITTEES.   All legislative bodies work by means of committees. Standing and select committees are the two most important types. *Standing committees* are permanent parts of formal organization and normally have a specific subject matter corresponding to executive departments. The most prevalent subject-matter committees include those for foreign affairs, defense matters, interior, appropriations, labor, economics, finance, and agriculture. British standing committees form a deviant case, reflecting the relatively weak position of parliamentary committees in that country. While three of the eight standing committees have specific topics (e.g., two for Scotland and one for Wales), the other five are known simply as A, B, C, D, and E. Each of these latter five committees consists of a core of permanent members, to which are added extra members with a special interest or expertise in the topic currently under examination.

Standing committees in the United States Congress probably represent the height in power; but French, Italian, and West German committees are also important. American committees are the graveyard of most bills, and they can operate surgically on other bills so that their final version bears little resemblance to the original. It is Italian standing committees, however, that provide the upper limiting case of the legislative power of committees. In a procedure known as *in sede deliberante* they have the direct capacity to make law. Though certain matters cannot constitutionally be handled in this manner and though there are ways to bring issues back to the whole chamber, most Italian laws have been passed *in sede deliberante*. Though purists decry this as a "usurpation" of Parliament's lawmaking prerogatives, a milder version of it exists in other parliaments. This is called the "vote without debate" or "unanimous consent" (in the United States). In such cases there is a general agreement not to oppose the reporting committee's findings and recommendations.

Select committees are formed ad hoc to investigate special topics not falling readily into the province of standing committees. Another reason for select committees is to lighten the burden of already busy standing committees. In Great Britain several select committees (e.g., those for Statutory Instruments, Estimates, and Public Accounts) are normally renewed each year so that they have become virtual standing committees. True select committees are disbanded after presenting their final report.

Frequent use and strong influence of select committees indicates a constitutional situation in which the legislature maintains considerable independence and initiative in relation to the Government. Select committees do not play much of a role in countries such as West Germany, Italy, Norway, and the Netherlands; although allowed in France, they are rarely used.

Joint committees are found in bicameral systems. Some of them are ad hoc, such as the House-Senate conference committees in the United States, which "iron out" the differences between the two houses' versions of the same bill. Other joint committees are permanent. In West Germany a Bundestag-Bundesrat mediation committee performs roughly the same job as American conference committees, except that its members do not change as in America.

FOLKWAYS.   In addition to the formal standing orders governing parliamentary procedures, most parliaments—especially the old established ones—have developed an informal set of rules and practices, or "folkways." If standing orders are analogous to a written constitution, the folkways of a legislative body can be compared to the "conventions" of the British constitution. Both folkways and conventions are unwritten and officially unenforceable. Though table 2.3 is derived from Donald Matthews' study of the United States Senate, similar folkways characterize other legislatures.[21]

An awareness of legislative folkways brings to mind a fundamental fact of legislative life: much parliamentary business is accomplished by procedures outside the range of both standing orders and formal organization. In Great Britain the expressions "through the usual channels" and "behind Speaker's Chair" relate to a host of informal mechanisms through which government and opposition come to terms about legislative matters. Cocktail parties, impromptu cloakroom conferences, the fabled "smoke-filled rooms"—all contribute in their way to the legislative process.

21. Donald Matthews, *U.S. Senators and Their World* (Chapel Hill: University of North Carolina Press, 1960).

TABLE 2.3. Matthews' Folkways of the American Senate

1. **Apprenticeship:** freshman senators are expected to deal with boring tasks without complaint, keep out of floor fights, show respect for "elder" senators, and more or less maintain a low profile.
2. **Legislative work:** a senator should willingly accomplish the dull pedestrian tasks involved in lawmaking and avoid "playing to the audience."
3. **Specialization:** a senator should choose a field of special interest and not be active on all issues.
4. **Courtesy:** a senator should be extremely courteous to other senators; this blunts disagreement and encourages compromise and cooperation. One manifestation of this is to never address another senator by name during debate; he is the Senior Senator from . . .
5. **Reciprocity:** senators are expected to reciprocate; this runs the gamut from the most blatant cases of "horse-trading" and "logrolling" to more subtle cases of cooperation and mutual aid.
6. **Institutional patriotism:** senators are expected to be demonstratively proud and attached to the Senate: this is seen in overt suspicion toward bureaucrats and the executive, as well as in a somewhat snobbish attitude toward the House of Representatives.

PARTIES. Ironically, the most salient structural feature of most parliaments, party organization, is rarely mentioned or is referred to only in the sketchiest terms in parliamentary standing orders. Nonetheless, all the other structural components of the parliamentary system feel the impact of parties. In two-party as well as multiparty systems, relationships between the parties dramatically affect the legislative process. Voting studies on parliaments generally reveal a rather impressive surface unity of the parties represented. Committees, which generally reflect the party strengths in the whole chamber, also operate under the strongest party influence. And, as we shall shortly see, the pattern of opposition and indeed all the "functions" of parliaments depend strongly on the behavior of parliamentary parties.

Thus, the internal party organization of parliamentary parties is of the highest importance in the legislative process. Most parties have a parliamentary leader who is aided by several *whips* (i.e., assistant leaders) in maintaining party discipline and unity. The strength of leadership, of course, varies according to the ideology, organization, and personal qualities involved. Though party leadership nowadays is generally quite strong and secure, occasional "revolts" do cause leadership or policy changes. Sometimes the security of a given leader is contingent upon his not making too many or too strict demands upon his followers.

In Great Britain there is even a leader of the House of Commons who helps the prime minister in "managing" the majority party.

The general meeting of all the members of a parliamentary party is known as the *party caucus*. Furthermore, there are usually a series of inner-party committees and study groups. Of special interest in this connection is the "1922 Committee" of the British Conservative party because it is formed by the party rank and file or "backbenchers" and acts as a sort of pressure group upon the party bigwigs, who sit on the front benches. This committee originated in 1922 as a backbench revolt that caused a decisive change in party policy and top leadership.

A final and most intriguing problem is the relationship between the parliamentary party and the external party organization. In the case of the old-fashioned *cadre party*, which originated as a faction within parliament and only later developed the rudiments of a true national organization, the parliamentary party is highly autonomous. Furthermore, its leaders generally dominate the external organization, such as it is. In the case of *mass parties*, which were often well organized *before* attaining significant representation in parliament, the situation is complicated by the possible competition of two distinct leadership groups: the group elected to parliament and the one prevalent in the external party organization. The same is true of modern *catchall parties*.[22]

The more extreme cases of parliamentary-external party relationships are easy enough to find. The Democrats and Republicans in the United States represent a pattern in which the national party organization is so weak that it is hardly worth the trouble of congressional party leaders to try to dominate it. The direct influence of the respective national committees upon legislative politics is, at best, marginal. In contrast, the two big British parties, Conservative and Labor, find their parliamentary leadership generally in control of the national party organization, and in this case there is something worth controlling. In fact, on several occasions the parliamentary leadership of the Labor party had to fight and fight hard to reverse policy stands taken by the Annual Conference of the whole party.

At the other extreme are parties like the French and Italian Communist parties, in which "democratic centralism" requires that the party members in parliament adhere strictly to the "party line" laid down by the external party hierarchy. This means that decisions on how to vote

22. See chapter 8 for more on these types of parties.

can be determined *outside* of parliament. A middle position between the Anglo-American and Communist patterns is seen in the parliamentary contingent of the Italian Christian Democratic party. Accordingly, two opposed tendencies in that party have been described: one which views "parliament as a place for the legislative ratification of decisions reached through party mechanisms, rather than as a place for the making of political decisions"; the other which is seen in "efforts of the parliamentary groups to maintain their own autonomy in relation to the party organs." [23]

A recent study has isolated several political factors influencing whether autonomy or subordination characterizes the relationship of a parliamentary party to its external organization.[24] Table 2.4 depicts the results.

TABLE 2.4. Factors Influencing the Autonomy/Subordination of Parliamentary Parties toward External Party Organs

---

1. **Level of ideology:** ideological parties, since they hope to implement a highly specific program, tend to tighten controls over their parliamentary contingents.
2. **Level of institutionalization of parliament:** in newer political systems legislative bodies may lack firm roots and widespread prestige and legitimacy, thus allowing strong national parties to be the decisive political force.
3. **Control over nomination of candidates:** if the national party organization exercises great control over the selection of candidates, it has a strong disciplinary weapon against members of parliament. On the other hand, if local groups dominate the nomination process, the elected M.P. can more readily defy the external party organization.
4. **Presence of the parliamentary leadership on the national directing boards of parties:** if the parliamentary leadership and external leadership of a party constitute an "interlocking directorate," a distinct pressure from the external party cannot be felt. To prevent this situation, some parties have limited the numbers of M.P.s that can serve on the national directing boards.

Functions of Modern Parliaments

Our survey of the structural aspects of modern parliaments has given us a kind of static anatomy of how parliaments look. We must now turn to what parliaments do, their physiology so to speak. The major functions of parliaments in the politics and governance of modern constitutional

23. Giorgio Galli and Alfonso Prandi, *Patterns of Political Participation in Italy* (New Haven: Yale University Press, 1970), pp. 260–61.
24. Malcolm E. Jewell, "Linkages between Legislative Parties and External Parties," in *Legislatures in Comparative Perspective*, ed. Allan Kornberg (New York: David McKay, 1973), pp. 203–34.

regimes include (1) formation and dissolution of governments, (2) legislation, (3) oversight of administration, (4) power of the purse, (5) forum for political education, and (6) institutionalization of opposition.

Formation and Dissolution of Governments

We have touched upon this problem several times already. Here we need only repeat that the old idea that sees a Government as merely "a committee of the parliament" nowadays misrepresents the actual balance between executive and legislative bodies. Nevertheless, in most constitutional regimes that same Government *is* elected by the parliament and is somehow "responsible" to it. While in most cases the vote of confidence has lost much of its former sting, it is still of some importance, and in Italy it is of great importance. Members of the Government in many regimes still retain parliamentary seats, and even where they have to resign those seats by law, they may well return to them at a future date. In other words, it may well be that Government policy does not originate in parliament, but Government personnel largely still does.

Legislation

Modern constitutions generally give legislatures a virtual monopoly in lawmaking. Unfortunately, this conclusion skirts the perplexing problem of *what counts as law* in the bureaucratic setting of the modern welfare state. There is a little, but not much, help in the classic distinction between *laws*, which are general in scope, and *decrees*, which concern specific or private matters. (The constitution of the Fifth French Republic maintains this distinction by assigning lawmaking to Parliament and decree powers to the Government.) The complexities and ambiguities of contemporary law can be seen in table 2.5, a classification of the types of laws passed by the Italian Parliament.

The vagueness surrounding the meaning of law has given rise to two opposite practical problems: *overlegislation* and *underlegislation*. The first problem has troubled constitutional experts in Italy. It emerges because of two factors: (1) the Italian Parliament has proven extremely jealous of its lawmaking prerogatives; (2) Italian M.P.s are much freer to introduce bills than their counterparts elsewhere. The overlegislation means that laws are made on matters that could be left to government decree or simple administrative action. The net results are badly

TABLE 2.5.   Types of Laws Passed by the Italian Parliament

1. Laws of general interest
2. Laws of sectional interest and limited importance
3. Budgetary laws
4. Laws authorizing or providing for budgetary variations
5. Laws confirming decrees that make demands on the reserve fund
6. Laws of ratification
7. Laws converting decree-laws into full laws
8. Laws delegating powers to administration

drawn-up legislation and time wasted on picayune issues without getting to important problems.[25]

The problem of underlegislation may be even more serious to friends of constitutional government. It refers to what is called "delegated legislation" in the United States, "statutory instruments" in Great Britain, and "executive orders" in West Germany. By this sort of procedure parliament passes legislation only in the broadest outlines and authorizes the Government or the bureaucracy to "fill in the details." The resulting provisions and regulations often have the force of law. Thus the real "meat" of delegated legislation is determined, not by elected representatives, but by appointed bureaucrats.

Since so many programs passed by legislatures originate in the executive bureaucracy anyway, the problem of delegated legislation seems to betoken wholesale legislative abdication. Those who deplore the "decline of parliaments" seem to find grist for their mill when they can point out that acts classifiable as delegated legislation far outnumber parliamentary laws in most constitutional regimes. Before rushing to any conclusions, we should look at some other functions of parliaments to see whether the "rubber stamp" label slapped on modern parliaments is truly justified.

Oversight of Administration

One of the traditional duties of parliaments is the oversight or supervision of the administrative-bureaucratic apparatus. Such a task also provides the opportunity for legislators to redress grievances of their

25. The Italians have been very slow, for example, in implementing basic provisions of their constitution, which require legislative action for their full implementation. Both these ideas and the basis for table 2.5 are found in S. Somogyi et al., *Il Parlamento Italiano 1946–1963* (Naples: Edizioni Scientifiche Italiane, 1963).

constituents and to pressure bureaucrats into special dispensations and favors. While the parliament's lawmaking powers are its ultimate weapon in the oversight of administration, three other techniques have been developed. These are (1) interpellations and questions, (2) investigation and inquiry, and (3) the power of the purse.

Interpellations, though often designed to embarrass the Government, can throw a searchlight on administrative abuses and shortcomings, and can lead in the end to corrective action. Interpellations were involved in a number of Government resignations in the French Fourth Republic (1946–58). Interpellation is the right to interrupt parliamentary proceedings in order to quiz a Government minister about any problem within the purview of his ministry. At the end of the minister's explanation, a vote is taken on whether to accept or reject the account. Since this is considered tantamount to affirming or withdrawing confidence in the Government, adverse votes in the case of the French Fourth Republic produced a grand total of eight resignations. Though interpellations are often double-edged, one edge can expose administrative malpractices.

Questions proper are best understood in the context of the British House of Commons because there the practice is so firmly institutionalized that several hours per week are set aside for them—the question hour. There are written and oral questions, as well as written and oral answers to them. Questions that are merely informational tend to be asked and answered in written form. Questions serve other purposes, however. Often the M.P. wishes to inform a minister of some difficulty within his jurisdiction. Oral questions may be asked after the member has failed to receive satisfaction in previous efforts to set the problem straight. Like the interpellation (though without the subsequent vote), the question, with its opportunity to embarrass the Government, has become an important opposition technique. But the question has a broader value than this. A leading authority on the British constitution has summed up the question's oversight function: "It compels the departments to be circumspect in all their actions: it prevents those petty injustices which are so commonly associated with bureaucracies. It compels the administration to pay attention to the individual grievance." [26]

The oversight effectiveness of parliamentary powers of investigation and inquiry is largely a function of the strength of committees. Thus, standing and select committees in the British House of Commons do not

26. Ivor Jennings, *Parliament* (2nd ed.; New York: Cambridge University Press, 1957).

possess strong investigatory capabilities as such. On the other hand, investigations of American congressional committees have achieved the highest political importance, as evidenced by the heights of controversy surrounding many of them. A favorite comparison of those being investigated and their supporters has been with the Spanish Inquisition. While executive officials generally appear before committees by "invitation," committees can subpoena witnesses and information; a particularly recalcitrant witness can be cited and tried for contempt of Congress. Both standing and select committees can be used for investigatory purposes, with the main concern of such investigations either information gathering for future legislation or the "watchdog" function of checking on administration.

Though similar concerns animate committees everywhere, we must recall that parliamentarism assumes a majority in support of the Government. Since the majority in a parliamentary house has the power to influence, if not dominate, the activities of committees, the ardor of committees to expose administrative abuses may be considerably dampened. This reservation loses some of its force if the pro-Government majority is a coalition made up of parties differing among themselves.

The Power of the Purse

The power of the purse has become an axiom of modern constitutionalism: it provides that the representative assembly has the final say on matters of taxation and expenditure. In theory, the power of the purse should endow legislatures, especially lower houses, with the means to control nearly every aspect of policy and administration. Since nearly all government agencies consume large and growing budgets, the ability of a parliament to cut down or stop these funds is a standing threat to bureaucrats. Two points indicate the importance parliaments attach to their financial powers. One is that finance committees are often the most powerful and prestigious of all. Another is that consideration of the Government's budget proposals often takes the lion's share of parliamentary business.

The theoretical omnipotence of parliaments in financial matters is not always translatable into practice. Alfred Grosser has found three reasons for this.[27] In the first place, the hypercomplexity of modern

27. Alfred Grosser, "The Evolution of European Parliaments," in *A New Europe?*, ed. Stephan Graubard (Boston: Houghton Mifflin, 1964), p. 230.

budgets is simply beyond the comprehension of most legislators. Second, since budgets normally run for a year, there is not enough time to give thorough consideration even to the main lines of expenditure, let alone to probe into details. Once approved, the basic elements of the budget are never subjected to real scrutiny. Third, the pressure of interest groups or constituents causes legislators to focus on special points and thus to ignore the broader features of the budget. All of this means that the real budget fight takes place before the proposals are submitted for legislative approval.

Forum for Political Education

Although some of the traditional lawmaking and oversight functions of parliaments may have been weakened somewhat,[28] constitutionalists take some consolation in the educational role of parliaments. In this view the broad span of parliamentary activities serves along with the press and formal education to raise public sophistication and knowledge. While broadcasting of regular parliamentary sessions is rare, reporting of some of their highlights is not. Many important ideas do filter down to various groups in the population. In fact, a frequent argument in favor of retaining the British House of Lords is that its nonelective basis and its restricted legislative capacity allows it to debate certain important issues more thoroughly than in the hard-pressed Commons and thus serve to educate the public.

Even more important, especially from the American viewpoint, are investigations conducted by standing and select congressional committees. Committee hearings lend themselves more to television than do parliamentary debates. They have moments of high drama and low farce capable of holding the attention of normally apathetic members of the mass public. While other countries have lagged behind the United States in exploiting the educational value of the parliamentary investigation, some change seems inevitable.

28. Students of comparative politics as well as specialists on America should ponder seriously Alfred Grosser's conclusion that "if one defines as 'parliamentary' no longer a political system where the administration is responsible to the legislature, but a system where the parliament as an institution exercises an important influence on political decisions . . . the European governments are clearly less 'parliamentary' than the government of the United States." Ibid., p. 242.

The Institutionalization of Opposition

Opposition is endemic to political systems. The nature of opposition reflects the type of state and government involved. In the present context our concern is limited to oppositions as they emerge and act in modern parliaments. Largely basing our analysis on the work of Robert Dahl, we can depict the major types of opposition found in parliaments as shown in table 2.6.[29]

TABLE 2.6. Types of Opposition in Parliaments

---

1. **Opposition to the socioeconomic order:** the opposition wishes to replace the economic system and the system of stratification in toto. While revolutionary violence might seem the natural strategy and outlet for such sentiments, there are often reasons for using parliament to further the cause of the movement (e.g., propaganda, immunity from prosecution).
2. **Opposition to the political order:** the opposition wishes to replace the existing setup of political institutions. Though this standpoint can and does produce a revolutionary posture, it can lead just as well to staying within the system in order to change the system.
3. **Opposition to Government policies:** the main outlines of both the socioeconomic and political systems are accepted, but major policies are opposed for reasons of principle, prudence, and interest.
4. **Opposition to the Government "team":** the main focus of opposition is on personnel. The Outs want to take the place of the Ins. The power and the perquisites of office are main stakes of opposition, though invariably some minor policy differences figure in.

CLASSICAL OPPOSITION. The mere existence of parties and groups corresponding to these four types of opposition is testimony to institutionalization of opposition. In the not too distant past parliamentary opposition was generally considered at best intransigent obstructionism and at worst outright treason. Institutionalization of opposition thus means that the function of criticizing the Government and its actions is accepted as a normal and useful aspect of modern government.

Such institutionalization suggests further that parliamentary organization and procedures should take pains to avoid crushing opposition

29. See Robert Dahl, "Patterns of Opposition," in *Political Oppositions in Western Democracies,* ed. Robert Dahl (New Haven: Yale University Press, 1966).

under the political weight of a pro-Government majority. Following such guidelines, we can confidently conclude that opposition is most highly institutionalized in Great Britain. There the parliamentary opposition —more precisely the largest party opposed to the Government—is called Her Majesty's Loyal Opposition. Its leader, probably a past or future prime minister, is even paid a special salary. Despite the streamlining of modern parliamentary procedure, every effort is made to ensure the opposition time to vent its views.

Thus the parliamentary agenda is arranged by the Government in consultation with the opposition leaders. Furthermore, the chairmanship of the Select Committee of Public Accounts, an important watchdog committee on government spending, goes to a member of the opposition.

These and other aspects of the relationship of government to opposition in Great Britain have prompted political scientists such as Otto Kirchheimer take it as a model for what they call "classical opposition." [30] The conditions of classic parliamentarism and the two-party system make for a "duellike" quality of the government-opposition confrontation. It is expected that the opposition will oppose, criticize, and vote against nearly all government bills. However, some of the hostility in this pattern is muted because the opposition leadership is an alternate or "shadow" government. It should be obvious that such a system can emerge only if opposition is predominantly of types 3 and 4 in our chart (see table 2.6).

OPPOSITION OF PRINCIPLE.   Kirchheimer distinguished a second major type of opposition, which he called the "opposition of principle." Here the opposition opposes on behalf of an ideology that rejects certain aspects of the existing order. One type (corresponding to type 1 in table 2.6) can be seen in the stance of many Socialist parties before World War I. Opposition of this type is both *expressive* and *instrumental*. Expressive opposition gives vent to moral and emotional repugnance against the status quo. Instrumental opposition tries to weaken the existing regime and gain converts.

A subtype (corresponding to type 2 in table 2.6) is convinced of the defective political organization of the state and attacks the "politicians," the "bureaucrats," or the "system." This sort of opposition usually falls on the right of the political spectrum. The mildest sort of opposition of

30. Otto Kirchheimer, "The Waning of Oppositions in Parliamentary Regimes," in *Comparative Political Parties,* ed. A. J. Milnor (New York: Thomas Y. Crowell, 1969).

principle attacks Government policies without necessarily rejecting the political or socioeconomic order. It could easily develop into opposition in the classical style.

The more extreme types of opposition of principle, on the other hand, follow a strategy of obstructionism and propaganda in parliament. They let no opportunity pass to hinder and delay the legislative process in order to embarrass the Government. The rules of parliament are bent to this purpose and the "folkways" are totally ignored. Debate becomes a forum for propaganda. These antisystem oppositions make the most of the "filibustering" potential of the assembly, and their rhetoric commonly has little to do with the subject under consideration. Sometimes extremists of the right and the left, who can hardly refrain from mutual violence in the streets, engage themselves in a kind of "unholy alliance" to maximize their respective obstructionism and propaganda.

FACTIONAL OPPOSITION.   Andrew Milnor and Mark Franklin have identified a third form of opposition, "factional opposition," in which "elected representatives will often be the most central actors, but within the legislature there will be a continual shifting of alliances and forces" in response to the changing pattern of political issues.[31] This ever-changing pattern of opposition is oriented toward type 3 in table 2.6. The United States Congress, in which the voting patterns of representatives and senators are highly personalized, presents the best example of factional opposition. The kind of logrolling, alliances, and vote-trading characteristic of Congress would be difficult in a different system where party discipline was strong and the government-opposition duel overwhelmed all other considerations.

CARTELIZED OPPOSITION. This pattern of parliamentary opposition emerges when the Government coalition, usually composed of two large parties, has a near monopoly of seats. The excluded groups, amounting to less than 10 percent of the seats, are too anemic to conduct a full-scale opposition. Though the distinction is sometimes tenuous, the cartelized situation should not be confused with the "Governments of national concentration" found during wartime and other grave emergencies.

The true cartelized situation means that opposition takes place *within* the parties of the Government coalition. This has practical consequences. First, the more blatantly contrasting views of the coalition partners are

31. Andrew J. Milnor and Mark N. Franklin, "Patterns of Opposition Behavior in Modern Legislatures," in *Legislatures in Comparative Perspective*, ed. Allan Kornberg (New York: David McKay, 1973), p. 425.

thrashed out and compromised before full governmental responsibility is assumed. Sometimes the compromise agreement is formalized in a published or secret written "pact of association." At other times, the "gentlemen's agreement" approach is preferred. A second consequence is that the parties in the cartel may "agree to disagree," allowing for differences to be expressed as divisive issues materialize. This means that a kind of opposition function is permanently operating, though critics charge that this sort of institutionalization of opposition perverts its essential purpose.

The longest and firmest experiment with cartelized opposition is in postwar Austria. There the Austrian People's party and the Austrian Socialist party have shared power through three decades. Two aspects of the Austrian pattern merit special emphasis. One is the *proportional rule,* which is a "system of two-party patronage exercised in proportion to the most recent election results" with respect to "government corporations only." [32] (Positions are parceled out among devotees of the two parties in the rough ratio of the election percentages.) The other is *jurisdictional opposition,* which involves "opposition to those aspects of the regime governed by the other partner, and vice versa." [33] (This takes the idea of agreeing to disagree to its most logical extreme.) A second cartelized system was tried in West Germany with the so-called Great Coalition of Christian Democrats and Social Democrats between 1966 and 1969. There it was felt that the small Free Democratic party was not an adequate force to provide the strong yet constructive opposition characteristic of genuine parliamentarism. After 1969 the Germans reverted to the pattern of having one of the two large parties in opposition. This time, however, it was the turn of the Christian Democrats, who were turned out of government responsibilities for the first time in two decades.

In this chapter we have developed our concept of constitutionalism as a type of regime that operates according to legally enforceable limits on the substance and procedure of government policy. This backdrop will carry over into the next chapter, where we examine presidentialism as the main constitutionalist alternative to classic or modern parliamentarism. Moreover, the notion of constitutionalism provides a contrasting frame of reference for our treatment of modern dictatorship in chapters 4 and 5.

32. Frederick C. Engelmann, "Austria," in Dahl, *Political Oppositions,* p. 264.
33. Ibid., p. 270.

STUDY QUESTIONS

1. What are the main causes and effects of the decline of parliaments?

2. How does the idea of the separation of powers relate to the overall notion of constitutional government?

3. What are the main obstacles in the way of developing a strong system of judicial review in European countries?

4. Contrast classic with modern parliamentarism on the issues of government by assembly and cabinet government.

5. Distinguish the role of the various types of committees in the lawmaking process.

6. How do the different types of opposition use their representation in parliaments to advance their political goals?

7. What are some of the main structural and functional differences between upper houses and lower houses in bicameral parliaments?

8. How can parliaments still "check," if not "balance," governments in the modern parliamentary system?

SUGGESTIONS FOR FURTHER READING

BARKER, ERNEST. *Principles of Social and Political Theory*. Oxford: Oxford University Press, 1967.

BIRCH, A. H. *Representative and Responsible Government*. Toronto: University of Toronto Press, 1969.

BLONDEL, J. *Comparative Legislatures*. Englewood Cliffs, N.J.: Prentice-Hall, 1973.

DAHL, ROBERT, ed. *Political Oppositions in Western Democracies*. New Haven: Yale University Press, 1966.

FRIEDRICH, CARL J. *Constitutional Government and Democracy*. 4th ed. Waltham, Mass.: Ginn-Blaisdell, 1968.

INTERPARLIAMENTARY UNION. *Parliaments*. New York: Praeger Publishers, 1962.

JENNINGS, IVOR. *Cabinet Government*. 3rd ed. Cambridge: Cambridge University Press, 1959.

———. *Parliament*. 2nd ed. Cambridge: Cambridge University Press, 1957.

KORNBERG, ALLAN, ed. *Legislatures in Comparative Perspective*. New York: David McKay, 1973.

LOEWENBERG, GERHARD. *Parliament in the German System.* Ithaca: Cornell University Press, 1966.

McILWAIN, CHARLES H. *Constitutionalism: Ancient and Modern.* Ithaca: Cornell University Press, 1961.

MACKINTOSH, JOHN P. *The British Cabinet.* Toronto: University of Toronto Press, 1962.

ROSSITER, CLINTON. *Constitutional Dictatorship.* New York: Harcourt, Brace & World, 1963.

VILE, M. J. C. *Constitutionalism and the Separation of Powers.* Oxford: Clarendon Press, 1969.

WHEARE, K. C. *Legislatures.* 2nd. ed. London: Oxford University Press, 1967.

————. *Modern Constitutions.* London: Oxford University Press, 1966.

WILLIAMS, PHILIP M. *The French Parliament: Politics in the Fifth Republic.* New York: Praeger Publishers, 1968.

WILSON, WOODROW. *Congressional Government.* New York: Meridian Books, 1969.

3

Presidentialism and the Administrative State

In this chapter we continue our discussion of modern constitutional regimes. In classic and transformed parliamentarism, the Government emerges and functions as a committee of the legislative body (at least according to constitutional theory). In presidential and quasi-presidential regimes (such as Fifth Republic France), the executive is more strictly separated from the legislature. Moreover, presidentialism in the narrow sense means that the president is not only ceremonial head of state but also the active head of government.

Our approach will be to take American presidentialism as a model for understanding since it has in fact played a model role for modern constitution writers, especially in Latin American countries. Then we will compare American presidentialism briefly to French and Chilean (to 1973) presidentialism to see the extreme variations possible on this theme. After this, we will briefly survey the "plural" or "collegial" executive of Switzerland because it is in many respects an interesting hybrid alternative of presidentialism and parliamentarism.

The chapter will close with a brief analysis of some of the problems of administrative decision-making and policy formation, since the "administrative state" or the massive growth of bureaucracy is the obverse side of the coin of the "decline of parliaments." While this material is included in a chapter on presidentialism for the sake of convenience, it is clear that the same problems relate to parliamentary regimes and in some cases to outright dictatorships.

PRESIDENTIALISM

The American Model

Choosing the American presidency as a model for the second major type of constitutional regime does not simply reflect its greater familiarity to readers. This model has been emulated in Latin America, where varieties of presidentialism are more common than in Europe or Asia. Fidelity to the model is, of course, another question.

To understand the importance and the unique features of the American presidency we should separate the presidency as a *cluster of roles* from the president as *leader and decision-maker*. The first refers to the various functions that the United States Constitution, public law in general, and the "constituencies" of the president attribute to the presidency regardless of the incumbent. In theory, these roles make the presidency appear to be an "imperial presidency" or near-dictatorship. In practice, the vagaries of presidential power and decision-making tell a rather different story.

Table 3.1 sums up the role cluster generally assigned to the institution of the presidency. Examination of each separate role is our first task. Then we can look at the president as an individual trying to cope with a hypercomplex leadership situation.

TABLE 3.1.   The Presidency as Cluster of Roles

---

1. Chief executive
2. Chief legislator
3. Commander-in-chief
4. Chief diplomat
5. Manager of prosperity
6. Party chieftain

THE PRESIDENT AS CHIEF EXECUTIVE.   The American president is both head of state and head of government. At present the latter role is our main concern, for in theory the president is the apex of the vast bureau-cratic pyramid called the "executive branch." Were we to take the orga-nizational chart literally, his command position would be the envy of Frederick the Great or Louis the XIV. But effectual presidential power is a very far cry from a general leading a superbly disciplined army. Many of the president's orders and directives are never realized in the way he wants, if they are realized at all. A recent student of the presidency tells us why this is so:

> Departmental personnel at bureau or division levels often believe that they know best how to run their own programs. Some cabinet positions are weak; some departments are even celebrated for their deviance from White House goals. Field personnel feel themselves closer to the problems and to local people. . . . Career professionals . . . do not believe that a president's generalist lieutenants possess the expertise they often, in fact, do. Special interest groups constantly press for separate agencies or departments to represent their areas of concern.[1]

THE PRESIDENT AS CHIEF LEGISLATOR.   The role reflects the growth of executive programs and policies since the New Deal. Though the Constitution prohibits the president or any executive official from per-sonally introducing bills in Congress, this is a rather minor disability. First of all, the State of the Union address and other messages to Con-gress inform legislators of his thinking. Second, members of the presi-dent's party and sometimes of the opposition can always be found to do the actual sponsoring of presidential legislation.

The chief-legislator role has certainly had its ups and downs, how-ever. The first year of the Roosevelt Administration (1933–34) and that of the Johnson Administration (1964–65) show the president getting strong congressional approval for ambitious social programs. On the other hand, when presidents have faced hostile congressional majorities (Truman from 1947 to 1949; Nixon after Watergate), the box score of presidential legislative successes plunges appreciably. But even the aver-age situation between these two extremes shows that the chief-legislator role of the president is a rather problematic one. Having stressed the strength of the American Congress in chapter 2, we can well appreciate Louis Koenig's conclusion that "in no other major nation is the program of the head of government more subject to rebuff in the legislature, to delay and crippling amendment, and to absolute, uncompromising rejec-

---

1. Thomas E. Cronin, *The State of the Presidency* (Boston: Little, Brown, 1975), p. 19.

tion. The President runs an obstacle course on Capitol Hill that other heads of government would find strange and even incredible." [2]

As a counterweight to congressional power to reject or emasculate legislation, the president has the direct veto. Also, in the last ten days of a legislative session he can simply fail to sign a bill and thereby "pocket veto" it. In addition to Congress's ability to override vetoes by two-thirds majorities in both houses, one other major feature of the presidential veto should be emphasized. That is, the president has a "blanket" rather than an "item" veto. He must veto the entire bill and cannot select certain parts (items) for exclusion. This allows Congress to tack on various amendments (called "riders") to bills whose core provisions are desirable or tolerable to the president. The president may thus find himself in the dilemma of either accepting the bill with its objectionable amendments or vetoing the whole thing including the desired core.

THE PRESIDENT AS COMMANDER-IN-CHIEF.   Since World War II the president's constitutional powers as commander-in-chief of the armed forces have been broadly interpreted, allowing him to intervene militarily in conflicts supposedly involving vital American interests. American actions ranging from the "quick hits" in Lebanon in 1958 and the Dominican Republic in 1965 to the protracted engagements in Korea and Vietnam were not accompanied by formal congressional declarations of war. Accordingly, many have questioned the constitutionality of such broad interpretations of the commander-in-chief role. Congress itself, in the War Powers Act of 1973, has attempted to circumscribe the president's ability to deploy American forces.

THE PRESIDENT AS CHIEF DIPLOMAT.   By styling the president as chief diplomat, we acknowledge that he both has the lion's share in the formation of foreign policy and conducts personally a good share of the negotiations involved—as with "summit diplomacy." Presidents Wilson, Franklin Roosevelt, and Kennedy best deserve the chief-diplomat label, because their respective secretaries of state were relegated to backstage in the formation of policy and the conduct of diplomacy. Strong secretaries such as Dean Acheson or Henry Kissinger have a much greater say in foreign policy and command some of the limelight generally reserved to the president.

Here too the prerogatives of Congress, if and when it chooses to ap-

2. Louis W. Koenig, *The Chief Executive* (New York: Harcourt Brace Jovanovich, 1975), p. 151.

ply them, can modify the president's foreign policy role considerably. Treaties have to be ratified by the Senate, though "executive agreements" have partially sidestepped this constitutional proviso. Moreover, in foreign as well as defense and domestic policy Congress has the money power. It can cut the ground from under foreign policy moves by withholding required funding. Furthermore, it can attach "riders" to various bills that can modify or subvert a president's current foreign policy initiatives.

THE PRESIDENT AS MANAGER OF PROSPERITY. This role, which lacks a direct sanction in the Constitution, has developed mainly since the New Deal. As Thomas Cronin puts it:

> The American people increasingly judge their president on whether he can cope aggressively with recession and inflation, whether he can offer effective economic game plans . . . and whether he can use the nation's budget as an instrument for insuring a healthy and growing economy.[3]

As if to confirm this conclusion, President Gerald Ford in his successful campaign to win the Republican nomination for the presidency in 1976 used the apparently improved economic picture as his chief claim to Republican support. Congress has given various recent presidents broad powers to intervene decisively in the American economy. The president is empowered to act both directly and indirectly in *fiscal* (spending/taxation) and *monetary* (currency/interest) policy.

THE PRESIDENT AS PARTY CHIEFTAIN. This is probably the least important of the president's roles. He is considered the titular leader of his party, but he is never formally elected to any such position. The luster of his position is tarnished a bit because on the national level neither major party has much organizational coherence or discipline. It was President Eisenhower who echoed the widespread feeling that there were as many Democratic and Republican parties as there were states. While congressional Democrats and Republicans do feel some pull of duty and pressure to support presidents from their party, nearly all presidents have complained about abandonment by party stalwarts on key occasions.

CONSTITUENCIES. A president is impelled to fulfill the role expectations of his office by constitutional and legal duty, as well as by the pressures and "anticipated reactions" of his various constituencies.[4] The president is entrusted by the Constitution to see to it "that the laws be

3. Cronin, *Presidency*, p. 15.
4. Carl J. Friedrich speaks of a "law of anticipated reactions" to refer to situations in which actors take the possible reactions of others into account when shaping their course of action.

faithfully executed." Though the Supreme Court has been somewhat more tolerant of presidential actions than of laws passed by Congress, presidents have seen the Court frustrate their designs in nearly all of their six roles. They have been held as exceeding their authority as commander-in-chief; their legislative programs have been derailed, as in the case of Franklin Roosevelt and the early New Deal; their power to remove officials has been curtailed; and some of their economic moves have been ruled unconstitutional.

The "constituencies" that push the president to act are not geographical, but rather are groups and individuals who look to the president for leadership in specific policy areas. One student of the presidency has singled out five major constituencies desirous of presidential attention and action.[5]

Figure 3.1. The President's Constituencies

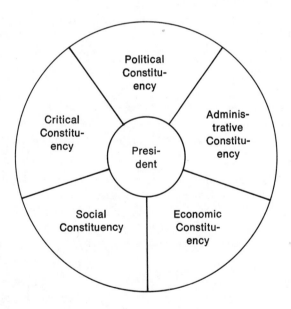

1. The political constituency includes the electorate at large, the two major parties, occasional third parties, Congress, governors and mayors, and foreign countries. Needless to say, demands and expecta-

5. Koenig, *Executive*, pp. 96–98.

tions of action stemming from such a wide array of sources will produce many discordant notes, to say nothing of occasional cacophony. The president desires support, benevolent neutrality, or at least a toning down of criticism from nearly all these political formations and thus must deliver some of the goods some of the time.

2. The administrative constituency of the vast and sprawling federal bureaucracy expects presidential conduct ranging from keeping his hands off their bailiwick to marshaling vast resources in campaigns against purported social evils. This constituency wants leadership but feels one can get too much of a good thing.

3. The economic constituency takes shape in the large organized pressure groups catering to business, labor, and agricultural segments of the economy. Trade unions such as the AFL–CIO, the Teamsters, and the auto workers; business groups such as U.S. Steel or General Motors, or trade associations such as the National Association of Manufacturers (recently merged with National Chamber of Commerce); farmers' organizations such as the National Farmers' Union, the National Farm Bureau Federation, and the Grange—all want something from the president.

4. The social constituency is made up of unorganized or poorly organized groups: minority groups, age groups, women, the handicapped or disabled. Because of their voting strength or the president's own values, he feels he must do "something" for group X.

5. The critical constituency embraces the various news media, the clergy, and the intellectuals. All these groups have claimed and have convinced others that they are a virtual conscience of the nation. Both as an important reference group for the president and as opinion-makers for the rest of society the media people, the clergy, and the intelligentsia figure prominently in the president's thoughts.

PRESIDENTIAL CHARACTER.   The precise use a president makes of the powers and prerogatives of his office depends largely on his character. The conventional wisdom about the American presidency speaks of "strong" and "weak" presidents. Theodore Roosevelt, Woodrow Wilson, Franklin D. Roosevelt, John F. Kennedy, and Lyndon Johnson were strong presidents, while William Howard Taft, Warren G. Harding, Calvin Coolidge, Herbert Hoover, and Dwight Eisenhower were weak—so the story goes. Unfortunately, such assessments betray a high correlation between the designation "strong" and the promotion of "liberal" or "progressive" policies. Likewise, weakness and conservative or standpat policies seem indissolubly linked. If the strong-weak dichotomy is tainted

by ideology, it nevertheless suggests some real differences among twentieth-century presidents.

Accordingly, James D. Barber has proposed a slightly more complex
way of assessing presidential performance that avoids narrow partisanship. Overall performance according to Barber is the resultant of three
basic *personality variables*. The first of these is *style*, which involves the
"president's habitual way of performing his three political roles: rhetoric, personal relations, and homework." [6] Rhetoric is the president's
mode of public and semipublic address—the phraseology and emphasis
in his speech. Perhaps surprisingly, recent presidents such as Eisenhower, Johnson, and Ford have lacked great oratorical gifts. On the other
hand Woodrow Wilson, Franklin D. Roosevelt, and John F. Kennedy were
accomplished public speakers. One wonders, given the premium placed
on oratory in parliamentary systems such as Great Britain, whether an
Eisenhower or a Ford could have risen to chief of government in a parliamentary system. Personal relations reflect the president's orientation to
others. Is he gregarious and open or is he withdrawn—the proverbial
loner? Presidential homework refers to the mass of technical detail that
a compulsive president might feel himself obliged to master. Does he
take pride in technical virtuosity, as did John Kennedy, or does he avoid
it like the plague, as did Dwight Eisenhower?

Worldview, the second of Barber's variables, refers to the president's
"primary, politically relevant beliefs, particularly his conception of social
causation, human nature, and the cultural-moral conflicts of his time." [7]
Though a president might be caught off guard if asked to itemize his
views on these topics, his worldview can be reconstructed from speeches,
written pieces, interviews, and more or less offhand remarks. Most
presidents evidently do not simply deduce a program from their fundamental worldview, but their attitudes toward policy choices are certainly
influenced by it.

Style and worldview are complemented by *character*, which Barber
defines as "the way the president orients himself towards life—not for
the moment, but enduringly. Character is the person's stance as he confronts experience." [8] As Barber sees it, character, worldview, and style
can be separated only for purposes of analysis because in the specific case

6. James D. Barber, *The Presidential Character* (Englewood Cliffs, N.J.:
   Prentice-Hall, 1972), p. 7.
7. Ibid., p. 8.
8. Ibid., p. 8.

they form "an integrated pattern." Barber's preoccupation is with character because this variable can show itself early on in the career of a future president. Not only can we *explain* successes and failures of past presidents in terms of character, we can also make predictions about future or would-be presidents through it, especially with respect to their reactions to highly stressful situations.

The personality variables of character, style, and worldview do not tell the whole story, however. To these we must add the *situational variables*, which include the power situation and the climate of expectations.[9] These two variables make up the political and social environment of constraints and opportunities within which the president must operate. Certain environments allow, while others impede, salient aspects of presidential character from manifesting themselves. Environmental triggering mechanisms are of special importance regarding "active-negative" presidents, for example.

Barber's typology of presidential character runs along two dimensions. The first regards activity-passivity and measures the type and extent of the president's involvement in his job. How long is his workday? Are his vacations always "working" vacations? Does he seek new areas to explore and act in? Does he refuse to delegate tasks that might seem better left to subordinates? The active president seems almost compulsive in his devotion to the work ethic. The passive president avoids new ventures and minimizes commitment to current ones. In extreme cases, lethargy, even laziness, seem to be involved.

Both activity and passivity can stem from various character sources. Chief of these is the president's positive or negative orientation toward his job, the second dimension of the character typology. Positive orientation means that he is enjoying the job. Inner needs of self-esteem (or perhaps some of Pareto's residues—see discussion in chapter 1) are gratified through the power and pageantry of the presidency. It is hard to escape the feeling that presidents like Franklin Roosevelt, Harry Truman, and John Kennedy were having fun during the less crisis-prone periods of their incumbencies. A negatively oriented president feels himself out of his element: the things he *has* to do are bothersome and even demeaning to him. Especially unsettling are the various conflicts and personal relationships flooding upon any president. He may be working more "and enjoying it less" as his term of office proceeds.

9. Ibid., pp. 8–9.

By combining the two dimensions Barber has produced a four-member typology, as shown in table 3.2.

TABLE 3.2.   Barber's Typology of Presidential Character

	Type	Examples
1.	Active-positive	Franklin Roosevelt, Harry Truman, John F. Kennedy
2.	Active-negative	Woodrow Wilson, Herbert Hoover, Lyndon Johnson, Richard Nixon
3.	Passive-positive	William Howard Taft, Warren G. Harding
4.	Passive-negative	Calvin Coolidge, Dwight Eisenhower

The active-positive president comes closest to meeting the ideal of admirers of a "strong" presidency. Personality and situation variables combine to produce an active, interventionist president. Because of his positive outlook the president feels a meshing between what he has to do and what he wants and likes to do. Following Barber we can depict the most salient traits of active-positive presidents, as shown in table 3.3.

TABLE 3.3.   Main Traits of Active-Positive Presidents

1. **Conviction of capacity:** these presidents have a sense of confidence, stopping short of infallibility, that they are qualified for the job.
2. **Investment without immersion:** they have the interest and capacity to learn but keep a sense of proportion about things. Humor sometimes at their own expense shows that their concern has not become a morbid obsession.
3. **Futuristic orientation:** they retain a pragmatic, open-ended perspective toward future actions and policies.
4. **Flexibility:** they can alter their style to meet different circumstances; they are not the prisoners of a set approach.
5. **Communication of excitement:** those around these presidents catch their infectious mood of confidence, joy, and excitement. They catalyze others to operate at peak levels.

The active-negative president suffers from a contradiction between "relatively intense effort and relatively low emotional reward for that effort." [10] Unlike the active-positive president, the active-negative type, as outlined in table 3.4, does not enjoy his commitment but follows through from an overdeveloped sense of duty. Barber's active-negative

10. Ibid., p. 12.

TABLE 3.4. Main Traits of Active-Negative Presidents

1. **Self-concern:** these presidents are obsessively concerned with the growth or decline of their power and with their virtue.
2. **Perfectionism:** they make extravagant demands upon themselves. They tend to view themselves and events in an all-or-nothing framework. They are at the heights or the depths with no in between.
3. **Denial of self-gratification:** these presidents seem to have the puritan's fear that there is something wrong with enjoyment; they think that virtue lies in hard work and extreme exertion.
4. **Control of aggression:** they strive to control aggressive impulses directed against real or imagined tormenters.
5. **Oscillation between fighting and quitting:** they shift from "standing up" against their enemies and throwing in the towel.
6. **A dangerous world:** they find the world threatening; people's, especially critics', motives are suspect. They are prone to see conspiracies of implacable enemies in league against them.

---

president is reminiscent of the heroes of classic Greek tragedy: though possessed of many admirable qualities they harbor a "fatal flaw"—a weakness that eventually casts them down from the heights.

Some major issue or conflict eventually emerges that ends in disaster for the active-negative president. He becomes rigid, incapable of changing his course or meeting critics halfway. Opponents now appear as personal enemies, just waiting for a pretext to destroy him. To give in now seems a sign of weakness; to compromise, immoral. The obvious examples are Woodrow Wilson's handling of United States' entry into the League of Nations, Herbert Hoover's reluctance to take measures against the depression, Lyndon Johnson's Vietnam policy, and Richard Nixon's Watergate cover-up.[11]

The passive-positive president, represented by William Howard Taft and Warren G. Harding, enjoys being president but feels rather overwhelmed about it all. Though he exerts little leadership, circum-

---

11. Before the outbreak of the Watergate affair, Barber wrote of President Nixon: "So far his crises have been bounded dramas, each apparently curtained with the end of the last act. The danger is that crisis will be transformed into tragedy—that Nixon will go from a dramatic experiment to a moral commitment, a commitment to follow his private star, to fly off in the face of overwhelming odds. That type of reaction is to be expected when and if Nixon is confronted with a severe threat to his power and sense of virtue" (ibid., p. 441). No better scenario of Nixon and Watergate could have been written after these events occurred.

stances will decide whether his incumbency will end disastrously, as with Harding, or show genuine though modest accomplishment, as with Taft. As Barber concludes, such presidents "are, in many ways, nice guys who finished first, only to discover that not everyone is a nice guy." [12]

The passive-negative president, represented by Calvin Coolidge and Dwight Eisenhower, is clearly annoyed by many of the responsibilities of the presidency. Rarely taking the initiative, Barber accordingly calls him a "responder." He is more concerned with restoring the prestige of the office than with extending presidential leadership. In his incumbency Congress reasserts itself and the cabinet or presidential aides move into the evident vacuum of power.

Although Barber's typology was designed with United States presidents in mind, it seems eminently applicable to top political leadership in all constitutional regimes. British prime ministers, Italian premiers, French presidents of the Fifth Republic, German chancellors, some Latin American chief executives, and so on would be appropriate candidates for Barber's pigeonholes. At least they would fit them as well as modern American presidents. Taking only the most famous examples, we could probably make a good case for ranking Winston Churchill active-positive and Charles de Gaulle active-negative. It seems only a matter of time before the Barber schema is applied to non-American heads of government of the past and present. We can conclude at any rate that full understanding of presidentialism requires a bifocal approach: one focus on the institutional-legal apparatus of the office, the other on the personality and character of the incumbents.

CONSTRAINTS AND SOURCES OF PRESIDENTIAL DECISION-MAKING.   We have surveyed the role expectations of the office of the United States presidency and made the important linkup with the personality-character variable. We understand better why different men exercise power so differently. We also see the president's constituencies bringing pressure on him to act (i.e., to use his power). However, it is equally important to appreciate how presidents encounter definite limits to their power-wielding and decision-making capabilities. In the first place, we share Richard Neustadt's well-known conclusion that the president's power to *command* may be unexpectedly limited, forcing him rather to *persuade* people to do as he wishes.[13] But persuasion may in turn in-

12. Ibid., p. 174.
13. Richard Neustadt, *Presidential Power* (New York: John Wiley, 1963).

volve bargaining in the technical sense of an exchange of valued items between two or more parties. To gain support or compliance the president may have to give something in return.

There are other constraints besides the need to persuade and bargain on the scope of presidential power and decision. There are the objective constraints which in a general way form limits to all sorts of institutional decision-makers. Ted Sorensen, who was a top Kennedy aide and nearly President Carter's first CIA director, has enumerated five "outer limits" of presidential decision, as shown in table 3.5.[14]

TABLE 3.5. Sorensen's Outer Limits of Presidential Decision

1. **Limits of permissibility:** these include law (constitutional, statutory, and even international); reactions of foreign powers; checks from the president's constituencies.
2. **Limits of available resources:** despite the enormous resource base of the federal government, the amount of time, money, and manpower at the president's disposal is limited.
3. **Limits of available time:** time constricts decision-making (a) by not allowing sufficient examination of alternatives and (b) by providing deadlines that undercut problem analysis.
4. **Limits of previous commitments:** these are many and various; given the stress on continuity of foreign policy since World War II, an incumbent president inherits a wealth of alliances and other commitments that he views as a burden. Programs already started have to be completed, and statements by the president himself, his aides, or party leaders may come back to haunt him.
5. **Limits of available information:** information shortfalls are both quantitative and qualitative. In the first case there simply is not enough information to ground a solid decision; in the second the information is false or distorted.

PATTERNS OF PRESIDENTIAL ADVICE AND ASSISTANCE.   At first glance the president's cabinet seems well situated to advise and assist the president in formulating policies and making decisions. In contrast to the large cabinets in parliamentary countries, it includes only twelve heads of departments—the departments in order of seniority are State; Treasury; Defense; Interior; Justice; Agriculture; Commerce; Labor; Health, Education, and Welfare; Housing and Urban Development; Transportation; and Energy. Certain other officials such as the ambassador to the United Nations are endowed with cabinet rank, if not with regular membership. In short, the cabinet does not exceed manageable committee proportions.

Despite its inclusion of the heads of main executive departments, the

14. Theodore C. Sorensen, *Decision-Making in the White House* (New York: Columbia University Press, 1963), pp. 22–42.

cabinet as a body has not contributed much to presidential decision-making in recent years. Richard Fenno attributes this in part to the cabinet's low institutionalization.[15] In other words, there has not developed a firmly established set of roles and functions for the cabinet as a whole. The Constitution mentions department heads reporting to the president, but not a definite collective body or cabinet. Thus the president has enormous leeway on how to utilize his cabinet. Utilization has historically ranged from frequent and serious consultation to virtual neglect.

One explanation of the cabinet's checkered career is the mode of its selection. While the president has a freer hand in selecting his cabinet than, say, a British or Italian prime minister, he too is under constraints. It seems highly unlikely, for example, that apart from his prominence in the Democratic party, William Jennings Bryan was really Woodrow Wilson's first choice as secretary of state. Similarly, certain departments such as Commerce, Labor, and Agriculture are generally headed by persons congenial to rather specific clienteles. Thus, potential advice-giving may rank rather low on the list of criteria for choosing members of the cabinet.

Another factor countering institutionalization of the cabinet as collective adviser is *departmentalism*.[16] This is the centrifugal tendency whereby each department head views things solely from a narrow departmental perspective. Cabinet meetings, if held, resemble more a congress of ambassadors from petty principalities than the board of directors of a large corporation. Each secretary jealously guards departmental independence and prerogatives. Department heads tend to become narrow specialists and cannot say much of value about outside areas. In some cases a new secretary is "captured" by the departmental orthodoxy defended by his ostensible assistants and subordinates. This problem is by no means confined to America. In fact, complaints like this are expressed in nearly all constitutional regimes, whether presidential or parliamentary.

The overall weakness of United States cabinets does not prevent certain members from achieving outstanding influence with the president. Occasionally a kind of "inner cabinet" of several cabinet members emerges that has a special relationship to the president. Both cause and effect of the cabinet's secondary position is the prodigious growth in size as well as influence of the White House staff. This has grown from over

15. Richard Fenno, *The President's Cabinet* (New York: Vintage Books, 1959).
16. Ibid., pp. 131–41.

40 with Roosevelt and Truman, to over 250 with Truman, Eisenhower, and Kennedy, and finally up to over 500 with Nixon, Ford, and Carter.[17] The staff itself has six subdivisions: (1) domestic policy and legislative program staff; (2) economic staff; (3) national security and foreign policy staff; (4) administrative staff; (5) White House and congressional relations staff; and (6) public relations.

In the Nixon Administration the more troublesome problems of a large and powerful presidential staff came to the surface. Not surprisingly, the large staff organization made many decisions that legally and constitutionally lay elsewhere. A chief casualty naturally was the cabinet, for as Thomas Cronin points out:

> The Presidential establishment has become, in effect, a new layer of government between the president and cabinet, and many of its members stand above most of the cabinet members in terms of influence with the president. The cabinet itself, as a council of government, has become somewhat of a relic. Continuous undercutting of the departments can cripple the capacity of cabinet officials to present policy alternatives and diminishes self-confidence and initiative within the bureaucracy.[18]

An overzealous and overprotective White House staff, especially "gatekeepers" like H. R. Haldeman, can surround the president with a *cordon sanitaire* that can cut him off from vital sources of both political and technical information.

The French Hybrid

As the constitution of the Fifth French Republic (1958–   ) was contrived by Charles de Gaulle and his associate Michel Debré especially to move away from the runaway parliamentarism of the Third and Fourth Republics, some ideas of de Gaulle's views of French presidentialism should precede our analysis. De Gaulle was in the Bonapartist tradition, which emphasizes a close relationship between the supreme national leader and the French people. Accordingly, parties, interest groups, and parliamentary factions are considered "intermediaries" standing between the people and its government. De Gaulle blamed the executive weakness and "government by assembly" of the Third and Fourth Republics for the weakness and collapse of those regimes. Never-

17. Cronin, *Presidency*, p. 119. Cronin also points out that the 500-plus figures may not reflect "borrowed" officials on temporary duty at the White House.
18. Ibid., p. 138.

theless, he did not establish a fullblown presidentialism: the Fifth Republic is a hybrid with the possibility of veering either toward presidential dominance or toward a more classic parliamentary system.

The first three presidents of the Fifth Republic—de Gaulle, Georges Pompidou, Valerie Giscard d'Estaing—have followed the Gaullist prescription of strong presidentialism. This has been possible because the majority in the National Assembly has always been favorable to the incumbent president. There is no guarantee, however, that this will be so in the future. Since the prime minister and his cabinet must enjoy the confidence of the National Assembly, the time may come when the president cannot pick and choose his prime minister and other ministers. The resultant constitutional crisis may displace power back toward the prime minister and the National Assembly. Bearing this in mind, the most economical approach is to compare the French presidency to the six roles of the American presidency.

THE PRESIDENT AS CHIEF EXECUTIVE.   There is no doubt that the French president in the Fifth Republic is the chief executive. The several prime ministers since 1959 have all stood in the shadow of the president. Presidents de Gaulle, Pompidou, Giscard have all exercised the powers of both head of state and head of government. The division of labor between president and prime minister, of course, reflects the style and personality of the two principals. Under de Gaulle (1959–69) the president with his preoccupation with French grandeur and foreign-defense policy allowed the prime minister and cabinet a certain discretion over domestic affairs. He may have paid a price for this neglect in the student uprising of May–June 1968 and his own resignation in 1969.

De Gaulle's successor, Georges Pompidou (1969–74), may have even been a more active chief executive than de Gaulle himself, because his six-year "training period" as prime minister provided him with profound knowledge of many administrative intricacies.[19] According to Roy Macridis, during the Pompidou presidency "relations between the French president and his cabinet resembled relations between the American president and his cabinet," [20] with the president frequently dealing directly with cabinet ministers over the head of the parliament. Even more suggestive is Macridis's further comparision with the American situation:

19. Roy Pierce, *French Politics and Political Institutions* (2nd ed.; New York: Harper & Row, 1973), pp. 58–59.
20. Roy C. Macridis, *French Politics in Transition* (Cambridge, Mass.: Winthrop Publishers, 1975), p. 29.

there was also a parallel growth of the "office" of the French Presidency. A select group of civil servants assisted the President in formulating policies and often in supervising their implementation. With responsibilities that often paralleled those of the Ministries and with special assignments to elaborate policies, they were not only the eyes and ears but also the brain and the nervous system of the President's office. . . .[21]

One slight difference is that in France certain categories of presidential acts must be "countersigned" by an appropriate minister. But as long as cabinet ministers remain virtual presidential appointees, this constitutional proviso is a mere formality.

THE PRESIDENT AS CHIEF LEGISLATOR.   Given the government's dominance over the legislative process and the president's dominance over the government, the French president merits the label "chief legislator" even more than his American counterpart. These powers are complemented by the broad decree powers granted to the executive by the French constitution. Though the French president has no full veto power, he can send bills back to the National Assembly for reconsideration within fifteen days. This is a kind of "suspensive veto." On the other hand, he has a power that many American presidents might covet: the power to initiate referendums. The president is the main force in bringing referendums about either constitutional amendments or broad policy issues to the French electorate. The president's legislative power and influence is also strengthened by his power to dissolve the National Assembly after consulting with the prime minister, president of the National Assembly, and Senate president.[22]

THE PRESIDENT AS COMMANDER-IN-CHIEF.   Little need be said about the role of the French president as commander-in-chief. Since General de Gaulle was military leader of the Free French Forces in World War II, it is no surprise that "his" constitution designates the president as "Chief of the Armies. He presides over the high councils and committees of national defense" (Article 15). Ironically, it was rebellious portions of the military that provided the severest threat to de Gaulle in the early years of the Fifth Republic when it became clear that the new president had other priorities than to "keep Algeria French."

THE PRESIDENT AS CHIEF DIPLOMAT.   In the area of diplomacy too the Gaullist design for a strong presidency has proven out. De Gaulle and his two successors have personally shaped and conducted much of

21. Ibid.
22. The National Assembly cannot be dissolved during a state of emergency or within one year of a previous dissolution.

France's foreign policy. The foreign minister's job has generally been that of administrative-political assistant to the president. Major foreign policy decisions, such as, first, the exclusion of Great Britain from the European Economic Community and, later, its admission, have been the province of the French president.

THE PRESIDENT AS MANAGER OF PROSPERITY.   Strong government involvement in the economy (called *dirigisme*) is even more firmly established in France than in the United States. The French public, like the American, looks to the president to secure prosperity and economic reforms.

THE PRESIDENT AS PARTY CHIEFTAIN.   With respect to political parties there are differences between French and American presidentialism. We have already mentioned de Gaulle's disdain for political parties. Accordingly, when a party devoted to him and his new republic, appropriately called the Union for the New Republic, formed in 1959,[23] de Gaulle maintained his distance and never joined, to say nothing of assuming formal leadership of the party. Pompidou likewise maintained formal aloofness from party politics, but was de facto chief of the Gaullist party—he handpicked its secretary-general. Valerie Giscard d'Estaing was the head of a small pro-Gaullist party, the Republican Independents, when he won a narrow victory in the presidential elections of 1974.

The Chilean Imitation

The political system of pre-Allende Chile is a good third point of comparison for modern presidentialism.[24] Many features of Chilean presidentialism before 1970 are found in other Latin American countries. In some of these, however, the balance tilts markedly toward dictatorship. In such pseudoconstitutional regimes, formal separation of powers along American lines has been weakened by total executive dominance. Legislatures and judiciaries have become rubber stamps, and presidents have sometimes subverted constitutions by becoming presidents for life— which in Latin American politics may not be very long at all.

23. The party is now called the Union of Republicans for Progress.
24. Salvador Allende served as president of Chile from 1970 to 1973. Although he lacked a mandate for thoroughgoing reforms of a socialistic nature, he nonetheless moved swiftly and methodically to transform radically the nature of Chilean society. Fearing that Allende's policies were the prelude to a full-scale revolution, the Chilean military launched a successful coup in the fall of 1973, in which Allende lost his life.

Reflecting the American model, the Chilean political system before 1970 had separation of powers with a popularly elected president and a bicameral legislature called Congress. There was also a Supreme Court, though its judicial review powers were quite restricted. The Chilean president was an even stronger figure than his American counterpart. He possessed "such wide political, administrative, legislative, and, on occasion, even judicial power that, in fact, the system might be described as 'legal autocracy.'" [25] Let us briefly survey his roles for comparative purposes.

THE PRESIDENT AS CHIEF EXECUTIVE.   The Chilean president exercised nearly all the prerogatives of a chief executive. He hired and fired members of the cabinet, who were uniquely responsible to him. He also appointed a vast number of public officials and had great say about salaries, tenure, and promotion. These powers even involved judicial officials. In these areas he appeared stronger than his United States counterparts, since presidential discretion in the United States is often limited by law and strict civil service regulations.

THE PRESIDENT AS CHIEF LEGISLATOR.   The Chilean president had extensive legislative powers. Endowed with powers that were supposed merely to supplement and reinforce laws passed by the Congress, Chilean presidents customarily employed their ordinance powers "in such a fashion as to make changes which affect[ed] not only the form but the spirit of the laws as well." [26] They also enjoyed both a general and an item veto, though overriding vetoes was easier for the Chilean than for the American Congress because only a two-thirds majority of those present rather than of the total membership was required.

Furthermore, the Chilean president could present legislation to the Congress by messages and could designate bills as "urgent" so as to guarantee their speedy consideration. He could call and, more significantly, prolong sessions of Congress. In budgetary matters his powers were even more considerable, because the failure of Congress to approve his proposals could lead to their automatic legalization after four months. This resembles the French practice rather than the American.

THE PRESIDENT AS COMMANDER-IN-CHIEF.   The Chilean president's role as commander-in-chief did suffer some legal limitations. These restrictions probably prevented Salvador Allende from purging the military before they ousted him in the coup of 1973.

25. Federico G. Gil, *The Political System of Chile* (Boston: Houghton Mifflin, 1966), p. 92.
26. Ibid.

THE PRESIDENT AS CHIEF DIPLOMAT.   The Chilean president was the main force in Chilean foreign policy.

THE PRESIDENT AS MANAGER OF PROSPERITY.   Pre-Allende Chile, as a fairly industrialized country, had developed many of the features of the modern welfare state. Its strong presidentialism thus entailed responsibility as manager of prosperity.

THE PRESIDENT AS PARTY CHIEFTAIN.   Chilean presidents were also party chieftains. One qualification is that in the Chilean multiparty system, the successful presidential candidate was a "front" coalition candidate. The coalitions that won were variously oriented toward the right, the center, or the left according to shifting political fortunes.

Discussing presidentialism in terms of the American model, the French hybrid, and the Chilean imitation shows us the variations that time and place produce in similar institutional setups. Despite the rather loose talk about the "imperial" American presidency, the United States Congress remains one of the strongest and most independent legislative bodies in the world, stronger by far than its French or Chilean counterparts.

The actual course and performance of the American presidency, as James Barber reminds us, depend on the times and the incumbent. To paraphrase the old nursery rhyme: when these are good, the presidency is very, very good; when these are bad, it is horrid. In other words, whenever we have able, balanced presidents working with the legislature in a cordial and cooperative way, presidentialism seems to avoid the instability and indecision that sometimes afflict parliamentary systems. On the other hand, when (as in the Nixon presidency) the president himself has personality problems and develops an almost adversary relationship with a politically hostile Congress, the weaknesses of presidentialism thrust themselves forward.

There seems little doubt that Nixon as prime minister in a parliamentary system would have been driven from office a year sooner than his ultimate resignation in August 1974. Moreover, the bitter stalemate of eight years with one party controlling the executive and another the legislative would by definition have been avoided in a parliamentary system. Given the collapse of Chilean presidentialism, the trauma of the later Nixon years, and the probable future crisis of French presidentialism, transformed parliamentarism looks increasingly attractive. This is especially so when we recall stabilizing features such as the German rule that when parliament removes a chancellor it must name his successor.

THE COLLEGIAL EXECUTIVE: SWITZERLAND

The Swiss political system represents the most successful constitutional alternative to parliamentarism and presidentialism, though it has similarities to both.[27] Switzerland is a federal system, made up of twenty-two cantons, of which some include half-cantons. The cantonal level of government is important, and in several small rural cantons a form of direct democracy—yearly political assembly of all the citizens similar to the New England town meeting—still survives. The Swiss national legislature is bicameral, with the Council of States representing the cantons (44 members) and the National Council representing the general population (200 members). The Swiss have a multiparty system.

TABLE 3.6.   **Party Strengths in Switzerland after 1975 Elections**

Party	Seats: National Council	% of Popular Vote
Social Democrats	55	25.4
Christian Democrats	46	20.6
Radicals	47	22.2
Swiss People's party	21	10.1
Independents	11	6.2
Liberal Democrats	6	2.3
Republicans	4	3.0
Communists	4	2.2
Evangelical People's party	3	2.0
National Campaign	2	2.5
Others	1	3.5

What interests us in terms of the present discussion is the seven-member Federal Council (*Bundesrat*), the Swiss executive, because in theory it represents the *collegial* principle of collective and collaborative decision-making. The Federal Council is elected by joint action of the National Council and the Council of States sitting together as the Federal Assembly. The whole Federal Council is reelected every four years and individual vacancies are filled by special elections. The Council differs from cabinets in parliamentary systems in that it does not resign if it receives an adverse vote in the legislature. (Federal councilors cannot be members of parliament.) However, the Federal Assembly of the two

27. Uruguay has also tried the collegial executive twice. The results have been far less successful than in Switzerland.

houses can express its feelings about the whole Council or its individual members at the quadrennial renewals or in the one-man replacement elections. Customarily, Council members are automatically reconfirmed in office with upward of 90 percent majorities. Particularly controversial councilors, however, have seen their majorities dip toward 60 percent.[28] When this happens the "message" is clearly understood by all concerned.

Each year the Federal Council chooses a president, who functions as head of state, and a vice-president. These two offices rotate among Council members, and the present vice-president will be next year's president. The Swiss president does not overarch his colleagues in the Council, as does a British prime minister, to say nothing about an American president. He is a "presiding officer" in the narrow sense of the term. Members of the Federal Council head the following seven departments: (1) Political (i.e., foreign); (2) Interior; (3) Justice and Police; (4) Finance and Customs; (5) Public Economy; (6) Posts and Railways; and (7) Military.

Formerly, there was considerable shifting of councilors from department to department, with the president automatically heading the Political department. Nowadays, in view of the more technical requirements of administration, the trend is for councilors to stay put. The Council, and especially the president, gets important administrative help from the federal chancellor, who despite his civil service status is also chosen by the Federal Assembly.

Although the composition of the Federal Council reflects regional and language considerations,[29] party representation is its most outstanding feature. In the last half of the nineteenth century the Radical party, with a secure majority in the Federal Assembly, monopolized the seven seats in the Federal Council. In 1891 a "bourgeois coalition" was formed of six Radical-Liberals and one Catholic Conservative (forerunners of the Christian Democrats). In 1919 this ratio was changed to 5:2. In 1929 a third coalition partner was incorporated—the Peasants, Artisans, and Bourgeois party (now the Swiss People's party). The new ratio was 4:2:1 (4 Radicals:2 Catholics:1 Peasant). In 1943 the bourgeois coali-

28. Klaus Schumann, *Das Regierungssystem der Schweiz* (Berlin: Carl Heymanns Verlag, 1971), pp. 189–90.
29. This means that some French-speakers, perhaps Italian-speakers, should be included. Likewise, the largest cantons should be brought in. Critics complain that such restrictions prevent selection of a Federal Council made up of the most truly qualified members.

tion formula was shelved, resulting in a ratio of $3:2:1:1$ (3 Radicals:2 Catholics:1 Peasant:1 Social Democrat [nonbourgeois]). In 1953 the bourgeois coalition was restored with a ratio of $3:3:1$ (3 Radicals:3 Catholics:1 Peasant). Since 1959 the Social Democrats have been brought back into the Government; and the new ratio, which the Swiss call the "magic formula," includes two councilors each from the Radicals, Social Democrats, and Christian Democrats, plus one from the Swiss People's party ($2:2:2:1$).

The "magic formula" of including the leading parties in the Federal Assembly in the Government has solidified certain transformations in the Swiss executive. Reserving fuller discussions of coalitions for a later chapter, we can here distinguish some differences between the Swiss approach and that of ordinary coalition governments. In the normal coalition situation where strong antisystem parties are lacking (as is also the case in Switzerland), the Government coalition confronts one or more opposition parties. Since the coalition includes some parties and excludes others, it can formulate some sort of program addressing social and political problems in a fairly decisive way. In the Swiss Federal Council, on the other hand, the virtual all-inclusiveness of the Government seriously limits its margin of maneuver. Decisions tend to reflect the lowest common denominator. Councilors from the different parties possess a virtual veto on some measures, and on others they quietly allow their party to vote against Council proposals in the Federal Assembly. In other words, there is virtual opposition *within* the governing coalition, with the Social Democrats usually cast in the main opposing role—this resembles the "cartelized opposition" discussed in chapter 2, especially the Austrian postwar experience.

Another tendency forwarded by this all-party coalition is the decline of true collegiality in the Federal Council. Rather than acting as a collective decision-maker over a wide range of issues, the Council has fragmented into seven more or less independent policy arenas. Since each councilor remains at his departmental post for an extended period, he becomes spokesman and advocate for departmental viewpoints. As in the United States cabinet, this departmentalism means the prevalence of centrifugal over unifying forces. But in Switzerland there is no strong president to counteract policy fragmentation. The growth of technical complexity and the mutual deference of federal councilors has weakened whatever collegiality existed in earlier times.[30]

30. Schumann, *Schweiz*, p. 195.

The actual political-administrative situation in Switzerland is still more complex than the seven quasi-autonomous departments would suggest. Within the public administration various sections, divisions, and bureaus have become "not only preparatory organs of departmental tasks, rather independent decision-makers." [31] Because of these and other considerations, Swiss reformers have proposed abandonment of the magic formula or even of direct popular election of the Federal Council. Up to now Swiss concepts of democracy, which require representation of major currents of opinion in the executive, have combined with the interests of possible losers from change to block such measures.

THE ADMINISTRATIVE STATE

It may well be that our brief speculations about the relative and respective virtues of parliamentarism are rather beside the point. Critics charge that the real rulers of the modern state are not the elected legislators and executives, but the "faceless bureaucrats" who operate behind the scenes. This problem is generally called the "administrative state," a system in which politicians conduct a kind of shadowboxing exhibition, while the real decisions are made elsewhere. The administrative state may not have replaced "politics by administration," as the old maxim has it, but it may have displaced both politics and policy away from legislatures, prime ministers, and presidents to the officials of the public administration.

Even if this last conclusion is too extreme, the problem of the administrative state afflicts all modern constitutional regimes. No one denies the growing impact of professional bureaucrats on the content and conduct of public policy. This counsels a somewhat closer examination of the problems of decision-making and policy formation from the angle of the administrative state. First, we should get a better idea of the basic types of public policy and the different problems of each type. Then we should explore alternative modes of decision-making, both because different administrators operate differently and because use of the "wrong" mode of decision-making may be responsible for the disheartening results of foreign and domestic policy decisions in a host of countries. Finally, we should see that even though the bogey of the administrative state can be exaggerated, a wide variety of relationships between bureaucrats and elected or appointed "political" officials exist.

31. Ibid., p. 199.

Public Policy

James E. Anderson defines *policy* as a "purposive course of action followed by an actor or set of actors in dealing with a problem or matter of concern." [32] A policy is a broad decision that implies other lower-level decisions: a kind of macrodecision made up of microdecisions. The latter relate to the various particular aspects of the policy. From a certain point of view "nondecisions" are also policies because by consciously choosing not to act we are, in effect, choosing to leave things as they are. Anderson further suggests that we distinguish *policy outputs*—"what a government does, as distinguished from what it says it is going to do" [33] from *policy outcomes*—"the consequences for society, intended or unintended, that flow from action or inaction by government." [34]

As an example of this most serious problem of modern government, we can cite United States government policy regarding the draft and higher education. The draft was instituted during World War II for obvious reasons and was retained during the 1940s, 1950s, and 1960s after the outbreak of the cold war. However, it was also government policy to grant deferments to students pursuing their higher education. What this resulted in, especially after escalated involvement in Vietnam, was the greatest boom for the colleges and universities that the country has ever known and, most likely, ever will know. This was neither the purpose of the draft nor of educational deferments nor yet of the Vietnam policy. Similarly, certain forms of aid to the poor were not designed to undermine family solidarity, but such was their outcome.

Following Theodore J. Lowi, we can be rather more precise about different types of public policy. Lowi divides public policy into three issue areas of increasing controversiality: distributive policies, regulatory policies, and redistributive policies.[35]

DISTRIBUTIVE POLICIES.   These are decisions that benefit rather specific groups and individuals in society. Special patronage and "pork-barrel" projects are cases in point. Distributive policies arouse a low degree of controversy because possible opponents are too scattered and

32. James E. Anderson, *Public Policy-Making* (New York: Praeger Publishers, 1976), p. 3.
33. Ibid., p. 5.
34. Ibid., p. 6.
35. Theodore Lowi, "American Business, Public Policy, Case-Studies, and Political Theory," in *Consensus and Conflict,* ed. James Young (New York: Dodd, Mead, 1972).

disorganized to offer much resistance. Says Lowi: "These are policies that are virtually not policies at all but are highly individualized decisions that only by accumulation can be called a policy." [36]

REGULATORY POLICIES.   These policies also have definite beneficiaries and losers. However, they are fashioned in more general terms than distributive policies and can be broken down so as to apply to rather specific social groups. Farmers, unions, businesses, professionals are those who feel the impact of regulations most closely. In Lowi's opinion, conflict over regulatory policies takes the form of interest-group competition along the lines of "pluralist" theory.[37]

REDISTRIBUTIVE POLICIES.   These relate to broad issues of redistributing political and economic power. Issues such as a *strongly* progressive income tax and socialized medicine fall into this category. Lowi further suggests that the "redistributive arena most closely approximates, with some adaptations, an elitist view of the political process." [38] As we will see in greater detail in chapter 6, the elitist view of politics stresses the domination of an organized minority over the political system. What Lowi has in mind here is that redistributive policies cut so deeply into the social or economic base of the dominant elite that they will come out into the open to defend their interests. Distributive and regulatory policies, since they affect the dominant elite only in superficial ways, may not lead to much action by the elite as a coherent political entity.

Distributive policies, because of their low controversiality and specific beneficiaries, are fairly easy for administrators to handle. Where (as in the United States) the legislature plays a major role in the budgetary process, the free hand of administrators to dish out specific benefits is somewhat curtailed. To handle the broadened involvement and controversy of regulatory policies, administrators resort to consultation and consultative committees, a development that is discussed in the next section. Redistributive policies, however, appear too "big" for administrators to push through on their own initiative. Administrative advocates of such grandiose measures would have to win over political leaders in legislative and executive posts, if they hope for success.

Administrators may be more successful in affecting redistributive policies in some contexts than in others, however. Hugh Heclo, for example, studied the development of regulatory and somewhat redis-

36. Ibid., p. 278.
37. Ibid., pp. 280–81. See chapter 6 in this text for fuller analysis of pluralism and elitism.
38. Ibid., p. 279.

tributive policies in Sweden and Great Britain in the areas of unemployment compensation and old-age security. He concluded that if "forced
to choose one group among all the separate political factors as most
consistently important . . . the bureaucracies of Britain and Sweden loom
predominant in the policies studied." [39] *Factors such as elections, political parties, and pressure groups were less crucial in ushering in new
policies than were administrators.*

Styles of Decision-Making

If Heclo is right about the impact of administrative decision-making upon
public policy, we must get a better idea of the nature of the decision-
making art. Theorists have distinguished three main styles of decision-
making: (1) the rationalist approach; (2) the pragmatist or incrementalist approach; and (3) the "mixed scanning" approach. The third is
a sort of compromise between the first two approaches. Each has been
offered both as a *description* of how decision-making sometimes occurs
and as a *prescription* of how effective decision-making ought to occur.

THE RATIONALIST APPROACH. This is the most ambitious and optimistic of the three styles of decision-making. In some versions it assumes
that for rational actors there is only "one best solution" for any problem
at hand. It assumes that social reality is a "system" that is knowable and
hence controllable. The chief problem for the rationalist is to clarify the
intentions of the group involved and to gather sufficient information
about the context of the problem. After doing this, a cost-benefit analysis
of various courses of action can be worked up and a decision made one
way or the other. If these preliminaries are done well, there is virtual
certainty that there will be a close symmetry between policy "outputs"
and final "outcomes," between what we want and what we get. A simplified version of the rationalist "model" is seen in table 3.7.[40]

THE PRAGMATIST APPROACH. This approach faults the rationalist
model on several counts.[41] The pragmatists charge that the rationalists
overestimate man's problem-solving capacities. For example, rationalists
underestimate the costs and difficulties in gathering and evaluating in-

39. Hugh Heclo, *Modern Social Politics in Britain and Sweden* (New Haven:
Yale University Press, 1975), p. 301.
40. See Anthony Downs, *Inside Bureaucracy* (Boston: Little, Brown, 1967),
chap. 15 for elaboration.
41. This discussion relies on David Braybrooke and Charles E. Lindblom, *A
Strategy of Decision* (New York: Free Press, 1970), chap. 3.

TABLE 3.7 Stages of Decision-Making in the Rationalist Model

1. **Definition of the problem:** the decision-maker can clearly mark off the problem area, where it begins, and where it ends. He knows what he wants to achieve through his action.
2. **Search for information:** having a decent sketch of the problem, the decision-maker gathers information about the specifics and subtleties missing in his original view.
3. **Assessment of alternatives:** having both clarity about goals and information about obstacles, the decision-maker can draw up several reasonable alternative courses.
4. **Selection of the best alternative:** after weighing the costs and benefits of various feasible alternatives, there is little puzzlement as to which is both most economical and effective.
5. **Implementation:** now the decision-maker can develop substrategies to effect the basic decision. The rationalist assumes that nothing is gained or lost by breaking the basic decision down into specific points.
6. **Feedback:** during implementation the decision-maker receives feedback about how things are working out. He may make minor adjustments to "calibrate" the decision, though the rationalist assumes that execution of steps 1–4 will keep this at a minimum.

formation. Furthermore, they fudge the issue of value judgments in decision-making. By overstressing the integration and interrelation of social reality, the rationalists grossly oversimplify the complexities and open-ended character of social life.

Instead of rationalism, Brayebrooke and Lindblom have offered a description of a *strategy of decision,* which they feel is prevalent in countries such as the United States. They call this "disjointed incrementalism" or "incrementalism," for short (see table 3.8).[42]

TABLE 3.8. Main Aspects of Incrementalist Decision Strategy

1. **Incremental change:** this strategy advocates what Karl Popper calls "piecemeal social engineering" (i.e., an attempt to deal with specific parts of social reality rather than to reconstruct the social system *en bloc*). The piecemeal social engineer does not have a "blueprint" of a complete new society before him; he deals with small and gradual changes.
2. **Serial approach:** we should not attempt to solve problems at one fell swoop, but return to them over and over again (i.e., serially). Each return to the problem adds a little more to the solution and allows for necessary adjustments.
3. **Remedial approach:** rather than constructing a flawless world according to plan, this strategy urges tackling of clear and present evils. In medical language, it is as much concerned with relieving symptoms as with curing the disease as such.

42. Ibid., chap. 5.

TABLE 3.8.   *(continued)*

4. **Social fragmentation:** "analysis and evaluation are socially fragmented, that is, they take place at a very large number of points in society. Analysis of any single given problem area and of possible policies for solving the problem is often conducted in a large number of centers." [43]

The pragmatist or incrementalist approach has in its turn been subject to searching criticisms. Its very cautiousness tends to exclude any attempt to make "structural reforms" in society. It thus becomes a kind of conservatism by default because unlike genuine conservatism it does not offer a principled defense of the existing order. Likewise, incrementalism steers clear of a coherent idea of the public interest that might cause us to relate low-gauge decisions to broad-gauge public concerns.

To counter these and other objections without resorting to the old rationalist approach, the sociologist Amitai Etzioni has proposed "mixed scanning" as a middle-of-the-road solution.[44] Mixed scanning distinguishes between broad-gauged and narrow-gauged issues. For the latter type incrementalism seems to work; for the broader issues, however, a broader perspective is necessary. Furthermore, there is a connection between the two levels of decision: "(a) most incremental decisions specify or anticipate fundamental decisions, and (b) the cumulative value of the incremental decisions is greatly affected by the underlying fundamental decisions." [45] In other words, fundamental decisions provide the context within which incrementalism can and must operate.

The contrast between the different styles or strategies of decision-making might be heightened by analogies from everyday life. Certainly, we all know people who are "well-organized," who plan out the day's or week's activities with almost compulsive and mathematical precision. They are our everyday rationalists. On the other hand, we know people who wait upon events before they respond. For them everything is to be done ad hoc: they figure that too much preplanning is more an obstacle than an aid to effective action. They are our everyday pragmatists or incrementalists. Those who fall in between would correspond to "mixed scanners."

Of special interest here is the relationship between a country's political culture and its prevalent mode of administrative and political decision-

43. Ibid., p. 104.
44. Amitai Etzioni, *The Active Society* (New York: Free Press, 1968).
45. Ibid., p. 289.

making.[46] Many observers, for example, have contrasted the "empirical" and "pragmatic" political cultures of Great Britain and the United States and the more "rationalistic" cultures of continental European countries such as France and Italy. In 1956 Gabriel Almond characterized the "Anglo-American political culture" as a "multi-valued political culture, a rational-calculating, bargaining, and experimental political culture." He further pointed out that to "a continental European this kind of political culture often looks sloppy. It has no logic, no clarity." [47] Knowing no more than this, we could legitimately infer that Continental decision-makers on the whole are predisposed toward the rationalist approach, while their counterparts in Great Britain and the United States are generally inclined toward incrementalism. Such a contrast, though less sharp now than a generation ago, has much to recommend it.

Politics and Administrators

In both parliamentary and presidential systems we commonly distinguish between the transitory "political" officials who head departments and the permanent civil servants who are technically their subordinates. Little imagination is needed to see that this relationship is both problematic and highly variable. Factors implicated range from the political culture, the laws and formal government organization, to personality variables. Here we can do little more than to present two analyses that do bring some order to the topic.

A crucial relationship, already touched upon in the last chapter, is that between government ministers and their aides in the permanent civil service. A study based upon British politics suggests that ministers can play five roles vis-à-vis their bureaucratic staffs (see table 3.9).[48]

All five types of ministers need some services from their top civil service staff. James B. Christoph's conclusions about the aid functions of the British higher bureaucracy clearly have broad comparative relevance here.[49] According to Christoph's analysis, administrators carry out, first,

46. For now we will merely define "political culture" as the politically relevant values and attitudes of a country's general culture. See chapter 10 in this text.
47. Gabriel Almond, "Comparative Political Systems," in *Comparative Politics*, ed. Roy Macridis (3rd ed.; Homewood, Ill.: Dorsey, 1968), p. 59.
48. Bruce W. Headey, "A Typology of Ministers: Implications for Minister-Civil Servant Relationships in Britain," in *The Mandarins of Western Europe*, ed. Mattei Dogan (New York: John Wiley, 1975), pp. 63–86.
49. James B. Christoph, "Higher Civil Servants and the Politics of Consensualism in Great Britain," in Dogan, *The Mandarins of Western Europe*, pp. 45–48.

TABLE 3.9.   Roles of Ministers in Relation to Their Staffs

1. **Policy initiators:** the minister dominates policy formation and the bureaucrats are expected simply to be responsive. This strong posture can rouse criticism in the ranks if the minister is overbearing and ignores his staff's recommendations totally.
2. **Policy selectors:** this type of minister restricts himself to choosing among alternatives presented by his subordinates. He does not get very involved in the preliminary stages of decision (e.g., stages 2 and 3 of the rationalist model).
3. **Executive ministers:** these are oriented more to the inner workings of the department than to its outside "constituency." They have a "management textbook view of their job." Absorption in organizational-managerial tasks and changes may cause them to "forego the role of defining policy objectives and reviewing alternative programs."
4. **Ambassador ministers:** this type is preoccupied with maintaining good relations with interest groups, local governments, and clientele groups. They are not well regarded by their staffs, though their "public relations" activities force them to delegate substantial policy-making to the staff.
5. **Minimalists:** these go through the motions of being active ministers, but their hearts (or their heads) are not really in it. They do accept responsibility and push for departmental budgetary and legislative proposals, but more to save face than to reach goals.

substantive policy implementation of projects determined by parliaments or other elected officials. We must bear in mind, however, that the role of administrators involves much more than passive follow-up operations, given the extremely broad guidelines of much legislation. Administrators also provide *political advice,* supplying one source of political information to the responsible minister. *Mutual political protection* occurs when the minister and the top officials exchange mutual political aid and comfort. The minister defends his staff from hostile political criticism, while they work to enhance his political image. The top bureaucrats cause the *advancement of clientele claims* by acting as a transmission belt for the demands of outside pressure groups. Finally, *conflict-management and consensus-making* is the attempt by administrators to conciliate the maximum number of pressure groups largely through what we will call in the next section "the politics of consultation."

GOVERNMENT BY COMMITTEE: THE POLITICS OF CONSULTATION

The Growth of Committees

Given the expansion of governmental tasks characteristic of our era, it is no surprise that public administration has tried new methods to cope with the vast problems involved. One such response is the enormous growth of administrative committees of all sorts and shapes. Their growth has been so prodigious that Winston Churchill once remarked that "we are overrun by them, like the Australians are by the rabbits." [50] Even if the reproductive process of committees is rather less than that of Australian rabbits, only recently have we fully recognized their political and administrative importance.

Though our concern here is with nonlegislative committees, much of the discussion, especially regarding the inner working of committees, can be applied to legislative committees as well. Administrative committees have grown apace with the growth of government. However, their advantages and disadvantages as a mode of decision-making have been hotly debated. Clichés about forming committees as the secret way to stifle an unpleasant topic, though having more than a grain of truth, cannot explain the complex political and administrative considerations that have sped their growth. Two main factors seem to lead to the growth of administrative committees: (1) the multifaceted nature of many administrative tasks; (2) the need to involve strategic groups from outside the administrative structure in policy formation.

Because of the many facets now involved in public administration, resort to committee-style decision-making responds to the need to widen the scope of information in policy formation. Modern industrial societies are more tightly interrelated than some earlier societies. Strikes in particular industries, for example, have profound and immediate effects in a host of related or dependent industries. Public policy in such complex societies must take into account many factors and points of view. It must gauge long-term as well as short-term impact of policy. Thus, at first glance at least, broadening the decision process beyond a one-man (monocratic) approach to the more inclusive committee approach seems one way to avoid the limits and biases of solo decision-makers.

Second, the growth of committees is symptomatic of the shift of policy initiative away from the legislative and toward the executive, which we discussed in chapter 2. This suggests that interest groups would be well advised to direct some of their concern away from the parliamentary stage to the preparliamentary and postparliamentary stages of policy. The preparliamentary stage in many countries is where the basic contours of legislation are really determined. Here the bureaucracy sets the basic guidelines for public policy. Likewise, even when parlia-

50. Quoted in K. C. Wheare, *Government by Committee* (Oxford: Oxford University Press, 1955), p. 1.

ment legislates, its outputs are often sketchy outlines whose details and specifics are filled in by administration, agencies, and bureaus. Thus special committees are often formed to formalize the focus of interest group concern and activity. This process at the preparliamentary and to a lesser extent at the postparliamentary stages is called the "politics of consultation."

According to one student of consultative committees, their main function is "to make possible the confrontation and reconciliation of the demands and the supports of social agents as well as the expansion of the wishes and policies of the political agents."[51] This is done by granting leadership to representatives of interest groups on the consultative committee. Many committees, for instance, might be *tripartite* and include representatives of the government, business, and trade unions. The avowed purpose would be to allow the interest groups to make "inputs" directly into the policy-making machinery. The bureaucrats would thus gain valuable technical and political information about the subject area of the committee. Bureaucratic isolationism would be cut down, and the level of public involvement would move closer to the ideals of traditional democratic theory. "Pluralistic democrats" could congratulate themselves.

The consultative committee seems to be a breakthrough in terms of bureaucratic information gathering, broadened participation in decision-making, and public accountability of officials. Leon Dion has given us a systematic representation of some of these possibilities, as shown in figure 3.2.[52] There is no doubt that consultative committees sometimes work according to this model, with bureaucrats shaping their policy largely in accordance with the information and the demands presented to them through the committee. However, one need not be a cynic to think that certain ulterior motives may also be involved. Chief of these is to forestall criticism by giving a show of real consultation. In such instances the bureaucratic members of the consultative committees, who usually retain ultimate legal responsibility, simply go through the motions of authentic consultation. Their real course of action has been decided beforehand. True, they may concede a detail or two to interest-group representatives, but this again is more for show than anything else. The bureaucrats hope that by such maneuvers they will have prevented the other

51. Leon Dion, "The Politics of Consultation," *Government and Opposition* 8 (Summer 1973): 335.
52. Ibid.

Figure 3.2.   Relationship of Consultative Committees to Political Forces

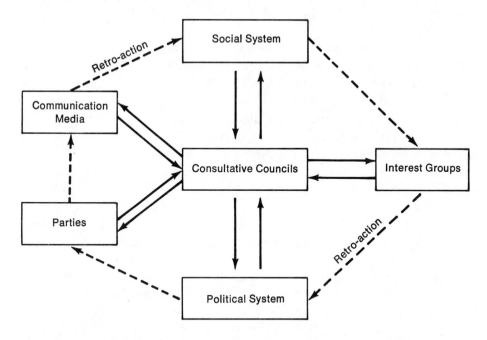

committee members and the groups they represent from later attacking the policy or decision involved.

Nonlegislative Committees

Committees found in public bureaucracies are of two major types: *advisory* and *administrative*. Advisory committees are empowered solely to make recommendations that require someone else's approval and implementation. Administrative committees, on the other hand, have the power to enforce their own or their superior's decisions. The problem here is the same one perennially confronted with so-called staff and line functions: [53] quite simply, staff officials often exercise line responsibilities. They issue orders to line people and these orders are followed. Similarly, a committee whose de jure function is merely advisory may be able

53. In administrative theory *staff* groups are confined to advising and otherwise supporting top decision-makers. *Line* officers are supposed to implement such decisions by actually commanding their subordinates to follow through.

to operate directly upon everyday activity. Nonetheless, as ideal types the distinction between advisory and administrative committees does point to some real differences.

Advisory committees within public administration are of two basic sorts: (1) *committees to inquire* and (2) *committees to negotiate*. The former type is given a more or less specific area to investigate. It is expected to produce a report which often contains specific policy recommendations. Circumstances may dictate that the recipient of the report follow it to the letter. On the other hand, K. C. Wheare has pointed out that certain advisory committees are actually committees to "delay or postpone." [54] In this case a committee is formed by some official or group to respond to a momentous public clamor. The new committee is supposed to appease these demands for action, but its real function is to "take the heat off" the officials involved. Hopefully, the issue that spawned the committee will fade away, and it in turn will die a quiet if inglorious death.

Committees to negotiate are formed to reconcile the diverse interests and demands of public and nonpublic groups. Government, labor, and management are called together to iron out their differences around the bargaining table. It may be that laws and regulations require the government to enforce the bargains struck by this committee. Even without such a legal basis, it would seem that the final report of a negotiating committee would be difficult for administrators to ignore. Their good faith would certainly be suspect, and this device would not be available to them in the future.

Internal Organization and Dynamics of Committees

Several aspects of committee structure and behavior are important to the student of comparative politics. For our purposes a "committee" can be defined as *a small, interacting face-to-face group of from three to about thirty persons who have been set up by some outside (parent) body to accomplish some more or less clear purpose*. This formal organization distinguishes the committee from the host of informal groups and cliques that honeycomb any large administrative structure. Most authorities agree that about thirty is the maximum for a true committee because large bodies cannot develop the appropriate intimacy. Of con-

54. Wheare, *Committee*, p. 90.

cern to us here are (1) committee leadership, (2) committee membership, and (3) committee decision-making.

Committees, like most human groups, exhibit and require leadership. Three or four types of leadership can be distinguished depending on how one defines leadership. *Formal leadership* generally consists of chairman (perhaps vice-chairman) and secretary. A chairman's leadership may be merely titular if he or she does not combine some informal leadership functions with it. The first of these informal leadership functions is *task leadership,* which involves the capacity to guide the committee through the nitty-gritty of its stated agenda. The task leader is one whose competence in the relevant area is recognized and respected by his committee colleagues.

Because a committee is also a small group made up of diverse personages and often dealing with highly controversial issues, many, if not most, committees can be hamstrung by conflicts of personality and principle. Anyone with the slightest committee experience knows that anything that Ms. X proposes will be strenuously resisted by Mr. Y and often vice versa. In order to avoid inefficiency or total breakdown of the committee's proceedings, the fortunate committee will cast up a leader who can carry out the second key informal leadership function, *social leadership.* The social leader's contribution is more in the way of smoothing the overall running of the committee than in any substantive area. Humor often is a most potent weapon. He or she can defuse a potentially explosive situation by an appropriate tension-reducing remark and can head off incipient personality clashes before they hamper the committee's work.

A chairperson who is neither task nor social leader would be a weak leader. A strong leader carries out one of these two leadership functions, but if he carries out both he would tend to dominate the committee. There is another important informal leadership role, though it is leadership in a different sense from task or social leadership. Many committees contain a type that could be called a *gadfly.* As the self-appointed "conscience" of the committee, the gadfly is often disliked and resented by most other members. His function is to recall the committee's attention to the moral dimensions of its task, its responsibilities and opportunities. He is impatient with the procedures often involved in committee behavior and is especially incensed when the "big issues" are obscured by nit-picking and petty details. While there is no doubt that an overabundance of gadflies can paralyze any committee, it is equally certain that the end product of a committee's work is often improved by their contribution.

How Committees Decide Things

Officially speaking, most committees decide according to the simple majority principle, sometimes with provisions for minority reports. The Italian political scientist Giovanni Sartori has warned us that such formal features mask the true dynamics of most committees. He states,

> How do committees actually work? Never, or hardly ever, on the basis of majority rule. Usually decisions are not brought to a vote. If they are, the vote generally is *pro forma*. As a rule, decisions in committees are unanimous—which comes very close to saying that committees decide by the principle of unanimity, but this is not because their members are of the same mind—they are not.[55]

Unanimity means literally *of one mind*, so that some clarification is necessary here. To begin with, we might distinguish between *positive* and *negative* unanimity. Positive unanimity refers to total agreement on principles and policy so that the "one mind" of the committee is demonstrably so. Negative unanimity is somewhat more complex. Here the members simply shelve the real objections they have to the emerging committee decision. They do this because an established committee has certain rules of the game, chief of which is *delayed mutual payoffs*.[56] By this arrangement committee members forego present objections to measures for the sake of similar future considerations for themselves and their proposals. Thus, there is a delayed payoff for not "making waves" about someone else's proposals. Since all members of the committee expect the same treatment, mutuality is the rule. The voting is reduced to ratifying the often tacit bargaining among the committee members. Unanimity prevails, but it clearly is negative and procedural, rather than positive and substantive.

In reality, committee decision-making is more complex than this analysis suggests. We can distinguish three types of decisions corresponding to three levels of integration and unity in the committee. These are known respectively as (1) upgrading common interests, (2) splitting the

55. Giovanni Sartori, "Will Democracy Kill Democracy? Decision-Making by Majorities and by Committees," *Government and Opposition* 10 (Spring 1975): 144.
56. Sartori says "deferred mutual compensations."

difference, and (3) lowest common denominator.[57] Upgrading common interests would seem to be quite rare with consultative committees and somewhat commoner with administrative committees. It presupposes dedication to an assured common interest of all the committee's members. The committee's finding or decision, if unanimous, would be genuinely or positively unanimous.

Splitting the difference assumes that some divergency of interest characterizes the committee. On the other hand, there is enough commitment to the whole to allow of some give-and-take and compromise. For example, let us assume a four-member committee deliberates concerning how much to spend on some project. Member A favors spending $5000; member B $4000; member C $3000; and member D $2000. Applying the splitting-the-difference principle literally, the committee would allocate $3500 to be spent.

With the lowest-common-denominator approach, the level of integration of the committee approaches zero. Each member of the committee possesses a virtual veto over its final decision. Thus in the case of the situation just described the only possible decision would be to expend $2000, the figure that is contained as the lowest common denominator in all the others.

In this chapter we have looked at several brands of presidentialism, the Swiss plural executive, and selected problems of policy formation and the administrative state. The overall lesson of this and chapter 2 has been the increasing power and importance of the executive and administrative aspects of government vis-à-vis the legislative bodies. However, we have encountered the intriguing paradox that although the American presidency has been the model for strong presidentialism, the American Congress remains the quintessence of a powerful legislative body. Indeed, it may have partially been the institutional and political *weaknesses* of the American presidency that prompted President Nixon to abuse his power. An "active-negative" president facing a Congress controlled by the opposition might be moved to save face and expand power by stretching the constitutional fabric to the tearing point.

If we perform another mental experiment and imagine Richard Nixon as a prime minister in a parliamentary system, two conclusions seem obvious. One is that the adversary relationship between the head of government and the legislature would be considerably toned down. This

57. Ernst B. Haas, *Beyond the Nation-State* (Stanford: Stanford University Press, 1964), p. 111.

might have cut down on strains and tensions that produced the worst aspects of the Nixon years. The other conclusion, which we have already suggested, is that ouster of Nixon as a parliamentary prime minister would have been far easier than forcing the first presidential resignation in American history.

Furthermore, while the situation during the Nixon years was aggravated by having different parties controlling the White House and Capitol Hill, the presidential approach has an inherent tendency to diffuse political responsibility. Who was responsible for the slowness in developing an energy policy in the United States? Several presidents have blamed Congress, and several Congresses have blamed recent presidents. Both are probably partially correct, but that is precisely the problem. In the parliamentary system, especially where the number of parties is small, it is generally clear who should be praised or blamed.

The weakness that advocates of presidentialism have seen in parliamentary systems relates to two major points: (1) the old idea of the difficulty of government by assembly, and (2) the instability of government. Regarding the first point, we have shown in chapter 2 that modern or transformed parliamentarism has strengthened the executive sufficiently to counter the threat of a body with several hundred members trying to exercise executive functions such as foreign policy. (Ironically, the initial response of many United States senators and representatives to the "imperial" presidency ostensibly revealed by the Watergate debacle was a movement toward a sort of "imperial Congress," against which Woodrow Wilson wrote in his *Congressional Government* nearly a century ago. For those who thought that Jimmy Carter's election would heal the partisan breach between legislative and executive and thus promote cooperation, the first year of the Carter incumbency must have been a disappointment. Strong majorities in both houses of Congress do not assure legislative productivity and harmony.) Regarding the second point on instability, we will see in chapter 8 that stability and parliamentarism can go along together if the party system contains two to five or six parties.

In discussing policy and administration we raised some of the key problems of modern constitutional governments. Public policy is a basic concern in the era of the welfare state, which is confronted with the enormous problems of technological change, population growth, pollution, inflation, and energy. At one time there was a virtual celebration of the idea that public policy in countries like the United States, Great Britain, and certain Western European states followed the pragmatist-incrementalist recipe of gradual, piecemeal, cumulative improvements. (This was one aspect of the theory known as the "end of ideology.")

However, in the late 1960s and the early and middle 1970s, the multitude and magnitude of social problems suggest to many that more comprehensive approaches to policy-making such as mixed-scanning or even a modified rationalism are necessary. The problem of energy, which ramifies throughout the length and breadth of any modern industrial society, seems to cry for highly complex yet integrated planning. In this connection it seems questionable whether British "muddling through" or American "pragmatism" is intellectually capable of grasping the problems, let alone solving or alleviating them.

STUDY QUESTIONS

1. What are some of the major differences between presidentialism and parliamentarism? Given the recent problems of American presidents, should the United States shelve presidentialism in favor of parliamentarism?

2. Why is it important to study not only the legal-institutional background of American presidentialism but also to explore the dimension of presidential character? What problems do your conclusions suggest about leadership in all political systems?

3. Does the Swiss collegial executive provide both an alternative to and a synthesis of parliamentarism and presidentialism?

4. Do you think that the problems of energy, economy, and ecology can be best handled by policies that emerge from the rationalist, pragmatist, or mixed-scanning approach to political and administrative decision-making?

5. Does the growth of government by committee in the form of consultative committees avoid or lessen the rigidities of the bureaucratic chain-of-command approach to governmental decision-making?

6. What are some results for effective policy-making that follow from the "inner politics" of consultative and administrative committees? Are policies reached by consensus always the best policies?

SUGGESTIONS FOR FURTHER READING

ANDERSON, JAMES E. *Public Policy-Making.* New York: Praeger Publishers, 1976.

BARBER, JAMES D. *The Presidential Character.* Englewood Cliffs, N.J.: Prentice-Hall, 1972.

CRONIN, THOMAS E. *The State of the Presidency.* Boston: Little, Brown, 1975.

DION, LEON. "The Politics of Consultation." *Government and Opposition* 8 (1973): 332–53.

DOGAN, MATTEI. *The Mandarins of Western Europe.* New York: John Wiley, 1975.

DOWNS, ANTHONY. *Inside Bureaucracy.* Boston: Little, Brown, 1967.

FENNO, RICHARD. *The President's Cabinet.* New York: Vintage Books, 1959.

GIL, FEDERICO G. *The Political System of Chile.* Boston: Houghton Mifflin, 1966.

HECLO, HUGH. *Modern Social Politics in Britain and Sweden.* New Haven: Yale University Press, 1975.

KOENIG, LOUIS W. *The Chief Executive.* New York: Harcourt Brace Jovanovich, 1975.

LOWI, THEODORE J. "American Business, Public Policy, Case-Studies, and Political Theory." In *Consensus and Conflict,* edited by James Young. New York: Dodd, Mead, 1972.

MACRIDIS, ROY C. *French Politics in Transition.* Cambridge, Mass.: Winthrop Publishers, 1975.

NEUSTADT, RICHARD. *Presidential Power.* New York: John Wiley, 1963.

PARKINSON, C. NORTHCOTE. *Parkinson's Law.* New York: Ballantine Books, 1968.

PIERCE, ROY. *French Politics and Political Institutions.* 2nd ed. New York: Harper & Row, 1973.

SARTORI, GIOVANNI. "Will Democracy Kill Democracy? Decision-Making by Majorities and by Committees." *Government and Opposition* 10 (1975): 131–58.

SIEGEL, RICHARD L., and WEINBERG, LEONARD B. *Comparing Public Policies: United States, Soviet Union, and Europe.* Homewood, Ill.: Dorsey Press, 1977.

SMITH, T. ALEXANDER. *The Comparative Policy Process.* Santa Barbara, Cal.: Clio Books, 1975.

WHEARE, K. C. *Government by Committee.* Oxford: Oxford University Press, 1955.

4
Authoritarian Dictatorship

In this and the next chapter we analyze dictatorship, the logical and historical alternative to constitutionalism. Naturally, the category of dictatorships covers a welter of regimes whose nature and moral worth vary enormously. We must first see the core differences between dictatorship and the constitutionalist regimes discussed in the last two chapters. Whatever their differences, all constitutionalist regimes are *limited by law:* the government is hemmed in by a set of operative procedural and substantive rules about the exercise of power. Dictatorships are not restricted in the same way or to the same degree by law. Here we run into the issue of sharp or even dichotomous distinctions: do all governments fall neatly into one of the two categories? The answer, alas, is no. Not only are there the familiar borderline cases, but we also find constitutionalist regimes "bending" constitutional rules on occasion. Likewise, existing legislation can even hamper the efforts of the most "totalitarian" dictatorship.

To understand these points we can set up two ideal types, perfect dictatorship and perfect constitutionalism, as the two extreme poles of a continuum (see figure 4.1). At point 0 we place perfect dictatorship to signify total absence of legal restrictions; at point 100 is perfect constitutionalism, with legalism pushed to almost straitjacket proportions. Neither pole is ever reached by an existing regime, and unfortunately all too many fall near the halfway point.

Figure 4.1. Dictatorship and Constitutionalism Continuum

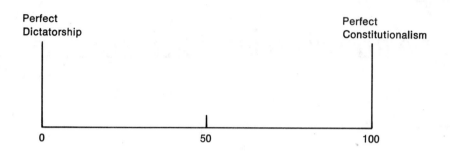

Moreover, the restrictive force of statute or customary law is only one way of limiting the power of governments. Obviously, they cannot avoid or annul the operation of physical and biological laws. They are also limited by a variety of social and political factors. The more moderate dictatorships, for example, must take care not to offend powerful social groups such as churches, big business, and landowners. Likewise, cultural and religious norms can prevent them (as well as constitutional regimes) from implementing desired policies. Thus our contrast between constitutionalism and dictatorship is not based on limits versus no limits, but on the relative strengths of legal limitations.

It is thus no paradox to assert that *many authoritarian regimes are actually "weaker" in certain respects than some constitutionalist regimes.* This means that despite its operative legal limitations, a constitutionalist regime can "by due process of law" do some things that are foreclosed to a weak authoritarian regime. The latter might encounter *extralegal* limitations to action that the former could forget about. Gabriel Almond and G. Bingham Powell have made our notion of the strengths of governments more concrete, with their five types of governmental capabilities, as shown in table 4.1.[1]

Clearly, governments differ substantially in their capabilities. What is not so clear is whether dictatorships in general or constitutionalist re-

---

1. Gabriel Almond and G. Bingham Powell, *Comparative Politics* (Boston: Little, Brown, 1966), chap. 7.

TABLE 4.1.   The Capabilities of Government

1. **Extractive:** the ability of a government to draw and mobilize resources of wealth and manpower from the society—taxes, tariffs, the draft, government monopolies.
2. **Regulative:** the ability of a government to guide and control the span of social activities—morality laws, regulation of business and labor, government standards in trades and professions, licenses, patents, fiscal-monetary policy, planning.
3. **Distributive:** the ability of a government to alter or maintain the existing balance of wealth, power, and status in the society. Most regulative functions can be turned to distributive purposes (e.g., high or low tariffs, progressive or regressive taxation, hard or soft money). (This point combines Lowi's distributive and redistributive policies of the last chapter.)
4. **Symbolic:** the ability of a government to mobilize emotional identification with the regime—idolization of the leader, pro-government parades and demonstrations, voluntary sacrifices of possessions, etc.
5. **Responsive:** the ability of a government to deliver when presented with demands and problems stemming from groups and individuals.

gimes in general have higher capabilities. While sometimes the five capabilities are interconnected and mutually supportive, governments commonly register different performances in each. Strong symbolic capability (often found in single-party regimes, for example) can ease but nowise guarantee strong extractive, regulative, distributive, or responsive performance. Nor does a strong distributive potential always go along with high extractive capability. And so on.

Though poor performance in these five capabilities has been both the explanation and the pretext for replacing constitutionalist by dictatorial regimes, a given constitutionalist regime may rank well above a given dictatorship in any or all capabilities. It is obvious that variables other than the form of government (e.g., political culture, level of economic development, the quality of leadership) play an important role in determining performance.

Our concern in the remainder of this chapter is with the major types of authoritarian dictatorship found in modern or modernizing societies. Though authoritarian dictatorships can be classified in terms of ideology, geography, and other variables, our basis of classification here is the political elite. What type of group is in power? The three main answers appear to be (1) the military rules (praetorian regimes); (2) a single-party rules (single-party regimes); and (3) a coalition of groups—possibly including the military and a single-party—rules (facade-party regimes).

PRAETORIAN REGIMES

American views toward praetorian regimes [2] reflect assumptions about the proper or "natural" relationship between civil and military authorities. It is equally evident that many foreign governments and publics do not share orthodox American views on this subject (which promote liberal or professional models for the military). Students of military politics have revealed three additional basic "models" of civil-military relations.[3] None of these models, partially excepting an antiquated aristocratic one, sanctions prolonged and direct military rule. And yet, military coups and regimes abound, especially in Latin America and Africa. Explanations of military political involvement focus on two sets of variables: (1) the general social and political conditions of coup-prone societies, and (2) internal factors governing the military. Figure 4.2 gives an exhaustive account of the pertinent variables, only some of which can we cover here.[4]

Praetorian Society

Many of the domestic social and political factors of the model in figure 4.2 are found in the theory of "praetorian society"—a type of society characterized by the high frequency of military coups. David Rappaport has characterized praetorian society in terms of four salient traits.[5] (1) There is a serious lack of consensus on the forms and functions of government. It seems likely that true constitutionalism presupposes a certain threshold of agreement on political fundamentals. A praetorian society does not agree on the proverbial rules of the game. (2) There is a naked struggle for wealth and power. While chapter 1 suggested that all political life is a sort of struggle for wealth and power, praetorian

2. The Praetorian Guard in the later days of the Roman Empire began as a kind of bodyguard for the emperors. Given their strategic position, they frequently assassinated emperors and sold the office to the highest bidder.
3. See Samuel P. Huntington, *The Soldier and the State* (New York: Vintage Books, 1957); and Alfred Stepan, *The Military in Politics* (Princeton: Princeton University Press, 1974), pp. 57–67.
4. Alan Wells, "The Coup d'Etat in Theory and Practice: Independent Black Africa in the 1960's," *American Journal of Sociology* 79, no. 4 (1974): 885.
5. David Rappaport, "A Comparative Theory of Military and Political Types," in *Changing Patterns of Military Politics*, ed. S. P. Huntington (New York: Free Press, 1970), p. 20.

Figure 4.2.   Factors in the Military Coup d'Etat

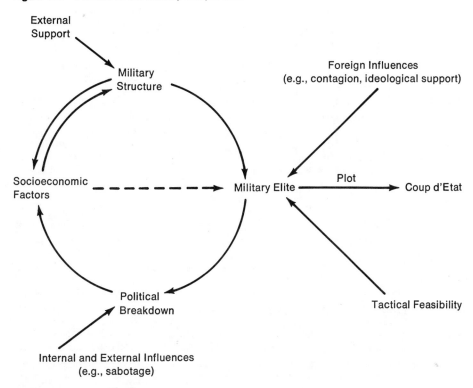

societies manifest this universal trait in a particularly ruthless, no-holds-barred manner. (3) A superrich minority faces a large poverty-stricken mass in a way that recalls Karl Marx's predictions about the final phases of capitalism. (4) There is a low level of institutionalization of political and administrative bodies because overall legitimacy is so low and overall instability is so high. With such low public morale, corruption and venality seem both the ends and means of political life. The military is tempted to intervene for two apparently opposed reasons: they want an end to the weak and corrupt civilian regime; and they want a bigger "piece of the action."

Samuel P. Huntington sees three basic types of praetorian regimes, which can succeed each other in certain societies: oligarchical, middle-class, and mass praetorianism.[6] A praetorian society is oligarchical when politicization of the masses is almost zero; middle class when it is moderate; and mass when it is high.

6. Samuel P. Huntington, *Political Order in Changing Societies* (New Haven: Yale University Press, 1968), chap. 4.

In *oligarchical praetorianism* the politically relevant public includes no more than traditional "notables"—aristocrats, upper clergy, upper middle class, big landowners, and top bureaucrats. Mass political action is rare and brief, taking the form of riots, revolts, and the like. Military coups in this setting have low stakes and aim more at changing ruling cliques than at reorienting long-range policy. The military's goals are narrow: power, money, promotion, better conditions. The traditional Latin American military coup displays this scenario.

In *middle-class praetorianism* full-scale military political activity "comes only with that differentiation of the officer corps as a semi-autonomous institution which goes with the rise of the middle class." [7] The military then becomes a crucial part, if not the vanguard, of the newly politicized and discontented middle class. The coup that dumps the oligarchical system in behalf of the middle class is a *reform coup*. Politically speaking, the reform coup is midway between the low stakes of the oligarchical period and the all-or-nothing stakes of a revolutionary coup.

The new government initiates orderly social change with land reforms, education, public works, and so on, without a full attack on the old order. Despite the reforms and the broadened participation, middle-class praetorianism still suffers from chronic military coups. The *anticipatory coup* actually occurs before the oligarchical system has been left behind. This tests out "support and opposition" as well as the strength of "the ruling monarchy or oligarchy." [8] Next comes the *break-through coup,* in which the reform-minded military seizes power. This in turn may be succeeded by a *consolidating coup,* in which radical officers push reforms to a point of no return to the old order. However, the opposite may occur with a *conservative coup* backed by upper-middle-class and oligarchical groups. These try to "put the brake on change, but they are seldom able to undo it." [9]

Mass praetorianism involves a relatively modernized and urbanized society with a generalized politicization. Change is advanced and threatens to go further. Since stable, effective, and legitimate political institutions lack deep roots, further mass participation poses a threat often met by a *veto coup.* The classic case is the military ouster of Juan Peron in 1955 in Argentina. Peron, a military man himself, enjoyed strong

7. Ibid., p. 201.
8. Ibid., p. 204.
9. Samuel P. Huntington, "Patterns of Violence in World Politics," in *Changing Patterns of Military Politics,* p. 36.

lower-class support. His demagogic political style and reforms were too much for the military.

This survey should indicate some of the diversity of the military variant of authoritarian dictatorship. Military coups and praetorian regimes run the range from reaction to reform to virtual revolution. Table 4.2 summarizes this diversity.

TABLE 4.2.   Typology of Military Coups

Type of Coup	Social Setting	Political Significance
Low stakes	Oligarchical praetorianism	Minor changes of personnel, division of spoils
Reform 　1.　Anticipatory 　2.　Breakthrough	Transition from oligarchic to middle-class praetorianism	The rise of middle-class groups into the political elite
Consolidating	Middle-class praetorianism	Prevents returns to old oligarchic patterns
Conservative	Middle-class praetorianism	Attempts to bring back the good old days of oligarchic rule
Veto	Mass praetorianism	Attempts to halt or reverse the trend to mass participation

Internal Military Factors

The theory of praetorian society explains military political behavior mainly by reference to factors external to the military. But inner dispositions also make the military succumb to outside pressures to act. Morris Janowitz speaks of four elements of a military "ideology," [10] which we prefer to think of as a mentality.[11] He sees hypernationalism, puritanism, collectivism, and antipolitics as particularly important in Third World countries.

Hypernationalism refers to the exaggerated nationalism found in

10. Morris Janowitz, *The Military in the Political Development of New Nations* (Chicago: University of Chicago Press, 1967), pp. 64–65.
11. Here we follow Juan Linz, for whom "mentalities are ways of thinking and feeling, more emotional than rational, that provide noncodified ways of reacting to different situations. . . . Mentality is intellectual attitude; ideology is intellectual content. Mentality is psychic predisposition, ideology is reflection, self-interpretation; . . . mentality is formless, fluctuating—ideology, however, is firmly formed." Juan Linz, "Totalitarian and Authoritarian Regimes," in *Handbook of Political Science*, ed. F. I. Greenstein and N. W. Polsby (Reading, Mass.: Addison-Wesley, 1975), 3:266–67.

many military organizations. The themes of national unity, nation-building, even revenge for national humiliations figure heavily in the mentality of many soldiers. This produces a fervent hope to transcend "primordial" ethnic and religious differences and merge all in a unity.

We can readily see why the military can attack a civilian government on nationalistic grounds. Perhaps the government did not defend the "national honor" vigorously enough. Or the government has come under foreign or alien influences. Maybe its efforts to unify domestic groups have miscarried or it has reneged on promises for greater defense expenditures.

Puritanism refers more to life-style than to specific policy issues. The military come to value a harsh and Spartan regimen with few luxuries and frills. They pride themselves on being harder and tougher than ordinary civilians. This is often accompanied by contempt and disgust when they view the corruption and luxury of civilian political leaders. They view such politicians as effeminate and flabby, a standing insult to themselves and the nation. Such corrupt officials do not deserve to rule. It is the "sacred" duty of the military to kick them out for good.

Collectivism Janowitz sees as the "acceptance of collective public enterprise as a basis for achieving social, political, and economic change." [12] To this we can in part attribute the popularity of a vaguely defined "socialism" (African or Arab) in a number of military regimes. One reason for this collectivism is that the military itself is a kind of "collective public enterprise." Since the military tends to consider itself the most effective organization around, it seems natural to conclude that what works for the military will also work in the economy. Furthermore, the collectivist idea of a "command economy" with a central planning board issuing plans and orders squares well with the dream of every hard-line officer.

Antipolitics refers to the military's largely negative evaluation of politics and politicians, as commonly understood. The military thinks of politics as petty and corrupt—wheeling and dealing, dirty deals, and double deals at the public expense. Even the few honest politicians are long on talk and short on action, while action is the military's strong suit. The military claims to stand "above politics" and heal the wounds of a people lacerated by divisions promoted and exploited by ambitious and unscrupulous politicians.

Other internal factors that condition the readiness of a military or-

12. Janowitz, *Military in Political Development*, p. 64.

ganization (or part of it) to strike or to rule are the social background of officers and the general condition of military life. If the military elite is recruited from social groups and strata that differ from those providing the social and economic elite, the chances for military intervention are heightened. If the recruitment base of the officers is higher than that of other elites, the coup will tend to be conservative or reactionary. If the recruitment base is lower, the coup will tend to be reformist or even revolutionary.

Also important in disposing the military toward intervention are mundane issues such as salaries, promotions, respect for the military, the size and distribution of the defense budget, and so on. As with most political action, military intervention involves a complex mixture of principle and gain, ambition and self-sacrifice. It may well be that broad theories of praetorianism or of military "ideology" and organization misplace the true explanatory emphasis. A recent student of the military in Africa complains, for example, that "insufficient weight is placed on the personal motives of ambitious or discontented officers, who have a great deal of freedom and scope for action in fragmented. unstructured, unstable political systems." [13]

The Military Regime and Modernization

The problem of evaluating the performance of praetorian regimes has produced a debate over the military as an "agent of modernization." We will examine the pros and cons of this issue because its very complexity and possible irrelevancy is highly instructive.

In the late 1950s and early 1960s some social scientists overcame liberal distaste for militarism to suggest that military rule in underdeveloped countries might sometimes provide the most viable political solution for those countries. More elaborately, the thesis held that military regimes might be the most effective custodians of modernization in the "transitional" situation between traditional and modern society. The following five arguments were made in behalf of the military's favorable impact on modernization.

1. *Military organizations are the epitome of modern organizations.*[14]

13. Samuel Decalo, *Coups and Army Rule in Africa* (New Haven: Yale University Press, 1976), p. 21.
14. Lucian Pye, "Armies in the Process of Political Modernization," in *The Role of the Military in Underdeveloped Countries*, ed. J. J. Johnson (Princeton: Princeton University Press, 1962), p. 62.

This argument assumes that the Weberian bureaucratic model is a main trait of modernity. Since armies in new states took World War II armies as their prototype, they also absorbed unity of command, functional division of labor, merit promotions, rational techniques, and the like. The military thus is a cluster of modern orientations and can serve as a center of diffusion for these attitudes. Traditional forms of corruption would be ruled out when the military ruled. (This argument presupposes the Weberian linkage of bureaucracy and modernity as discussed in chapter 1.)

2. *Armies are easier to create and develop than other forms of modern organization, such as parties and bureaucracies.*[15] The cold war made this development of armies "easier" because the Soviets, the Americans, and to a lesser extent the Chinese were rather prodigal in dispensing technical assistance and military hardware. Their pocketbooks were somewhat tighter when it came to funding political and administrative institutions.

3. *The military sense the need for change.* Change is the logical prerequisite for modernization and the normality of change is one token of modernity. Lucien Pye sees the military's pro-change outlook coming from two sources.[16] First, the military must keep one eye abroad so that its capabilities are not outstripped by foreign adversaries. Second, its semiisolation from the rest of society improves the military's sensitivity to the need for change.

4. *The military is an instrument of social mobility.* Increased social mobility is usually considered both a cause and an effect of modernization. Bringing new people into higher social, economic, and political positions unleashes forces that crack the "cake of custom." Modern armies supposedly cast their recruitment nets deeper into the social structure (even for high officers) than do traditional armies. Edward Shils finds that wherever low social mobility, low economic growth, and low educational opportunity prevail, the "army tends to recruit into its officer ranks the brightest and most ambitious young men of the small towns and countryside." [17]

Furthermore, the military is "ubiquitous, it recruits from all parts of the country, and, most important of all, it is national in its symbol-

15. Ibid., p. 74 .
16. Pye, "Armies"; see entire article.
17. Edward Shils, "The Military in the Political Development of New States," in Johnson, *Role of the Military,* p. 17.

ism." [18] From the Pye-Shils perspective, the military not only raises up new men with new ideas, but it also makes inroads on the "primordial sentiments" of ethnicity, religion, tribalism, and localism that are the flies in the ointment of most theories of modernization.

5. *The military is unified.* When the social differences just mentioned have a high potential for political conflict, they are called "cleavages." The unified military, it is held, can provide the only effective counter-weight to the centrifugal tendencies of the various cleavages.

Understandably, this rosy estimate of the military's modernizing potential has roused substantial criticism. The following four arguments represent the most important critical themes.

1. *Armies tend to bureaucratic and social conservatism.* This argument suggests that "bureaucratic sclerosis" soon afflicts even the most reform-minded military organization. Parkinson's law finds the military bureaucracy growing to unmanageable size, because new bureaus proliferate to justify the officers' positions. The "Peter Principle" suggests that a military organization declines in effectiveness because officers are promoted to their level of incompetence. [19] These inbuilt tendencies toward caution and inertia jibe well with the ideas and interests of established social groups.

Eric Nordlinger points to two other negative influences on the military's modernization potential. First, since there is a strong correlation between military takeovers and inflated military expenditures, the evidence suggests that the military rulers "actively pursue their corporate interests and that they do so in a way that detracts from economic and social change." [20] By grabbing a larger chunk of the national budget, the military leaves precious little for reform projects.

Second, Nordlinger feels that the mainly middle-class background of officers makes their reformist pledges largely irredeemable. The growing conservatism of praetorian regimes does not result from a "change of heart" among the officers, nor from new perspectives that power brings. It is rather that "they were not convinced reformers to begin with; they simply used the call for economic and social change for the realization of their own class and status interests." [21]

18. Ibid., p. 32.
19. Lawrence J. Peter, *The Peter Principle* (New York: Bantam Books, 1972).
20. Eric A. Nordlinger, "Soldiers in Mufti: The Impact of Military Rule upon Social and Economic Change in the Non-Western States," *American Political Science Review* 64 (December 1970): 1135.
21. Ibid., p. 1148.

2. *The military is not necessarily unified politically, nor is it a true "melting pot" of the nation.* The military's internal political differences may be just as serious as those among civilian politicians. Since these differences can lead to coups and counter-coups, the argument about the military bringing stability seems refuted. To avoid this conflict may require wishy-washy compromises that destroy the original justification for military rule.

Likewise the military's melting pot function may be more mythical than real. The ethnic and other differences are papered over by the army, not overcome. The recent history of Pakistan, Nigeria, Uganda, and other states provides eloquent testimony on this score. The military's obsession with a facade of unity may ironically create a pressure-cooker situation, with no benefit from a safety valve to air political and social controversy. At a certain point the whole thing may blow.

3. *The military cannot create viable political institutions to handle increasing mass participation.* Henry Bienen suggests that "armed forces can be more concerned with control than with modernization." This is due not only to the caution and inertia mentioned in point 1, but also to the failure of the military "to gain consent as a ruling group." [22] The problem is that a military organization is good at some things and not so good at others. One weak point is mobilizing mass civilian support for the government and its tasks; another is using ideology to create legitimacy.

4. *Military regimes are not notably less corrupt and more efficient than the civilian regimes they replace.* While the shock of a military takeover may temporarily cut down corruption, it soon reappears and often involves the same military leaders who previously denounced it. What Samuel Decalo finds about African military regimes has been echoed by specialists on the Middle East, South and Southeast Asia, and Latin America:

> Once in power military leaders have not been able to resolve the socio-economic and political issues facing them; many are linked to external factors outside their control; others are either intractable or not amenable to simple solutions; and still others require social and fiscal policies contrary to the army's inclinations or incompatible with stable military rule.[23]

Deciding who is right about the military's modernizing potential may prove impossible for two reasons. First, the concepts of *modernization*

22. Henry Bienen, "The Background to Contemporary Study of Militaries and Modernization," in *The Military and Modernization,* ed. H. Bienen (New York: Atherton, 1971), p. 19.
23. Decalo, *Army Rule,* pp. 36–37.

and *political development* may be too vague to allow decent comparisons between praetorian and nonpraetorian regimes. Second, even if we get our concepts straight, the two sorts of regime may not show any consistent pattern.

Modernization and Political Development

While there are many theories of modernization, most of them agree that modernization is the transition between traditionalism and modernity. Some of these theories view modernization in terms of various subprocesses. Table 4.3 can be considered a "syndrome" of modernization.

TABLE 4.3.   The Subprocesses of Modernization

---

1. **Economic growth:** modernization involves a gross national product (GNP) that continuously expands and produces a more diversified economy.
2. **Growth of science:** modernization involves spread of scientific knowledge and methods at the expense of traditional lore.
3. **Technological advance:** modernization involves establishment and growth of industrial centers and their attendant technical paraphernalia.
4. **Secularization:** modernization involves decline of the role and influence of organized religion and theological conceptions upon social, cultural, and political affairs.
5. **Growth of the modern state:** modernization involves increase in the state's capabilities and development in bureaucratic administration.
6. **Growth of nationalism:** modernization involves spread and intensification of the sentiment that all the people in a certain territory belong to one nation.
7. **Democratization:** modernization involves decline of status inequality; growth of egalitarian claims in law and politics; demands for broader participation; increased social mobility.

To place these seven subprocesses under the umbrella term "modernization" raises the most serious questions.[24] Not only do some of the subprocesses emerge without the others, but even if they emerge together they may be out of phase and contradictory. While economic growth and growth of the state, for example, have often been mutually reinforcing, many cases could be cited of their working at cross-purposes. Likewise, religiously oriented forms of nationalism have certainly delayed secularization.

The expression "political development" has usually suggested that

24. We will also make use of the problematic relationship of these seven subprocesses of change in discussing the long-term causes of revolution in chapter 7.

aspect of overall modernization that produced a "modern polity." There should be no surprise then if the concept is elusive and controversial.[25] Such slipperiness has led Samuel P. Huntington to offer a more modest but more manageable concept of political development, divorced from grand theories of progress and modernization.[26] Instead of the latter he speaks more broadly of *social change*. Political development he virtually equates with institutionalization—a concept we have repeatedly employed in a general way. Huntington employs four pairs of opposites, in this case to suggest the difference between high and low levels of institutionalization. We have alluded to "institutionalization" before in a general sense. Now it is time to firm the concept up because it will be useful to us here and in later chapters.

1. *Adaptability-rigidity*. A highly institutionalized structure is highly adaptable. It can adjust itself and cope with changing pressures from its environment. It can take on new tasks without paralysis or collapse. It is flexible and resilient. A poorly institutionalized structure is rigid, unable to confront new situations without enormous strain. In the face of change and new tasks, its fate is either disintegration or survival as a mere ornament.

2. *Complexity-simplicity*. A highly institutionalized structure has divided and subdivided itself into specific functional areas. This allows it to benefit from the division of labor and to adapt with ease to new tasks. Simple organizations cannot readily take on new tasks nor can they maximize utilization of existing resources. The simplicity of an organization indicates that it has not really settled on its goals and procedures.

3. *Autonomy-subordination*. As an organization becomes more institutionalized it becomes more autonomous. It is no longer in the shadow of some "parent organization." Autonomy means that an institution's leaders are more or less free to run the organization as they see fit. Subordination means that the organization is an appendage of something else; its leaders are no more than errand boys for some outside group.

25. Lucian Pye once catalogued the following definitions or parts of definitions of "political development": (1) the political prerequisite of economic development, (2) the polity typical of industrial societies, (3) political modernization, (4) the operation of a nation-state, (5) administrative and legal development, (6) mass mobilization and participation, (7) the building of democracy, (8) stability and orderly change, (9) mobilization and power, (10) an aspect of complex social change. Quoted in Samuel P. Huntington, "The Change to Change: Modernization, Development, and Politics," *Comparative Politics* 3 (April 1971): 301.
26. Ibid.

4. *Coherence-disunity.* A highly institutionalized organization can be vast and complex and yet retain a sense of fundamental unity. Disunity prevails with low levels of institutionalization because each component group wants to "go it alone." The organization seems composed of little organizational "fiefdoms" ready to break off from the parent body at the slightest provocation or good opportunity.

Even if we substitute "social change" for "modernization" and "institutionalization" for "political development," our original problem may be no nearer solution. It may really be impossible to give a general answer to the question of the modernizing potential of praetorian regimes. The conclusions of a recent study are somewhat discouraging in terms of the original promilitary and antimilitary debate.[27] First, in terms of performance military regimes do not form a distinct category of modern regimes.[28] Second, the diversity found among military regimes is not basically different from that found among civilian regimes. Third, the amount of similarity or difference between military and civilian regimes changes when we look at different issues. Finally and most importantly, the study finds that "the nature of military regimes cannot be adequately understood either in terms of assisting or inhibiting modernization or in terms of a typology based on a simple distinction between military and civilian regimes.[29]

Even if this last conclusion is a bit drastic it serves to remind us of the difficulties of creating an adequate typology of modern dictatorships. It also suggests that our focus on the ruling group, despite its old-fashioned quality, is one of the least troublesome approaches.

SINGLE-PARTY REGIMES

The second major type of authoritarian dictatorship is the single-party regime. When considering this type of regime, several initial problems must be cleared up, for, as Giovanni Sartori points out, the expression

27. R. D. McKinlay and A. S. Cohan, "A Comparative Analysis of the Political and Economic Performance of Military and Civilian Regimes," *Comparative Politics* 7 (October 1975): 1–30.
28. Performance in this study was related to such things as degree of constitutionalism, parliamentarism, freedom of parties, proportion of the military in cabinet posts, banning Communist parties, executive tenure. Economic factors included the GNP, the budget, production, export-imports, investments. Military factors included the size of the military and of the defense budget.
29. McKinlay and Cohan, "Military and Civilian Regimes," p. 23.

"one-party" is often applied to three different situations.[30] First of all, there is the pure one-party or *monopolistic party* situation, where no other parties are tolerated. Their suppression is either required by law or accomplished by extralegal procedures. Next is the situation of the *hegemonic party*, where "other parties are permitted to exist, but as satellite parties for they are not permitted to compete with the hegemonic party in antagonistic terms and on an equal basis." [31] From our point of view the differences between the monopolistic and the hegemonic parties can be ignored, and we will call both "single-party regimes."

Unfortunately, a third rather different situation has been confused with the previous two. This is the *predominant party* situation, where one party always captures the overwhelming majority in parliament, if not necessarily the near-totality of the votes. Here, "other parties are not only permitted to exist, but do exist as legitimate—if not necessarily effective—competitors of the predominant party. The minor parties are truly independent antagonists of the predominant party, and all parties have an equal start." [32] Rather than a single-party political system, the predominant party system is really a plural party system with traits of a multiparty system.

The three situations just described can be stages of a country's political history. A familiar pattern in some African countries in the 1950s and 1960s began with a nationalist predominant party faced with weak but genuine competitors. Then this party became hegemonic by depriving the weaker parties of real independence and potential for challenge. The third step of a monopolistic party system was taken in places like Ghana and Tanzania by outlawing all other parties.[33]

Even with these clarifications, authoritarian single-party regimes present striking differences. Ideology, centralization, party-state relationships, traces of true constitutionalism—all these differences make one despair of doing more than treating each case as unique. Nevertheless, typologies exist that will serve our purposes, even if they sometimes miss the specific mark. Two broad concerns underlie most of these typologies: (1) relation of the party to society; and (2) relation of the party to the government.

30. Giovanni Sartori, "The Typology of Party Systems—Proposals for Improvement," in *Mass Politics*, ed. E. Allardt and S. Rokkan (New York: Free Press, 1970), p. 327.
31. Ibid.
32. Ibid.
33. Aristide R. Zolberg, *Creating Political Order* (New York: Rand-McNally, 1966).

TABLE 4.4.   Mobilizational and Pluralistic Patterns of the Single-Party

The Mobilizational Pattern	The Pluralistic Pattern
1. **Participation:** the party is interested in activating broad mass participation.	1. The party is not concerned with mass participation; rather it appeals to leaders of established groups so long as they are not too hostile to the party.
2. **Ideology:** such mobilization is both cause and effect of the party's commitment to clear and distinct, programmatic ideology.	2. Though the party may espouse some sort of ideology, it is rather vague and held with minimum intensity. There is an adjustment of theory to practice, not vice versa.
3. **Centralization and discipline:** to spread the ideology and mobilize the masses requires a strong military-type organization.	3. The party is more a coalition of locally powerful notables than a monolithic hierarchy. Bargaining and negotiations play a larger policy role than simple orders from the top.
4. **Movement:** the party wants to change society, perhaps revolutionize it, more or less in terms of the ideology.	4. The party reflects existing social forces and is committed more to gradual reformism than to drastic social surgery.
5. **Auxiliary organizations and activities:** the party develops an elaborate infrastructure of social, recreational, sportive, cultural groups in order to control members and win new members.	5. The party may have links with outside groups, but these are hardly satellites or fronts of the party. They preserve considerable autonomy.

There are two patterns of party-society relationships: the *mobilizational* and the *pluralistic* (see table 4.4).[34] As there are two opposed patterns of party-society relationships (shown in the mobilizational-pluralistic dichotomy), we find two opposed patterns of party-government relationships. When the party has the upper hand over the government and administration, it is *dominant;* when the government controls the party organization, the latter is *subordinate.* Samuel P. Huntington suggests three standards of party dominance (and subordination).[35]

1. *Legitimation of the political system.* Does the political system as a whole derive its legitimacy (such as it is) from the single-party (and its

34. The following analysis and the chart related to it are a synthesis of views contained in James S. Coleman and Carl G. Rosberg, Jr., "Introduction," in *Political Parties and National Integration in Tropical Africa*, ed. J. S. Coleman and C. G. Rosberg, Jr. (Berkeley: University of California Press, 1966); and David Apter, *The Politics of Modernization* (Chicago: University of Chicago Press, 1965).
35. Samuel P. Huntington, "Social and Institutional Dynamics of One-Party Systems," in *Authoritarian Politics in Modern Society*, ed. S. P. Huntington and C. H. Moore (New York: Basic Books, 1970), p. 6.

ideology?) or from other sources? The party's legitimizing role is part of its dominance over the government. Contrarily, if institutions such as a traditional monarchy or church have a substantial legitimizing function, the likelihood of a subordinate place for the party is increased.

2. *Recruitment of political leadership.* Since legislatures in most single-party systems are little more than organized cheering sections, recruitment is mainly for executive-administrative posts. The judiciary may be included in this category in certain regimes. Are these top posts manned by officials who have climbed up the party ladder? Or does the leader choose nonparty bureaucrats, soldiers, and "notables" for most of these offices? Or does he choose people, who, to be sure, are formally party members, but whose service and loyalty to the party is highly limited? In the latter two cases party dominance would be hard to conceive. In short, true party dominance demands that most top posts fall to key party figures.

3. *Interest aggregation and policy-making.* A truly dominant single-party is the leading influence in the policy-making process—"the authoritative allocation of values." It aggregates interests by being the main funnel and filter of demands arising from social groups. It makes itself the champion and spokesman for some types of demands, while rejecting or repressing others. Furthermore, the party guides the translation of acceptable demands into policy outputs. Its top members supervise all stages of policy formulation and implementation, even if detail work is left to nonparty personnel. A subordinate party dominates policy only rarely and in selected areas.

On the three fronts of legitimation, leadership recruitment, and policy, the single-party may face serious competition from power rivals. The dominant party is able to outdistance them for the most part; the subordinate party may find itself a distant second, third, or fourth. Table 4.5 identifies the main types of power rival.[36]

Putting our two factors together, we can generate a four-member typology including   (1) the dominant-mobilizational single-party regime; (2) the subordinate-mobilizational single-party regime; (3) the dominant-pluralistic single-party regime; and (4) the subordinate-pluralistic single-party regime. A closer look at Fascist Italy and Franco's Spain in the next two sections will help us to evaluate the strengths and weaknesses of this typology, as well as to gain a deeper understanding of authoritarian regimes.

36. Based on Huntington, *Authoritarian Politics.*

TABLE 4.5. Power Rivals of the Single-Party

1. **Personalistic actors:** charismatic or personal leaders
2. **Traditional actors:** the church or monarchy
3. **Bureaucratic actors:** the public administration
4. **Parliamentary actors:** national assemblies, local government bodies
5. **Functional socioeconomic actors:** groups such as peasants, workers, managers, businessmen, technicians, and intellectuals

FASCIST ITALY

Some scholars consider it wrong to include the regime that coined the expression *lo stato totalitario* in the category of mere authoritarian dictatorships.[37] Despite Benito Mussolini's rhetoric about "everything within the state and nothing outside the state," however, Fascist Italy fell considerably short of true totalitarianism. The influence of the monarchy—King Victor Emmanuel III reigned throughout the whole Fascist era of 1922 to 1943—and of the Roman Catholic church are only the most visible instances of failure to carry through totalitarian rule.

Looking to legitimation by the single-party, it is clear that the Italian Fascist party, or Partito Nazionale Fascista (PNF), provided only part of the legitimacy of Mussolini's regime. For some, Mussolini's original appointment by the king to the post of prime minister was the source of legitimacy of an otherwise questionable regime. For others, Mussolini's 1929 Concordat with the Roman Catholic church promised more cordial church-state relations than had been seen for decades.

While any attempt to divide the history of Fascist Italy into distinct stages is hazardous, several decisive turning points exist, as shown in table 4.6. Unavoidably the more than twenty years of the regime produced changes in the role of the Fascist party.

The PNF began in 1919–22 as an authentic movement of mobilization. Though its ideology was inchoate, it harbored some potentially revolutionary notions. The "irrationalism" its critics attacked was at least a dynamic, activist irrationalism. The stage seemed set for a dictatorship based on a dominant-mobilizational single-party. This seemed the trend of events through the mid-1920s.

But the circumstances of Mussolini's original appointment as govern-

37. Cf. Dante Germino, *The Italian Fascist Party in Power* (Minneapolis: University of Minnesota Press, 1959).

TABLE 4.6. Stages in the History of Fascist Italy

1. 1922–25: legal takeover of power and period of quasi constitutionalism
2. 1925–28: emergence of an authoritarian regime and the destruction of serious opposition
3. 1928–39: development of an only moderately strong single-party with the creation of authentically Fascist institutions
4. 1939–43: completion of the corporative order and increasing subordination of the regime to Nazi Germany

ment leader are the key to later developments. Instead of leading a movement dedicated to destroying the whole institutional setup, Mussolini was appointed prime minister, later head of government, while the king remained titular head of state. To attain and retain power Mussolini compromised with traditional groups and institutions. Unlike Hitler, Mussolini was unable or unwilling to shake off his early deals. Right off, some of the potential for dominance and mobilization of the PNF had to be curtailed for pragmatic reasons.

The weakening of the PNF, with sporadic attempts at recovery, continued through the late 1920s and the 1930s. The party became more subordinate and if it never became wholly pluralistic, much of its mobilizational drive fizzled out. Alberto Aquarone thus speaks of a "process of depoliticization, of reduction to a prevalently choreographic role," which overtook the party in the 1930s.[38] Responsibility for this goes to the Duce himself, "who more or less consciously tended increasingly to make Fascism more into a personal regime than a party regime."[39] The personalistic dictatorship not only forestalled a true party-state, but also hamstrung fascism's experiment in economic reorganization: the corporative state.

The negative impact of Mussolini's personalism on party dominance was ironically reinforced by the statism of Fascist ideology. Though never fully realized, this statism demanded that the state penetrate and animate all social institutions. Admirers of poetic justice might find solace in the fact that this principle was also applied to the PNF, the original bearer of statist ideology. In the Duce's own words:

> "If in Fascism all is in the state, the Party as well cannot avoid such inexorable necessity, and must therefore cooperate subordinately with the organs of the state.

38. Alberto Aquarone, *L'organizzazione dello stato totalitario* (Turin: Einaudi, 1965), p. 182.
39. Ibid.

"We must not confuse the [PNF], which is the primordial political force of the regime with the regime itself, which coinvolves, embraces, and harmonizes this political force and all the others of various natures." [40]

The other political forces Mussolini refers to we have called "political rivals" of the single-party. Let us survey their role in Fascist Italy.

Political Rivals

Mussolini himself was a rival of the single-party. It is hard to avoid the label "charismatic" with respect to Mussolini, considering him as a personalistic actor. He refused to subordinate himself or his policies to the PNF. Many Italians distinguished Mussolini sharply from the party. While they supported or tolerated the man, fascism itself symbolized violence and rowdiness beneath their contempt. If they could have voted in these terms, it probably would have turned out: Mussolini Si, Fascismo No! No one was more aware of this than the Duce of fascism.

Regarding traditional actors, we have mentioned the survival and popularity of the monarchy throughout fascism. This must have been a serious disappointment to those party members who dreamed of a revolutionary "fascistization" of the Italian political system. The Concordat restored privileges to the Catholic church, denied to it in the previous decades of Liberal rule. Catholic organizations continued to operate, despite controversies with party and government authorities. Factors such as these made fascism's self-proclaimed totalitarianism rather ludicrous.

In terms of bureaucratic actors, the fascistization of the administration, the police, and the military left much to be desired. Many bureaucrats remained outside the party fold, and suggestions from party militants to purge them in favor of party loyalists were squelched by Mussolini. Many bureaucrats, of course, joined the PNF—some through conviction, more for opportunistic reasons. Promotion was generally easier for PNF members.

But Giovanni-come-lately Fascists were no substitute for the massive purge and reorganization necessary to make the party master of the bureaucracy. That the Duce did not share Hitler's disdain for bureaucracy is seen in his wearing so many ministerial hats. At one point he was head of government, minister of foreign affairs, minister of corporations, minister of interior, minister of war, minister of marine

40. Quoted in ibid., p. 164.

(naval affairs), and minister of air. Though he later gave up some of these posts, the real result of his apparent tirelessness was to make the permanent undersecretaries the true decision-makers.[41]

As in some other single-party regimes, the PNF had its own party militia, the Voluntary Militia for National Security (MVSN). However, the militia was a far cry from, say, Himmler's SS in Nazi Germany. There the SS became a vast and powerful secret political police. The MVSN on the contrary was relegated to a secondary role, useful to Mussolini more to check other police units than to launch a full-scale attack on fascism's political enemies.[42]

Since the MVSN also posed no serious threat to the military, they along with the police exhibited the same mixture of support and aloofness vis-à-vis fascism as the bureaucracy. Thus the three bureaucratic actors—military, police, administration—enjoyed a good strategic position to compete with the PNF for power and influence. Often the competition produced serious clashes in various spots in Italy, at least until the full domestication of the party in the mid-1930s.

In the early years Parliament was a thorn in the side of the PNF, because both non-Fascist and anti-Fascist parties were still represented. After 1928, with a PNF monopoly in the lower house of Parliament—called the Chamber of Deputies from 1928 to 1939, and the Council of Fasci and Corporations from 1939 to 1943—the "rubber stamp" stereotype (as we will see below) is essentially appropriate. The Senate, however, which was made up of appointees for life, always contained a shrinking number of non-Fascists. Now and then the sounds of opposition would emanate from its chambers.

In the case of social and economic groups, the Fascist corporative state (see below) was set up to absorb the various business, labor, agricultural, professional, and cultural organizations in the political structure of the state. The main business organization was the Fascist Confederation of Industry. The non-Fascist trade unions were disbanded and Fascist organizations took their place. But how far these various organizations were under the direct and complete control of the PNF is another matter entirely. Though the expanded Fascist unions were an integral part of the "movement" and monopolized legal union activity, Mussolini prevented any serious independent action through government controls. The business confederations supported the regime, if

41. Ibid., p. 305.
42. Ibid., p. 256.

somewhat tepidly, but were Fascist in name only. Though the formal institutions of the corporative state were truly "fascistized," much of political and economic importance transpired outside them. Direct negotiations of the relevant groups under governmental rather than party auspices was the norm in certain sectors.

Mussolini's Government

Alberto Aquarone describes the evolution of the PNF in terms of "clientelistic bureaucratization" and "depoliticization." In the terms of our typology, this means that the PNF became much more pluralistic and much less mobilizational as time went on. Aquarone explains this by reference to the "incapacity of Fascism to create for itself a ruling class of the highest level. This is typical of every authoritarian regime with a prevalently personal character. . . ." [43] This must be kept in mind as we take a look at the government structure, the PNF organization, and the corporative structure in turn. Figure 4.3, though simplified, depicts the political structure as rather like a web woven by a neurotic spider.

One way to understand Mussolini's government is to view it as the survival, subversion, and transformation of institutions of the Liberal era of 1861–1922. If the monarchy was a figurehead institution under Mussolini, so it was in the earlier system. The relationship between the head of government and the head of state, though sometimes tense, was generally proper. Mussolini tried by tokens of respect and deference to compensate the king for his political weakness. Sometimes he even modified a policy because of kingly objections.

Mussolini was appointed prime minister in October 1922. In December 1925 the office of head of government (*Capo del governo*) was created and the government virtually removed from parliamentary control. Its responsibility was theoretically to the king. Ironically this new arrangement paving the way for dictatorship was closer to the letter of the Italian Constitution—the so-called Albertine Statute. In the cabinet Mussolini towered over all its other members, able to hire, fire, and shift them around at will. He was the main force in policy-making, and the cabinet followed the common pattern of dictatorships as a *group of administrative assistants for the leader*. Naturally, some members had more influence with the Duce than others for a variety of personal and political reasons.

43. Ibid., p. 301.

Figure 4.3.   Political Structure of Fascist Italy (c. 1932)

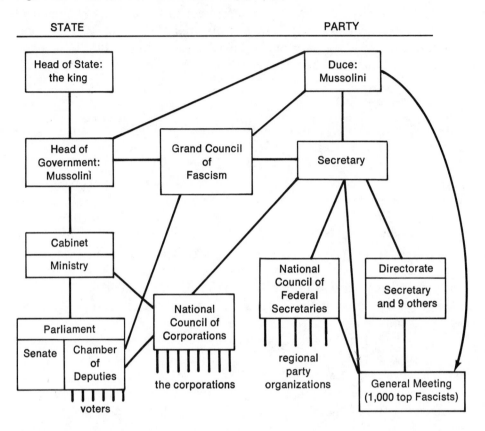

The Fascist "Parliaments"

In spite of the talk of "totalitarianism" and a "revolution," the regime maintained the facade of classic parliamentarism until 1939. As early as 1923 the "Acerbo reform" so doctored the electoral law that the party with at least 25 percent of the popular votes would get two-thirds of the seats in the Chamber of Deputies. Following this procedure the 1924 elections returned an overwhelming Fascist majority. Reforms in 1928 altered the composition of the Chamber almost beyond recognition. The new all-Fascist Chamber abandoned geographical constituencies and was reduced in size to four hundred. The selection procedure involved several steps.

First, thirteen National Confederations, representing business and labor in areas such as agriculture, commerce, transportation, banking, and the like, nominated a grand total of 800 candidates. An additional

200 nominations were made by 23 different educational, cultural, veterans, and social organizations. Next, the list of 1000 was presented to the Grand Council of Fascism, which would screen the list and narrow it down to a new list of 400.

Finally, the Italian electorate was given the chance to accept or reject the entire list of 400 nominees. In 1929 the list was approved by a vote of 8,500,000 to 135,000. The 1934 "elections" had similar results. There was a proviso for a second list should the first be rejected, but this remained a dead letter. Also noteworthy is that the new law cut down the electorate by a substantial 24 percent.

In 1939 another more decisive step away from parliamentarism was taken. By then the apparatus of the much-heralded corporative state had been set up. The Chamber of Deputies was abolished and with it any trace of direct popular elections. In its place emerged the Council of Fasci and Corporations, composed totally of ex officio or appointed members from three previously distinct organizations. Table 4.7 analyzes its membership.[44]

TABLE 4.7.   Composition of the Council of Fasci and Corporations

---

1. The Grand Council of Fascism (18 members)
2. The National Council of the Corporations (525 members)
    a. Members of the Corporative Central Committee, including all ministers and undersecretaries
    b. Councilors representing the PNF, professional associations, and Fascist cooperative organization
3. The National Council of the PNF (139 members)
    a. The PNF secretary, national directorate
    b. Federal secretaries and other PNF officials

To characterize the legislatures in Fascist Italy (and other single-party situations), we have used phrases like "rubber stamp" and "organized cheering section." But we need a more subtle understanding of the Fascist legislatures in order to have a better general understanding of their role in dictatorships. Before the big reorganization of 1939, G. L. Field pointed to four main traits of the Fascist legislatures, as mentioned in table 4.8.[45]

44. Based on Aquarone, *L'organizzazione*, pp. 276–77.
45. G. Lowell Field, *The Syndical and Corporative Institutions of Fascist Italy* (New York: AMS, 1968), p. 56.

TABLE 4.8.   Characteristics of the Italian Fascist Legislative Process

1. The large share of decree-law ratifications among the bills considered—the Chamber reduced to approving decrees of Mussolini's government; lawmaking initiative virtually monopolized by the Government (rubber stamp at work).
2. The lack of *expressed* opposition in the Chamber to the passage of bills (the rubber stamp again).
3. Frequent subservient declarations of thanks to the Government for being allowed to approve their bills (the organized cheering section).
4. Frequent passage of a group of bills without discussion (the rubber stamp).

While the Chamber's voting statistics support such conclusions, they also suggest that not only in the incompletely Fascist Senate,[46] but also in the all-Fascist Chamber, *most bills did arouse some opposition in the form of a small number of negative votes.* That the range for no's was only 1–8 votes out of over 350 voting does not change the fact that "the passion for unanimity" found in all totalitarian and some authoritarian regimes was stymied in Fascist Italy.

In the Senate the no's could read more than 20 out of around 280 votes. Another glowing cinder of constitutionalist opposition is seen in the Government's withdrawal of 35 of its 3213 bills.[47] While some of these withdrawals no doubt reflected the Government's own reconsiderations, the rest may have resulted from intense reactions among the deputies. The survival of the Senate and the Chamber (until 1939), however much a caricature of genuine parliamentarism, raises the general question of the functions of such institutions in single-party systems. Table 4.9 shows some possible answers.

The Organization of the PNF

What Aquarone call the party's largely "choreographic" role was not always the case and may have been avoidable. The year 1929 seems to have been a turning point so that by 1932 the new party constitution called the PNF a "civil militia under the orders of the Duce, in the service of the Fascist State." [48] Such an official description of the single-

46. Here we should point out that had the Senate given Mussolini more trouble than it did, he could have asked the king to name large numbers of Fascist or pro-Fascist senators.
47. Field, *Institutions*, p. 56.
48. "Statute of the National Fascist Party," in Benito Mussolini, *Fascism: Doctrine and Institutions* (New York: Howard Fertig, 1968), p. 198.

TABLE 4.9.   Functions of Legislatures in Single-Party Authoritarian Regimes

---

1. **To enhance the symbolic capabilities of the regime:** single-party regimes often indulge in great outpourings of pomp, pageantry, and political ritualism. These may reflect authentic strategies of mass mobilization or be a kind of substitute gratification—let them eat symbols!—for the regime's failures in policy. The leader's coming before parliament and the elections thereto—however rigged—create a festive atmosphere beneficial to the regime.
2. **To improve the form, if not the content, of legislation:** though basic policy is determined authoritatively, a legislative body, especially through its committees, can help the Government with details and legal forms.
3. **To give the Government a forum in which to announce new policies:** speeches before parliament may provide maximum access to foreign and domestic information media. Also political bigwigs are likely to be on hand.
4. **To provide a domestic feedback mechanism:** modern dictators are not unconcerned with public opinion, quite the contrary. Given the tendency to tell the leaders good news rather than bad, the existing information services may not accurately estimate the state of public opinion. The functions of parliament, especially the more secretive ones, may allow certain ideas ultimately to reach the dictator and his entourage.
5. **To serve as a kind of national honorary society:** the honor of being an M.P., even if the parliament is a political cipher, can be a potent reward or incentive for regime supporters.

---

party would have been impossible either in Stalin's Russia or Hitler's Germany. Figure 4.4 is a simplified organizational chart of the PNF, followed by a brief account of the more important party organs.

THE DUCE.   Mussolini's personal dominance over the PNF was virtually unshaken until the very end of the Fascist regime. His powers to appoint and remove party officials were virtually absolute. The only pro forma restrictions were the king's assent and the party secretary's act of appointment. The PNF was the Duce's creature and its progressive debilitation was his own doing. As the party's chief ideologist and policy-maker, he was able to quell incipient rebellions and mediate the factional warfare that lurked behind the facade of party unity.

THE PNF SECRETARY.   This important official was named by the king upon the Duce's proposal. Besides being administrative chief of the party and Mussolini's right-hand man for PNF affairs, he had an inordinate number of other offices and tasks. They included secretaryship of the PNF Grand Council; occasional participation in the Council of Ministers; membership in the Supreme Defense Council, the Superior Council of National Education, the Council of the National Fascist Institute of Culture, and the top corporative institutions; presidency of a reserve officers' group and of an employment group; and high office in youth

Figure 4.4.   Main Organs of the PNF

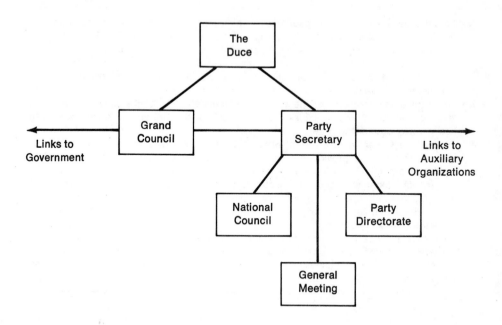

and university groups. In his spare time the secretary was a liaison man with the Corporations, the Senate, the Chamber, the MVSN, and other groups.

Though some of this Herculean job description was merely ceremonial, the secretary's near omnipresence is a residue of the original drive for totalitarian party control. On the other hand, this very immersion in bureaucratic and ceremonial routine sapped the revolutionary dynamic of the PNF. In fact, several secretaries resigned in the late 1920s because they sensed that strengthening the state meant weakening the party and betrayal of its "mission." The relative ease of their stepping down, however, was further testament to Mussolini's domination over the party.

THE GRAND COUNCIL OF FASCISM.   In the 1920s the Grand Council of Fascism seemed capable of realizing true party dominance in Italy. Originally a party organization, the Council was "constitutionalized" in 1929 to give it governmental powers as well. It was the link that—next to Mussolini himself—would best represent the intimate connection of party and state. Cut down in size in 1929, Grand Council membership included the head of government; the PNF secretary; the Quadrumvirs [49] for life; ex officio members such as the Senate and Chamber presidents, important ministers (Foreign Affairs, Interior, Justice, Finance, Education, Agriculture, and Corporations), heads of the Corporations and other officials; others appointed by Mussolini for special merit.

As a hybrid group with both party and governmental duties, the Grand Council had a great power potential, as seen in table 4.10. The

---

TABLE 4.10.   Dual Functions of the Grand Council of Fascism

Party Functions	Governmental Functions
1. Discussion of the constitution and general activities of the PNF	1. Drawing up the final list for elections to the two Chambers that served before 1939
2. Appointment and dismissal of the PNF secretary, administrative secretary, vice-secretaries, and others in the PNF directorate	2. Right to be consulted on powers and succession to the crown; on its own composition and functions and those of the Senate, the Chamber, and head of government; on decree laws, executive powers, corporative organization, church, etc.

---

fate of the Grand Council illustrates the general problem of advisory bodies, which becomes acute in dictatorships. In the late 1920s it operated as an authentically deliberative organ, whose opinion weighed heavily with Mussolini. Its secret sessions discussed important projects before they were revealed to wider circles of the party, the regime, and the public.

Nevertheless, one crucial constitutional proviso pulled the rug from under its broad policy jurisdiction: "The meetings of the Council are called by the Head of the Government whenever he deems it necessary." Its merely advisory role and Mussolini's freedom to convoke it or not explain its decay as an institution. Its meetings became more infrequent and were transformed into a "passive audience for the speeches and reports of the Duce." [50] The Grand Council ceased meeting altogether after December 1939, with the one exception when it met clandestinely on July 23–24, 1943, to plot Mussolini's ouster.

OTHER INSTITUTIONS.   Other PNF institutions were yet weaker than the Grand Council: their prevalently "choreographic" role was even

---

49. The Quadrumvirs were Mussolini's four top lieutenants at the time of the March on Rome of October 1922.
50. Aquarone, *L'organizzazione*, p. 184.

more evident. The *Party Directorate* was the "secretariat" of the PNF and included the secretary, vice-secretary, and seven others. As a collective body it had little political initiative. The *National Council* was an assemblage of all the federal (i.e., provincial) secretaries of the PNF. The federal secretaries were directly responsible to the PNF secretary. Every province had a *Directorate* of eight members, including the federal secretary. Subordinated to the provincial organizations were the local party groups called *Fasci di combattimento*. These had their own secretaries, directorates, and sometimes other subunits. The PNF's *General Meeting* of about one thousand members included all those mentioned above and certain local leaders.

The Corporative State

Because of its rejection of liberal individualism, the Fascist regime could not rest content with a system of representation that, however transmogrified, still implied "one man, one vote." The final remedy was taken only in 1939 with creation of the Council of Fasci and Corporations, composed completely of appointed members. Though the "corporative state" had been proclaimed in the Labor Charter of 1927 and the Corporations were set up only in 1934, one suspects that Mussolini burned with less than full ardor for the whole thing.

The underlying principle of the corporative system was simple enough: *to overcome the conflict between labor and capital by bringing both into institutions that are organs of the state.* Both sides would be equally represented and the centrifugal tendencies of bringing all these forces within the orbit of government were to be offset by the PNF and the executive. The basis of the corporative system was the 22 Corporations, which covered the main branches of the economy such as cereals, construction, glass, metallurgy, sea and air transport, textiles, chemicals, and so on. Each Corporation had its own council, including from 15 to 68 members. Each had representatives from labor, management, and the PNF—the vice-presidents of the Corporations had to be PNF representatives. All councilors together constituted the General Assembly of the National Council of Corporations (822 members). See figure 4.5.

Both the corporative law and Fascist propaganda endowed the Corporations with extensive powers. They were supposed to "regulate economic relations and the unitary discipline of production." Each specific Corporation was given the power to fix "salary scales for the work

Figure 4.5.   The Corporative Organization

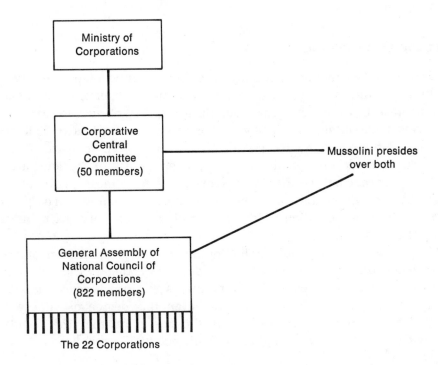

and economic services of producers carrying out their activity in the field under the jurisdiction of the Corporation." But here too we see the familiar pattern of taking away with the left hand what was given with the right: the corporative law made approval of the head of government mandatory on all important actions. Mussolini had no intentions of creating a political Frankenstein monster that could turn on its master.

It is also no surprise that the mammoth 822-member General Assembly was quickly reduced to ceremonies and ratifications. Its real work was done by the 50-member Corporative Central Committee. Even here the presence of PNF representatives, ministerial officials, and the Duce himself ensured that the regime's obsession with hierarchy and Mussolini's power was not jeopardized.

With such inbuilt constraints we can see why the promise of the corporative state as an alternative to liberal capitalism and Communist collectivism was not matched by performance. Major economic decisions were still taken outside the corporative structure, which merely ratified them or worked out details. The government bureaucracy headed by Mussolini guided the negotiations of interest groups to ensure their satisfactory outcome.

FACADE-PARTY REGIMES

Surprisingly few regimes nowadays are totally devoid of parties. Even military regimes generally set up some "union" or "alliance" to extend the political base of the regime. Our third category of authoritarian regimes is made up neither of military nor authentic single-party dictatorships. Yet these regimes too can display a "party." These "parties" are so weak or so dependent that we can properly speak of "facade-party" systems. Facade-parties are formed by a regime almost as an afterthought, after the regime is established or during a civil war. The party is an entirely new creation or is a merger of previously distinct political formations.

Organizational and political life of the facade-party are under the complete control of the government leaders. Even though the PNF was subordinated in Italy, party militants always retained a sense of independent mission. With a facade-party, even this degree of vitality is excluded. Of course, there is always the possibility that the facade-party can develop into an institution with potential for mobilization or even dominance.

Franco's Spain

A look at the role of the Falangist party in Franco's Spain (1939–75) will help us better understand the facade-party. We should be able to see important differences from a party like the PNF in Mussolini's Italy, which at certain points made serious efforts at dominance and mobilization. As with the PNF, let us follow the party-dominance framework suggested by Huntington.

LEGITIMATION OF THE POLITICAL SYSTEM.   The Falangist party (Falange Espanola Tradicionalista y de los Juntas de Offensiva Nacional-Syndicalista), as its monstrous name indicates, developed from a merger. The needs of the Spanish Civil War (1936–39) counseled the amalgamation of certain right-wing forces. General Francisco Franco, together with his military and political advisers and associates, decided to deck out their rebel regime with the trappings of a broad-based political movement. The Falange was the result.

Even after the merger the Falange kept traces of the semirevolutionary drive of some of its component groups. These, however, were swamped even more decisively than in the PNF by moderate, conservative, and reactionary elements. So long as the Nazi and Fascist regimes existed (i.e., until 1945), Falangist militants nourished hopes of transforming Spain into a single-party regime along Fascist lines. After World War II the party resembled less and less a "select, energetic political movement" and more and more a "grand national honorary society." [51]

The Falange and its ideology was a source of legitimacy for only a minority in Franco's Spain. Monarchists, for example, were pro-Franco on a wholly different basis, especially when Spain was declared a monarchy with Franco as permanent head of state. The full "restoration" of the monarchy, however, was shelved for nearly thirty years until Franco died in 1975. If Franco's procrastinations denied him the full devotion of all Spanish monarchists, it certainly toned down their hostility. His staunch Catholicism and generally good relations with the Spanish church also won him support in a country where many viewed the Civil War as a crusade against Anti-Christ. This was so because in this particularly brutal war some of the anti-Franco Loyalists vented their hostility by killing clergy and destroying church property.

For other Spaniards it was "performance" rather than "principles" that won grudging respect for the Franquista regime. The main successes were in preserving order with (given twentieth-century standards) only moderate repression and, since the 1950s, rapid economic growth. Franco also had a strong personal appeal with people who disliked the regime and despised the Falange.

RECRUITMENT OF POLITICAL LEADERSHIP.   Here as well the Falange performance is a cut or two below the PNF. Military men, nonpolitical bureaucrats, and others far outnumbered Falangists in high public office in Franco's Spain. Extremely revealing are some data gathered by the Falange secretary-general in 1956 and outlined in table 4.11.[52] These figures run much lower than the corresponding ones for Fascist Italy.

INTEREST AGGREGATION AND POLICY-MAKING.   The Falange's limited membership and appeal precluded a preeminent role in these two areas. Since the Franco regime involved what Juan Linz calls "limited plural-

---

51. Stanley Payne, *Falange* (Stanford: Stanford University Press, 1961), p. 201.
52. Source of chart: Juan Linz, "From Falange to Movimiento-Organizacion: the Spanish Single-Party and the Franco Regime 1936–1968," in Huntington and Moore, *Authoritarian Politics*, p. 203.

TABLE 4.11. Falangists in Public Office (c. 1956)

Offices	Total Number of Officeholders	Number of Falangists
Cabinet members	16	2
Provincial governors and party heads	50	18
Mayors of provincial capitals	50	8
Legislators (Cortes)	575	137
Provincial deputies	738	133
Mayors	9155	776
Municipal councilors	55,960	2226

ism," certain policy areas have been the special preserve for each of the main groups in the pro-Franco coalition. The Falangist preserve has been the Sindicatos, the Spanish version of the Fascist Corporations. Linz includes among the functions of the Sindicatos: "serving as a channel of pressure group activity for economic interests and as an arena for more or less muted social protest . . . , [providing] assistance in the case of industrial grievances at the plant level, and some of the direct services in the fields of sports, leisure, labor training, and . . . since 1958 collective bargaining." [53] The Sindicatos, whose head doubled as Falange secretary-general, have been the most active, well-heeled part of the Falange.

Political Rivals

The facade character of the Falange comes out most clearly regarding political rivals. Franco was a strong personalistic actor and therefore, like Mussolini, was a rival of the party he headed. Officially the head of the Falange, he seemed bent on preserving an almost Gaullist position "above all parties." Franco, known as the Caudillo, or highest leader, felt that his "constituency" stretched far beyond the Falange and he acted accordingly.

Traditional actors such as the church and the monarchy (in absentia) competed often successfully with the Falange for Franco's favor. The Caudillo, a virtuoso at the divide-and-rule strategy, played these groups off against each other. In the occasional clashes between the church and the Falange over education, the Falange won some and lost some. Franco was regarded so highly by the church leaders that he was given a legal voice in the selection of Spanish bishops.

53. Ibid., p. 152.

The bureaucracy, the army, and the police asserted and maintained essential independence from the Falange. Though individuals in these organizations were sometimes Falange members, their level of party identification was generally low and hardly influenced their conduct in office.

The Spanish Cortes or parliament naturally displayed many aspects of the "rubber stamp–organized cheering section–honorary society syndrome." Nevertheless, there were several differences from Fascist Italy. First, with only about a quarter of the members, there was no "ruling party" monopoly of the legislature. Second, in the closing years of the Franco regime, committee debates in the Cortes were "lively and even heated" and "a number of government bills" were "shelved or drastically changed." [54] Moreover, there were "public negative votes and abstentions even in plenary sessions." All in all, the Spanish Cortes manifested a degree of independence which, though much lower than in a constitutional regime, was measurably higher than in Fascist Italy, to say nothing of Hitler's Germany or Stalin's Russia.

Regarding socioeconomic groups, the limited pluralism of Franco's Spain emerged rather clearly. The Sindicatos, despite formal subordination to the Falange, were far more effective than the Fascists' unions and Corporations. Moreover, toward the close of the Franco period, supposedly illegal labor groups were not only allowed to form more or less openly, but also had some impact upon government policy.

Perhaps the Falange's most serious competitor at the highest political levels was the Opus Dei. Basically a Roman Catholic fraternal-religious organization with branches outside Spain, Opus power is distinct from that of the church hierarchy. Its penchant for secrecy has earned it such labels as "a holy mafia" or "a Catholic Masonry." In Franco's last two decades an increasing number of cabinet and other high officials came from Opus ranks. While Opus members had ideological disagreements, their influence on Franco and his aides stressed economic growth through reduced government controls and increased technological advance. Such economic "liberalization" was not necessarily matched, however, by a strong desire to "liberalize" the political system rapidly.

Political Institutions of Franco's Spain

The institutional structure of the Franco regime bears some formal resemblance to Fascist Italy (see figure 4.6).

54. Ibid., p. 205.

Figure 4.6.   Political Institutions of Franco's Spain

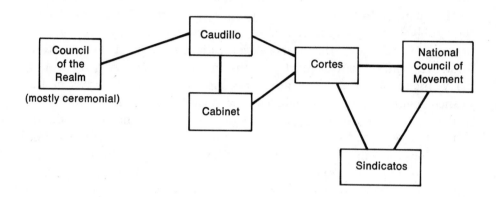

THE CAUDILLO.   In one respect Franco outdid Mussolini: even with the monarchic "restoration" of 1947 he was head of state as well as head of government and party. Particularly important also was his position as commander-in-chief of the army. Franco could appoint and remove all cabinet ministers, all fifty provincial governors, the heads of the (twenty-four) Sindicatos, top military officers, and (directly or indirectly) many members of the Cortes. Though he obviously dominated policy-making for most of four decades, toward the end old age caused him to delegate considerable power to certain cabinet members.

TABLE 4.12.   Composition of the Cortes under Franco

1.	150 members from Sindicatos
2.	115 members from local groups (indirect election)
3.	108 members elected by family heads and married women
4.	102 members representing the National Council of Falange
5.	23 members representing professional organizations
6.	25 named by the state (Franco)
7.	19 ministers and high officials
8.	18 university rectors and other educational officials
9.	6 representatives from cultural organizations
	566 total

THE CABINET.   While the typical pattern of the cabinet as a "group of administrative assistants" prevailed in the Franco regime, some institutionalization did occur in the final years. There was even a sort of "prime minister" and, except for the absence of parliamentary responsibility, the relationship between this official and Franco resembled that between the French premier and de Gaulle. Studies of the cabinet show the eclectic nature of the regime as a whole: included were Falangists, soldiers, traditionalists, monarchists, Opus members, technocrats, and others.[55]

THE CORTES.   We have already mentioned that the Cortes under Franco was a little bit more than the game of charades found in most dictatorships. Its composition is of interest for three reasons: (1) it combined geographic with "functional" representation; (2) it blended direct and indirect election; and (3) like the Italian Council of Fasci and Corporations it included high party organs (see table 4.12).[56] Category 3 was considered a step in the direction of "democratization" of the political system.

Most observers agree that since the end of World War II, the Franco regime evolved into a "milder" form of dictatorship than that of Fascist Italy. One indicator of this is that Juan Linz could discriminate between different degrees of opposition, which ran from relative tolerance to outright repression on the Government's part. Linz's typology (see table

---

TABLE 4.13.   Types of Oppositions in Authoritarian Regimes

---

1. **Illegal opposition:** groups that hope to overthrow the regime. In a country like Spain *some* Communists and anarchists fit in this category, as do separatist groups like Basques and Catalans. Because of their underground and sometimes terroristic activities, the government is implacably hostile toward them.
2. **Alegal opposition:** groups that lack a real legal basis for their activities, although the activities may not contravene any specific law. The activities run counter to the spirit, if not the letter, of the law. The government varies in its hostility and actions against the alegal groups.
3. **Semiopposition:** groups outside the government which are willing to participate under certain conditions "without fundamentally challenging the regime." This diversified opposition includes people who favor different policies from the government's—elite dissidents who have some ideological point to make, wish to realize earlier promises, or want to promote or retard certain trends. Some of these groups are so close to the rulers that they can be called a "pseudo-opposition."

---

55. Ibid., p. 170.
56. Linz, "Falange to Movimiento," p. 169.

4.13), though based on Spain, has obvious relevance for the milder sort of dictatorship.[57]

While the Falange as a facade-party represents a lower level of political power and importance than the PNF, there are still other so-called single-parties that are weaker. Such, for example, is the Arab Socialist Union in the United Arab Republic (Egypt). One student sees the ASU as a prime case of the "collaboration movement" whose subservience to the government is total.[58]

We have remarked above on the recent tendency to play down the differences among authoritarian regimes of the praetorian, single-party, and facade-party varieties. Certainly there is much to recommend this outlook if we glance at constitutionalism as one contrast and totalitarianism as another. Yet, before rushing to the conclusion that the formal structure of an authoritarian regime is of cosmetic rather than deep political significance, several factors should be mentioned. While it is true that the African experience has chastened the hopes of advocates of *both* praetorian and single-party regimes as agencies of effective modernization, some differences nevertheless remain.

In those rather rare instances where the single-party ranks high in the scale of dominance and mobilization, it shows a real capability to spread an ideology and hasten social change. Likewise its state-building and (to a lesser extent) its nation-building performance is relatively high. The problem is that many observers have taken the rhetoric of regime leaders at face value and have mistaken parties that were subordinate-pluralistic at best and mere facades at worst for dominant-mobilizational parties.

Praetorian regimes, on the other hand, seem more adept in general at preserving order and defending tradition than at engineering important structural reforms. Here, too, categorical judgments are tricky. The political role of the military in Portugal and Ethiopia in the mid-1970s can hardly be described as traditionalist or conservative.

57. Juan Linz, "Opposition to and under an Authoritarian Regime: The Case of Spain," in *Regimes and Oppositions,* ed. R. Dahl (New Haven: Yale University Press, 1973).
58. Iliya Harik, "The Single Party as a Subordinate Movement: The Case of Egypt," *World Politics* 26 (October 1973): 80–105.

STUDY QUESTIONS

1. Are external or internal factors more important when we try to explain why military organizations launch coups d'etat?

2. Is a praetorian regime likely to perform well in Third World countries when it comes to modernization?

3. How did the political system of Fascist Italy differ from a typical praetorian regime?

4. How did Mussolini's personalistic dictatorship stand in the way of the PNF becoming a fully dominant-mobilizational single-party?

5. Compare the role of the PNF in Mussolini's Italy to that of the Falange in Franco's Spain.

6. Discuss the functions of legislative bodies in authoritarian regimes. Is the corporative state a genuine alternative to the representative system of presidential and parliamentary systems?

7. What are the key power rivals to the single-party in authoritarian dictatorships? Why do certain dictators actually promote a sort of limited pluralism of important veto groups?

8. Compare the role of Mussolini and Franco as political leaders.

SUGGESTIONS FOR FURTHER READING

BIENEN, HENRY, ed. *The Military and Modernization*. New York: Atherton, 1971.

COLEMAN, JAMES S., and ROSBERG, CARL G., JR., eds. *Political Parties and National Integration in Tropical Africa*. Berkeley: University of California Press, 1966.

DAHL, ROBERT, ed. *Regimes and Oppositions*. New Haven: Yale University Press, 1973.

DECALO, SAMUEL. *Coups and Army Rule in Africa*. New Haven: Yale University Press, 1976.

FIELD, G. LOWELL. *The Syndical and Corporative Institutions of Fascist Italy*. New York: AMS, 1968.

FINER, HERMAN. *Mussolini's Italy*. New York: Grosset & Dunlap, 1965.

FINER, S. E. *The Man on Horseback*. Baltimore: Penguin Books, 1976.

GERMINO, DANTE. *The Italian Fascists in Power*. Minneapolis: University of Minnesota Press, 1959.

HUNTINGTON, SAMUEL P., ed. *Changing Patterns of Military Politics*. New York: Free Press, 1962.

————. *Political Order in Changing Societies*. New Haven: Yale University Press, 1970.

————. *The Soldier and the State*. New York: Vintage Books, 1957.

HUNTINGTON, SAMUEL P., and MOORE, CLEMENT H., eds. *Authoritarian Politics in Modern Societies*. New York: Basic Books, 1970.

JANOWITZ, MORRIS. *The Military in the Political Development of New Nations*. Chicago: University of Chicago Press, 1967.

JOHNSON, JOHN J., ed. *The Role of the Military in Underdeveloped Countries*. Princeton: Princeton University Press, 1962.

LINZ, JUAN J. "An Authoritarian Regime: Spain." In *Mass Politics*, edited by E. Allardt and S. Rokkan. New York: Free Press, 1970.

————. "Totalitarian and Authoritarian Regimes." In *Handbook of Political Science*, edited by F. I. Greenstein and N. W. Polsby. Vol. 3. Reading, Mass.: Addison-Wesley, 1975.

MEDHURST, KENNETH N. *Government in Spain*. New York: Pergamon Press, 1973.

NORDLINGER, ERIC A. *Soldiers in Politics*. Englewood Cliffs, N.J.: Prentice-Hall, 1977.

PAYNE, STANLEY. *Falange*. Stanford: Stanford University Press, 1973.

SCHAPIRO, LEONARD, ed. *Political Opposition in One-Party States*. London: Macmillan, 1972.

STEPAN, ALFRED. *The Military in Politics*. Princeton: Princeton University Press, 1974.

WOOLF, S. J., ed. *The Nature of Fascism*. New York: Vintage Books, 1969.

ZOLBERG, ARISTIDE R. *Creating Political Order*. New York: Rand-McNally, 1966.

5
Totalitarian Dictatorship

The problem of totalitarianism well illustrates the thematic structure of this book: regimes, movements, and ideologies. For some students of politics, the movement and its evolution give true insight into the dynamics of totalitarianism.[1] For others, the main concern is with the ideology associated with a totalitarian movement and regime. The concern here is with totalitarianism as a regime—variously called "totalitarian dictatorship," "totalitarian rule," "totalitarian domination," or sometimes "the totalitarian state." Nevertheless, constant reference must be made to the movement and the ideology if we are to understand totalitarian dictatorship.

THE CLASSIC TOTALITARIAN SYNDROME

As the literature on totalitarianism is vast, complex, and highly controversial and spreads back over five decades, the most economical approach is a critical analysis of the "totalitarian syndrome." This approach was formulated by Carl J. Friedrich and Zbigniew K. Brzezinski over

1. Among those who stress the movement aspect are Hannah Arendt, *The Origins of Totalitarianism* (New York: Harcourt, Brace & World, 1966); William Kornhauser, *The Politics of Mass Society* (New York: Free Press, 1963); and Emil Lederer, *The State of the Masses* (New York: Howard Fertig, 1967).

twenty years ago.[2] Their syndrome presupposes four controversial claims:

1. Totalitarian dictatorship is a novel and unique type of political system.
2. Fascist and Communist totalitarian dictatorships are basically, though not wholly, alike.
3. There is an unplanned quality to the full emergence of totalitarianism.
4. While a set definition of totalitarianism may be unattainable, its basic identifying traits can be put into a six-point syndrome.

The "novel and unique" claim involves two separate arguments. The novelty argument, which stresses the unprecedented quality of totalitarianism, maintains that while earlier tyrannies, despotisms, and autocracies share certain traits with totalitarianism, the novel differences outnumber the classic similarities. Modern technology offers possibilities for social control and manipulation unavailable to previous rulers. Especially crucial are breakthroughs in mass communications and social psychology. Moreover, the successes of the industrial revolution have inflated the claims of some twentieth-century ideologies to unprecedented heights.

The uniqueness argument stresses the differences between totalitarian and other modern dictatorships. Critics understandably have attacked its claim that totalitarianism is the keynote political phenomenon of the present century. Robert Tucker, for example, argues that the truly unique political form is "the revolutionary mass-movement regime under single-party auspices." [3] According to this interpretation, totalitarian dictatorship is demoted, being only one variety of the general class of "movement-regimes," which includes the single-party dictatorships of the last chapter.

Nevertheless, the claim for the novelty and uniqueness of totalitarian dictatorship has an historical basis. Not only do earlier tyrannies and autocracies lack modern technological instruments, but they also lack the framework of the modern state—the indispensable backdrop for a

2. Carl J. Friedrich and Zbigniew K. Brzezinski, *Totalitarian Dictatorship and Autocracy* (New York: Praeger Publishers, 1956). This book has had many critics, including the authors themselves. Some of this criticism is contained in a second edition, revised by Friedrich alone in 1965. However, the original 1956 edition, because of its hard-hitting quality, will be our reference here.
3. Robert Tucker, *The Soviet Political Mind* (New York: Praeger Publishers, 1963), p. 7.

truly totalitarian regime. Totalitarianism can develop only through its enigmatic encounter with modern bureaucracy.

There are many and complex reasons for refusing to catalogue totalitarianism as just another single-party regime. No doubt moral revulsion explains why some early theorists of totalitarianism made a rigid separation. Still, less value-laden and emotional reasons exist for the special place of totalitarian dictatorship. In a sense the argument of the preceding chapter and this are a justification of the uniqueness thesis.

The second Friedrich-Brzezinski claim—that Fascist and Communist totalitarian dictatorships are "basically alike"—is rather more troublesome. The two political scientists have admitted that there were some important differences between Communist and Fascist ideologies and that the pre-takeover movements appealed to different groups and attained power differently. Their point was that, starting from divergent backgrounds, the two sorts of regime converged on the same six key points of the syndrome; this is the basis for the strong resemblance of these two regimes and for their common differences from past and nontotalitarian regimes.

One objection to the "basically alike" claim is presented in our conclusion of chapter 4 that the Italian Fascist regime, despite its own pretensions and its critics' credibility, was never truly totalitarian. Moreover, the original (1956) Friedrich-Brzezinski theory made communism and totalitarianism inseparable, suggesting that all regimes ruled by Communist parties were doomed to remain totalitarian. This outlook took account neither of diversity among Communist states nor of possible "detotalitarianization."

The third claim of the Friedrich-Brzezinski approach holds that totalitarian dictatorships were born less as carefully planned systems than as the unintended result of certain processes and decisions—a product of "the political situations in which the anticonstitutional and antidemocratic revolutionary movements and their leaders found themselves." [4] This seems valid, as there is no "blueprint for a totalitarian state," except in the minds of science-fiction writers.

The fourth claim is about the six-point syndrome itself. This asserts that we can call a regime totalitarian if, and only if, all six elements of the syndrome are present. Table 5.1 is a simplified account of the syndrome. We will follow it by a point-by-point critical analysis.

4. Friedrich and Brzezinski, *Dictatorship*, p. 5.

TABLE 5.1. The Friedrich-Brzezinski Totalitarian Syndrome

1. **An official ideology:** this is characterized by its attempt to cover nearly all aspects of human existence (totalism) and by the projection of a utopian goal that compels total rejection of the status quo.
2. **A single, elite-directed mass party:** the party is headed by the dictator, is somewhat restrictive, and does not exceed 10% of the population. The party contains a hard core of militants dedicated to realizing the ideology. It is either superior to the government bureaucracy or "commingled" with it.
3. **A system of terroristic police control:** this assists the party but can be turned against it. Terror is applied not only against open oppositionists, but against arbitrarily singled-out groups of the population. The secret police uses the latest scientific techniques.
4. **A near-complete monopoly of control over the media of mass communication:** this monopoly affects press, radio, and motion pictures, and is carried out by the party and its servants.
5. **A party-dominated monopolistic control over all means of "effective armed combat":** in short, this is a weapons monopoly.
6. **A centrally controlled and directed economy:** this involves a "command economy" in which the central authorities control basic economic decisions and priorities.

An Official Ideology

The official ideology of the totalitarian regime is "totalistic" and "utopian." Totalism means that no realm of social life is free of ideological imperatives. The ideology *prescribes* what is true, good, right, proper, and permissible not only in politics, but in morals, art, science, and human relations as well. While it is enormously difficult to get even partial compliance with this all-inclusive goal, illustrations taken from art and science in Stalin's Russia and Hitler's Germany might show how serious is the attempt.

There are few more treasonable utterances in the totalitarian setting than "art for art's sake." The ideology and the regime's rendition of it supply a whole set of principles for judging good and bad art. Good art furthers the regime's mission, while bad art contradicts it or, just as seriously, is irrelevant to it. So it is with the Soviet doctrine of Socialist Realism, the theory of art criticism mandatory for artists and art critics since the 1920s. Roughly speaking, its cardinal tenet is the partisan nature of art: art must take sides. In the Soviet context it must actively help to achieve a "socialist" and ultimately a "communist" society in the USSR and the world. This means depicting and exhorting the proletariat's "heroic struggle" to defeat capitalism and build the new society.

Accordingly, themes such as overfulfilling a plant's production quota or finding new labor-saving techniques are suitable themes for both graphic and plastic art. Purely personal experiences such as romantic love are dismissed as "bourgeois sentimentality" or mere "subjectivism." This explains why Boris Pasternak's Nobel-Prize-winning novel *Doctor Zhivago* was officially denigrated in the USSR. It was not that it was anti-regime or anti-Communist, but that it focused on one man's experience in a world set adrift by war, revolution, and civil war. Since it did not deal with the collective struggle of the Russian proletariat, it was "bad art."

In Nazi Germany "good art" was "Aryan" art—freed of all alien, in particular Jewish, influences. Joseph Goebbels, the Nazi minister of propaganda, once declared:

> The purging of the cultural field has been accomplished with the least amount of legislation. . . . The German artist has his feet on a solid, vital ground. Art, taken out of its narrow and isolated circle, again stands in the midst of the people and from there exerts its strong influences on the whole nation.[5]

Here too the Nazi ideology or *Weltanschauung* (literally: view of the world) was the touchstone of artistic orthodoxy.

Science too is encompassed within the totalist ideological claims. Understandable in the social sciences, which overlap in concerns with political doctrines, the claim is extended also to the natural sciences, especially biology. Biology, after all, has much to say about man, his nature, and potentials. Thus, biology was subjected to great ideological constraints in both the USSR and Germany in the 1930s.

On the Soviet side, biology was expected to confirm the optimistic "environment is more important than heredity" implications of revolutionary Marxism-Leninism. Only if environment is the key factor in human behavior can the ideological assertion of a future "classless society" be vindicated. Accordingly, the strongly environmentalist biological doctrines of Trofim D. Lysenko were enshrined in the USSR in the 1930s as the compulsory approach to biological research. Opposing biological schools of thought were condemned, and their spokesmen harassed or worse. One practical result was that vast northern areas were sown with wheat in the confidence that they would simply adapt themselves to the new colder environment. The resultant fiasco led to

5. Joseph Goebbels, "Freedom and Organization," in *Nazi Culture*, ed. G. L. Mosse (New York: Grosset & Dunlap, 1968), p. 154.

a change in front, and Lysenko was subsequently disgraced (though he later made something of a comeback).

Nazi ideological views about biology were diametrically opposed to environmentalism. Nazi racism teaches that hereditary, genetic differences between peoples are the root of their differing ("higher" and "lower") cultures. For this reason, environmental factors must be downplayed to almost zero in biological research. A work of the time on the role of biology in German education reached the strange-sounding conclusion that "if the emphasis on the ideology of the biotic community creates a feeling of belonging to our people and state, then racial eugenics creates the will to struggle, body and soul, for the growth and wealth of this biotic community." [6] Likewise, certain trends in modern physics were tabooed in Nazi Germany because Jews like Albert Einstein had developed them. "Jewish science" obviously had no insights for an "Aryan Folk Community"!

Nevertheless, we should not conclude that Nazi or Communist ideologies were so complete that the totalitarian leaders could simply deduce the proper ideas in art, science, and morals down to the minutest detail. It is more a question of specific applications in the overall spirit of the ideology. Since the leader monopolizes interpretation of the ideology, flexibility, opportunism, and manipulation find their way into the situation. The totalitarian elite may have been "prisoners of ideology," but they were not in solitary confinement.

The second major aspect of the totalitarian ideology is its utopianism. It envisages a genuine community to come, where the conflicts between and within men are totally and irreversibly resolved. Reaching this perfect end-state will come through a combination of will and determinism. The party and the leader have a special mission to guide people toward the promised land.

In fact, parallels to religion occur so often in the totalitarian attitude toward ideology that many view communism or national socialism as "secular religions." The themes of salvation and redemption, and the blissful end-state are certainly there in totalitarian ideology. In addition, from an anthropological perspective the totalitarian ideology "functions" like some traditional religious manifestations. But such resemblances are mere analogies, not identities. The "secular religion" theory of totalitarianism requires the greatest caution.

6. Paul Brohmer, "The New Biology: Training in Racial Citizenship," in Mosse, *Nazi Culture*, p. 88.

A Single Mass Party

The second element of the syndrome is the single elite-dominated mass party, dedicated to the ideology and largely subservient to the "charismatic" leader or dictator. In the syndrome and in most other theories of totalitarianism the totalitarian party is depicted as fully dominant and fully mobilizational. Sigmund Neumann in 1942, for example, attributed three major functions to the "dictatorial party": (1) "it creates the political elite"; (2) "it controls and educates the masses"; and (3) "it maintains communications between state and society." [7] These three factors boil down to the question: does the party really dominate the government?

One answer with much to recommend it is that only in the USSR did the party truly dominate the government. Fascist Italy (which was originally considered totalitarian) showed the opposite pattern, with government dominant over party. Nazi Germany occupied a middle position hard to characterize.[8] Reserving a fuller treatment for later, we must here observe that full party dominance is something more than a virtual monopoly of higher governmental offices by members of the party. Nor does the "interlocking directorate" system, in which the same individuals have the highest positions in the party and the government, give us the whole story. The crucial factor is *the status of the party as an institution.* Does the party organization have enough autonomy, adaptability, complexity, and coherence to determine consistently what government policy will be?

That full party dominance may not distinguish the totalitarian regime is even suggested by Friedrich and Brzezinski. They admit that due to the "total dependence of the party as a following upon the leader," it "does not possess any corporate existence of its own." [9] The personalistic elevation of the leader above all institutional structures including the party accounts for the noted "formlessness" and "fluidity" of totalitarian rule. Unfortunately, this line of thought is hard to reconcile with the different assertion by Friedrich and Brzezinski that the victorious party "becomes the vehicle for transforming the entire society in its image." [10]

7. Sigmund Neumann, *Permanent Revolution* (New York: Praeger Publishers, 1965), p. 126.
8. Franz Neumann, *Behemoth* (New York: Octagon Books, 1963), p. 67.
9. Friedrich and Brzezinski, *Dictatorship*, p. 29.
10. Ibid., p. 28.

A recent student of totalitarianism sees a solution to the dilemma just posed. The party emerges as the key factor in the early phases of the regime after the seizure of power (here we can speak of a "monopolistic party regime"). But later on, the party is "subject to a *process* of institutional degeneration." [11] Taking this a step farther, the pretotalitarian period may be characterized by single-party dominance, while under full totalitarianism all power centers possibly presenting an institutional challenge to the leader's preeminence—including the party itself—are pulverized. Thus, the party becomes one of several competitors for the leader's grace—divide-and-rule in still another form. As Martin Jänicke puts it:

> That the party besides the propaganda, mobilization, and recruitment functions remaining to it, forms the "monolithic" formal structure, as well as the framework of tradition and legitimacy, of the "totalitarian" system changes nothing. In fact, it has forfeited its "leading role" as institutional brace of the system of domination—i.e., as monopolistic control center . . . not subject to any extra-party control power. [12]

Figure 5.1 depicts the kinds of groups that leap into the breach created by the party's loss of institutionalization.

Competition in totalitarian regimes differs from that in a single-party authoritarian setup. In the latter the competitors ("power rivals") are highly institutionalized formations, some with deeper roots than the regime itself. With totalitarianism we find organizations that have been created or taken over by the totalitarian elite—Huntington's traditional, legislative, and functional actors are a dead letter (see chapter 4). Which groups are up and which down varies with the leader's changing assessments of power and policy. Once again, in Jänicke's words, the fact that "party members play a leading role in all power and control apparatuses says little in this secondary phase about the 'leading role of the Party' as an institution." [13]

A System of Police Control

Given the Nazi and Stalinist experiences, we can see why terror and the secret police loom large in theories of totalitarianism. Hannah

11. Martin Jänicke, *Totalitäre Herrschaft* (Berlin: Duncker & Humblot, 1971), p. 44.
12. Ibid., p. 148.
13. Ibid., p. 156.

Figure 5.1.   Instrumentalities of Power in the Totalitarian Dictatorship

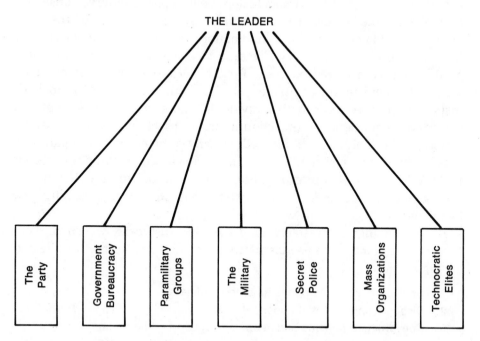

Arendt, in fact, considered the "symbiotic relationship" of ideology and terror the quintessence of totalitarian rule.[14] Terror on such a grand scale made observers think that the goal of terror went far beyond cowing actual or potential oppositionists. In Arendt's view totalitarian terror was divorced from such purposes and became an end in itself. Its application became wholly arbitrary, directed against seemingly random groups of the society.

The most visible embodiment of this runaway terrorism were the Stalinist and Hitlerian secret police formations. The early GPU and later the NKVD and MVD under Stalin were secret police organizations that were above and beyond the law. Citizens had virtually no recourse against their assaults. Torture, executions, and unexplained disappearances all took place beyond public view. In time, with the operation of vast labor and concentration camps, the Nazi and Soviet secret police played an essential role in the national economy.

Despite this evidence, we can still ask whether Hitler-Stalin style terrorism and secret police are an inescapable facet of totalitarian rule. If

14. Arendt, *Totalitarianism*, chap. 13.

so, Communist China probably cannot be considered a totalitarian regime. Before we accept that conclusion, several points deserve consideration. First, some "revisionist" critics maintain that in view of the overarching position of the totalitarian dictator, personal quirks, not essential to maintaining the regime or pursuing ideological goals, account for a good part of terroristic excesses. Robert Tucker asserts that not only were Hitler and Stalin complete autocrats, but also that (1) "in both instances we have to do with individuals whose personalities would be classified somewhere on the continuum of psychiatric conditions described as paranoid; and (2) in both instances the needs of the paranoid personality were a powerful motivating factor in the dictatorial decision-making." [15] While this interpretation can be pushed too far, it reminds us that the precise intensity and extensity of the terror is conditioned by the dictator's personality.

Before linking terror solely to personality disorders, we should not forget the rational means-ends calculation that uses terror for the following purposes:

1. Neutralizing actual opponents of the regime
2. Discouraging potential opponents
3. Converting opponents and neutrals to support of the regime
4. Maintaining a state of tension and enthusiasm among regime supporters

The composite goal of terror is *positive conformity* to the regime's ideology, policy, and leadership. This is an inordinately ambitious and difficult goal, and secret police terror seems one route to attain it. The question is: is terror the only way or the best way?

A negative answer seems to come from the Chinese Communist experience. Though widespread terrorism erupted in the late 1940s, more recently the Communists have generated high levels of positive conformity without an overinflated terroristic secret policy along Hitler-Stalin lines. Through the years the Chinese have developed various techniques called "thought reform" or "rectification." Using social and group pressures as intimidation, they have made great headway with former opponents, intellectuals, and ordinary peasants and workers. The means employed create an artificial, surrealistic environment in which the subject is induced to repudiate his past and to accuse himself of real or imagined "crimes against the people." Then he humbly resolves to make amends by faithful service to the regime. There are

15. Robert Tucker, "The Dictator and Totalitarianism," *World Politics* 17 (1965): 566.

obviously themes of Chinese political culture that make such contrived experiences more successful as conversions than Westerners might appreciate.[16]

Monopoly Control Over Media

A virtual monopoly of the means of mass communications seems mandated by the totalist and utopian "project" of the totalitarian ideology. Positive conformity—what Friedrich and Brzezinski call the "passion for unanimity"—requires the wholesale indoctrination of the public. Control of communications is essential for two reasons: (1) to screen out messages in the media that run against the ideology and current policies; and (2) to reinforce, by constant reiteration, ideas and attitudes wanted by the regime. These goals imply a "saturation" approach to the media.

Censorship of the printed word is neither new nor peculiar to totalitarian dictatorships. Normal censorship or "postcensorship" occurs *after* publication of the offensive material. The government authorities then confiscate whatever of the books, pamphlets, or newspapers they can lay their hands on and prosecute the authors, publishers, and others involved. While totalitarian regimes sometimes do this, they generally make it unnecessary by using "precensorship." In this form of censorship, government or party representatives screen material *before* it reaches the public.

But the term "censorship" suggests something negative: the keeping out of information. The significance of the monopoly of communications, on the other hand, is positive: the structuring and alteration of public opinion. Totalitarianism uses its strategic monopoly to *in-doctrinate*, to implant the official ideology and its ramifications in the minds of the people. It uses propaganda or the techniques of manipulating symbols, gross oversimplification, and tireless repetition to create the appropriate "mental set" among the public.[17]

A Weapons Monopoly

The syndrome's fifth element, an almost total monopoly of control over weapons, appears to be superfluous to distinguish totalitarianism.

16. Robert Jay Lifton, *Thought Reform and the Psychology of Totalism* (New York: W. W. Norton, 1963), p. 414, where the author points out that "thought reform achieves a degree of psychological control over the individual as strong as any yet devised."
17. See chapter 9 for more on propaganda.

This is because all modern states tend toward such a monopoly. States that allow powerful "private armies" or "paramilitary" formations are generally short-lived. The syndrome is better served either by a more general or a more specific feature. In the first case we can simply repeat the point made earlier that the modern state is the framework within which totalitarianism operates. The narrower point is that in a totalitarian dictatorship the military is highly politicized and subject to strict party controls. This factor at least would highlight the differences between praetorian and totalitarian regimes.

A Centrally Controlled Economy

The final element of the syndrome, a centrally controlled and directed economy, was an important addition to the syndrome.[18] If the totalitarian ideology is totalist and utopian, and if the regime is committed to the ideology, how could the economy be left out of the system of control? No totalitarian regime could allow such a vital aspect of social life to be determined mainly by market factors and by owners' and managers' decisions.

The easiest control mechanism for such a regime would be some type of collectivism with public ownership of the means of production and exchange. Factories, farms, mines, retail outlets, credit institutions, medical and educational facilities, would all be owned by the public and operated by government officials. There would be tight central planning of the entire economy. All this, in fact, is an accurate description of the Soviet economy under Stalin.

Though there was no full-scale collectivism of this sort in Nazi Germany, Friedrich and Brzezinski find that methods of reward and intimidation employed by state and party did produce a command economy. Even though most industry was privately owned, the Nazi government succeeded in making plans and reorienting German business to suit its own goals. The remaining areas of "free enterprise" remained because the regime was unwilling, not unable, to reshape institutions and priorities. It was not because big business dominated the Nazi regime or was a powerful veto group.

Since Hitler's foreign policy aims required a strong economy for re-

18. Friedrich began with a five-point syndrome in his "The Unique Character of Totalitarian Society," in *Totalitarianism,* ed. C. J. Friedrich (Cambridge, Mass.: Harvard University Press, 1954), pp. 47–60. The sixth element, on the centralized economy, was added in the first edition of *Totalitarian Dictatorship and Autocracy.*

armament policies, his brand of totalitarianism at first proceeded cautiously on economic matters. There are strong signs, however, that more drastic economic reorganization would have followed a Nazi victory in World War II.

GENERAL CRITICISMS OF THE CONCEPT OF TOTALITARIANISM

In discussing the totalitarian syndrome, we have made criticisms of the details of one general approach to the concept of totalitarianism. Now we must survey some more fundamental objections to the concept itself.

A first critique denies the usefulness of the concept of totalitarianism because it allegedly is an ideological weapon of the United States in the cold war.[19] In this view the term "totalitarianism" has been indelibly tainted through its use as a counter-ideology to Soviet communism. Thus, a rigid moral dichotomy is made between the virtuous "free world" and the vicious Communist "totalitarianism" of the East. In this regard the critics charge that Friedrich and Brzezinski's "basically alike" thesis is ideological because it virtually equates the Communists with the hated Axis enemies of World War II.

This critique, while serious, is by no means fatal. First, there is hardly a term in the political lexicon that has not been flagrantly abused and misused by ideologists. Abandonment of these terms would surely impoverish both social science and rational discussion in general. If some of the rhetoric used by students of totalitarianism has been too combative, the fault is corrigible and in many cases has been corrected.

A second critique concerns the obsolescence of the concept of totalitarianism. In this case the critics, while admitting the past application of the theory to the Soviet Union, protest that since Stalin's death no truly totalitarian regimes have existed. This argument seems valid (leaving China aside) because many theorists of totalitarianism have in fact dragged their heels on admitting the significance of far-reaching post-Stalin changes; and they were moved to this attitude out of a conviction that a totalitarian regime could develop only in one direction: *toward more totalitarianism.* This is clearly a weakness in some views of totalitarianism.

Even if the concept of totalitarianism is no longer applicable to the Soviet Union, as these critics suggest, that does not mean we should

19. Benjamin R. Barber, "Conceptual Foundations of Totalitarianism," in *Totalitarianism in Perspective: Three Views,* Benjamin R. Barber, Carl J. Friedrich, and Michael Curtis (New York: Praeger Publishers, 1969).

stop talking about it. Furthermore, there are grounds for thinking that Communist China has developed its own unique brand of totalitarianism, though Chairman Mao's death in September 1976 may be a crossroads in this respect.

A third type of critique accuses the theory of totalitarianism of wholesale exaggerations. One version of this critique is the pluralist argument, which charges that the theory of totalitarianism oversimplifies the power structure and policy process in so-called totalitarian regimes. By using descriptive terms such as "total," "monopolistic," "monolithic," "uniformity," "unanimity," "coordination" (*Gleichschaltung*), the totalitarianism theory approach overestimates the centralization of the regime and underestimates its susceptibility to outside group pressures. As one of the more careful pluralist critics points out, however, even a non-totalitarian account of the Soviet power structure "could not be described as genuine pluralism; it appeared rather to be a kind of *imperfect monism* in which, of the many elements involved, one—the party—was more powerful than all others but was not omnipotent." [20]

Three responses can be made to the pluralist critique. First, it may not be so much a critique of the concept of totalitarianism as it is of those who persist in applying it to the Soviet Union and other Communist states. Pluralist research has been mostly on the post-Stalin era, and until it is pushed backward in time, it will not succeed in refuting the totalitarian model. Second, as we have already seen, it is not at all clear that the notion of totalitarianism actually goes so far as to involve a "single-party, itself free of internal conflict," which "imposes its will on society, and on all social groups," [21] as it has been described by pluralist H. Gordon Skilling. Finally, there is a recognition, in Friedrich and Brzezinski at least, that there is some diversity within totalitarian systems. Their concept of "islands of separateness" will allow us to judge better if the pluralist charge of oversimplification and exaggeration is warranted.

Totalitarianism and Islands of Separateness

The idea of "islands of separateness" acknowledges that the monopolistic or monolithic character of totalitarian regimes has serious limits.

20. H. Gordon Skilling, "Interest Groups and Communist Politics: An Introduction," in *Interest Groups in Soviet Politics*, ed. H. G. Skilling and F. Griffiths (Princeton: Princeton University Press, 1973), p. 17. Italics added.
21. Ibid.

These islands are *areas of social life that resist (passively, rather than actively) penetration, coordination, and transformation by regime-controlled "intruders."* They include the church, the family, academia and the scientific community, the military, ethnic groups, and local groups.

The church is in trouble in totalitarian regimes for two main reasons. First, as a dispenser of religion the church (or its Jewish or Muslim equivalents) presents a view of the world, a morality, and a cultural ethos that differ dramatically from the totalitarian ideology. For that reason the teachings of the church run against the totalist and utopian claims of the ideology. Second, as an autonomous organization (perhaps with an international character), the church resists the totalitarian impulse to transform all permitted organizations into "transmission belts" of the regime.[22] Thus, for both power and ideological reasons, traditional organized religion is incompatible with the *ultimate* goals of totalitarianism.

Despite this last point, neither Hitler nor Stalin, who were not noted for excessive caution, launched a full-scale, sustained campaign to eradicate all traces of organized religion from the fabric of social life. Constant harassment coupled with occasionally intensive conflict was the fate of the churches in both regimes. Indeed, on occasion both dictators had to compromise with church authorities. Stalin, for example, relaxed some of the restrictions on the Russian Orthodox church in exchange for full support in the war effort.

The "islands of separateness" metaphor evokes an enclave where nonregime thought and behavior is in a wholly defensive position. It does not in the least resemble the situation in certain authoritarian regimes where the church is part of the power structure or at least is an important pressure group.

Another resistant nodule to assimilation and incorporation in the totalitarian system is the family. Despite some early talk of abolishing the family as an "outmoded bourgeois institution," the Stalinist regime made no frontal assault on the family. In Nazi Germany the family had an even more positive place in the ideology, though Nazi practices call this into question somewhat.

Indirectly, family life was threatened by the totalitarian regime. There is the famous story of the 1930s, for example, of the Soviet lad who was killed by neighbors after denouncing his parents to the authorities. The regime made him into a kind of martyr, though most Soviet citizens probably had a somewhat different view of him. Likewise, there

22. The phrase is Lenin's.

was some encouragement from the Nazi regime for having babies out of wedlock to provide more Aryans to stave off the threat of "alien, inferior" hordes. This could be viewed as an oblique attack on the traditional family.

Nonetheless, the family remained largely intact as an institution that provided an intimate retreat where attitudes and behavior uncongenial to the regime might find expression.

In calling academia and scientific activity islands of separateness, Friedrich and Brzezinski do not mean that they are "free." Rather, they pose a serious dilemma for the totalitarian regime. If the regime allows too much latitude, the scientific and academic communities can be centers of political criticism and opposition. On the other hand, if ideological conformity is too tightly imposed, the scientific and technical capabilities of the regime will be lowered. While certain forms of scientific activity can operate successfully in highly repressive environments, the unmitigated enforcement of ideological and political orthodoxy can have diminishing returns—for instance, the Lysenko affair mentioned earlier.

If the regime wants results it will simply have to soft-pedal its control of academic and scientific institutions. This will naturally encourage a spirit of inquiry and sense of community that pose problems for the current party line.

What is true of the military as an island of separateness is partially applicable to any formal organization with some sense of unity. We have seen in the last chapter that the military as an institution and professional organization tends to think itself the foremost guardian of national independence. It may also combine its patriotism with a pragmatic, nonideological style and self-image. Thus, the military can develop a certain imperviousness to the regime's ideological appeals. As such it constitutes a permanent problem and perhaps a threat for the regime. Stalin was so frightened of a military coup that he viciously purged the military in 1938. Hitler had to work by degrees to wear down the army's independence and succeeded only in the midst of World War II. Mao, too, had various bouts with the military.

Ethnic groups can also form a stumbling block for a totalitarian elite. This applies with special force to the Soviet Union as a multinational state. The Communist party has never recruited proportionally among all the varied groups in the country. Some groups have been overrepresented; other groups have been underrepresented. In the early prerevolutionary days minorities such as the Jews had more than their share of party members. With the rise of Stalin, ethnic Great Russians have provided the bulk of truly militant Communists. On the other side of the coin, certain minorities are conspicuous by their lack of enthusiasm.

Even if a particular ethnic group has its share or more of party members, this does not say much about the whole group's commitment to communism and the regime. Ethnic groups with a distinctive traditional culture may be hard nuts to crack for regime goals. This is especially the case when ethnicity is conjoined with strong religious attachments as with the Georgians, Armenians, Jews, and certain Muslim groups in Soviet Central Asia.

The lingering influence of localism also calls into question any excessively centralistic concept of totalitarianism. Local areas often develop a kind of machine-style politics within the orbit of the totalitarian regime. Such localism acts as a distorting prism for directives coming from central government or party headquarters. Even under Stalin the party organizations of large Soviet cities were slightly out of step with the Moscow central. In Nazi Germany, the Gaue, the geographical subdivisions of the Nazi party, embodied a centrifugal force too. "In their loyalty to Hitler and his principles, the Gauleiter [party chiefs of the Gaue] openly resisted his government, continuously, and, toward the end, so successfully that the government of Berlin was turned over to them." [23]

Before reaching any final conclusions about the usefulness of the notion of totalitarianism, we must survey three major regimes to see their specific similarities and differences: the Soviet Union under Stalin, Hitler's Germany, and Mao's China.

THE SOVIET UNION UNDER STALIN

The Bolshevik coup that ushered in the second phase of the Russian Revolution took place in November 1917. Shortly thereafter, the new Soviet regime headed by V. I. Lenin (1870–1924) was plunged into the Civil War, punctuated by foreign intervention. The war was essentially over by early 1921. Previous to this, Lenin had banned all parties but his own. Originally known as the Bolshevik party, it became the Russian Communist party in 1918 and later the Communist Party of the So-

23. Edward N. Peterson, *The Limits of Hitler's Power* (Princeton: Princeton University Press, 1969), p. 434. *Gau* is singular; *Gaue* is plural. There simply is no translation of this term.

viet Union (CPSU). Lenin, by firmly establishing the Communist party and prohibiting openly organized factions within it, had created a dominant-mobilizational single-party that ruled an authoritarian state. Though he paved the way for totalitarianism, Lenin's rule itself was not totalitarian. It is an open question whether or not, had he lived, the Soviet Union would have become totalitarian.

The power struggle to succeed Lenin began before his death. The leader had become seriously ill in 1921 and was unable thereafter to exert sustained direct control over political affairs. The two main power contenders were Joseph Stalin (1879–1953) and Leon Trotsky (1877–1940). Stalin was helped in his ultimate victory by holding the originally modest office of secretary-general of the party. Using this office to build up an infrastructure of loyal supporters in party lower echelons, Stalin clearly outmaneuvered Trotsky and other possible rivals.

One of Stalin's favorite tactics was to portray his own policy position as the middle ground between the extremist or "deviationist" views on the right and left wings of the CPSU. This paid off handsomely because by 1928 Trotsky had been kicked out of the CPSU and later out of the country. The Georgian's triumph was complete.[24]

The totalitarian aspects of the Stalinist regime, however, did not result solely or directly from his successful struggle for autocratic power. Of crucial importance is the decision taken late in 1929 to abandon Lenin's New Economic Policy (1921). That policy had determined a slowdown and even a reversal of the attempt to develop the country rapidly into a full-fledged socialist industrial society. Especially important were concessions to private enterprise and a market economy in agriculture. Lenin reasoned that the country needed a respite from the high pressure of War Communism (1918–21). Reconstruction of the badly devastated economy seemed a higher priority than experiments inspired by Marxist ideology.

By 1929 considerable recovery had occurred, but the USSR was actually more a mixed economy than a truly socialist system. Many observers, then and later, maintain that an authoritarian single-party regime with a gradualist approach to economic development and social change was a perfectly viable alternative for the Soviet future. It would seem that ideology more than any other factor prompted Stalin and his

24. Stalin was not an ethnic Russian. His homeland was Georgia, a small country in the Caucasus. Stalin always spoke Russian with a slight accent, and some biographers feel that he overcompensated for a sense of ethnic inferiority by stressing the supremacy of the Great Russians.

lieutenants to launch what many call the "second revolution." This involved forced-draft industrialization and especially the collectivization of the independent peasant farms.

The peculiar aspects of Soviet totalitarianism are principally a result of the decision to collectivize and industrialize and of Stalin's personal response to the massive and profound controversy spawned by this decision. The divide-and-rule technique was the foundation of the Stalinist system. Such a technique will only work under the aegis of a supreme leader of Hitler's, Stalin's, or Mao's stature. Contrary to the view that totalitarian rule automatically becomes "more totalitarian" with time, this dependence on a charismatic leader shows the fragile and transitory nature of such a system. Only the leader has the personal authority to keep the system from collapsing and the personal qualities to master the Byzantine power struggle among his subalterns.

Stalinist totalitarianism rested on four organizational pillars, which Stalin succeeded in keeping in a weird sort of equilibrium (see figure 5.2). These four pillars—Communist party (CPSU), government, army, and secret police—were not necessarily of equal strength. Stalin would favor one or more of them while he was purging one or more of the others. Though an institution is something different from its component individuals, the purge can wreak institutional havoc by the frenetic replacement of personnel. This lowers the level of institutionaliza-

Figure 5.2.   Four Pillars of Stalinist Totalitarianism

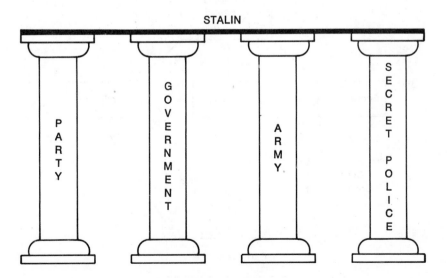

tion and gives that impression of social "atomization" that struck early students of totalitarianism.

The Party

It is ironical that the institution that sped Stalin to power should also have suffered most at his hands in both institutional and personal terms. In the 1930s Stalin purged all echelons of the party of everyone who did not blindly support his policies. Terror from incarceration and torture to murder was the fate of people who failed to show the required degree of enthusiasm. Especially hard hit were the "Old Bolsheviks," comrades of Lenin, who were bizarrely charged with being spies, traitors, and foreign agents. Forced confessions and "show trials" were supposed to "prove" that the colossal difficulties of collectivization and industrialization were their doing. With such "spiders, bloodsuckers, and vampires"—to use a memorable phrase of Stalin's—no wonder "wrecking activities" and "sabotage" undermined the succession of Five-Year Plans.

The extent of Stalin's onslaught against the party can be seen in a brief look at its organization in the 1930s (see figure 5.3).

The *party congress* is the "legislature" of the CPSU and still exists

Figure 5.3. Main Organs of the CPSU in the 1930s

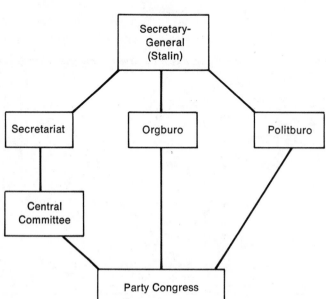

today. In Lenin's time the party congresses were lively arenas of discussion and political conflict. Toward the close of the 1920s the Stalinist pattern of the organized cheering section was beginning to prevail. Party congresses became occasions to praise the great leader and to ratify decisions already taken and policies already implemented. The main function of the party congress was to elect the Central Committee, but under Stalin these elections simply put the rubber stamp on previous selections.

Yet, this apparently was not enough for Stalin, since of the 1966 voting and nonvoting delegates at the 17th Party Congress (January–February 1934), "no less than 1108, or more than half, were arrested on charges of counter-revolutionary crimes." [25] Moreover, according to the party constitution, congresses were supposed to meet at least once every four years. Despite this, the lag between the 18th Party Congress (1939) and the 19th (1952) was over thirteen years. We can understand why the four war years (1941–45) did not permit such a conclave, but the postwar delay of more than seven years is just another symptom of the sorry state of CPSU institutions under Stalin.

The *Central Committee* of the CPSU was a smaller group of slightly over one hundred full members in the 1930s. It seemed a natural place for the top party elite to decide key issues. To some degree this promise was realized under Lenin, but here again the Stalinist purges had a devastating effect on institutionalization. Out of 139 members and candidate members elected at the 17th Party Congress, about 70 percent were ultimately shot or arrested.[26] Like the party congresses, the Central Committee met less and less from the late 1930s on, and did less and less.

The three small organs, which were also formally chosen by party congresses, showed the same pattern of purge and institutional weakness. These were the *Politburo* (Political Bureau), the *Secretariat*, and the *Orgburo* (Organization Bureau). As these small groups consisted more and more of blindly devoted or thoroughly browbeaten followers of Stalin, the leader could grant them a small share in policy-making and implementation. Nonetheless, of the fifteen members of the "Stalinist" Politburo chosen at the 17th Party Congress, seven were purged before the end of the decade.[27] The Politburo contained the sixteen top

25. Leonard Schapiro, *The Communist Party of the Soviet Union* (New York: Vintage Books, 1964), p. 417.
26. Ibid.
27. Robert J. Osborn, *The Evolution of Soviet Politics* (Homeward, Ill.: Dorsey Press, 1974), p. 214.

Communists. Stalin's top lieutenants were permitted to meet and discuss the key issues of the day. Under Stalin, however, it never reached its potential as a kind of "party cabinet," and was relegated to a background position in his final years. The Central Committee Secretariat was since 1922 Stalin's special province. Its members and staff were his most loyal subordinates. Other organs such as the Orgburo would spring momentarily into activity when Stalin used them to purge or discipline other segments of the Party. Afterwards, their powers were stripped away.

Two recent students point to three techniques by which Stalin preserved his hegemonic position from institutional challenge.[28] The first was the "dictator's tolerance of the most distinctive feature of Soviet rule at all periods—the local clique." The territorial expanse of the USSR allowed the formation of local cliques that were strong enough to rule locally, but were too weak to pose a real threat to Stalin's hegemony. If any of them proved troublesome, he could always bring in other organs like the secret police to crush resistance. Each local clique had "vertical" links reaching up to Stalin himself, but was prevented from establishing "horizontal" links to form a network beyond Stalin's control.

The next technique was employment of the clique or "Mafia system" at the national level. This involved (1) "taking decisions in *ad hoc* committees of two or three selected leaders," and (2) the "use of agents of personal rule in addition to his all-powerful personal secretaries, to operate outside the framework of the Party and State institutions." [29] As we will see later in the chapter, much of this description could also be applied to the Nazi regime.

The use of the secret police was Stalin's third technique for preserving his position. In the 1930s the OGPU (later the NKVD), which previously had been concerned with non-Communist oppositionists, was increasingly directed against CPSU members. To the task of purging suspected party members by jailings and executions were added the operations of vast labor camps. It should cause no surprise by now if we recall that two prominent victims of secret police purges were two successive chiefs of the secret police, Yagoda and Yezhov.

28. Leonard Schapiro and John W. Lewis, "The Roles of the Monolithic Party under the Totalitarian Leader," in *Party Leadership and Revolutionary Power in China*, ed. John W. Lewis (New York: Cambridge University Press, 1970).
29. Ibid., p. 127.

The Soviet Government under Stalin

In 1936 a new constitution known as the "Stalin Constitution" was proclaimed in the USSR. It declared the country a "socialist" society and set up the formal government structure that still exists today. Not surprisingly, it also declared the CPSU the only legal party.

Figure 5.4. Organs of Soviet National Government under Stalin

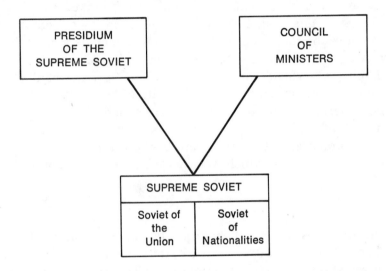

In theory the basic organ of Soviet government was (and is) the bicameral Supreme Soviet. The Soviet of the Union was elected in districts drawn according to one deputy for every 300,000 people. The Soviet of Nationalities was chosen both in terms of the federal structure (fifteen or so Union-Republics) and according to national minorities (autonomous republics and national areas, etc.). This meant that even in the 1930s the whole Supreme Soviet counted more than one thousand deputies. On paper the supreme lawmaker and appointer of government officials, the Supreme Soviet under Stalin was the paradigm case of the rubber-stamp–organized-cheering-section stereotype. Things have not changed very much since his passing.

The Supreme Soviet chose a small board called the Presidium of the Supreme Soviet to carry on the parent body's functions when it was not in session, i.e., most of the time. The Presidium had many of the functions of a collective chief executive and its chairman was considered the head of state or "president" of the USSR. This office has usually been reserved for elder statesmen or political "lightweights," although Leonid Brezhnev once served as president. His springboard to power, however, lay in the party and not in the Presidium. Brezhnev surprised some observers by reassuming this office in 1977.

Also emanating from the Supreme Soviet was the "cabinet," known until 1946 as the Council of People's Commissars and since then as the Council of Ministers. It selected a chairman, who was the Soviet prime minister, and several vice-chairmen. Stalin rarely served as prime minister, delegating this office to his most loyal subordinates, such as V. M. Molotov. Since the Council of Ministers grew to include many ministries and other agencies, there emerged yet another Presidium (of the Council of Ministers), which was the true or "inner" cabinet of the system. Ministries were of two sorts in the Council: (1) Union-republic ministries had separate organizations at both the national (Moscow) and the republican levels; (2) All-union ministries existed only at the national level and operated directly everywhere in the country. There were also republic-level ministries, which were not included in the national Council of Ministers.

The Soviet Army

The third main instrument of Stalin's rule was the military. The Soviet Army (Red Army until 1945) showed pretty much the same pattern as the other institutions. Stalin's dramatic collectivization drive in 1929 presupposed the solid loyalty of the Red Army. However, toward the end of the 1930s the purge engulfed the army itself. In June 1937 Marshal Tukhachevsky, Deputy Defense Minister Gamarnik, and other top generals were executed for treason. This inaugurated a "large-scale purge of the Soviet High Command and the top Party apparatus in the Army." [30] The near-calamitous results of this purge for Soviet performance in World War II was acknowledged by Nikita Khrushchev in his famous "anti-Stalin" speech at the 20th Party Congress in the fall of 1956: "Very grievous consequences, especially in reference to the beginning of the war, followed Stalin's annihilation of many military commanders and political workers during 1937–41 because of his suspiciousness and through slanderous accusations." [31]

30. Merle Fainsod, *How Russia Is Ruled* (Cambridge, Mass.: Harvard University Press, 1953), p. 405.
31. Nikita Khrushchev, "Secret Speech," in *The Anti-Stalin Campaign and International Communism,* ed. Russian Institute of Columbia University (New York: Columbia University Press, 1956), p. 48.

From the time of the Civil War (1918–21) party leaders had dispatched "political commissars" to the army to watch over the political reliability of military commanders of non-Communist backgrounds or inclinations. This parallel system continued even when the top commanders were increasingly members, often of long standing, of the CPSU. Since Stalin was forced to relax some of the pressures on the military during World War II, tendencies toward professionalism and national mission were naturally strengthened. After the war, however, the familiar steps of putting the army "in its proper place" were retraced:

> When there were signs that Marshal Zhukhov was becoming too prominant a figure, he was promptly removed from the limelight. . . . Ideological indoctrination of the army, which had been relaxed during the war, was revived and intensified. The Party leadership tightened its grip on the army. The officer corps was not only expected to be efficient; it was required to demonstrate unswerving devotion to the regime.[32]

The Secret Police

The fourth and final instrument of Stalin's rule was the secret police. The Soviet secret police first emerged during the Civil War of 1918–21 as the "Cheka," the Russian acronym for "Extraordinary Commission to Fight Counterrevolution." In 1922 the Cheka was replaced by the GPU (State Political Administration), which a few years later became the OGPU. In the late 1930s the OGPU was absorbed into a ministry, the NKVD, or People's Commissariat of Internal Affairs. After World War II, when Stalin dropped the revolutionary-sounding "people's commissariat" as the official name for his ministries, the NKVD became known simply as the MVD, or Ministry of Internal Affairs. Shortly after Stalin's death in 1953, the secret police was demoted in status: instead of being a full ministry, it became a mere committee—the KGB, or Committee of State Security.

Destalinization and Detotalitarianization

Our suggestion above that Stalin's character had much to do with fundamental traits of Soviet totalitarianism does not imply that without him no form of totalitarianism would have emerged in the Soviet Union. Nor does it exclude the possibility that a modified form of totalitarianism

32. Fainsod, *Russia,* p. 408.

could have emerged after his death in March 1953.[33] This did not happen. Though the post-Stalin USSR still suffers from a kind of "totalitarian hangover," the change that has occurred is enough to make the totalitarian model inapplicable. Though official "destalinization" commenced only with the 20th Party Congress more than three years after Stalin's death, the actual process began when Stalin took his last breath. In this sense destalinization is equivalent to Soviet "detotalitarianization." Table 5.2 summarizes the gist of this process, whose features will be briefly covered below.

TABLE 5.2.   Main Traits of Destalinization

1. Decline of the secret police and emergence of "socialist legality"
2. Resurgence of the CPSU and strengthening of its institutions, such as the Central Committee
3. Emergence of collective leadership at the expense of the cult of personality
4. Development of a more flexible economic system

The precipitous decline of the secret police (then called the MVD, or Ministry of Internal Affairs) after Stalin's death reflects the power struggle during the "succession crisis." L. V. Beria, head of the secret police for over nineteen years (and like Stalin, a Georgian), acted as if he were planning to make himself his countryman's heir. Before the end of 1953 not only were Beria and his henchmen executed, but the secret police had lost its ministry status. Many of its functions were transferred elsewhere or stopped outright. In place of a massive lawless police apparatus, there developed some rudimentary due process safeguards called "socialist legality."

While the term "police state" has some relevance for the Soviet Union today, the physical survival of regime critics contrasts starkly to Stalin's day, when they doubtless would have perished without a trace. Allowing someone like Alexander Solzhenitsyn to emigrate to the West would have been unthinkable a generation ago. As Frederick Barghoorn contends: "The Party apparatus and its police allies still dominate Soviet Russia.

---

33. Among attempts to reformulate totalitarianism so as to fit the USSR since Stalin, see Allen Kassof, "The Administered Society: Totalitarianism without Terror," *World Politics* 16 (July 1964): 558–75; and Zbigniew K. Brzezinski, *Ideology and Power in Soviet Politics* (New York: Praeger Publishers, 1962), chap. 1.

However, their dominance is not as overwhelming as it once was." [34] The "imperfect monism" that H. Gordon Skilling talks about (see above, under "General Criticisms of the Concept of Totalitarianism") is neither totalitarianism nor pluralism (full or limited); it is a rigid authoritarianism.

We must bear in mind that even during Stalin's harshest attacks on CPSU organizations and personnel, Soviet ideology and propaganda never flagged in proclaiming the supremacy of the party. The main agent and original beneficiary of closing the gap between ideology and practice with respect to the party in the post-Stalin era was Nikita S. Khrushchev. First secretary of the party from 1953 to 1964 and prime minister from 1958 to 1964, he assumed the former post after Georgi Malenkov gave it up to take the prime ministership—which he held to early 1955. As Beria's death symbolized the downfall of the MVD, Malenkov's 1955 ouster signaled the subordination of the government bureaucracy to the party leadership.

Later in 1957 when Khrushchev's enemies, the so-called antiparty group that included Malenkov, counterattacked and tried to remove him from the first secretaryship, he relied on the army for support and rewarded them for it. This dependence too was short-lived, and party hegemony was reaffirmed. The removal of Marshal Zhukhov as defense minister in late 1957 and the firing of Marshal Bulganin as prime minister in 1958 were symptomatic of this shift.

The role of the Central Committee both in strengthening Khrushchev's power in 1957 and taking it away in October 1964 shows that his personal victories did not make him a new Stalin. Khrushchev was bound to the party as an institution, and when he was dumped it was partly because his "harebrained schemes" of party reorganization (as the new leadership dubbed them) had alienated party bigwigs at the Central Committee level. Though the Brezhnev-Kosygin era differs from the days of "Mr. K.," the strengthening of the party and its institutions has, if anything, increased.

While Khrushchev's peak years (1958–62) represent something less than fullblown collective leadership, no cult of personality revolved around him as with Stalin. Khrushchev lacked the borrowed charisma of being a lieutenant of Lenin—always a key to Stalin's authority. Further, his personal style of chummy boorishness was miles away from

34. Frederick C. Barghoorn, "The Security Police," in Skilling, *Interest Groups*, p. 128.

the awesomeness of a Hitler, Stalin, or Mao. He may simply have been too sane to play the superleader soaring above all institutions.

While it is clear that since 1964 Leonid Brezhnev has been the leading figure in Soviet politics, he has not added the prime ministership to his post as head (general-secretary) of the CPSU. Furthermore, there appear to be definite rules that limit what he or any other top leader can do. Basing ourselves on Robert J. Osborn, we can put these in a chart, as shown in table 5.3.[35]

TABLE 5.3.   Rules of the Game in Recent Soviet Politics

1. The leader does not commit the Politburo and the Central Committee without discussion and consultation.
2. The purging of policy opponents is excluded.
3. Reorganization will not be used as a disguised purge.
4. Policy opponents will not be charged with "Stalinism."
5. The functions of party organs will not be undermined.
6. Khrushchev's ideas about "the regularity of party work, the faithful observance of party rules" are still in force.

As a final step in the process of "destalinization" a more flexible economic system had to be developed. The Soviet economy under Stalin was an extremely rigid, highly centralized affair. It was indeed a command economy because the State Planning Commission (Gosplan) in Moscow set rigid production targets for the whole economy. The plan was so detailed that a given factory might receive production targets well above its reach. Little feedback to the Moscow center was allowed so that targets could be readjusted to economic realities. Complaints were virtually taboo, and failure to meet the often arbitrary targets could result in the severest punishments.

Because of the rigidities and penalties, various ways of avoiding difficulties were concocted. Though these were illegal and often punished, the government tacitly acknowledged their necessity. One such expedient was the "fixer," who came into the picture because Soviet factories had little flexibility in their "inputs"—resources coming in. Thus, a given factory might not have enough nails allotted to it to produce enough chairs to meet plan requirements. Even if there was a nail factory (perhaps needing chairs for its staff) across the street, cash or barter

35. Osborn, *Evolution*, pp. 191–92.

deals were ruled out. By law, any exchange would have to be cleared by the appropriate ministry or ministries back in Moscow. This generally meant intolerable delay or no deal at all.

To surmount such a snag, the "fixer" of the chair factory would make a deal with his opposite number at the nail factory. The purchase or trade would be made outside the law. The fixer either had a sinecure position in the firm or one with nothing to do with his fixer role.

"Economic destalinization" refers to various approaches to decentralization in the post-Stalin economy. Khrushchev initially tried to decentralize on a regional basis in 1957, setting up over one hundred regional economic councils (Sovnarkhozy). Their number was cut down over the next few years, and finally this system was shelved. More recently, decentralization has been at the firm level, with factory managers given far looser guidelines as to how to achieve quotas.

Even profitability, which for years was thought synonymous with "capitalist exploitation," has been rehabilitated as an indicator of efficiency. The changes mean greater freedom for managers, greater mobility for workers, and greater product choice for consumers. These things contribute to the overall loosening of controls which betokens the transition from totalitarian to an authoritarian regime.

HITLER'S GERMANY

On January 30, 1933, Adolf Hitler was appointed chancellor (prime minister) of the German Republic. His party, the National Socialist German Workers Party—NSDAP, or Nazi, for short—was the largest, but not the majority, party in the Reichstag (lower house of parliament). Though prepared and accompanied by violence, Hitler's advent to power was an essentially legal event. The Great Depression after 1929 had combined with widespread extremism on left and right to sap confidence in German constitutionalism. After 1930, normal parliamentarism had given way to constitutional dictatorship authorized by the aged president Paul von Hindenburg. The last three pre-Hitler chancellors—von Brüning, von Papen, and von Schleicher—failed to generate enough support to handle massive inflation, crippling unemployment, and burgeoning extremism.

Thus, Hitler was called in to head a "government of national concentration," with a cabinet that initially contained only three Nazis. The conservative-rightist majority was supposed to restrain Hitler and the revolutionary rumblings that had been associated with the NSDAP since the early 1920s. The new chancellor had promised powerful interests such as big industrialists and the army to do nothing to endanger their position in the "new" Germany. The dozen-year history of the Third Reich records how all these promises were broken.

However, this turnabout was not taken overnight. As with Mussolini, there are certain stages and turning points in the expansion of Hitler's power and the emergence of totalitarianism. The three main stages are: 1933–34, takeover and consolidation of power; 1934–37, period of relative moderation; and 1938–45, intensification of the totalitarian dynamic. In the first stage Hitler used constitutional dictatorship to destroy German constitutionalism. Since the constitutional structure was never formally abolished and superseded by a new Nazi constitution, the Third Reich operated as if in a perpetual state of emergency. But an emergency cannot really be perpetual, and this self-contradictory expression symbolizes rather well totalitarian formlessness and lack of institutionalization.

Among the institutions subverted and transformed by this process, the most important are (1) the presidency, (2) the chancellor and his cabinet, (3) the Reichstag, and (4) the federal system.

Since Hitler was appointed chancellor by President von Hindenburg, he was temporarily outranked in the ceremonial order of the state. So long as the senile president lived, his popularity stood in the way of Hitler's plans. When Hindenburg obliged by dying in August 1934, the cabinet decreed merger of the offices of president and chancellor. Afterward Hitler never used the title of "Reich President" and was known officially as "Führer and Chancellor of the German People." By this he wished to show that his legitimacy did not derive from institutions or constitutions.

Hitler's cabinet quickly ceased to operate as a collegial body. Though completely "Nazified" only in 1937, somewhat earlier it had ceased voting and authentic debate. Hitler increased the cabinet's size at the same time he cut down its importance as an institution. Brought in were Rudolf Hess, the Führer's party deputy—exemplifying the mixture of party and state which is one of the riddles of totalitarianism. Other top administrators were brought in too, such as the army chief of staff and the head of the Four-Year Plan (Hermann Goering). Despite its list of important members, Hitler's cabinet soon fell into the typical pattern of dictatorships. For example, its meetings were more and more infrequent: twelve in 1935, four in 1936, six in 1937. The single session for

1938 was the last for the whole cabinet.[36] In addition to the chancellor himself, the Führer's deputy, army (Wehrmacht) chief, and head of the Four-Year Plan, the cabinet in 1939 included three separate categories of officials. First, there were ten holdover ministries from the pre-Hitler government organization: Foreign Affairs, Interior, Treasury, Justice, Economic Affairs, Nutrition-Agriculture, Labor, Communications, Posts and Telegraph, and Forestry. Then there were five new Nazi ministries: Propaganda and Popular Enlightenment, Aviation, Church Affairs, Science and Education, Arms and Munitions. (These new ministries are highly indicative of Nazi totalitarian concerns!) Finally there were six other administrative posts brought into the cabinet, such as the head of the Reich Chancellory.

Martin Broszat points out that the cabinet became degraded into "an apparatus of execution of the Führer's will" and remarks that this development was bound "to a further withdrawal of Hitler from the daily exercise of the Reich government." [37] Hitler, especially after the start of the war, thus ceased to be chancellor in the sense of day-to-day supervision of policy and administration. This job was delegated first to Hans Lammers, head of the Reich Chancellory. Later Martin Bormann took over. Bormann, using both his position as chief of the Party Chancellory and dominant figure in the Führer's headquarters, became ultimately a "superminister and control minister, while Lammers simultaneously declined to a messenger of Bormann's." [38]

The composition of the Reichstag reflected the Nazis' speedy elimination of all other political parties. By mid-1933 all leftists had been purged from the body and in November the first all-Nazi Reichstag was "elected." What had taken Mussolini nearly seven years Hitler accomplished in a little more than seven months. If anybody truly deserved the rubber stamp–organized cheering section label it was the Nazi Reichstag. As a national honorary society, it was expanded from about six hundred to more than eight hundred members in this most ceremonial of modern dictatorships.

Weimar Germany was divided into a number of provinces or Länder, each of which had a government elected independently from the national government. If the term "coup d'etat" cannot be applied to Hitler's appointment as chancellor, it certainly is hard to avoid use of it regard-

36. Martin Broszat, *Der Staat Hitlers* (Munich: Deutscher Taschenbuch Verlag, 1969), p. 350.
37. Ibid., p. 353.
38. Ibid., p. 394.

ing the Nazi takeover of several Land governments. In Bavaria, for example, Nazi leaders "seized the initiative and forced their way into power, assured that the national government would support them and that the army would not interfere." [39] By threats of force Ernst Röhm, head of the SA, or Storm Troopers, secured the appointment of a Nazi general as commissar for Bavaria. This meant virtual suspension of the legal government and ushered in the period of full Nazi control. By similar actions elsewhere German federalism was laid to rest. While the Länder and their officials were never formally abolished, the realities of Nazi rule were those of a unitary state.

Hitler's Style of Leadership

The vacuum created by the weakening or destruction of constitutional institutions had to be filled with something. Since the Nazis viewed Hitler's legitimacy as independent from institutions, he obviously was not accountable to them. Hitler sought self-justification in his ideological mission—he often spoke of being sent by "Providence" and of his deep sense of the true interests of the people, or *Volk*—and in occasional plebiscitary approval. As a charismatic leader, the authority of all subleaders should ultimately derive from him. Nevertheless, the total renovation of all laws and institutions implied by this concept of leadership was not, and could not have been, instantly realized in Nazi Germany.

The result was a basic *dualism* or contradiction in the Nazi dictatorship.[40] On the one hand was the survival of rational-legal authority and procedures in the government bureaucracy, some of the courts, and even the military. On the other was the revolutionary dynamic of a movement unconditionally obedient to the will, whims, and wishes of its Führer. For a while in 1933–34 the second aspect seemed to be heading Germany toward a full-scale revolution. Later, in the mid-1930s, the claims of a bureaucratic state, alien to true totalitarianism, seemed on the verge of victory. The final phase after 1938 revealed a stronger attempt to dispense with solid institutions, bureaucracy, and remaining legalism.

Hitler considered continuance of traditional bureaucracy an evil, but for the time being a necessary evil. Since it was not a suitable instru-

39. Peterson, *Hitler's Power*, p. 158.
40. Ernst Fraenkel, *The Dual State* (New York: Oxford University Press, 1941).

ment for realizing many of his cherished goals, he resorted increasingly to what today would be called "task forces." Reflecting his ideas of leadership, he set these up with one "strong" leader (the Führerprinzip). This individual would be personally responsible to Hitler and empowered to cut through the red tape of bureaucratic routine.

That these special deputies and new agencies trespassed on ground supposedly assigned to other bodies did not bother Hitler in the least. He believed that the ensuing competition would result in the survival of the fittest—the person or group who could get things done. Moreover, by unleashing competition and complicating the administrative picture, Hitler's position as supreme arbiter and decision-maker would be guaranteed. This approach to government has been aptly described as an "organizational jungle." [41] A jungle is not only complex and disorderly, but things also grow more quickly there.

The fragmentation of power fostered by Hitler might have been more orderly had be been willing to supervise his subordinates closely. His aversion for systematic and sustained administrative routine caused him to oscillate between periods of intense, even frenetic activity, and periods of sullen, lethargic withdrawal. Though Hitler's power was in many ways the most autocratic of any ruler of a large modern state, he often failed to make use of it. He avoided many decisions entirely, delegated many, and procrastinated before making still others.

"Polycracy of Agencies"

The highly complex, fluctuating structure of Hitler's government has been called a "polycracy of agencies" by German scholars. Figure 5.5 represents a simplified analysis because more than forty government agencies were ostensibly under Hitler's direct control (i.e., their heads were supposed to report directly to him).

In addition to the cabinet and the Reichstag, three distinct groups of government authorities were subordinated to Hitler: (1) special high-level offices and councils involved with rearmament and economic mobilization (e.g., head of the Four-Year Plan, Ministerial Council of National Defense); (2) chancellories under Hitler in his quadruple capacity as Reich chancellor, head of state or president, head of party (NSDAP), and Führer of the German People; and (3) special agencies entrusted by

41. Broszat, *Staat*, p. 439.

Figure 5.5. The Structure of Hitler's Government

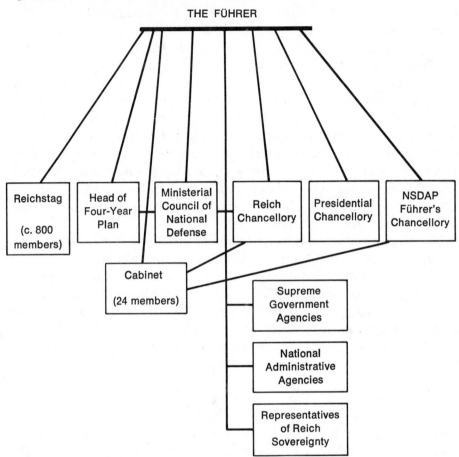

Hitler with important duties and projects. What no organizational chart can really show is the crisscrossing jurisdictions and overlapping functions of these bodies.

Hitler's appointment of his designated successor, Hermann Goering, as head of the Four-Year Plan in 1938 represents the peak of the latter's influence. Goering's failure to become "economic czar" of Nazi Germany was probably due to his characteristic inability to make the most of his power opportunities. This fact may also explain why the Nazi Four-Year Plan did not become, like the Soviet Five-Year Plans, the basis of a strongly planned economy. For a while, however, Goering's several hats made him the only one besides Hitler who could issue orders to government, party, and military authorities—he was also chief of the Air Force (Luftwaffe). The Ministerial Council of National Defense, also headed by Goering, included party, military, and government officials. More of a staff than a line agency, it soon declined as Hitler named an increasing number of special deputies.

The Reich Chancellory was the personal administrative staff of the chancellor. For a while this office was important because its chief, Hans Lammers, served as an intermediary between Hitler and his numerous subordinates. The combination of the Führer's awsome authority and his shirking of responsibility explains how a "mere secretary" can wield enormous, even if derivative, power. Does an official really know if it is the leader or merely his mouthpiece who has spoken? Can he risk finding out for sure?

We have already mentioned Lammers' replacement by Martin Bormann, another "mere" secretary, who began as staff leader in the office of the Führer's deputy (Rudolf Hess). After Hess flew to England in 1940, Bormann became the alter ego of Hitler. The deputy's Chancellory also acted as the party chancellory (since Hitler was chief of the NSDAP). Since Bormann's rise was due to personal closeness to Hitler rather than to any official position, "The party Chancellory . . . under Bormann remained far removed from the position of the Communist Politburo. The personalistic nature of the National Socialist leadership principle . . . obstructed the emergence of an all-powerful bureaucratic leadership central."

Filling in the complicated picture of Hitler's mode of governance were the special agencies. Supreme Government Agencies, created mostly after 1933, were technically below cabinet rank. They included the inspector of roads and highways, the youth leader, and other offices. Ranked lower were the National Administrative Agencies, such as that headed by Heinrich Himmler as "Reich Commissar for Strengthening German Nationality." Its job was to settle Germans on conquered Polish territory. Finally, the "Representatives of Reich Sovereignty" were the rulers of annexed or occupied areas. The general rule was that if an appointee was close to Hitler or his task area attracted Hitler's attention, he could become more powerful than his supposed administrative superiors.

The Nazi Movement

Evaluating the role of the Nazi party (NSDAP) in the Nazi regime is complicated by the loose usage of the term "party." If we have all the groups and institutions associated with the NSDAP in mind, the Nazi "party" is a classic case of a dominant mobilizational single-party. But this conclusion (gained from definitional vagueness) is not likely to find support in the facts. For this reason, we must distinguish between the *party proper* and the *movement*. The party included all Germans who formally joined the NSDAP and belonged to one of its geographical sub-divisions. The hierarchy embracing them was called the Political Organization (PO). The movement, on the other hand, included a variety of

Figure 5.6.   Organizations in the Nazi Movement

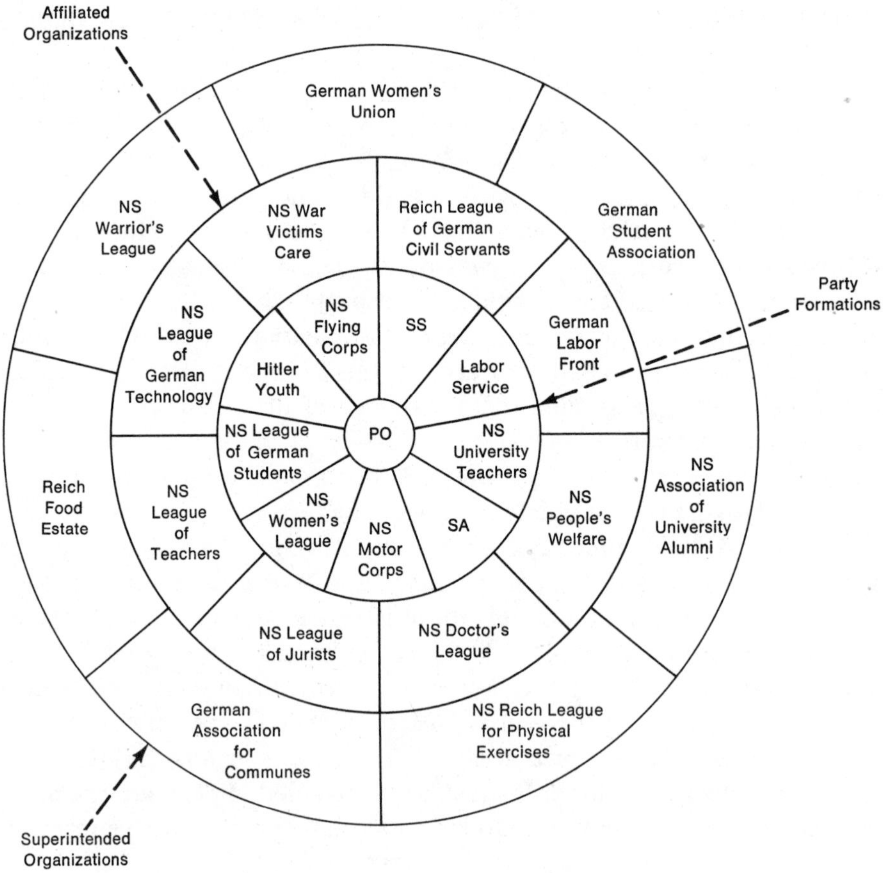

groups whose leaders, to be sure, were party members, but which by no means were controlled by the PO.

One way to visualize this is to think of the Nazi movement as a series of concentric circles with the PO at the center (see figure 5.6). In the circles nearest the center are those organizations that are technically most closely bound to the party (Party Formations). The next circle represents looser affiliation with the party (Affiliated Organizations). The final circle involves the loosest bonds of all (Superintended Organizations). Most Party Formations originated before 1933, while takeover or establishment of the others came after the seizure of power.

Let us begin from the inner circle of the PO and select only the most important of the other organizations for brief treatment.

THE POLITICAL ORGANIZATION.   The organizational core, if not always the predominant power factor, in the Nazi movement was the PO. As Hitler after 1933 had less time for party affairs, he appointed Rudolf Hess as his deputy for the party. Though the latter developed his own office into a number of administrative subdivisions, his drive to become a kind of secretary-general along Soviet or even Italian Fascist lines was quickly frustrated. The ambitions and jealousies of other party leaders stood in his way as did the quasi-independent regional party leaders, the Gauleiter. Accordingly, in contrast to the SS, the PO never became an organization with strict centralized control and a "hierarchically organized apparatus." [42]

The Gaue, as mentioned earlier, were the largest geographical subdivisions of the PO. They numbered thirty-two in 1933 and forty-two by 1941.[43] The political bosses of the Gaue, the Gauleiter, were the "old fighters," and as such always maintained a special and personal relationship with Hitler. For this reason they were never fully subjugated either by the PO or (later) by the SS. If they were particularly strong or power-hungry, they often achieved strong control in their Gaue.

In the early 1930s the Gauleiter often served as government chiefs in the still retained Länder. Later on, when some of these "personal unions" of party and government office were dissolved, the Gauleiter were compensated with special tasks such as jobs as wartime defense commissars. The position of the Gauleiter shows that absolute political centralization

42. Ibid., p. 201.
43. Each Gauleiter was at the head of a geographical hierarchy. Under him were a number of district leaders (Kreisleiter). Each district leader was set over a local group leader (Ortsgruppeleiter), of which there were over 20,000. Responsible to the local group leader were several cell leaders, of whom there were about 70,000.

is not necessary to the notion of totalitarianism. In fact, one study of the Gauleiter concludes that on certain occasions "Gauleiter politics contradicted the discipline of the totalitarian regime represented by the SS as well as the centralistic order-principle of the Reich government. It illuminated the centrifugal and anarchistic undercurrents of National Socialist domination, the fragility of its hierarchy." [44]

THE SA.   As a Party Formation the SA (Sturmabteilung), known also as the Storm Troopers or Brownshirts, were a Nazi paramilitary force dating back to the early 1920s. They had taken part in Hitler's abortive attempt to seize power in Bavaria in 1923—the famous Munich Beer Hall Putsch. In the first eighteen months of Hitler's rule the SA, led by Ernst Röhm, were the most unruly and "revolutionary" force in the Nazi movement. Their dream to replace the regular army endangered Hitler's early compromises with the High Command. For these reasons and others, on June 30, 1934, Hitler had the SS carry out a violent purge of the SA top leadership. Röhm and others were executed, and the SA never recovered its prominence as a political force. It was never abolished, however.

THE SS.   The SS (Schutzstaffel, or security squad) grew from the humblest origins as a subdivision of the SA assigned to guard Hitler. From this point (1925) the organization grew to where the expression "the SS state" has often been applied to its power position. Heinrich Himmler was appointed head of the SS in 1929 with the title of "Reichsführer SS." Henceforth the character of the SS changed rapidly. Even before the takeover of 1933 it had become an inner-party security or police force.

By 1936 Himmler had risen to the post of chief of the German Police, which office was technically under the jurisdiction of the minister of the interior. Since this additional post gave him command of the Gestapo, or Secret State Police, he held the reins of the two main security organizations in Nazi Germany. The SS and associated groups were assigned control over the concentration camps, which grew from modest beginnings in the 1930s to the mammoth proportions of the death camps during the war.

Still another dimension of the SS is seen in Himmler's desire to bestow SS rank and honors on key political figures. This obviously served his plan to make the SS the Führer's most potent and loyal weapon. Furthermore, the SS was to be the recruitment and proving ground of a new

44. Peter Hüttenberger, *Die Gauleiter* (Stuttgart: Verlags-Anstalt, 1969), p. 165.

"racially pure" Aryan elite, which would rule the "New Order" after victory in World War II. To this end special training, and even breeding, centers were instituted under the aegis of the SS. While the traditional term "state within the state" is easily abused when it comes to Nazi Germany, the inflated and multipurpose apparatus of the SS seems to demand such a phrase.

After 1936 the SS was a hybrid organization, being in one sense a Party Formation, yet in another an appendage of the state. Soon Himmler's subordination to the minister of the interior became an empty formality. Since Himmler was in one sense a direct subordinate of Hitler, in cases of conflict over police leadership "the Reich Minister of the Interior could appeal neither to the legal competence of his department, nor apply his authority against his personal and immediate 'subordinate,' because by doing so he would assail the authority of the Führer." [45]

After the war broke out, the direct military contribution of the SS grew prodigiously. By the end of 1940 SS military units, the Waffen-SS, comprised 150,000 troops; and by late 1944 over 900,000.

THE LABOR FRONT.   In the circle comprising Affiliated Organizations (figure 5.6), the German Labor Front (DAF) stands out because of size and political importance. The Labor Front was headed by Dr. Robert Ley, who also was a top figure in the PO as "Reich Organization Leader." This huge organization of over 25 million members from both labor and management was the Nazi substitute for the unions they had crushed in 1933. With the usual pretext of "overcoming the class struggle," strikes and lockouts were outlawed. Thus, the officials of the Labor Front conducted considerable labor-management arbitration. There were even "courts of social honor" to try those guilty of lowering the "dignity of labor." There was also the exotic-sounding Strength through Joy organization, an offshoot of the Labor Front, whose main job was to arrange travel, recreational, and cultural activities at rates workers could afford.

Dr. Ley's plans for the Labor Front were so ambitious that many Nazis in the PO felt he was trying to replace the NSDAP with his own organization. This explains why Hitler never took the apparently logical step of appointing Ley minister of labor.

THE GERMAN FOOD ESTATE.   In our fourth circle of Superintended Organizations (figure 5.6) the Reich Food Estate draws attention. The early Nazi ideology had hailed the virtues of the peasantry, but the

45. Hans Buchheim, "Die SS-Das Herrschaftsinstrument," in Hans Buchheim et al., *Anatomie des SS Staates* (Olten und Freburg in Breisgau: Walter-Verlag, 1965), 1: 61.

regime's efforts and achievements in the area of food production were less impressive than elsewhere. In itself the Food Estate under Walter Darré was a somewhat cumbersome association of German farmers. It too was criticized as a "state within the state" by the more totalitarian Nazis. Though theoretically outside the party, the Food Estate was closely bound to the agriculture apparatus of the NSDAP. It ran into serious conflicts with the NSDAP, the SA, and the Labor Front. "Competence battles and organizational rivalries were thus often the expression of differences of opinion on social and economic policy as well as conflicts of interest." [46]

Even this cursory and incomplete survey of organizations that, loosely speaking, could be called parts of the NSDAP, shows that factionalism and diversity are not annihilated in the totalitarian regime. It also suggests caution in estimating the exact role of the "party" in such a regime. Understood in the narrowest and most manageable sense as the PO and its geographical subdivisions (the Gaue, etc.), the NSDAP had enormous troubles controlling some of the groups in the Nazi "movement." The entire movement depended on Hitler, and Hitler often pursued a "hands off" policy.

MAO'S CHINA

The Communist victory in China in late 1949 culminated one long and tortuous process and started another. The Chinese Communist party (CCP), formed in 1921 by Mao Tse-tung and others, assumed an active revolutionary strategy only after 1927 when Chiang Kai-shek, previously an ally of the Soviet and Chinese Communists, and the Nationalists struck against them. For some time the CCP was divided between advocates of urban insurrection by the party-led workers and those like Mao who argued that the peasantry was the "driving force" of the Chinese Revolution. By the mid-1930s the Maoist strategy had won out, and the Communists controlled certain rural and remote regions ("base areas").

According to one controversial view, without the Japanese invasion of 1937, the Communists would not have achieved victory as early as they did, if at all.[47] The Japanese onslaught triggered latent peasant nationalism. Since the CCP depicted itself as the most resolute "anti-Japanese" military-political force, it gained both members and legitimacy.

46. Broszat, *Staat*, p. 239.
47. Chalmers Johnson, *Peasant Nationalism and Communist Power* (Stanford: Stanford University Press, 1962).

A somewhat different theory does not discount this entirely, but stresses instead the Communists' skill in expressing and remedying deep-seated peasant grievances and problems. Their ability not only to "outfight," but also to "outadminister" their Nationalist rivals was the decisive factor, according to this theory.[48]

The Chinese Communist regime, the People's Republic of China (PRC), has provided challenging problems for students of both revolution and totalitarianism since its inception in 1949. The prevalence of totalitarian features in this regime has been episodic and the forms distinctly Chinese. Even the most confident theorists of totalitarianism have hedged their bets considerably in characterizing the regime. This is because its totalitarian features have been more pronounced at some times than at others. Thus we have to make some distinctions. In this regard, one recent student distinguishes two "models" of ideology, policy, and power that have operated over the last three decades in China.[49]

The *transformation model* involves commitment to the imperatives of a "comprehensive" (totalist?) ideology. The regime's policy is militantly revolutionary and egalitarian. Power accrues to the "supreme" (charismatic?) leader who relates directly to various "mass movements" more than to established institutions such as the party.

The *consolidation model* stresses practice over ideology by treating ideology as emerging from specific problems rather than as providing a blueprint for constructing a new society. The former is called "operational ideology." Since the policy priorities are development and efficiency, bureaucratic organization is used to tackle the problems of economic development and administration of a vast socialist state. The party bureaucracy is the ruling body and its institutions are strong.

If totalitarianism figures at all in recent Chinese history, it is in periods of transformation. Consolidation periods represent a "retreat from totalitarianism" strongly reminiscent of the post-Stalin USSR.[50] Similarly, leading CCP figures have favored one or another of these models. Mao was a transformer, while his one-time successor, Liu Shao-chi (purged in 1966), was a consolidator. On the other hand, the late Chou

48. See Eqbal Ahmad, "Revolutionary War and Counterinsurgency," in *National Liberation*, ed. N. Miller and R. Aya (New York: Free Press, 1971); and Mark Seldon, *The Yenan Way in Revolutionary China* (Cambridge, Mass.: Harvard University Press, 1972).
49. Byung-joon Ahn, "The Cultural Revolution and China's Search for Political Order," *The China Quarterly*, no. 58 (April–June 1974): 249–85.
50. This "wavelike" pattern contradicts those concepts of totalitarianism that suggest its uniform increase over time.

En-lai, though a consolidator by inclination, was flexible enough to support Mao's transformation campaigns.

Table 5.4 represents the oscillations between transformation and consolidation.[51] Of course, none of these periods is "pure" in the sense of excluding one of the models completely. In the early 1960s, for example, Mao tried in vain to launch transformative efforts. It was only when these were frustrated that he later unleashed the far riskier Cultural Revolution.

TABLE 5.4.   Transformation and Consolidation in China since 1949

Period	Type of Phase	Major Development
1949–53	transformation	rehabilitation, land reform
1953–55	consolidation	nation-building; First Five-Year plan
1955–60	transformation	collectivization, "100 Flowers" Campaign, Great Leap Forward
1960–66	consolidation	economic recovery, Socialist Education Movement, PLA Emulation Campaign
1966–69	transformation	Great Proletarian Cultural Revolution
1969–	consolidation	rebuilding the state and the party

The Cultural Revolution

The Great Proletarian Cultural Revolution illuminates much about Chinese communism. Advocates of power interpretations of politics see it as Mao's personal attempt to recapture power he lost to Liu Shao-chi in the 1960s. After the disappointments of the Great Leap Forward (1958–59), which tried to speed up industrialization and social change by tapping human enthusiasm, Mao resigned as chairman of the People's Republic (PRC). His policies were quietly, but nonetheless effectively, shelved. Doubtless, Mao and his supporters viewed the Cultural Revolution in part as a golden opportunity to settle old scores and recover lost positions. In short, the launching of the Cultural Revolution was an "attempt on the part of Mao Tse-tung to reassert his personal authority over all aspects of party policy and over all levels of party organization. . . ."[52]

Power politics, however, is only one dimension of the complex phenomenon of the Cultural Revolution. Ideology too played a major role.

51. Table based on Ahn, "Cultural Revolution," pp. 249–85.
52. Charles Neuhauser, "The Chinese Communist Party in the 1960's: Prelude to the Cultural Revolution," in *China in Ferment*, ed. R. Baum and L. B. Bennett (Englewood Cliffs, N.J.: Prentice-Hall, 1970), p. 34.

Mao and his cohorts did not want a highly bureaucratic, elite-dominated "pragmatic" regime as China's destiny. In this view, the Cultural Revolution embodied "Mao's radical, utopian communism, which preaches the attainment of the same communist goals by means of shortcuts replacing economic and political rationality with a blind belief in doctrine and reliance on force and the power of the human will." [53]

The power and ideological interpretations of the Cultural Revolution focus on factions and personalities at the vertex of the CCP hierarchy. There is, however, some sense in viewing the Cultural Revolution as a movement "from below." Since Mao increasingly saw the CCP apparatus as an obstacle, he outflanked it by mobilizing the youthful Red Guards and other extraparty formations. These were urged in 1966 to seize party headquarters all over China and to assail the "establishment" of the PRC. That this was a genuine "social movement" is proven by Mao's eventual moves to bring it back under control.

The Cultural Revolution also reveals that the main political actors in China have been the CCP itself, the People's Liberation Army (PLA), and various mass movements. This situation diverges from other totalitarian patterns because of the relative weakness of the government bureaucracy and the security police. However, the PLA and the Red Guards and "revolutionary rebels" of the late 1960s can be understood as "functional equivalents" of a terroristic secret police. They were used to enforce the leader's will, and when they went too far they were severely disciplined. Both the PLA and the mass organizations were involved in mobilization-purge campaigns typical of totalitarianism. And both were temporary beneficiaries when Mao attacked the institution of the party.

Taking these three political actors—the PLA, the CCP, and the mass organization—as his basis, one scholar contrasts three different types of regime in China since the early 1960s, as shown in table 5.5.[54]

Government Organization of the PRC

On January 17, 1975, the 4th National People's Congress of the PRC adopted a new constitution superseding the old one of 1956. While the new political structure resembles its predecessor, several key innovations need analysis.

In an innovation unprecedented for Communist regimes, the new con-

53. Franz Michael, "The Struggle for Power," in ibid., p. 52.
54. Ahn, "Cultural Revolution," pp. 249–85.

TABLE 5.5.   Three Types of Regime in Communist China

1. **An institutionalizing regime under the party:** this operated from 1962 to 1966 and less clearly from 1971 onward. The CCP dominates the regime; institution-building is advancing; and the level of mass participation (according to Chinese standards) is low.
2. **A movement-regime under the supreme leader:** this corresponds to the first phase of the Cultural Revolution in 1966–67. Institutions are attacked and the leader mobilizes the masses. Here totalitarianism prevails.
3. **A praetorian regime:** the PLA dominates the system, as in 1967–71. Institutionalization and mobilization are at a standoff. The top military leadership becomes the top political leadership. A praetorian regime cannot be truly totalitarian.

stitution makes the chairman of the Central Committee (until his death in September 1976, Mao himself) of the CCP commander of the country's armed forces. This striking reform is obviously a reaction to the "praetorian regime" mentioned above. This move exemplified more clearly than ever before the old Maoist dictum that "the Party commands the gun."

The office of chairman of the PRC has been abolished. This Chinese version of a head of state had only two incumbents: Mao Tse-tung (1954–59) and Liu Shao-chi (1959–66). They both had been elected by the National People's Congress. The office lapsed with the purge of Liu in 1966. However, the chairman of the Standing Committee of the National People's Congress may wind up as titular head of state, when the post-Mao setup is clarified. The new constitutional structure is shown in figure 5.7.

Following a typical Communist pattern the *National People's Congress* is ostensibly the sovereign base of the Chinese state. Just as typically, its size and composition make it a ratifying-ceremonial rather than an initiating body. On paper its powers impressively include constitutional amendment; legislation; appointing and removing (with the important proviso of Central Committee proposal) the premier; and approval of plans, budgets, and public accounts. The *Standing Committee* of the National People's Congress, like the Presidium of the Supreme Soviet in the USSR, is a small "steering committee" with numerous political and diplomatic functions. Most important are interpreting laws, issuing decrees, and calling sessions of the People's Congress.

The *State Council* is the cabinet and includes the premier, vice-premiers, and other ministers. Theoretically responsible to the National People's Congress and its Standing Committee, its real responsibility is

Figure 5.7. National Political Structure in the PRC

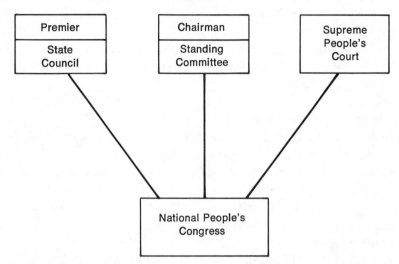

"horizontal" toward the highest party organs, especially the Central Committee. The new constitution endows the State Council with broad supervisory, administrative, and planning functions. It issues orders to regional and local administrative bodies. The *Supreme People's Court* is the highest legal organ in the PRC. It has little autonomy and enforces policy decisions made elsewhere.

The PLA

The People's Liberation Army includes all of China's land, sea, and air forces. Its political role in the late 1960s goes beyond that of the Red Army under Stalin and the Wehrmacht under Hitler. In the PRC's first decade the PLA was "apolitical" in the sense of engaging in no active intervention in Chinese politics. The PLA kept more or less aloof from factional squabbles and the few military dissidents were removed with ease by CCP authorities. In the early 1960s things began to change, with a gradual broadening of political involvement. This eventuated in "large-scale intervention and a takeover of civil functions by the military in the closing stages of the Cultural Revolution." [55] The third and present stage is marked by a "reversal of the trend toward military predominance and a gradual disengagement of the military from politics." [56]

55. Ellis Joffe, "The PLA in Internal Politics," *Problems of Communism* 24 (November–December 1975): 1.
56. Ibid.

The PLA's political rise began in the early 1960s when Mao secured the cooperation of Lin Piao, head of the army, for his goals of change. One result was that the PLA was hailed as a model revolutionary organization from which the rest of the nation should "learn." Another was to give Mao a powerful ally in the factional disputes that had temporarily diminished his political role.

It took the Cultural Revolution to catapult the PLA (and Lin Piao) to the heights of political influence. With Mao's attack on the CCP bureaucracy, there was no dike against the revolutionary upsurge of mobilized masses like the Red Guards. When the Cultural Revolution seemed out of control, Mao reluctantly and hesitantly called on the PLA to restore order. Military authorities moved into the power vacuum created by the Cultural Revolution. Lin Piao was rewarded for his collaboration by being made minister of defense and, more importantly, Mao's official successor.

With the influx of PLA men into higher CCP and government offices, the PRC seemed to have become a "praetorian" regime. Clearly, this outcome did not square with Mao's ideological vision or his reasons for launching the Cultural Revolution in the first place. The tension created climaxed with the report that in September 1971 Lin Piao had been shot down in an escape flight to the USSR, after instigating an abortive coup against Mao. That there was more involved in all this hazy affair than a personal grab for power is seen by the subsequent "disengagement" of the military from full-scale political activity. Ellis Joffe finds three main features in this (gradual) process: (1) "a scaling down of the army's excessive involvement in civil affairs"; (2) "a reaffirmation of professional values within the army at the expense of extreme politicization"; and (3) "a reduction of the army's position of strength in the national and regional organs of political power." [57]

The CCP

The Cultural Revolution's assault on the CCP as an organization is surprising only in contrast to the regime's previous exaltation of it. It also appears inexplicable if we identify Communist regimes with the dominant-mobilizational single-party. If we view the Cultural Revolution as in part an episode of totalitarianism, however, most of the mystery disappears. Stalin, too, attacked the party organization without destroying it,

57. Ibid., p. 9.

and though Hitler did not purge the PO of the NSDAP, he allowed the SS, and sometimes even the government bureaucracy, to supersede it.

Before the Cultural Revolution, the CCP bureaucracy was crystallizing as a force largely outside Mao's control. As we saw, power was not the only factor involved: the leading "anti-Mao" factions in the CCP apparatus had a divergent vision of China's future. Mao used first the Red Guards and later the PLA as counterweights and substitutes for the beleaguered party organization.

If 1971 marked a shift toward the political "disengagement" of the PLA, it *ipso facto* meant a "reengagement" for the CCP. Mao's strengthening of the party organization in the last few years of his life ironically had to reactivate and reinforce those same trends toward moderation and bureaucratization that originally had spurred him to attack it. As long as he lived, however, there was no question of simply returning to the pre-Cultural Revolution status quo. At the time of his death there was a precarious equilibrium between the "radicals," who want faster change, and the "moderates," who want more deliberate action.

The 10th Party Congress (August 1973), which lessened the PLA's political role, also modified the structure of the CCP. Though the pattern represented in figure 5.8 resembles the Soviet (and general Communist) pattern, two peculiarities should be noted. The party Secretariat, which disappeared during the Cultural Revolution, was not reinstituted by the 10th Congress. Second, there was a move toward "collective leadership" with the naming of five vice-chairmen of the Central Committee. Before his death in 1971 Lin Piao had been the sole vice-chairman.

While it is too soon to give a definitive verdict, present trends in China suggest a most serious defeat for the radicals and a provisional victory for the moderates. Although such categories oversimplify somewhat, we can interpret the political meaning of the moderate victory (symbolized by the disgrace of Mao's widow, Chiang Ching, a radical leader) by using some of the categories explained above. First, the "consolidation" policy seems to have gotten the upper hand over the "transformation" policy. With the disappearance of the charismatic leader and his top lieutenants, as well as the gradual depoliticization of the PLA, there seems little political alternative to the reemergence of an "institutionalizing regime under the party." This development should mute, if not drown out entirely, whatever totalitarian features characterized the Maoist period.

In this latter connection, it is hard for observers to avoid talking of "demaoization" roughly along the lines of "destalinization" in the USSR

Figure 5.8.   National Organization of the CCP after 10th Party Congress

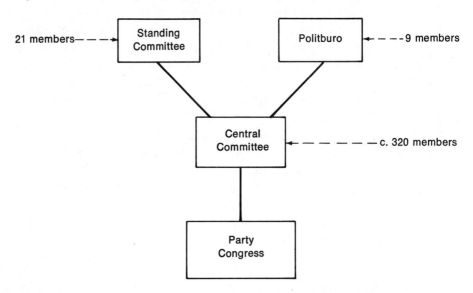

and Eastern Europe. However, there are important differences in the two cases. Mao was not only China's Stalin, but also its Lenin. Just as the Soviets have never denigrated Lenin's myth and memory, future Chinese leaders will not publicly, or even semipublicly, attack the words and deeds of Chairman Mao. Indeed, his authority will be invoked even for policies that most likely would have disturbed him greatly. Without Mao, transformationist efforts such as the Great Leap Forward or the Cultural Revolution seem unlikely.

THE PROBLEM OF TOTALITARIANISM

Our survey of several reputedly totalitarian regimes should help to resolve the problem of whether the original Friedrich-Brzezinski syndrome or some modification of it is the best way to defend or rescue the notion of totalitarianism from its critics. Historically, there have been two main trends or emphases in concepts of totalitarianism: some have stressed the *total state;* others have stressed the *total revolution* (see table 5.6).[58]

Of the two, the total-revolution approach is clearly superior, because the total-state idea is so easily exaggerated. This latter approach makes us think of an omniscient, omnipotent, and omnipresent bureaucracy,

58. This discussion and the following chart are based on Jänicke, *Herrschaft,* chaps. 1–2.

TABLE 5.6.   The Two Main Approaches to Totalitarianism

The Total State Approach	The Total Revolution Approach
1. Marked by static orientation.	1. Marked by dynamic orientation.
2. Marked by structural emphasis.	2. Marked by process emphasis.
3. Borders blurred between state and society.	3. Means a monopoly of power without necessarily penetrating all social sectors.
4. Based on Communist experiences.	4. Based on Fascist experiences.
5. Stresses hypertrophy of bureaucracy and impacted institutions.	5. Stresses antibureaucratic "movement" aspect of the regime and weakness of institutionalization.

but, as Martin Jänicke points out, "no study of totalitarianism has yet furnished proof that the gapless, centralistic coordination [*Gleichschaltung*] and control of a society (perhaps according to the model of Orwell's *1984*) has even been realized." [59] The total-revolution approach stresses the impact of revolutionary dynamism within the framework of a modern state.

Such was the thrust of Sigmund Neumann's approach to totalitarianism in 1942. Then he wrote, "The first aim of totalitarianism is to perpetuate and *institutionalize revolution.* Paradoxical though it is to put revolution on a permanent basis, the conscious creation of quasi-institutional structures is the most significant political feature. . . . It is exactly this fact that distinguishes the present-day dictatorships from earlier forms of despotism." [60] Z. K. Brzezinski, modifying somewhat his earlier views, has a similar stress to Neumann's:

> the totalitarian movements holding power do not aim to freeze society in the status quo; on the contrary their aim is to institutionalize a revolution that mounts in scope, and frequently in intensity, as the regime stabilizes itself in power. The purpose of this revolution is to pulverize all existing social units in order to replace the old pluralism with a homogeneous unanimity patterned on the blueprints of the totalitarian ideology. [61]

Pondering the Neumann-Brzezinski total-revolution approach and our look at specific regimes, we can see that the totalitarian syndrome presented earlier is too rigid to encompass the different patterns of totalitarianism. A syndrome approach implies that all the factors mentioned are *necessary conditions,* which must be present before we can group a

59. Ibid., p. 184.
60. Neumann, *Revolution*, p. xii.
61. Brzezinski, *Soviet Politics* (note 33, above), p. 15.

specific case under a general concept. The points we have found most troublesome are party-dominance and the terroristic secret police.

To avoid such rigidities, another approach to totalitarianism might first define it broadly along the lines proposed by Neumann and Brzezinski. Then, instead of a syndrome of necessary traits, we could draw up a list of what the philosopher Ludwig Wittgenstein called *family resemblances*. These are the sum of features that characterize the whole class of things under study (say, totalitarian dictatorships), but are not all found in each specific case (e.g., no terroristic secret police in China). A simplified way of understanding this is to think of five regimes and six traits that make up the family resemblances. Then we could suggest that possession of four of these traits is enough for us to call a regime "totalitarian." Let us call the five regimes I, II, III, IV, and V; and the six family traits A, B, C, D, E, F. Now let us diagram a possible situation:

Regime I has traits	Regime II has traits	Regime III has traits	Regime IV has traits	Regime V has traits
A, B, C, D.	A, B, C, E.	A, B, D, E.	B, C, E, F.	A, C, D, F.

It is clear from this illustration that no one of these traits is found in all totalitarian regimes. And yet the whole group of them draw from the same "bank" of traits, a bank that (hopefully) is categorically different from the one for authoritarian, to say nothing of constitutional, regimes.

At any rate, our argument should show that the difference between totalitarian and authoritarian dictatorship is categorical. Totalitarianism flourishes with a totalist and utopian ideology, while ideology in authoritarian regimes is rather half-baked or is a mere "mentality" as in many praetorian regimes. Totalitarianism aims at "internal conformity" of citizens: it wants them to believe and feel enthusiastically that the regime's goals are foreordained by history and its leaders are infallible guides in a great historical mission. An authoritarian regime is basically satisfied with "external conformity": if citizens refrain from public criticism and opposition to the regime, they are generally left alone.

Moreover, the totalitarian regime is concerned with mass mobilization, while many authoritarian regimes, despite protestations to the contrary, seem to relish mass apathy. At the level of the political elite, political conflict (which is very bitter in a totalitarian regime) stems from factionalism. In other words, it has to do with power struggles and policy disputes within one and the same totalitarian elite. All factions acknowledge the leader's hegemony and the ideology's validity. Political conflict in an authoritarian regime, on the other hand, reflects a limited pluralism, which allows a variety of social groups and institutions to have some impact on policy. The church, the military, the single-party, the business community, the unions, the large landowners—these and other groups can act as "veto groups" which can generally stop policies inimical to their vital interests.

STUDY QUESTIONS

1. Do the major criticisms of the notion of "totalitarianism" make it useless as a term of political analysis?

2. What problems do the case studies of Stalin's USSR, Hitler's Germany, and Mao's China raise for the Friedrich-Brzezinski six-point totalitarian syndrome?

3. What light do the Nazi and the Chinese experiences cast on the important distinction between the party proper and the totalitarian movement?

4. What is distinctive about totalitarian ideology? Did ideology really play the same role in our three totalitarian regimes?

5. How do totalitarian regimes differ from authoritarian regimes?

6. Are the outstanding traits of the three totalitarian regimes presented in this chapter basically the results of the (often disturbed) personalities of the totalitarian leaders?

7. Realizing that a personal attack on the memory of Mao Tse-tung in China along the lines of Soviet "destalinization" is unlikely, some institutional "demaoization" is probable. What shape are these changes likely to take?

SUGGESTIONS FOR FURTHER READING

ARENDT, HANNAH. *The Origins of Totalitarianism.* New York: Harcourt, Brace & World, 1966.

ARON, RAYMOND. *Democracy and Totalitarianism.* New York: Praeger Publishers, 1969.

BARBER, BENJAMIN R.; FRIEDRICH, CARL J.; and CURTIS, MICHAEL. *Totalitarianism in Perspective: Three Views.* New York: Praeger Publishers, 1969.

BRACHER, KARL D. *The German Dictatorship.* New York: Praeger Publishers, 1972.

BUCHHEIM, HANS. *Totalitarian Rule.* Middletown, Conn.: Wesleyan University Press, 1972.

CASSINELLI, C. W. *Total Revolution.* Santa Barbara, Cal.: Clio Books, 1976.

FRIEDRICH, CARL J., ed. *Totalitarianism.* Cambridge, Mass.: Harvard University Press, 1954.

FRIEDRICH, CARL J., and BRZEZINSKI, ZBIGNIEW K. *Totalitarian Dictatorship and Autocracy.* New York: Praeger Publishers, 1956.

LEWIS, JOHN W., ed. *Party Leadership and Revolutionary Power in China.* New York: Cambridge University Press, 1970.

LIFTON, ROBERT J. *Thought Reform and the Psychology of Totalism.* New York: W. W. Norton, 1963.

NEUMANN, FRANZ. *Behemoth.* New York: Octagon Books, 1963.

NEUMANN, SIGMUND. *Permanent Revolution.* New York: Praeger Publishers, 1965.

PETERSON, EDWARD N. *The Limits of Hitler's Power.* Princeton: Princeton University Press, 1969.

SCALAPINO, ROBERT A., ed. *Elites in the People's Republic of China.* Seattle: University of Washington Press, 1972.

SCHAPIRO, LEONARD. *The Communist Party of the Soviet Union.* New York: Vintage Books, 1964.

SCHURMANN, FRANZ. *Ideology and Organization in Communist China.* Berkeley: University of California Press, 1971.

SKILLING, H. GORDON, and GRIFFITHS, FRANKLIN, eds. *Interest Groups in Soviet Politics.* Princeton: Princeton University Press, 1973.

UNGER, ARYEH. *The Totalitarian Party.* New York: Cambridge University Press, 1974.

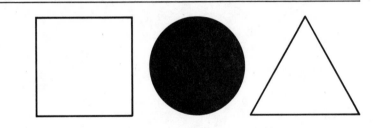

PART **2**

Movements

INTRODUCTION

Part 1 of this book has dealt with political regimes in a somewhat formalistic way. We have laid great stress on the structure and function of the official or legal institutions in modern and not-so-modern states. But all along we have made some references to things like political parties, social groups, interest groups, social movements, and currents of opinion. These provide the political systems with much of the work they have to do. They are the politically relevant segments of society, whose demands, needs, and activities breathe life into the formal political institutions. We call such segments the "movement" aspect of politics to emphasize their dynamic role.

The four chapters of part 2 cover the social roots of political life, hopefully without reducing politics to a mere play of social groups or economic interests. Chapter 6, the most broadly focused chapter in this part, is a kind of prelude to the rest. Its main goal is to explore how social inequality or, more precisely, social stratification produces distinct groups and types of conflict that are either resolved or repressed by the political system. But since the precise relationship between social stratification and political power is a highly controversial issue, we look instead to the three main ways social scientists and others view the power structure of contemporary societies, a subject that is more manageable.

Generally associated with conservative political views is an elitist approach to political power, which suggests that some sort of minority (not necessarily economic) will inevitably monopolize political power. Many theorists who tend to be liberal in their political views accept a pluralist vision of the power structure that stresses open competition among a large number of interest groups. To their left stand radical critics with a neo-Marxist vision of the power structure that sees a constant conjunction of economic and political power. The latter parts of chapter 6 go beyond the elitist–pluralist–neo-Marxist debate and delve into social stratification and the types of political conflict rooted in it. Finally, select groups called "crisis strata" are treated because of their pivotal role in contemporary politics.

The first half of chapter 7 deals with social movements in the narrow sense. These arise because of the conflicts and problems that trouble the social groups and crisis strata discussed in chapter 6. Such movements are important since they often capture political power, producing distinctive sorts of regimes. Even where they avoid or fail to achieve this goal, they provide either needed support or alarming opposition to the existing regime. When social movements settle down and become well-organized, they can take the shape of political parties (chapter 8) or interest groups (chapter 9). The second half of chapter 7 deals with that most dynamic and movement-oriented of political phenomena, revolution. The main problems considered are the nature, causes, and phases of revolution considered as a movement or, more exactly, as a convergence of movements.

Chapter 8 covers competitive parties and party systems. It assumes some knowledge of the social roots of politics discussed in chapters 6 and 7, since it is hard to grasp the origins and actions of modern political parties without reference to social stratification and social movements. The parties and party systems of chapter 8 are especially relevant to the constitutionalist regimes of chapters 2 and 3. The first part of chapter 8 presents a typology of the main sorts of parties found in competitive systems. The second part deals with the dynamics of party systems (i.e., the two-party and the multiparty systems). The chapter not only points back to its two predecessors in part 2 on social stratification and social movements, but also points ahead to the discussion of political culture and ideology in part 3. Perhaps chapter 8, since it deals with the crucial topic of political parties, illustrates better than any other the linkage of our trilogy of regimes, movements, and ideologies.

Chapter 9 is concerned with interest groups, which pluralists see as the main actors in the political process. Especially important are pressure groups, which most assuredly seek to influence political decisions. The types of pressure groups and the strategies they employ are important here. The latter part of the chapter is devoted to the important and elusive idea of public opinion. Its changing currents are, as the image implies, a key dynamic or movement aspect of politics.

6
Society and Polity

The problem of this chapter is the relationship of social structure to political power. The previous four chapters (2–5) have dealt with how political power is expressed through political institutions and less formal political organizations. Now we must turn to problems raised in chapter 1 and examine who rules and who benefits from rule. In the first section of this chapter we examine three main approaches or "methodologies" in the study of the power structure of contemporary societies: elitism, pluralism, and neo-Marxism. The second section, on social stratification and political power, builds upon the elitist, pluralist, and neo-Marxist approaches while showing their weaknesses. The final section discusses certain social groupings called "crisis strata," which have been of pivotal significance in the political conflicts of our time.

ELITISM, PLURALISM, AND NEO-MARXISM

Elitism

The classic elitist theory of Gaetano Mosca and Vilfredo Pareto has two main interconnected themes. The first involves a critique of the classic democratic principle of majority rule, which will be discussed in chapter 11. Our present interest is rather in the second theme, the empirical hypothesis that a small minority controls the state, indeed, all human organizations. We will base our present discussion on Vilfredo Pareto, Guido Dorso, and the American James Burnham.

Pareto's basic assumption was that men differ enormously in intelligence, talent, industry, ambition, moral worth, and aesthetic sensitivity. In his terms, society is therefore "heterogeneous." This means that for any sector of social activity—be it art, science, business, teaching, sports, politics, or manual labor, even crime—we will find tremendous differences in performance. Crudely speaking, there are those who perform well, those in a mediocre category, and those who perform miserably. In each of these activities we can call the minority who excels an *elite* and all the rest a *nonelite*. A multiplicity of elites therefore emerges made up of all the highly talented and capable people in various activities. This composite of elites becomes for Pareto the "elite of society"; the composite of nonelites becomes the "nonelite of society."

Pareto then divides the elite of the society into the *governing elite* and the *nongoverning elite,* arguing that only a minority of the minority is in actual charge of the political affairs of the whole society. In his own words "every society, however little developed, possesses a hierarchy and is governed by a small number of men, even when the government apparently seems in the hands of the greatest number." [1] Pareto's theory thus can take pyramidal form, as shown in figure 6.1.

Figure 6.1.   Pareto's Model of Social Stratification

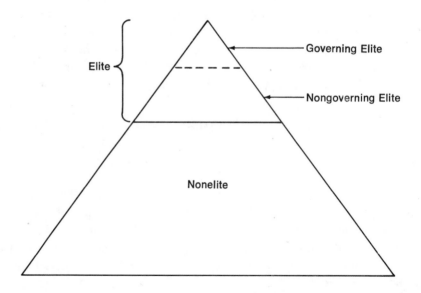

1. Vilfredo Pareto, *Scritti Sociologici* (Turin: U.T.E.T., 1966), p. 353.

Now, if the elite-nonelite distinction were the whole story, human society would have long ago crystallized into a rigid unchangeable castelike structure. That this has not happened Pareto attributes to the fact
that both elites and nonelites change. For reasons that Pareto could not
fully explain, elites tend to "decay" and nonelites tend to produce potentially elite elements. History is thus "a graveyard of aristocracies." The
principle of "circulation of the elite" operates to prevent the old elite
from destroying the whole society with its decline. The circulation of
elites involves, quite simply, the "demotion" of decadent elements of the
elite into the nonelite and the "promotion" of worthy elements from the
nonelite into the elite (see figure 6.2).

Figure 6.2.   Circulation of the Elite

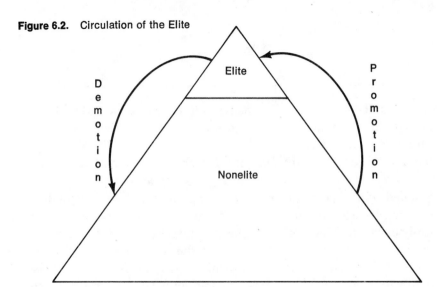

Had human societies found a perfect mechanism of elite circulation,
man's whole history would be one of perfect stability and gradual
evolutionary development. For a while stability seems assured because a
gradual but steady circulation is taking place. We can call this "piecemeal circulation of the elite." Sooner or later, however, the channels of
circulation are clogged by an old, entrenched elite that foolishly forbids
"new blood" from entering its ranks. Though Pareto did not use this precise expression, a "counterelite," which wishes to enter the elite or replace it, emerges at the head of the nonelite. This counterelite does not
openly declare its ambition to merge with or eliminate the old elite. It
masks its real intention by appealing to slogans of equality, democracy,
freedom for all, and the like, in order to win over the nonelite. When the

Figure 6.3.   Formation of a Counterelite

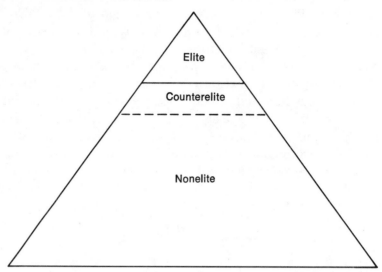

counterelite aided by the nonelite masses succeeds in ousting and replacing the old elite, we can call this process "wholesale circulation of the elite" or simply, *revolution*.

What about the fate of the old elite in a successful revolution? To be sure, many of its members (especially the "decadent" ones) are either killed, jailed, exiled, or sink into social obscurity among the nonelite. Others, however, follow a different tack, since no elite is completely and uniformly decadent. These save themselves by becoming traitors to their class and often occupy leading positions in the revolutionary movement. Pareto concludes that the main net result of revolutionary change is a new elite with some admixture from the old one. The nonelite nevertheless do benefit, at least temporarily, from the new regime. Ousting the old decadent elite results in a period of economic prosperity. Full equality and democracy remain as chimerical as ever, and the cycle leading to the next revolution soon is under way.

Guido Dorso, an Italian political theorist (1892–1947), attempted to remedy some of Pareto's defects and omissions by incorporating ideas of Karl Marx and Gaetano Mosca into the concept of elitism. It was Dorso who further refined the familiar dichotomy of the *ruled* and the *ruling* classes. The latter he defines as the "organized power that has the political, intellectual, and material leadership of society."[2] He further

2. Guido Dorso, *Dittatura, classe politica, classe dirigente* (Turin: Einaudi, 1955), p. 127.

distinguishes the "political class," which is the "technical instrument" of the ruling class, from the rest of the ruling class. This relationship becomes problematic when the political class becomes corrupt and pursues its own selfish interest at everyone else's expense. It is the ruling class's job to prevent or correct this situation. If it can do neither, its days as a ruling class are numbered.

Dorso subdivides the political class still further into the Ins, i.e., the "government political class," and the Outs, i.e., the "opposition political class." Under modern conditions political parties seem to regulate the relationships between government and opposition factions of the political class. The power structure of modern society can be depicted as in figure 6.4.

Figure 6.4.   Dorso's View of the Modern Power Structure

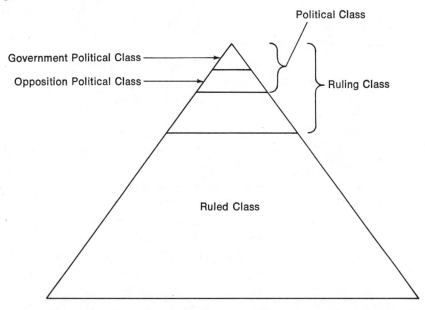

Dorso shares Pareto's concern with "circulation of elites," but speaks more specifically of "exchange" between different segments than of general circulation. There are three main exchange mechanisms whose smooth operation means stability, and happiness for society: [3]

1. Exchange between the government and opposition segments of the political class. Simple two-party systems such as England and the United States are definitely in Dorso's mind as illustrations.

3. Ibid., pp. 123–36.

2. Exchange between the political class and the rest of the ruling class. This reinvigorates the political class and prevents it from becoming a closed corporation.

3. Exchange between the ruled class and the ruling class. This is Pareto's "circulation" and corresponds to what social scientists call "vertical social mobility."

If some or all of these exchange relationships are disrupted, either revolution or wholesale decline is inevitable. "Political revolution" occurs when the governing political class becomes a *camarilla,* which hoards and abuses power. In this case the opposition political class enlists the aid of factions in both the ruled and ruling classes and purges and disciplines the camarilla. The political system is altered, but the social structure, the relation between the ruled and ruling classes, remains more or less intact. Sometimes, however, the ruling class cannot do the job, and the ruled class with its leaders overturns the entire social hierarchy—Dorso calls this "social revolution."

James Burnham's theory of the "managerial revolution" provides a variant of elitism. It sets out from two assumptions found in other theorists, principally Karl Marx and Thorstein Veblen. The first assumption holds that *economic organization is the key to political power,* and the second stresses *the increasing separation of ownership and control in modern industry.* Following these ideas Burnham maintained that the "capitalist" epoch in human history was virtually closed. But unlike Marx, and like Pareto and Mosca, he argued that the new epoch would not involve a classless, egalitarian society. Instead there would emerge a new "ruling class" of managers. The transition to that new "managerial society" Burnham called the "managerial revolution."

Burnham followed Marx in asserting that in the capitalist period, which reached its peak a century ago, the capitalists were the true rulers because *they owned and hence controlled the basic means of production and exchange.* Burnham argued, however, that control, not formal ownership, is the strategic factor. Control over the economy means virtual control over the life chances of the whole population.

Since the "managers" (in the broadest sense of the term) have the essential skills to run a technologically advanced economic system and the capitalists lack them, the latter would retreat before the former. Burnham envisaged only a short time before managerial society would cover the whole planet. Thus he saw the rise of fascism, communism, and the welfare state as instances of the same process: "There is, in truth, not a formal identity, but a historical bond uniting Stalinism (communism), Nazism (fascism), and New Dealism. Against differing developmental backgrounds and at different stages of growth, they are all *managerial* ideologies: They all have the same historical direction: away from capitalist society and toward managerial society." [4]

Although the claims of Burnham's theory have not as yet been confirmed, many theorists speak of "technocracy" in modern society. Technocracy suggests that the tasks of modern politics, administration, and economics are so complex that only highly trained specialists can deal with them. Technology is in the saddle, and technocrats within and without the government are the real rulers of the modern state. The takeover is not so blatant and complete as Burnham foresaw, but behind the facade of capitalist owners and elective officials real decision-making power lies with the technocrats.

Managerial revolution or technocracy approaches are frequently applied to the Soviet Union. Some scholars have even suggested that the great purges of the 1930s paved the way for a new elite of managerial and technical specialists interested more in organization and production than in ideology and revolution. Studies of the Politburo and Central Committee of the CPSU suggest an influx of technocratic-managerial types.[5] Whether they really have the political upper hand over the party professions, or *apparatchiki*, has not been finally settled.

Pluralism

The theory of pluralism has both a negative and a positive dimension: the former criticizes shortcomings in the elitist and neo-Marxist theories, while the latter offers a distinct image of its own of the power structure of modern societies.

Pluralist criticisms of elitism stress either sociological or methodological problems. The sociological critique challenges the distinctiveness and the coherence of the ruling elite postulated by elite theories. James Meisel, for example, finds the characteristics imputed to ruling elites to be the weakest link in the elitist argument. "To put it in a facile formula,"

---

4. James Burnham, *The Managerial Revolution* (Bloomington: Indiana University Press, 1960), p. 196.
5. See, for example, Michael P. Gehlen and Michael McBride, "The Soviet Central Committee: An Elite Analysis," in *Man, State and Society in the Soviet Union*, ed. J. L. Nogee (New York: Praeger Publishers, 1972), pp. 113–29.

he writes, "all elites shall be credited . . . with what we would call the three C's: group consciousness, coherence, and conspiracy." [6]

Meisal and other pluralists complain that elitists solve the problem by definitional fiat. They do not offer empirical evidence about the amount of consciousness a ruling elite possesses and seem to move from superficial evidence about coherence to suppositions about an almost conspiratorial central command. This criticism seems hard to maintain, however, especially regarding Pareto. The latter was highly critical of those who "conceive the governing class almost as a single person or at least a concrete unity, and suppose that it has a single will and that through logical measures it effectuates preconceived designs." [7] Instead of a straw man such as this, Pareto suggests:

> Governing classes like other collectivities perform logical and non-logical actions, and a principal part of the phenomenon is the organization, not the conscious will of individuals, who in certain cases can be dragged by the organization where their conscious will would not lead them. [8]

Robert Dahl's pluralist critique focuses on the *methodology* of proof involved in the claim that a ruling elite exists. He argues that the burden of proof is upon all those who allege that a ruling elite somehow dominates decision and policy in modern democratic polities. Thus a ruling elite would be a "minority . . . whose preferences regularly prevail in cases of differences of preference on key political issues." [9] This minority, however, should not be "a pure artifact of democratic rules." [10] In other words it should not be a product of the distortions of electoral mechanisms, such as the single-member district system, which can operate in a way so as to produce governments that stem from a minority rather than a majority of the votes. [11]

Thus, proving the existence of the ruling elite would require that dissensus rather than consensus is evident. Only then could we measure whether or not the views of our supposed ruling elite prevail on a regular basis.

6. James Meisel, *The Myth of the Ruling Class* (Ann Arbor: University of Michigan Press, 1962), p. 4.
7. Vilfredo Pareto, *Trattato di sociologia generale* (Milan: Edizioni di Communita, 1964), para. 2254.
8. Ibid.
9. Robert Dahl, "A Critique of the Ruling Elite Model," in *Political Power*, ed. R. Bell et al. (New York: Free Press, 1969), p. 37.
10. Ibid.
11. See chapter 8 in this text for more on the distortion of electoral systems.

Dahl admits that a ruling elite can be suspected if we observe a minority group with "high potential for control." [12] But to call such a group an actual "ruling elite" would be to decide according to circumstantial evidence because high potential for control may go along with low potential for unity. As Dahl puts it, "The actual political *effectiveness* of a group is a function of its potential for control *and* its potential for unity." [13] To measure the political effectiveness (i.e., the power) of the group in question we must, according to Dahl, examine a "series of concrete decisions." [14] These decisions should include all or a representative sample of key or controversial decisions. Only after careful scrutiny of the generative process of these key decisions are we entitled to conclude that a ruling elite does exist. Dahl and other pluralists find that no such ruling elite exists today in democratic systems either at the local or national level.

Dahl's and the general pluralist critiques of elitism have themselves encountered serious criticism in recent years. This countercritique does not necessarily support the elitist contention that minority rule is an inescapable factor of social organization. However it implies that elitism's basic premise is not damaged by evidence drawn from democratic or pluralistic industrial societies. Representative of this viewpoint is an objection as to whether research can "overlook the chance that some person or association could limit decision-making to relatively noncontroversial matters, by influencing community values and political procedures and rituals, notwithstanding that there are in the community serious but latent conflicts." [15] In other words, issues are developed in terms of the existing rules of the game (i.e., the accepted patterns of the political culture). Such rules and patterns, however, may constitute a "political formula," which in part legitimizes and in part disguises the hegemony of a ruling elite. Only certain kinds of issues—those of a noncrucial character—filter through the screening process. Thus, "nondecisions" reveal as much or more about the political system as the actual decisions taken, because a ruling elite could tolerate considerable flexibility concerning these noncrucial decisions that do not affect its vital group interests.

Pluralism focuses on the interest group as the main political actor.[16]

12. Dahl, "Critique," p. 38.
13. Ibid.
14. Ibid.
15. Peter Bachrach and Morton S. Baratz, "The Two Faces of Power," in Bell, *Political Power*, p. 96.
16. Definitional problems of interest groups will be discussed in chapter 9.

By rejecting the existence of a simple ruling elite or ruling class, pluralism views the power structure as fluid or "polymorphic": it assumes many forms that change continually. No interest group or coalition of interest groups always gets all of what it wants. No interest group or coalition of interest groups is always a loser. Winners and losers vary from issue to issue. This idea can be represented graphically. Let us consider a simple system of six interest groups: A, B, C, D, E, F. According to pluralist theory, the configuration of winners and losers will alter from issue to issue, as depicted in table 6.1.

TABLE 6.1.   The Pluralist View of the Power Structure

	Winners	Losers	Neutrals
Issue 1	A, B, C	D, E, F	
Issue 2	B, C, D	E, F	A
Issue 3	C, D, E, F	A, B	
Issue 4	D, E, A	B, C	F
Issue 5	F, A	D	B, C, E

Pluralists of course are not so naive as to think that all interest groups are of equal power and influence, even in the "pluralist" democracies of the West. Their point is rather that the relatively weak interest group can enter into coalitions or alliances with other groups for the furtherance of common or compatible goals. Political power is not concentrated, as elitists or neo-Marxists contend. Rather it is broadly shared or dispersed. The main political function of interest groups is to articulate the interests of their clienteles by making demands upon the political system.

Since no interest group or coalition of interest groups is predominant, the natural strategy is a combination of bargaining and compromise. The interest group begins by publicly proclaiming a "maximalist" policy that demands a high level of consensus in the group. In reality, it is prepared to accept a "minimalist" return or payoff, and hopes to achieve something between the maximalist and minimalist positions.

In the pluralist view, government as an institution plays a somewhat more passive role than in some competing theories. As Arthur F. Bentley, the founder of American pluralism, put it in 1908:

> The interest groups create the government and work through it; the government, as activity, works "for" the groups; the government from the viewpoint of certain of the groups may at times be their private tool; the

government from the view-point of others of the groups, seems at times their deadly enemy; but the process is all one, and the joint participation is always present. . . .[17]

Government cannot be considered the defender of the "public interest" against the "vested interests," since there is no monolithic public able to possess or express a single coherent interest.

Pluralists like to use such words as *umpire, arbiter, balancer* to describe the main role of government. This suggests that formal executive and legislative decisions are merely the visible tip of the iceberg, while lying submerged is the complex of group interactions that give rise to the decisions. The government's function is more to register and implement the compromises of interest groups than to frame policies in the mythical public interest.

The goal of interest groups is what David B. Truman calls "effective access," the ability to "reach" the appropriate government centers and have them listen seriously. "Governmental decisions are the resultant of effective access by various interests of which organized groups may be only a segment." [18]

Though Bentley, Truman, Dahl, and most American pluralists have been concerned with the United States and other Western "democracies," pluralism has been applied in recent years to Soviet politics as a critique of the totalitarian model. One problem with this is that there is, going back to Bentley, a tendency in pluralism to play down ideology in favor of interests, and governmental institutions in favor of group pressures. Thus even though we can agree with pluralists that the totalitarian model is exaggerated and inapplicable to recent Soviet politics, their interpretation of the role of the Communist party is inadequate. Pluralists tend to reduce the party to a sort of clearinghouse of group demands from all over the Soviet social system. This underestimates the dominance of the party elite.

Furthermore, as the foremost spokesman of the pluralist approach to Soviet and communist politics admits, Western pluralist theory has been mainly concerned with "associations" (i.e., groups that are formally organized and legally sanctioned). On the other hand, "the paradox of the Soviet situation is that loose associations of individuals are more likely to

17. Arthur F. Bentley, *The Process of Government* (Cambridge, Mass.: Harvard University Press, 1967), p. 270.
18. David B. Truman, *The Governmental Process* (New York: Alfred A. Knopf, 1958), p. 507.

be active exponents than organized groups, and more likely to assert demands for government or party actions." [19] Such "latent" or "potential" groups have always taken the backseat (if not the rumble seat) in Western-oriented pluralist theory. The question thus emerges: how can Western pluralist theory be applied to systems that forbid truly independent associations? Depending on how one stretches the term, all political systems to a greater or lesser extent are "pluralistic." But one sort of "pluralism" may differ dramatically from another: some interpreters of Soviet politics have not understood this.

Neo-Marxism

Since neo-Marxist [20] theorists still employ the term "ruling class," they clearly reject the pluralist idea of the polymorphic and fluid nature of the power structure. They consider pluralism merely a version of "bourgeois ideology" covering up capitalist domination of the power structure. According to neo-Marxists, pluralists fail to see that some "interest groups" are vastly more powerful than others. They also miss the point that pluralism operates only on minor issues of detail and that issues challenging the system are suppressed.

While neo-Marxists agree with elitists on these and other shortcomings of pluralism, the agreement stops there. Because classic elitism was highly critical of Marxism, neo-Marxists consider elitism to be yet another version of "bourgeois ideology." It is no surprise, then, that they find recent elite theories such as that of the "managerial revolution" or "technocracy" false or misleading. Neo-Marxists argue that the separation of ownership and control in modern capitalist industry is (1) less widespread than elitists think and (2) less significant than the elitists think, where it does in fact occur.

Ralph Miliband, for example, argues that shareholders (owners) and directing personnel (managers, etc.), whatever their differences, share

19. H. Gordon Skilling, "Interest Groups and Communist Politics," in *Interest Groups in Soviet Politics*, ed. H. G. Skilling and F. Griffiths (Princeton: Princeton University Press, 1973), p. 30.
20. The term "neo-Marxist" refers to theorists who claim intellectual descent from Karl Marx and who have observed the workings of Communist states in the USSR and elsewhere. Such theorists analyze and criticize Western capitalism from a Marxist perspective and are often critical of Soviet and other brands of communism. They claim to represent the true Marx, before the Communists came to distort his meaning.

one overriding concern: *maximizing profit for their firm*.[21] Adding this factor to the similar social and educational background of owners and managers, Miliband finds that the "separate elites" constitute a "dominant economic class, possessed of a high degree of cohesion and solidarity, with common interests and common purposes which far transcend their specific differences and disagreements."[22] In a similar vein, T. B. Bottomore argues that though "managers, especially top managers" make up an "important functional group" in modern societies, they are not "independent of the upper class of property owners, and they are not becoming a new 'ruling class.' "[23]

Neo-Marxists like Miliband and Bottomore agree on the uselessness of looking for the key to the power structure elsewhere than in the class structure. Their view of the class structure of advanced capitalist societies looks something like that shown in figure 6.5.

Figure 6.5.   The Neo-Marxist View of the Class Structure of Advanced Capitalism

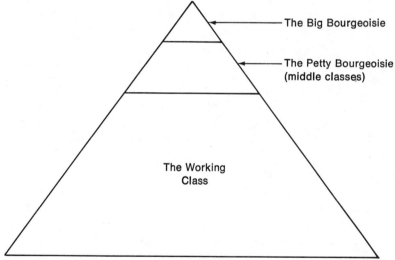

- The Big Bourgeoisie

- The Petty Bourgeoisie (middle classes)

The Working Class

The "big bourgeoisie" or capitalist ruling class owns the lion's share of a country's mines, large farms, factories, banks, insurance and investment companies, large wholesale and retail firms, and so on. They

21. Ralph Miliband, *The State in Capitalist Society* (New York: Basic Books, 1969), p. 34.
22. Ibid., p. 48.
23. T. B. Bottomore, *Elites and Society* (London: C. A. Watts, 1964), p. 76.

also dominate "nonprofit" institutions such as universities, foundations, and charitable organizations.

The "petty bourgeoisie" or "middle classes" include four strata with various roles in the process of production. (1) Professional people such as doctors, lawyers, higher educators, and others are either "self-employed" or have some skill that brings them greater income and prestige than ordinary workers. (2) Owners of small- or medium-scale enterprises do not belong in the big capitalist category. Since prices and public policy respond more to the machinations of giant corporations than to the interests of small businessmen, the latter are in effect "exploited" by the former.[24] (3) The "petty bourgeoisie" is the remnant of the "old middle class" of shopkeepers, artisans, and small family farmers. Though industrialization and the rise of the working class have seriously threatened the basis of this grouping, it shows remarkable resilience. (4) The white collar or "service" class feels itself above the workers in status, even though wage differences are often in favor of the working class.

Despite its diversity, the "working class" is the main counterpoint to the capitalist rulers. Neo-Marxism sees the political process as something of a duel between these two protagonists. Other actors on the scene, such as the middle classes or the holdovers from the old "feudal" aristocracy, complicate, but do not destroy, the worker-capitalist dichotomy. If the working class in Western countries appears to have little interest in casting off the "capitalist yoke," this results from the strength of "bourgeois ideology" and the conservatism of the privileged workers or "labor aristocracy."

In the neo-Marxist theory, the working class despite internal differences sells its "labor power" on a market whose basic conditions are dictated by capitalist interests. For this reason, neo-Marxists argue that "exploitation" is not alleviated by rising living standards of certain workers. On the one hand, poverty is not an occasional or marginal feature of advanced capitalism, but a necessary one. On the other hand, wealth appears even more concentrated than in previous generations: the rich have given way to the "superrich."

Thus, neo-Marxist theory analyzes the power structure in two steps: (1) it strives to show that the topmost economic groupings form a coherent "class"; and (2) it attempts to link the functioning of the state

24. John K. Galbraith, *Economics and the Public Purpose* (Boston: Houghton Mifflin, 1973).

to protecting and defending the interests of this class. Step 1 has been easier than step 2, since many neo-Marxists seem content with repeating Marx's dictum that the "state is the executive committee of the ruling class."

Some neo-Marxists, however, claim to demonstrate how the state in capitalist society is the state of the capitalists. Ralph Miliband cites four grounds for such a conclusion: [25]

1. Businessmen constitute a significant portion of the "state elite."
2. Businessmen and the state elite are drawn predominantly from the same upper- and upper-middle-class groups.
3. The ideology of the state elite, especially the bureaucracy, is highly "conservative" and pro-capitalist.
4. Government policy, even with social democratic or reformist governments, is invariably supportive of the capitalist system.

There are in capitalist governments countless examples of what Guido Dorso would call "exchange between the political class and the ruling class." The early Eisenhower cabinet was recruited almost exclusively from the ranks of big business. In France the reverse movement finds many high civil servants resigning to take top jobs in business.

Neo-Marxists argue rather plausibly that businessmen do not doff and don their "class interests" upon entering and leaving government service. While they may be forced by law to divest themselves of certain shares in businesses, ex-businessmen will not readily divest themselves of friendships, associations, and patterns of thought and behavior. These things will influence the public behavior of the "state elite."

Miliband's second argument looks to the common social background of businessmen and the state elite. Even if few ex-businessmen hold public office, the common "socialization" experience of the two groups will "pre-program" a convergence of views between business and governmental leaders. The conservatism of these views ensures that top civil servants will be "the conscious or unconscious allies of existing economic and social elites." [26]

Ideology also makes the state benefit the capitalists. Neo-Marxists use the term "ideology" in the broad sense of deeply held beliefs. Ideology thus is not so much an explicit, programmatic set of guidelines, but a vague and diffuse view of things that closes off some options while leaving others open. This approach underlies Miliband's conclusion that "the fact

25. Miliband, *The State*, chaps. 3–5.
26. Ibid., p. 123.

that governments accept as beyond question the capitalist context within which they operate is of absolutely fundamental importance in shaping their attitudes, policies, and actions." [27]

The proof of this set of arguments, according to Miliband, is in policy. The mode of political recruitment and the pervasive influence of ideology virtually guarantee policies that strengthen the reigning capitalist system. In the neo-Marxist view, openly conservative governments, reformist governments with "socialistic" overtones, and "fascist" governments all pursue pro-capitalist policies. Despite political variations the fundamental class and economic reality of these regimes is for all intents and purposes identical.

Certain neo-Marxists have even applied these ideas to the Soviet Union with mostly critical results. Some set out from Leon Trotsky's thesis that Stalinism represented a stalling point of the Russian Revolution. The wearing down of revolutionary enthusiasm and energy in the mid-1920s allowed a new "bureaucratic caste" to usurp the place of the working class as ruler of Soviet society. Nonetheless, Trotsky maintained to the end that the USSR was a "workers' state" just waiting for someone (like himself) to come along and get the revolution moving again.

More recent neo-Marxists have gone beyond Trotsky's analysis, as did Milovan Djilas, vice-president of Yugoslavia in the early 1950s, in his book *The New Class* (1957). Djilas distinguished between "revolutionary" and "dogmatic" communism. Revolutionary communism characterizes the struggle for power and the period right after victory. Dogmatic communism follows the consolidation of power, when a "new class" emerges as the ruler of Communist societies. This group is not wholly identical with the Communist party, though the party is its "core" and "base." Though its exact borders are indeterminate, it includes all those who "have special privileges and economic preference because of the administrative monopoly they hold.[28]

Djilas's theory can be considered Marxist, because it defines the new class in economic terms and talks of a "new form of property" peculiar to Communist societies.

> The ownership of private property has, for many reasons, proved to be unfavorable for the establishment of the new class's authority. . . . The new class obtains its power, privileges, ideology, and its customs from one

27. Ibid., p. 72.
28. Milovan Djilas, *The New Class* (New York: Praeger Publishers, 1957), p. 37.

specific form of ownership—collective ownership—which the class administers and distributes in the name of the nation and society.[29]

Those outside the new class are exploited just like the masses in classic capitalism, according to Djilas. The Communist ideology serves the same cover-up function as does "bourgeois ideology" in old-fashioned capitalism. In fact, these and other similarities have prompted some neo-Marxists to describe the Soviet and Communist economies in general as "state capitalism." This is not "true socialism," because the state has simply replaced the class of capitalists as the exploiter of the masses.

SOCIAL STRATIFICATION AND POLITICAL POWER

Though elitism, pluralism, and neo-Marxism provide insights about the relationship between society and polity, each theory has weaknesses. Pareto's elitism oversimplifies the complexities of social stratification and hence of its relationship to political power. His stress on the psychology of elites underestimates the importance of socioeconomic structures and institutions. Pluralism—with its concern for social differentiation rather than for stratification—is better at showing the exaggerations of competing theories than at explaining power. Neo-Marxism reminds us of the role of economics, but in an exaggerated way that loses the historical variability of modes of social stratification.

Fortunately, the sociology of Max Weber provides us with a more subtle and historical understanding of these problems. Before going on to his analysis of social stratification, let us first recall that mere *social differentiation* means no more than the fact of a division of labor, different age and sex roles, and of various groupings whose behavior reflects cultural differences. From this standpoint all these differences are on the same plane: mere social differentiation gives us no standards by which to rank some of these groups higher or lower than others. They are just different.[30]

Social stratification is a form of social differentiation, but with something added. Any stratification model is based on some value or quality (or set of these) that allows us to place certain groups higher and others lower on a scale like the pyramid models we have already used. The mental image is of different layers or strata ("stratum" is the singular form), which are ranged one on top of another. A simple economic model would

29. Ibid., pp. 74–75.
30. The pluralist theory is at its best regarding social differentiation.

simply place utterly destitute people in the lower strata, those with median incomes in the center strata, and millionaires and billionaires in strata at the summit of the pyramid.

Max Weber spoke of three main modes of social stratification. First we have economic stratification, in which the strata are called *classes*. These can be termed upper, middle, and lower, or can be subdivided still further into upper middle, lower middle, and so on. Or we can name the classes as do the Marxists with bourgeoisie, petty bourgeoisie, and proletariat. The second mode of social stratification is based on status, and the strata involved are called *status groups*. In particular societies the status groups are termed "estates" (as in France before 1789), "castes" (as in India), or by their specific ethnic designations wherever race or ethnicity is the main status criterion. Political stratification, the third mode, refers to the unequal distribution of political power, and while Weber preferred the term "party," we will look to Pareto for names for the strata: *governing elite, nongoverning elite, counterelite,* and *nonelite*.

Before examining these three modes of stratification in more detail, let us clarify the problem of their interrelationship. To visualize this, we can use a three-strata pyramid for each mode of stratification. Let us further think of three groups of individuals: A, B, and C. In an imaginary society the people in group A are in the top stratum for economic position, the middle stratum for status, and the lower stratum for political power. The people in groups B and C also figure in three different posi-

Figure 6.6.   Social Stratification: Dispersed Inequalities

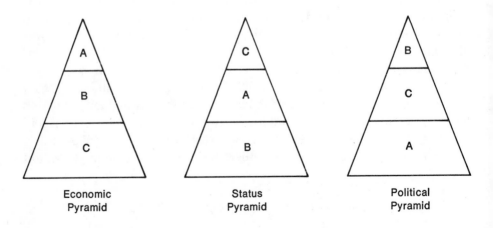

| Economic Pyramid | Status Pyramid | Political Pyramid |

tions in the three pyramids as shown in figure 6.6. We call this situation one of "dispersed inequalities." [31]

In another imaginary society we find just the opposite picture, with the same stratification pattern holding for all three pyramids (figure 6.7). In this society all the pyramids could be superimposed upon each other. In effect, there is one pyramid because inequalities are "cumulative" (i.e., inequality in one respect means inequality in all respects). We have called our two societies "imaginary" because perfect dispersal and cumulation of inequalities seems unlikely. The stratification patterns of actual historical societies fall somewhere between the two extreme cases.

Figure 6.7.   Social Stratification: Cumulative Inequalities

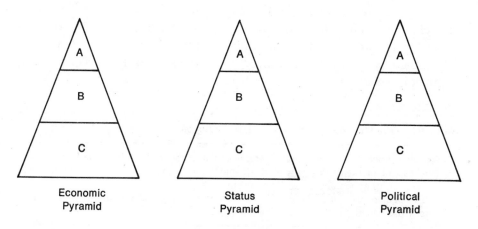

Economic	Status	Political
Pyramid	Pyramid	Pyramid

Given the complexity suggested by this last conclusion, especially when more than three strata are involved, we can feel the temptation to cut the Gordian knot and proclaim one mode as primary and determinant of the other two. Economic determinism teaches that class is the primordial reality so that political power and status are functions of the class variable. Elitism tends to think that political power is the golden road to status and wealth. However, none of these one-way street theories is historically justified, for, as a distinguished French historian points out, most of the time "rank attracts power and money. Power is the generator of prestige and fortune. Riches give power and rank." [32]

31. Robert Dahl, *Who Governs?* (New Haven: Yale University Press, 1963).
32. Roland Mousnier, "Introduction: Problemes de Stratification Sociale," in *Deux Cahiers de la Noblesse* (1649–51), ed. R. Mousnier et al. (Paris: Presses Universitaires de France, 1965), p. 47.

Classes

Despite their importance in contemporary societies, economic classes are not the most prevalent historical unit of stratification. Unfortunately, many people persist in calling all kinds of social strata "classes." Max Weber avoided this by linking the emergence of classes to the specific situation of a *market economy*. The market is a system of exchanging goods and services (including labor), and a market economy is one where most production is done for sale on the market. In Weber's theory, class membership is determined by the individual's relationship to the market.

More specifically, Weber set down three conditions for considering a group of people members of the same class (table 6.2).[33] The term "life chances" refers to possibilities of consumption, mobility, and access to status and power. A class has common life chances, which are determined by the wealth and income it derives from its market position as buyer or seller, employer or employee.

TABLE 6.2. The Weberian Syndrome of Class Affiliation

1. A group of people have in common an important aspect of their "life chances."
2. This aspect of their life chances relates to their economic interests regarding the possession of goods and possibilities for income.
3. This aspect of their life chances is also determined by the operations of the commodity (i.e., goods) and the labor market.

While markets have existed since the earliest recorded times, only with the expansion of Western "capitalism" since the Renaissance has the market dominated economic and other relationships between people. It is thus misleading to speak of classes in premodern times, except where a market dominated a regional economy. In certain ancient and medieval urban centers, however, a class system of sorts did provide a contrast with the different stratification in the countryside.

Whether or not a particular class can assume a strong and unified political stance is determined by at least four factors: (1) cross-cutting cleavages; (2) level of organization; (3) state of communications; and (4) attitude of the regime.

33. Max Weber, *Economy and Society* (Totowa, N.J.: Bedminster Press, 1969), 2:927.

The presence of cross-cutting cleavages, such as ethnic and religious differences, can prevent the emergence of a common class front. One reason why a strong labor or Socialist party representing a unified working class never developed in the United States is the accentuated ethnic and religious diversity of this country. Level of organization refers to the transformation of a class from a mere category to a group with a number of organizational expressions, and thus a stronger political stance. Strong political parties, unions, various business and farmers' organizations all express the growth of class solidarity. The state of communications, including transportation, also influences the organizational potential of social classes. Similarly the attitude of the regime plays a role in the politicization of a class. Sometimes, repression can retard the growth of political consciousness and organization; other times, repression can boomerang and serve only to strengthen the determination of those leading the movement toward class political action.

Levels of antagonism between classes can be identified. Following T. H. Marshall, we can identify three intensities of conflict found in class relationships (figure 6.8).

Figure 6.8. Levels of Antagonism in Class Relationships

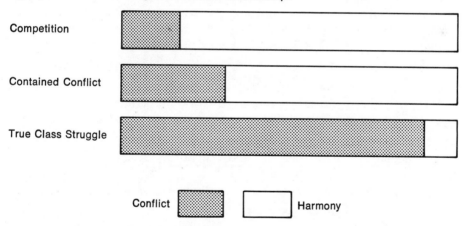

In the competitive situation the classes have different interests but accept the basic rules governing competition. Contained conflict emerges when the stakes rise to include "the terms on which cooperation is to take place." [34] The problem area to be resolved is broader than with mere

34. T. H. Marshall, *Class, Citizenship and Social Development* (Garden City, N.Y.: Doubleday, 1964), p. 165.

competition, but the groups involved share enough to expect eventual agreement. True class struggle, on the other hand, implicates the whole system "upon which the allocation of functions and the distribution of benefits are based." [35] In this type of situation "the common interest shared by the rivals dwindles to a vanishing point." [36]

The three levels of antagonism correspond to three levels of politicization. Mere competition involves almost no politicization. Compromise and collective bargaining among organizational leaders of the various class-based organizations are the main means of resolving disputes. Contained conflict entails a higher degree of politicization because legislative, judicial, and administrative action are often brought in to effect change. True class struggle is highly politicized because the antagonistic classes seek to control political power in order to impose a one-sided solution.

Status Groups

Status stratification differs importantly from class stratification. The hierarchy of status groups displays

> each one distinct from the other and organized not according to the wealth of their members nor their consumption capacity, nor yet by their role in the process of production . . . but according to the esteem, honor, and rank that society attributes to social functions that can have no connection at all with the production of material goods.[37]

The esteem according to a high status group also involves numerous *privileges, perquisites, and prerogatives* of rank. The members can do things and enjoy things denied to the lower groups. The three Ps of rank include such things as monopoly of high political or military positions, special tax dispensations, and special services performed by the lower orders.

The three Ps of high rank, however, do involve a certain price, for "status honor is normally expressed by the fact that above all else a specific *style of life* is expected from all those who wish to belong to the circle." [38] A high-status group is excluded from doing some things and en-

35. Ibid., pp. 165–66.
36. Ibid., p. 167.
37. Roland Mousnier, *Social Hierarchies* (New York: Schocken Books, 1973), p. 23.
38. Weber, *Economy,* p. 932.

joying some things permitted the lesser ranks. Members may be debarred from marrying whom they please, engaging in the trade or profession of their choice, or generally acting as they please. Taboos and prohibitions, often legally enforced, keep the various descriptions in their "proper places."

Status stratification presupposes a general agreement on basic values because the value system determines and legitimizes a group's position in the hierarchy. This usually means an "organic" conception of society which considers the different status groups as essential but unequal collaborators in the common business of society. Some functions are inherently nobler, more essential to a good society: groups associated with these "higher" functions naturally enjoy higher status. If the military virtues are highly prized and beyond the reach of the common man, a military aristocracy is likely to arise. If religion is a predominant concern, priests will generally receive high-status rank.

Three main types of status stratification are found in history: the estate system, the caste system, and the racial system. They differ in terms of mobility, social distance, intermarriage, type of privileges, and supposed moral justification. Estate stratification prevailed in Europe from the Middle Ages to early modern times and still has strong traces in certain European countries. In prerevolutionary France the clergy was the First Estate, the nobility was the Second Estate, and the overwhelming commoner majority was the Third Estate. Each of these groups, moreover, was stratified into a number of higher and lower ranks.

An estate system is somewhat less rigid than caste or racial systems. While birth determines estate membership in general, there is at least the possibility of "ennoblement." The crown could usually grant titles of nobility to "worthy" commoners. Sometimes this "worthiness" was gauged by the new noble's financial generosity to the royal treasury. Nonetheless, in many cases the most enormous wealth was not enough to allow a commoner to jump status barriers.

Though often applied to extremely rigid status groups, the term "caste" is of dubious relevance outside the Indian context. The rigidity of the caste system is rooted in the Hindu religion. Actually the term "caste" is applied either to the four main caste divisions or Varna (Brahmans, Kshatriya, Vaisya, and Sudras) and to the hundreds of subdivisions (jatis) of the Varna. Such "subcastes" have been defined as a

small and named group of persons characterized by endogamy, hereditary membership, and a specific style of life which sometimes includes the pursuit by tradition of a particular occupation and is usually associated with a more or less distinct ritual status in a hierarchical system.[39]

Ritual status distinguishes a caste from an estate system, as each caste occupies a special niche in a gradation of religious purity. The extreme of this is seen with the "untouchables," who are not supposed to come into physical propinquity with the "twice-born" Brahmans.

Racial or ethnic stratification has certain resemblances to the two previous status types. The principle of distinction here, however, follows from observed physical differences between the so-called higher and lower groups. Naturally these physical differences are associated with cultural differences that supposedly endow the "superior" group with the right to rule and privilege. The "inferior" race is relegated to being the "hewers of wood and drawers of water" of the society. This often means enslavement or enserfment. Ethnic or racial stratification has existed in nearly every continent. The Arabs dominated black Africans in certain parts of East Africa, and those of Spanish descent (Ladinos) have lorded it over pure-blooded Indians (Indios) throughout Latin America.

Closer to home, the "peculiar institution" of black slavery in the United States is a good example of the extremities of racial stratification. Later, "Jim Crow" legislation enshrined the status inferiority of black Americans. Even today, racial status differences have a lingering importance in various parts of the United States.

Conflicts between status groups cannot be called class struggles, even though economic factors can be involved. We can speak more appropriately of "status resentment" when serious tensions affect the relations of different status groups. Status resentment can take two different forms: (1) when a lower group resents the privileges and arrogance of a higher group; (2) when a higher group resents the attempt of a lower group to narrow or ignore the differences between them.

Even though Western societies can no longer be called estate societies, the politics of status has by no means disappeared. Many political parties and movements have made political capital by articulating the status concerns of higher social strata.

In a somewhat broader sense women's liberation has to do with status inequalities. Feminists argue that holdover inequities from the days when women were clearly and legally second-class citizens still keep women back from full achievement. They hope to eradicate all such "sexist"

39. Andre Betaille, *Caste, Class and Power* (Berkeley: University of California Press, 1971), p. 46.

status differentials. People should be ranked according to performance, not according to irrelevant biological criteria.

Political Elites

Though Max Weber realized that class and status considerations often determined the power structure, he wisely reserved some autonomy for the realm of politics. He chose the term "party" to designate any association within the state that sought power without itself being a class or a status group. Relationships between parties on the one hand and social strata on the other were open and variable:

> In any individual case, parties may represent interests determined through class or status situation, and they may recruit their following respectively from one or the other. But they need be neither purely class nor purely status parties; in fact, they are more likely to be mixed types, and sometimes they are neither.[40]

As Weber's notion of party was loose, we can replace it with our idea of a political elite without much fear of confusion. Thus we can develop a new typology of political elites in terms of the other modes of stratification, as depicted in table 6.3.

TABLE 6.3.   Relationship of Political Elites to Classes and Status Groups

1. **Class-oriented political elites:** the political elite is the agent of a class.
2. **Status-oriented political elites:** the political elite is the agent of a status group.
3. **Mixed political elites:** the political elite mixes classes and status groups.
4. **Autonomous political elites:** the political elite is too heterogeneous to be described as any of the above.

The *class-oriented political elite* is less frequent than commonly thought, since class stratification is relatively modern. This elite recruits the vast bulk of its members from one class, and its ideology and policy are geared to promoting that class's values and interests. Such elites will often take the organizational form of a party. Thus, nineteenth-century "liberal" political elites and parties were spokesmen for middle-class groups in most European countries. Similar linkages could be made for some working-class and peasant elites and political parties. However, we must always bear in mind Roberto Michels's "iron law of oligarchy,"

40. Weber, *Economy,* p. 938.

which teaches that a strong separation will always emerge between the elite level and the mass base of any organization.[41]

The *status-oriented political elite* emerges in its pure form in estate, caste, or racially stratified societies. Monopoly of key political positions in this elite is a perquisite of high rank. Social beliefs support the idea that rule by a certain status group is "natural" or "sacred." Such a political elite is found in both feudal and patrimonial polities. Quite often in this setting the monarch elevates "new men" without the traditional status credentials, but personally loyal to him, into the political elite. This will allow him a freer hand in ruling and represents a step toward a more mixed or autonomous political elite.

The British political elite has always been highly status-oriented; yet, it has been increasingly permeable to new recruits from lower strata. Higher aristocrats were joined by the "gentry" in the seventeenth and eighteenth centuries. The nineteenth century saw the rise of middle-class people of business background. All three groups are overrepresented in the contemporary elite, though the trade unions and the Labor party have funneled some working-class people up into the political elite.

The *mixed political elite* refers to three distinct situations: a mixture of classes, a mixture of status groups, and a mixture of classes and status groups. The first type naturally finds its home in a class society. This does not mean that political elites in Western societies have a mixed class composition accurately reflecting the distribution of classes in the global society. As neo-Marxists remind us, the curve of distribution is skewed in favor of the upper and the upper-middle classes.

Elites that mix status groups naturally flourish where status stratification is still strong. The long-term broadening of the British political elite exemplifies this. This is especially clear in the history of the Conservative (Tory) party. Likewise the ruling Congress party, which ruled India for thirty years, appeals to different castes in elite recruitment. Elites that mix individuals from both classes and status groups are mostly found wherever class is displacing status as the main type of stratification. This situation is captured by Weber's idea of "rule by notables." [42]

41. See Roberto Michels, *Political Parties* (New York: Dover Publications, 1959).
42. Weber considers notables as "persons who first, are enjoying an income earned without, or with comparatively little labor, or at least of such a kind that they can afford to assume administrative functions in addition to whatever business activities they may be carrying on; and who second, by virtue of such income, have a mode of life which attributes to them

The *autonomous political elite* is either one whose composition is too complex to show a pattern or one that has broken the bonds of previous social background. Elites of *declassé* intellectuals, what Karl Mannheim called the "socially-unattached intelligentsia," fit this description.[43] Revolutionary and totalitarian elites with heavy contingents of intellectuals seem able to get beyond some, if not all, of the preferences and prejudices of their social background. Ideological passion can wrench people out of the grooves of behavior scored by their social past.

CRISIS STRATA

Sigmund Neumann used the expression "crisis strata" to designate a "shifting new middle class, a restless unemployed, and a militia of irregulars" who provided the mass basis of European fascism in the 1920s and 1930s.[44] Here we extend his meaning to social strata (or parts of them) that become politically mobilized because their livelihood, social status, or scheme of values is imperiled by existing conditions and trends. Only rarely do whole classes or status groups become politicized. But subgroups of them often play a decisive political role as crisis strata. We will discuss three of the most important modern crisis strata: peasants, intellectuals, and the petty bourgeoisie.

Peasants

Though controversy rages as to who is and who is not a peasant, George Foster's approach seems to cover the important features of a true peasantry:

> When settled rural peoples subject to the jural control of outsiders exchange a part of what they produce for items they cannot themselves make, in a market setting transcending local transactions, then they are peasants. We see peasants as a peripheral but essential part of civilizations, producing the food that makes urban life possible, supporting (and subject to) the specialized classes of political and religious rulers and the other members of the elite.[45]

This notion of a peasantry excludes nomadic and pastoral peoples, as

---

the social 'prestige' of a status honor and thus renders them fit for being called to rule." *Economy*, p. 950.

43. Karl Mannheim, *Ideology and Utopia* (New York: Harcourt, Brace, 1936).
44. Sigmund Neumann, *Permanent Revolution* (New York: Praeger Publishers, 1965), p. 116.
45. George M. Foster, "Introduction: What Is a Peasant?," in *Peasant Society: A Reader*, ed. J. Potter et al. (Boston: Little, Brown, 1967), p. 6.

well as tribes without steady contact with cities and markets. It also suggests that peasants are politically subjected to outside groups and that peasant culture is interdependent with urban culture and that of "higher" social strata.

Though peasants are agriculturalists, they are not just "farmers." For farmers, agriculture is a *livelihood;* for peasants, it involves a *way of life.* This means that the peasant does not produce solely for the market, as a pure capitalist would do. The rules of peasant economy are different: "the objective arithmetic calculation of the highest possible net profit in the given market situation does not determine the whole activity of the family unit: this is done by internal economic confrontation of *subjective evaluations.*" [46] Thus, a peasant household may stop producing marketable goods when its own needs are met. From the standpoint of the profit-oriented capitalist firm, its behavior is "irrational."

Peasants, however, are found in quite a variety of rural economic settings, and this variety can have important consequences for different types of peasant political behavior, as table 6.4 suggests. [47]

Several of these five major types of rural economic organization may coexist in a given country. In one region we may find the latifundia prevalent, in another the peasant family farm. Various transitions from one type to another can take place: a traditional latifundial estate may end up (1) parceled out among peasant families, (2) broken up into modern family farms, (3) "modernized" in a large capitalist industrial farm, and (4) collectivized after a revolution or radical land reform. Such possibilities suggest two features of modern rural life: the crisis-inducing potential of change, and the stratification and differentiation among groups in rural society.

Many theorists have tried to link internal peasant stratification to political behavior. Lenin, for example, distinguished between *poor peasants* who were prorevolutionary, *rich peasants* (or kulaks) who were counterrevolutionary, and *middle peasants* who "wavered" between the previous two groups. Eric Wolf accepted the rich, middle, poor scheme of Lenin, but saw the middle peasant as the most likely to take independent political action. [48]

46. Quoted in Basile Kerblay, "Chayanov and the Theory of the Peasantry as a Specific Type of Economy," in *Peasants and Peasant Societies,* ed. T. Shanin (Baltimore: Penguin Books, 1971), p. 153.
47. Based on Boguslaw Galeski, "Social Organization and Rural Social Change," in ibid., pp. 115–37.
48. Eric Wolf, *Peasant Wars in the Twentieth Century* (New York: Harper & Row, 1969).

TABLE 6.4. Types of Rural Economic Organization

1. **Peasant family farm:** generally a small unit run by family labor but sometimes with seasonal hired help. The peasant may live on the farm or in a nearby village. The peasant household is a cultural entity, not just a business. The farm can be owned outright or be held on a tenant (rent) or sharecropping basis.
2. **Modern family farm:** a small unit that is restricted to a narrowly economic role in the farmer's life. The owner is a small rural businessman who thinks like other businessmen. His life style is not so distinct from nonagricultural groups as is peasant culture.
3. **The latifundial farm:** a very large operation in which traditional and status-oriented ideas are dominant. The landowner is not just the employer of his peasants, but their master as well. His control extends to moral, legal, and political matters. The owner-peasant relationship is supposedly "paternalistic" as the owner is supposed to guide and protect his underlings as expressed in the term "padrone."
4. **The large industrial farm:** a large-scale operation in which modern business attitudes replace paternalism. The owner- (rural) worker relationship is based more on contract than on the status of the parties. The rural worker is much freer than his peasant counterpart on the latifundia.
5. **The collective farm:** a medium or large operation found mostly in Communist countries. The total membership of the collective "owns" the land and implements, and remuneration of the members is determined by a complex calculation based on total production. There are usually "private plots" assigned to peasants, whose produce they can sell on the "open market."

In Wolf's view the rich peasants were beneficiaries of the existing order and thus were precluded from mounting a challenge against it. The poor peasants, on the other hand, were too cowed and dominated by large landowners to dare any politically defiant action. This left the middle peasants, who were exposed to serious damage from the increasing commercialization of agriculture and had just enough independence to form a political movement.

Lenin's and Wolf's schemes of peasant stratification and political behavior are rather crude, however. H. Alavi, for example, objects to considering rich, middle, and poor peasants simply as top, middle, and bottom rungs of a ladder based on wealth. He maintains instead that rather than the middle peasants standing "between" the rich and poor peasants, "they belong to a different sector of the rural economy." [49] We put his more subtle views in table 6.5.

Alavi's suggestions, plus an awareness of the history of peasant move-

49. Hamza Alavi, "Peasants and Revolution," *The Socialist Register 1965*, ed. R. Miliband and R. Saville (New York: Monthly Review Press, 1965), p. 74.

TABLE 6.5. Main Groups of the Rural Economy

1. **Capitalist farmers:** "rich peasants," who employ workers but often participate in farm work themselves
2. **Landlords:** owners of the latifundia, who do not follow modern capitalist practices on their estates
3. **Farm laborers:** workers who are paid a contractual wage and are often included as part of the poor peasantry
4. **Sharecroppers:** workers who do not own the land they work, but share the proceeds with the true owner
5. **Independent small-holders:** these are the true "middle peasants," who own the land and work it themselves without much outside help

ments, leads to one firm conclusion: what specific rural group becomes a politicized crisis stratum depends on specific historical conditions.[50] Though the middle peasants have often been the spearhead of political action, other situations find capitalist farmers, sharecroppers, or farm laborers as the politically hyperactive group.

Peasant political behavior runs the gamut of what we can call the four Rs of peasant politics: *reaction, revolt, reform, and revolution.* The first two (and to some extent the third) political actions reflect the so-called innate conservatism of peasants. This conservatism involves specifically "an intense attachment to native soil; a reverent disposition to habitat and ancestral ways; a restraint on individual self-seeking in favor of family and community; a certain suspiciousness, mixed with appreciation of town life; a sober and earthy ethic." [51] These are some of the reasons why Karl Marx considered peasants as incorrigibly reactionary and antirevolutionary. Thus, reaction, the stubborn resistance to change, has some basis in traditional peasant attitudes.

Such attitudes also play a prominent role in the peasant revolts that figure in early modern Europe as throughout the millennia of Chinese history. As we shall see in the next chapter, revolts are not innovative movements that did not quite make it, but are backward-looking attempts to restore an earlier, supposedly more satisfactory, condition. Peasants in revolt are violently protesting against changes they consider as disruptive of their way of life.

50. See Roland Mousnier, *Peasant Uprisings in Seventeenth Century France, Russia, and China* (New York: Harper & Row, 1971); Edward E. Malefakis, *Agrarian Reform and Peasant Revolution in Spain* (New Haven: Yale University Press, 1970).
51. Robert Redfield, *Peasant Society and Culture* (Chicago: University of Chicago Press, 1965), p. 140.

Reform, however, is a growing concern with peasants as we approach modern times. Land reform distributing large estates in parcels to peasants is particularly important. Though much has been said of late about the role of peasants in revolution, several qualifications must be registered. Peasant response to the revolutionary situation is quite variable. These responses can be graded and put on a continuum, as depicted in figure 6.9.

Figure 6.9.   Peasant Responses to Revolutionary Situations

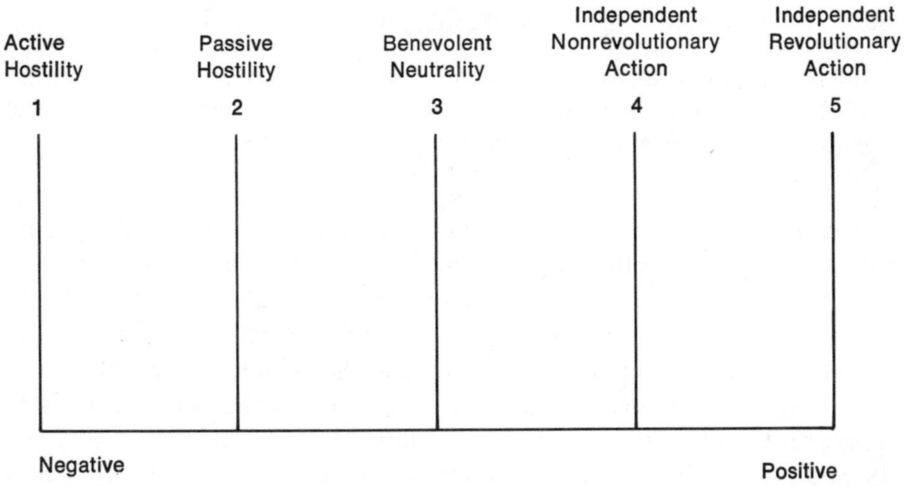

Active Hostility	Passive Hostility	Benevolent Neutrality	Independent Nonrevolutionary Action	Independent Revolutionary Action
1	2	3	4	5

Negative   Positive

Responses 4 and 5 often coincide with another political possibility. Here an independent peasant movement for change or protest is taken over by an outside revolutionary movement. With the imposition of a new ideological and organizational format, however, the question is raised as to how far the revolutionary movement is still a peasant movement.

Intellectuals

The intellectuals or intelligentsia form a crisis stratum of great importance in twentieth-century politics. Intellectuals have a special relationship to culture in the sense of "higher culture." Seymour Martin Lipset considers three intensities of this relationship: (1) creators of culture, (2) distributors of culture, and (3) appliers of culture.[52] Art-

52. Seymour M. Lipset, *Political Man* (Garden City, N.Y.: Anchor Books, 1969).

ists, scientists, writers, composers, philosophers, and architects fall in the first category. Academics and some teachers, clergymen, journalists, and performing artists belong in the second. Doctors, lawyers, military officers, indeed nearly all "professional people" are placed in the third. In some countries university students would be considered intellectuals, but qualitative and quantitative aspects of American higher education make their inclusion risky here.

Though many intellectuals would be loath to admit it, they are in some respects lineal descendents of the priests, prophets, and devotees of the traditional higher religions. The French word *clerc* means both priest and intellectual. As Edward Shils put it,

> Intellectual work arises from religious preoccupations. In the early history of the human race, it tended, in its concern with the ultimate or at least with what lies beyond the immediate concrete experience, to operate with religious symbols.[53]

This helps to explain the prophetic and messianic tone assumed by many intellectuals. There is thus a pronounced tendency among intellectuals to look down upon those whose horizons are more mundane.

In line with this is the self-appointed role of conscience of society congenial to many intellectuals. Like the Old Testament prophets, intellectuals in open societies condemn the powers that be, the general public, and, quite often, other intellectuals, for derogation of duty. Such alienation from their society seems an occupational, or perhaps an avocational, disease for many intellectuals. This tendency toward excess and exaggeration can culminate in political extremism.

Lewis Feuer, perhaps overstating his case, grounds the critical antagonism of intellectuals toward their society in basic psychological or biological needs. The inability of intellectuals to translate their ideas and ideals into practice produces high frustration. Frustration occurs because the biological process from inner thought to outer action is short-circuited by the intellectuals' powerlessness. Thus Feuer concludes that the "frustration of inaction tends to make ideas into a displaced means of aggression. An extremist ideology is an idea suffused with displaced aggressive energy. The situation of the intellectual tends to make him into an ideologue." [54]

53. Edward Shils, *The Intellectuals and the Powers and Other Essays* (Chicago: University of Chicago Press, 1972), p. 16.
54. Lewis S. Feuer, *Marx and the Intellectuals* (Garden City, N.Y.: Anchor Books, 1969), p. 61.

Whether crisis produces critics or critics the crisis, social criticism is the strong suit of intellectuals. Raymond Aron has discerned three stages or types of criticism voiced by intellectuals, as outlined in table 6.6.[55]

TABLE 6.6.   Stages of Social Criticism by Intellectuals

1. **Technical criticism:** this operates within the framework of the existing order, but suggests ways of attenuating existing evils. The attitude is more "pragmatic" than it is ideological.
2. **Moral criticism:** this expresses outrage at the existing order. It denounces the status quo in the light of a noble ideal, but the ideas remain essentially vague and diffuse.
3. **Ideological and historical criticism:** this gives a systematic indictment of the present order and "sketches out the blueprint of a radically different order in which man will fill his true vocation."

Modern intellectuals have acted to formulate the ideologies of our time and to lead social and political movements dedicated to their realization. Both as a barometer and promoter of social crisis and change, intellectuals are a crisis stratum with influence well beyond what their numbers would suggest.

The Petty Bourgeoisie

The petty bourgeoisie is a composite group, including small farmers, small businessmen and merchants, and independent artisans. Because of its historical roots in preindustrial societies, the petty bourgeoisie is as much a status group as a class. Economically, it is marked by small-scale operations and ownership of the "means of production"—land, shops, tools. A petty bourgeois is proud of the status difference between himself and ordinary wage-earners. He is a "rugged" individual, not just one member of a faceless mass.

All three petty bourgeois groups have been threatened by industrialization. Industrialization gives an advantage to massive economic organizations, which can achieve economies of scale and mass production. Thanks to this, they can undersell and outproduce their small competitors. Large-scale farming makes certain techniques beyond the reach of small farmers highly profitable. Department stores and chains can

55. Raymond Aron, *The Opium of the Intellectuals* (New York: W. W. Norton, 1962), pp. 210–11.

often undersell and outadvertise small shopkeepers, as when supermarkets drive neighborhood grocers out of business. Cheap goods, mass produced in huge factories, have forced the wood or metal products of skilled artisans—carpenters, cabinetmakers, silversmiths, tinsmiths—off the market.

While the economic position of the petty bourgeoisie has gone downhill, that of unskilled or semiskilled workers has improved. Through trade unionism and the welfare state, the gap in the standard of living between workers and the petty bourgeoisie has narrowed and sometimes disappeared altogether. The status resentment of the "little man" of the petty bourgeoisie has three main targets: big business, big government, and big labor. In fact, the petty bourgeoisie is driven to think that big business, government, and labor are in a conspiracy against it.

For these reasons the petty bourgeoisie in most industrialized countries has been susceptible to the appeals of right-wing protest movements. Movements such as poujadism in France, the Wallace movement in the United States, and Social Credit in Canada have articulated the fears and resentments of the small independent person. Ironically, the Nazi party in its early phases made special appeals to small farmers and merchants. In power, however, the Nazis did little to redeem its promises to these groups.

This chapter has set the stage for the next three chapters, which discuss social movements, parties, and interest groups respectively. We now sense better that a full and deep understanding of politics requires us to go somewhat beyond the institutional structures of part 1. The institutional structures are but one aspect, however important, of the power structure that gives real meaning to various political regimes. For better or for worse, there is little agreement among social scientists and others as to the power structure of certain types of society or as to that of a given society, say, the United States. The three basic methodologies of elitism, pluralism, and neo-Marxism have been discussed at length for two reasons: first, to allow students to make up their own minds about the best one; and second, to prepare them for the divergent perspectives of writers on politics and economics.

The inadequacy of the three methodologies as simple and universally valid theories of power is the justification for an elaborate study of social stratification. Since political regimes, parties, and movements are influenced by social structure, we have to grasp Max Weber's three primary modes of social stratification: economic, status, and political.

Classes, status groups, and political elites are different sorts of social and political entities. Their goals and motivations differ, as do the political expressions of them. Class struggle differs from status resentment and both can diverge from the struggle for power.

Furthermore, general theories of class or status politics are often too broad-gauged to capture the real social background of movements, parties, and interest groups. For this reason, the more refined concept of crisis strata comes in to highlight the narrower groups, whose specially intense problems launch them into political hyperactivity. Various groups of peasants, the petty bourgeoisie, and the intelligentsia have been politically decisive forces at certain historical moments. This justifies the time we have spent on them.

STUDY QUESTIONS

1. How would pluralists criticize the elitist and neo-Marxist views of the power structure of modern industrial societies? How would elitists criticize the pluralist and neo-Marxist views of the power structure of modern industrial societies? How would neo-Marxists criticize the elitist and pluralist views of the power structure of modern industrial societies?

2. What would it mean to say that a society was a classless society and yet retained considerable social and political inequalities?

3. Why does the notion of "crisis strata" give us a more precise idea of social stratification and its influence on political life?

4. What are peasants and what are their distinctive modes of political behavior?

5. Why do the petty bourgeoisie get involved in right-wing protest movements?

6. Why do intellectuals play a disproportionately strong role in the politics of many countries? What about their role in the United States?

SUGGESTIONS FOR FURTHER READING

ARON, RAYMOND. *The Opium of the Intellectuals*. New York: W. W. Norton, 1962.
BELL, RODERICK; EDWARDS, D. V.; and WAGNER, R. H., eds. *Political Power*. New York: Free Press, 1969.

BENDIX, REINHARD, and LIPSET, SEYMOUR M., eds. *Class, Status, Power.* 2nd ed. New York: Free Press, 1966.

BENTLEY, ARTHUR F. *The Process of Government.* Cambridge, Mass.: Harvard University Press, 1967.

BÉTEILLE, ANDRÉ, ed. *Readings in Social Inequality.* Baltimore: Penguin Books, 1969.

BOTTOMORE, T. B. *Elites and Society.* London: C. A. Watts, 1964.

BURNHAM, JAMES. *The Managerial Revolution.* Bloomington: Indiana University Press, 1960.

DAHL, ROBERT. *Who Governs?* New Haven: Yale University Press, 1963.

DAHRENDORF, RALF. *Class and Class Conflict in Industrial Society.* Stanford: Stanford University Press, 1965.

GIDDENS, ANTHONY. *The Class Structure of the Advanced Societies.* New York: Harper & Row, 1973.

MARSHALL, T. H. *Class, Citizenship, and Social Development.* Garden City, N.Y.: Doubleday, 1964.

MICHELS, ROBERT. *Political Parties.* New York: Dover Publications, 1959.

MILIBAND, RALPH. *The State in Capitalist Society.* New York: Basic Books, 1969.

MOSCA, GAETANO. *The Ruling Class.* New York: McGraw-Hill, 1939.

MOUSNIER, ROLAND. *Social Hierarchies.* New York: Schocken Books, 1973.

PARETO, VILFREDO. *Sociological Writings.* Edited by S. E. Finer. New York: Praeger Publishers, 1966.

PARRY, GERAINT. *Political Elites.* New York: Praeger Publishers, 1969.

SHANIN, TEODOR, ed. *Peasants and Peasant Societies.* Baltimore: Penguin Books, 1972.

TRUMAN, DAVID B. *The Governmental Process.* New York: Alfred A. Knopf, 1958.

7

Social Movements and Revolution

This chapter builds upon the knowledge of social structure gained in chapter 6 in order to develop further our theme of part 2 on the "movement" or dynamic aspects of political life. It deals specifically with social movements and with a most important kind of social movement, revolution. The next two chapters on parties (8) and on interest groups (9) deal with the more institutionalized movement aspects, while the present chapter deals with political phenomena having a low level of institutionalization. There is a connection between these topics insofar as many political parties and interest groups have originated as social movements. Moreover, we should recall once more that many regimes, especially dictatorships, are also the direct result of social movements.

Discussion of social movements and revolution generally gets short shrift in most introductory textbooks in political science or comparative politics. This is unfortunate because these interrelated topics are not only among the most intriguing of political phenomena, but they are also among the most important. Some notion of the basic concepts involved is necessary to complement knowledge of more conventional forms of political behavior. Indeed, we could subtitle this chapter "unconventional political behavior."

We will first deal with the problem of crowds as a basic form of collective behavior. Crowds, after all, have brought down many governments, whether this resulted in a mere change of personnel or inaugurated a time of actual revolution. The so-called politics of confrontation that reached its peak in the late 1960s, discussed here, makes some inroads on crowd phenomena. Then we will deal more expansively with the theory of social movements, looking at some examples to bring home some key points. Let us recall that communism, nazism, fascism, nationalism, and the like can be viewed as social movements.

Finally, we will cover at some length the topic of revolution. The complexity of revolution is not the only reason why it has so often been left out in the cold in introductory textbooks. Sometimes the reason has been ideological distaste, but sometimes it has been a methodology that makes revolution look too eccentric or bizarre for discussion. Nonetheless, the large number of ostensibly revolutionary regimes and movements in the present century make it essential to have some comparative knowledge of these topics even at the fundamental level of an introductory text.

COLLECTIVE BEHAVIOR AND SOCIAL MOVEMENTS

The study of collective behavior is a branch of social science that deals with forms of group action where the level of institutionalization is low. Thus it specializes in some of the more erratic and dramatic types of group behavior. At the opposite pole from organization theory, which deals with bureaucracies and other highly structured bodies, collective behavior embraces such things as panics, crazes, crowds, and social movements. Among types of collective behavior panics (e.g., people fleeing a fire) represent a low point in institutionalization, while social movements represent a high point. Crowds (e.g., lynch mobs or revolutionary crowds) are somewhere in the middle (see table 7.1).

Since the field of collective behavior developed out of early crowd

TABLE 7.1. Types of Collective Behavior

Panics and Crazes	Crowds	Social Movements
Disorganization		Organization
Spontaneity		Planning
Expressive function		Instrumental function
Transitory		Enduring
Leaderless		Strong leadership

psychology, we will discuss briefly some ideas of the French sociologist Gustave Le Bon (1841–1931), a pioneer in the latter area. Le Bon developed an extreme version of the *contagion* theory of crowds. He taught that people virtually lose their personal identity when immersed in a crowd situation. Crowd contagion eliminates all the cultural and educational differences among the members of the crowd, who are reduced to the lowest common denominator. By joining an "organized crowd, a man descends several rungs in the ladder of civilization. Isolated, he may be a cultivated individual; in a crowd, he is a barbarian—that is, a creature living by instinct." [1]

One result of the contagion is *suggestibility*, whereby the crowd becomes highly susceptible to the most absurd fictions. Faith completely overwhelms reason. Along with some idea or ideology that takes hold, the chief beneficiary of suggestibility is the leader, who can impose his will upon the crowd. This does not mean that the leader himself is a cynical manipulator, as he has "most often started as one of the crowd. He himself has been hypnotized by the idea, whose apostle he has since become." [2] With characteristic exaggeration Le Bon attributed special qualities to crowd leaders: they are "especially recruited from the ranks of the morbidly nervous, excitable, half-deranged persons who are bordering on madness." [3]

Never one for understatement, Le Bon's theories have provoked criticism and new interpretations of crowd behavior. Some of these deemphasize contagion in favor of *convergence*.[4] In this view crowds attract specific types of people disposed to act in the wayward way of crowds. In other words, the crowd attracts untypical "barbarians," rather than transforming Caspar Milquetoast into Alley Oop. Still more recent theories soft-pedal the irrational and atavistic aspects of crowds and suggest that crowd behavior is merely a modification and extension of normal group behavior.[5] "Emergent norm theory," for example, sees crowds as far more organized, rational, and purposive than earlier theories suspected. The crowd is seen as a group of people who are groping toward a new consensus on norms of conduct.

1. Gustave Le Bon, *The Crowd* (New York: Viking Press, 1960), p. 32.
2. Ibid., p. 118.
3. Ibid.
4. See Floyd Allport, *Social Psychology* (Boston: Houghton Mifflin, 1924), p. 313.
5. See Stanley Milgram, "Crowds," in *Handbook of Social Psychology*, vol. 4, ed. G. Lindzey and E. Aronson (2nd ed.; Reading, Mass.: Addison-Wesley, 1969).

Many social movements have originated as crowd phenomena. Conversely, they often give rise to crowd activity both as spontaneous outbursts and as planned tactics. Hans Toch defines a social (or mass) movement as a "spontaneous large group constituted in support of a set of purposes or beliefs that are 'shared' by the members. Psychologically defined, a *social movement* represents an effort by a large number of people to solve collectively a [common] problem." [6] Social movements thus are more definite and organized than mere trends and tendencies. For example, we can call the broad long-term developments toward greater liberties and opportunities for women a trend or a tendency. However, the various organizations and groups involved in women's liberation are parts of an authentic social movement.

Causes and Development of Social Movements

Students of social movements have reached some agreement about their general causes and development. Neil J. Smelser, for example, advocates a six-factor approach, in which the first five factors can be thought of as actual stages the movement goes through (table 7.2).[7]

TABLE 7.2.   Six Factors in the Growth of Social Movements

1. Structural conduciveness
2. Structural strain
3. Spread of a generalized belief
4. Precipitating factors
5. Mobilization of participants for action
6. Operation of social control

Structural conduciveness refers to the possibilities for the growth of social movements. Is the social structure so stratified and differentiated as to make the emergence of social movements likely? For example, an ethnically complex society is more likely to produce ethnic social movements than a society where ethnicity has given way to total assimilation. Social movements develop more readily in "open" societies than where the government is willing and able to use repressive force. Many incipient social movements have been nipped in the bud by jittery but

6. Hans Toch, "Social Movements," in Lindzey, *Handbook*, p. 584.
7. Neil J. Smelser, *Theory of Collective Behavior* (New York: Free Press, 1962), pp. 12–17.

strong governments. The strength of religious and other cultural characteristics also influence structural conduciveness.

Structural strain emerges as the result of some sort of change. Some group sees its way of life, view of the world, social position, or economic security called into the most serious question. Smelser sees "ambiguities, deprivations, conflicts and discrepencies" as the major types of structural strain.[8] Groups and individuals find life losing all meaning and coherence, a condition that Emile Durkheim called "anomie." Conflicts of the type discussed in chapter 6 begin to get out of hand.

Structural strain prepares the ground for the *spread of the generalized belief,* which "identifies the sources of strain, attributes certain characteristics to this source, and specifies certain responses to the strain as possible or appropriate."[9] This process provides instant diagnosis and remedy for the social malaise. Before the generalized belief came upon the scene, troubled individuals suffered in virtual ignorance and isolation. Now the cause or causes of their present discontents are revealed and they find a (generally simplistic) recipe for counteraction. A social movement is on the verge of forming.

The notion of *precipitating factors* is important in explaining the final outbreak of large-scale social phenomena such as movements, wars, and revolutions. Involved are specific events, which might normally pass without great stir, but which in the supercharged atmosphere of the general belief, have strong causal impact. The precipitant—whether a riot, a killing, an economic bust, or something else—provides "concrete, immediate substance" for the generalized belief. The social movement now takes shape in an apparently spontaneous manner.

Mobilization of participants for action means that without the active intervention of leaders, social movements or other collective behavior would probably fizzle out very quickly. The crucial importance of leadership is clear when we recognize that many acts of collective behavior which seem wholly spontaneous have been carefully orchestrated by behind-the-scenes leaders. Social movements need different types of leaders, some of which prevail at given stages in their history.

The *operation of social control* is not confined to a special phase of the movement. Social control consists of "those counter-determinants which prevent, interrupt, deflect, or inhibit" those factors producing the social movement.[10] Social control comes first into the picture when repressive

8. Ibid.
9. Ibid., p. 16.
10. Ibid., p. 17.

actions or timely reforms preempt the emergence of a full-scale social movement. A second type of social control operates once a movement has surfaced, so to speak. Do the authorities crack down ruthlessly, but swiftly and effectively? Do they temporize and vacillate, giving strength to the movement by their own indecision? Or do they institute timely and significant reforms that take some or all of the wind out of the sails of the movement? Several factors are at work here: (1) the nature of the movement itself; (2) government perception of attitudes toward the movement; and (3) the attitude of key social groups toward the movement. Stated differently, it is the real or imagined radicalism of the movement that determines its reception in society and polity.

Smelser's analysis brings us to the appearance of the movement but not beyond. His first four factors can be called an *incubation period* and his fifth factor an *action period*.[11] Many students point to a third period of *adaptation or institutionalization,* in which the movement loses much of its drive or elan and becomes a fairly tame, even bureaucratized organization. A successful social movement is prone to such institutionalization because of the difficulty in maintaining hypertensive mobilization once the early objectives have been won. Also an enduring movement will spawn a "second generation" of leaders who are less concerned with militancy than with administration as usual.

Leaders and Followers in Social Movements

Impressed by the incubation-action-institutionalization sequence of many social movements, students have related a particular type of leader to each of the three stages. Thus does Eric Hoffer speak of (1) the *men of words,* whose task is the "readying of the ground for a mass movement" through their "skill in the use of the spoken or written word"; (2) the *fanatics,* whose "temperament and talents" assist the "hatching of an actual movement"; and (3) the *practical men of action,* who are concerned with the "final consolidation of the movement."[12]

Hoffer's men of words have also been called "intellectuals" or "ideologists."[13] Their role is to express the symptoms of structural strain

11. Paul Meadows, "Sequence in Revolution," *American Sociological Review* 6 (October 1941): 702–8.
12. Eric Hoffer, *The True Believer* (New York: Mentor Books, 1958), p. 120.
13. See Lewis M. Killian, "Social Movements," in *Handbook of Modern Sociology,* ed. R. E. L. Faris (Chicago: Rand-McNally, 1964); and Harold D. Lasswell, *Pyschopathology and Politics* (New York: Viking Press, 1960).

in intellectual terms and to give some coherence to generalized belief. Ideologists are generally well-educated persons hailing from middle and upper social strata. Hoffer sees four elements in how ideologists or men of words prepare the way for the coming of a social movement. First, they undermine the existing beliefs and institutions. Second, they indirectly promote a "hunger for faith" in susceptible people. Third, they weaken the beliefs of the "better people," who thus are neutralized when the "new fanaticism" shows its face. Fourth, they provide the "doctrine and the slogans of the new faith." [14]

While sometimes the men of words proffer a comprehensive, systematic ideology, they frequently propagate a less coherent, highly emotive myth. As the revolutionary French journalist Georges Sorel (1847–1922) always preached, it is difficult, if not impossible, to mobilize masses of men by appealing to purely rational principles. A successful social movement must stimulate deep-lying emotional responses in the human psyche. Since the myth is a symbolization of these emotions, it alone can tap human sentiments of courage, enthusiasm, and sacrifice.

Sorel denied that a "utopian" ideology, however effective with select intellectuals, could animate a broad mass movement. Intellectuals tend to use logic and empirical observation—things totally irrelevant to the strength of a myth. As Sorel said: "A myth cannot be refuted, since it is, at bottom, identical with the convictions of a group, being the expression of these convictions in the language of movement; and it is, in consequence, unanalysable into parts which could be placed on the plane of historical descriptions." [15] Utopias, on the contrary, presuppose the occurrence of certain events and trends, which are subject to intellectual tests.

The ideology or myth, of course, must be brought home to the movement's mass base, and this is where the fanatic or agitator comes in. It is up to him to "translate" the ideology or myth into terms graspable by people under stress. Many students see the agitator as a distinct personality type; some go as far as to depict him as definitely pathological. Lewis Killian expresses a common denominator when he describes the agitator as "bold, even impulsive, given to the dramatic and the stirring appeal to emotions. He is both prophet and agitator." [16]

Since the agitator is more adept at getting things moving than at

14. Hoffer, *Believer*, p. 128.
15. Georges Sorel, *Reflections on Violence* (Glencoe, Ill.: Free Press, 1950), p. 58.
16. Killian, "Movements," p. 441.

setting them in a pattern, he is oftimes displaced by the practical man of action or administrator in a movement's later stages. Success brings the movement increased size and complexity. It becomes an organization and this is reflected in a new leadership style. Coordination of the various branches and activities of the swollen movement requires leaders with a taste and capacity for administrative and practical routines. The administrator's concern with consolidating existing gains before striding forward is likely to generate opposition from the "old guard" of ideologists and agitators. It is hard to deny the considerable truth in their charges that the administrator is betraying the original ideals or goals of the movement.

Since the three types of leadership call upon rather different traits, we generally find different sets of persons in the three roles. However, on occasion movement leaders have acted interchangeably in ideological, agitational, and administrative work. Revolutionary leaders such as Lenin and Mao Tse-tung fall into this category.

Beneath the leadership level, social movements, like political parties, have different degrees of participation (figure 7.1). Following the leader, there is his immediate entourage of disciples or "adepts" (i.e., those who have inner knowledge of the message of the leader). Next comes the militant following, and finally the more or less passive sympathizers.

Figure 7.1.   Degrees of Participation in Social Movements

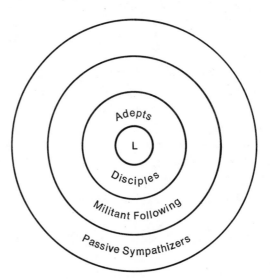

The disciples or adepts present two major problems for the leader. First, they may collectively or individually pose a threat to his supremacy: more than one original leader has been transformed into a figurehead. Second, jealousies and rivalries amongst the disciples may sap the energies of the movement and lead to splits. However, our discussion of Hitler and Stalin shows that the leader may actually encourage such strife. In any case, perfect harmony is hard to imagine in view of the different types of leadership that will coexist in any stable movement.

There is considerable controversy over the nature of the militant following of social movements. The *orthodox* approach finds that social movements attract followers who are deeply disturbed in the psychological sense. According to this view, such persons' mental balance has been warped. They are essentially creatures of unreason looking for some bogus salvation or what Sigmund Freud called a "crooked cure" for their neurotic or psychotic symptoms.

Proponents of the orthodox view such as Eric Hoffer consider that objective social and economic factors play only a secondary role in the genesis of social movements. Hoffer's list of the "disaffected" who are the prime recruits of movements includes not only the sociological categories of the poor, the outcasts, and minorities. Also included are the moral-psychological categories of misfits, adolescent youth, the ambitious, those in the grip of some vice or obsession, the impotent in body or mind, the inordinately selfish, the bored, and the sinners.[17]

Since these latter eight types refer to highly individualized experiences, Hoffer naturally sees relief from personal frustration as the main motive for joining a movement: "A rising mass movement attracts and holds a following not by its doctrine and promises but by the refuge it offers from the anxieties, barrenness and meaninglessness of individual existence." [18] The social movement does not give its followers an absolute truth or solution of social problems. Rather it frees them from their "ineffectual selves," by "enfolding and absorbing them into a closely knit and exultant corporate whole." [19]

Hoffer's view of social movements as sanitoria leads him to the conclusion that "mass movements draw their adherents from the same types of humanity and appeal to the same types of mind." [20] This means

17. Hoffer, *Believer*, pp. 30–56.
18. Ibid., p. 44.
19. Ibid.
20. Ibid., p. 26.

first of all that social movements are *competitive* because the number of possible recruits is limited. The gains of one movement are losses for others. Second, it means that social movements are *interchangeable* because nationalist, religious, or revolutionary movements can be transformed into the other two. Interchangeability can occur on the individual level as well. Extremists of the left often end up as extremists of the right, and vice versa. However, Hoffer's claims about the competitiveness and interchangeability of social movements also seem a little on the extreme side. To think that all religious, nationalist, and revolutionary movements can change their skins like snakes is feasible only by defining religion, nationalism, and revolution with unpardonable looseness.

These and other problems with the orthodox view of social movements have provoked some *revisionist* interpretations. Revisionists see movements more as collective responses to objective problem situations than as a melange of personally frustrated oddballs. Such collective problem-solving occurs because "respectable society offers no redress or solution to the dominant concerns of the individuals involved." [21] Instead of recruiting exclusively among the "poignantly frustrated," social movements "contain a wide range of humanity, but . . . within social movements particular kinds of people may be overrepresented: different kinds of people tend to be overrepresented in different kinds of movements. . . ." [22]

Not only do revisionists like Hans Toch stress the differences among social movements, they also defend their rationality. Certain social movements only appear irrational and "crackpot" because they deviate from reigning social norms. But when we look at them as collective attempts to cope with social problems, social movements may well be as rational as any other response.

The revisionist approach to social movements, like most other revisionist theories, may react too far in the opposite direction from orthodoxy. However, it makes us aware of the complexities of motivational factors. To help us on this score, Rudolph Heberle has applied Max Weber's typology of motivation to social movements. Heberle's motivation types are value-rational motivation, traditional motivation, emotional-affectual motivation, and purposive-rational motivation.[23]

Value-rational motivation operates when the individual actor is com-

21. Toch, "Social Movements," p. 584.
22. Ibid., p. 588.
23. Rudolph Heberle, *Social Movements* (New York: Appleton-Century-Crofts, 1951), pp. 95–99.

mitted to some supposedly universal value or set of values. His action is dictated by desire to realize the goals of the value system. Here the pure appeal of religion or ideology attracts the actor to the movement, and his joining is rational as a logical consequence of the religious or ideological value-system.

Traditional motivation operates when the actor follows the prescriptions of immemorial tradition. Membership in the movement may itself be traditional or, more likely, the movement appears as both an expression and defense of traditional values and cultures. This motivation is strong in certain peasant and nativistic movements.

Emotional-affectual motivation resembles Hoffer's account of the frustrated joiners of movements. As Heberle puts it, "resentment and enthusiasm are probably much more frequent types of motivation among participants in a social movement than a clear conception of the ultimate goal and its benefits for society." [24]

Purposive-rational motivation involves action in terms of achieving personal goals such as "safety, power, income, and deference." The joiner of a movement may care precious little for its ideology or myth, and his "alienation" from the general society may be minimal. He sees the movement as a golden opportunity to advance his career prospects. Such persons are not usually among the movement's founders, but join when it appears to be getting somewhere—the typical bandwagon effect.

By now it should be almost needless to point out that with typologies of this sort it is not excluded that more than one of the above "pure" motivations may operate in any given individual. Likewise a person can change so that his earlier motivation will be replaced by something different. An idealist moved by value-rational motivation may end up as a cynic playing the movement for all it is worth—purposive-rational motivation.

Some Varieties of Social Movements

Rather than elaborating a full-fledged typology, we will instead take a closer look at three kinds of movements because of their historical and contemporary interest: the millenary-messianic, youth, and nativistic.

MILLENARY MOVEMENTS.   Millenary movements are inspired by biblical prophecies about Christ's "second coming" to earth to inaugurate a

24. Ibid., p. 96.

new kingdom that will last a thousand years (i.e., a millennium). The destruction of the world as we know it will be the prelude to "a new heaven and a new earth." Millenarism differs from orthodox religion because it promises an earthly rather than a heavenly paradise. It often repudiates the powers that be in both church and state. The rich and the powerful may be threatened because millenarians teach that "the first shall be last and the last shall be first." Accordingly, there is a rigid contrast between the "elect" (or the "saints" or the "chosen ones") who are divinely called to join the movement and the others, the "damned" or the "sinners," who will be destroyed in the process of spiritual resurrection.

Messianism is the chief form of millenary social movement. It fastens upon a charismatic leader or messiah who is deemed the mouthpiece of God, or sometimes the Deity himself. The messiah is at the core of a new community, whose rules deviate sharply from those of the rest of society. Messianic movements can run from extreme puritanism to extreme permissivism or can show bizarre mixtures of these opposed moral postures. Communalism may develop, with the abolition of private property and even marriage and the traditional family structure. Some of the more energetic messiahs set up virtual harems, though banning such ventures with the rank and file.

Maria Pereira de Queiroz distinguishes between three rather different types of messianic movements: reform, subversive, and national liberation. Reform messianic movements are essentially moderate and can, if allowed, reach a modus vivendi or compromise with the existing order. Their basic goal is a "revitalization" of traditional values, though this probably also involves changes in leadership. Regarding messianic movements of reform in Brazil, Pereira concludes that "they assist in the rise and fall of the local political leaders . . . in the hierarchy of political positions, without discussing in any way the very principle of this hierarchy. They were an added element in the circulation of sociopolitical elites. . . ." [25]

Subversive messianic movements are considerably more extreme. On the surface at least, their denial of the social and religious order is total and uncompromising. A good example is the Fifth Monarchist movement during the English Revolution of the 1640s and 1650s. The

25. Maria Isaura Pereira de Queiroz, *Historia y etnologia de los movimientos messianicos* (Mexico City: Siglo XXI Editores, 1969), p. 121.

so-called Fifth Monarchy was supposed to have been established by the return of Jesus Christ to set up the kingdom of his "saints" in a paradisiacal community. Moreover, members of the movement

> saw existing society as the creation of the antichristian Fourth Monarchy. In looking forward to the millennium, they demanded that its whole structure should be remodeled in accordance with the pattern laid down in the Bible. . . . Their belief was a declared readiness to destroy by force the kingdoms of the world, and thereafter to be rulers of the earth.[26]

Messianic movements of national liberation emerge after a people has been conquered or subjected or when a state based on one ethnic group has virtually fallen to pieces. Thus, the movement "unleashed by the myth of the national hero has the reestablishment of a nation in its old condition of independence or integrity as its function." [27]

YOUTH MOVEMENTS.   To consider youth movements as social movements presents some problems. Sometimes the phenomena so described are trends and tendencies rather than true social movements. Only when the generation gap is wide enough to produce well-structured youth organizations do we find the genuine article. Another problem is illustrated by student movements, a specific type of youth movement. According to Lewis Feuer, student movements tend to attach themselves to "a carrier movement of some more major proportions—such as a peasant, labor, nationalist, racial or anti-colonial movement." [28] The problem is how far a youth movement retains its identity in this coalescence.

The German youth movement flourished in the two decades before World War I. It tended to reject the "mediocrity" and "conformity" of the "bourgeois society" of the time. Because of its preference for hikes and camping in the German countryside over political action, it seemed more escapist than most social movements. Nonetheless, the romantic and nationalist ideas nurtured in the youth movement paved the way for any conversions to national socialism in the 1920s. The Nazis, however, changed the basic character of the youth movement: "From a loose federation of fellowships, it was converted into a centralized organization, the very opposite of what the movement had been trying to practice.

26. B. S. Capp, *The Fifth Monarchy Men* (London: Faber & Faber, 1972), p. 130.
27. Pereira, *Historia*, p. 155.
28. Lewis S. Feuer, *The Conflict of Generations* (New York: Basic Books, 1969), p. 8.

From a romantic and somewhat anarchistic federation . . . it was converted into a huge paramilitary organization." [29]

If the German youth movement moved to the right, other youth and student movements lean to the left. However, underlying similarities of such movements make the ideological labels seem superficial. Youth movements tend to espouse a romantic critique of existing society that considers it repressive and hypocritical. Not only are the lower strata kept in subjection, but true human feelings and sentiments are repressed under a covering of stereotyped conventions, fraudulent pretense, and phony morality. Youth leaders call for a more honest, more open, more authentic system of human relations. Since the older generation is irredeemably corrupted by the "system," the mission of social regeneration falls by default to the youth.

The rise of student radicalism—the so-called New Left—in the 1960s is an example of the differences between revisionist and orthodox views of social movements. Following revisionist guidelines we can see the New Left movement as a response to three objective social problems: (1) widespread poverty in the midst of an affluent society; (2) the frustration of some American blacks with the slow pace of change—the shift from "civil rights" to "black power"; and (3) the quicksand United States involvement in Vietnam.

On the other hand we can follow the more orthodox views of Lewis Feuer and see instead that "it is the state of mind and feeling which impels a person to the revolutionary experience for its own sake. . . . Thus impelled, students turn from doctrine to doctrine, from cause to cause, ideology to ideology. . . ." [30] One wonders, however, whether the choice between the two approaches really has to be made. It may just be a question of different levels of analysis, both of which are necessary for a truly comprehensive explanation.

A good test case that seems to show that both revisionist and orthodox approaches contribute something to our comprehension of youth movements is the French Student Revolt of May–June 1968. The events themselves were remarkable enough. Disturbances had begun in late 1967 concerning a variety of student grievances at the University of Nanterre. The disputes took on a political cast as they were associated with protest against the Vietnam war. In the winter and spring of 1968 student strikes and demonstrations increased. They provoked the clos-

29. Heberle, *Social Movements*, p. 138.
30. Feuer, *Conflict*, p. 36.

ing of the Faculty of Letters at Nanterre, which caused the protest movement to spread to the Sorbonne. When militants occupied the latter on May 3, the police were called in. This seems the point of no return in the dispute. Henceforth occurred a widening spiral of clashes, arrests, negotiations, and concessions.

However, what distinguished the May Days of 1968 from other student revolts before and after was the involvement of certain elements of organized labor. On May 13 the unions carried out a general strike with massive demonstrations. The Sorbonne was reoccupied. Two days later, workers, especially young ones, began to take over factories. The Gaullist government was seriously troubled as student-worker solidarity was punctuated by more strikes and joint demonstrations through the latter half of May. Much of the labor activity was of the wildcat variety, since the French Communist party and its union affiliate, the General Confederation of Labor (CGT), advised moderation and ruled out a violent insurrection. The Communists wished to use the government's troubles to score an electoral win.

To the surprise of some and the chagrin of others, by the end of May the real brunt of the crisis had been weathered. Workers began returning to their jobs and pro-government demonstrations drew even larger crowds than anti-government ones. The Communists condemned student militancy, but their attempt to do some political fishing in troubled waters allowed President de Gaulle to raise the specter of "totalitarian communism." His party won a crushing majority in the elections at the end of June.

While there is no doubt that May–June 1968 constituted a serious crisis in French politics, its very meteoric quality suggests that it was not really an abortive revolution.[31] As Jacques Ellul points out, "Contrary to what was proclaimed, the government was never for a moment in danger, and there was no 'vacancy of power.' "[32] That some students and workers can be termed "revolutionaries" does not make a revolutionary situation. The exhilarative, festive atmosphere may be unforgettable to participants, but such feelings were too diffuse and were shared by too narrow a cross section of French society to have constituted a revolution.

31. For a contrasting interpretation, see Mostafa Rejai, *The Comparative Study of Revolutionary Strategy* (New York: David McKay, 1977), chap. 6.
32. Jacques Ellul, "The Psychology of a Rebellion—May–June, 1968," in *Struggles in the State*, ed. G. A. Kelley and Clifford W. Brown, Jr. (New York: John Wiley, 1970), p. 497.

The grievances of students and others were real and many, but their attempt to move beyond remedying these to a reconstruction of the whole society was quixotic in the extreme. Significant is the disproportionate strength of students in certain disciplines at the vanguard of the movement. Particularly impressive were the contingents from philosophy, sociology, and psychology. To sympathizers this simply reflected the greater political sensibility and acquaintance with social problems of students in these fields. Ellul has suggested an equally probable explanation: "philosophers (in France at least), sociologists and psychologists are the 'fifth wheel of the cart'; they are not really of any use, their knowledge is a false science, they have no hold over society and they feel useless." [33]

It is not just the problem of joblessness that exists for such people, but also the feeling that a society producing such problems forces alienation and protest. Two particular factors allowed the French Student Revolt of 1968 to go as far as it did: (1) the aesthetic-moral critique of the modern "consumer society" it offered in contrast to the traditional leftist socioeconomic critique of capitalism did find a response among nonrevolutionary elites; and (2) no really serious threat against the system was involved, which caused the Gaullist government to avoid rapid, ruthless repression for fear of creating sympathy and martyrs for the movement. This seems clearer if we recall that repression of the revolutionary Paris Commune of 1871 may have cost as many as twenty thousand lives, while hardly any were lost in the spring of 1968.

NATIVISTIC MOVEMENTS. Nativistic movements are the product of culture contact and conflict. They typically emerge when representatives of one culture dominate the representatives of another culture socially, economically, and politically. Three- or four-sided relationships, however, are not uncommon (e.g., the British, Muslims, and Hindus in Imperial India before 1947). Though sometimes found among dominant groups, nativistic movements usually break out among subordinate groups as in the typical colonial situation. Ralph Linton defines a "nativistic movement" as "any conscious, organized attempt . . . to revive or perpetuate selected aspects of [a] culture." [34]

There are at least two major forms of nativistic movement. The first,

---

33. Ibid., p. 502.
34. Ralph Linton, "Nativistic Movements," in *Reader in Comparative Religion*, ed. W. A. Lessa and E. Z. Vogt (Evanston, Ill.: Row, Peterson, 1958), p. 467.

revivalist nativism, is characterized by extreme xenophobia (i.e., total repudiation of the alien and his culture). The idea is to purge one's own culture of all foreign encrustations and go back to some "golden age" that supposedly predated the alien intruder. With the importance of religion in traditional society, revivalist nativism may well assume a religious, even millenary, aspect. The Ghost Dance cult among the American Indians, the Boxer Rebellion in turn-of-the-century China, and the Mau-Mau in Kenya after World War II all show the traits of nativistic movements.

In such cases, however, we must beware that "the image of the ancient culture to be revived is distorted by historical ignorance and by the presence of imported and innovative elements." [35] Nativistic movements in central Africa illustrate this with their fusion of "imported" Christian themes and traditional cultural and religious motifs.[36]

Reformative nativism, on the other hand, is the attempt of a "subordinated group to attain a personal and social reintegration through selective rejection, modification, and synthesis of both traditional and (alien) dominant cultural components." [37] As an attempt to "get the best of both worlds," reformative nativism is less militant and violent than revivalist nativism. Moreover, when the reformist elements loom large enough in a movement, it has· probably crossed the somewhat hazy border between nativism and modern nationalism.

Social movements are important features of political life. They have built up and cast down regimes. Governments have to keep a watchful eye on them, especially on the more flamboyant and aggressive movements. Of special interest is the movement that has become a regime, as is the case with totalitarian and some authoritarian dictatorships. After taking power the movement's leaders will begin to act differently from the old days of struggle. Some see an illustration here of the Actonian maxim that "power tends to corrupt," but personal corruption may play only a minor part in the transformation. A movement out of power is one thing; the movement's leaders governing a country is another.

No movement leader who has become chief of government has been exempt from charges of treason to the movement and its ideals. But be-

35. Anthony F. C. Wallace, "Revitalization Movements," *American Anthropologist* 58 (April 1956): 276.
36. Vittorio Lanternari, *The Religions of the Oppressed* (New York: Mentor Books, 1965).
37. Fred W. Voget, "The American Indian in Transition: Reformation and Accommodation," *American Anthropologist* 58 (April 1956): 250.

fore we whisper "corruption" let us admit the natural gap between promising something and delivering it. Reaching the pinnacle of power may be a sobering as well as an exhilarating experience. The new government chief has a broader perspective; his constituencies have multiplied beyond the movement's original devotees. New needs and claims must be balanced off against the old ideals of the dynamic movement. This means postponement, if not abandonment, of the movement's original program. There are virtually no exceptions to this rule of political life.

REVOLUTIONS

Revolutions can be studied under a number of categories: social change, political violence, and so on. Here we will consider them as a special type of social movement. Thus, much of our discussion above on social movements could be used in the analysis of the French Revolution of 1789, the Russian Revolution of 1917, and the Chinese Revolution from the late 1920s on. In reality, most major revolutions comprise several rather distinct social movements, whose convergent impact brings down the old order and launches society on the uncharted and often stormy waters of revolutionary change.

Collective Violence and Revolution

The word "revolution" is a popular, even glamorous, word nowadays. Thus many people overwork it until it loses all definite meaning. Accordingly, broad-based, drawn-out, sociocultural changes such as the Reformation or the Industrial Revolution have evoked the label "revolution." Even political breakthroughs—the Jacksonian "Revolution" or the New Deal "Revolution," or new economic policies such as the Keynesian "Revolution"—have been so christened. From the standpoint of political science, *revolution* is somewhat more specific and can be defined as

> an acute, prolonged crisis in one or more of the traditional systems of stratification (class, status, power) of a political community, which involves a purposive, elite-directed attempt to abolish or to reconstruct one or more of said systems by means of an intensification of political power and recourse to violence.[38]

38. Mark N. Hagopian, *The Phenomenon of Revolution* (New York: Dodd, Mead, 1974), p. 1.

Such a definition of revolution is designed to fulfill several purposes: (1) to distinguish revolutions from subrevolutionary forms of collective political violence such as coups d'etat, revolts, and secessions; (2) to stress the importance of social stratification; (3) to highlight the role of ideology and leadership; (4) to relate revolution to social change; and (5) to show the importance of power and violence.

DISTINGUISHING REVOLUTIONS FROM SUBREVOLUTIONARY FORMS. We have already discussed some of the dynamics of coups d'etat in chapter 4. The term means literally a blow at the state and connotes a violent, illegal attempt to seize or expand political power. Its basic form is the *simple* coup d'etat, which aims at changing top leadership, perhaps with some "cosmetic" shifts in policy, but little more. In other words, the simple coup does not seriously alter the fundamental political, social, or economic institutions of a country. The stakes of the simple coup are mainly personal power and some of its fringe benefits in wealth or status.

TABLE 7.3.   Typology of the Simple Coup d'Etat

1. **Palace revolution:** conspiracies revolve around the throne, usually involving members of the royal family, a rival family, or top officials in the royal court.
2. **Executive coup:** the chief of state employs force to seize full power or to perpetuate his rule.
3. **Military coup:** the military assumes the government by ousting "corrupt" or ideologically unacceptable civilian leaders.
4. **Paramilitary coup:** paramilitary organizations launch a putsch to seize power.

The simple coup is distinguished by who makes it. Table 7.3 distinguishes coups on this basis. Though the military are the prime movers only in military coups, their neutrality or tacit support seems essential to the success of the other three types. Other important factors are, of course, the attitude of the politically relevant public and of foreign governments. Initially successful coups have been reversed due to domestic or foreign opposition.

In a revolutionary context, however, a coup assumes greater political significance. First, it can signify the start of an authentic revolution. Second, a coup can mark transitions between different phases or turning points of a revolution. Finally, a coup can be counterrevolutionary either by forestalling an imminent revolution or by overthrowing a partially successful one. In such cases the real importance of the coup lies in its role within the broader constellation of revolution or counterrevolution. In no case, however, is a coup, whether simple or complex, to be identified with a full revolution.

Revolts (as already noted in the discussion of peasants in chapter 6) are oriented very differently from true revolutions. This goes against the widespread idea that revolts are merely *revolutions that failed.* Failure, however, can be gauged only in terms of goals, and the goals of revolt are categorically different from those of genuine revolution. Put simply, a revolution aims to reorganize parts of or the whole of the social stratification systems (see section on stratification in chapter 6.) A revolt, on the other hand, aims more to restore a bygone condition, to revitalize traditional institutions, and to punish those responsible for deviating from custom. The violence of a revolt is largely *expressive:* it is an outlet for the anger of people who feel wrongfully deprived of their rights. While revolutionary violence too has its expressive side, it emphasizes an element of directed "creative destruction" to clear the way for innovations.

While all revolts tend to be retrospective, they differ in terms of the specific actors and interests involved. Borrowing some ideas from the present and the previous chapter, table 7.4 develops a typology of revolts.

TABLE 7.4. The Major Types of Revolt

---

1. **Jacqueries (peasant revolts):** jacqueries are outbursts of peasant violence, mostly against landlords. Peasant revolts are less purely expressive and are aimed against trends and policies threatening peasant livelihood and way of life.
2. **Revolts of the urban mob:** these are violent outbursts in the pre-industrial city, which are triggered usually by the high cost of bread. Minimal economic concessions generally placate the participants.
3. **Nativistic revolts:** these occur when revivalist movements consider violent expulsion of the alien the only way to restore the threatened cultural values.
4. **Millenary-messianic revolts:** subversive or national liberation movements are likely to resort to violence. Their extreme goals and the rigid distinction between "insiders" and "outsiders" make conflict inevitable.
5. **Aristocratic revolts:** these occur when an aristocracy loses some of its privileges to the benefit of a king and his "commoner" allies. The revolt is in a dilemma because by going too far it might threaten the whole system.
6. **Slave revolts:** uprisings of slaves as in the Spartacus rebellion in ancient Rome or the rebellions in the South before the American Civil War.

Revolts can be simple as in each of the six above types or they can be complex, with several aspects—for instance, the Fronde in France from

1648 to 1653 had elements of aristocratic, peasant, and urban mob involvement.

Though revolts are not revolutions, they can contribute to conflict and discontent and thus encourage a revolutionary onslaught. The aristocratic "prerevolution" of 1787–88 in France was a virtual revolt to restore aristocratic privileges. Many historians consider this confrontation a necessary prelude to the Revolution proper.

Secessions have also been mistaken for true revolution. A simple secession occurs when part of a sovereign state breaks off and establishes a new state or joins another state. This part is usually territorial. Sometimes a region breaks off, as the South did in 1861; and sometimes it is a colony, as with the thirteen American colonies in 1776. In addition to regional and colonial secession, we can have secessionism based on religion and ethnicity.

Certain secessionist movements, however, can become revolutionary. This depends on the severity and duration of the government's anti-secessionist measures and other factors. A colonial secessionist movement, for example, may adopt a revolutionary strategy not only to wage a "war of liberation," but also because state-building, nation-building, and economic development seem to require the most radical measures.

SOCIAL STRATIFICATION AS A FACTOR IN REVOLUTION.   The importance of social stratification as a factor in revolution is the second major emphasis in our definition. This emphasis allows us to understand the

Figure 7.2.   Intensities of Revolutionary Change

	Negligible Change	Moderate Change	Radical Change	Total Abolition
Class System				
Status System				
Power System				

differences between revolutions in a more rigorous way. Thus we can consider revolutions as attempts to change one or more of the systems of stratification discussed in chapter 6. In figure 7.2 we have distinguished four intensities of change from negligible to complete abolition. By filling in the appropriate boxes for each specific revolution, we could compare their "scores" and thus have a better idea of how they differ.

THE ROLE OF IDEOLOGY AND LEADERSHIP.   Ideology is another way of distinguishing genuine revolutions from subrevolutionary political violence.[39] Revolutionary ideology has three major dimensions. In its first dimension, ideology as *critique* provides a systematic indictment of the existing order—taking up what is wrong and why. Rather than vague complaints, the ideology itemizes the defects of society, polity, or economy and explains why the system cannot reform itself. The "bad men" theory can serve a revolt, but not a revolution.

Second, since revolutions are built on "hope," as the saying goes, the ideology must have the additional dimension of *affirmation*. This shows that a superior political or social system is possible, and if the ideology is deterministic, how the coming of the blissful future society is "inevitable." Revolution is required merely to speed up the process. If the ideology furthermore depicts a final stage of utter social harmony free of poverty, ignorance, vice, exploitation, conflict, and aggression, we can call it "utopian."

Over the last century the third dimension of revolutionary ideology, *strategy*, has assumed a foremost position.[40] Since the critical and affirmative aspects of ideologies will occupy us further in later chapters (see part 3), a brief characterization of six major revolutionary strategies follows next. The first four are urban strategies; the last two are rural strategies.

1. *The Blanquist strategy.* This advocates revolution by a small conspiratorial clique with the tightest and most disciplined organization

39. The type and level of ideology is one basis for distinguishing true revolutions from subrevolutionary political violence. Let us recall our definition of *ideology:* "a programmatic and rhetorical application of some grandiose philosophical system (a *Weltanschauung*) that arouses men to political action and may provide strategic guidance for that action."

40. *Strategy* is the general plan by which we seek to achieve our goals or objectives. *Tactics* consists of the narrow actions done to implement the strategy. Tactics are therefore more flexible and adaptable than the broader strategic principles. It is helpful to recall that the term "strategy" is related to the ancient Greek term for "general in the army." See Rejai, *Comparative Study of Revolutionary Strategy.*

possible. It assumes that the masses have been fooled into acceptance of the status quo or are otherwise unable to engineer their own liberation. In the words of Auguste Blanqui, a French revolutionary of the nineteenth century: "There must be no more of these tumultuous uprisings of ten thousand isolated heads, acting randomly, in disorder, with no thought of the whole, each in his own corner and according to his own fantasy." [41] Probably the best contemporary examples of Blanquists are radical military leaders who make a coup d'etat, not to defend their own military corporate interests or the social and political status quo, but to gain power in order to make a revolution from "above." Ethiopia and Portugal come closest to this.

2. *The Leninist strategy.* This resembles the elitism of the Blanquists but establishes closer links with the masses. The party is the vanguard of the revolutionary masses, but the masses do act during the insurrection. The party, which leads and "educates" the masses, acts like the general staff of an army. Lenin spoke of the need for "iron discipline" among the members of the revolutionary organization. During and before the Russian Revolution of 1917 Lenin organized the Bolshevik party according to this strategy. During the 1920s, 1930s, and 1940s most Communist parties in the Western world tried to follow the path of an elite of professional revolutionaries, who would lead the urban masses in revolution when the right moment came.

3. *The urban guerrilla strategy.* This approach advocates a multitude of separate violent acts to create a revolutionary situation and bring it to a climax. Assassination, kidnapping, robbery, and bombings will force the government to further repressive acts, which will gain sympathy for the cause of revolution. The final victory of the revolution "will depend on the combination of a guerrilla force of several hundred men who will attack everywhere in order to disarm and weaken the enemy, giving cover to the regular formations of the people deployed on semi-mobile fronts. . . ." [42]

4. *The general strike strategy.* This shows the "anarcho-syndicalist" mistrust of political parties and favors instead the direct revolutionary action of the militant trade unions through a general strike. Such

41. Auguste Blanqui, "Instructions for an Uprising," in *Revolutionaries on Revolution*, ed. P. B. Springer and M. Truzzi (Pacific Palisades, Calif.: Goodyear, 1973), p. 148.
42. Abraham Guillen, *The Philosophy of the Urban Guerrilla* (New York: Morrow, 1973), p. 249.

a strike, which involves the entire labor force, will polarize the country into friends and enemies of the revolution and trigger the violence that will decide the fate of the revolution. In the words of Georges Sorel: "With the general strike . . . the revolution appears as a revolt, pure and simple, and no place is reserved for sociologists, for fashionable people who are in favor of social reforms, and for the intellectuals who have embraced the *profession of thinking for the proletariat*."[43] This strategy has not registered great successes. Many general strikes do not have truly revolutionary goals. Those that do seem easy enough to crush if the forces of order combine patience with selective repression. Spain in the 1920s and 1930s witnessed a number of abortive revolutionary general strikes.

5. *The people's war strategy.* This looks to the peasantry to come to the aid of revolutionary rural guerrillas. Starting out with simple hit-and-run tactics against government, the guerrilla movement expands until it controls large chunks of the hinterland. It ceases to be a purely military operation and becomes a virtual state within the state. As one theorist puts it, "A revolutionary guerrilla movement which does not have these administrative concerns and structures to fulfill its obligations to the populace would degenerate into banditry."[44] The people's war strategy is a generalization of Mao Tse-tung's successful revolutionary strategy in China. It is not for impatient revolutionaries, since Mao pursued it for over twenty years before the ultimate victory of 1949. The revolutionary guerrilla movement expands from one or more base areas in rural or remote regions, until most of the country is under its de facto political control. As Mao put it, "The countryside will encircle the cities."

6. *The guerrilla "foco" strategy.* This eschews the strong party organization and "base areas" of the people's war. It looks to a minuscule corps of dedicated revolutionary fighters. It thus resembles the urban guerrilla approach except for its rural setting. According to Regis Debray, French radical and disciple of the late Cuban revolutionary leader Ernesto "Che" Guevara, the revolutionary group or "foco" differs from the Blanquist-type minority because it "aims to win over the masses before and not after the seizure of power. . . . This minority establishes itself at the most vulnerable zone of the national territory, and then slowly

---

43. Sorel, *Reflections*, p. 157.
44. Eqbal Ahmad, "Revolutionary Warfare and Counterinsurgency," in *National Liberation*, ed. N. Miller and R. Aya (New York: Free Press, 1971), p. 157.

spreads like an oil patch propagating itself in concentric ripples through the peasant masses, to the smaller towns, and finally to the capital." [45]

The foco theory supposedly reflects Fidel Castro's successful overthrow of the Batista dictatorship in Cuba in late 1958. However, Castro's triumph was largely attributable to the inner rot and collapse of the Batista regime. When "Che" Guevara tried to export the foco strategy to the backwashes of Bolivia in 1967, he was killed and the insurgency aborted. A strategy that "works" in one set of conditions will not necessarily succeed in other times and places.

Although the concept of strategy implies leadership, the precise role of leadership in revolution is rather controversial. Two simplistic answers are given by the "conspiracy theory" and the theory of "mass explosion." The first, generally championed by enemies of revolution, sees revolutions as the work of tiny elites who manipulate men and events from behind the scenes. This hidden group plots the downfall of the old order, and after the carefully engineered downfall of the old regime they leap into the breach and set up a revolutionary regime according to plan.

The theory of mass explosion is espoused by friends of revolution, because it portrays the revolution as the work of the "people" or the "masses" alone. Since in some theories the people or the masses can do no wrong, the fact that the revolution is their doing legitimates it. The imagery is of explosion or spontaneous combustion, in which the people, oppressed for so long, suddenly rise up in righteous indignation and throw off their yoke.

These two theories are probably equidistant from the truth. A better approximation to the truth is to consider leadership as a catalyst, lacking which a successful revolution is impossible. In this view leadership does not create the complex web of revolutionary discontents, but weaves them into the pattern of a revolutionary movement. Leadership of revolution, as with any social movement, must shape an ideology, agitate the masses, and run the revolutionary government. Revolution means increasing organization, and this means increasing oligarchy. No one knows for sure if the majority of people support that oligarchy. We do know that the revolutionary oligarchy enjoys significant support among strategic crisis strata.

REVOLUTION AS SOCIAL CHANGE.   Nearly everyone agrees that revo-

45. Regis Debray, "Castroism: The Long March in Latin America," in *Struggles in the State,* ed. G. A. Kelly and C. W. Brown (New York: John Wiley, 1970), p. 453.

lution is a form of social change. The question is, what is it in or about society that changes? Marx saw revolutions as the displacement of an old ruling class tied to an outmoded economic system, by a new class championing advanced technology. For Pareto, revolutions occurred when an old elite made up mostly of crafty but cowardly "foxes" was overthrown by a new elite composed of daring but dull "lions."

These and other approaches have merit, though they seem more appropriate to some revolutions than to others. For this reason our definition is somewhat noncommittal on the focus of revolutionary change. Though the possible targets of change are the three stratification systems, each specific revolution has a unique pattern of change. If we compare the English Revolution of the 1640s and '50s with the Chinese Communist Revolution, we can see that the intensity and amount of change is lower in the English case.

THE ROLE OF POWER AND VIOLENCE.   Our view of revolution rejects the possibility of a nonviolent revolution. Revolutions necessarily involve violence because the types and pace of change they involve cannot be instituted without generating violent opposition. A revolution makes a breach in the legal continuity of a society, which affords an opportunity for violence that is nonlegitimate in terms of the old regime. Violence is used by revolutionaries to mobilize supporters and frighten opponents. There is no substitute for violence in the revolutionary process.

The Causes of Revolutions

Modern social science teaches that highly complex events such as revolution are caused by many factors and not by a single factor. Monocausal theories stressing economics or conspiratorial elites persist, however. Our own approach will be to give a rough idea of the multiple factors whose interaction produces the revolutionary situation, which is then precipitated into the outbreak of revolution. The total package of factors leading to outbreak can be called the "antecedent conditions." This package includes social trends as well as the mental state of people.

Such trends and states of mind result from change, but change of a special sort. Since the problem is that, in the case of the revolutionary situation, the different aspects of change are somehow out of kilter, we will call this special sort of change "discordant change." *It is not so much the swiftness of change per se as the discordance among the various processes and types of change that is conducive to revolution.*

Some social scientists prefer to express this general idea through the notion of "equilibrium." A society is in equilibrium when the changes stay within a certain framework. Minor disturbances to the system can be handled by various adjustment mechanisms so that the whole functions more or less stably. Disequilibrium means that the society is more susceptible to "fall apart" in revolution.[46]

We can make the relationship between revolution and discordant change clearer. R. M. MacIver divides society into three analytically distinct orders (see table 7.5), within which and between which the drama of social change is played out.[47] Though the cultural, technological, and social orders are somewhat interdependent, change can lead in one while lagging in the others. This is how change becomes discordant.

TABLE 7.5.   The Three Orders of Human Society

1. **Cultural order:** this includes the patterns, interactions, and trends of values, norms, and goals as seen in the mores, folkways, traditions, faiths, fine arts, philosophies, the play-activities, and the way of life of various social groups.
2. **Technological order:** this includes the processes by which men gain their livings from nature. Industry, engineering, design, economic production and distribution, the military, and government are seen in this order.
3. **Social order:** this includes all that we have discussed under social stratification and social differentiation, including what we will cover in the chapters on parties and interest groups.

In eighteenth-century France, for example, cultural values changed rapidly in favor of the modern secular and liberal beliefs. Nevertheless, many forms of social organization—the system of three estates, for example—survived, which had their roots in the medieval feudal system. As the gap between the cultural and social realms grew more pronounced, so did the idea that some dramatic breakthrough was necessary to narrow it.

Though there are three "locations" of change—in the three orders of human society—we distinguish only two "forms" of change: linear and cyclical. Linear change is so called because it moves, so to speak, in a straight line. It is change that (1) moves to further the process originally initiated; (2) is stengthened by earlier success (the "snowball effect");

46. See Chalmers Johnson, *Revolutionary Change* (Boston: Little, Brown, 1966).
47. R. M. MacIver, *Social Causation* (New York: Harper & Row, 1964), p. 273.

and (3) once made, cannot be unmade. Many think that scientific and technological change is linear over the long run.

Cyclical change refers to phenomena that seem to recur in a definite rhythm. Seasonal change causes recurrent patterns of behavior in all societies. Certain economic processes such as business and trade cycles also obey rhythms that are partially predictable. An important difference between linear and cyclical change lies in their impact on government. While a government can take measures to slow down linear processes and cushion their social impact, they cannot stop them altogether. Governments may be able to stop or reverse certain cyclical processes, on the other hand.

Figure 7.3. Linear and Cyclical Change

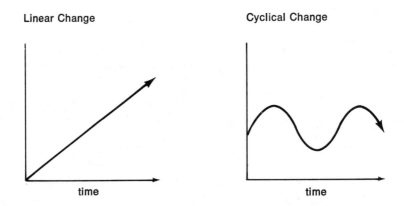

Let us think, for example, of a business downturn that might have serious social consequences. If this is a cyclical development, the government might (1) be able to foresee it and provide against its worst ravages, (2) keep its nerve in the knowledge that things will eventually swing up again, (3) treat the symptoms of the downturn vigorously and effectively.

LONG-TERM CAUSES OF REVOLUTION.   Long-term causes begin their destabilizing work several generations more or less before the outbreak of revolution. Middle-term causes begin to operate several decades in advance of it. Naturally, some of the latter are themselves generated by the long-term causes, or at least speeded up by them. Table 7.6 gives some idea of the complexities involved.

TABLE 7.6.   Overview of the Causal Nexus of Revolutions

Long-Term Causes	Middle-Term Causes
1. Economic growth 2. Technological innovation 3. Growth of science 4. Democratization 5. Secularization 6. Growth of modern state 7. Growth of modern nationalism	1. Economic depression 2. Alienation of intellectuals 3. Division and ineptitude of ruling class 4. War 5. Government financial crisis

Long-Term Causes } + Middle-Term Causes } = Revolutionary situation

This scheme does not mean that all the long-term and middle-term causes are at work in all revolutions. Moreover, George Pettee may well be right when he points out that "there are enough possible factors to cause revolutions on entirely different sets of causes." [48] Using some ideas we applied to the problem of totalitarianism, we can say that our lists of long- and middle-term causes do not form a *syndrome* of necessary causal conditions, but a group of *family resemblances* culled from study of a number of separate revolutionary experiences. A discussion of the long-term causes follows.

1. *Economic growth.* Our normal inclination would be to think that economic growth produces stability rather than revolution. Though this often is its result, in some circumstances economic growth increases the discontent of certain segments and makes them crisis strata. Since economic growth is measured in aggregate figures such as the gross national product (GNP), it tells us virtually nothing about the actual distribution of income among social groups.

Thus, as Mancur Olsen points out, there can be losers as well as winners in the process of economic growth.[49] Absolute losers would be those whose jobs, professions, and businesses were made obsolete by the changes associated with economic growth. Relative losers are people with rising incomes who feel themselves losers because the economic posi-

48. George Pettee, *The Process of Revolution* (New York: Harper & Row, 1938), p. 30.
49. Mancur Olsen, "Rapid Growth as a Destabilizing Force," in *When Men Revolt and Why*, ed. J. C. Davies (New York: Free Press, 1971), pp. 215–27.

tion of some other group rose still faster. Economic winners might become discontented because their high economic position was not matched by high status or political position. In short, economic growth is liable to increase class struggle, status resentment, and political conflict as well as to raise popular expectations.

2. *Technological innovation.* Such advances can first of all stimulate the socially ambivalent process of economic growth. It certainly speeds the decline or demise of certain sectors of the economy. Technological advance has another, more subtle, influence on the prerevolutionary climate of opinion. It makes some people, especially intellectuals, think that a kind of social engineering could remedy the defects and drawbacks of the existing social and political order. Since this appears impossible under the old regime, a revolutionary conclusion is easy to draw.

3. *The growth of science.* Despite the contemporary convergence of science and technology, these become more and more distinct the farther back in time we look. Until the nineteenth century science was the preserve of persons of high social standing and their protégés, while technology was relegated to lower-lying artisans and entrepreneurs. The growth of science, however, has a similar result to the growth of technology: it induces the idea that scientific method can and should be applied to the solution of social problems, or perhaps to the construction of new society. It was no accident that Karl Marx called his doctrines "scientific socialism."

In another vein, we must recall that many traditional societies have been legitimated by appeals to divine sanction. Whether the "divine right of kings" in early modern Europe or the "mandate of Heaven" in Imperial China, the common idea is that the social and political hierarchy reflects a divine model. Now, scientific advances, and especially hasty conclusions drawn from them, have eroded many cherished theological dogmas and beliefs. This not only makes a regime's legitimacy doubtful, but it also may create a spiritual void that can be filled by a revolutionary ideology.

4. *Democratization.* Democratization is a lengthy and gradual process of leveling social differences—though more regarding status barriers than economic or political inequalities. In the West this change has resulted in a movement from medieval feudalism to the looser estate society of early modern times to the "bourgeois" society of the last two centuries. Its main results are increased social mobility and the stripping away of the privileges of high status. In the last century Sir Henry Sumner Maine described democratization as a shift from a society based on

"status" to one based on "contract," in which individuality replaces kinship as "the unit of which civil laws take account." [50]

As in the case of economic growth, there is a certain irony in that lowered status barriers do not necessarily mean greater stability and contentment. The higher status groups may bitterly resent the rise of lower groups, and the latter may feel that the change is too little, too late. Moreover, lowering status barriers does not guarantee equality for rich and poor, and social frustration may actually increase.

5. *Secularization.* Secularization means the declining role of organized religion in culture and society. Having already discussed the impact of secularization on regime legitimacy, we can now stress the role of the church as an organizational pillar of the old regime. Any slide in its influence will weaken the forces in favor of the status quo. Religious thinkers are quick to point out the relationship between the decline of religion and the rise of revolutionary movements.

6. *Growth of modern state.* We have discussed the modern state in chapter 1. Its development is important for us because our modern idea of revolution is unthinkable without it. If the revolutionaries are to seize power, that power is lodged in the central governmental institutions. If revolutionaries wish to transform society, they must resort to the apparatus of the modern state.

Moreover, the emergence of the modern state involves certain growing pains. In prerevolutionary England and France, for example, many of the early opponents of the crown were incensed at its state-building endeavors. That the revolutionary process helped by their opposition created an even stronger state is not the first nor the last case of political action that has boomeranged.

7. *Growth of modern nationalism.* Nationalism is one of the most important general causes of revolution. Nationalism is a social movement that spreads from a small nucleus of the intelligentsia, then involves the middle classes, and finally engulfs the lower strata. Two traits of nationalism help to explain why its spread may have revolutionary consequences: ethnocentrism and egalitarianism. Ethnocentrism is an intolerant preference for one's own group and its ways, which causes a low regard for other groups and cultures.

The culture of aristocracies and upper classes has often seemed "foreign" to those below. (See section on nationalism in chapter 11 for il-

50. Sir Henry Sumner Maine, *Ancient Law* (Gloucester, Mass.: Peter Smith, 1970), p. 163.

lustrations of revolutionary implications of nationalism.) Quite frequently, it does contain elements borrowed from outside cultures. In some cases the higher groups consider themselves ethnically different from the common people. When conditions such as these prevail, the ethnocentrism of growing nationalism makes the alien or foreign aspects of the rulers' culture seem strange and intolerable. This undermines the legitimacy of the existing order and makes some people look to revolution.

Nationalism is egalitarian in the sense that it considers the individual an integral part of the whole, regardless of his social or economic position. Depending on how literally this egalitarianism is taken, a particular nationalism may go beyond removal of status differences and promise political or economic equality for all members of the nation. Revolution may seem the only way to attain such goals.

MIDDLE-TERM CAUSES OF REVOLUTION.   The following account of five middle-term causes of revolution does not claim to be exhaustive but to represent some consensus among theorists and historians.

1. *Economic depression.* The idea that a sudden economic downturn following a long period of growing prosperity will likely produce a revolutionary situation is linked to James Davies's J-curve of actual need satisfaction.[51] This theory presupposes the notion of *Relative Deprivation*, or RD. In simple terms RD is the ratio between what people want and expect and what they actually get.[52] Davies prefers to speak of "expected need satisfaction" and "actual need satisfaction." He finds that revolution is likely under two conditions: (1) expectation of need satisfaction increases continuously, and (2) a sudden dramatic decline of actual need satisfaction occurs. This rapidly widening gap between expectations and actual satisfactions produces generalized frustration, which in turn produces aggression directed against the government (i.e., revolution).

Originally Davies came close with his theory to a single-factor explanation of revolutions. Later he put the J-curve in a larger framework, as when he said about the French Revolution that "more or less independently of frustrated rising expectations in the eighteenth century,

---

51. It is called a J-curve because the curve measuring actual need satisfaction dips down drastically resembling a letter J tipped on its side. See James C. Davies, "Toward a Theory of Revolution," in Davies, *When Men Revolt.*
52. Ted R. Gurr in the most rigorous and comprehensive account of RD and politics speaks of "value capabilities" and "value expectations." *Why Men Rebel* (Princeton: Princeton University Press, 1971).

French society was already deeply fragmented." [53] If we recognize that different crisis strata become the main protagonists in different revolutions, it seems clear that different patterns of RD dispose different groups to revolutionary propaganda and mobilization. Figure 7.4 illustrates some alternative patterns of RD.

Figure 7.4. Some Patterns of Relative Deprivation

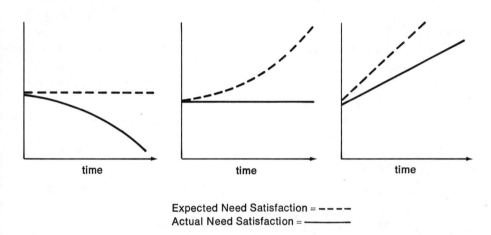

Expected Need Satisfaction = – – – –
Actual Need Satisfaction = ————

If we take pattern 1 we see that expected need satisfactions remain constant over time, while actual need satisfaction goes downhill. In other words, a group's basic ideas of what it expects from life do not change, but their standard of living or what they own or enjoy declines markedly. This type of RD seems to square best with our earlier notion of revolt, rather than with revolution. However, revolts can coincide with and speed up revolutions, as happened with the Mexican peasants before the outbreak of the Revolution of 1910. Pattern 2 suggests a group undergoing a "revolution of rising expectation," but whose standard of living remains relatively constant. This might characterize groups in the Third World or in remote regions of a country that are newly exposed to communications that show them how the other half lives. When they look away from the new models of consumption or freedom to their own

53. James C. Davies, "The J-Curve of Rising and Declining Satisfactions as a Cause of Some Great Revolutions and a Contained Rebellion," in *Violence in America: Historical and Comparative Perspectives*, ed. H. D. Graham and T. R. Gurr (New York: Bantam Books, 1969), p. 700.

unchanging condition, the gap of RD widens. Pattern 3 sees the group improving their actual need satisfaction, but at a pace that falls behind their rising expectations. It is the old story of "give them an inch and they'll take a mile."

2. *Alienation of intellectuals*. This commonly observed prerevolutionary trend sees intellectuals moving away from support or neutrality toward the existing order to a critical and revolutionary posture.[54] The impact of long-term and some middle-term revolutionary causes upon intellectuals leads to two main results: (1) the intellectuals weaken support for the regime through their influence on public opinion; and (2) the intellectuals found or join revolutionary sects, parties, and movements.

These things do not happen overnight, however. The intellectuals' criticism is initially apolitical. There grows a "literature of exposure" which bemoans the general moral laxness, hypocrisy, vulgarity, superciliousness, and selfishness of the high and the mighty. Satire is extremely corrosive of the regime's strength, for a "ruling class can survive even though it knows itself to be tyrannical. It cannot survive if it is made to appear foolish in its own sight." [55] In a second phase criticism becomes politicized and revolutionary ideologies take shape. Now we can speak of a true and proper revolutionary movement.

3. *Division and ineptness of ruling class*. An insight as old as Plato's *Republic* is that "in any form of government revolution always starts from the outbreak of internal dissension in the ruling class. The constitution cannot be upset so long as that class is of one mind, however small it may be." [56] In addition to the problem of defining the "ruling class," two qualifications to Plato's finding must be entered. First, a united "ruling class" must count on the loyalty of the military, because "whatever government or party has the full allegiance of the country's armed forces is to all intents and purposes politically impregnable." [57] Second, Plato's thesis may not hold where the "ruling class" is of a different race

---

54. Lyford P. Edwards calls this "transfer of the allegiance of the intellectuals" in his *The Natural History of Revolution* (Chicago: University of Chicago Press, 1970); while Crane Brinton prefers "desertion of the intellectuals" in his *The Anatomy of Revolution* (New York: Vintage Books, 1960).
55. Edwards, *Natural History*, p. 106.
56. Plato, *The Republic*, trans. F. Cornford (New York: Oxford University Press, 1960), sec. 546.
57. Katharine Chorley, *Armies and the Art of Revolution* (London: Faber & Faber, 1943), p. 16.

from the ruled classes. In such a case ruling-class unity may not be enough to hold back a tide of outraged "inferiors."

Many historians have portrayed the prerevolutionary ruling class as hopelessly "decadent," and we have seen Pareto make this the heart of his own theory. The symptoms of decadence are vague, but obsolescence, irresponsibility, and isolation turn up in most lists of charges. According to this view, the ruling class is obsolete because it is too tied to the past to handle present challenges. The ruling class is irresponsible because it shirks its duties and prefers, ostrichlike, its life of luxury while its world crumbles around it. The ruling class is isolated and loses touch with the masses. This causes its members to espouse ideologies that idolize the "downtrodden" and to lose faith in themselves.

While some of these charges seem amply justified, the whole scenario is too much like a morality play whose theme is "the wages of sin is death." Not all "decadent" ruling classes have been overthrown by revolution. Moreover, even a decadent ruling class "is not all and equally and uniformly decadent however. Different factions of it are more and less devoted to the old myth, more and less receptive to innovation, more and less dissolute." [58]

4. *War.* War is important in bringing on revolutions. It is at least doubtful whether the Communists could have succeeded in Russia and China without World Wars I and II. Unsuccessful wars can topple regimes because the people resent the sacrifices and destruction of war. Abortive revolutions such as the Paris Commune of 1871 and the Russian Revolution of 1905 followed military disasters. Another problem is that war governments are tempted to promise all manner of reforms in order to shore up the war effort. The failure to deliver when peace comes can lead to revolution. War can also have a more delayed impact by raising government indebtedness.

5. *Government financial crisis.* Many prerevolutionary governments have suffered financial woes before their collapse or overthrow. This has several destabilizing results. First, it appears to prove the government's incompetence and corruption—a theme critics have been hammering away at for some time. Second, the government may be unable to pay its civil servants and, most crucially, its soldiers. Should the government resort to extraordinary taxation, the resulting protest may reach revolutionary proportions. Money cannot buy everything, but a shortage of it can sometimes bring on a revolution.

58. Pettee, *Process*, p. 58.

Precipitants. Having already discussed precipitants in regard to social movements, we can now merely distinguish planned from unplanned precipitants in revolution. *Planned precipitants* are provocative actions taken by revolutionaries to force the revolution to break out. *Unplanned precipitants* are incidents that trigger a much wider response than anyone could have foreseen. There also seems to be a middle category, which occurs without foreknowledge but is exploited by revolutionaries just waiting for such a chance. Finally, since all revolutionary situations do not culminate in actual revolutions, there is the possibility of an "antiprecipitant," which can be defined as "some action or event" that "thwarts or balks the operation of the intrusive factor." [59]

A good instance of a planned precipitant would be the general strike strategy or the establishment of one or more guerrilla focos. The classic example of the unplanned precipitant is the storming of the Bastille, an almost empty Parisian fortress, by an angry mob on July 14, 1789. If our interpretation of the meaning of the military coup against the Allende government in Chile in 1973 is correct, it served as an antiprecipitant in the developing revolutionary situation in that country.

Phases of Revolution

It is widely held that revolutions have to traverse three clear and distinct phases. The idea is based upon the course of the French Revolution of 1789, which has served as a paradigm for so much theorizing about revolution. The Edwards-Brinton three-phase model is the best rendition of this approach.[60] It sees phase I as the *rule of the moderates*, phase II as the *rule of the radicals*, and phase III as the *"Thermidor" or downturn in the revolutionary process.*

THE MODERATE PHASE.   Phase I is inaugurated more by the collapse of the old regime than by its overthrow. Thus, the old regime's inherent weaknesses as much or more than external revolutionary pressures account for the early victories of the revolution. Initial beneficiaries of the collapse are the moderates, who are chiefly drawn from the upper and middle social strata. Their background disposes them to view the revolution in essentially political terms and to reject grandiose plans of social reorganization. This caution along with their scruples against needless bloodshed prevents them from acting decisively against the revolution's inner and outer enemies.

59. MacIver, *Causation*, p. 179.
60. See the works cited in note 54.

The moderates proceed to lose control over the situation, since they "always try to govern the army by political instead of military methods. The results are uniformly and universally disastrous. The army is demoralized and defeated. The revolution is put in jeopardy." [61] Given their dismal performance and the desire of many to push the revolution on further and faster, a split occurs in the revolutionary coalition. While the moderates temporarily retain control over the formal machinery of government, their opponents, the radicals, establish a virtual counter-government. This "dual power" situation finds the radicals strong in the army or at the capital.

THE RADICAL PHASE. The moderate phase is terminated by a coup installing the radicals in power. The high point of the radical phase in the Edwards-Brinton model (phase II) is the Reign of Terror, another term taken from the French paradigm. Why the Terror emerges is disputed. For those (like Lyford Edwards) friendly to revolution, the Terror is a rational strategic move necessitated by domestic and foreign assaults on the revolution. The Terror is a carefully orchestrated scheme for scaring people. Its goal is to discourage or eliminate counterrevolutionaries, mobilize the halfhearted, and test the mettle of self-proclaimed revolutionaries.

Other interpretations of the Terror are more critical. In the conservative tradition the Terror is seen as a logical result, but not as a rational act. Two factors explain it: (1) since the revolution has rejected traditional norms and institutions, the violent passions of men are allowed a field day; and (2) the Terror stems from the radicals' attempt to realize hopelessly utopian goals and their search for scapegoats when these goals prove, as they must, illusory. Crane Brinton occupies a middle position between Edwards and the conservatives when he speaks of a Reign of Terror *and Virtue*. According to Brinton, the radicals wish to cleanse society of the seamier and more corrupt forms of human behavior. Certain forms of pleasure and entertainment are to give way to a puritanical revolutionary ethic.

As a system of rule, the radical phase is a dictatorship that goes well beyond the Terror in the narrow sense. We can encompass the more salient traits of the radical dictatorship within three major points. The first is increased political and economic *centralization*. The radicals tend to concentrate political power in the capital city at the expense of the periphery. This is understandable since the capital city is generally the

61. Edwards, *Natural History*, p. 146.

epicenter of the revolution, which contains the most ardent (i.e., radical) revolutionaries. Enthusiasm for the revolution (at least in Western-style revolutions) tends to shade off as one gets farther and farther away from the center. Certainly, Paris in the French Revolution of 1789 (as well as those of 1830, 1848, and 1871), London in the English Revolution of the 1640s and 1650s, and Moscow and St. Petersburg in the Russian Revolution of 1917 follow this stereotype.

In a somewhat different sense, the radicals institute greater centralized controls over the country's economy. Greater economic controls may come in part from ideology, but they also stem from the need to ensure that food and other supplies are enough to keep the capital city and other revolutionary centers alive. Peasants in the countryside may not be overly sympathetic to the revolution and will hold back supplies unless forced to deliver.

A second major trait of the radical dictatorship is the *heightened social conflict* generated by the revolution and the *revolutionary justice* that deals with that conflict (and perhaps throws still more oil on the fire). Because of its political and economic measures, the radical dictatorship succeeds willy-nilly in raising the level of conflict between classes and strata. "Aristocrat" became a term of abuse during the French Revolution as did "bourgeois" in the Russian and other Communist revolutions. We have already mentioned that regional attitudes toward a revolution can vary considerably. The radical dictatorship does not like fence-sitting and forces the various parts of the country to make a decision for or against the revolution and, more narrowly, for or against the radicals.

Most revolutionary civil wars (e.g., the Russian, Chinese, English, Mexican, and Spanish) display interesting political maps characterized by distinct zones for and against the revolution. However, it is more than a suspicion that many people, perhaps a numerical majority, reject both the revolutionary side and the counterrevolutionary side.

Finally, religious conflict rages because the radicals are ideologically or politically hostile to the old-time religion. Their ideology may be agnostic or atheistic or they may view the church as one of the pillars of the old regime they are trying to destroy. But religion and the religious die hard, and thus the radicals must fight a war on this political front too.

With all this internal conflict and the possible threat of outside military intervention, we can understand to a degree how due process of law seems a needless and dangerous luxury to the radicals. Instead, there emerges revolutionary justice, which acts most severely against clearly recognized enemies of the revolution. Since the rules of evidence are often scrapped, however, large numbers of people are convicted and punished (sometimes by death) on the flimsiest hearsay. What this sometimes amounts to is that some radical supporters use the campaign against counterrevolutionaries as a pretext for settling old scores and realizing purely personal vendettas. (Of course, much the same thing goes on on the other side of the barricades or combat lines, when counter-revolutionaries get their hands on real or alleged revolutionary activists or sympathizers.) While two wrongs don't make a right, they certainly complicate the moral equation.

A final and most intriguing feature of the radical dictatorship is the *emergence of the ultrarevolutionaries*. These are sects of revolutionary purists, who accuse the radicals of betraying the "true" revolution. Ul-trarevolutionaries generally appeal to some of the lowest strata of society because they consider the radicals as a closed clique, perhaps no better than the defunct ruling class of the old regime. They demand a revving up of the revolutionary engine and instant delivery of some of the grandiose promises that originally justified the upheaval.

We have already mentioned the Fifth Monarchy men who attacked Oliver Cromwell (a radical in the context of the English Revolution) as the betrayer of the true religious or millenary meaning of the revolution. The French Revolution too had its share of ultrarevolutionaries, who accused the radical government of Maximilien Robespierre of doing too little and going too slow even during the high pressure of the Terror of 1793–94. In the Russian Revolution of 1917 factions such as the anarchists and "left Communists" charged Lenin and the Bolsheviks with shortchanging the proletariat. Since the ultrarevolutionaries are willing to act on their beliefs, the radicals may end up fighting not only the counterrevolutionaries on the right, but also the ultrarevolutionaries on the left.

THE TERMINAL PHASE.   Phase III or the terminal phase of revolution is generally called the Thermidor after the month in the French revolutionary calendar when Robespierre, the radical leader, and his closest associates were removed from power and executed. More broadly, the Thermidor is considered a decisive downturn in the revolutionary process. The "symptoms" of Thermidor include ouster of the extreme radicals, "rehabilitation" of moderates and other political purge-victims, deemphasis on "revolutionary virtue," loosening of government controls and pressures, and increased bureaucratization and institutionalization.

Two outstanding factors contribute to this winding down of revolution.

One is the mental and moral exhaustion produced by the revolutionary crisis itself. Civil war, foreign war, the Terror, hardship and privation—these push people to the verge of physical and mental collapse. The movement for more revolution has simply run out of steam, and some backsliding is inevitable. The second factor is the emergence of a new elite. There is a great temptation for the new holders of political and economic power to defend their gains and to forget about advancing the revolution. As Gaetano Mosca once put it, "Love for the instrument becomes stronger and more active than for the end that should be reached through the instrument." [62]

Since the three-stage model is based on Western revolutionary experience, it should come as no surprise that non-Western revolutions do not fit it. Revolutions such as the Chinese and the Cuban do not show a neat three-stage trajectory. It is thus better to think of two opposed tendencies at work in all revolutions: one pushes the revolution further and faster, the other pushes to wind it down and institutionalize it. The first can be called the "law of revolutionary hypertrophy," an umbrella term that covers a variety of radicalizing trends. The increased social conflict, for example, produces a dynamism making for change. Revolutions also tend to produce factions that try to outbid each other in advancing the revolution to new and more ambitious goals.

The opposite tendency, which we can call the "law of revolutionary entropy," is also an umbrella concept. It encompasses the wear and tear of revolutionary turmoil, the emergence of new "vested interests," and the routinization of the revolutionary organization. The entropic forces work against the hypertrophic ones, producing a pattern of phases that may or may not be threefold. Revolutionary leaders such as Mao with the Great Leap Forward and the Cultural Revolution may be able temporarily to counteract entropic forces. However, in the long run it appears likely that entropic forces will get the upper hand in all revolutions. They will wind the revolution down to a point where a new "establishment" rules in relative tranquillity. Literally understood, the term "permanent revolution" is self-contradictory.

In this chapter we have examined the important topic of social movements and revolutions. (Social movements, at least most of them, are actually political movements, but we have stuck with the traditional

62. Gaetano Mosca, "Il principio aristocratico e il democratico," *Partiti e sindacati nella crisi della regime parlamentare* (Bari: Laterza, 1949), p. 29.

terminology.) Our study of these topics has also revealed something about political science and social science in general: their controversiality. The dispute between the orthodox and revisionist views of social movements, as well as that between conspiracy and "mass explosion" theories of revolution, is not just a dispute about the "facts." Such disputes concern the perspective within which to place the facts to get their meaning. Unfortunately, the perspective problem can involve moral and ideological choices and often does. Hopefully, our giving some play to both sides in some of these disputes will give readers a chance to make up their own minds.

At any rate, our conviction has been that the theory and practice of social movements and revolutions are appropriate material for an introductory textbook. Unconventional political behavior is as much political behavior as more conventional forms, such as those treated in the next two chapters on parties and interest groups. Social movements and revolution often create political regimes in their own image, though considerable distortion of this image inevitably occurs over time.

Moreover, public policy in many regimes is concerned with how to deal with the demands of social movements and how to counter the possible threat of revolution. Environment, women's liberation, minority problems are not merely abstract items of a government's policy agenda; each involves a corresponding social movement, whose militancy might annoy, if not alarm, governmental leaders.

STUDY QUESTIONS

1. Compare the orthodox and revisionist views of social movements. Is one of these views superior to the other? Why or why not?

2. How do youth movements differ from the other categories of social movements? Was the French Student Revolt of May–June 1968 an abortive revolution or not?

3. Why are coups d'etat, revolts, and secessions often mistaken for true revolutions? Why do the simple forms of these political activities fall short of the revolutionary threshold?

4. What is wrong with the statement: "revolutions are always the upheaval of the lower classes against the upper or ruling class"?

5. Is it important to discuss long-term causes of revolution or can you just start with middle-term causes? Why?

6. What is the three-phase pattern that many think characterizes revolutions? What are the weaknesses in this theory?

7. How can economic phenomena figure in the causal pattern of revolutions? Does the notion of relative deprivation (RD) help much in understanding revolution and other forms of political violence?

SUGGESTIONS FOR FURTHER READING

ABEL, THEODORE. *The Nazi Movement.* New York: Atherton Press, 1966.

ALMOND, GABRIEL. *The Appeals of Communism.* Princeton: Princeton University Press, 1954.

BRINTON, CRANE. *The Anatomy of Revolution.* New York: Vintage Books, 1960.

BURKS, R. V. *The Dynamics of Communism in Eastern Europe.* Princeton: Princeton University Press, 1961.

COHAN, A. S. *Theories of Revolution.* London: Nelson, 1975.

COHN, NORMAN. *The Pursuit of the Millennium.* New York: Oxford University Press, 1970.

DAVIES, JAMES C., ed. *When Men Revolt and Why.* New York: Free Press, 1971.

EDWARDS, LYFORD P. *The Natural History of Revolution.* Chicago: University of Chicago Press, 1970.

GREENE, THOMAS H. *Comparative Revolutionary Movements.* Englewood Cliffs, N.J.: Prentice-Hall, 1974.

GREGOR, A. JAMES. *Interpretations of Fascism.* Morristown, N.J.: General Learning Press, 1974.

GURR, TED R. *Why Men Rebel.* Princeton: Princeton University Press, 1971.

HAGOPIAN, MARK N. *The Phenomenon of Revolution.* New York: Harper & Row, 1974.

HEBERLE, RUDOLPH. *Social Movements.* New York: Appleton-Century-Crofts, 1951.

HOFFER, ERIC. *The True Believer.* New York: Mentor Books, 1958.

KORNHAUSER, WILLIAM. *The Politics of Mass Society.* New York: Free Press, 1963.

LANTERNARI, VITO. *The Religions of the Oppressed.* New York: Mentor Books, 1965.

LE BON, GUSTAVE. *The Crowd.* New York: Viking Press, 1960.

MERKL, PETER. *Political Violence Under the Swastika.* Princeton: Princeton University Press, 1975.

REJAI, MOSTAFA. *The Comparative Study of Revolutionary Strategy.* New York: David McKay, 1977.

SMELSER, NEIL J. *Theory of Collective Behavior.* New York: Free Press, 1962.

SOREL, GEORGES. *Reflections on Violence.* Glencoe, Ill.: Free Press, 1950.

8

Competitive Parties and Party Systems

This chapter is concerned with the role of political parties in competitive systems. In contrast to the one-party regimes of chapters 4 and 5, in competitive systems several parties contest elections in relative freedom. Competition is thus compatible both with a highly restricted suffrage where perhaps 2 percent of the total population vote and with a situation where one of the parties controls the government for extended periods and has huge legislative majorities. It was the lack of competitiveness in single-party regimes that caused Sigmund Neumann to deny that the single party was a party in the true sense of the term.[1] For Neumann a party is a "part," which can be understood only in connection with other parts or parties.

As there is little consensus on what a political party really is, some prefer to term "parties" all those groups that so consider themselves. One problem with such an operational definition is that many political parties, especially French ones, have rejected the label "party" in favor of "rally," "union," "movement," and "section." There are two main tendencies among nonoperational definitions of party: one based on ideology, the other on power.

1. Sigmund Neumann, "Toward a Comparative Study of Political Parties," in *Modern Political Parties*, ed. S. Neumann (Chicago: University of Chicago Press, 1956), p. 395.

British statesman Edmund Burke in 1770 represented the ideological approach when he defined a party as a "body of men united, for promoting by their joint endeavors the national interest, upon some particular principle in which they are all agreed." [2] A little thought should show that Burke's assumption of ideological consensus tends to be less true the larger a party is and the more it moves toward the middle of the road.

Max Weber considered parties to exist in nearly all formal organizations. The goal of a party thus is "to secure power . . . for its leaders in order to attain ideal or material advantages for its active members. These advantages may consist in the realization of certain objective policies or the attainment of personal advantages or both." [3] Weber thus stressed power, leaving open the question of ideological versus selfish purposes. This suggests a simple dichotomy contrasting parties of "principle" with parties of "patronage."

Basing our own definition on Burke and Weber, we can define a "political party" as *an association formed to influence the content and conduct of public policy in favor of some set of ideological principles and/or interests either through direct exercise of power or by participation in elections*. This somewhat ungainly definition should embrace minor or "splinter" parties that do not seriously lust after power and exclude mere interest groups that exert political influence in more oblique ways. Political parties wish to influence public policy: the major parties, through the direct exercise of power involved in actually taking part in government; the minor parties, through participation in elections influencing the public and the policy-makers. In reality, we find a continuum of motivations with some parties leaning toward ideology, others toward interests, still others in between (see figure 8.1).

PARTIES IN COMPETITIVE SYSTEMS

Types of Parties

If we ask organizational and sociological questions in addition to the ones about ideology and power, five different types of parties have been found in competitive systems. These are (1) proto-parties, (2) cadre

2. Edmund Burke, "Thoughts on the Cause of the Present Discontents," *Burke's Works* (London: Geo. Bell & Sons, 1893), 1:375.
3. Max Weber, *Economy and Society* (Totowa, N.J.: Bedminster Press, 1968), 1:284.

Figure 8.1. The Continuum of Party Motivations

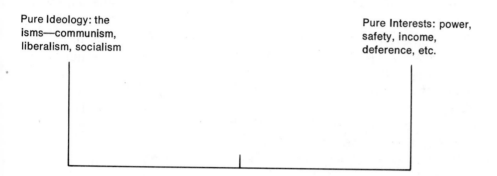

Pure Ideology: the
isms—communism,
liberalism, socialism

Pure Interests: power,
safety, income,
deference, etc.

parties, (3) mass parties, (4) dictatorial parties, and (5) catchall parties.

PROTO-PARTIES. Full-fledged political parties are a more recent phenomenon than many realize. History speaks, to be sure, of the oligarchic and democratic "parties" in the Greek city-states, of Guelphs and Ghibellines in the late Middle Ages, and so on. But such formations—factions is the best name for them—lacked the apparatus of modern political parties. As one political scientist points out, "until well into the nineteenth century . . . the terms 'party,' 'faction,' and 'interest,' were used interchangeably to mean any kind of identifiable current of opinion or set of common goals, organized or unorganized . . . bearing on public authorities." [4]

We can learn something about proto-parties if we examine the controversy about the Whigs and Tories in eighteenth-century England. In one view, both of these groups had enough organizational substance and ideological distinctiveness to qualify as true political parties. Thus the eighteenth-century dualism of Whigs and Tories appears the direct ancestor of the nineteenth-century dualism of Liberals and Conservatives, and the twentieth-century version of Labor versus Conservatives.

The historian Sir Lewis Namier, however, finds this line of thought anachronistic since it reads later developments back into earlier history. Instead of a precocious two-party system, he finds "three broad

4. Austin Ranney, "The Concept of 'Party,' " in *Political Research and Political Theory*, ed. O. Garceau (Cambridge, Mass.: Harvard University Press, 1968), p. 146.

divisions, based on type and not on party" in the eighteenth-century House of Commons."[5] In the first group were the "followers of Court and Administration . . . *par excellence* a group of permanent 'ins.'" Some of this group, sometimes called the "King's Friends," supported the government by reason of patronage and a host of "corrupt" practices. Others felt it was their duty to support the king and "his" government. Pitted against this group were the "independent country gentlemen, of their own choice the permanent 'outs.'"[6] In between the "ins" and the "outs" was another group that "occupied the centre of the arena" and attracted the "attention of the public and of history." This middle group was composed of the "political factions contending for power, the forerunners of a parliament based on a party system."[7] Namier further suggests that there was a blurriness as to where one group started up and another left off.

Namier's whole analysis suggests that extreme caution should be used in talking of full-scale political parties before the middle and late nineteenth century. The amorphous aggregates he describes can be called "proto-parties" because they foreshadow true parties without being so themselves.

CADRE PARTIES. The second type of party, the cadre party,[8] is the next stage in the evolution of parties—appearing in the last several decades of the last century. Representing an advance in organization and ideology, this type of party is dominated by notables, people of high status who have sufficient leisure to devote to politics. Formed before the broadening and final universalization of the suffrage, the cadre party depends on upper- and middle-class electorate, membership, leadership, and financial backing. Cadre parties begin as proto-parties (i.e., as rather vague groupings in parliament). However, they are led to form the barest rudiments of an organization outside parliament to help elect M.P.s. Still, the organizational and ideological level of the cadre party is low, largely because the party qua organization has little to do. Through their association with the higher social strata, the politics of cadre parties runs from extreme conservatism to moderate reform-

5. Sir Lewis Namier, *Personalities and Power* (New York: Harper & Row, 1965), p. 21.
6. Ibid., p. 22.
7. Ibid.
8. *Cadre* means "framework" in French. Thus the original connotation of this term refers to the party organization as a whole. (The Chinese Communists, however, have popularized a usage of "cadre" that relates to individuals. Their use suggests "political activist" or lower-level leaders.)

ism. They are basically content with the existing order and approve of the general direction of change. Thus, they have beliefs, but not much ideology in the sense of deep criticism and ambitious plans and programs. Likewise, there is no need for a big organization to mobilize the masses. In the nineteenth century the masses did not vote, and for many nineteenth-century cadre parties, this was how things should be.

Leadership in the cadre party is provided by the *caucus*, (i.e., the meeting of the party's parliamentary contingent). Discipline is lax, some historians say, because of the "rugged individualism" and middle-class types that dominate the party. The weapon of expulsion is hard to use against renegades, when the concept of membership is virtually nonexistent. The cadre party is more like an informal club than a disciplined army on a war footing. This organizational looseness is what Maurice Duverger calls *weak articulation*.[9]

While the traditional cadre party had no need for vast sums for "media blitzes," it obviously needed some funds for campaigning, which sometimes amounted to virtual bribery of the small local electorate. The method of party financing bears directly upon the political behavior of the party itself. The financial formula for the cadre party is a *small number of large contributions*. It can cover its limited expenses with the assistance of a small group of wealthy patrons. One does not have to be an economic determinist to see how this sort of funding will diminish a party's zeal to "bust the trusts" or otherwise damage the interests of its benefactors.

Though the heyday of the cadre party is long past, it still has survivals in contemporary party systems. Many small Liberal parties, as in Italy or in the Netherlands (People's Party for Freedom and Democracy), defend similar principles, have a similar organization, and appeal to similar groups as their counterparts a century ago. The difference is that a century ago such parties could capture a majority of the votes, while today 5–10 percent seems a difficult target.

Perhaps the best recent example of the cadre party is the French Radical-Socialist party of the Third, Fourth, and early part of the Fifth French Republics.[10] The party is also instructive on how misleading party names can be. The official title taken back in 1901 was *Parti républicain*

9. Maurice Duverger, *Political Parties* (New York: John Wiley, 1963), pp. 40–52.
10. This analysis relies heavily on Philip M. Williams, *Crisis and Compromise: Politics in the Fourth Republic* (Garden City, N.Y.: Anchor Books, 1966), chap. 9.

radical et radical-socialiste. Despite this flamboyant leftist symbolism, the party behaved far more moderately, and even conservatively, than its name suggested. The party after World War II was radical in no modern sense and was still less a socialist party. It had a kind of split political personality or, as critics put it, its members' "hearts were on the left," but their "pocketbooks were on the right."

Still more disparaging were those observers who found that the Radicals were "without a program, without an organization, without leadership, and without any membership to speak of." Nonetheless, this ethereal organization could be described as virtually dominant in the Third Republic (1871–1940) and as of strategic importance in the Fourth Republic (1946–58)—nine of the twenty-one premiers of that republic were Radicals.

If any party was a loose coalition of notables, it was the Radical-Socialist party. While on paper it had a federal-type organization, the accent was definitely on local autonomy, where the notables of small-town France held sway. "The lowest territorial unit was the committee (comité) based on the commune or canton [i.e., towns or local units], and above it were departmental and sometimes regional federations. . . . The committees differed from the sections of other parties in being entirely self-sufficient. . . . The federations enjoyed full independence in choosing candidates and election tactics. . . ." [11] This independence of electoral strategy meant that in some districts the Radicals made electoral alliances with the Socialists on the left, while in others they did the same thing with Conservatives on the right.

No central party authority could approve or disapprove of these opportunistic maneuvers. Indeed for several years in the early Fourth Republic many Radicals actually belonged to two parties: one, the Radicals proper; the other, the Gaullist R.P.F., or Rally of the French People. This "bigamy" as it was called at the time was justified under the pretext that the Gaullists were a "rally" (in French, *rassemblement*) and not an ordinary political party. Understandably, party indiscipline and factionalism were rampant in parliament. It was common practice for the Radical party to take part in no-confidence votes that brought down governments headed by premiers from the Radical party.

MASS PARTIES. According to Duverger, mass parties represent the true embodiment of the party principle. Their emergence is both cause and effect of broadening of voting to include literally all adults.

11. Ibid., p. 128.

Since the United States achieved white manhood suffrage relatively early, Americans are wont to forget that universal or even manhood suffrage is essentially a twentieth-century phenomenon. The previous century is a series of steps toward that goal. In some countries the steps were larger and came sooner than in others. In the Netherlands, for example, the electorate in 1800 included about 12 percent of adult male population; by 1890 this was up to 27 percent; by 1900 it reached 47 percent; by 1910 63 percent. Full suffrage came for men in 1917 and for women two years later.[12]

Mass parties were thus a political and organizational response to a broadened suffrage and were the champions of a further broadening. Their origin, in sharp contrast to proto-parties and cadre parties, was outside of parliament. Based on the lower strata, mass parties assumed the character of social movements looking toward workers, peasants, or religious groups. Much of their organization was developed before they scored electoral victories and won many seats in parliament. Their successful agitation for wider suffrage brought them into the parliament with considerable strength. In most European countries true mass parties espoused some brand of socialism and appealed to urban workers. Their success was contagious because peasant and religious parties then tried also to adopt the mass-party format. Even cadre parties made some gestures in this direction.

On almost all counts the mass party is the opposite of the cadre party. The level of ideology, for example, is much higher in the mass party. Ideology is used for political mobilization, which has been the prime task of mass parties. Given the humble social background for the mass base, the ideology naturally has tended to criticize or reject the existing order. However, for many early socialist parties the militancy in words was often combined with moderation in practice.

Mobilizing the masses and working for ideological goals are tasks requiring organization. Instead of a parliamentary caucus of party notables, the mass parties have developed a bureaucratic hierarchy based on *branches*. As these branches throughout the country have been tightly controlled by the party central, the mass parties have had what Duverger calls *strong articulation*. While the cadre party's leaders came from relatively high social strata, those of the mass party have often been of working-class background. Duverger relates all these points by con-

12. Arend Lijphart, "The Netherlands," in *Electoral Behavior: A Comparative Handbook*, ed. R. Rose (New York: Free Press, 1974), p. 230.

cluding that "the branch is not only working for success in the elections, but to give its members a political education, and thus to form an elite proceeding directly from the masses and capable of acting in their name." [13]

To reach such ambitious goals the mass party sets up a number of *auxiliary organizations* for sportive, recreational, cultural, and other activities. The aim is to create and reinforce a sense of togetherness and camaraderie that marks the "movement" off from outsiders. Newspapers and other periodicals are founded to spread the party's views and support the ideas of the faithful. In contrast to the limited and intermittent commitment of the cadre party, the involvement of the active mass-party member is expected to be total. The distinction between private and political life loses its meaning.

Quite naturally, membership is formalized and regularized in the mass party. One takes out a membership card and pays regular dues. The formula for party finance is *a large number of small contributions*. This is followed both to reduce dependence on wealthy notables and to demonstrate the "faith" of ordinary members. If party leaders are elected to parliament, they often have to hand over part of their salaries to the party treasury. This too has a dual purpose: to get money for the party and to show that personal gain has no place in the party.

While membership in the cadre party is *direct*—one simply joins a local party organization, the situation with the mass party is more complex. While there is direct affiliation with a local branch, there can also be *indirect membership*. In this latter case one becomes a party member by virtue of membership in some intermediate organization such as a trade union. Even today the vast bulk of the members of the British Labor party are indirect members, because their unions are organizationally connected with the party.

The French Socialist party (PS, or *Parti socialiste*), known for most of its history as the SFIO, for *Section Francaise de l'Internationale Ouvrière*, is a good example of a traditional mass party that almost became a cadre party. Numbering more than 335,000 members in 1945, it fell steadily throughout the Fourth Republic to 120,000 members in 1955. In the early days of the Fifth Republic both its members (79,000 in 1960) and voters continued to decline. However, the early 1970s saw not only a new name and reorganization of the party, but also a recovery of members back toward the 1955 figure. Moreover, the party's leader,

13. Duverger, *Parties*, p. 35.

Francois Mitterand, was but narrowly defeated by Valerie Giscard d'Estaing in the presidential elections of 1974. Mitterand was a front candidate of the French left, which included the powerful Communist party.

Before the recent reorganization, the grassroots-level organization of the party was the *section*, which grouped together members from cities, towns, and villages. Sections were placed together in departmental federations, each of which had a secretary with considerable powers and autonomy. On the national level the base organization was the National Congress, which met once a year. Chosen by the large National Congress was the typical steering committee, called the Directing Committee. Also following the typical mass party format was the proviso that only a minority of the Directing Committee could be M.P.s. The head executive board of the party was the Bureau of ten members, which was empowered to make decisions on policy, tactics, discipline, and so forth. The party was capped by a general secretary, and there was also a National Council composed of the secretaries of the departmental federations.

In the postwar period the French Socialists have proven to be a moderate Marxist-oriented party, which has rejected violence and preached the attainment of the workers' goals through peaceful parliamentary methods. In the late 1940s and early 1950s they were considered part of the "third force," which sought to preserve the parliamentary system against the threat of Gaullist authoritarianism on the right and that of Communist revolution on the left. Later, the Socialists went into opposition, a position they have essentially maintained throughout the Fifth Republic.

Throughout the postwar era the French Socialists—as also the Italian Socialists—have had to contend with a strong Communist party, which could claim to be more truly a socialist and a workers' party. Nonetheless, the revitalization of the 1970s has led to unity-of-action agreements with the Communists, a situation that hearkens back to the Popular Front government of the late 1930s. That the Socialists are something more than weak junior partners of the Communists is suggested by three major recent developments.[14] First, the party leader (Mitterand) and the leadership in general have been strengthened. Second, the party has increased its membership and has its strongest and most dynamic

14. Vincent Wright and Howard Machin, "The French Socialist Party in 1973: Performance and Prospects," *Government and Opposition* 9 (Spring 1974): 125.

organization in many years. Finally, the party's appeal has spread to nearly all segments of French society.

DICTATORIAL PARTIES. These parties, which Duverger terms "devotee parties," are called "dictatorial parties" here because their victory would lead to a regime along the lines of those discussed in chapters 4 and 5. Organizationally they appear an accentuated version of the mass party and, save for their historical importance, might be treated as a subtype of the other. The dictatorial party has a more rigid and radical ideology than the mass party does. Its revolutionary rhetoric carries a greater degree of conviction. The party head and the top leaders exercise the most stringent controls over all ranks of the party. Ironically, active control may be stronger before the seizure of power than afterward, because in the later situation the leaders are saddled with many new governmental tasks. These obviously cause a time-drain away from party work, narrowly speaking.

The dictatorial party is more selective in membership recruitment than is an ordinary mass party. This type of party wants time to test a prospective member's loyalty and ideological orthodoxy. The Communists call this probationary period "candidate membership." Rather than stressing the branch, as does the mass party, the dictatorial party pyramids up from the cell (Communists) or the militia (Fascists) to the top party organs, more or less on the patterns discussed in chapters 4 and 5.

Clearly, large Communist parties like those of France and Italy in the first decade or so after 1945 followed the model of the dictatorial party, champing at the bit to overthrow constitutionalism in favor of a Soviet-style dictatorship. The issue in the 1970s is much more complex: it has been called the issue of Eurocommunism. What scholars, politicians, and journalists are debating is whether or not the French and Italian (and the recently legalized Spanish) Communist parties have shaken off their Stalinist pasts.

According to one school of thought, the French and Italian parties are wolves in sheep's clothing. Their leaders are Leninist revolutionaries who pay lip service to the ideals of constitutionalism and democracy in order to throw other factions off guard. These critics point to the rigid discipline of Communist parties, which exceeds that of all other major parties. Furthermore, despite occasional criticisms of Soviet policy, such as the invasion of Czechoslovakia in 1968, Communist parties (in particular, the French) are extremely defensive about the USSR, which remains a hard-line dictatorship.

On the other side, there are observers of both French and Italian Communist parties who consider them mass parties in which enthusiasm but not fanaticism reigns. Ideology has been watered down by a large dose of political compromise and pragmatism. Georges Lavau, a French political scientist, denies that the French Communist party is a threat to the political system of the Fifth French Republic.[15] On the contrary, the party has performed important functions that actually work in favor of stabilizing the system. The first of these is "legitimation," not in the sense of total, enthusiastic support of all aspects of polity and society, but in the sense of a partial acceptance of the fundamental rules of French politics. According to Lavau, "The party does not merely adhere to the gamut of values and principles of the political system. It adds something to them and accepts them on condition that they be developed. To the panoply of Republican principles it adds socialism, and the role of the working class as protagonist in the class struggle."[16] As Lavau points out, these ideas also have deep roots in the French political culture.

The second function of the French—and one could also add the Italian—Communist party is to be the "tribune of the people." In this role, party spokesmen keep a sharp eye out for political and economic abuses and shortcomings, and their victims. Since such are easy enough to find in any modern industrial society, the Communists become bold champions of the insulted and the injured. This sometimes vociferous defense of groups, which are usually outside the standard Marxist category of "progressive" classes and strata, may even help to defuse problems before they reach a critical stage.

Finally, the party is the largest and strongest opposition group. In chapter 2 we discussed the institutionalization of opposition in the context of modern parliaments. We found that one type of opposition combats the socioeconomic order, while another, milder type merely rejects the regime. If Lavau is correct, the French Communist party has toned down these two types of opposition and, despite its rhetorical outbursts, has confined its effective opposition to government policies and personnel. Evidence for such a conclusion is found in "all the steps the PCF has taken in recent years to prove its sincerity, its attachment

15. Georges Lavau, "The PCF, the State, and the Revolution: An Analysis of Party Policies, Communications, and Popular Culture," in *Communism in Italy and France*, ed. D. Blackmer and S. Tarrow (Princeton: Princeton University Press, 1975), pp. 87–139.
16. Ibid., p. 97.

to the rules of liberal and pluralistic democracy, its internal democratization, its independence from the Communist Party of the Soviet Union, and its desire to avoid its dominance over its political allies." [17]

For these and other reasons many feel that participation of the French and Italian Communists in their respective governments, instead of being harmful, would be positively beneficial to the cause of constitutionalism and reform. In Italy, this whole project is called the "historical compromise," which would entail a coalition government of Communists, Socialists, left-wing Christian Democrats, and perhaps other "progressive" forces. Indeed, preliminary steps to this end appear to have been taken, since the present governmental formula, though not a full-fledged coalition, involves what we will call below a "negative coalition." In France, the next elections will determine whether the experiment will be tried in that country as well.

CATCHALL PARTIES. While most modern political parties fall under one of the previous types, some do not. Frank Sorauf, for example, looking to Duverger's basic dichotomy of cadre and mass parties, found that the American major parties must be considered a "hybrid" form.[18] While they are something more than old-line cadre parties, the Democrats and the Republicans are something less than European-style mass parties. Otto Kirchheimer went further and questioned the relevance of the traditional labels to postwar trends in European political parties. He saw a convergence toward a new form, which he called the "catchall people's party"—"catchall" for short.[19] The convergence is from the two directions of the mass party and the cadre party.

From the mass party side come parties previously dedicated to full socialism, such as the British Labor party or the German Social Democratic party. From the cadre party side come such parties as the British Conservatives, the French Gaullists, and the German Christian Democrats. At the heart of the catchall phenomenon is a simple desire: *to win elections.*

As the twentieth century wore on, European Socialist parties with their unadulterated ideology and mainly working class voters ran into a problem of diminishing returns. In Germany before Hitler, this was

17. Ibid., p. 107.
18. Frank Sorauf, *Political Parties in the American System* (Boston: Little, Brown, 1964), pp. 44–48.
19. Otto Kirchheimer, "The Transformation of the Western European Party Systems," in *Political Parties and Political Development*, ed. Joseph La-Palombara and M. Wiener (Princeton: Princeton University Press, 1966), pp. 177–200.

called the "one-third barrier" because the Social Democrats grew rapidly to about one-third of the votes and then stopped. The general dilemma of European socialism became this: either to preserve ideological and social traits and lose, or to modify or abandon some of these in order to win.

Cadre parties (or newly founded parties that hailed back to defunct cadre parties) had a similar problem. In order to do well with a mass electorate, certain ideological and organizational shifts were necessary. If the German Christian Democratic party had appealed exclusively to the Catholic middle classes as did its ancestor, the old Center party; if the British Conservatives had appealed mainly to the "establishment"; if the Gaullists since 1958 had confined themselves to the clerical and antirepublican right wing—none of these parties could have registered the substantial successes that they have achieved since 1945.

Both types of catchall party—former mass and former cadre—have hit upon the same solution on how to win: *to catch all, that is, to appeal to the maximum number of social groups, barring none or very few of them.* This involves soft-pedaling ideology in favor of group benefits. With the former Socialist mass parties, this means "deradicalization" and "demarxification": abandoning classic socialism and embracing the welfare state with its large private sector. With the former Liberal or Conservative cadre parties, the adjustment involves shelving old-fashioned laissez-faire capitalism and accepting, however reluctantly, the idea of a mixed economy.

Steering clear of ideological abstractions, the catchall strategy aims at specific rewards to a variety of broad interest groups. All catchall parties promise better conditions for businessmen, higher wages and better social insurance for workers, good prices and supports for farmers, security for the aged, help for small businessmen, better education and jobs for the youth, and the like.

Because of its preoccupation with voters, the catchall party lacks the mass party's concern with members. The leaders have no wish to create an indoctrinated, disciplined phalanx pointed toward the promised land of some ideology. Rather, they want to fashion the party's image and that of its candidates in a way to maximize votes. The primacy of electioneering involves stressing public relations techniques such as polling, television, and advertising.

The transition to the catchall format may not be easy and is certain to be controversial. This was the case with the German Social Democratic party, known as the SPD (*Sozialdemokratische Partei Deutschlands*).

Twenty years ago and still today an articulate left-wing minority recalls the party to its old socialist ideals and working-class constituency. In the 1945–52 period, SPD policy and strategy was dominated by its leader, Kurt Schumacher.[20] Sticking to a hard-line working-class and socialist approach, he stressed such ideas as nationalization of industry and a "neutralist" foreign policy. Schumacher's hard line may have been influenced by his long stay in Hitler's prisons, which ruined his health.

In the late 1950s, however, there occurred a decisive turning point in SPD history. Indeed, we can pinpoint the party congress of 1958 at Bad Godesburg as the critical stage. Here the party made an agonizing reappraisal of its ideological ballast and its electoral strategy and found them both wanting. As one student interpreted the results of the congress: "The significance of the *Godesburgerprogramm* is that it has no ideology. The party has changed enough so that an ideological program is no longer appropriate." [21] More broadly, this turning point involved a change in the party's perception of the public, which was no longer viewed as a "great thinking being which has to be rationally convinced with sophisticated arguments or inspired by the vision of a new society." Instead, the dominant approach—along catchall lines—was to "see the party's essential role vis-à-vis the public as offering a series of well-founded, concrete plans, which can be accepted or rejected depending on the voter's interests." [22]

Clearly the new approach worked, since the SPD's share of the popular vote increased for the next four elections (1961, 1965, 1969, 1972), although it has never won more votes than its main rival, the Christian Democratic party. However, its growth allowed it to form a coalition with the smaller Free Democratic party, which has controlled the chancellorship (Willy Brandt, Helmut Schmidt) since 1969.

Degrees of Affiliation and Motivation

The concept of party membership is much easier to handle with non-American political parties than it is with the Democrats and Republicans. Is a member of the latter two parties someone who votes for the party, or someone who registers to vote in a party primary, or someone

20. See Lewis J. Edinger, *Kurt Schumacher: A Study in Personality and Political Behavior* (Stanford: Stanford University Press, 1965).
21. Douglas A. Chalmers, *The Social Democratic Party of Germany* (New Haven: Yale University Press, 1964), p. 67.
22. Ibid., p. 83.

TABLE 8.1.   Main Traits of Political Parties

	Proto-Parties	Cadre Parties	Mass Parties	Dictatorial Parties	Catchall Parties
Social Appeal	upper classes and aristocracy	upper classes and middle classes	lower classes: workers and peasants	diverse: workers in communism	nearly all strata and groups
Level of Ideology	very low	very low	high	very high	low
Ratio of Members to Voters	low	low	high	medium to high	medium to low
Articulation	weak	weak	strong	very strong	moderate
Centralization	low	low	high	very high	medium
Membership	tiny	small	large	medium	medium to small
Leadership	aristocrats and notables	notables	new men and upper-class traitors to their class	new men and upper-class traitors to their class	middle class and lower middle class

who is active in the party's behalf? Fortunately for mass parties, dictatorial parties, and catchall parties in Europe and elsewhere, the concept of membership is clear: a member is someone who joins the party by taking out a membership card and paying dues.

Beyond this simple finding, we still can ask important questions about degrees of affiliation to political parties. Following Duverger's analysis, figure 8.2 represents this problem by a series of concentric circles.

The *inner circle* is the top elite of the party. In some parties this inner circle is dominated by legislators and other officeholders. In the mass and dictatorial parties regulations usually ensure that people outside parliament occupy some top posts. Not unexpectedly, the powers of the inner circle vary considerably if we compare cadre or catchall parties on the one hand, with mass or dictatorial parties on the other. While the inner circle always tends to dominate the party rank and file, the inner circle of mass or dictatorial parties dominates more aspects of members' lives more intensively. In a cadre or catchall party occasional "revolts" from below do succeed; with mass or dictatorial parties they almost never do.

The *militants* (or "activists") make up the second highest level of involvement in the party. Militants do something special for the party.

Figure 8.2.   Degrees of Affiliation to Political Parties

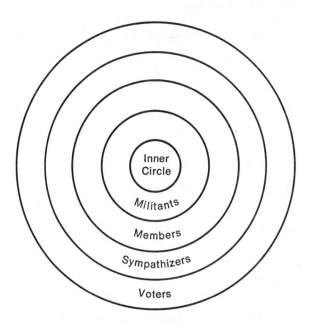

They not only go to meetings and read the party press, but they also spread the word on every possible occasion. They are missionaries for the party and perform many thankless, routine tasks for the party. Militants, however, can be motivated in different ways. One type of militant can be called the "true believer" (borrowing from Eric Hoffer) because of his faith in the mission and ideology of the party. This type for obvious reasons is most prevalent in mass and dictatorial parties. In catchall parties true believers are usually parts of a disgruntled left or right wing, bemoaning the loss of ideological purity caused by the catchall formula.

The polar opposite of the true believer is the "careerist," who joins and works for the party in order to advance his own prospects. His motivation falls into the Weberian category of purposive-rational action, in which desires for safety, income, deference, and the like are more important than principles. Many militants rank neither as unblemished true believers or complete careerists. The precise blend of motivations varies both as between different militants and over time in the same individual.

The concept of incentives helps to break down motivations of party

TABLE 8.2.   Incentives to Party Militancy

1. **Patronage:** one becomes a party militant in order to obtain an appointive public job for himself, his family, or his followers.
2. **Preferments:** one becomes a party militant in order to influence the awarding of government contracts or special government services to one's business interests or those of friends, relatives, etc.
3. **Political career:** one becomes a party militant to launch a career that should lead to elective or appointive public or party office.
4. **Economic rewards:** one becomes a party militant in order to make contacts that will sooner or later benefit one's private business or profession.
5. **Personal rewards:** one becomes a party militant because it gratifies a number of personal desires for personal involvement, public acclaim, friendship, and excitement.
6. **Policy-making:** one becomes a party militant so as to influence public policy for the sake of interest or principle.
7. **Ideology:** one becomes a party militant because the party embodies some cherished ideology and is a vehicle for spreading it.
8. **Identification:** one's militancy is reinforced through an emergent loyalty to the organization as such, whatever were the original incentive(s) for joining.

militants still further. Table 8.2 summarizes the findings of an American political scientist on specific reasons that make people show extraordinary commitment to political parties.[23] The incentives are by no means exclusive: a wide variety of incentive patterns are found with different militants.

Naturally different types of party differ regarding which incentives they offer the prospective militant. The ideologist will find little comfort in the cadre or catchall party. Patronage and preferments will be scarce commodities in a mass or dictatorial party seeking to overturn the status quo. On the other hand, someone after "personal rewards" like a sense of deep belonging should choose a mass or dictatorial party instead of a cadre or a catchall party.

The third circle consists of ordinary *members*. They are simple people who through pressures, subtle or otherwise, or through vague ideological conviction, have formally joined the party. Many members serve mainly to inflate party membership figures. Others, of course, attend meetings and rallies, talk politics, and engage in other activities that fall short of genuine militancy. Furthermore, there is movement back and forth, with formerly passive members turning militant and former militants falling back to a passive role.

23. Based on Sorauf, *Political Parties*, pp. 82–87.

The fourth circle includes party *sympathizers,* or supporters—individuals who prefer and defend the party without taking the final step of joining. Various reasons account for such reluctance. Sometimes, the sympathizer would like to join the party but fears that some action might be taken against him. He might lose his job, friends, family affection, or even suffer physical harm. In other cases the decision not to join is more purely voluntary. The sympathizer wishes to preserve his independence instead of undergoing the rigid discipline of the prospective party. The example of Communist "fellow-travelers" among American and European intellectuals is most instructive here.

Figure 8.2, since it implies that sympathizers have less party commitment than do members, is somewhat misleading. Actually, many sympathizers are more valuable man-for-man to a party than many of its regular members. Some sympathizers are so sympathetic that they are hard to tell from party militants. One difference, however, concerns dictatorial parties: when the party abruptly changes its "line" the sympathizers may yell "foul," while the old-time militants are expected to overcome negative feelings. Auxiliary organizations may be set up to gather in the maximum number of sympathizers. Some of these are formed to bring in people who side with the party in some issues, but not others. When the party tries to conceal its involvement in an organization, the latter can be termed a "front organization."

The outer circle of party affiliation encompasses the *voters.* Why people vote for and identify with parties is a complex problem. Several conclusions seem firm, however. First, voters tend to be less moved by ideology than those in the narrower circles of party involvement. This suggests, in general, that voters tend to be more moderate (i.e., more oriented toward the middle of the road) than are the militants and top leaders of their chosen party. There are, however, some cases, as perhaps Dutch politics from 1945 to 1965, in which top party leaders seem more moderate and pragmatic than their partisan voters.[24]

The act of voting is influenced by various factors. Table 8.3, based on a study of American voting, seems to summarize voter motivation on a cross-national basis.[25] The percentages in each category would, of course, vary from country to country and from time to time.

24. Arend Lijphart, *The Politics of Accommodation: Pluralism and Democracy in the Netherlands* (Berkeley: University of California Press, 1975).
25. Based on Angus Campbell et al., *The American Voter* (New York: John Wiley, 1963), pp. 124–44.

TABLE 8.3.   Influences on Party Choice in Voting

1. **Ideology and near-ideology:** voters either follow a full-fledged political ideology and vote for the party that best embodies it, or have a somewhat vaguer set of beliefs in which some ideological themes enter (near-ideology).
2. **Group benefits:** this general motivation focuses on the voter's group identification and his perception of the party's performance regarding "his" group. Opinion surveys often evoke responses such as "The Communists are for the worker"; "The Conservative party (Great Britain) is good for businessmen like myself"; "The Democrats help the common people like us."
3. **Nature of the times:** this category of voter constitutes something of a "swing-vote." They support the governing party (or one of the coalition partners) when their general feelings of social or economic well-being is positive. They punish them when things take a downward turn in their personal fortunes.
4. **No issue content:** this miscellaneous category includes voter motivations that elude the above categories. One subgroup has a party-orientation that seems to rest on tradition or habit—"My family has always voted for the X party." Another subgroup votes for a particular candidate: their vote for the party is a side effect of their basic motivation.

Types and Degrees of Centralization

Duverger suggests four dimensions of centralization in political parties: local, ideological, social, and federal.[26] Local centralization involves the balance of power between the center and the periphery of the party organization. How strong is the national organization, usually headquartered in the capital city, in relation to local organizations? In parties of the center and moderate right, generally cadre or catchall parties, party organization is quite decentralized. Local autonomy is considerable, and the local constituency organization can often buck the candidate choice of the central party authorities.

Ideological centralization concerns the "wingspread" of the left and right wings of a party. Every party has a right and left tendency, as well as a center or intermediate tendency. Whether these wings become organized *factions* is another question, as we will see below. Some ideological decentralization is likely in a catchall party, which pivots right and left from the center of the political spectrum. Parties whose main bond is religious or ethnic are also likely to harbor people of varying ideological persuasions. The German and, especially, the Italian Chris-

26. Duverger, *Parties*, pp. 52–60.

tian Democratic party, for example, include both "socialists" and devotees of "free enterprise."

Social centralization refers to the social base of a party. A party appealing solely to one social stratum is centralized, while one appealing to many strata would be socially decentralized. Very few parties, of course, remain content with a narrow basis. Some, like the catchall variety, try to attract new groups. Here too religious or ethnic parties may be able to cut across the horizontal lines of social stratification.

Federal (or national) centralization is a dimension that is significant mainly in the context of a strong federal system. Party organization in such a system responds to two distinct governmental hierarchies: national and provincial (or state). Some party politicians will have a national focus; others will look to the lower units. Attempts of the national party central to dominate the provincial parties may be frustrated. The classic example of this, of course, is the United States, where the national party organization exercises appreciable control only once every four years. If a political maverick retains the support of his state party, his political position is virtually unassailable.

Functions of Political Parties

Political parties perform a variety of functions that contribute to the stability and effectiveness of political systems. Looking at these functions does not mean (1) that all parties perform them all, (2) that all parties perform them uniformly well, and (3) that no "functional alternatives" could take the place of parties. Table 8.4 lists the functions most often discussed in the literature on parties. While certain of these functions overlap somewhat, each is distinct enough to merit a brief account.

1. While many people vote from a general sense of duty and others

---

TABLE 8.4.   The Functions of Parties in Competitive Systems

1. Mobilization of voters
2. Education of the public
3. Political socialization
4. Policy-making
5. Interest aggregation
6. Political recruitment
7. System integration
8. Communications conduit

as an act of protest, some people are pushed over the line from abstention to voting by political parties. Parties are constantly asking, sometimes cajoling, people for their votes. Party "platforms" or policy statements and candidates are selected with a view toward maximizing votes. In countries where nonvoting is high, such as the United States, parties search for strategies to mobilize nonvoters in behalf of their candidates. Much of the work of party militants is devoted to getting out the vote.

2. Parties are a source of education and information for many citizens. The pronouncements of party leaders, articles in the party press or elsewhere, as well as more informal methods of spreading ideas, help to raise the general public's level of information. This remains true despite the partisan and biased nature of much of this information. In a competitive system there is at least a chance for counter-information and rebuttal. The realistic situation very often does not lie between receiving biased and unbiased information, but between receiving biased information and none at all.

3. Political socialization differs from the educational role of parties because it involves, more than the latter does, the inculcation of the fundamental values and norms of the system.[27] Though the issue is controversial, many social theorists consider a certain minimal consensus on values essential to the survival of any society. Parties, at least those basically supportive of the existing order, play a considerable role in maintaining, if not creating, that consensus. By following certain rules of the game, a party spreads knowledge of those rules and contributes to their acceptance and legitimation.

4. Though American major party platforms are a notorious counterinstance, political parties sometimes deliver on their policy promises. An exceptionally successful case of this was the Labor Government in England from 1945 to 1950. Exceptionally unsuccessful instances were registered in the Fourth Republic in France from 1946 to 1958, where the weakness and volubility of coalition governments gave over much policy initiative to the bureaucracy.[28] More generally, Anthony King has suggested great reservations about the policy impact of political parties. Even outside the United States, party organizations have not been

> particularly successful in imposing their will when their own leaders have either formed the government or participated in a governing coalition. The

27. See chapter 10 for more on political socialization.
28. See Herbert Leuthy, *France Against Herself* (New York: Meridian Books, 1960).

past decade or so in Europe provides several examples of new governments, mainly radical ones, pursuing much the same policies as the governments they replaced, and of existing governments executing abrupt policy shifts without prior warrant from the party organizations . . . and sometimes in the face of strong party opposition.[29]

While it would be wrong to neglect the role of political parties in policy formation, King's conclusions suggest that the performance may vary much from time to time and place to place.

5. In any complex society, if all the possible interest groups deluged the government with all their possible demands, the political system would most likely be overloaded and break down. Parties, especially catchall parties, are able to lighten this problem somewhat by combining, coordinating, and refining demands before they reach the formal political institutions. This cuts the load on the system and allows it to work better.

6. Political systems need leaders. Certainly most legislators and most cabinet officers in constitutional regimes have borne a party label. However, not too much should be made of this raw fact, since, as we found with the single-party, party membership is not the whole story about leadership. Someone who rises into the political elite and, almost as an afterthought, joins a political party is a different sort of leader from someone with a long apprenticeship in the party organization. With this reservation in mind, it is no exaggeration to call the role of political parties in leadership recruitment "crucial."

7. Parties, at least "pro-system" parties, serve the function of integration by managing conflict and mobilizing support. In the first case they provide a forum for certain conflicts of interest and principle. According to Guido Dorso, parties serve the cause of social integration by counteracting the fissiparous potential of class divisions:

> Their essential characteristic is to be interclass organizations, which organize vast human formations on the basis of the ideological struggle. They are composed of factions of the ruling and ruled classes and all the strata of both.
>
> .　　　.　　　.
>
> Through the struggle of parties, there occurs a contraposition between factions of the same social stratum which is determined by ideological

29. Anthony King, "Political Parties: Some Skeptical Reflections," in *Comparative Politics*, ed. R. Macridis (4th ed.; Homewood, Ill.: Dorsey Press, 1972), p. 248.

divergencies. Even when these latter are justified with class arguments, they end in the long run by altering the functioning of classes.[30]

In the second case, by supporting a pro-system party, the citizen gives an indirect vote of confidence in the system as a whole.

8. Communications is involved at all stages and in all aspects of the political process. Political parties can serve as a two-channel conduit of communication. In simpler terms, this means that communications flow upwards from the grass roots, and downward from the government to the public. The political party is the link, the conduit, between the two units.

FACTIONALISM IN POLITICAL PARTIES

A somewhat neglected aspect of the anatomy and physiology of political parties is factionalism. We have mentioned the ideological tendencies of left and right and center. Factions, though they may be based on such tendencies, go beyond them in important respects. Richard Rose defines a *tendency* as a "stable set of attitudes, rather than a stable group of politicians. It may be defined as a body of attitudes expressed in Parliament about a broad range of problems; the attitudes are held together by a more or less coherent political ideology." [31]

TABLE 8.5.   Types of Factions in Political Parties

I.   POLICY FACTIONS
    A.   Ideological factions
    B.   Strategy factions
II. SOCIOPOLITICAL FACTIONS
    A.   Regional factions
    B.   Ethnic factions
    C.   Religious factions
    D.   Economic factions
    E.   Age factions
III. PERSONALISTIC FACTIONS
    A.   Leader-oriented
    B.   Oligarchic

---

30. Guido Dorso, *Dittatura, classe politica, classe dirigente* (Turin: Einaudi, 1955), p. 173.
31. Richard Rose, "Parties, Factions, and Tendencies in Great Britain," in *Political Parties,* ed. R. Macridis (New York: Harper & Row, 1967), p. 107.

A *faction,* on the contrary, is a "group of individuals based on representatives in Parliament who seek to further a broad range of policies through consciously organized political activity." [32] The distinguishing trait of a faction is organization; the best organized party factions have an infrastructure that includes special funds, press outlets, and physical facilities. Table 8.5 shows three major types of factions, each with a somewhat different basis.

Policy Factions

Policy factions can stress either ideology or strategy, though sometimes the distinction between them is less than clear. An ideological faction revolves around a serious ideological difference from the rest of the party. It is a "spiritual" tendency embodied in a specific group of men. Ideological factions tend to upbraid the rest of their party brethren for violating the "true" principles of the party. The left wing of the British Labor party, centered around Aneurin Bevan in the 1940s and 1950s, bitterly complained that the party's overall moderation and pro-Americanism betrayed basic "socialist" principles.

A strategic faction does not disagree with its comrades on ultimate principles, but favors distinctive strategies and tactics. This concerns such questions as collaboration or alliances with other parties, going into a proposed government coalition, appealing to this rather than that bloc of voters, and so forth. While Communist parties prohibit organized factions, they often contain groups that favor a hard-line "left" strategy or an accommodationist "right" approach.

Sociopolitical Factions

Though sociopolitical factions clothe themselves in ideology, they reflect the impact of the country's social, cultural, and economic structure upon the party's own structure. Southern Democrats in the Congress were for years a coherent and distinctive faction. Ethnic factions, such as the present-day black caucus in the House of Representatives or the German, Hungarian, Jewish, and various Slavic factions in the Social Democratic party of the old Austro-Hungarian Empire before 1918, can be of considerable political importance. Religious factions will probably emerge in the Netherlands if plans for a merger of Catholic and Protestant parties into a Dutch Christian Democratic party ever materialize.

32. Ibid., p. 106.

Economic factions are based on large outside interest groups such as trade unions and farmers' organizations. Large catchall parties are likely to sport this type of faction. Age factions emerge when the younger members of a parliamentary contingent revolt against the party "gerontocracy."

Personalistic Factions

Leader-oriented factions are held together by loyalty to a particular leader. Examples are the Fanfaniani and Morotei in the Italian Christian Democratic party, looking to former premiers Amintore Fanfani and Aldo Moro, respectively. Some personalistic factions naturally involve ideological and other policy considerations, but the real basis is personal loyalty. Of course, there is the fervent hope that the devotee will receive his "just" reward of office, patronage, preferments, and the like.

Oligarchic factions resemble leader-oriented groups save that there is no single outstanding personality present. A few notables and their clienteles form the base of this sort of faction.

TABLE 8.6. Factors Concerning the Political Strength of Party Factions

---

1. **Size:** a large faction, capable perhaps of gaining a plurality at various party conclaves, has a better chance than a small faction to enter the coalition that rules the party.
2. **Position:** a faction whose political center of gravity is close to that of the party as a whole is strategically better placed to exercise influence than an extremist faction.
3. **Composition:** a faction that backs up its M.P.s with extraparliamentary leaders and "cadres" is more solid and effective than a faction with no extraparliamentary organization.
4. **Organization:** a faction that need not rely on official party channels to communicate with actual or possible sympathizers is better off than a faction so dependent.
5. **Extension:** a faction with support throughout the country in local or regional governments or party organizations can absorb local defeats without endangering its national position.
6. **Control of voters and recruitment:** a faction with its own electoral support and base of militants has a very strong bargaining weapon: the threat to secede from the party.
7. **Leadership:** the organizational coherence of a faction is seriously weakened when the leadership is so divided that the faction is really a coalition of "mini-factions."
8. **Stability:** a faction which loses very few members and may even gain a few must be taken most seriously when it comes to forming inner-party coalitions and dividing the "spoils" of office.
9. **Rigidity:** a faction cannot be very influential—unless it is very large—if its inflexibility prevents it from making politically advantageous alliances.

The importance of all such factions depends on a number of variables. "Success" must be measured differently for policy, sociopolitical, and personalistic factions. Table 8.6, based on the Italian experience, seems to exhaust the relevant factors.[33]

Giovanni Sartori has reached several interesting conclusions on the likelihood and importance of factionalism in parties.[34] First he finds that the electoral system plays a role in determining the number of factions. The single-member plurality system works to decrease the number of factions, while proportional representation or PR—see the next section, "Party Systems"—encourages their proliferation. A second issue concerns the relation of factions to the number of parties. Ideological factions decrease when there are many parties, but increase when there are fewer parties. Factions of "interest," however, vary independently of the number of parties in the system.

A final finding of Sartori's maintains that factions, ideological or not, tend to increase if the "structure of opportunities" makes it rewarding to form them. This resembles Parkinson's law that work expands to fill the time allotted to it: so long as a group of party members have something to gain by forming a faction, they will not let the opportunity to form one slide past.

PARTY SYSTEMS

The expression "party system" implies competition between two or more political parties. While the following typology of party systems stresses the number of parties, we will see that much more than this is involved. The primary numerical distinction runs between (1) *the simple two-party system*, (2) *the moderate multiparty system* (3–5), and (3) *the extreme multiparty system* (6–?). According to Giovanni Sartori, the politically important difference is between types 1 and 2 on the one hand, and type 3 on the other.[35] He further points to four features that operate somewhat differently in the three types of party system. These are the number of

33. Based on Giovanna Zincone, "Accesso autonomo alle risorse: le determinanti del frazionismo," *Rivista Italiana della Scienza politica* 5 (April 1972): 139–60.
34. Giovanni Sartori, *Parties and Party Systems* (Cambridge: Cambridge University Press, 1976), chap. 4.
35. Much of the following is inspired by Giovanni Sartori, "European Political Parties: The Case of Polarized Pluralism," in *Political Parties and Political Development*, ed. J. LaPalombara and M. Wiener (Princeton: Princeton University Press, 1966).

poles in the party system, the ideological distance between the parties, the "drives" of the system, and the relationship between government and opposition(s).

The number of poles refers to the number of attractive centers in the political spectrum. The simple two-party system by definition has two poles, one for each party. Likewise the moderate multiparty system has two poles, which may be constituted either by two *groups* of parties or by one large party facing a coalition of parties. The extreme multiparty system has at least three poles (right, center, and left) and possibly more.

Ideological distance is a feature that tells how far apart are the right and left extreme parties represented in parliament. For example, the gap between Nazis and Communists in the German parliament in 1932 was much wider than that between conservative Republicans and liberal Democrats in the United States Congress then or today. Wide ideological distance suggests that the extreme parties are implacably anti-system, since no system could possibly satisfy them both. Narrow ideological distance means an agreement on fundamentals, to which all important parties subscribe.

The "drives" of a party system are basic tendencies toward the center and moderation, or toward the extremes and radicalism. These can be called "centrist" and "extremist" drives, respectively.[36]

The three types of party system normally tend to produce three characteristic patterns of government and opposition (see table 8.7). The simple two-party system leads to *alternative governments*, where the two major parties periodically exchange the role of government and opposition. The moderate multiparty system tends to produce *alternative coalitions*, where various coalitions made up of different parties succeed each other. Sometimes, however, one large party "goes it alone," confronting an opposition coalition. The extreme multiparty system pro-

---

TABLE 8.7.   Main Traits of Party Systems

	Poles	Ideological Distance	Drives	Type of Government
Simple two-party system	2	very small	centrist	alternative governments
Moderate multiparty system	2	small	centrist	alternative coalitions
Extreme multiparty system	3 or more	great	extremist	marginal turnover

---

36. Sartori uses "centripetal" for centrist and "centrifugal" for extremist.

duces *marginal turnover*, where the same parties dominate the government over long stretches, with occasional additions and subtractions to the government coalition.

The Simple Two-Party System

The two-party system has been extolled as a model of political stability. Its British and American versions, in particular, are considered to be sources of continuity and compromise in those countries. Though it has been shaken in recent years, many Englishmen and Americans still see the two-party approach to politics as the most "natural" and fair. Proponents of the two-party system, however, sometimes neglect certain preconditions of the stability, moderation, and effectiveness they see in this system.

A key issue here is the distribution of opinions among the politically relevant public. A successful two-party system presupposes a unimodal distribution of opinions (figure 8.3). This means that the largest number

Figure 8.3.   Unimodal Distribution of Public Opinion

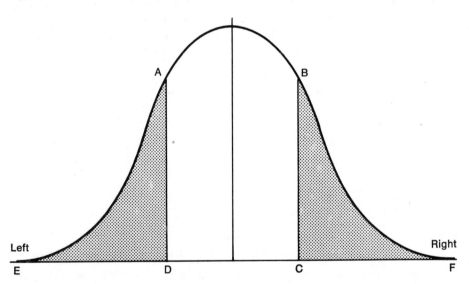

of individual opinions are bunched at one point along a spectrum of divergent views. From this point the numbers slope off rather drastically both to the left and the right. The center vertical line is the one *mode* of this curve, hence *unimodal*. The vast bulk of opinions are found within the area ABCD. Very few opinions are contained in the two areas ADE and BCF.

The main result of this unimodal distribution pattern is that both major political parties find their main support in ABCD. Thus the drives are centrist because that is where the votes are. If one party launches an ideological appeal skewed toward the extreme right or left, it will lose and lose badly. Correctly or incorrectly, Republican presidential candidate Barry Goldwater was perceived as "too right-wing" in 1964, while George McGovern was seen as "too left-wing" in 1972. Both lost and lost badly.

If we change the scenario and assume a bimodal distribution with two modes appearing toward the extreme left and right, things change dramatically (figure 8.4). Now we have two large camps of extremists,

Figure 8.4.   Bimodal Distribution of Public Opinion

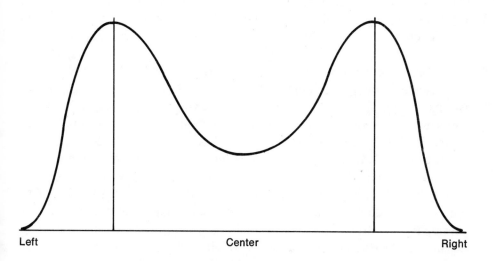

Left   Center   Right

who by definition do not agree on fundamentals. So far apart are their ideologies that an orderly alternation in power is out of the question. Victory of one party will lead to the destruction of the other.

Even if we alter the situation a bit and assume that the two modes fall one on the center and one on an extreme, the preconditions for a two-party system are seriously disturbed (figure 8.5). Clearly, the party

Figure 8.5.   Bimodal Distribution Skewed to the Right

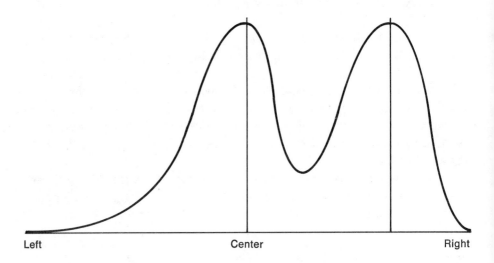

Left   Center   Right

oriented to the center mode can never give up the government, lest the rightists set up a dictatorship. The same holds if one of the modes is on the extreme left. Thus, the alternation of two parties presupposes basic unimodalism.

Unfortunately for the neatness of theory, the British and American party systems deviate somewhat from a simplistic understanding of the two-party approach. If we think that the two parties should be roughly equal in the two-party system, that they should alternate frequently in power, and that almost every election is "up for grabs," the American experience is likely to disappoint us. Samuel Lubell pointed out a generation ago that instead of being a relationship of two roughly equal competitors, the relationship between the two American parties has been that of dominant to dominated.[37] That is, one party has repeatedly won the presidency, controlled the Congress, won most governorships and state legislative majorities, and elaborated public policy during its dominance.

To highlight this disparity, Lubell calls the dominant party the *sun party,* and the dominated party the *moon party.* The sun party predominates because of its timeliness: it is able to express policies and project an "image" that appeals to social groups that are on the rise. It thus fashions a coalition of groups that delivers the vote. According to Lubell the

37. Samuel Lubell, *The Future of American Politics* (Garden City, N.Y.: Anchor Books, 1956).

moon party is a "party of nostalgia," anchored to past glories, unable for the present to remodel its basis of appeal.[38]

British politics deviates from a pure two-party model because of the strength of third parties in their system. If we take as a measure of deviance a third party in the House of Commons with more than 10 percent of the seats, we find no pure two-party system after the 1886, 1892, 1895, 1900, 1906, 1910, 1918, 1922, 1923, and 1929 elections. Moreover, in terms of popular votes, the elections of 1918, 1922, 1923, and 1929 show less than a 10 percent spread between the first- and third-place finishers.[39]

Actually, Great Britain looked most like a pure two-party system in the first two decades after World War II. The elections of 1945, 1950, 1951, 1955, and 1959 could be fairly viewed as a duel between the Conservative party and the Labor party. However, the 1964 elections saw a revival of the Liberal party, which, at least in terms of popular votes, has carried over into the 1970s. More recently, the resurgent Scottish National party and the Welsh nationalists have considerably complicated the picture. In recent elections such as that of October 1974, Labor and the Conservatives have garnered almost exactly 75 percent of the popular vote. At that time the Liberals received over 18 percent.

Nevertheless, as we shall see below, the British electoral system favors the largest parties, so that the Labor and Conservative parties have well over 90 percent of the seats in the House of Commons. This would suggest that parliamentary politics would be two-party, even if that of the whole country is not. But since neither big party had a majority, the resulting Labor Government had to turn to the Liberals for support.

The Moderate Multiparty System

This system strongly resembles the two-party system. The chief difference between them, of course, is the number of parties. This situation may promote or reflect a somewhat wider ideological distance, since parties have to distinguish themselves from their competitors. The Scandi-

38. Examples of dominance include the Democratic dominance in the two generations before the Civil War, the Republican dominance from the 1870s to the 1920s, as well as the clear Democratic dominance from 1932 to the present. The Democrats since 1932 have controlled Congress over 90 percent of the time.
39. Enid Lakeman, *How Democracies Vote* (London: Faber & Faber, 1970), p. 31.

navian countries give us the best example of the operation of the moderate multiparty system (figure 8.6). The five major parties in the Swedish Parliament (Riksdag), since 1969 a unicameral body, have been the Conservative party, the People's party, the Center party, the Social Democrats, and the Communists. The Norwegian party system is similar, with the Christian People's party replacing the Communists as the fifth party with parliamentary representation.

The Swedish and Norwegian party spectrums resemble nothing so much as each other. The weakness of both the extreme left and right is clear in both countries, as is the dominance of the moderate left in the guise of the Swedish Social Democrats and the Norwegian Labor party.[40] On the right both countries have fairly strong conservative parties, but "conservative" more in the sense of twentieth-century America, not nineteenth-century Europe. Both countries have liberal parties and farmers' parties. The main difference is the strength of the Norwegian Christian People's party, whose Swedish counterpart (Christian Democrats) is very weak.

These two systems fulfill Sartori's criteria for moderate multiparty systems. There are two poles: one provided by the Socialists and the other by the coalition of Liberals, Conservatives, and Agrarians. Moreover, the ideological distance has narrowed rather steadily among the major parties over the last four or five decades. Alternative coalitions have not been found in Sweden until very recently, though this has been a frequent pattern in its neighbor Norway.

A closer look at figure 8.6 shows two rather interesting developments, however. First, Social Democratic predominance and control of the Swedish government has been really broken for the first time in over four decades. In September 1976, Social Democratic Prime Minister Olof Palme stepped down, and Thorbjörn Fälldin, leader of the Center (formerly Agrarian) party formed a coalition government with the People's party and the Moderates. This historic turning point nonetheless corresponds to the alternative coalition formula of the moderate multiparty system. This is especially so since the Social Democrats had actually been in coalition with the Communists.

The Norwegian pattern of change, however, may suggest a movement toward an extreme multiparty system, or at least toward a less moderate multiparty system. We see an increase from five to eight in the number of parties represented in parliament. Moreover, big winners

40. Recently the dominance of the Swedish Social Democrats for over forty years has been broken and a "bourgeois" coalition is in power.

Figure 8.6. The Swedish and Norwegian Party Spectrums

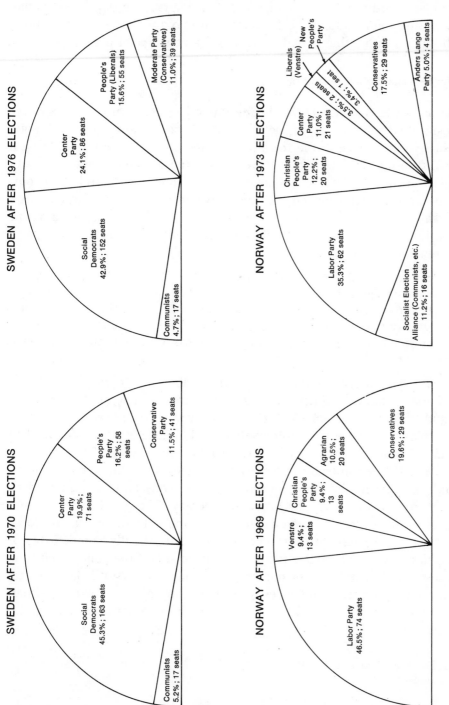

SWEDEN AFTER 1976 ELECTIONS

Moderate Party (Conservatives) 11.0%; 39 seats

People's Party (Liberals) 15.6%; 55 seats

Center Party 24.1%; 86 seats

Social Democrats 42.9%; 152 seats

Communists 4.7%; 17 seats

NORWAY AFTER 1973 ELECTIONS

Liberals (Venstre) New People's Party

3.5%; 2 seats

3.4%; 1 seat

Conservatives 17.5%; 29 seats

Anders Lange Party 5.0%; 4 seats

Christian People's Party 12.2%; 20 seats

Center Party 11.0%; 21 seats

Labor Party 35.3%; 62 seats

Socialist Election Alliance (Communists, etc.) 11.2%; 16 seats

(Percentages refer to popular vote)

SWEDEN AFTER 1970 ELECTIONS

Conservative Party 11.5%; 41 seats

People's Party 16.2%; 58 seats

Center Party 19.9%; 71 seats

Social Democrats 45.3%; 163 seats

Communists 5.2%; 17 seats

NORWAY AFTER 1969 ELECTIONS

Conservatives 19.6%; 29 seats

Agrarian 10.5%; 20 seats

Christian People's Party 9.4%; 13 seats

Venstre 9.4%; 13 seats

Labor Party 46.5%; 74 seats

were the "extremists" of the Socialist Electoral Alliance (including Communists) and the Anders Lange party (a poujadist group—see chapter 12). Still, the results of the 1973 election may prove to be a momentary aberration rather than a real transition to a new type of party system.

The Extreme Multiparty System

According to Maurice Duverger, multiparty systems run counter to the basic "dualist" tendency in politics. This is so because "political choice usually takes place in the form of a choice between two alternatives. A duality of parties does not always exist, but there is almost always a duality of tendencies." [41] This dualism stems from the natural dichotomy between order and movement, and between conservatism and change.

Thus Duverger is forced to conclude that the center is not a viable political force in the political life, especially in extreme multiparty systems:

> There may well be a center party but there is no center tendency, no center doctrine. The term "center" is applied to the geometrical spot at which the moderates of opposed tendencies meet. . . . The center is nothing more than the artificial grouping of the right wing of the left and the left wing of the right. The fate of the center is to be torn asunder, buffeted and annihilated. . . .[42]

The dualist pattern based on a bimodal distribution of opinions has many historical examples. Such polarization occurred in Italy after World War I and in Germany from 1929 to 1933. However, it is not a "law" of politics. Not only do we have unimodalism and bimodalism, but trimodalism and still more complex patterns are also possible (figure 8.7).

The left in a trimodal pattern is represented by revolutionary socialism and anarchism, the right by old-fashioned conservatism and modern fascism, and the center by liberal democracy. There is in trimodalism, therefore, a center and even a center "doctrine": liberal or constitutional democracy. Whether this center is dominant, equally competitive, or hopelessly weak vis-à-vis left and right depends on the political culture, history, and institutions of the country in question. If there is a general rule about political tendencies, it is that they are *triadic* rather than dualistic: someone can always say that both extremes are far from the mark.

41. Duverger, *Parties*, p. 215.
42. Ibid.

Figure 8.7.   Trimodal Distribution of Public Opinion

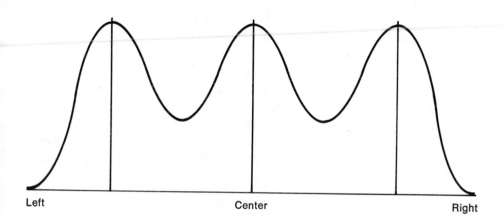

Left   Center   Right

An extreme multiparty system is multipolar: there are at least three poles of attraction. This is so because the distribution of opinion is itself trimodal (though more modes may exist, we will assume three for simplicity's sake). Why then are there not three parties in the system? While some of the answer comes in the next section, we can refer here

Figure 8.8.   Parties in a Trimodal System with Wide Ideological Distance

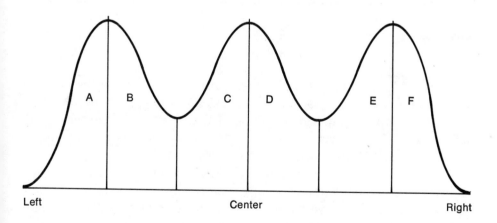

Left   Center   Right

to ideological distance and extremist drives as a partial answer. Since the modes and poles are so far apart, it pays off in votes for some parties to keep them apart. Figure 8.8 shows how wide ideological distance will give more than three parties. If the spread within each hump is itself wide, we can thus end up with six parties. Party A will be an extreme left party; Party B will be a moderate left party; Party C will be a left-center party; Party D will be a right-center party; Party E will be a moderate right party; and Party F will be an extreme right party.

Another way to understand the importance of ideological distance between parties is to compare the spectrum of the United States Congress in recent decades with that of the Italian Parliament of the same period (figure 8.9). In specific terms, on the left of the Congress (i.e.,

Figure 8.9.   Ideological Distance in the United States and Italy

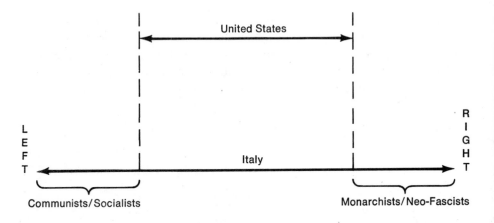

the "liberal" Democrats) there was virtually no one with views akin to Italian Communists and Socialists—parties which had around a third of the seats in Parliament. On the right in Congress (i.e., "conservative" Republicans and Southern Democrats), few, if any, legislators had views similar to Italian Monarchists and neo-Fascists.

The extreme multiparty system has many important political consequences. One is a tendency to irresponsibility. Since the extreme parties can never, or almost never, be brought into the government, they can criticize the government without letup or restraint and can promise the electorate the moon. As permanent "outs" they never have to deliver on their promises. Ideology is at a premium; bargaining and compromise are superfluous. This general situation is both a cause and an effect of the marginal turnover in government coalitions in this system.

To understand the dynamics of marginal turnover, let us imagine a nine-party system (figure 8.10). Since Parties A and I are virulently

Figure 8.10.   Marginal Turnover in Extreme Multiparty Systems

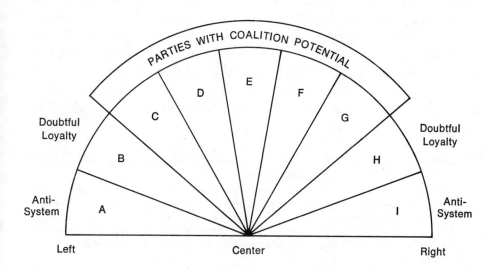

anti-system, they are permanent outs. Parties B and H will likely also be excluded from the government coalition because the extremist drives of the party system push them toward A and I. This leaves Parties C, D, E, F, and G as parties with a *coalition potential* because of their overall support for the existing system. In the Fourth French Republic we saw that these parties were known collectively as the "third force," as against the other two forces of the far left (Communists) and right (Gaullists).

Marginal turnover occurs among the parties with coalition potential. Only rarely, however, will there be a "grand coalition" or a government of national concentration, embracing all five parties C, D, E, F, and G. The more common coalition pattern will be to exclude C or G and sometimes both, though this latter situation may narrow down policy support too much. C and G tend to be mutually exclusive, because the wide ideological distance even affects them. Under noncrisis conditions, policy differences between C or G keep them from cooperating, despite their overall pro-system attitude.

All of this suggests that Parties D and F have a very high likelihood of government participation and that Party E is virtually indispensable, especially if it has better than 10 percent of the seats in parliament. At the dead center of the system, Party E will play a pivotal role in government coalitions.

Attempts to break out of the marginal turnover situation have rarely been successful. The "Popular Front" government in France in the late 1930s, which included Socialists, Communists, and left-liberal elements was short-lived. Its counterpart in Spain was the prologue to civil war. Likewise, Italian attempts to form a center-right coalition including neo-Fascists failed in the 1950s because it was too controversial.

Whatever the formula of the marginal turnover situation in extreme multiparty systems, the exact pattern of the coalition relationship can vary. Table 8.8 shows this.

TABLE 8.8.   Patterns of Coalition Relationship

---

1. **Direct coalition:** cabinet and other posts are divided among the coalition partners roughly in proportion to their strength in parliament.
2. **Indirect coalition:** at least one of the parties involved does not have officials in the Government, but regularly and by agreement supports and votes for the Government in parliament.
3. **Negative coalition:** the cooperating party neither joins nor votes for the Government, but abstains on votes of confidence and other important issues.

Electoral Systems and Party Systems

One of the longest and hottest debates in political science concerns the relationship between electoral systems and party systems. Before we can assess the various claims and counter-claims in this debate, we must learn something about different electoral systems.

Perhaps the simplest electoral system is the *single-member plurality system* for legislative bodies. The country is divided up into separate districts and constituencies, each choosing one legislative representative. The winner of the seat is the candidate with the largest number of votes. In other words one needs a *plurality*, not an absolute majority, to win. Thus, the system is called the "first-past-the-post" system, though thinking of it as an endurance test seems a better idea than thinking of it as a horse race.

Of course, if there are only two candidates, the winner will get a majority of valid votes. Since there are often more than two candidates, however, certain problems arise. We can see this in an extremely improbable illustration. Let us say that we were given the total national percentages of four parties who ran candidates in all 500 districts. Party A got 26 percent, Party B got 25 percent, Party C got 25 percent, and Party D got 24 percent. The logical possibilities here as to party representation in the legislature are enormous. On the one hand there could be perfect correspondence, with Party A getting 130 seats, Parties B and C getting 125 seats each, and Party D getting 120 seats. On the other hand, the other extreme logical possibility could happen and Party A could win all 500 seats. In this latter case Party A would squeak past the post with narrow margins, just getting enough more than the second highest party in all 500 districts. While it *wasted* no votes to speak of, the other three parties wasted all of theirs.

Though this latter nightmare has only the tiniest real chance of happening, the single-member plurality system does tend to "distort" results. That is, the party strengths in the legislative body do not faithfully reflect party preferences among the electorate. In Great Britain in 1951, for example, the Conservative party totaled 13,718,069 votes, while the Labor party got 14,878,626.[43] Nevertheless, the Conservatives won the election with 321 seats in the House of Commons as against Labor's 304. Another "distortion" works against third and fourth parties by awarding them far fewer seats than their national share of popular votes would seem to warrant. In 1929 the British Liberal party finished third in total national votes with 23.5 percent; however it received only 10 percent of the seats in the Commons. Things got worse in both 1964 and 1966 when the third-place Liberals got 11 percent votes to 1.4 percent seats, and 8.5 percent votes to 2 percent seats, respectively.

These and other types of distortion have prompted reformers to reject the single-member plurality system in favor of a fairer and more "democratic" electoral system. The leading alternative, which is found with variations in many European countries, is called *proportional representation* (PR). Though exploration of all the niceties of PR is beyond our concern, we can at least get a general idea of it. The core of it is make the legislature into a mirror image of public opinion.

43. Lakeman, *Democracies*, p. 40.

While PR could work by making the whole country one giant constituency, it has seemed more practicable to divide the country into a number of multimember districts. Twenty-five twenty-member districts would equal the 500 seats we worked with above. Thus in a particular district where five parties were competing, the result might be as follows:

	% of Voters	Number of Seats
Party A	20	4
Party B	10	2
Party C	30	6
Party D	30	6
Party E	10	2

A party's total parliamentary contingent would be the sum of its representatives in all 25 districts.

This example is obviously rigged for simplicity: voters themselves do not dispose their votes in multiples of 10 percent. Thus, even in a PR system parties might "waste" some votes that are more than enough for certain seats, but not enough to get one more seat in another situation. One way of handling this problem is to total the "wasted" votes of all the parties in all the 25 constituencies and then parcel out some seats proportionally from a special "national" constituency. The legislative body might therefore hold 520 rather than just 500 members.

Another feature of most PR systems is the *list system*. This means that each party running in one of our fictitious 25 districts would present the electorate there with a list of 20 candidates for the 20 seats available in the district. Each voter would thus vote for the list of the party of his choice. Since it is highly unlikely that any party will monopolize the votes in a district, where a candidate is positioned on the list is crucially important. Only the candidates near the top of the list stand a real chance of getting elected so that party bigwigs cluster in the top spots.

In Italy, however, the voter is allowed to indicate his preference for particular candidates and move them up on the list if desired. The list system can also allow for two (or more) parties to collaborate on a joint list. This list then has a new, rather vague name that differs from those of the cooperating parties in the district. One variation on this, called *apparentement,* was used with great success by the Third Force parties (Socialists, Radicals, Christian Democrats, and Independents) in the French general elections of 1951. Serious losers, since they could not make profitable deals, were the Gaullists and the Communists.

While it seems hard to dispute claims about the greater fairness of PR, critics have called it the "trojan horse of democracy" because of its potential to destroy democracy.[44] The case against PR has been most ably and forcefully stated by F. A. Hermens. Before tackling the issues raised by such a critique, we can see its basic thrust in figures 8.11 and

Figure 8.11. PR as the Trojan Horse of Democracy

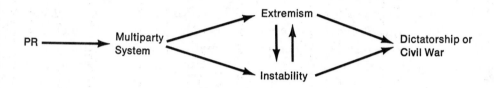

8.12. The other side of the coin of this argument looks like this:

Figure 8.12. The Two-Party System

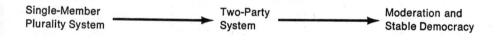

The key assumption of Hermens's theory is that the electoral system plays a dynamic and decisive role in the emergence of party systems. The list system of PR encourages many parties for the same reason that the single-member system discourages them. PR also makes it much

44. F. A. Hermens, "The Dynamics of Proportional Representation," in *Comparative Politics*, ed. D. Apter and H. Eckstein (New York: Free Press, 1964).

easier for new, small parties to rise up and gain a foothold in the system because it gives them at least a few parliamentary seats.[45] Moreover, this parliamentary base can be used for propaganda and attention-getting. The single-member system, on the other hand, makes it hard for small, new parties to concentrate enough votes in specific districts to gain a plurality. Voters are thus disinclined to waste their votes, while they feel that in PR their votes count for something.[46]

In the Hermens scenario, PR not only multiplies parties, it also radicalizes them. Secure with some seats, extremist parties make virulent attacks on the government at the same time they make extravagant claims for themselves. It often takes no more than an economic calamity to transform the extremists from criers in the wilderness into the fastest growing political force in the country: "The more incensed the voters are by reason of the distressed condition . . . and the apparent failure of the government . . . the more they will be inclined to fall into the well-placed nets of the extremists." [47] In a typical vicious-circle situation, the growth of extreme parties makes it still harder for the government to implement a decisive program.

In addition to the self-destructiveness of PR, Hermens sees a whole series of political drawbacks flowing from it. Table 8.9 summarizes these.

Quite naturally, defenders of PR and others have denied some or all of these charges. While no balance sheet is possible here, Hermens seems to have oversimplified some of the political dynamics involved. After surveying the number of parties in European parliaments before and after PR, Enid Lakeman concluded that PR "does not encourage the formation of parties but only reflects in the parliament whatever tendencies toward fusion or division may exist . . . at the time of the election." [48]

More broadly, Hermens has exaggerated the importance of electoral mechanisms and underestimated that of social cleavages. Let us imagine a society with a trimodal opinion distribution where the three humps

45. Looking at results from a pre-Hitler German PR district, Hermens even concluded that it is "eight times easier to succeed with a new party under proportional representation as it is under the majority system." Ibid., p. 255.
46. To counter the proliferation of tiny parties some PR systems set a threshold below which a party is denied all representation. In the 1953 electoral law in West Germany (which is half PR and half single-member), a party which failed to register 5 percent of the total vote would get no seats at all, unless it won at least one single-member constituency.
47. Hermens, "Dynamics," p. 258.
48. Lakeman, "Democracies," p. 161.

TABLE 8.9.   Possible Drawbacks of PR

1. **Change in party structure:** Parties become ideological fortresses, cut off from outsiders.
2. **Emergence of interest-based parties:** PR allows the rise of small parties, which are glorified interest groups. These are narrow and selfish and contribute little to solving broad problems.
3. **Deterioration of the political elite:** PR favors the selection of lackluster candidates beholden to the bosses who draw up the party lists.
4. **Destruction of inner-party democracy:** because of the party list, local candidates have no real political base from which to challenge the party oligarchs. Likewise party discipline will be stronger in parliament.
5. **Loss of vitality:** PR excludes that head-on confrontation of candidates which invigorates the political process by producing strong, dynamic political leaders.
6. **Discrimination against youth:** older politicians have little incentive to step aside since it is so easy to retain one's place on the list. Younger candidates have to kowtow to the party oligarchs to win a place on the list.
7. **Political stagnation:** PR produces parliaments that change little from one election to the next. Parties reach a certain level and rarely rise above or dip below it. This further curtails the circulation of new blood.
8. **Weak governments:** PR cuts down majorities so much that fragile and short-lived coalitions become the order of the day. Decisive action is replaced by immobilism.

favor a full-fledged socialist economy, the modern welfare state, and old-fashioned free enterprise. Assuming voter "rationality," we have the basis for a three-party system. Let us further assume a rigid "cross-cutting" cleavage between pro-church "clericals" and anti-church "anti-clericals." Since these two groups cannot abide each other, we will have a split resulting in six parties: (1) anticlerical socialists, (2) clerical socialists, (3) anticlerical welfarists, (4) clerical welfarists, (5) anti-clerical capitalists, and (6) clerical capitalists.

Let us go further and assume that the society is divided into two equal but hostile ethnic groups: the Dacians and the Thracians. This cleavage cuts across the other two so that what results is a twelve-party spectrum as seen in figure 8.13. While things never work out exactly as our fanciful example suggests, it shows that complex, deeply divided societies have a predisposition toward multipartism regardless of the electoral system. Thus, PR may be as much a result of cleavages as their cause. PR does not create ethnic, religious, and cultural differences, even though it probably facilitates their translation into the party system.

In the light of this analysis it seems best to take a middle position between Hermens's thesis on the single-factor importance of the electoral system and Lakeman's conclusion that the electoral system makes no profound difference. Maurice Duverger seems to take a middle road

Figure 8.13.   The Impact of Social Cleavages on the Number of Parties

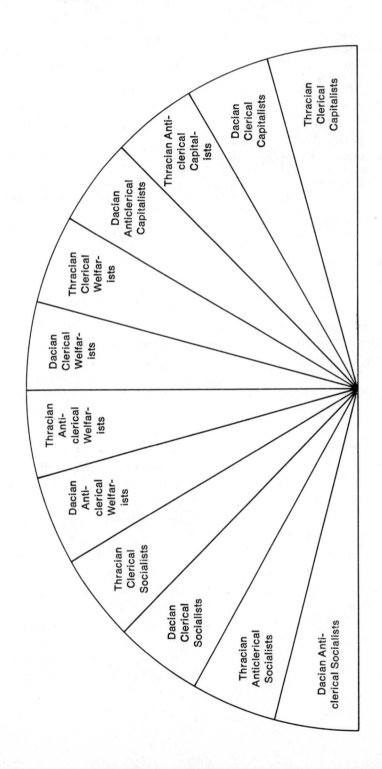

when he finds that the main effect of introducing PR is to retard the development of a two-party system. He does concede, however, some slight multiplying effect on the number of parties, though this "does not seem as great as is sometimes suggested, and above all it takes place in certain well-defined directions." [49]

Giovanni Sartori goes still farther than Duverger, however, in diluting the *positive* impact of PR. Sartori agrees with Lakeman that the introduction of PR does not increase the number of parties where a multiparty system already exists. Instead of multiplying parties, it simply "does nothing to prevent the fragmentation of a party system." More specifically, this means that PR has no positive impact, but rather a negative one in so far as it removes "a previous impediment (i.e., a plurality electoral system that did serve to impede party fragmentation)." [50]

In this chapter we have done two basic things. First, we have developed our typology of political parties in competitive political systems. Proto-parties, cadre parties, mass parties, dictatorial parties, and catchall parties seem to exhaust the possible categories. We have made little, however, of a distinction that may appear of prime importance to American readers: major vs. minor parties. Our reticence follows from the extreme relativity of such a distinction. Parties that would be classified as minor, according to the size principle common in this country, have played important, even pivotal roles in other countries. A case in point would be the tiny Republican party in Italy (2–3 percent of the popular vote), which has contributed needed parliamentary support and cabinet personnel to Italian governments in the 1960s and early 1970s.

Regarding American minor parties, V. O. Key seems to have hit the mark when he divided them into "transient" parties that come and go rapidly, and parties "of long duration" that have considerable staying power.[51] Transient minor parties in America are of two types: parties of "economic protest" (e.g., the Populists of the 1890s), which reflect the hard times of particular socioeconomic groups; and "secessionist" parties, which break off from one of the major parties (e.g., the Bull Moose Progressives of Teddy Roosevelt from the Republicans in 1912).

49. Duverger, *Parties*, p. 249.
50. Sartori, "European Parties," p. 173.
51. V. O. Key, Jr., *Politics, Parties, and Pressure Groups* (5th ed.; New York: Thomas Y. Crowell, 1964), chap. 10.

The minor parties of long duration also dispose themselves into two major categories: the "ideological" (usually Marxist) parties (e.g., the Communist party, the Socialist party, or the Socialist Labor party); and the "one-issue obsessionist" parties, which push one leading idea with almost fanatical zeal (e.g., the Prohibitionists, the Vegetarians). Such categories might work also in non-American contexts, but only with two-party or moderate multiparty systems, in which it is relatively easy to agree on which parties are truly "minor."

The chapter's second major concern has been with party systems. We have gone into some detail on the simple two-party system, the moderate multiparty system, and the extreme multiparty system. We have discussed not only the structural features and inner dynamics of these systems, but have also raised some questions about the causes of these systems (electoral system vs. political culture, and so on). One dimension that has been soft-pedaled is that of change from one type of system to another. One of the most striking of such shifts has occurred in the Federal Republic of Germany since the first postwar elections of 1949.

In that year the returns suggested a likely reincarnation of the pre-Hitlerian extreme multiparty system—a system whose collapse inspired Hermens's attack on PR. In 1949 eleven parties succeeded in winning seats to the German parliament (Bundestag), compared to fifteen in 1928.[52] Moreover, the largest party, the Christian Democrats with 31.0 percent, did scarcely better than the largest party of 1928, the Socialists (29.8 percent). This suggested that stability might stand beyond the reach of the West Germans.

However, even in 1949 there were some encouraging differences from the 1920s. If we look at the performances of the three largest parties in 1928 and 1949, we find that in 1928 the three largest parties got 56.1 percent of the popular vote and 58.7 percent of the parliamentary seats, while in 1949 the three largest parties (Christian Democrats, Social Democrats, and Free Democrats) attained 72.1 percent of the vote and over 80 percent of the seats. This implied that the possibilities for fragmentation in 1949 were distinctly fewer than in the pre-Hitler era. Not only did things not worsen, but they improved so that in the 1953 elections only six parties found their way into parliament. In 1957 this figure sank to four, and the elections of 1961, 1965, 1969, 1972, and 1976 have all resulted in three parties being represented in parliament. Not

52. Gerhard Loewenberg, "The Remaking of the German Party System," in *European Politics: A Reader*, ed. M. Dogan and R. Rose (Boston: Little, Brown, 1971), pp. 259–80.

only has West Germany passed out of the extreme multiparty category, it has a moderate multiparty system that just misses being a two-party system. (This borderline case has caused some to speak rather misleadingly of a "2.5 party system" in Germany.) If we look at the last four elections, we see that the two largest parties, the Christian Democrats and Social Democrats, have totaled as follows: 1965 with 86.9 percent; 1969 with 89 percent; 1972 with 90.7 percent; and 1976 with 91.2 percent.

The question remains: why has this happened? We can divide explanatory factors into our two familiar categories: the nature of the electoral system and the political culture. The electoral system does make a difference. West Germany elects the Bundestag half by PR and half by single-member constituencies. This cuts down on whatever multiplier effect on the number of parties that PR has. Moreover, parties must get at least 5 percent of the national popular vote or win at least one single-member seat to qualify for any seats at all through PR. This makes it very difficult for splinter parties to get any real foothold in the party system. Finally, the Federal Constitutional Court has ruled some small extremist parties, such as the neo-Nazis in 1952 and the Communists in 1956, unconstitutional. (In recent years these bans have been rescinded, however.)

The electoral system is by no means the whole reason for the transformation of the West German party system. We have spoken in the chapter of ideological cleavages, ethnic and religious divisions, and for Germany we could add regional diversity as cultural predispositions toward a multiparty system. The point here is that up to now the salience of these factors has declined significantly in contrast to their strength in pre-Hitler times. Important changes include the following: (1) Nazi totalitarianism ironically contributed to the "modernization" and homogenization of German society. Its very destructiveness performed a kind of positive function by eliminating some of the roots of many parties (e.g., sharp status differences and pronounced regionalism).[53] (2) The French, British, and American occupation (1945–49) pursued policies that discourged extremism and favored the precise three parties that have survived in parliament after 1961.[54] (3) Since the eastern part of Germany is a Communist regime (the German Democratic Republic), the western part is a more homogeneous society. (4) The "economic miracle" of the 1950s and early 1960s took the wind out of the sails of

53. This thesis is elaborated in Ralf Dahrendorf, *Society and Democracy in Germany* (Garden City, N.Y.: Doubleday, 1965).
54. This point is especially stressed by Loewenberg. "German Party System."

extreme political movements. (5) The leaders of the three major parties have displayed political talents and a willingness to cooperate that seem far above that of their predecessors of the 1920s.

A still deeper study of the German case would illustrate the validity of our party and party-system typologies. Proto-parties, cadre parties, mass parties, dictatorial parties, and catchall parties stretch back into the German nineteenth century. Germany also gives us good examples of both the extreme and moderate multiparty system. Moreover, if the Free Democratic party declines much further, we will see a full-fledged two-party system in operation.

This brings us to the point of discussing still another movement aspect of politics, interest groups, which is the concern of chapter 9. Interest groups and parties are related and are sometimes hard to distinguish clearly. Some people even think that certain pressure groups are more effectual political organizations than political parties in certain countries. Let us see if this is true.

STUDY QUESTIONS

1. Contrast the role of ideology in cadre, mass, dictatorial, and catchall parties.

2. What are the main sources of factionalism in modern political parties?

3. Would getting rid of political parties constitute an improvement in the quality of statemanship and public policy in democratic countries?

4. Why do cadre parties fall mostly on the right of the political spectrum, catchall parties toward the middle, and mass parties on the left?

5. Is political culture or the nature of the electoral system the decisive factor in determining whether a country develops an extreme multiparty system?

6. Discuss the major problems of forming and sustaining a coalition government in an extreme multiparty system.

7. Compare the pros and cons of the single-member plurality system vs. PR.

SUGGESTIONS FOR FURTHER READING

ALLARDT, ERIC, and ROKKAN, STEIN, eds. *Mass Politics.* New York: Free Press, 1970.
BLACKMER, DONALD, and TARROW, SIDNEY, eds. *Communism in France and Italy.* Princeton: Princeton University Press, 1975.

CHALMERS, DOUGLAS A. *The Social Democratic Party of Germany.* New Haven: Yale University Press, 1964.

DUVERGER, MAURICE. *Political Parties.* New York: John Wiley, 1963.

GALLI, GIORGIO, and PRANDI, ALFONSO. *Patterns of Political Participation in Italy.* New Haven: Yale University Press, 1970.

HENIG, STANLEY, and PINDER, JOHN, eds. *European Political Parties.* London: Allen & Unwin, 1969.

LAKEMAN, ENID. *How Democracies Vote.* London: Faber & Faber, 1970.

LAPALOMBARA, JOSEPH, and WIENER, MYRON, eds. *Political Parties and Political Development.* Princeton: Princeton University Press, 1966.

LAWSON, KAY. *The Comparative Study of Political Parties.* New York: St. Martin's, 1976.

LIPSET, SEYMOUR M., and ROKKAN, STEIN, eds. *Party Systems and Voter Alignments.* New York: Free Press, 1967.

MACRIDIS, ROY C., ed. *Political Parties.* New York: Harper & Row, 1967.

McDONALD, NEIL A. *The Study of Political Parties.* New York: Random House, 1955.

McKENZIE, ROBERT. *British Political Parties.* 2nd ed. London: Mercury Books, 1964.

MILNOR, ANDREW J., ed. *Comparative Political Parties.* New York: Thomas Y. Crowell, 1969.

NEUMANN, SIGMUND, ed. *Modern Political Parties.* Chicago: University of Chicago Press, 1956.

ROSE, RICHARD, ed. *Electoral Behavior: A Comparative Handbook.* New York: Free Press, 1974.

RUSTOW, DANKWART. *The Politics of Compromise: A Study of Parties and Cabinet Government in Sweden.* Princeton: Princeton University Press, 1955.

SARTORI, GIOVANNI, *Parties and Party Systems.* New York: Cambridge University Press, 1976.

SORAUF, FRANK. *Political Parties in the American System.* Boston: Little, Brown, 1964.

9

Interest Groups

In various previous chapters we have talked about interest groups and the theory of political pluralism. Devoting a special chapter to interest groups is not to endorse pluralism as a general approach to politics. Nevertheless, the decisions and policies that emerge out of the encounter of interest groups and modern government are important, if not cataclysmic. Economic growth, social welfare, equality, the "quality of life" issue—all these are problem areas in which the machinations of interest groups make an appreciable and concrete difference in daily life. This is more than enough to justify the strong concern of modern political science in the political role of interest groups. Even if elitists or neo-Marxists are right about the power structure, there is a considerable margin of maneuver in that structure within which interest groups can operate with effect.

NATURE AND TYPES OF INTEREST GROUPS

Although considerable controversy exists regarding the concept of the interest group, most political scientists would agree that the place to begin is with David B. Truman's 1951 formulation. For Truman, an interest group is "any group that, on the basis of one or more shared attitudes, makes certain claims upon other groups in the society for the establishment, maintenance, or enhancement of forms of behavior that are implied by the shared attitudes." [1] The shared attitude or attitudes serves to distinguish interest groups from merely statistical aggregates such as people with the same blood type. A group becomes an interest group, however, only if it makes claims based upon the shared attitude. Not all groups do this.

We should distinguish further between political and nonpolitical interest groups. Because of its demands, the former would be involved in more or less regular contact with some level of government. The latter would lack such involvement. Instead of such a simple dichotomy, we see a continuum running from a small number of virtually apolitical groups to a larger number of totally politicized interest groups (see figure 9.1). Given the expansion of government in the modern welfare state, it is difficult for interest groups to keep totally aloof from political involvement. Even if some groups would prefer that government stay out of "their" affairs, group conflict forces the government to intervene as an "umpire" or defender of the public interest.

Figure 9.1. Level of Politicization of Interest Groups

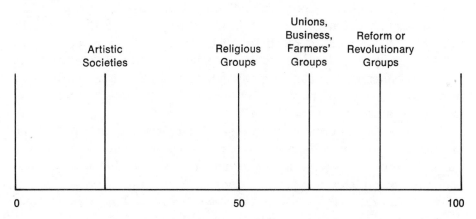

Gabriel Almond has offered a widely used classification of interest groups: (1) associational interest groups, (2) nonassociational interest groups, (3) institutional interest groups, and (4) anomic interest groups.[2]

1. David B. Truman, *The Governmental Process* (New York: Alfred A. Knopf, 1958).
2. Gabriel Almond, "Introduction: A Functional Approach to Comparative Politics," in *The Politics of the Developing Areas*, ed. G. Almond and J. Coleman (Princeton: Princeton University Press, 1960), pp. 33–38; and Gabriel Almond and G. Bingham Powell, *Comparative Politics: A Developmental Approach* (Boston: Little, Brown, 1966), chap. 4.

While there are problems with some of these categories, discussion of them will pave the way for a more adequate typology.

Associational Interest Groups

"Associations" are the privileged child of modern interest-group theory. (Sociologists call them "voluntary organizations" or "secondary groups.") Associations are groups that one joins, and they are marked by one or more avowed purposes plus any number of informal purposes. Informal purposes include such things as giving the leaders and employees of the organization safety, income, deference, and the like. The formal organization of an association involves an official hierarchy and a division of labor, often along Weberian bureaucratic lines. Associations also have an informal organization of factions and friendship groups that can deviate sharply from the formal organization. The "staff" of an association can run the gamut from a few volunteers up to a Leviathan of hundreds of full-time employees and specialists.

Associations are also likely to have meetings at stated intervals—once a year, for example—where the whole membership or their representatives assemble. Often carried out with the trappings of the "majority principle," these plenary meetings choose the top leaders and affirm the main lines of association policy. Depending on the organization involved, these conclaves can resemble either a rambunctious parliament in an extreme multiparty system or the rubber stamp-organized cheering section model of a dictatorship.

The more affluent organizations promote an elaborate information (or propaganda) activity. Some of this is for members only, but the rest takes the form of widely circulated newsletters, pamphlets, brochures, books, radio and television presentations.

The organization of associations takes many and complex forms. Though some have a unified, almost bureaucratic setup, many have a federal structure, which groups many local and/or "functional" units. Some are in fact "federations of federations," like the AFL–CIO, which contains dozens of national unions, in turn subdivided on a local craft-oriented or an industry-wide basis. In the early 1960s the AFL–CIO had about 130 national unions representing about 70,000–80,000 locals.[3] The top federations are also called "peak organizations," for ob-

3. V. O. Key, *Politics, Parties and Pressure Groups* (5th ed.; New York: Thomas Y. Crowell, 1964), p. 63.

vious reasons. Discipline and effective centralization tend to decline as an organization embraces a wider and wider clientele. Likewise, narrow ideological coherence is difficult to preserve because of the diversified base of a peak organization.

Figure 9.2.   Federal Structure of Associations

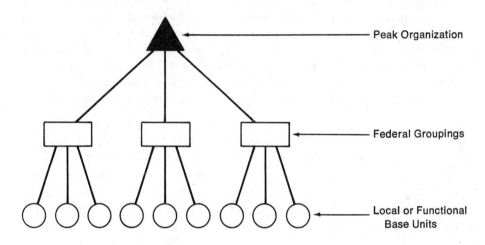

Peak Organization

Federal Groupings

Local or Functional Base Units

Nonassociational Interest Groups

Almond's second major category is "nonassociational" interest groups. This choice of terms reveals a certain indecisiveness about how this type really fits into group theory. It includes "kinship and lineage groups, ethnic, regional, religious, status and class groups that articulate interests informally, and intermittently, through individuals, cliques, family and religious heads, and the like." [4] Thus, many nonassociational interest groups are broad social categories or "natural" communities, which are represented by no single formal organization. In Almond's view the process of modernization involves replacement of nonassociational groups by associations as the main agents of interest articulation.

As with any concept that is defined as "not something else," there is danger that it is a residual category containing things that do not really belong together. Apples and oranges are not peaches, but clearly we

---

4. Almond, "Introduction," p. 33. It should be noted that by including class and status groups in this category Almond makes an end-run around the stratification problems dear to elitists and neo-Marxists. The superiority of pluralism is thus "proven" by definition.

can do better than "nonpeaches" as our category. Almond's nonassociational category includes small traditional formations such as kinship and local groups along with broad categories such as ethnic, religious, class, and status groups.

These broad categories have been termed "quasi-groups" by the sociologist Morris Ginsberg.

> Not all collectivities or aggregates form groups. Groups are masses of people in regular contact or communication, and possessing a recognizable structure. There are other aggregates or portions of the community which have no recognizable structure, but whose members have certain interests or modes of behavior in common, which may at anytime lead them to form themselves into definite groups. To this category . . . belong such entities as social classes, which, without being groups, are a recruiting field for groups. . . .[5]

There are countless examples of such quasi-groups becoming a "recruiting field" for associational interest groups. American blacks, for example, are a quasi-group with differing views on a wide array of issues. As a recruiting field, blacks give support to many associations such as the NAACP, the Urban League, CORE, the Black Panthers, the Southern Christian Leadership Conference, and others.

Figure 9.3.   Quasi-Groups as Recruiting Fields for Associations

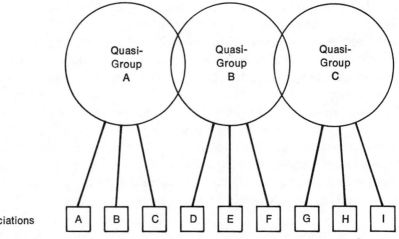

5. Morris Ginsberg quoted in Ralf Dahrendorf, *Class and Class Conflict in Industrial Society* (Stanford: Stanford University Press, 1965), p. 180.

Membership in more than one quasi-group is frequent, as in the case of a wealthy black Catholic businessman from the South. The more general situation can be represented graphically. Other examples of quasi-groups are youth, women, and aged persons. Each of these generates associations claiming to defend the interests of the whole original quasi-group.

Quasi-groups also have a more indirect, but still important impact on the political process. In the sense of Carl J. Friedrich's "law of anticipated reactions," politicians and administrators shape their positions and policies by anticipating the possible reactions of certain quasi-groups. Voting is one way in which this works, but another is the emergence of new associations recruited from quasi-groups affected by government policy. Sometimes politicians and administrators have promoted such groups for their own selfish or unselfish purposes.

Institutional Interest Groups

Almond finds institutional interest groups emerging in "legislatures, political executives, armies, bureaucracies, churches, and the like." [6] Such institutional bodies or segments of bodies may be found to champion their own interests or those of some external groups. Churches are highly important institutional interest groups and raise no conceptual problems for us. But legislatures, executives, bureaucracies, and armies are formally within the aegis of the state. One wonders if Almond's calling legislative blocs "interest groups" is not just another attempt to validate the pluralist approach by definitional fiat. Perhaps when legislators grant themselves a big pay raise, there is some sense in speaking of "interest articulation," but when a legislative bloc represents "the interest of groups in the society" [7] it seems better to think of them as agents or parts of that outside group, and not as a separate "institutional" interest group.

Moreover, if legislatures, executives, and bureaucracies can all be interest groups, the usual pluralist idea of groups presenting demands before the government appears inoperative. The very notion of the state dissolves into a congeries of forces pulling every which way. If the concept of the institutional interest group is pushed too far, the resultant image of the political process seems more appropriate to feudalism than to a modern state.

6. Almond, "Introduction," p. 33.
7. Ibid.

Anomic Interest Groups

Almond considers anomic interest groups as "more or less spontaneous penetrations into the political system from the society, such as riots, demonstrations, assassinations, and the like."[8] Almond admits that "much of what passes for anomic behavior is really the use of unconventional or violent means by organized groups."[9] Nevertheless, he still wants to include under the anomic interest-group category spontaneous explosions "where explicitly organized interest groups are not present, or where they have failed to obtain adequate representation of their interests. . . ."[10]

It is doubtful, however, whether this category really holds up under analysis. The riot, demonstration, or violent deed is either an instrumental action of an association or quasi-group or it is an expression of their frustration. Thus it cannot be considered a special autonomous, spontaneous type of interest group or, at least, it would not be an interest group in Truman's sense. Such a group would lack the shared attitudes or the structures of the other types of interest group.

Other Classifications

We are now in a position to understand why the association dominates research and theory on interest groups. The other types of interest group are far more difficult to get a conceptual handle on. For this reason our further discussion will assume the association, unless otherwise indicated. The French political scientist Jean Meynaud has divided (politi-

---

TABLE 9.1.   Meynaud's Three Types of Interest Groups

1. **Political cliques:** these groups would like to take political power, but cannot for organizational reasons be considered as political parties.
2. **Opinion groups:** these operate on the level of elite or mass opinion, rather than directly on political institutions.
3. **Pressure groups:** these seek to influence the conduct and content of public policy through "pressure" at key points of political institutions.

---

8. Almond and Powell, *Comparative Politics*, pp. 75–76.
9. Ibid., p. 76.
10. Ibid.

cal) interest groups into three main types according to the "role and mission" of the group, as outlined in table 9.1.[11]

Because of the sinister sound of "pressure" and "pressure group," many political scientists substitute the more neutral and generic "interest group." Since "pressure" seems to say something more specific and can be exercised for positive as well as negative purposes, however, we will retain the term "pressure group." While the various forms of this pressure will be discussed in the next section, table 9.2 follows, while modifying, Meynaud's tripartite classification of pressure groups.

TABLE 9.2.   Three Types of Pressure Groups

1. **Business-institutional groups:** these are groups that exercise pressure on government for their own narrow gain, profit, or enhancement. A business might lobby for government contracts; a church for school subsidies; or a university for tax privileges.
2. **Category-defense groups:** these are formed to defend and promote the welfare of broad categories (quasi-groups) of the population. Unions, farmers' organizations, veterans' groups, business federations (not individual firms), professional, ethnic, and religious formations are good examples.
3. **Promotional groups:** these groups promote a cause that does not bring them any immediate or tangible reward. They consider themselves "altruists" advancing some cause that is truly in the "public interest." Pacifist, consumer-protection, or anti-capital punishment and other groups figure in this category.

Naturally, we will encounter groups that seem hard to place in only one of these categories, especially when taking into account the frequent gap between avowed formal purposes and real informal purposes. Many pressure groups that are in categories 1 and 2 try to give the impression of selfless altruism and dedication to the public interest (i.e., to don the mantle of a promotional group).

BUSINESS-INSTITUTIONAL PRESSURE GROUPS.   These are so diversified that no single example could represent very much of the universe of such groups. Companies such as General Motors or Exxon in this country, Fiat or Montedison in Italy, or British Petroleum or Unilever in Great Britain are large and powerful enough to articulate and defend their own interests in myriad ways. Moreover, many pressure groups that appear to be category-defense or even promotional groups are, in reality, fronts for one or several big businesses. Furthermore, some of these businesses are so-called multinationals, which have considerable political clout in a number of countries.

11. Jean Meynaud, *Nouvelles etudes sur les groupes de pression en France* (Paris: Librairie Armand Colin, 1962), pp. 128–37.

CATEGORY-DEFENSE PRESSURE GROUPS.   Our example of this type of group is drawn from Germany. Most capitalist countries have organizations that defend the interests of big business. The German version of this type of association is the Federation of German Industry (BDI, for *Bundesverband der Deutscher Industrie*).[12] The BDI is the heir to previous business organizations going back into the nineteenth century. However, its present structure and overall approach reflect serious reorganization after the downfall of the Third Reich in 1945. Organizationally, the BDI is a federation of federations, made up in the 1960s of nearly forty federations that covered some seven hundred base organizations. These in turn included over ninety thousand German employers, or better than 90 percent of German industrialists.[13]

The BDI's national organization involves a president, presidential board, executive board, and a large number of committees, departments, working groups, and regional offices (13). Like most formal organizations, real power tends to flow from the top down. However, Gerard Braunthal has compared the BDI with some of its counterparts in the following terms:

> A comparison of the BDI with the Federation of British Industries shows parallels in their power structure. In the FBI, as in the BDI, policy is made by the president and his official advisors, the professional staff, and the commissions. The French counterpart of the BDI, the Conseil National du Patronat Francais, is structured similarly. . . . The NAM [National Association of Manufacturers (USA)], reflecting the strong federalist tradition of the United States, is an exception to the oligarchical and centralist pattern found in the other organizations.[14]

As with most business organizations, the BDI employs a variety of techniques to maximize its direct and indirect impact on public policy. Set up jointly by the BDI and another business group is the Institute of German Industry, which is supposed to "give the point of view of industry to the public and its own members in the most favorable light." [15] The Institute engages in expensive research and publicity campaigns involving an impressive assortment of publications and news releases. Other public relations efforts call upon radio, television, and motion pictures.

12. Our brief analysis relies heavily on Gerard Braunthal, *The Federation of German Industry in Politics* (Ithaca: Cornell University Press, 1965).
13. Ibid., p. 31.
14. Ibid., p. 61.
15. Ibid., p. 72.

The BDI is also involved directly in the German political process. Quite naturally, the BDI has looked with greatest favor upon the Christian Democrats and the Free Democrats as the parties most favorable to the free enterprise system. In the early 1950s the BDI was quite hostile to the Social Democrats, whose "socialism" was obviously anathema to them. As the Social Democrats have mellowed, relations between them and the BDI have grown correspondingly more cordial. In terms of financial aid to political parties, especially to the Christian Democrats and Free Democrats, the BDI operates indirectly rather than directly. That is, a number of associations have been set up for which the BDI personnel have provided leadership and coordination.

Moreover, BDI officials have run for public office, often serving in the German parliament. From this base, BDI views reach the heart of the legislative process. Nor is the executive ignored: Chancellor Konrad Adenauer (1949–63), for example, maintained friendly and mutually beneficial relationships with BDI leaders. Lower down, the bureaucracy was subjected to the usual lobbying techniques of any well-heeled category-defense group. Nonetheless, the BDI has suffered bitter disappointments, even in the "golden age" before the Social Democrats entered the Government as junior partners in 1966 and later as senior partner after 1969.

PROMOTIONAL PRESSURE GROUPS.   The Italian Catholic Action, which has been closely associated with the ruling Christian Democratic party since the end of World War II, is an example of a promotional pressure group. Still powerful today, the heyday of Catholic Action political influence was probably the decade of the 1950s. While we have classified Catholic Action as a promotional group, it is clearly more than that. Given its large numbers (over 3 million at its height) and its adherence to a worldview (Catholicism), if not an ideology, it has many of the aspects of the social movement, as discussed in chapter 7. Moreover, during the 1950s and early 1960s it was a most powerful political organization. Indeed, Joseph LaPalombara agreed with the sentiment that Catholic Action was the "single most powerful interest group operating in the [Italian] political system." [16]

Any organization, even one dedicated to a "spiritual" mission, can be strengthened by the ability to dispense patronage and to participate in recruiting the political and administrative elite. A former Catholic Action member once suggested that "Catholic Action is immensely pow-

16. Joseph LaPalombara, *Interest Groups in Italian Politics* (Princeton: Princeton University Press, 1964).

erful in the bureaucracy because it is increasingly able to influence bureaucratic appointments, determine who will be awarded major academic chairs . . . place its own people on state-owned radio and television organization, and receive its quota of appointments to the directive boards of the state-controlled industries." [17]

And yet, behind the high-pressure opportunism of Catholic Action, there is a cause to be promoted. That cause is broadly that of Catholic "integralism," the view that society must be permeated with influences stemming from Roman Catholic church, its dogmas, doctrines, and teachings. As LaPalombara puts it: "If the society is shot through with evil, evil itself must be eradicated wherever it is found; if the Catholic Church is beseiged by enemies, they must be sought out and combatted wherever they may lurk; if the message of the Church is total, applying to every facet of human existence, there is no section of social organization and behavior that should remain ignorant of it." [18] This means that Catholic Action continually finds itself in the cockpit of such controversial issues as pornography, censorship, divorce (until recently illegal in Italy), abortion, aid to parochial education, and so on.

Before World War II, Catholic Action had four main branches, for male and female adults and for male and female young people. [19] In 1946 there were added special movements for university students, university graduates, and elementary teachers. The organization has the closest ties with the Catholic church at all levels. Moreover, "the hierarchy and the clergy maintain a tight control over Catholic Action, which is their devoted army and instrument." [20] As a political force, Catholic Action in certain parts of Italy is much stronger than the Christian Democratic party organization itself. Though ostensibly prohibited by the Concordat of 1929 from engaging in direct political action, Catholic Action operates in electioneering through an organization of "civic committees" first formed in 1948. This organization is "a cover for Catholic Action and was manned entirely by Catholic Action personnel." [21]

The 1960s saw a decline in the political importance of Catholic Action. The policies of the organization had always lain considerably to

17. Ibid., p. 350.
18. Ibid., p. 421.
19. Giorgio Galli and Alfonso Prandi, *Patterns of Political Participation in Italy* (New Haven: Yale University Press, 1970), p. 175.
20. Ibid., p. 175.
21. Ibid., p. 176.

the "right" of major elements of the Christian Democratic party. The early 1960s, however, were the period of the "opening to the left," an attempt by Christian Democratic leaders to wean the Italian Socialist party away from its long-term alliance with the Communists. Since the party leaders looked one way while Catholic Action looked another, a considerable cooling of relations was inevitable.

This trend was reinforced in the first part of the decade since the opening-to-the-left strategy seemed to work. However, the late 1960s and early 1970s showed that one major goal of the opening-to-the-left strategy had failed: the Communist vote continued to grow, election after election. Moreover, the passage of a law allowing for divorce by the Italian parliament and its subsequent affirmation by a popular referendum showed that, like the old gray mare, Catholic Action was not what it used to be.

We can clarify the differences between the three types of pressure groups by recalling Theodore Lowi's three types of public policy: distributive, regulatory, and redistributive.[22] Accordingly, we can establish different frequencies of involvement in the three issue areas for each of the three types of pressure group, as outlined in table 9.3.

TABLE 9.3.   Frequency of Involvement of Pressure Groups in Policy

	Distributive	Regulatory	Redistributive
Business-institutional groups	very frequent	occasional	rare
Category-defense groups	rare	very frequent	occasional
Promotional groups	never	frequent	frequent

DIRECT ACCESS TO THE POLITICAL SYSTEM

"Access" refers to the ability of a pressure group to reach important centers of political decision. Without access there can be no pressure. Access is such a scarce resource and so unequally distributed that one

22. It will be recalled that distributive policies concerned very narrow issues such as local highways, etc.; regulatory policies concerned fairly extensive sectors of society; while redistributive policies concerned very broad issues affecting the political and economic structure of society. See chapter 3 for a fuller discussion.

critic of pluralism maintains that *"pressure politics is a selective process, ill designed to serve diffuse interests. The system is skewed, loaded, and unbalanced in favor of a fraction of a minority."* [23]

We can consider access as both *direct* and *indirect*. Direct access means immediate communications between pressure group agents and legislators, bureaucrats, and judges. Indirect access (taken up in the closing two sections of the chapter) involves the mediating role of political parties and public opinion. Direct access can occur at three stages of policy: preparliamentary, parliamentary, and postparliamentary.

Preparliamentary Access

In chapters 2 and 3 we discussed why pressure groups have come to shift much attention away from legislatures and toward executives and bureaucracy. Especially where "transformed parliamentarism" prevails, the main guidelines of policy are set by the government and its bureaucracy before bills come to parliament. Virtually no pressure group can therefore afford to ignore the preparliamentary stage of policy. Thus such groups often concentrate their pressure tactics upon particular departments or agencies of the government.

When the relationship between a government department or agency and a specific pressure group becomes especially intimate, we have a *clientele relationship*. More technically, Joseph LaPalombara sees this relationship emerge when a government agency considers a group "the natural expression and representative of a given social sector which, in turn, constitutes the natural target or reference point for the activity of the administrative agency." [24]

This is an apt description of the relationship between the American Farm Bureau Federation and the United States Department of Agriculture. During the Eisenhower administration (1953–61) the Farm Bureau's "friends occupied high posts in the Department, and the Administration's farm legislative recommendations followed lines congenial to it." [25] This is the more remarkable because the Farm Bureau, though the strongest farm pressure group, was by no means in a monopoly posi-

23. E. E. Schattschneider, "The Scope and Bias of the Pressure System," in *Readings in Political Parties and Pressure Groups*, ed. F. Munger and D. Price (New York: Thomas Y. Crowell, 1965), p. 142.
24. LaPalombara, *Italian Politics*, p. 262.
25. V. O. Key, *Pressure Groups*, pp. 34–35.

tion. Other organizations such as the National Grange and the National Farmers' Union also have a strong farmer representation.

We can easily imagine the advantages that close personal relationships brings to both sides of the clientele relationship. And yet, this is not the whole story. The Italian Ministry of Industry and Commerce, typical of many ministries, suffers from a shortage of information. As one of its officials complained, "Every time we need a single datum, we have to turn to Confindustria [the Italian Confederation of Industry] or the other professional associations. We are completely dependent on them and literally at their mercy." [26]

One does not have to be a cynic to question the unblemished objectivity of information passed on by pressure groups. Even statistical information can be less than divinely revealed truth, for as the old maxim has it, "Figures don't lie, but liars sure do figure." Data may be incomplete or presented in a questionable manner. On the other hand, the prevalence of pressure groups in public policy may be less a matter of collusion than of default.

In chapter 3 we spoke of the "politics of consultation" as one way of bringing interest groups and pressure groups into the preparliamentary phase of policy formation. We can see a most highly institutionalized form of this in the Economic and Social Council of the Fifth French Republic. Founded in 1945 under the Fourth Republic, the Council survived into the Fifth Republic and still exists, somewhat less actively, today. It was a consultative body of 200 members grouping together representatives of labor, business, agricultural, and other organizations.[27] The 42 labor representatives were spread among the three large unions (Catholic, Communist, and Socialist in political tendency) and two smaller groups. The 47 business representatives grouped 40 representatives from eight various organizations of big and small business, plus 7 from nationalized industries. Eleven farmers' groups contributed a total of 32 members. Further Council seats numbering 69 went to several cooperative and other organizations. Of the total 200 the Government named 59 members.

In addition to a president, secretary-general, and a Bureau, the main organization subdivision of the Economic and Social Council was the section. Each section was originally given a topic, and its membership

26. Quoted in LaPalombara, *Italian Politics*, p. 283.
27. J. E. S. Hayward, *Private Interests and Public Policy* (New York: Barnes & Noble, 1966).

was intended to reflect the composition of the entire Council. The sections were as follows:

1. Social Activities
2. Technical Research and Economic Information
3. Foreign Economic Expansion
4. Economic Regionalism
5. Overseas Development and Technical Cooperation
6. Investment and Planning
7. Conjuncture and National Income
8. Finance, Credit, and Taxation
9. Agriculture
10. Industrial Production and Power
11. Public Works, Transport, and Tourism [28]

The Council's machinery could be activated by four stimuli: the Government, one of the organizations represented in the Council, a section, and the Council's directing Bureau. Some Council business involved mere studies, but other parts involved reports and recommendations to the Government in sensitive issues. The actual policy impact of the Economic and Social Council was somewhat checkered. In the early de Gaulle period with its general deemphasis of parliament, it made a significant input into Government policy. Later on, the Council declined somewhat in impact. This should cause no surprise since merely consultative bodies are at the whim of those who consult. Henry W. Ehrmann has pointed to another explanatory factor: "Being less useful, the larger and less technical committees have also less weight. This explains in part why the various Economic Councils have never fulfilled the expectations of pluralists and administrators who hoped that the councils would, by combining the advantages of expertness and publicity, relieve the pressure of the lobbies." [29]

Parliamentary Access

The parliamentary stage of policy and legislation is the traditional locus of pressure group activity. The transfer of so much initiative elsewhere

28. Ibid., p. 36.
29. Henry W. Ehrmann, "Interest Groups and the Bureaucracy," in *European Politics: A Reader*, ed. Mattei Dogan and R. Rose (Boston: Little, Brown, 1971), pp. 339–40.

has naturally caused changes in pressure group strategy. Nonetheless, legislatures still have important powers in all constitutional regimes, and in countries like the United States and Italy they can overwhelm the executive. For this reason pressure groups have developed a variety of strategies to maximize their legislative influence. The most important of these are lobbying, support for candidates, alliances, and logrolling.[30]

Lobbying, though the expression is an Americanism, is a common practice wherever legislatures rise above the rubber-stamp category. Lobbying in general is simply the attempt of pressure group agents to influence the outcome of legislation. The techniques of lobbying run from outright bribery to less blatant modes of "winning friends and influencing people." Persistence and friendliness can be sometimes as effective as more questionable practices such as campaign contributions, wining and dining, and the like. In certain cases the lobbyist may be little more than a source of information to the legislator, though here the same reservations about objectivity must be entered as with information transmitted to bureaucrats.

A student of British pressure groups finds that personal lobbying involves three different techniques.[31] The first is the *mass assault,* in which a number of excited people literally swamp the legislator or have him come to some noisy meeting arranged to impress him. The *steady trickle,* on the other hand, suggests a small but steady stream of visitations by those who wish to win over the legislator. The *deputation* is a sort of intermediate form, in which a small group presents its "case" to the legislator. When a pressure group is mobilized for a "campaign," it is likely to use all three approaches, in addition to letter and telegram avalanches.

Support for candidates, financial and otherwise, is a frequent technique of pressure groups in their quest for legislative influence. Business, labor, and farmers are especially active in this area. In the United States in 1960, for example, "union financial support went to 194 Democratic House candidates but only to 6 Republican House candidates." [32] In West Germany business activity was more indirect, but no more subtle. So-called sponsors' associations were formed in the 1950s, which

30. Discussion of these strategies follows Truman's account in *Governmental Process* closely.
31. J. D. Stewart, *British Pressure Groups* (Oxford: Oxford University Press, 1958).
32. Key, *Pressure Groups,* p. 63.

were "designed to act as intermediaries between the parties on the one hand and individual firms on the other." Although "firms had the right to designate the party to which they wished their contributions to go," it was not always clear "whether the contributions thus earmarked were deducted from the general pool before its distribution to the parties. . . ." [33]

In many cases, pressure group officials are directly elected to parliament. In Great Britain it is not considered improper for M.P.s to accept retainers from outside organizations. In Italy, and to some extent wherever there are Christian Democratic parties, the Roman Catholic church helps candidates in a number of ways. Such moral support can sometimes be as effective as the material support received by rival parties.

Forming alliances is another way in which pressure groups seek to maximize their legislative influence. An alliance is a fairly long-term cooperative arrangement between legislative representatives of different groups for the sake of common political objectives. Farmer-labor alliances in certain American states have been frequent, as have alliances between some business and farmer groups in Congress. In France and Italy, where the labor movement was for a long while divided into three main political strains, recent trends show strong alliances for common goals. This shows that an alliance presupposes some degree of ideological congruence between the allies as well as a common perception of enemies. In France and Italy this has been achieved by the Catholic unions moving to the left somewhat and the Communist-dominated unions sliding toward the right.

An alliance means that legislative "friends" of the allied groups use all possible opportunities to advance the common cause. Votes, committee sessions, debates, amendments, and other parliamentary devices are exploited to help the alliance.

Logrolling represents another type of working arrangement. Its motto is "You scratch my back and I'll scratch yours." More elegantly, a logrolling arrangement finds two or more sets of group representatives helping each other in a series of measures, each of which is a pet project of one group. It is a cynical type of vote-trading and help-trading. A frequent outcome of logrolling ventures is what Americans have come to call "pork barrel" legislation. The latter produces a shower of dams, roads, bridges, and other construction projects in the logrollers' dis-

---

33. U. W. Kitzinger, *German Electoral Politics* (Oxford: Oxford University Press, 1960), p. 208.

tricts. In countries where the Government dominates the legislative process, however, logrolling and even alliances are much less effective.

Postparliamentary Access

We have suggested in previous chapters that action by the legislature often provides only the broadest outlines of actual government policy— the problem of delegated legislation. Actual policy implementation is left to special bureaus and regulatory commissions. This presents an important opportunity for postparliamentary interest group intervention. Suppose, for example, that a business group gets wind of a possible government regulation that could cut its profits. Previous campaigns and consultations at the preparliamentary stage, and lobbying and other activities at the parliamentary stage, have failed to quash the legal foundation of the forthcoming regulation. There is a broad legal basis for it.

Nevertheless, this same broadness allows the government bureau that is empowered to act a considerable leeway as to the timing and severity of the ultimate regulation. A big delay might allow the business time to rake in its present high profits. Similarly a half-hearted enforcement of the final regulation can lead to continued high profits. A frequent complaint about "independent" regulatory commissions in the United States such as the Federal Trade Commission (FTC) has been that they have been "colonized" by the very groups they are supposed to regulate.

Another type of postparliamentary pressure group activity involves the judiciary. Organizations often go to court (litigation) in order to get rid of laws or administrative measures they do not like. In countries with strong judicial review, pressure groups have had some striking successes. In the United States, for example, the NAACP (National Association for the Advancement of Colored People) has had a long series of legal victories that have whittled down the pattern of racial segregation.[34] In contrast, the NAACP in its early days could expect no help from state legislatures, very little from Congress, and not much more from the president. In certain European countries "supreme administrative courts," known often as the Council of State, hear cases about pressure-group complaints over administrative actions.

34. Clement Vose, "Litigation as a Form of Interest Group Activity," in *Readings in American Political Behavior*, ed. R. Wolfinger (Englewood Cliffs, N.J.: Prentice-Hall, 1966).

Figure 9.4.   Modes of Pressure-Group Intervention in the Flow of Public Policy

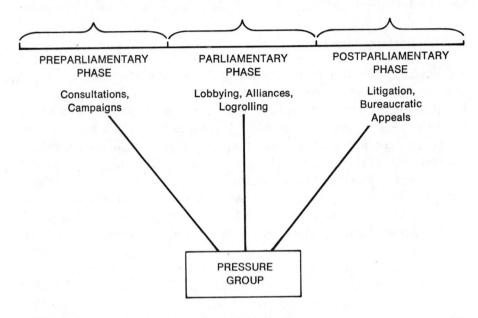

INTEREST GROUPS AND POLITICAL PARTIES

We have already seen that political parties have a special position in pluralist theory. In some pluralist accounts political parties are merely a special type of interest group or perhaps are no more than a "coalition" of such groups. In a milder approach political parties are seen to "aggregate" the interests of pressure groups and quasi-groups. These groups condition their support of a party on how far the party champions their "demands." [35] The relationship between interest groups and political parties is rather more complex than this, however. Following Meynaud, we can see the five patterns of table 9.4.[36]

TABLE 9.4.   Relations between Interest Groups and Parties

1. Full neutrality
2. Shifting support
3. The privileged relationship
4. Party formation
5. Party domination of interest groups

35. Almond and Powell, *Comparative Politics*, chap. 5.
36. Meynaud, *groupes de pression*, pp. 123–27.

Full neutrality is a far, far rarer thing than the claims of nonpartisanship voiced by pressure-group leaders would suggest. Full neutrality involves abstaining from both official and unofficial support for parties. In such a situation the dealings of pressure-group leaders with public officials would be free of ideology and partisanship. The leaders would refrain from influencing the partisan choices of the group rank and file. Neutrality is all the harder to maintain because certain parties are closer in ideology and style to the group than others.

Shifting support means that a group "shops around" for suitable parties and candidates to support. As Meynaud puts it, "This is the result of a pragmatic conception of politics which attaches itself to the content of the activity and not to the ideological label of the representative." [37] But even here there may be an element of illusion, because a pressure-group leaders' professions of open-mindedness about parties and candidates may mask a foregone conclusion. This is a kind of insurance policy whereby the leaders want to make sure that their favorite parties and candidates do not take them for granted.

The privileged relationship means that a pressure group has chosen one party as its own party. In Italy, such a relationship is found between numerous organizations of the "Catholic world" and the Christian Democratic party. Joseph LaPalombara calls this *parentela*, a word suggesting kinship among the groups and the party.[38] Organizations such as Catholic Action (a promotional group advocating Christian principles), the CISL (the Catholic Trade Union), and the Direct Cultivators (a Catholic farmers' group) have provided direct and indirect support to the Christian Democrats. In the United States it is no secret that the AFL–CIO strongly favors the Democrats, while many business groups prefer the Republicans.

Forming their own party is one way pressure groups try to assure themselves an input into the policy process. The British Labor party, for instance, is largely the creature of the unions. An even clearer case is the Poujade movement in the closing years of the Fourth French Republic (1953–58).[39] Formed initially in the fall of 1953, the movement set out as a dissident association of small merchants and artisans, called the Union for the Defense of Merchants and Artisans (UDCA). It was clearly a protest organization of petty bourgeois groups in southern

37. Ibid., p. 124.
38. LaPalombara, *Italian Politics,* chap. 9.
39. Stanley Hoffman, *Le Mouvement Poujade* (Paris: Librairie Armand Colin, 1956).

and western France. Resenting the bigness of business, government, and organized labor, the UDCA and its dynamic leader Pierre Poujade focused their attack on "unfair" taxes.

In time Poujade and his lieutenants began to broaden the base of the movement and to stress extreme nationalism. Something like an ideology began to take shape. By scheduling early elections, the Government forced the hand of the Poujadistes, who decided to run lists of candidates for the 1956 elections. The results for a "party" formed a matter of weeks before an election in a multiparty system were rather remarkable: 9.2 percent of the votes and fifty-two seats in the National Assembly.[40]

Party domination of interest groups is best exemplified by the relationship of the French and Italian Communist parties to a wide network of auxiliary organizations of economic, cultural, recreational, and related character. It should be observed, however, that sometimes this domination was less than complete and that since the 1960s these "mass organizations" have become more independent. Such, for example, is the change in the relationship of the French Communist party and the General Confederation of Labor (CGT)—the largest French trade union. In the words of George Ross: "The PCF no longer meddled openly in trade-union affairs. Instead, it stood exclusively as a political party whose main concerns were to strengthen its electoral position and engineer an alliance with parties. . . ." On the other side of the coin, the CGT "almost totally depoliticized its actions, becoming strictly trade unionist in outlook." [41]

INTEREST GROUPS AND PUBLIC OPINION

Despite the improvement in polling techniques and other forms of measurement, the concept of public opinion remains controversial and elusive. Only rarely is the attention of the whole public so concentrated as to have a single opinion. It is more common to speak of a series of "publics" related to changeable issues. There also seems to be a distinction between *static* and *dynamic* public opinion. Static public opinion is the state of opinions at any given moment: what is the range of attitudes on China, abortion, politicians, etc.? Dynamic public opinion

40. Ibid., p. 189.
41. George Ross, "Party and Mass Organization: The Changing Relationship of PCF and CGT," in *Communism in Italy and France*, ed. S. Tarrow and D. Blackmer (Princeton: Princeton University Press, 1975), p. 537.

implies that a particular public has been mobilized and that its views are changing political decisions.

Whether our concern is with static or dynamic opinion, we must follow most students in their stress on the opinion stratification of the public.[42] James Rosenau suggests a three-layer model made up of *opinion-makers* and two distinct groups of *opinion-holders*. As figure 9.5 shows, opinion-holders constitute the vast bulk of the population: they possess opinions but cannot influence the views of those beyond a very narrow circle of acquaintances. Opinion-holders are divided into the very large *mass public* and the much smaller *attentive public*. Let us analyze this pyramid from the base upward.

Figure 9.5. Opinion Stratification of the Public

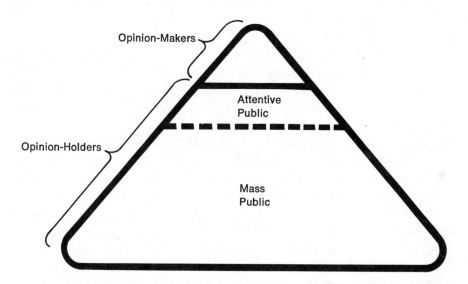

The Mass Public

The mass public may include more than 90 percent of the population. Its members are distinguished by the relative opaqueness and incoherence of their views. Their level of information on important issues is low. One of the favorite ways of showing this is to ask people the names of high officeholders. There are numbers of people even in "advanced" societies who do not know who their presidents or prime ministers are, to

42. Much of the following is inspired by James N. Rosenau, *Public Opinion and Foreign Policy* (New York: Random House, 1964).

say nothing of lower echelon legislators. The low coherence of mass public opinions can be stated negatively: members of the mass public are not ideologists, at least according to a tight definition of ideology.[43]

If we roughly designate ideologies as radical, liberal, and conservative, we find that many members of the mass public seem to pick and choose radical, conservative, and liberal elements at random. Their views are thus weirdly "eclectic" and leave logical consistency out of consideration.

This is why many consider the mass public governed more by "mood" than by structured opinions. Its outlook on issues is conditioned less by accurate information and firm principles than by vague and fickle waves of emotionalism. A good example is the oscillation between internationalism-interventionism and isolationism in public attitudes toward United States foreign policy in this century. Likewise British public attitudes toward European unity have had their ups and downs. Another example is the roller-coaster curve of the popularity of American presidents and other chief executives.

We should not conclude, however, that mass public opinion is a negligible, indeterminate, or wholly manipulable quantity. Quite the contrary, mass public opinion has become a salient political force, and with the expansion of polling and other survey techniques it may become more important still. We have come to expect political leaders to be embarrassed, if not contrite, when told that their policies or proposals register strong negative results in public-opinion polls. Few serious candidates for high office are without their own pollsters, and political consultant firms are a "growth industry" in recent years.

Voting counts, and the mass public makes up the bulk of voters. Foreknowledge of the shifting currents of mass public opinion would thus seem a prerequisite to a successful political strategy. Which issues should be stressed and which shelved or played down are largely determined by estimates of the state of mass public opinion.

Aside from voting in elections, the broad political function of the mass public is to set "the outer limits within which decision-makers and opinion-makers feel constrained to operate and interact."[44] Because of the breadth of these "outer limits" and the normal passivity of the mass public, "it is the more structured and informed opinions of the attentive and opinion-making publics that usually determine the context within

43. See chapter 10 for the distinction between loose and tight definitions of ideology.
44. Rosenau, *Foreign Policy*, p. 36.

which the opinion-policy relationship functions." [45] This is the normal situation, but at times of crisis or instability segments of the mass public can exercise a more direct influence on policy. The terms "public out-cry" and "the politics of confrontation" suggest an extraordinary mo-bilization of mass opinions.

These outer limits define the range of policies that can be advocated or implemented without seriously disturbing an underlying *consensus*. Consensus on fundamentals is another way of saying that the distribu-tion of opinions is unimodal. Given the importance of consensus, it is well to follow V. O. Key's fourfold analysis of consensus. [46]

1. *Supportive consensus*. Here the mass public overwhelmingly sup-ports a particular line of governmental action. This may result from a spontaneous convergence of mass opinion trends and government pol-icy, or it may be due to the government's carefully preparing the ground for positive acceptance of a new policy. Still another situation finds the government changing its mind and adopting a course more in keeping with prevalent views.

2. *Permissive consensus*. With permissive consensus, the link between public opinion and public policy is considerably loosened. The govern-ment has broad discretion as to whether and when it can go ahead with a certain policy. Once it decides to act, however, it knows it can count on the *general* support of mass public opinion.

3. *Consensus of decision*. This involves a fairly rapid and widespread crystallization of public attitudes on a given issue. Up to the point of this consensus, there had been serious divergencies among the public. But some event, perhaps, has precipitated a rapid convergence of views. The government accordingly feels wholly confident in taking de-cisive action.

4. *Multiple consensus*. Multiple consensus means that the various component publics of the general public have reached a basic consen-sus, [47] perhaps following a period of dissensus. The bulk of opinion in all the key publics is for or against the policy at hand. The argument that these component publics can be considered "veto groups" is sug-gested by Key's conclusion that "a policy supported by a numerical ma-

45. Ibid.
46. V. O. Key, *Public Opinion and American Democracy* (New York: Alfred A. Knopf, 1961), pp. 28–39.
47. These "component publics" are roughly equivalent to the "quasi-groups" mentioned above.

jority that is faced by the determined opposition of organized labor, organized religion, organized business, or some other such center in society may rest on shaky foundations." [48]

The Attentive Public

The attentive public, like the mass public, is by definition outside the orbit of decision-making and opinion-making. However, most of its members would like to enter those charmed circles if they only could. Moreover, the opinions of the attentive public are better informed, more coherent, more easily classifiable in terms of ideologies than those of the mass public. There are also sociological differences between the two groups of the opinion-holding public. Members of the attentive public tend to be better educated, wealthier, and to have more prestigious jobs. In short, there is considerable correspondence between the status and economic pyramids, and the opinion pyramid.

If we lacked the time to give a "depth interview" to an individual to see if he or she belonged in the attentive public, there is a reliable, if not foolproof, indicator of this: does this individual consistently expose himself or herself to the "quality press"? We could make a checklist of periodicals and say that frequent reading of several items of the list indicates attentive-public status. Newspapers such as the *New York Times,* the *Times* of London, *Le Monde* in France, *Corriere della Sera* in Italy, the *Neue Zuricher Zeitung* in Switzerland would figure in the lists of their respective countries.

Members of the attentive public are also activists and militants in parties and pressure groups, though not their top leaders. Thus, active participation in such organizations would be another shorthand indicator of membership in the attentive public. Because of these positions, the attentive public acts as a communications link between opinion-makers and the mass public. Thus, opinion-makers communicate both directly and indirectly with the mass public. It should be pointed out, however, that indirect communications through the medium of the attentive public involve a "filtering process" which is liable to distort the original "message." Because of this distortion, members of the attentive public can sometimes be considered secondary opinion-makers.

The attentive public can sometimes provide a more rigorous check

48. Key, *American Democracy*, p. 37.

Figure 9.6. Communications between the Opinion-Makers and the Mass Public

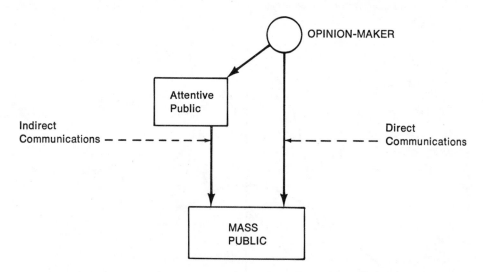

than the mass public on the actions of decision-makers. They are the vanguard of the mass public, since their reactions to public controversy are likely to stimulate mass responses. A key problem here is the distribution of opinions among the attentives. Does the distribution follow a unimodal, bimodal, or multimodal pattern? Does the curve of distribution follow the same pattern as that for the mass public or is it skewed to one or both sides?

The degree of asymmetry between the two curves varies from country to country and from time to time. Since the attentive public includes intellectuals, we should recall that our discussion in chapter 6 of intellectuals and extremism suggests asymmetry on one or both ends of the curve. Figure 9.7 therefore shows a unimodal or bell curve for the mass public, while that for the attentive public has a lower mode and slopes more gently toward the extremes. In other words, the mass public is more moderate than the attentive public. This suggests, on the one hand, that the attentive public would tolerate a greater range of alternatives from opinion-makers and decision-makers.

On the other hand, we can readily understand how the attentive public can be a serious check on decision and opinion-makers. In the first place, many decision-makers emerge from the attentive public or keep close ties with it. Thus, the reference groups of decision-makers are located within the attentive public. Very few politicians or administrators

Figure 9.7. Asymmetrical Distribution of Opinions between
the Mass and Attentive Publics

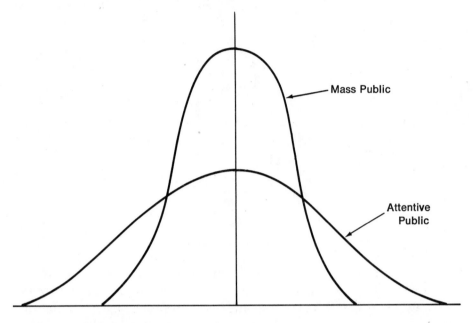

can burn all their bridges behind them. Currents of opinions in the attentive public carry more weight with these decision-making elites than do mass opinions.

The Opinion-Makers

James Rosenau defines *opinion-makers* as people who "occupy positions which enable them regularly to transmit, either locally or nationally, opinions about any issue to unknown persons outside of their occupational field or about more than one class of issues to unknown professional colleagues." [49] Rosenau distinguishes thus between two basic types of opinion-maker. The first has a position that gives him something of a captive general audience. The position is so powerful or prestigious that people listen almost automatically to the pronouncements of the present incumbent. His successor will enjoy similar possibilities. The second sort of opinion-maker is more limited: his audience is not so much captive as "won over." He has so impressed his professional colleagues that they take him seriously on issues which have

49. Rosenau, *Foreign Policy*, p. 45.

nothing to do with his expertise. Both types of opinion-maker can diversify their utterances and pontificate on morals, art, religion, politics, and everything else from soup to nuts.

While Rosenau's stress on the *position* of the opinion-maker is well taken, we must also bring in personality. Position gives one an opportunity to influence others; personality determines the use a person makes of this opportunity. An extraverted, loquacious, or "committed" person will make maximum use of his chances; an introverted, reticent, or cynical person will let most of them lie dormant. This is why change of personnel seems to alter the actual opinion impact of one and the same position.

James Rosenau sees four basic categories of opinion-makers: *governmental, associational, institutional,* and *individual* (see table 9.5).[50] These can be national or local in scope and can range from affecting a single issue to a multitude of them.

TABLE 9.5. Types of Opinion-Makers

1. **Governmental opinion-makers:** legislators, executives, important bureaucrats, judges, and politicians. Because of their importance and notoriety, all these types have an inside track into our minds. Perhaps Max Weber was correct when he spoke of the "charisma of office."
2. **Associational opinion-makers:** the top officials of opinion groups and pressure groups. The more powerful the group, the better are the possibilities for its leaders to be effective opinion-makers.
3. **Institutional opinion-makers:** leaders of institutions such as large businesses, universities, churches, and foundations.
4. **Individual opinion-makers:** various people, who, though they may be affiliated to associations and institutions, do not owe their opinion-making notoriety to them. Individual accomplishments, perhaps of a scientific, artistic, or intellectual nature, have gained these people renown.

Propaganda

Despite the efforts of social scientists to use the term "propaganda" neutrally, it retains an unsavory connotation, not far removed from lying. The good guys dispense information, the bad guys spread propaganda. Rather than argue at length here for a neutral usage, we will simply suggest that propaganda is everywhere and that causes dear to each of us will occasionally resort to propagandistic techniques.

50. Ibid., pp. 58–73.

"Propaganda" may be defined as *any organized attempt to manipulate opinions by words, images, or acts*. This does not necessarily mean that the new or changed opinions are false. "Manipulation" here simply means that the propagandist does not fully reveal his purposes and techniques to the target group or public. In fact, many propagandists are convinced that their long-term goal is to replace ignorance or error by knowledge or truth. Other propagandists are, of course, cynical through and through.

Governments, parties, movements, and interest groups use propaganda. They use it, most students agree, for both specific and general purposes. In the first case the propagandist wishes to alter the target group's opinions regarding some precise and current project. A pressure group, for example, might wish to gain support for a specific piece of legislation; it thus mounts a propaganda campaign to demonstrate the "need" for it. General propaganda serves to build up general acceptance and support for the pressure group and its goals. This "reservoir of good will" will be tapped at some future date when the group makes specific demands.

According to David B. Truman, propaganda has three different goals, which sometimes can be seen as "stages" in a propaganda effort. They are, in increasing order of difficulty:

1. Ensuring reception of the message
2. Stimulating favorable preexisting attitudes
3. Changing attitudes [51]

The first goal of the propagandist is to ensure that the target group receives the message. While the easiest of the three propaganda goals, it is by no means automatic. Time, money, and other resources may be too scarce for many groups to be very successful in hitting their projected targets. Propaganda can be face-to-face or can utilize the mass media.

No target group is completely virgin territory for the propagandist. It is a congeries of attitudes, prejudices, preferences, tastes, interests, and so forth. The second goal of the propagandist is to strike the right notes in behalf of his group. In the words of a popular song of the 1940s, he must "accentuate the positive" and "eliminate the negative" associations of his message. Thus, a group favoring a revolution in the United States would be wiser to associate a modern revolution with 1776 than with the Russian Revolution of 1917.

51. Truman, *Governmental Process*, p. 226.

The propagandist must show that what he is advocating is "really" compatible with, if not derived from, the prevailing positive attitudes of the target group or public. Such "putting one's best foot forward" is distortion, insofar as it selects only certain aspects of the project of the propagandist for presentation.

The third stage or goal of propaganda, attitude change, is extremely difficult to engineer. Even if claims about the "innate conservatism" of people are simplistic, there are reasons why people cling to the tried and the true, why basic assumptions ingrained early in life are never seriously challenged, and why objective interests come to reinforce subjective preconceptions. Graham Wallas, British political theorist of the early twentieth century, suggested as much in 1908 when he said that "most of the political opinions of most men are the result, not of reasoning tested by experience, but of unconscious or semiconscious inferences fixed by habit." [52]

A disciple of Wallas, Walter Lippmann, even considered "stereotypes" as the main type of mental habit.

> The systems of stereotypes may be the core of our personal tradition, the defenses of our position in society.
>
>   They are an ordered, more or less consistent picture of the world to which our habits, our tastes, our capacities, our comforts and our hopes have adjusted themselves. They may not be a complete picture of the world, but they are a picture of a possible world to which we are adapted.[53]

The propagandist aiming at attitude change wants to disturb, even to uproot, the habitual, the system of stereotypes, in the target group. Although prohibitionists in America were able to change the Constitution regarding the sale and manufacture of alcoholic beverages, their inroads on people's moral attitude toward drinking were far more limited, and thus their ultimate failure can be considered a propaganda failure.

Certain techniques have been developed to attain the three goals. Reception of the message means getting the attention of members of the target group or public. One way to do this is using *attention-getting symbols*. Many symbols have something to do with the message intended by the propagandist. They "stand for" some quality or abstraction that the propagandist cannot or will not (because of its vastness, complexity, or abstractness) present to his target group. Thus, we can readily under-

52. Graham Wallas, *Human Nature in Politics* (1908; reprinted ed., Lincoln: University of Nebraska Press, 1962), p. 122.
53. Walter Lippmann, *Public Opinion* (New York: Macmillan, 1961), p. 95.

stand why the Italian Christian Democratic party chose a shield with a cross on its emblem. There is, of course, the obvious generic association with Christianity. The shield is a symbol of defense (against communism?) and, more subtly, recalls the crusades against the infidels of the Middle Ages.

The Communists have fastened upon the hammer and sickle to represent the alliance between the proletariat (hammer) and peasantry (sickle). Some attention-getting symbols, on the other hand, have little or nothing to do with the content of the propagandist's message, but are surefire for attention-getting. Their symbolism is diffuse, evoking favorable associations. Babies and beauties are quite effective in this respect. Color combinations are helpful too: red, white, and blue are "good" colors in the United States, as red, white, and green are "good" in Italy.

A second and superficially simple technique of propaganda is *repetition*. If an assertion is repeatedly drummed into our heads, it can leave an unconscious residue even though a conscious mind is unaware of it. One proof of this is seen in the controversy over "subliminal advertising." This technique flashes images upon a television or movie screen so rapidly that viewers are not aware that they have been so exposed. Later, tests will show that they have indeed perceived the message.

Thus the manifest rejection of a message may well mask latent retention of it. This is why slogans are important in both politics and advertising: they are easy to remember and have a way of popping back into awareness with the slightest stimulus.

A third major propaganda technique is *gross oversimplification*. This means leaving out important information that may seriously qualify, if not completely contradict, the conclusions desired by the propagandist. In advertising, this sometimes takes the form of favorable (or unfavorable) comparisons that mysteriously leave out the second term of the comparison. For example, the claim that "Blinko Beer is 40 percent milder" sounds good, until we ask "milder" than what: Brand X, sulfuric acid, or the "old" Blinko. It may well be that the standards used are so minute that a 40 percent difference between new Blinko and, say, old Blinko does not register in the amateur beer-drinker's palate.

Gross oversimplification is very frequent in political propaganda. One example is fairly frequently used by certain opponents of the welfare state. As we shall see in more detail in chapter 11, the concepts of the welfare state, socialism, and communism refer to rather different things. Nevertheless, it makes for good propaganda somehow to link these things, since socialism and communism seem alien and forbidding to most Americans. Accordingly, the gross oversimplification takes the crude form: welfare state = socialism = communism. From this perspective anyone who favors expanded social security, expanded government medical services, and the like appears as an apostle of Communist revolution. In a more subtle version, welfarism is not equated with socialism and communism, but is portrayed as the first step of an inexorable process culminating in socialism-communism:

welfare state————→socialism————→communism.

As these examples illustrate, gross oversimplification may achieve its desired impact by "begging the question" (i.e., by assuming certain things are true when their truth is highly questionable). Another type of gross oversimplification asserts that mere correlations are in fact cause-and-effect relationships. From the fact that phenomena X and Y occur together, the propagandist may wish to convey that X is the cause of Y. But the truth of the matter is that both X and Y are effects of a more basic underlying cause (or set of causes), Z.

For example, it is tempting to conclude that poverty is the decisive cause of certain types of crime because of the close correlation of the two phenomena. Maybe someone wants to use such data as propaganda for a more aggressive "war on poverty." However, it may be the case that both poverty and the crimes considered are products of a syndrome of factors left out of the equation. The propagandist may be aware of these complexities, but since his goal is to convince, rather than to demonstrate logically and empirically, he sweeps them under the rug.

Given these techniques of attention-getting symbols, repetition, and gross oversimplification, it might seem that the propagandist has everything in his own favor. But a moment's thought should dispel any such illusion. We have already mentioned some limits on propaganda in changing attitudes. The point is that no target group or public is completely open to the messages of each and every propagandist. This is so because each member of a target group has a virtual "perceptual screen" that determines which propaganda messages reach the individual and which do not.

The perceptual screen means that a given individual is more likely to receive propaganda from sympathetic than from antagonistic sources. A militant Communist, for example, is not likely to expose himself to the periodicals or other propagandistic ventures of centrist or rightist political groups. He will expose himself mainly to Communist propaganda

Figure 9.8.   The Perceptual Screen of Individuals

that reinforces his original beliefs and commitments to the point of saturation. Hence he has no "room" for countervailing messages. As this situation holds for nearly all political positions, the "outside" propagandist may quickly feel that he is butting his head against a stone wall.

In this chapter he have covered types of interest groups, their political behavior, and the broad problem of public opinion and the means of influencing it. As usual, much of our discussion points to topics in earlier and later chapters. Our typology of business-institutional, category-defense, and promotional pressure groups seems most relevant to the constitutional regimes of chapters 2 and 3, though some of the politics of authoritarian regimes (chapter 4) involves such groups. One does not have to be a full-fledged pluralist (chapter 6) to see that interest groups play a significant role in the formulation of Lowi's distributive and regulatory policies.

Acknowledging the importance of interest groups is compatible with the notions of social stratification developed in chapter 6. Some interest groups, such as business federations, are upper-class oriented, while most trade unions lean toward the lower classes of society. Professional groups and many promotional groups can be loosely described as middle class. At certain points our discussion also meshes with the treatment of social movements in chapter 7. In Almond's classification, for instance, social movements can be considered nonassociational interest groups. Our own preference is to think that social movements become interest groups only when the action stage has given place to adaptation.

The middle part of the chapter deals with types of access that interest groups pursue to reach centers of political decision. This involves analysis of the preparliamentary, parliamentary, and postparliamentary stages of the policy-making process. Interest groups deal with executives, bureaucrats, legislators, judges, and party politicians. There is a whole gamut of techniques, ranging from bribery to direct seeking of public office, available to interest group representatives to influence policy.

The final part of the chapter deals with public opinion from the vantage point of an interest group propagandist. An essential notion here is the stratification of the public into the three layers of opinion-makers, attentive public, and mass public. Whatever the target group of the propagandist, he will generally strive to get the attention of his target, to stimulate favorable attitudes, and (he hopes) to change attitudes. Such techniques as attention-getting symbols, repetition, and gross oversimplification are the stock-in-trade of the propagandist, as they are of his first cousins, the public relations man and the advertising consultant.

We concluded with the point that, despite these techniques, the propagandist often butts his head against a stone wall because his target group may have a perceptual screen of ingrained stereotypes, prejudices, and preferences. Even in totalitarian regimes, as we found in chapter 5, propaganda has notable failures.

This chapter concludes our section on movements in the broad sense. Parties, social movements, and interest groups, however, espouse certain beliefs and ideologies. It is the job of part 3 to explore the content of these beliefs and ideologies in greater detail.

STUDY QUESTIONS

1. Relate the idea of a quasi-group to that of a pressure group. Distinguish interest groups from political parties, and then survey the possible relationships between these two forms of political organization.

2. How would a typical pressure group operate in its attempt to influence policy in the preparliamentary, parliamentary, and postparliamentary stages?

Would you see any basic differences in the strategy of a promotional group as compared, say, to a business-institutional group?

3. Identify the various strata in the public and distinguish the role of each in the formation of public opinion. Is the vast improvement in polling techniques a boon or a bane to the cause of democracy and good government?

4. Discuss the basic goals of the propagandist and the techniques used to achieve them.

5. Discuss the various sorts of obstacles that prevent or limit the success of most propagandists.

SUGGESTIONS FOR FURTHER READING

BEER, SAMUEL H. *British Politics in the Collectivist Age.* New York: Alfred A. Knopf, 1965.

BRAUNTHAL, GERARD. *The Federation of German Industry in Politics.* Ithaca: Cornell University Press, 1965.

DUVERGER, MAURICE. *Party Politics and Pressure Groups.* New York: Thomas Y. Crowell, 1972.

EHRMANN, HENRY W., ed. *Interest Groups on Four Continents.* Pittsburgh: University of Pittsburgh Press, 1960.

HAYWARD, J. E. S. *Private Interests and Public Policy.* New York: Barnes & Noble, 1966.

HOROWITZ, DANIEL L. *The Italian Labor Movement.* Cambridge, Mass.: Harvard University Press, 1963.

KEY, V. O. JR. *Politics, Parties, and Pressure Groups.* 5th ed. New York: Thomas Y. Crowell, 1965.

————. *Public Opinion and American Democracy.* New York: Alfred A. Knopf, 1961.

LaPALOMBARA, JOSEPH. *Interest Groups in Italian Politics.* Princeton: Princeton University Press, 1964.

LIPPMANN, WALTER. *Public Opinion.* New York: Macmillan, 1961.

MUNGER, FRANK, and PRICE, DOUGLAS, eds., *Readings in Political Parties and Pressure Groups.* New York: Thomas Y. Crowell, 1965.

ROSENAU, JAMES N. *Public Opinion and Foreign Policy.* New York: Random House, 1964.

SCHATTSCHNEIDER, E. E. *The Semi-Sovereign People.* New York: Holt, Rinehart & Winston, 1960.

SKILLING, H. GORDON, and GRIFFITHS, FRANKLIN, eds. *Interest Groups in Soviet Politics.* Princeton: Princeton University Press, 1973.

STEWART, J. D. *British Pressure Groups.* Oxford: Oxford University Press, 1958.

TRUMAN, DAVID B. *The Governmental Process.* New York: Alfred A. Knopf, 1958.

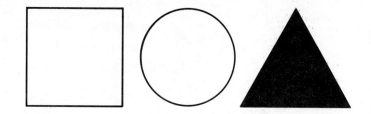

PART 3
Ideologies

INTRODUCTION

Now we come to the third part of our trilogy of regimes, movements and ideologies. Our concern in part 3 is with the norms and values, programs and projects characteristic of both regimes and movements. As will soon become clear, our position is that ideas and ideologies play an important role in political life. Thus we will have to argue against certain attempts to "reduce" political ideas and ideologies to being mere by-products of economic interests, psychological drives, and power struggles.

Chapter 10 first develops a tight definition of ideology that stresses its systematic, programmatic, activistic, and rhetorical aspects. Less coherent ideas and collections of ideas, however, also have considerable political importance by contributing to the distinctive political culture of specific societies. If ideologies often give specific direction and policy suggestions to political regimes and movements, the more diffuse impact of political culture helps to explain what sorts of movements will emerge in certain societies, as well as what sorts of regimes can succeed and what sorts will fail.

Chapter 11 tackles some of the broad themes found in more than one modern ideology. This is why we call them "crosscutting" themes: progress, utopia, democracy, freedom, socialism, and nationalism are ideas that are not confined to any small segment of the left-to-right ideological spectrum. Many regimes and movements find sustenance in these themes and proclaim themselves their champions.

Another major goal of chapter 11 is to show how the themes of freedom, democracy, and the like, take on a different coloration and meaning when interpreted by different ideologies. Everybody loves freedom, but the policies and institutions that various ideologies associate with it have nothing or little in common save the name. Thus one ideology sees "freedom" only in the destruction of the state; another sees "freedom" only in an economy in which the state owns and manages all economic institutions. For some "freedom" means escape from social control; for others it means total merger of the individual with the collectivity. The same polyvalent quality attaches to the other themes in chapter 11.

Chapter 12 covers the specific ideologies that nowadays are linked to regimes and movements. It surveys the major ideological strains such as anarchism, communism, social democracy, Christian democracy, liberalism, conservatism, poujadism, fascism, and racism. Though we follow here the traditional left-to-right approach, the last part of the chapter points to some of the difficulties underlying our traditional labels "left" and "right." One such problem is the lack of symmetry between the general ideological spectrum and the actual party spectrum to be found in countries with competitive parties. The cohabitation of several ideological strains in a single party helps us to understand why factionalism and similar tendencies are likely to plague all but the tiniest microparties.

10

Ideology and Political Culture

This chapter is concerned with two interrelated themes that set the stage for the more substantive analyses of chapters 11 and 12. These themes are ideology and political culture. For some "loose" definitions of ideology —we will shortly criticize these—there is little sense in distinguishing between ideology and political culture. However, we prefer to think of ideologies as very explicit, often highly systematic, patterns of political belief. Political culture, on the other hand, is the far more complex and diffuse set of political beliefs found in a whole country. Only rarely, as in totalitarian regimes, is the attempt made to infuse the whole political culture with the values and beliefs of a single ideology. Thus, the usual case is that a country's political culture is a composite—almost a mosaic —that includes not only several competing ideologies, but also belief systems (subcultures) too vague to qualify as ideologies.

The first part of the chapter deals with the notion of ideology. Since this is a highly controversial topic, some attempt is made to survey and criticize alternative formulations. Of special concern are those general theories (which we will call "reductionism") that attempt to explain away or minimize the role of ideas and ideologies in political life. While sometimes correct in describing specific historical cases, these reductionist theories suffer from serious shortcomings.

The second part of the chapter is concerned with the broader arena of political culture, within which ideologies often compete. Study of political culture helps to tell us which ideologies can or will take hold in specific societies; it also indicates why certain types of regimes and movements flourish in some places and languish in others. The political culture is a kind of soil that is hospitable to some plants, but kills others sooner or later.

IDEOLOGY

In our various encounters with the concept of "ideology," we have treated it as *a programmatic and rhetorical application of some grandiose philosophical system, which arouses men to political action and may provide strategic guidance for that action.* Before exploring some of the implications and applications of such an approach to ideology, we must examine how this "tight" definition of ideology differs from widespread "loose" definitions of it.

Loose definitions of ideology tend to equate it with "belief system." Accordingly, political ideology is seen as any set of political beliefs that characterize any individual, group, political party, government, social class, or entire nation. Polls and surveys of such political actors would ostensibly reveal their ideologies. The "system" of belief system is not taken very seriously by loose approaches, in other words. What makes the system is that the beliefs in question are found to cluster together. Moreover, logical coherence, the mutual implication of the different component ideas of the ideology, goes completely by the board with loose concepts of ideology.

Situated between loose and truly tight approaches to ideology is the approach taken in the classic study *The American Voter* (1960). There the authors distinguish between an "attitude structure" and an ideology. An attitude structure emerges "when two or more beliefs or opinions held by an individual are in some way or another functionally related." [1] This functional relationship can be of means to ends or of some analogy between things. An ideology, however, goes beyond an attitude structure, since it is a "particularly elaborate, close-woven and far-ranging structure of attitudes." [2] While this explanation tightens things up considerably, the criteria of elaborateness, close-wovenness, and far-rangingness are still too vague to distinguish ideologies.

1. Angus Campbell et al., *The American Voter* (New York: John Wiley, 1964), p. 110.
2. Ibid., p. 111.

Table 10.1 gives us a sampling of how some social scientists point toward a more definitive and useful notion of ideology.

TABLE 10.1.   Tight Definitions of Ideology

Joseph LaPalombara: Ideology "involves a philosophy of history, a view of man's present place in it, some estimate of probable lines of future development, and a set of prescriptions regarding how to hasten, retard, and/or modify that developmental direction." [3]

Raymond E. Reis: "In its more active form, the insistence that knowledge must act as an instrument of social change is known by the term 'ideology.' The force of ideology is the force of passion and commitment to an idea. An ideology provides its possessor with self-justification and with a claim to action. It is something to believe in and give orientation to one's life and experience. Ideology has a function analogous to religious commitment." [4]

Robert A. Haber: "Ideology as an intellectual production has several elements: (1) a set of moral values, taken as absolute, (2) an outline of the 'good society' in which those values would be realized, (3) a systematic criticism (or . . . affirmation) of the present social arrangements and an analysis of their dynamics, (4) a strategic plan of getting from the present to the future. . . ." [5]

Willard A. Mullins: Ideology is a "logically coherent system of symbols which, within a more or less sophisticated conception of history, links the cognitive and evaluative perception of one's social condition—especially its prospects for the future—to a program of collective action for the maintenance, alteration or transformation of society." [6]

Structure and Functions of Political Ideology

These and other tight definitions of ideology involve some definite claims about the structure and functions of political ideology. The emphasis on structure suggests that the content of ideologies is more specific than with mere belief systems. The main structural aspects are (1) relationship to a grandiose philosophical system; (2) the program that derives from that system; and (3) the strategy of realizing programmatic aims. The functional aspect—what the ideology does in the realm of politics— lies in the rhetorical element that motivates action to realize both program and strategy.

IDEOLOGY AND A GRANDIOSE PHILOSOPHICAL SYSTEM.   A political ideology is related to a grandiose philosophical system, though the ideol-

3. Joseph LaPalombara, "Decline of Ideology: A Dissent and Reinterpretation," in *The End of Ideology Debate*, ed. Chaim I. Waxman (New York: Simon & Schuster, 1969), p. 320.
4. Raymond Reis, "Social Science and Ideology," in ibid., p. 283.
5. Robert A. Haber, "The End of Ideology as Ideology," in ibid., p. 186.
6. Willard A. Mullins, "On the Concept of Ideology in Political Science," *American Political Science Review* 66 (1972): 510.

ogy is not the system itself. The ideology tries to apply and make concrete such abstract philosophical principles as theism and atheism; idealism (the doctrine that "mind" is the essence of reality) or materialism (the doctrine that material substance is the bedrock of reality); rationalism or romanticism; evolutionism and the like. While it is doubtful how far these grandiose systems point to specific political conclusions, most of them have undergirded various ideologies of the right, left, or center. Nonetheless, each particular ideology claims to embody the "true" political implications of the grandiose doctrine. This aspect of ideology helps it to gain respectability among intellectuals, whose predilections toward ideology we have already discussed.

Perhaps a brief look at rationalism and romanticism will give us a better idea of how broad philosophies relate to specific ideologies. Rationalism as it developed in Europe in the seventeenth and eighteenth centuries was a grandiose philosophical system. It taught that the essential structure of reality was rational and that we could know reality through right reason. The universe was a monumental system ordered by God in a rational pattern. Reason had to be the key to all valid knowledge and the foundation of morality (e.g., as in the doctrine of Natural Law). In this view we could reach specific philosophical and moral truths by "deducing" them as conclusions from a few "self-evidently true" universal ideas.[7] To extend our knowledge, all that was necessary was to apply logical deduction to ideas that were clear, distinct, and "adequate."

If rationalism were simplistically applied to politics (perhaps in an ideology), it might fit Michael Oakeshott's stereotype of the rationalist in politics:

> His mental attitude is at once sceptical and optimistic: sceptical, because there is no opinion, no habit, no belief, nothing so firmly rooted or so widely held that he hesitates to question it and judge it by what he calls his "reason"; optimistic, because the rationalist never doubts the power of his "reason" (when properly applied) to determine the worth of a thing, the truth of an opinion or the propriety of an action.[8]

A simplistic rationalist ideology would claim to "have all the answers."

---

7. Note the rationalistic phraseology of the American Declaration of Independence: "We hold these truths to be self-evident, that all men are created equal and are endowed by their Creator with certain inalienable rights. . . ."
8. Michael Oakeshott, *Rationalism in Politics* (New York: Basic Books, 1962), pp. 1–2.

When the rationalist compares his rationalistic model of a "good society" to the existing order, he is tempted to conclude that the latter's manifest irrationality is the work of ignorance or deliberate deception.

Many of the political doctrines of the French Enlightenment of the eighteenth century could be considered rationalistic in this sense. As the Marquis de Condorcet (1743–94), a political theorist and activist in the first years of the French Revolution, expressed this type of ideology: "That general philosophy which embraces in its views, goals, and achievements the principles, effects, and totality of human knowledge— that general philosophy which is only reason expanded and fortified by study—will necessarily become the common attribute of enlightened men in all countries where human intelligence has reconquered its rights and its liberty." [9] The last part of Condorcet's panegyric to reason does imply a kind of program to "reconquer" the freedom necessary for human intelligence to flourish.

Romanticism is much less a systematic doctrine than rationalism. Indeed it is a view of the world that tends to reject any and all systems. What the various schools of romanticism seem to agree on is the *primacy of feeling*. Whether the matter of concern is art, morality, or human relations, truth and authenticity are to be found in passion, emotion, and sentiment. Thus, the romanticist critic of society is apt to attack the status quo for being too rationalized, too logical. He bemoans the rigid forms of social convention, as well as the rationalized and bureaucratized technology and organization of society. These, he feels, stifle the true creativity that people harbor within them. He wants, therefore, to liberate these repressed or dormant feelings. This is the only sure road to human greatness and happiness.

While at one point in the nineteenth-century romanticism could be linked with ideologies of the right and rationalism with those of the left, too much intellectual water has passed under the dam for this to be true today. German romanticism provided much of the intellectual origins of Nazi ideology. However, the "ideology" of the American New Left in the 1960s also contained strong strains of romanticism.[10]

IDEOLOGY, PROGRAM, AND STRATEGY.   Ideologies are programmatic: in Lenin's words they tell us "what is to be done." A grandiose philosophi-

---

9. Keith M. Barker, ed., *Condorcet: Selected Writings* (Indianapolis: Bobbs-Merrill, 1976), p. 291.
10. See Fritz Stern, *The Politics of Cultural Despair* (Garden City, N.Y.: Anchor Books, 1965), and Herbert Marcuse, *An Essay on Liberation* (Boston: Beacon Press, 1969), for insights on how romanticist ideas have influenced both right-wing and left-wing ideas.

cal system may remain merely "descriptive," telling us how things are and perhaps why they are that way. An ideology becomes "prescriptive" when it tells us either what is good about the status quo and why we should preserve it, or what is bad about it and why we should change it. The ideology heralds the grandiose philosophical system as the ultimate source of the values that condemn or condone the existing order. The program of an ideology can range from vague hints to a comprehensive blueprint of the desired social condition.

Our discussion of revolutionary strategies in chapter 7 should give us some insight about this dimension of ideology. Strategic issues include such problems as violence vs. nonviolence, rapid change vs. gradualism, "going it alone" vs. collaborationism, maximum vs. minimum demands, fighting elections vs. boycotting them, compromise vs. intransigence, and the like.

IDEOLOGY AND RHETORIC.   With the rhetorical, action-oriented dimension of ideology, controversy enters social science. Some social scientists and philosophers take exception to the critical or "pejorative" approach to ideology. They object that the "truth content" of ideology can be very high or that dichotomies such as truth vs. ideology, or science vs. ideology, underestimate the considerable overlap between the categories. Since all human thought is in some sense "ideological," it is wrong, they charge, to single out political ideologies as particularly distorted or erroneous.

The reason why we cannot fully agree with such attempts to rehabilitate political ideologies is that a main "function" of ideologies is to exhort people to take political action. While calm, dispassionate, logical argumentation has been known to win isolated converts to social movements and political parties, it has not often gained their mass followings. An ideology thus involves certain techniques that appeal to the passions, feelings, and emotions of its devotees. One way to understand this is by looking at the classic Aristotelian distinction between logic and rhetoric.

Logic is the science of right reasoning: it employs the *syllogism* both to conclude and convince. The syllogism is the three-step process of reasoning of major premise, minor premise, and conclusion. The traditional example of the syllogism is:

> Major Premise: All men are mortal.
> Minor Premise: Socrates is a man.
> Conclusion: Socrates is mortal.

Rhetoric is the art of persuasion; as such it may omit certain stages of an argument in order to gain assent. Aristotle himself felt that rhetoric was ethically neutral: it could be used for good as well as evil purposes. It deserved moral reproof only when unscrupulous teachers of rhetoric called "sophists" used rhetoric "to make the weaker argument appear the stronger." Aristotle's analysis of the three techniques of rhetoric can also serve to throw light on three aspects of ideology. The three persuasive techniques of rhetoric (and ideology) are "(1) to reason logically, (2) to understand human character and goodness in their various forms, and (3) to understand the emotions—that is, to move them and describe them, to know their causes and the way in which they are excited." [11] It is when the third technique is used that morally dubious aspects of rhetoric may emerge. Accordingly, Aristotle distinguished between "good" and "bad" rhetoricians: the good do not abuse rhetoric, the bad do.

Appeal to emotions is the substitute for fullblown logical argumentation. This is what causes ideologies to distort reality, at least to some degree. The use of logic implies carefully constructed conclusions with all the relevant ideas and assumptions made explicit. The more ideologies present a logical analysis of the complexities and subtleties of social reality, the less becomes their force of persuasion. Ideologies are not tissues of barefaced lies: it is rather that they omit certain things and exaggerate others. This is done to heighten the emotional impact of the ideology.

Reductionist Theories of Ideology

Our conception of ideology assumes that it is often an *independent variable,* that is, that ideology has an independent causal impact on politics. There are theories that deny this and claim that ideology is instead a smokescreen or camouflage for the true underlying motives of political actors. Because of the influence of these theories in social science and because the situations they describe often do occur, we must give them serious consideration. Theories that "reduce" ideologies to symptoms of something more basic fall into three main categories: power reductionism, economic reductionism, and psychological reductionism.

POWER REDUCTIONISM.   Power reductionism or "political realism" sees political power as the independent variable and ideology as the depen-

11. Aristotle, *Rhetorica* in *The Basic Works of Aristotle,* ed. Richard McKeon (New York: Random House, 1941), p. 1330.

dent variable in political life.[12] Power is seen as the chief ends and means of politics; ideology is used to mask the real power intentions of political actors. This masking is done to throw adversaries off guard and to make sure that neutrals stay neutral or perhaps come over to the side of the power seekers. Ideology is thus manipulated cynically: its spokesmen do not really believe their own professions.

Such a view of ideology squares with ancient views of politics, such as that which the ancient Greek historian Thucydides puts in the mouth of speakers in his great *History*. At one point he has some Athenian diplomats articulate the two main principles of power reductionism in a discussion with the inhabitants of a neutral island (Melos). First: "For of the gods we believe, and of men we know, that by a law of their nature wherever they can rule they will." [13] Second—the ideological smoke-screen: "Of all men whom we know they [the Spartans] are the most notorious for identifying what is pleasant with what is honorable, and what is expedient with what is just." [14]

The power reductionist is highly suspicious of all the "isms" that have cluttered the ideological landscape of the last few centuries. If ostensibly ideological disputes erupt in a party, he will instead see a personal power struggle as with Stalin and Trotsky in the USSR of the 1920s, and with Mao and Liu Shao-chi in China in the early 1960s. In international politics the power reductionist finds "national interest," in terms of the maintenance or enhancement of a state's power position, as fundamental. Here too ideological assertions are so many traps set for the unwary.

ECONOMIC REDUCTIONISM.   This theory sees economic interests as the true foundation of ideologies. The economically privileged groups, according to this theory, are inexorably drawn toward conservative or status quo ideologies. The economically marginal groups gravitate toward reformist or revolutionary ideologies. The economic reductionist will, of course, allow for a certain amount of confusion. Segments of the wealthy sometimes espouse ideologies of change, while the poor are occasionally "deluded" into conservatism.

Economic reductionism can take various forms. The simplistic approach makes a direct one-to-one linkage between economic interests and

12. See Hans Morgenthau, *Politics Among Nations* (3rd ed.; New York: Alfred A. Knopf, 1960).
13. Thucydides, "The Peloponnesian War," in *Selections from the Greek and Roman Historians*, ed. C. A. Robinson (New York: Rinehart, 1959), p. 104.
14. Ibid.

political ideologies. If we know the economic interests of a given group, we can predict its ideological manifestations. Some forms of Marxism try to avoid simplism by assuming a more complex relationship between economic groups or classes and the various ideologies current in a society. George Plekhanov, for example, sees these ideologies arising from the "mentality of men living in society." [15] This mentality results from two interrelated factors: first, the direct impact of the "economic conditions"; second, the indirect impact of the "entire sociopolitical system that has arisen on that foundation." [16]

Figure 10.1.   The Two Forms of Economic Reductionism

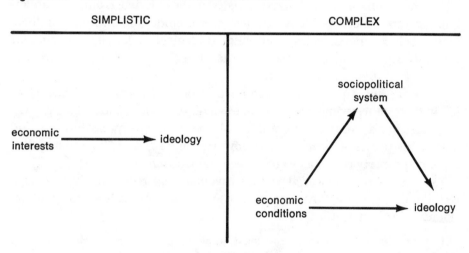

A good example of economic reductionism of the more complex variety is the judgment on liberalism rendered by the great British Socialist theorist, Harold J. Laski (1893–1950). In Laski's view, "The idea of liberalism . . . is historically connected in an inescapable way, with the ownership of property. The ends it serves are always the ends of men in this position. Outside that narrow circle, the individual for whose rights it has been zealous has always been an abstraction upon whom its benefits could not, in fact, be fully conferred." [17]

PSYCHOLOGICAL REDUCTIONISM.   This is a theory that sees ideologies

15. George Plekhanov, *Fundamental Problems of Marxism* (New York: International Publishers, 1969), p. 80.
16. Ibid.
17. Harold J. Laski, *The Rise of Liberalism* (London: Unwin Books, 1962), p. 15.

rooted in mental traits and dispositions. We can illustrate this sort of theory by recalling Pareto's theory of "residues," discussed in chapter 1. Pareto's six classes of residues were the relatively constant mental forces manifested in human societies. They included forces for combination, group persistence, individual self-expression, defense of one's self and possessions, sociality, and sexuality. Distributed in different proportions in different individuals, the residues are supposed to be the true motivating forces for the bulk of social and political behavior.

In the Paretian theory, men are rarely aware of the true wellsprings of their thoughts and actions. Instead they rationalize their attitudes and actions in terms of some general principle or doctrine. Pareto calls all such rationalizations "derivations," as they derive from the underlying psychological residues. Derivations include such things as theological beliefs, moral codes, and political ideologies. These, in particular the last, are not objective assessments of reality, but are outward projections of individual character.

For example, a person characterized strongly by group persistence is likely to embrace some sort of collectivistic or nationalistic ideology. On the other hand, someone dominated by the need to express himself and defend his possessions would lean toward some form of "liberalism" that stressed property rights as well as personal freedom.

An interesting attempt at virtual psychological reduction is seen in a well-known study of American conservatism. According to political scientist Herbert McCloskey:

> Conservatism, in our society at least, appears to be far more characteristic of social isolates, of people who think poorly of themselves, who suffer personal disgruntlement and frustration, who are submissive, timid, and wanting in confidence, who lack a clear sense of direction and purpose, who are uncertain about their values, and who are generally bewildered by the alarming task of having to thread their way through a society which seems to them too complex to fathom.[18]

Regarding the pessimistic view of man found in conservatism (see chapter 12), McCloskey further suggests that "expressed as political doctrines, these projections of aggressive personality tendencies take on the respectability of an old and honored philosophical position." [19]

While attempts to link specific political ideologies to specific personal-

18. Herbert McCloskey, "Conservatism and Personality," in *Politics and Social Life*, ed. R. A. Dentler, N. W. Polsby, and P. A. Smith (Boston: Houghton Mifflin, 1963), p. 225.
19. Ibid., p. 228.

ity types can be a valid study, one suspects that some ventures in this direction are fancy versions of the commonplace idea that "anyone who disagrees with me has got to be mad."

Broad Functions of Ideology

While it would be senseless to deny the role of power, economic, or psychological factors in the rise and spread of ideologies, single-factor theories of politics based on them are equally misleading. Ideologies play a role that is hard to reduce to any of the three factors. Despite, and sometimes because of, their distorting aspect, ideologies can serve to (1) justify political institutions, (2) mobilize political movements, and (3) provide some mental organization for the frequent confusion of political life.

JUSTIFICATION.   We have seen that legitimacy involves a basic sense of the "rightness" of movements or regimes to issue commands. These commands can be law or more informal rules.[20] In many societies vague systems provide answers to the question: "Why should I obey the laws and the government?" In modern times, however, the "political formulas"—to use Mosca's phrase—of regimes and movements are often full-blown ideologies. Why does the group in power have legitimacy? An ideology may answer by pointing to some "historic mission" that this elite has been called upon to perform. A Communist ideology claims that its party is the "vanguard" of the workers, leading them towards the inevitable goal of the "classless society." A Fascist ideology claims that only under the guidance of the charismatic leader and his followers can the "chaos" of liberal democracy and the ossification of communism be avoided.

MOBILIZATION.   Ideologies mobilize by playing on the hopes and fears of regime or movement followers. They promise greatness and social renewal or lash out against the debilitating forces that are dragging society down. These messages, which are spread through the propaganda techniques of symbolism, repetition, and gross oversimplification, find a ready response. This is especially so with groups and individuals whose distress and aspirations no longer find consolation or fulfillment in traditional beliefs.

An ideology provides answers, generally simple answers, for people with neither the time nor the inclination to fathom the complex forces

---

20. Indeed, according to the influential legal philosophy of legal positivism, law is nothing more than "the command of the sovereign."

that enmesh them and seem to doom them to unmerited suffering. Most importantly, an ideology identifies the enemy or enemies behind most of the bad things that are happening. In addition, it has a scheme for exorcising or neutralizing that enemy. The capitalists, the kulaks, the Jews, the infidels, the foreign devils, the inferior races, international finance, the church, the state, the parties—some or all of these can become scapegoats for devotees of an ideology.[21]

MENTAL ORGANIZATION. Students note a third major function of ideology: the mental organization of political reality. This factor is a partial explanation of why people perceive the significance of political facts, events, and trends so divergently. At the end of chapter 9 we spoke of a perceptual screen that filtered out some propagandistic messages aimed at the individual, while letting others reach him. By both conscious and unconscious mechanisms people tend to tune in ideas with which they already sympathize and to tune out dissonant, conflicting ideas. In this context ideology is not merely a set of abstract principles that we trot out in order to make value judgments about social and political reality. Rather, it provides "constitutive principles" according to which the ideologue "sees" the world around him. Thus, the daily experience of the ideologue tends to confirm his ideological faith. In other words, experience and ideology are mutually reinforcing. The ideology sensitizes its devotees to see things that others may miss and to endow them with special significance. Where an impartial observer may see no connection at all between discrete events, an ideologue sees them as "causally" related—perhaps the work of a hidden, heinous conspiracy.

Though the ideologue by definition sees reality less clearly than the "impartial scientific observer," in a given situation the latter may be absent. Thus, the ideologue's understanding of that situation may be better than that of an unsophisticated person. The latter has virtually no conceptual framework on which to hang reality. Political reality for him is the "bloomin', buzzin' confusion" that William James in a somewhat different context spoke about.

Moreover, it is certainly the case that the distortion factor varies considerably from one ideology to the next. Some ideologies may be quite insightful regarding certain problems, while having blind spots on others; other ideologies seem impervious to any light at all.

21. It is possible that such groups may sometimes play a less than beneficial role. However, their total eradication usually does not bring permanent relief to the troubled and resentful populace. As so often is the case in politics, the cure may be worse than the disease.

Esoteric vs. Exoteric Ideology

One argument offered by reductionist theories to disparage the importance of ideology concerns the "gap" between elite and mass levels of ideology. Here the reductionist focuses on the power drives of political elites. He concludes that the ideology "fed" to the masses is so crude and simplistic that the elite could not possibly follow or swallow it. Motivated solely by power and its fringe benefits, the elite is nonideological and uses ideology to delude the benighted masses into submission.

While such a scenario has countless past and present examples, it is sheer dogma to apply it to every case. To do so would short-circuit the real explanation of the elite-mass ideological gap. Instead of the cynical elite bamboozling the masses through ideology, two distinct levels of one and the same ideology may be involved. *Esoteric ideology,* as the term implies, is a level of ideology that requires study and meditation. Clearly only a small number of intellectuals and political militants have the time or mental equipment to grasp the finer points of certain modern political ideologies.

This is especially the case where the linkage to a grandiose philosophical system is more apparent. Moreover, the works of Marx and Lenin and even Mussolini embrace dozens of volumes. Marx's *Das Kapital* is a complex and lengthy work, written for the most part in a turgid style. While Hitler's *Mein Kampf* poses less difficulty, some of the theoretical tomes on modern racism are bulky and even erudite works.

To convey the main points of an ideology to a mass following, a certain measure of simplification, translation (faithful and otherwise), omission, and addition is necessary. Thus emerges the *exoteric ideology,* ideology for mass consumption. The esoteric ideology contains qualifications and reservations—the proverbial "if's, and's, and but's" of human discourse. These are too much for the plain person, who prefers a no-holds-barred, all-or-nothing approach. For example, while the esoteric ideology allows for multiple factors to explain social phenomena, the exoteric ideology is prone to single out one factor as solely responsible. The esoteric ideology may look to "impersonal forces" as producers of social evils; the exoteric ideology makes a scapegoat group guilty of all the troubles.

Preformed vs. Ad Hoc Ideology

Change or growth in ideologies is also cited as evidence for a reductionist view of ideology. Since ideologies in both movements and regimes are subject to (sometimes considerable) change, many leap to the conclusion that raw power is the real motivation of leaders. But we prefer to see power and ideology in a mutually interdependent or "symbiotic" relationship. Power without some ideological justification is hard pressed to maintain itself in the modern world. On the other hand, ideologies require political power to reach their goals. Within the basically symbiotic relationship between ideology and political practice, however, two rather distinct formats emerge. These are preformed and ad hoc ideology.

Preformed ideology means that a movement or regime has a ready-made and comprehensive ideology. Though the ideology suggests certain broad policies, it does *not* rigidly predetermine every strategic or tactical twist and turn. If the importance of ideology were to be confirmed by the rigid predetermination of every strategic move, reductionism would be confirmed by evidence of any flexibility at all. To avoid this we must allow for a certain margin of maneuver as to how, and how faithfully, movements and regimes pursue their ideological goals. We can go still further and conclude that *all politically successful regimes deviate somewhat from their preformed ideology, if they have one.*

In some cases we have little preformed ideology, only the "shared attitudes" of a politicized interest group or the "generalized belief" of a nascent social movement. In time, however, the movement, especially after coming to power, sees the need for a more coherent ideology. We can call this *ad hoc ideology* because it emerges through a series of encounters and experiences in the life history of the movement.

While there were definite ideological roots to the Fascist movement founded by Mussolini in 1919, it was only some time after the takeover of 1922 that something like an authentic ideology was discernible. That this ideology consisted of ad hoc accretions to a somewhat general basis does not deprive Fascist doctrine of a certain explanatory force in Italian politics to 1943.

The emergence of Castroism is quite similar. There seemed to be precious little preformed ideology beyond "nationalism" and hatred for the Batista dictatorship when Fidel Castro launched his revolutionary onslaught in 1956. Moreover, Castro was in power many months after January 1959 before he revealed (or discovered?) that he was a Marxist-Leninist. Ideology in the case of Castro's brand of communism seems something of an afterthought. Its emergence when Castro was cottoning up to the Soviet Union and trying to extend his influence in

Latin America suggests that more than a dose of what the Germans call *Realpolitik* was involved.

But before taking the reductionist route and writing off Castro's ideological effusions as window dressing, here too we must acknowledge a more complex alternative. Once an ideology takes shape, even if its growth is somewhat suspicious, it assumes a force of its own. This usually leads to a reinterpretation of the early history of the movement that endows events and ideas with an ideological significance they lacked previously. The official ideology becomes so firmly entrenched that even the regime leaders find it a burden. Not only is hypocrisy the homage that vice plays to virtue, it is the homage that power pays to ideology.

It is thus our conclusion that political ideology can be an independent force in generating political movements and regimes. This does not exclude that in given circumstances power, economic, and psychological motives can be of greater moment than ideological principles. Common dedication to Marxism-Leninism did not prevent the Sino-Soviet dispute from breaking out in the 1960s. Nor need we deny that liberalism historically reinforced the interests of the rising bourgeoisie. And there is some correlation between personality and ideology. But in almost every case the growth and influence of an ideology cannot be wholly explained by combining power, economic, and personality motives. We must allow for broader cultural influences and the autonomy of human reason to help explain why apparently disinterested and sane people reach drastically different conclusions about the good society.

POLITICAL CULTURE

"Political culture" has become an increasing concern of political science and comparative politics over the last two decades. The term broadly refers to all those aspects of a country's general culture that bear more or less directly on political processes and institutions. It is thus an analytical construct that exists in its pure form only in the minds of observers. Accordingly, political culture is a mosaic of attitudes, ideologies, traditions, customs, beliefs, and myths that influence political life. Recent concepts of political culture overlap somewhat with the older idea of "national character," which has been abandoned by many social scientists because of its vagueness or its tendency to stereotype. The "authoritarian" Germans and the "inscrutable" Orientals are merely the worst cases of such stereotypy.

Political culture is an important variable because it helps to determine which form of government a country is likely to develop and sustain. The French political philosopher Montesquieu in the mid-eighteenth century had something like this in mind when he concluded that the "government most conformable to nature is that whose particular disposition relates best to the disposition of the people for whom it is established." [22] Montesquieu's finding suggests that political institutions and constitutions will "work" best, if at all, where the country's political culture is such to support them.

The best way to grasp this general point is to examine some recent political history. After World War II the great saga of decolonization began. In Africa and Asia former French, British, Belgian, Dutch, Italian, and later Portuguese colonies gained formal independence. The question naturally arose as to what political forms these newly independent countries would and should adopt. Quite often the initial choice was made to set up constitutions and institutions based upon French, American, British, and other Western models. The nationalist elites of Third World countries were often educated in Western Europe or America and were thus attracted to the political values and institutions found there. Even where these elites remained home, their education and broader learning processes were influenced by ideas from the metropolitan countries.

Thus, ambitious Western-style constitutions replete with separation of powers, due process guarantees, and so on, were introduced in a host of Asian and African countries. In most cases, however, these constitutions did not work, and the floundering constitutionalist regimes gave way to the single-party or military regimes discussed in chapter 4. Considerable responsibility for these fiascoes lies in political culture.

Let us recall that the ideas and institutions that contributed to Western constitutionalism did not grow up overnight. They evolved over generations in close relationship to changes in religion, economy, family structure, social stratification, and the like. To think that Western constitutionalism could be exported to areas with dramatically different political cultures was, to say the least, naive. The terrain simply had not been prepared sufficiently for such alien imports. Moreover, constitutional regimes seem securest when "national unity" characterizes the population of a state. Where there is no nation, or several competing

22. Baron Montesquieu, *L'Esprit des lois*, in *Oeuvres complétés* (Paris: Éditions du Seuil, 1964), p. 532.

ones, attempts to introduce Western-style constitutionalism are likely to abort. This is not to say that more modest and gradualist attempts to interweave Western legal and constitutional ideas and practices were equally doomed to failure. But the first decade or so after World War II was a time when "modernization" was equated with "westernization," and the West (especially after the defeat of the Fascist and Nazi dictatorships) was identified with liberal or constitutional democracy.

Almond and Verba call the problem raised here one of congruence between political culture on the one hand and political institutions on the other.[23] "Congruence" refers to the degree of appropriateness between the institutional setup and the congeries of public attitudes we have called "political culture." To understand this problem better we must look at the Almond-Verba theory more closely.

An Individualistic Theory of Political Culture

The Almond-Verba approach to political culture is *individualistic:* it considers the total political culture to be the sum of the political attitudes or "orientations" of all of the members of the community. These individual attitudes are grouped into three analytic categories: (1) knowledge attitudes, (2) emotional attitudes, and (3) value attitudes.[24]

Knowledge attitudes refer to the quality and quantity of information an individual possesses concerning the enveloping political system. Does he know about the major political institutions of his country, how they work, the holders of high office? Answers to such questions can be graded and compared. Not only will different individuals score differently; so also will different groups (e.g., the attentive vis-à-vis the mass public). Moreover, despite the difficulties of precise comparison, different countries will show different average scores, if samples of the respective populations are asked roughly equivalent questions.[25] Thus, knowledge attitudes diverge both among individuals and whole political cultures.

Emotional attitudes refer to the individual's degree of psychological identification with and commitment to a regime. Is he filled with pride

23. Gabriel Almond and Sidney Verba, *The Civic Culture* (Princeton: Princeton University Press, 1963), pp. 21–23.
24. The terminology has been altered here for the sake of simplicity.
25. Indeed, *The Civic Culture* itself was the result of an elaborate survey of political attitudes in five countries: the United States, Great Britain, West Germany, Mexico, and Italy.

about the country's political institutions? Does the symbolism of the regime arouse a positive response in him? Or is he neutral or even negatively charged toward the system?

Value attitudes refer to the individual's value system. How does the regime measure up to the standards set by his hierarchy of values? Is he an advocate of democracy or dictatorship, socialism or free enterprise, permissivism or law-and-order? What is his view of justice and the good society? Does he get his values from a transcendent religion or does he believe that "pleasure and pain" are the basis of all morality? Is the individual an ideologue or not?

Almond and Verba apply these three types of attitudes to four different aspects of political life: (1) the system as a whole, or *regime;* (2) *inputs*—that is, demands and supports—going into the system; (3) *outputs*—that is, policies or decisions taken by a government; and finally (4) the *self* as a "political actor." Thus the perfectly politicized individual would have twelve separate attitudes, as in figure 10.2. To avoid the complexities of this twelvefold division of attitudes, Almond and Verba collapse the knowledge, emotional, and value aspects into

Figure 10.2. The Perfectly Politicized Individual

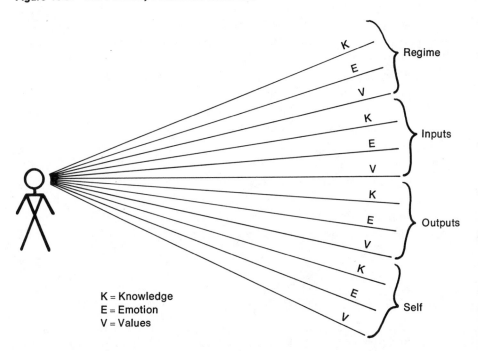

K = Knowledge
E = Emotion
V = Values

one composite orientation. This allows them to discriminate between three major types: (1) the participant, (2) the subject, and (3) the parochial.

The participant possesses definite attitudes on all four aspects of political life. He knows about, reacts to, and judges the regime, its inputs, its outputs, and his own role as a citizen. He is called "participant" precisely because his attitudes make him think that he can and should play an active role in the political process. He seems to be preprogrammed in favor of some sort of grass-roots democracy, although in a system of restricted voting he might be part of the select few. He is, in short, the ideal citizen of classic democratic theory.[26]

The subject has discernible attitudes about the regime as a whole and about the outputs of the political system. He is on the receiving end of public policies and knows it makes a difference to him what they are. On the other hand, he feels excluded from the political elite or at least from the politically relevant public. What he wants, his demands (and those of people like him), seem to him to have little or no impact on public policy. He thus has only the weakest of attitudes concerning the input aspect of politics and his own political role. These weak attitudes are generally called a "low sense of political efficacy."

The parochial, finally, lacks strong attitudes toward any of the four aspects of political life. He may not even know about the political system under whose aegis he technically exists. This is easy enough to appreciate with tribal groupings remote from centers of "civilization." But even in advanced societies there are some people who are in total darkness about politics and government, and probably prefer it that way.

When we move from the individual level of analysis to that of a whole political culture, however, problems besetting any purely individualistic approach emerge. One such problem is that though it seems easy enough to find individuals who are clearly participants, subjects, or parochials, no historical political culture can be so simplistically described. Total parochialism would exclude the notion of politics; it would resemble the "state of nature" hypothesized by philosophers such as Hobbes and Rousseau. Total participation may be an equally fanciful ideal. The total-subject political culture—perhaps some sort of oriental despotism decked out with modern communications—would be blemished by participatory attitudes in the court clique and lingering parochialism in the periphery.

Almond and Verba clearly see some aspects of this problem, since

26. See chapter 11 for views on the role of the citizen in a democracy.

they consider historical political cultures as complex "mixes" of the three fundamental attitude-sets. One such mix, the "civic culture," Almond and Verba found highly "congruent" with the institutions of a modern liberal democratic state. In the civic culture

> many individuals are active in politics, but there are also many who take the more passive role of subject. More important, even among those performing the active political role of the citizen, the roles of the subject and parochial have not been displaced. The participant role has been added to the subject and parochial roles. This means that the active citizen maintains his traditional, nonpolitical ties, as well as his more passive political role as a subject.[27]

In other words, the civic culture mixes not only "pure" participants, subjects, and parochials, it also mixes the attitudes in the same individuals.

Nevertheless, while all actual political cultures are mixes, some mixes are more congruent with certain types of political systems than with others. Hence we are dealing with more than an abstract scheme of classification. The theory has some explanatory and predictive power. It can help us to understand what has happened and to suggest what will happen. The congruence problem bears directly on two crucial political issues: (1) political stability and (2) the capabilities of political regimes.[28] Thus, a high level of congruence between culture and regime should promote stability and maximization of regime capabilities. Low congruence should tend to produce instability and a weakening of regime capabilities.

For example, it seems likely that the type of civic culture democracy described by Almond and Verba would be menaced by an overgrowth of any of the three attitude-sets. Too much participation would cause strain on the system, while too much subject orientation or parochialism would lead to a narrow elite-directed regime. A traditionalist dictatorship would also seem to thrive on widespread subject attitudes and parochialism. If demands for participation grew beyond a certain critical threshold, however, the dictatorship would seem destined for trouble. Only the personal leadership of Francisco Franco could keep the lid on such trends in the last decade and a half of his rule in Spain. With his passing the balked participation orientation has emerged with a possibly explosive force.

Almond and Verba see three different versions of the congruity-in-

27. Almond and Verba, *Civic Culture*, p. 474.
28. See chapter 4 on capabilities of government: extractive, regulative, distributive, symbolic, and responsive.

congruity problem. Here too we distinguish how knowledge attitudes, emotional attitudes, and value attitudes relate to the whole regime. However, we can simplify the Almond-Verba approach a bit by omitting knowledge attitudes, since knowledge is presupposed by the other two attitudes—you first have to know about something before you can react to it or judge it. Thus we can specify positive, negative, and neutral/indifferent attitudes within the emotional and value orientations. Table 10.2 represents three different patterns of individual attitudes toward the regime: allegiance, apathy, and alienation.

TABLE 10.2. Allegiance, Apathy, and Alienation

	Allegiance	Apathy	Alienation
Emotional attitudes	positive	indifferent/neutral	negative
Value attitudes	positive	indifferent/neutral	negative

In reality the situation is not so clear as this chart implies. There are positions between allegiance and apathy, and between apathy and alienation, that appear to be politically significant. In other words, the span from total allegiance to total alienation is a continuum wherein we could add further categories, as figure 10.3 shows. This type of scale is frequent in social science and could be put into practice by appropriate questionnaires.

Figure 10.3.   A Continuum of Political Loyalty

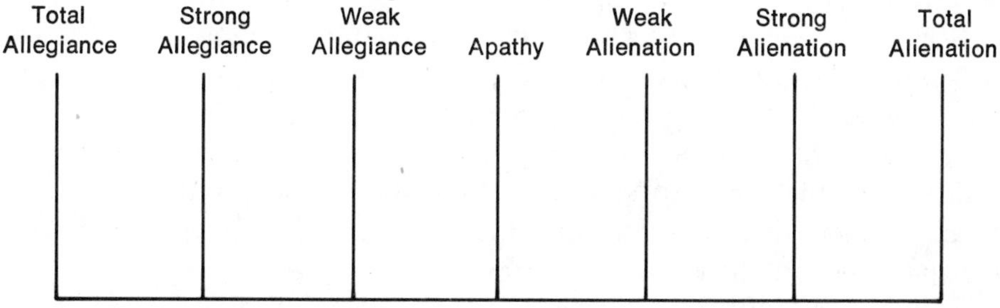

| Total Allegiance | Strong Allegiance | Weak Allegiance | Apathy | Weak Alienation | Strong Alienation | Total Alienation |

Political Culture and Subculture

One of the chief shortcomings of the Almond and Verba approach is its failure to do full justice to political subcultures. This weakness results from the shifting back and forth of their approach from the micro-level of the individual to the macro-level of the whole culture. Thus, political subcultures figure in only indirectly through their impact on specific individuals or on the sum of all individuals.

However, Almond and Verba's ideas on the "mixed" quality of actual political cultures suggests the possibility of political subcultures. Here we will define a "political subculture" as *any part of the general political culture that leads significant numbers of people to think and behave in politically distinct ways.* Obviously large and complex societies will be likely to display a large array of political subcultures. We have encountered the problem of political subcultures in several guises in previous chapters (e.g., with respect to "cleavages" in parties and the "base" of quasi-groups). Five major types of subculture are of key importance in modern politics: (1) regional, (2) ethnic-linguistic, (3) socioeconomic, (4) religious, and (5) age.

Regional subcultures derive from ecologically distinct parts of the country. That is, regional identity is not just a matter of latitude and longitude. Climate, soil, terrain, and other factors contribute to economic differences that affect the whole way of life of a genuine region. Since the overall culture is distinctive, it is no surprise that political attitudes and behavior follow suit. The solid Democratic South for nearly a century after the American Civil War and the Red Zone in central Italy are two examples. Of course, ethnic-linguistic and religious factors may sometimes reinforce regionalism so that it is difficult to gauge the independent force of the regional variable.

Ethnic-linguistic subcultures focus on ethnicity and/or language. The political manifestations of this type of subculture run the gamut from secessionist movements to separate political parties to voting trends.

Socioeconomic subcultures derive from status groups and classes. Status groups and classes produce different life-styles along with specific interests that play an important political role. The resulting divergencies will naturally be more serious when the stratification pyramid is very high, since the gap between the topmost and bottommost strata is likely to accentuate subcultural differences. These will inevitably spill over into the realm of politics.

Religious subcultures arise because religion is an all-permeating aspect of culture. Religion can constitute an in-group, and its influence on morality will influence both the ends and means of politics. In many respects religious subcultures resemble ethnic-linguistic ones.

Age subcultures are less frequent and pervasive in impact than the other types. However, the political significance of the generation gap has been recognized since ancient times. Plato in the *Republic,* for example, makes divergent values and attitudes between the older and the younger generation a main ingredient of his concept of political change. In a more contemporary context, we have already discussed one manifestation of age subcultures in chapter 7, where we treated youth movements.

Political Socialization

Political socialization is the process of shaping those attitudes that contribute to the political culture. It operates in all regimes, but in widely different forms. In totalitarian dictatorships the process can be called *indoctrination*, the centrally controlled attempt to structure political attitudes according to ideological precepts. In more "open" societies, political socialization operates in a more slapdash manner. Yet the controversies over grammar school and high school texts in history and other "sensitive" subjects shows that the formation of political attitudes is an important concern even in the United States.

The concept of political socialization in social science is almost as controversial as the reality of political socialization in societies. One viewpoint considers it a necessary function of all political systems: it helps create the minimum consensus required for political systems to work. Another viewpoint considers that political socialization implants views that hide and defend the domination of a "ruling class." No doubt political socialization has this dual aspect, as does all politics. It serves needs of the whole community, but in a prejudicial way that favors some parts of the community more than others.

Also controversial is the time-frame of political socialization. One school follows the basic Freudian dictum that personality—in particular, "political personality"—is basically set before the onset of adolescence. We can call the proponents of this school the "Freudians." The alternative approach envisages a more open process, in which adolescent and postadolescent influences still have an impact on political attitudes and behavior. We can call this numerous school of thought the "developmentalists."

THE FREUDIAN APPROACH.   The essential teaching of the Freudian approach is that early childhood experience is decisive for the formation of political attitudes. Moreover, it is the family whose influence is crucial, especially the relation between male children and their fathers.

This is called the problem of the Oedipus complex. While full discussion of this technical subject is out of the question here, we can give some idea of it in ordinary language. In the Freudian view unsuccessful coping with the male child's natural resentment of his father (because of the father's claims on the mother for love and affection) can leave deep psychological wounds that hurt the individual for the rest of his life. Various types of neurosis will plague the individuals so affected.

Freudians have conducted their political research and speculations at two levels. One concerns political leaders of various types; the other deals with the political attitudes of ordinary citizens (or at least with political followers rather than leaders). The Freudian approach to leadership sees the political activism of leaders as a projection and compensation for their damaged personalities. Psychobiographies have been written of such people as Hitler, Stalin, Robespierre, Woodrow Wilson, Richard Nixon, Mao Tse-tung, Gandhi, and others. There is a remarkable sameness about these psychobiographies because the authors somehow always relate the adult political behavior to the ambivalence (love-hate) toward the father.[29]

At the nonleadership level, the Freudian approach has been concerned largely with the formation of "extremist" political attitudes. The most famous venture in this area was *The Authoritarian Personality* in 1950. Though concerned largely with ethnocentric and anti-Semitic attitudes, part of this study was concerned with an "anti-democratic" or "potentially Fascist" personality.[30] After developing a test (the F-scale) that purportedly measures fascistic tendencies in personality, the authors found that particularly rigid family patterns were correlated with "high scorers" on the F-scale. Particularly implicated were the rigid and aloof "authoritarian father" and the warm but "submissive" mother. Since this is the Freudian recipe for personality disorders, the

29. See, for example, Gustav Bychowski, *Dictators and Disciples* (New York: International Universities Press, 1969); E. Victor Wolfenstein, *The Revolutionary Personality* (Princeton: Princeton University Press, 1971); and Sigmund Freud and William C. Bullitt, *Thomas Woodrow Wilson* (Boston: Houghton Mifflin, 1967).
30. See T. W. Adorno et al., *The Authoritarian Personality* (New York: John Wiley, 1964), chap. 7. This study was marred by the authors' inability or unwillingness to define "fascism" in ideological terms or to make any real allusions to fascism in Italy. Moreover, their scales were so constructed that even the most dogmatic Stalinist would have been a low scorer on authoritarianism. For a study that overcomes some of these weaknesses, see Milton Rokeach, *The Open and Closed Mind* (New York: Basic Books, 1960).

authors naturally concluded that the "potential fascism" of some of their subjects was symptomatic of mental illness.[31]

THE DEVELOPMENTAL APPROACH.   The developmental approach considers political socialization an ongoing process—the family is important, but rarely decisive. Socialization is a learning process, and learning never really stops, though it may slow down to a crawl. Since such learning occurs outside the family, we can speak of additional agents of political socialization. Figure 10.4 depicts the influence of all these agents upon the individual's political personality.

Figure 10.4.   Agents of Political Socialization

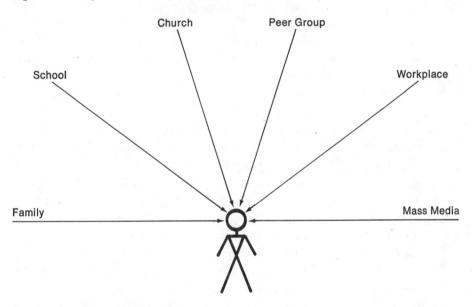

1. *The Family.* Despite some weakening, the "nuclear" family of mother, father, and children is an important agency of political socialization. The family has a virtual monopoly over shaping the triad of knowledge, emotional, and value attitudes in the earliest childhood years. Quality and quantity of information, emotional nourishment and

31. "When we consider the childhood situation of the most prejudiced subjects, we find reports of a tendency toward rigid discipline on the part of the parents, with affection which is conditional rather than unconditional, i.e., dependent upon approved behavior on the part of the child. Related to this is a tendency apparent in families of prejudiced subjects to base interrelationships on rather clearly defined roles of dominance and submission." Adorno, *Authoritarian Personality*, p. 482.

malnutrition, and basic training in values—the family is prime mover in all these things in the first years of life. As Robert E. Lane puts it: "The family is the microcosm of society. The history of a nation may, in considerable measure, reflect the changes in the ways children and parents . . . struggle to get along with one another. Some of the characteristics of a nation's politics may rest on the resolution of these struggles." [32]

2. *The School.* The school is an important source of attitude formation, though we should distinguish between the manifest and the latent political socialization it provides. Manifest political socialization refers to conscious attempts to create "proper" attitudes among students. Involved are the content and information of course and text material. Latent political socialization involves the relationship of teachers to students. Is the classroom organized in an authoritarian manner with the teacher considered virtually omniscient and omnipotent? Or is the teacher removed from the pedestal and converted into a friend and helper of the student? Is discipline relaxed somewhat and a more democratic atmosphere prevalent in the classroom?

Higher educational institutions also play a role in this process, especially regarding manifest political socialization. Substantial numbers of university youth are drawn, temporarily at least, to more extreme causes than those supported by their parents or by nonuniversity youth. Many of these revert to more moderate political views sooner or later, thus raising the question whether they are returning to earlier patterns or responding to the new experiences of their postuniversity life.

3. *The Church.* Religion and politics are never far apart. As with the school, church attendence has both a manifest and latent impact on political socialization. In the first case, that of manifest impact, the church seeks to promote definite political attitudes and ideologies. We have already mentioned this regarding highly politicized churches, such as the Roman Catholic church in Italy. The second case, latent impact, concerns church organization: some churches are more authoritarian and hierarchical; others are more flexible and democratic. While any simplistic relationship is out of the question, there does seem to be some historical correlation between the first type of organization and conservative views, and between the second and liberal or even leftist views.

32. Robert E. Lane, "Fathers and Sons: Foundations of Political Belief," in *Learning About Politics*, ed. Roberta S. Sigel (New York: Random House, 1970), p. 128.

4. *The Peer Group.* The peer group is the individual's circle of friends and acquaintances. This can run from neighborhood gangs to that other type of neighborhood gang, the country club. All such groups exercise subtle and not so subtle pressures on their members for conformity. Political attitudes and ideologies provide no exception to this. While having less impact, perhaps, than other agents of political socialization, the peer group can reinforce views and attitudes absorbed elsewhere. Sometimes the peer group runs counter to the basic socialization pattern of the individual, producing what is known as "cross-pressures." The resulting ambivalence in the individual sometimes causes him to defer or avoid making a political commitment.

5. *The Workplace.* The workplace, and the union or professional organizations stemming from it, also play a role in the ongoing process of political socialization. Workers in England are under certain pressures to favor the Labor party and its policies, though a substantial number resist them. In business firms there likewise are pressures to eschew causes and parties associated with the political left. Sometimes the individuals absorb the views of the work environment so slowly that they are unaware how much they have changed. Another kind of workplace is provided by military service, voluntary and otherwise. This unfortunately understudied process is especially important with professional military men. We would want to know the amount of, and the reasons for any asymmetry between, the views of the military and those of the general public. Even in the United States the political views of the higher officers are skewed somewhat to the right of their fellow citizens.

6. *The Mass Media.* The full impact of the massive growth of communications is difficult to gauge. Suffice it to say that television has probably diminished the importance of the family as a general socializing agent. The long hours spent before the TV screen by American and other children since the late 1940s have possibly vast behavioral consequences. Television and motion pictures provide us all with conscious and unconscious models and stereotypes. The media supply us not only with information, they help condition our emotions and shape our values. Many controversies show that everyone is aware of this. Some people complain that the news is politically slanted—such complainants have included presidents and vice-presidents of the United States. Others object to the stereotypy of different groups, ethnic, professional, or others. New Left critics charge that the media is brainwashing the American public to accept the "capitalist system."

In this chapter we have surveyed two concepts—ideology and political culture—crucial to the understanding of all political life. By stressing the philosophical background, the programmatic aspect, and the rhetorical functions of ideology, we have hopefully distinguished ideology from the broader and looser idea of belief system. An ideology, of course, is a belief system, but a belief system of a particular sort. Its structure is far more coherent and systematic than any garden variety of belief system. Likewise, its function of political mobilization is far easier to see than in the case of ordinary belief systems.

We have also spent time examining challenges to the relative autonomy and effectiveness of political ideas and ideologies. Power, economic, and psychological reductionism—each fails as a general theory of political behavior. Moreover, each form of reductionism, perhaps ironically, can serve an ideological function by being used to impugn the credibility of the ideologies of political adversaries. We have seen that it is convenient for antiliberals to portray liberalism as a thinly disguised justification of the social and economic position of the bourgeoisie. We have also suggested that anticonservatives welcome the finding that conservatives are a bit daft. And we might add now that radicals and revolutionaries have had their ideologies explained away as covers for what St. Augustine called the *libido dominandi*, the desire for domination.

The second major theme of the chapter has involved political culture, which can be defined as the sum of all the political beliefs, ideological and otherwise, that characterize a country's political life. The notion of congruence suggests that sometimes there is a kind of hand-in-glove fit between political culture and political system. But it also alerts us that this often is not the case. In the latter case, we can expect a large measure of indifference (apathy) or hostility (alienation) toward the regime. Widespread allegiance is the reverse side of the coin of close congruence between culture and system.

With slight modifications we have followed the Almond-Verba approach in analyzing political culture. By focusing on knowledge, emotional, and value attitudes as the basis of political culture, we developed three ideal types of political culture and personality: the participant, the subject, and the parochial. Realizing that every actual political culture is a unique blend of the three elements, we arrived at a more modern and more rigorous idea of the ancient wisdom that a country's political culture and its political system are mutually interdependent.

Finally, we briefly explored the process known as political socialization, whereby people come to learn and internalize the values, norms, and attitudes characteristic of their political culture (or subculture). Among the agencies of political socialization are the family, school, church, peer group, workplace, and the mass media. Of relevance to all these agencies is the distinction between manifest (i.e., conscious, planned) and latent (i.e., unconscious, spontaneous) aspects of the political socialization process.

Our overall analysis should be germane to all the preceding chapters, since political culture (including the special topics of ideology and political socialization) is the matrix of political life. Moreover, our discussion justifies the fairly elaborate treatment of ideological themes and specific ideologies found in the last two chapters of this book.

STUDY QUESTIONS

1. How does a "tight" definition of ideology differ from a "loose" one?

2. Is ideology always and simply a distortion of reality? Why or why not?

3. Evaluate the three reductionist theories that try to minimize the autonomous role of ideas and ideologies in political life.

4. What functions can an ideology perform for a regime or a movement?

5. How would you conduct a survey to uncover the main features of a country's political culture? What sorts of questions would you ask?

6. Relate the ideas of citizen allegiance, apathy, and alienation to the idea of congruence between political culture and political system.

7. What are the main agencies of political socialization? Which do you think is most important? Why?

SUGGESTIONS FOR FURTHER READING

ADORNO, T. W.; FRENKEL-BRUNSWIK, ELSE; LEVINSON, DANIEL J.; SANFORD, R. NEVITT. *The Authoritarian Personality*. New York: John Wiley, 1964.

ALMOND, GABRIEL, and VERBA, SIDNEY. *The Civic Culture*. Princeton: Princeton University Press, 1963.

APTER, DAVID E., ed. *Ideology and Discontent*. New York: Free Press, 1964.

BARTH, HANS. *Truth and Ideology*. Berkeley: University of California Press, 1976.

BELL, DANIEL. *The End of Ideology*. New York: Collier Books, 1961.

CHRISTENSON, REO M., et al. *Ideologies and Modern Politics*. 2nd ed. New York: Dodd, Mead, 1976.

COX, RICHARD H., ed. *Ideology, Politics, and Political Theory*. Belmont, Calif.: Wadsworth, 1969.

LICHTHEIM, GEORGE. *The Concept of Ideology and Other Essays*. New York: Vintage Books, 1967.

LIPSET, SEYMOUR M. *Political Man*. Garden City, N.Y.: Anchor Books, 1963.

MANNHEIM, KARL. *Ideology and Utopia*. New York: Harcourt, Brace, 1936.

OAKESHOTT, MICHAEL. *Rationalism in Politics*. New York: Basic Books, 1962.

PLEKHANOV, GEORGE. *Fundamental Problems of Marxism*. New York: International Publishers, 1969.

PYE, LUCIAN W., and VERBA, SIDNEY, eds. *Political Culture and Political Development*. Princeton: Princeton University Press, 1965.

REJAI, MOSTAFA, ed. *Decline of Ideology?*. Chicago: Atherton, 1971.

ROKEACH, MILTON. *The Open and Closed Mind*. New York: Basic Books, 1960.

ROSENBAUM, WALTER A. *Political Culture*. New York: Praeger Publishers, 1975.

SELIGER, M. *Ideology and Politics*. New York: Free Press, 1976.

WAXMAN, CHAIM I., ed. *The End of Ideology Debate*. New York: Simon & Schuster, 1969.

II

Crosscutting Themes in Modern Ideologies

This chapter discusses themes that cut across the ideological spectrum of modern politics. Certain ideas seem to prevail in a variety of ideological positions. Very few people will be found to oppose "progress," "democracy," or "freedom." But the same verbal expression can stand for radically different things. Agreement about progress or democracy, for instance, may prove to be merely verbal when we explore the substance behind the common phraseology. Exploration of the main crosscutting themes will make our brief analysis of ideologies in the next chapter easier and more profitable.

PROGRESS AND UTOPIA

"Progress" and "utopia" are analytically distinct terms, as we shall see. Nevertheless, they share some common emphases. For example, some theories of progress point to a utopian society to come at the end of the historical process. A theory of progress thus suggests that a future society will be immensely superior to the present one. Similarly, a utopia portrays a society that is far, far better than our own, whether the time-frame of this society is past, present, or future. Such overlap between the two notions of progress and utopia is our rationale for placing them together in this chapter. As will become clearer below, however, many utopias are "static" and thus could never "progress" beyond their present condition.

Progress

"Progress" is a well-worn term: Americans have it dinned in their ears virtually from the cradle to the grave. Only recently have some of the theoretical ambiguities and practical costs of progress come in for reassessment. However, the term is so well ensconced in the American political culture that few bother to examine the logical grounds of progress as an idea. First, we must distinguish progress from mere change. Progress, of course, presupposes change but adds a value dimension absent from the simple idea of change. Progress is thus a special kind of change: namely, *a change over historical time that finds an increase in value*. Progress means betterment, and anything that is better logically presupposes a standard of good.

Figure 11.1. A Simple Theory of Progress

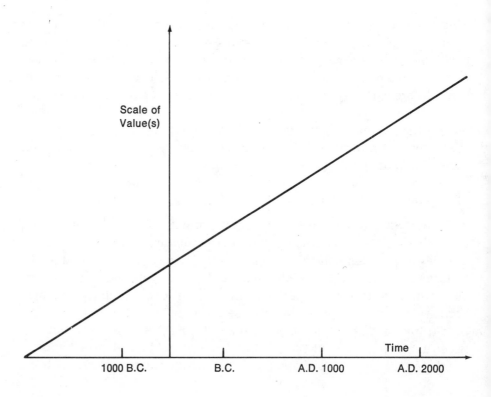

Figure 11.1 shows how a simple theory of progress would look if we tried to chart human history. Any serious theory of historical progress suggests that humanity advances in the sense of realizing more and more of the value (or set of values) championed by the theory. Possible values are such things as freedom, justice, equality, morality, altruism, democracy, knowledge, technology, happiness, harmony, peace, material abundance, order, creativity, and other things. Some theories of progress will select one of these as its sole or core value, while others have a kind of package-deal theory including some or all of the value items.

The German philosopher G. W. F. Hegel (1770–1831), for example, saw the meaning of history as the growth of freedom. While a full understanding of his notion of freedom involves metaphysical concepts outside our interest, in one of its more mundane aspects freedom involves the growing rationality of our obedience to the state and its laws. After excluding much of the world from the compass of true history, Hegel saw three grand stages in the progressive growth of freedom.

In the Oriental World of the Near and Far East, only one was free, the despotic ruler. His subjects were unfree. In the Classical World of the Greeks and the Romans, some were free, the full citizens. Slaves and foreigners were unfree. In the modern Northern European World (which Hegel called the "Germanic," but not the German, world), all were free, as equal citizens before the law. They obeyed in the full awareness of the basic rationality of the state and their place in it. Hegel did not feel, however, that this freedom he described required a democratic state.

Figure 11.2.   Unilinear and Wavelike Theories of Progress

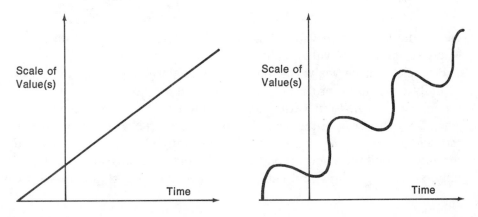

Alternative theories of progress show significant variations on the actual pattern of history and the values involved. Some theories are *unilinear;* that is, they assume a straight-line pattern of progress with steady, undisturbed increase of the value or values involved. Other more cautious theories admit that progress has its ups and downs, that temporary setbacks might actually decrease the amount of value being realized over a certain stretch. These *wavelike* theories of progress, however, assume that eventually the tempo of progress will pick up and things will roll on.

Still another contrast exists between *infinite* and *plateau* theories of progress. In infinite theories progress is without bounds: there is no

Figure 11.3.   Infinite and Plateau Theories of Progress

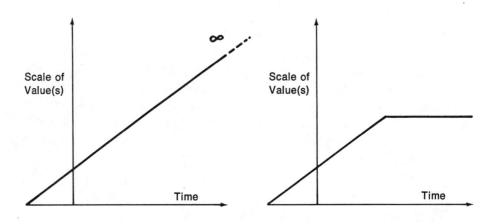

end to the increase in value. Plateau theories see an optimal end-state where the amount of value realized levels off.

Progress is a pervasive theme of most modern ideologies. But what actually constitutes progress and what must be done, if anything, to attain it are spelled out with dramatic differences in competing ideologies. Does progress entail equalization or hierarchy? Does it involve individual freedom or tighter social organization? Is progress reached through revolution or evolution? Does it grow gradually and incrementally, or by large leaps and bounds? In fact, the idea of progress is so flexible that it figures both in status quo and radical ideologies. It makes sense to say either that progress requires the gradual improvement of existing institutions or that these same institutions are roadblocks that have to be removed.

Utopia

We have already discussed utopian thinking as projecting a future or possible society characterized by complete social harmony and the eradication of scourges like poverty, ignorance, aggression, crime, and unhappiness. The term "utopia" comes from the fanciful tale of the English humanist and statesman Sir Thomas More (1478–1535). More used the term "utopia" since it derived from the ancient Greek for no-place. More's story was related by a fictional traveler who had sojourned with the utopians, inhabitants of an island where all social problems had been overcome. Henceforth the terms "utopia" and "utopian" have been applied to all such imaginary perfect societies and, more broadly, to detailed blueprints for total social reorganization.[1]

Utopias serve two major functions. "Utopias of escape" or diversion attempt to entertain or edify the reader. They are not intended, at least consciously, to produce any specific political reorientation or action. They are merely a literary type, though they may have an impact beyond that envisaged by the author. "Utopias of reconstruction" (so called by Lewis Mumford) involve the "vision of a reconstructed environment which is better adapted to the nature and aims of the human beings who will dwell in it than the actual one; and not merely adapted to their actual nature, but better fitted to their possible developments."[2]

Some utopias of reconstruction are presented seriously as blueprints for the future of mankind. Their authors descend with quasi-mathematical precision into the minutiae of humans living together. Other utopias are more suggestive than definitive: they provide a standard by which to criticize the status quo as well as some hints about the future.

Most utopias, whatever the range of their specific plans, share certain

1. Some of the more important classic utopias include Plato's *Republic;* Tommaso Campanella's *City of the Sun;* Francis Bacon's *New Atlantis;* Edward Bellamy's *Looking Backward;* William Morris's *News from Nowhere;* and B. F. Skinner's *Walden II.*
2. Lewis Mumford, *The Story of Utopias* (New York: Viking Press, 1971), p. 21.

broad assumptions and involve certain implications. The most crucial of these regard human nature. The utopian believes that the bulk of crime, conflict, aggression, frustration, failure, self-destruction, sadism, exploitation, and vindictiveness that characterize human society are not due to traits inherent in human nature. Such deplorable human conduct is the result of defective social institutions and false values. In the utopian view, either there is no "human nature" (in the sense of stable traits of the human mind), or human nature is basically good (i.e., benevolent and sympathetic). The utopian's problem is either to shape a new human nature or to release those benevolent impulses presently warped or repressed by bad social and political institutions.

Perhaps the main feature of a utopian society is the absence of social conflict. As Ralf Dahrendorf puts it, "Conflict over values or institutional arrangements is either impossible or simply unnecessary. Utopias are perfect—be it perfectly agreeable or perfectly disagreeable—and consequently there is nothing to quarrel about." [3] If we recall our discussion of politics as conflict resolution (chapter 1), utopias involve the abolition of politics—politics is replaced by administration. Since utopia makes conflict over the ends and means of politics superfluous and obsolete, it merely remains for the experts to determine the steps necessary to reach the agreed-upon goals. Thus, many utopias have an elitist flavoring since the experts are selected through specialized procedures instead of through democratic election.

Utopian theories see the "maldistribution" of wealth in existing societies as the root cause for most crime, poverty, and suffering. But they tend to deal with the problem of wealth in two different ways. *Utopias of abundance* envisage a technology so advanced that all possible human needs can be readily met. Not only will basic physical needs be satisfied, technology will cater to needs that are presently the luxuries of a small minority. Automation in some form or other is the foundation of this sort of hedonistic paradise.

Utopias of frugality, on the other hand, handle the problem of frustrated needs in another way. Their guiding principle is that many "needs" that consume so much of our present resources, including human labor, are not true human needs at all. Rather, they are luxuries and frills that a "leisure class" (and its imitators) demand to show off

---

3. Ralf Dahrendorf, *Essays in the Theory of Society* (Stanford: Stanford University Press, 1966), p. 109.

their privileged position to the less affluent mass of society. They are, in Thorstein Veblen's eloquent phraseology, examples of "conspicuous consumption" and "ostentatious waste." [4]

What the utopia of frugality proposes to do is to eliminate the leisure class and its "corrupt" system of values. This will destroy those artificial needs associated with the leisure class and redivert production to truly social purposes. People will learn that true material needs are few and simple and that true happiness lies in humane, religious, or aesthetic pursuits in which wealth is more an impediment than an advantage. Technology will be used to eliminate inherently unpleasant tasks instead of creating a superabundance of creature comforts.

Though utopias are generally associated with ideologies of the left, the authoritarianism, elitism, and stabilization of some utopias are compatible with right-wing ideas. This is why Karl Mannheim spoke of a "conservative counter-utopia" that serves as a kind of antidote to Communist and Socialist utopianism.[5] Though Karl Marx coined the expression "utopian socialism" in order to criticize the naiveté of those Socialists who believed that the beauty and rationality of their utopian projects would "convert" the capitalists and make revolution unnecessary, his own vision of the classless society of communism is no less utopian.

DEMOCRACY

Very few modern ideologies completely reject the term "democracy." Yet the movements and regimes that espouse these ideologies differ radically in policy and organization. Clearly there is enormous diversity under that umbrella term "democracy," and unless we have more information we are in almost total darkness as to what different people mean by it.

While our concern in the rest of this section is with political democracy, some ideologies stress instead what can be called "societal democracy." The latter looks more to social and economic organization than it does to the state. In other words, it downplays the political dimension in favor of a "general equality of condition." Societal democracy would seem to point toward the classless society or toward "workers' control"

4. Thorstein Veblen, *The Theory of the Leisure Class* (New York: Funk & Wagnalls, n.d.; originally published in 1899).
5. Karl Mannheim, *Ideology and Utopia* (New York: Harcourt, Brace, n.d.; originally published in 1936).

of economic institutions. Societal democracy preaches that political democracy without complete social equality is meaningless or merely "formal" democracy. "True" democracy is accordingly an all-pervasive ideal of human brotherhood.

The origins of the term "democracy" itself, however, give us some rationale for our preoccupation with its more narrowly political meaning. Democracy comes from the ancient Greek words for "people" (*demos*) and "to rule" (*kratein*). Democracy thus was the rule of the people in direct contrast to the rule of one man or a few men. The Greeks, however, believed in pure or direct democracy, where all the citizens assemble in one spot to determine what law and policy would be. Something of this idea is preserved in the New England town meeting and in the popular assemblies of the small Swiss cantons.

For obvious reasons, then, it was assumed for centuries that democracy was suitable only for very small states. Large states, political philosophers agreed, would have to set up some sort of monarchy. Such monarchies could be aided by assemblies of "estates," representing the various status groups, though not the people as a whole. Toward the close of the eighteenth century, however, theorists resurrected the idea of democracy and freed it from its association with tiny states. They came up with the idea of indirect or representative democracy. The people did not have to make law in person; instead they would elect officials to represent them, their wishes and interests, in the national legislature.

This immediately raised the question of the proper role of the representative, and two opposed theories soon emerged. One is called the *mandated delegate theory*, because it has the people give the representative definite instructions—a mandate—as to what he can and cannot do. The representative is thus a sort of mouthpiece or errand boy for his constituents. He is to follow their instructions to the letter, and when in doubt he must consult with the people back home for further instructions. Should the representative deviate too sharply from the express wishes of his constituents, some mechanism for recalling him from office and replacing him with a more reliable person will be invoked.

While the mandated delegate seems close to the original democratic idea of *re*-presenting the people, many see serious drawbacks to this approach to representation. First of all, it is difficult for representatives to check with their constituencies when unexpected, perhaps unprecedented, problems arise. Should a representative really have his hands tied by rigid instructions that might prevent or delay his action? Perhaps a more important question is: what type of person would be content with the errand boy role of the mandated delegate? It would seem that mediocrities would be typecast for it.

The mandated delegate theory more or less defined the problem of political leadership out of existence. If knowledge and wisdom are indeed concentrated in the mass of the citizenry, the representative should be little more than a conduit from the "grass roots" to the center of political decision. The Burkean *theory of the "discreet representative"* is more pessimistic about the people's having ready-made solutions to pressing problem.[6] Burke sees the representative pulled in two different, perhaps opposite, directions. On the one side he owes his constituents concern for their welfare, wishes, and interests. On the other side, he is part of a "national" assemblage, the legislative body entrusted with pursuit of the "national interest." Accordingly, he must have discretion and some latitude in which to make his own assessment of where that national interest lies. He should not therefore be bound by an iron-clad set of instructions: these would upset the delicate moral balancing act he has to perform. Required is a person of some independent vision and strong character—someone unlikely to seek the role of mandated delegate.

It is difficult to say which of these two concepts of representation has won out in representative systems. The growth of parties and proportional representation (PR) has altered some of conditions for the whole debate. With strong party discipline the individual representative is a mandated delegate, to be sure, but the question is who gives the mandate, the electorate or the party organization? PR also muddies the waters because people usually vote for the party list rather than the individuals on the list.

The United States with its weak party discipline and single-member districts should provide a better testing ground for this question con-

6. Edmund Burke based his theory on the following assumption: "Parliament is not a *congress* of ambassadors from different and hostile interests, which interests each must maintain, as an agent and an advocate, against other agents and advocates; but Parliament is a *deliberative* assembly of *one* nation, with *one* interest, that of the whole—where not local purposes, not local prejudices, ought to guide, but the general good, resulting from the general reason of the whole." "Speech to the Electors of Bristol" (excerpt) in *The Philosophy of Edmund Burke*, ed. L. I. Bredvold and R. G. Ross (Ann Arbor: University of Michigan Press, 1967), pp. 147–48.

cerning representation. Unfortunately, the results seem quite variable. Some congressmen have their fingers very close to the pulse-beat of their constituency and spend much time literally doing errands for constituents. Others, assured of reelection because of family or wealth or party, can afford to "do their own thing," sometimes to the chagrin of many constituents. On occasion this may even result in an even-handed approach to the public interest.

Individualist vs. Collectivist Democracy

In classic democratic theory the rule of the people is transposed into majority rule. Theorists differ, however, as to precisely why majority rule is ethically superior to minority rule. Two main schools of thought exist, which we can call "individualist" and "collectivist" theories of democracy. Individualist (or liberal) democratic theory understands society as an aggregation of free and equal persons. "Society" is merely a name for the separate individuals who make it up. Concepts such as the public interest or the common good are no more than the mathematical sum of the interests or goods of the members of society.

In such a perspective, a "one man, one vote" system of majority rule seems the only just solution to the problem of government. Each individual has his peculiar interests, and there is no standard by which to rank some interests as "higher" or "nobler" than others. Thus the goal of public policy becomes in Jeremy Bentham's famous phrase "the greatest happiness of the greatest number." What policy will produce this result? The individualist democrat answers, "Ask all of the people and take the majority decision as definitive." The person on the receiving end of public policy is best situated to gauge its effect on him.

Collectivist democracy justifies majority rule on a somewhat different basis. First of all, the collectivist considers society to be an entity in its own right—it is not just a name for a grouping of individuals. As such, society is a moral whole, for which there is an "objective public interest" above and beyond the petty interests of selfish individuals and pressure groups. The problem of politics becomes that of discovering that objective public interest.

We can appreciate these ideas better by a look at the views of French philosopher Jean-Jacques Rousseau (1712–78). Rousseau felt that people could be truly free only in a political order where the individual's welfare was indistinguishable from that of the community. In the common run of societies people tend on the contrary to follow their narrow, selfish interests, that is, their "particular will." They can even reach haphazard compromises and crude bargains on the national level, what Rousseau called "the will of all." However, the particular will and the will of all represent a caricature of humanity's potential for freedom and democracy.

Only in a tightly integrated society free of the conflicts and divisiveness caused by rigid class differences, religious polarities, and greedy interest groups can the individual and collective welfare converge. Rousseau called the identification of the objective public interest with the individual's interest "the General Will." The only problem was to have this General Will express itself. Rousseau answered without hesitation that wherever unanimity was lacking, the majority is the infallible guide to the General Will. A vote will be taken, and policy will follow the majority decision.

What about the dissenting minority? Here Rousseau used language that appears paradoxical and ominous to liberals and other individualists: the minority "must be forced to be free." In other words, they must swallow their objections and go along with the majority's decision. Some of the paradox, if not the ominousness, of Rousseau's position can be lightened by remembering that the ultimate goal of all members in this society is identical: the prevalence of the General Will.

If the majority has the inside track into the General Will, then the minority is simply mistaken—mistaken not about the goal, but merely about the means. Even if we have to nudge them a bit to see this, it is no abridgement of their freedom. Likewise, some of the ominousness is dissipated if we realize that Rousseau's errant minority is a numerical minority, not a "minority group," an ethnic or religious community. Members of the present errant minority can easily change places with members of the correct majority, perhaps on the next vote.

Democratic Elitism and Participatory Democracy

Despite these important differences, individualist and collectivist theories of democracy share several crucial traits: (1) majority rule is the only legitimate basis for governments; (2) democracy requires political equality in the sense of one man, one vote; and (3) democracy involves the full-fledged participation of all citizens in order to work properly. These three principles are the core of classic democratic theory. All of them were most harshly challenged by the classic elitists Gaetano Mosca,

Vilfredo Pareto, and Robert Michels. In contrast to traditional antidemocratic thought, which considered democracy "undesirable," elitism simply charged that it was "impossible." [7] Majority rule cannot be realized.

Having covered elitism in chapter 6, just a few points need be added here. The essential elitist argument is that the majority cannot rule because the minority of necessity does. Owing to the imperatives of human organization and the fundamental differences between men, there will always be a *governing elite* (Pareto), a *ruling class* (Mosca), or an *oligarchy* (Michels). While the theories of Pareto and Michels became more implacably antidemocratic, Mosca's mellowed considerably. Instead of seeing a monolithic, castelike ruling class confronting an atomized and dominated majority, Mosca made some reservations that paved the way for a synthesis of elitism and democratic theory.

If the later Mosca represents a softened attitude of elitism toward the idea of democracy, the views of others represent a rapprochement with it. As another Italian writer put it:

> Notwithstanding the current opinion . . . the theory of *elites* and the great truth upon which it is founded are not intimately antidemocratic. They require, however, a definition of the meaning and scope of the concept of democracy, that makes a clean slate of a number of utopian and demagogic exaggerations which have misled and envenomed two centuries.[8]

It is with the great economist Joseph Schumpeter (1883–1950) that most associate the reconciliation of democracy and elitism, namely, in *democratic elitism*. Schumpeter criticized classic democratic theory because it mishandled the "vital fact of leadership." [9] A realistic conception of democracy would not shrink from the inexorable fact of elites, but turn it to the advantage of democracy itself. Schumpeter redefined democracy as an "institutional arrangement for arriving at political decisions in which individuals acquire the power to decide by means of a competitive struggle for the people's vote." [10]

7. David Spitz, *Patterns of Anti-Democratic Thought* (New York: Free Press, 1965).
8. Filippo Burzio, *Essenza e attualitá del liberalismo* (Turin: U.T.E.T., 1945), pp. 49–50.
9. Joseph Schumpeter, *Capitalism, Socialism, Democracy* (New York: Harper & Row, 1962), p. 270. Schumpeter considers that the classic idea of democracy was that "institutional arrangement for arriving at political decisions which realizes the common good by making the people decide issues through the election of individuals who are to assemble in order to carry out its will" (p. 250).
10. Ibid., p. 269.

Such a revision of democracy gives up some of the core values in classic democracy in favor of a method of choosing governments. Democracy is no longer popular sovereignty with the majority finding the general interest. Instead, it is a kind of marketplace where competing elites display their wares to the consuming public. The people can select between the rival elites as they can between rival brands and commodities, but the actual "product" (i.e., policy) is made by the elites.

Democratic elitism also revises classic democratic theory's emphasis on participation, according to which political apathy indicates sickness in a truly democratic polity. In individualistic theories, apathy is seen as preventing the assertion of interests that figure in calculating the greatest happiness of the greatest number. In collectivist theories, apathy works to short-circuit the emergence of a true democratic political will. John Dewey reflects the collectivist stress on participation when he points out that "each individual has something to contribute, whose value can be assessed only as it enters into the final pooled intelligence constituted by the contributions of all." [11]

According to democratic elitism, apathy, if it does not go too far, can have definite positive results.[12] It can, for example, be the indicator of the successes rather than the failures of a democratic polity. Apathy emerges as a "passive vote of confidence" in the system, while outbursts of activism indicate that something is rotten in the state of. . . . Thus, activism betokens discontent; apathy betokens satisfaction. Moreover, apathy has the further "positive" function of providing a kind of ballast that steadies the state. As Bernard Berelson points out, "The apathetic segment of America probably helped to hold the system together and cushioned the shock of disagreement, adjustment, and change." [13]

Not everyone accepts democratic elitism as an adequate rendition of the democratic idea. Theorists complain that the Schumpeterian stress on leadership has emasculated the original moral ideal underlying democracy. Democratic elitists have lost the classic democratic tradition's teaching on the moral growth potential of mass participation. This further means that democracy has been transformed from a critical standard and ultimate goal to a description and justification of "that political system which actually exists in various countries, such as the

11. John Dewey, *Problems of Men* (New York: Philosophical Library, 1946), p. 60.
12. Bernard Berelson, "Survival through Apathy," in *Frontiers of Democratic Theory*, ed. Henry Kariel (New York: Random House, 1970).
13. Ibid., p. 76.

United States, Britain, Canada, and the like." [14] Democracy, historically the most radical of political ideas, has been denatured by democratic elitism into a rather insipid defense of the status quo.

Such critics of democratic elitism advocate *participatory democracy*. John Dewey revealed the core of this doctrine when he highlighted twin principles of democracy:

> First, the opportunity, the right and the duty of every individual to form some conviction and to express some conviction regarding his own place in the social order, and the relation of that social order to his own welfare; second, the fact that each individual counts as one and one only . . . so that the final social will comes about as the cooperative expression of the ideas of many people. [15]

Participatory democrats clearly hearken back to the classic approach to democracy; they find "democratic elitism" too much elitist and too little democratic.

This comes out in ideas regarding the true meaning of political apathy. Though Jack Walker, a critic of democratic elitism, admits that purely personal factors such as personal inadequacy and lack of interest are causes of some apathy, he suggests that it may also have "roots in the society's institutional structure, in the weakness or absence of group stimulation or support, in the positive opposition of elements within the political system to wider participation; in the absence, in other words, of appropriate spurs to action, or the pressure of tangible deterrents." [16] Widespread political apathy thus may not indicate general confidence in the system, but sullen withdrawal and resentful alienation. Democratic elitism papers over these gross shortcomings by defining them out of existence.

On the more positive side, participatory democrats wish to expand mass participation. Since the existing channels of political access seem clogged by entrenched elites and powerful pressure groups, they consider "unconventional" techniques as a revitalizing force for a dormant democracy. One such tack is the "politics of confrontation" where sit-ins, voter registration drives, minority representation, petitions, letter writing, protests, demonstrations, telegrams, telephone calls, and appeals to the media (especially television) are used to change the political

14. Peter Bachrach, *The Theory of Democratic Elitism* (Boston: Little, Brown, 1967), p. 24.
15. Dewey, *Problems*, p. 36.
16. Jack L. Walker, "Normative Consequences of 'Democratic' Theory," in Kariel, *Frontiers*, p. 236.

process. While these approaches work outside the normal institutional framework, the hope is that the "new politics" will itself be eventually institutionalized.

FREEDOM

"Freedom" is another sacred cow for nearly all groups on the ideological spectrum. Each feels that it has a corner on "true" freedom, while its adversaries make a travesty of it. While surveying all the dozens of varying conceptions is beyond our range here, we can at least give some analysis of "negative" and "positive" freedom, for most theories are variants of these two broad ideas.

Negative Freedom

Negative freedom is easier to understand, since it seems closer to a commonsense view of freedom. It is called negative freedom because it suggests an *absence*—a negative term—of restraints, restrictions, and impediments to movement, thought, and action. The imagery is of a body moving through space without any external disturbances to its motion. In political terms negative freedom would maximize the individual's ability to do as he wishes and think as he pleases.

An extreme version is seen in individualistic anarchism, which denies the legitimacy of all laws and institutions that derive from the state. The individual is truly free only when he can do what he wants to do unobstructed by laws, regulations, and officials. Some individualistic anarchists refer to a "higher law," which should regulate interpersonal relations, but they vest interpretation and application of that law in each specific person. Others deny that there is any principle that overrides the momentary whim or desire or feeling of the sovereign individual.

More moderate versions of negative freedom admit the necessity for political institutions with coercive powers. A classic statement of this view is John Stuart Mill's *On Liberty* (1859). Mill's defense of individual liberty has two main thrusts: one based on "social utility" and the other on the basic dignity of the human personality. Only the latter is of concern in the present context. Mill's dilemma is to defend maximum individual liberty without denying certain rights of self-defense to society as a whole. He thus needs a principle by which to judge when interference with the individual's conduct is permissible and when it is not.

Mill's solution divides our actions into two basic types. Some affect only ourselves, our bodies and minds—these Mill calls "self-regarding" actions. Others of our actions discernibly affect other people and are hence "other-regarding" actions. The general rule should be obvious: the community may not interfere coercively with self-regarding actions, while it may interfere with our other-regarding actions. Since our other-regarding actions have a direct impact on the community for good or evil, in the latter case the community is justified in constraining us. Such constraint can be legal-political, working through laws and public officials. Or it can be moral-social, working through subtle social norms and group pressures. The killer, the robber, the arsonist, the swindler, and the counterfeiter can be forcefully stopped and punished by due process of law.

Self-regarding actions, however, are another matter. These actions pertain to the individual himself, and "over himself, over his own body and mind, the individual is sovereign." [17] Mill further concludes that coercion for the individual's own sake is illegitimate:

> the only purpose for which power can be rightfully exercised over against any member of a civilized community, against his will, is to prevent harm to others. His own good, either physical or moral, is not a sufficient warrant. He cannot rightfully be compelled to do or forebear because it would be better for him to do so, because it will make him happier, because, in the opinions of others, to do so would be wise, or even right.[18]

Mill concedes that these are "good reasons" to advise or implore the individual to mend his ways, but not for coercing or punishing him. The drug abuser, for example, can be coerced only if his actions constitute a clear and present danger to the public. Moral or aesthetic revulsion is no grounds for cracking down on him.

Positive Freedom

Theories of positive freedom deny that a mere absence of restraints is what freedom is all about. Such emptiness or vacancy is mere license. Whatever their differences, theories of positive freedom envisage some substantive value that must be realized before someone can be truly free. Thus we are free, not when we follow mere whims or inclinations, but when some moral condition prevails in our lives. There are two main

17. John Stuart Mill, *On Liberty* (Chicago: Gateway Books, 1955), p. 14.
18. Ibid., pp. 13–14.

approaches to achieving this moral condition that makes us free: the *individualistic* and the *collectivist*.

In individualistic theories of positive freedom, there is usually a dichotomy between our "higher" and "lower" selves. People thus have two routes they can follow in their lives, but only one will lead to true freedom. The lower self is the self of passion, desire, and emotion. To succumb to the pressures of these internal forces destroys our freedom, even if there is no coercion by others. As Rousseau himself put it, "The impulsion of appetite alone is slavery."

The higher self, on the contrary, is the self of reason, morality, or true humanity. In this view we are free only when reason governs our conduct, when morality is reflected in it, or when humanity gets the best of our animal nature. Achieving such goals is not automatic—if it were, we could embrace negative freedom and let things take their natural course. The theorist of positive freedom may suggest assistance to guide individuals toward freedom. Poverty, oppression, ignorance, and corruption may be seen as obstacles to self-realization. Public action may be necessary to advance individuals to the goal of freedom.

In some theories of positive freedom such help is minimal. This can be seen in the philosophy of T. H. Green (1836–82), who represents a transition from the classic liberalism of Mill to the modern liberal position. Green admits that the state must do more to usher individuals along toward the goal of free moral growth, but offers the reservation that "the effective action of the state, i.e., the community as acting through law, seems necessarily confined to the *removal of obstacles*." [19] (Italics added.) To do too much for the individual is to abandon liberalism and adopt some sort of "social paternalism." [20]

Just this last step is taken by George Santayana's version of positive freedom. Santayana rejects negative freedom, which he calls "vacant liberty," because it cannot bring happiness to the vast majority of men. Since happiness is the highest moral goal, we are free when we have attained the happiness appropriate to our given natures. When this condition is realized, Santayana speaks of "vital liberty." Since Santayana

19. T. H. Green, *Lectures on the Principles of Political Obligation* (London: Longman, 1960), pp. 208–9.
20. "Social paternalism" suggests that the state or some elite does things for the masses, who are deemed incompetent to do them for themselves. Like the father-child relationship, the authorities may have to push the masses along, even against their momentary wishes.

has a low opinion of the common man's ability to achieve vital liberty wholly on his own, he advocates the rule of a paternalistic elite:

> For every man who is governed at all must be governed by others; the point is that the others, in ruling him, shall help him to be himself and give scope to his congenial activities. When coerced in that direction he obeys a force which, in the best sense of the word, *represents* him, and consequently he is truly free. . . .[21]

Collectivistic theories of positive freedom teach that the individual is truly free only when he merges his identity with that of the political community. Such theories, in fact, consider both freedom and individuality meaningless outside the context of the state. As Hegel put it: "Since the state is mind objectified, it is only as one of its members that the individual himself has objectivity, genuine individuality, and an ethical life." [22] Moreover, "In the state as something ethical . . . my obligation to what is substantive is at the same time the embodiment of my particular freedom. This means that in the state duty and right are united. . . ." [23]

SOCIALISM

The term "socialism" has the same chameleonlike quality as the others treated in this chapter. The Soviets call their society "Socialist," but so too do the Chinese and the Yugoslavs, who sometimes deny the Soviet claim. The Nazis called their ideology National *Socialism,* and both admirers and critics of Sweden speak of its "socialism." Other examples would only confirm that sometimes "socialism" symbolizes all that is good and hopeful, and sometimes it is a catchall epithet for envy, leveling, regimentation, and decadence.

Rather than tackle the Herculean labor of itemizing all the variations of "socialism," we hope to uncover some core that characterizes the more coherent Socialist doctrines. Since the meanings of terms are often clarified by reference to the terms most used as opposites to them, the most likely candidate is something called "capitalism." Ordinary usage suggests that socialism and capitalism represent two contrasting modes of economic organization. An essential, though not exhaustive, trait of

21. George Santayana, *Reason in Society* (New York: Colliers, 1962), p. 134.
22. G. W. F. Hegel, *Hegel's Philosophy of Right* (Oxford: Oxford University Press, 1958), p. 156.
23. Ibid., p. 161.

capitalism is *private ownership of the means of production and exchange.*[24] From this standpoint, the core idea of socialism is that it is *an economic system based on public ownership of the means of production and exchange.*

Naturally a fullblown Socialist ideology will contain either an historical explanation of why such an economy will eventually emerge (e.g., Marxism) or a moral justification of why it ought to emerge (e.g., "utopian" socialism)—perhaps both. However, we must here explore the rather vague term "public ownership." We know that it means that the whole people somehow owns the key aspects—sometimes called the "commanding heights"—of the economy, but this says little about the administrative organization and the distributive principles involved. In terms of the first problem area there seem three main solutions: (1) collectivist socialism; (2) functional socialism; and (3) localist socialism.

Collectivist Socialism

This is a system in which the basic industries are "socialized" or "nationalized" and come under central government control. The best historical examples are found in the Soviet Union and other Communist states. As this brand of socialism embraces nearly the whole economic production, central planning is essential. Such planning is called "preceptive" or "imperative" since its provisions have the force of law. The central plan is broken down at various administrative levels until each factory, farm, or shop gets its specific plan for the year. The technical term for this is "disaggregation," and it can be done according to geography or economic sector (agriculture, mining, electronics, etc.).

Collectivist socialism ideally would have a number of ministries in the capital city, which would work closely with the central planning board to formulate the national plan for one or more years. The ministries would have regional branches that reach down to the local level. Their organization would be hierarchical along Weberian bureaucratic lines. The higher levels would issue orders and expect reports and accounts from the lower levels.

If men were perfect, knowledge complete, shortages and overproduction unheard of, the total national plan could be implemented en bloc.

24. The means of production include such things as energy resources, land, raw materials, tools, machines, and factories. The means of exchange include transportation and communications facilities, wholesale and retail outlets, banking and credit institutions, etc.

Figure 11.4.   Organization in Collectivist Socialism

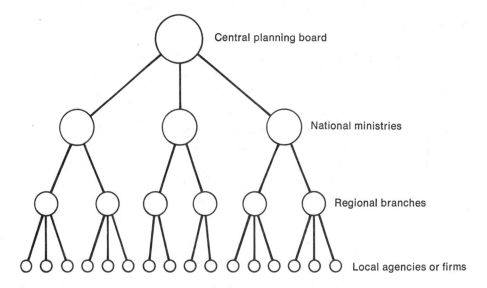

Every ministry, every regional branch, every subregional branch, every local group, and every specific firm would simply implement its own chunk of the total national plan. There would be virtually no need for feedback and readjustments of the plan.

Since such perfection has not as yet been achieved, despite the computer revolution, various types of decentralization have been tried in collectivist socialism. *Regional decentralization* and *enterprise decentralization* are attempts to avoid the bottlenecks and rigidities of extreme centralization. Regional decentralization uses existing geographical units or creates new ones, and the central planning board gives these units only the broadest planning goals and targets. It is up to the regional planning units to assign goals to subregional and still lower groups. Centralization thus remains, but in the regions instead of the whole system.

Enterprise decentralization gives the managers of factories, farms, and retail outlets broad choice as to how much and precisely what they should produce. This allows market elements, usually associated with capitalism, to figure in the managers' decision-making about the quality and quantity of their goods and services. Thus, consumer choice, which usually receives short shrift in collectivist socialism, can play a rather important economic role. Nevertheless, there are limits to the amount of decentralization collectivist socialism can tolerate before it changes into something else.

Functional Socialism

Functional socialism sees functional groups as the basis of social and economic organization. In functional socialism, the trade unions are by far the most important of these groups. *Anarcho-syndicalism* and *guild socialism*, the two leading varieties of functional socialism, agree on the importance of the unions, but diverge on political strategy and the role of the state.

"Anarcho-syndicalism," as the term implies, has two main thrusts. As a variety of anarchism, it views the state as the antithesis of human freedom. Whether it is a capitalist or a Socialist state makes little difference. Thus, the anarcho-syndicalists consider collectivist socialism just another type of despotism. The syndicalist aspect reflects the faith placed in the trade unions.[25] Not only are the trade unions to be the spearhead of the revolutionary movement against capitalism, they are the nucleus of future social organization. This involves enormous expansion of union responsibilities. They will not only protect the rights of workers; they will also manage the enterprises now controlled by the capitalists. How the complexities of coordinating a modern industrial economy are to be handled has been left more or less open in anarcho-syndicalism.

The British doctrine of "guild socialism" followed a middle course between the centralization of collectivism and the disorder of anarcho-syndicalism. English economist G. D. H. Cole (1889–1959), the chief theoretician of guild socialism, saw the solution to the latter dilemma "in a division of functions between the State as the representative of the organized consumers and the trades unions, or bodies arising out of them through industrial unionism, as the representatives of the organized producers."[26] Such an arrangement would result in "democratization" of all levels of government and a "sharing of industrial control between producers and consumers. The State should own the means of production: the guild should control the work of production."[27]

Localist Socialism

This type of Socialist doctrine vests formal ownership, or at least control, of the means of production in the local community. It shares functional

25. The French word for trade union is *syndicate;* the Italian, *sindacato.*
26. G. D. H. Cole, "Collectivism, Syndicalism and Guilds," in *Self-Management,* ed. Jaroslav Vanek (Baltimore: Penguin Books, 1975), p. 64.
27. Ibid.

socialism's mistrust of the highly centralized state. Indeed most advocates of localist socialism are anarchists, in the sense of advocating the abolition of the modern state. While Guild Socialists looked to the medieval guilds as something of a model for the future, anarchists like Russians Michael Bakunin (1814–76) and Peter Kropotkin (1842–1921) were impressed by the autonomy and relative self-sufficiency (Autarchy) of the medieval town or "commune." Accordingly, Bakunin saw socialism beginning at the grass roots of the commune: "A truly popular organization begins . . . from below, from the association, from the commune. Thus, starting out with the organization of the lowest nucleus and proceeding upward, federalism becomes a political institution of Socialism, the free and spontaneous organization of popular life." [28] Federalism would allow socialism to achieve significant (voluntary) coordination without reintroducing the state in another guise.

Socialism, Distribution, and the Welfare State

To this point we have looked to but one of two major economic dimensions of the notion of socialism, the organization of production. Now we must explore the problem of *distribution:* who will get what under socialism. Early Socialist doctrines in fact stressed distribution much more than production. They wanted to pool all or most private property and then distribute it according to some fair and just principle. One simple scheme is absolute equality, which gives every member of society an equal share of the "total social product." This could be done, for example, by giving everybody the same amount of "credits," which they could spend as they saw fit, or by a complicated system of rationing that allotted identical portions of things to each individual.

Karl Marx discussed alternative schemes of distribution. First he distinguished between distribution in the "lower" and the "higher" stages of Communist society. In the lower, immediately postcapitalist stage, distribution is affected by the fact that society is "in every respect, economically, morally, and intellectually, still stamped with the birthmarks of the old society from whose womb it emerges." [29] Thus, distribution in the lower stage, though much more equitable than under capitalism,

---

28. Michael Bakunin, *The Political Philosophy of Bakunin*, ed. G. P. Maximov (New York: Free Press, 1964), p. 273–74.
29. Karl Marx, "Critique of the Gotha Program," in *Marx & Engels: Basic Writings on Politics and Philosophy*, ed. L. Feuer (Garden City, N.Y.: Anchor Books, 1959), p. 117.

would still be basically unequal. The individual would be compensated according to his labor time: "The same amount of labor which he has given to society in one form he receives back in another." [30] Lenin later put this into a slogan, "From each according to his ability, to each according to his work." He also called Marx's first stage "socialism" as distinct from the second stage of "communism."

In the higher stage of Communist society, Marx saw the principle of distribution as, "From each according to his ability, to each according to his needs." Marx reasoned that absolute equality was unjust because different people have different needs. To give them identical portions would be to give too much in some cases, too little in others. Justice would be better served by allowing all members of society to determine their own needs and to take the appropriate things from the common product of society.

Given the plethora of organizational and distributive ideas associated with socialism, it is no surprise that the *welfare state* has been called "socialism" or at least "socialistic." This is misleading, however, because the welfare state does not resort to full-scale public ownership of the means of production. Despite some nationalization, most business and industry remain in private hands. The confusion emerges because the welfare state does try to achieve some of distributive aims of classic socialism.

In doing this, it departs in significant ways from old-fashioned laissez-faire (leave things alone) capitalism—that is why the welfare state seems hardly indistinguishable from socialism to its critics. The welfare state does redistribute some wealth and tries to provide a basic minimum standard of living for all citizens. The point is that these goals are pursued in an economy in which the "private sector" still outdistances the "public sector." We can thus speak of a "mixed economy" of two large sectors, but not of authentic socialism.

The modern welfare state uses government regulation and public policy to provide goods and services to various categories of the population. Table 11.1 will give us some idea of the key policies of the welfare state.

NATIONALISM

We have frequently dealt with nations and nationalism in this book. However, as early as chapter 1, we took pains not to identify nationalism

30. Ibid., p. 118.

TABLE 11.1.   Key Policies of the Welfare State

---

1. **Progressive taxation:** a soak-the-rich taxation policy allows more money to go into the public treasury which can be used to fund programs and projects that benefit mainly the poorer segments of the population.
2. **Social and health insurance:** the government mandates far-reaching unemployment and retirement programs. These are funded by required employer and employee contributions, but as more people draw on them, the money tends to be increasingly drawn out of general public funds. Health insurance can run from modest assistance programs to "socialized medicine," whereby nearly all medical costs are covered by the government.
3. **Fiscal and monetary policy:** here government uses its policies in taxation and government spending to direct the economy into socially desirable directions. Monetary policy concerns the rate of interest for borrowing, as well as the "hardness" and "softness" of the currency. These policies have a significant influence on how fast an economy grows, and on the rate of unemployment and inflation.
4. **Indicative planning:** since the government is assigned responsibility for national prosperity, it projects the overall trend of the economy for the next few years or so. It then acts upon this data to shore up weak spots in the economy or speed up socially desirable trends. Indicative planning is far less comprehensive, definitive, and compulsory than the imperative planning of collectivist socialism.
5. **Government regulation:** the government intervenes frequently and significantly in the economy regarding such things as hours and wages, product quality, business standards and policies. "Consumerism" illustrates the gap that separates the modern welfare state from the "let the buyer beware" philosophy of old-fashioned capitalism.
6. **Special programs:** the government becomes involved in a variety of programs and projects designed to aid certain groups—especially the "disadvantaged." It becomes active in education, nutrition, drug rehabilitation, housing, and other areas that previously were left to private groups and individuals.

---

with *national sentiment,* that is, the sense of common identity that marks off members of one nation from outsiders. We also found that there was no objective syndrome of a nation: language, ethnicity, and religion suffered too many exceptions. We thus have some cause to distinguish national sentiment from nationalism. While there can be no nation without national sentiment, there may well be nationalism without a nation and nations without nationalism.[31]

Anthony Smith resolves these apparent paradoxes because he sees nationalism essentially as an ideology, or better, as an "ideological movement." The nationalism-without-a-nation paradox dissolves wherever a small cadre of a nationalist movement confronts a population divided by the primordial sentiments of race, religion, region, and tribe. This

31. Anthony D. Smith, *Theories of Nationalism* (New York: Harper & Row, 1972), p. 175.

hodgepodge is a "potential nation," at least in the eyes of the nationalist elite. The latter's goal is welding these groups together, that is, nation-building.

The nations-without-nationalism paradox refers to long-established nation-states. Since the nation is already built or grown and has its own state, much of the rationale for a nationalist movement is lacking. The nation can go for long periods, running so to speak on national sentiment instead of the highgrade fuel of nationalism.

Smith unfortunately operates with a loose concept of ideology. Thus, though he admits that nationalism "unlike Marxism, does not furnish a complete theory of social change or political action," he calls it an "ideology." We prefer instead to see nationalism as an attitude-set. At any rate, Smith speaks of a "core nationalist doctrine," which appears in the nationalist movements of the last two centuries. Table 11.2 represents this.[32]

TABLE 11.2.   The Core Nationalist Doctrine

1. Nations are a "natural" division of mankind.
2. Each nation is unique.
3. The nation is the source of political legitimacy.
4. To gain freedom and self-realization men must identify with a nation.
5. Nations require their own state.
6. Loyalty to the nation-state is the true primordial loyalty.
7. The world will be free and harmonious by strengthening the nation-state.

Based upon this core nationalist doctrine or attitude-set, Smith's definition of nationlism is of "an ideological movement, for the attainment and maintenance of self-government and independence on behalf of a group, some of whose members conceive it to constitute an actual or potential 'nation' like others." [33] Smith further sees a set of "logical corollaries" from this goal. They can be considered a kind of program and include such things as equality and fraternity for members of the nation, return of lost nationals to the "fatherland," enhancement of the nation's cultural distinctiveness, autarchy and self-sustaining growth, expansionism, and structural reforms to strengthen the nation.[34]

32. Based on ibid., p. 21.
33. Ibid., p. 171.
34. Ibid.

Survey of Nationalist Movements

Based on the work of Anthony Smith and Louis Hartz, a complex yet serviceable typology of nationalist movements can be offered. Its very complexity suggests the difficulty of calling nationalism an ideology. Like the concepts of democracy or progress, it is much too diffuse for an ideology. Table 11.3 shows the main features of the typology.[35]

TABLE 11.3.   A Typology of Nationalist Movements

---

1. Territorial movements:
   a. Heterogeneous movements
   b. Fragment movements
2. Mixed movements
3. Ethnic movements
   a. Secessionist movements
   b. Diaspora movements
   c. Irredentist movements
   d. Pan-movements

HETEROGENEOUS MOVEMENTS.   Territorial nationalist movements obviously have a geographical basis. One type—heterogeneous movements—emerges in the colonial situation. Within the colonial territory is a variety of groups with little in common. Territorial movements are apt to become revolutionary because of the enormity of their self-appointed role as nation-builder. Given the frequent colonialist strategy of dividing and ruling by maintaining or even exacerbating the primordial differences among the involved groups, nationalist movements have their work cut out for them.

FRAGMENT MOVEMENTS.   The second type of territorial nationalist movement can be called "fragment movements." [36] These occur in colonies were the dominant settler population dominates the native peoples, usually in numbers as well as in politics. Despite strong language and cultural ties with the mother country, these colonies seek self-government and independence. The new nations exist as fragments of a wider European culture, as in British and French Canada, the United States, Dutch (Afrikaner) and British South Africa, Australia, New Zealand, and Latin America.

35. Based on Smith, *Nationalism*, and Louis Hartz, *The Founding of New Societies* (New York: Harcourt, Brace & World, 1964).
36. Hartz, ibid.

According to Louis Hartz, the nationalist movements in these countries are indelibly stamped by a sort of cultural birthmark. Being founded as colonies at a specific point in history, they persist in the cultural traits of the original settlement: "For when a part of a European nation is detached from the whole of it, and hurled out on to new soil, it loses the stimulus toward change that the whole provides. It lapses into a kind of immobility. . . ."[37]

Thus, when nationalism emerges in the fragment culture before or after independence, that nationalism is wedded to a definite political culture, if not to a fullblown ideology. In the United States the fragment culture embodies the seventeenth- and eighteenth-century English liberal tradition. Australian nationalism is colored by the more "radical" democratic ideas of Victorian England. The French culture of Quebec and the Spanish culture of Latin America reflect the aristocratic, corporativist ethos of prerevolutionary Europe.[38]

MIXED MOVEMENTS.   These correspond to a situation where "the projected 'group' is composed of one, or more, 'strategic' cultural groups, and some minority groups."[39] They differ from the heterogeneous movements mainly in the smaller number of groups involved.

SECESSIONIST MOVEMENTS.   Ethnic movements are quite numerous. Their base is a single ethnic group that has achieved or is close to achieving full national awareness. Each of the four subtypes corresponds to a somewhat different situation of the group's members. The ethnic group in secessionist movements is contained within a large political unit, such as a "multinational" empire. As we found in chapter 7 the ethnic nationalist movement wants to break away, either to form its own state or to join its compatriots in an already existing state. The German majority in the Sudetenland in pre-World War II Czechoslovakia, for example, longed to join the German Reich.

DIASPORA MOVEMENTS.   These nationalist movements find members

---

37. Ibid., p. 3.
38. Howard J. Wiarda describes the Iberic-Latin tradition of corporativism in the following terms: "a hierarchically- and vertically-segmented structure of class and caste stratifications, social rank orders, functional corporations, estates, juridical groupings and *intereses*, all fairly well-defined in law and in terms of their respective stations in life, a rigid yet infinitely adaptable scheme whose component parts are tied to and derive legitimacy from the authority of the central state or its leader." In "Toward a Framework for the Study of Political Change in the Iberic-Latin Tradition: The Corporative Model" (Paper delivered at the Annual Meeting of the American Political Science Association, Chicago, Ill., September 1971), p. 3.
39. Smith, *Nationalism*, p. 218.

of the ethnic group scattered in a number of different countries as small or tiny minorities. The movement advocates "back to . . . ," by projecting a return to the ancestral homeland. There is usually a nucleus of people in that homeland, but they may be outnumbered by "interlopers" who have to be driven out. The best example of this, of course, is Zionism, which issued a clarion call for all Jews to return to Palestine.

IRREDENTIST MOVEMENTS.   These resemble diaspora movements in that they find the members of their group residing in one or more states. However, they "do not stop at advocating the ingathering of co-nationals into the main area," but also wish to "add the territory on which their several kinsmen reside." [40]

PAN-MOVEMENTS.   These movements are the most ambitious of all nationalist movements. In a certain sense they are "supranationalist" movements because the one big nation they wish to create or reunite involves the absorption of both states and peoples already equipped with their own narrower national feelings. Among the more important examples are (1) Pan-Germanism, which hoped to unite all the German groups from all over Central and Eastern Europe; (2) Pan-Slavism, which hoped to unite Russians, Ukrainians, White Russians, Poles, Czechs, Slovaks, Croats, Serbs, Slovenes, Lithuanians, Bulgarians, and other smaller groups; (3) Pan-Turkism, which envisaged a vast Turkic state stretching from the Dardanelles through Soviet Central Asia up to the gates of China; and (4) Pan-Arabism, which had similar aspirations for all the Arab peoples around the southern and eastern coasts of the Mediterranean Sea.

Nationalism and Ideology

Even this brief survey of nationalist movements should suggest that nationalism itself cannot be considered an ideology. The problems of the seven types of movement are so divergent that a wide variety of ideological positions can be joined to the basic nationalist impulse. The clinching proof of this is that *the nation itself can be defined ideologically.* In other words, the nationalist movement may resort to nonethnic and nonlinguistic principles to separate members of the nation from nonmembers. Indeed these principles may override ethnic, linguistic, and other similarities when certain groups are extruded from the nation. This happens when class or status criteria, for example, are used to limit membership

40. Ibid., p. 222.

in the nation. What is important is that principles and criteria of inclusion and exclusion are taken from a distinctive ideology.

As an example, let us consider that French society before the Revolution of 1789 was legally a society of "estates." The First Estate was the clergy; the Second Estate was the nobility; and the Third Estate was everyone else, rich or poor, powerful or powerless. In his *What Is the Third Estate?* (1789) the Abbé Sieyès virtually demanded expulsion of the first two estates from the French nation. He wrote: "It is not enough to have shown that the privileged, far from being useful to the nation, can only weaken and injure it; we must prove further that the nobility is not part of our society at all: it may be a *burden* for the nation, but it cannot be part of it." [41]

To some degree parts of the French nobility of this period "led with their chin" by defending their privileged position on the "right of conquest." Aristocratic apologists of the early eighteenth century made much of the idea that the aristocracy were the descendants of the Franks, who had subjugated the "Gallo-Roman" ancestors of the Third Estate at the start of the middle ages. As Sieyès asked, somewhat rhetorically, "Why should it [the Third Estate] not repatriate to the Franconian forests all the families who wildly claim to descend from the race of the conquerors and to inherit their *rights of conquest?*" [42]

Something similar has occurred in the history of Chinese communism, where nationalism has had an important though controversial role. In 1939 Mao Tse-tung, by then ideologist-in-chief, summarily excluded the landlords and the "big bourgeoisie of a comprador [local capitalists who work for foreigners] character" from the Chinese nation.[43] All other classes were included. Later on, however, some of those who were tolerated in 1939, such as the "national bourgeoisie," were placed on the "outsider" list. However, this ouster of whole classes did not exclude the possibility that members of them could eventually go through "self-criticism" and be rehabilitated to rejoin the nation. Here too Marxist-Leninist ideology as interpreted by Mao helped to define the nation.

This chapter has examined several themes—progress and utopia, democracy, freedom, socialism, and nationalism—whose variant mean-

41. Emmanuel Joseph Sieyès, *What Is the Third Estate?* (New York: Praeger Publishers, 1964), p. 57.
42. Ibid., p. 60.
43. Mao Tse-tung, "The Chinese Revolution and the Chinese Communist Party," in *Selected Works of Mao Tse-tung* (New York: International Publishers, 1954), 3: 88.

ings are so diverse that we cannot call them "ideologies" in the narrow sense of this book. Versions of each theme are found sprinkled throughout the world's political cultures and the specific ideological systems treated in the next chapter. One lesson from our analysis should be an alertness to the different connotations that contemporary regimes and movements give to all of our basic themes.

If this were a text in political theory rather than a comparative introduction to political science, we would have been harsher in dealing with some of the more vacuous or misleading renditions of the five major themes. However, our goal was to expound the various alternatives so as to allow students to make up their own minds about the "true" meaning of democracy, freedom, and the rest. Nevertheless, it has been necessary to impose some order, especially regarding the notions of progress, socialism, and nationalism. In these cases we have tried to mine our way to a core of viable meaning. For example, we have handled socialism more as an economic concept than a moral one and we have separated nationalism from mere national feeling or sentiment. This means that our treatment of these themes would probably arouse more controversy than our surveys of freedom and democracy. Looking ahead to the next chapter, our exertions here should help us to understand that communism and Christian democracy view democracy quite differently. Likewise, we should appreciate better how the anarchist and the liberal have a different view of freedom and the state.

STUDY QUESTIONS

1. Many theories of human progress culminate in a utopian society of perfect social harmony. However, some utopias have features that would seem to exclude further progress. Discuss these problems.

2. Many people consider freedom and democracy as virtually indistinguishable. But this follows only if we define the two ideas in certain ways. Explore some concepts that might place freedom and democracy in partial or even total opposition.

3. Is a fairly substantial degree of apathy harmful or beneficial to the attainment and maintenance of a modern democratic order?

4. Does the welfare state lead inexorably to full-scale socialism? Why or why not?

5. Many consider democracy to be impossible or imperfect without socialism. State the assumptions of this argument and evaluate them.

6. How does nationalism differ from mere national feeling or sentiment? How can ideological assumptions affect who is and who is not considered a member of the nation?

7. Is there some intimate connection between nationalism and democracy? Will national liberation necessarily bring about political freedom?

SUGGESTIONS FOR FURTHER READING

BACHRACH, PETER. *The Theory of Democratic Elitism*. Boston: Little, Brown, 1967.

BERKI, R. N. *Socialism*. New York: St. Martin's, 1975.

BERLIN, ISAIAH. *Four Essays on Liberty*. New York: Oxford University Press, 1969.

BURY, J. B. *The Idea of Progress*. New York: Dover Books, 1955.

DAHL, ROBERT. *A Preface to Democratic Theory*. Chicago: University of Chicago Press, 1956.

DAVIS, HORACE B. *Nationalism and Socialism*. New York: Monthly Review Press, 1973.

DAWSON, CHRISTOPHER. *Progress and Religion*. New York: Image Books, 1960.

DOWNS, ANTHONY. *An Economic Theory of Democracy*. New York: Harper & Row, 1957.

KARIEL, HENRY, ed. *Frontiers of Democratic Theory*. New York: Random House, 1970.

KATEB, GEORGE. *Utopia and Its Enemies*. New York: Schocken Books, 1972.

MANUEL, FRANK, ed. *Utopias and Utopian Thought*. Boston: Beacon Press, 1967.

MILL, JOHN STUART. *On Liberty*. Chicago: Gateway Books, 1955.

MUMFORD, LEWIS. *The Story of Utopias*. New York: Viking Press, 1971.

SARTORI, GIOVANNI. *Democratic Theory*. New York: Praeger Publishers, 1965.

SCHUMPETER, JOSEPH. *Capitalism, Socialism, Democracy*. New York: Harper & Row, 1962.

SMITH, ANTHONY D. *Theories of Nationalism*. New York: Harper & Row, 1972.

SPITZ, DAVID. *Patterns of Anti-Democratic Thought*. New York: Free Press, 1965.

12
The Left-Right Ideological Spectrum

This final chapter deals with the major positions found on the left-right ideological spectrum: anarchism, communism, social democracy, Christian democracy, liberalism, conservatism, poujadism, fascism, and racism. Why we speak of "left" and "right" is something of an historical accident. It just so happened that after the French Revolution the different political factions simply sat in different locations in the semicircular legislative chamber. The most radical, republican, democratic, the egalitarian elements sat together on the left side of the chamber, while the most conservative, monarchist, antidemocratic, and aristocratic elements—as if to avoid contamination—sat together on the right side. The more moderate, middle-of-the-road groups had no choice but to occupy the center seats.

Since party labels did not mean much in those days, the three "spiritual families" in France became known as the left, center, and right. Then the labels were applied to groups or currents of opinion outside parliament, and finally the whole scheme was exported to all other European countries. At that time the right-center-left approach had another important feature: it was essentially quantitative. In other words, something increased (or decreased) as we moved from the left to the right. Actually two and possibly more things were involved; the groups on the

450

far left wanted considerable social change and maximum equality, while those on the far right wanted no changes and maximum inequality. There was thus a *spectrum* effect as we moved from left to right—one of continuous decrease in the demand for change and equality.

Whether the spectrum idea and the old left-center-right division makes any sense at all regarding twentieth-century ideologies can be judged only after making a survey of these ideologies. We will return to the general problem at the close of this chapter.

ANARCHISM

Anarchy means no rule, no "state" in the modern sense of term. Anarchism is thus an ideology that preaches the abolition of the state. The anarchist sees the state as the negation of human freedom, an albatross around the neck of humanity. The state is an excrescence and parasite that must be removed as early as possible. As Michael Bakunin put it: "It is the sacrifice of natural liberty and the interests of everyone—of individuals as well as of comparatively small collective units, associations, communes, and provinces—to the interests and liberty of all, to the prosperity of the great whole." [1]

No change in the formal organization of the state can really help matters. The modern "democratic state" is no less despotic than the state of "absolute monarchy." In fact, it is worse because it hypocritically covers up its authoritarian and exploitative character with the slogans and trappings of popular sovereignty. As long as the state exists, an unholy alliance of priests, bureaucrats, soldiers, and businessmen will be the prime, if not the sole, beneficiaries of the institutionalized violence we call the "state."

The anarchist denies that state and government are "functional" necessities of human societies. The human being existed before the rise of the state and will reach full human potential only after its demise. The state persists only because certain groups have a vested interest in it. There is nothing in "human nature" or "social organization" that requires the state.

Most forms of anarchism share the above ideas, but diverge on several important issues. There seem to be three broad schools of anarchist

1. Michael Bakunin, *The Political Philosophy of Bakunin*, ed. G. Maximov (New York: Free Press, 1964), p. 206.

thought, however: individualist anarchism, collectivist anarchism, and anarcho-syndicalism.

Individualist anarchism wants anarchy for the sake of individual freedom. Some versions of this argue for an essentially negative concept of freedom. This is seen in flamboyant form in the ideas of German thinker Max Stirner (1806–56). Stirner's first principle was the absolute uniqueness and value of each individual or ego. Since the ego is the highest good, no form of morality has any claim against wishes or whims of the sovereign individual.

> Morality is incompatible with egoism, because the former does not allow validity to *me*, but only to the Man in me. But, if the State is a *society of men*, not a union of egos each of whom has only himself before his eyes, then it cannot last without morality, and must insist on morality.
>
> Therefore we two, the State and I, are enemies. I, the egoist, have not at heart the welfare of this "human society," I sacrifice nothing to it, I only utilize it. . . .[2]

Stirner wished to annihilate the state and replace it with the "union of egoists."

Some individualist anarchists on the other hand work with a positive concept of freedom. Robert Paul Wolff's recent defense of anarchism uses a notion of freedom that derives from the idea of autonomy of German philosopher Immanuel Kant (1724–1804). Autonomy means literally "following one's own law." Autonomy stands in contrast to "heteronomy," which means following the law of another. For Kant, heteronomy involved either subjection to someone else's command or to one's own passions, drives, or sentiments. In the Kantian perspective, freedom or autonomy is the right and duty of each human being as a creature of reason. An individual is thus autonomous or free who does something because he or she knows it is right and is willing to make a general moral rule binding on all other people in a similar situation.

The problem for Wolff is how to reconcile this primordial right and duty of autonomy with the state's claim to our rightful obedience. Wolff rejects the solutions proposed by democratic theory as defective. In particular he finds Rousseau's paradox about "forcing men to be free" to be a stumbling block. No matter how large a majority is found in favor of a law or rule, the minority, even a minority of one, is wrongfully deprived of its autonomy when forced to go along. Since the state cannot avoid

2. Max Stirner, *The Ego and His Own* (New York: Libertarian Book Club, 1963), p. 179.

infringements on someone's autonomy, its authority lacks a truly moral foundation.

Wolff's defense of anarchism is rather negative and provisional. He leaves us with the following choice:

> Either we must embrace philosophical anarchism and treat *all* governments as non-legitimate bodies whose commands must be judged and evaluated in each instance before they are obeyed; or else, we must give up as quixotic the pursuit of autonomy in the political realm and submit ourselves (by an implicit promise) to whatever form of government appears most just and beneficient at the moment.[3]

Collectivist anarchism stresses society as much or more than the individual. According to Bakunin, for example, the "individual, his freedom and reason, are the products of society, and not *vice versa:* society is not the product of individuals comprising it. . . ."[4] This is a very different view from a Stirner or even from a Wolff. It means that the collectivist anarchist is especially concerned with how people will organize themselves to cooperate after the state is destroyed.

Bakunin's collectivist approach naturally leads him to advocate "socialism" as the basis of the future anarchist order (i.e., an order based "exclusively upon collective labor, under economic conditions that are equal for all—that is, under conditions of collective ownership of the tools of production."[5] Bakunin admits that this goal is the same as the "Communist" followers of Karl Marx. These latter, however, move toward the common goal by taking over political power in the state—state socialism. Such a tactic is the kiss of death for true human freedom, since a new oppressive elite will shortly emerge even in a "Socialist" state. "The Communists are the partisans of the principle and practice of authority, while revolutionary socialists [i.e., anarchists] place their faith only in freedom."[6]

Having discussed certain aspects of anarcho-syndicalism in the last chapter, we need to make just one or two points now. The general anarchist abomination for the state comes out especially in the anarcho-syndicalist strategy and tactics. Anarchists reject the normal political process because it is tainted through association with the state. Thus no anarchist grouping can bring itself to don the label "party," since parties

3. Robert Paul Wolff, *In Defense of Anarchism* (New York: Harper & Row, 1970), p. 71.
4. Bakunin, *Political Philosophy*, p. 158.
5. Ibid., p. 300.
6. Ibid.

seek to capture political power in the state. Anarcho-syndicalists instead pin their hopes on the trade unions, which are the main attack force against the hated capitalist order.

COMMUNISM

Marx

As an ideological term "communism" refers to Marxism-Leninism and its variants. Accordingly, we must briefly discuss the basic ideas of Karl Marx (1818–83) and his collaborator Friedrich Engels (1820–95), V. I. Lenin (1870–1924), Joseph Stalin (1879–1953), and Mao Tse-tung (1893–1976).

Karl Marx was a great synthesizer.[7] He combined ideas from different sources in a doctrine he variously called "scientific socialism," "historical materialism," or "dialectical materialism." One main source was British political economy as practiced by such classic economists as Adam Smith and David Ricardo. This tradition taught Marx that economic life could be studied "scientifically." However, Marx criticized "bourgeois" political economy because it made the economic "laws" it discovered absolute and unchangeable. A second source was the French Socialist tradition, which taught Marx that the future social organization had to abolish private ownership. However, these Socialist theorists were naive and utopian because they failed to grasp the need for revolution. A final source was German philosophy, especially that of G. W. F. Hegel, which inspired Marx's insight into the process of change. Hegel, however, had erred in making ideas and culture into independent forces of change.

While Hegel strayed into idealism, Marx insisted on the materialistic character of his own philosophy. Materialism is an ancient philosophy; indeed Marx's own doctoral dissertation was on the ancient Greek materialists or "atomists." Materialism teaches that the world is made of matter and that all that goes on in it results from matter-in-motion. What this meant to Marx was that material needs and interests, how men feed, clothe, and shelter themselves, are the real stuff of life. Ideas,

---

7. We will treat Marx and Engels together. Recently scholars have stressed philosophic differences between the two. While there is some merit in doing this, it is sometimes exaggerated.

ideals, and theories thus have force only if they are connected with the basic needs of life.

Marx tried to fuse his materialism with the "dialectic," a complex idea of questionable usefulness and one which requires further examination. Both Marx and Hegel thought that the dialectic was the key to change— revealing the pattern, sequence, and rhythm of change. In the dialectic change, especially historical change, involves three basic stages: the thesis, the antithesis, and the synthesis.[8] The thesis is the original condition or situation of anything. Each thesis produces an opposite or contradiction, the antithesis. Out of the opposition of thesis and anti- thesis comes the third stage, the synthesis. Things do not stop here, however, since the synthesis acts as a new thesis, which produces its own antithesis, and the cycle is traversed again.

The dialectical approach to change has many implications. First, the third phase or synthesis represents both the destruction and the preser- vation of thesis and antithesis. Thus, the synthesis is *novelty,* but a novelty that was partially foreshadowed in the earlier stages. A common- sense way of grasping this is to think of three glasses, one of which con- tains sugar and water; the second, tabasco sauce and water; and the third, a mixture from the first two glasses. If we taste the first, then the second, we will note "sweet" and "bitter" respectively, that is, opposites. When we try the third glass, we find a "bittersweet" taste different from the first two, and yet, it recalls something of both.

Another feature of dialectical change is *abruptness.* Change is not manifest through gradual, peaceful, evolutionary growth. Rather, we find a buildup of contradictions beneath the surface of things. At a cer- tain point, however, the contradictions break down and suddenly and drastically we leap well ahead to a new stage. Thus, there is a kind of

---

TABLE 12.1. Marx's Uses of the Dialectic

1. **Class struggle:** this is a prime mover of history.
2. **Contradiction between the "mode of production" and the "relations of production":** the inevitable tension between the way things are produced and who has formal ownership of the "productive forces" will bring the old order down.
3. **Contradiction between ideology and social reality:** this tension will eventually lead to revolution.

---

8. Neither Hegel nor Marx often used these terms. However, they do help in beginning to deal with dialectical thinking.

breach or discontinuity of change, as when water suddenly becomes steam at 212° F. This point is the "nodal point" and suggests that social change takes place through revolution.

Marx applied the dialectic to history and society in order to highlight two key ideas: (1) the interdependence of social phenomena; and (2) the importance of social conflict ("contradictions") in causing change. Table 12.1 depicts some of the ways in which Marx used dialectical contradictions.

As a theory of society Marxism tends toward *economic determinism*. This theory holds that the economy basically determines the general shape of politics and culture.[9] Marx thus distinguished between the *substructure* (i.e., the "economic base") and the *superstructure* of society. As Figure 12.1 suggests, the former basically determines the latter. The

Figure 12.1.   The Relationship between Substructure and Superstructure

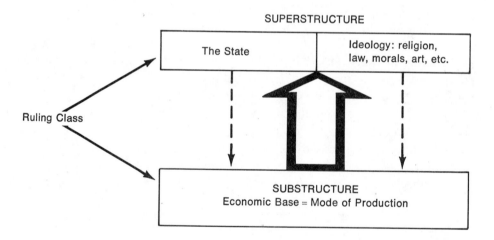

linkage between the two levels of society is provided by the ruling class, which owns and hence controls the means of production and exchange.

Through its economic dominance the ruling class makes the state into its "executive committee." The state serves to repress lower-class challenges to the hegemony of the ruling class. Physical force is not enough, however. The ruling class needs to justify its position in the sight of the

9. See the discussion of neo-Marxism in chapter 7 for more on this subject.

ruled classes. Thus arises "ideology," Marx's catchall term that includes nearly all aspects of culture:

> The ideas of the ruling class are in every epoch the ruling ideas: i.e. the class which is the ruling material force of society, is at the same time its ruling intellectual force. The class which has the means of material production at its disposal, has control at the same time over the means of mental production, so that . . . the ideas of those who lack the means of mental production are subject to it.[10]

In Marx's view all aspects of culture or ideology work to implant a "false consciousness" in the masses. This prevents them from seeing how the ruling class "exploits" them and how easy it would be to shake off this yoke. This is why, for example, Marx considered religion "the opiate of the people." Like an opiate, religion dulls sensitivity and prevents action. This is so because religion teaches "otherworldliness" and "turning the other cheek"—attitudes that favor passive resignation in the face of oppression.

With so much in its favor it would seem that the ruling class could go on indefinitely. Marxism is also a *philosophy of history,* however, which explains the comings and goings of different ruling classes. The explanation of the changing of ruling classes lies in a simple principle: *technological advance can be slowed down, but not stopped.* This fact brings about the downfall of all ruling classes. Such a fate is not accidental or premature since "no social order ever perished before all the productive forces for which there is room in it have developed; and new, higher relations of production never appear before the material conditions of their existence have matured in the womb of the old society itself." [11]

Every ruling class becomes obsolete when technological advance makes the old mode of production obsolete. Meanwhile, a new rising class, more attuned to the new technology, emerges which will replace the old ruling class. Eventually it too will suffer the same fate of obsolescence and ouster. More specifically, Marx saw five main stages to world history, the middle three of which were characterized by specific types of ruling classes (see figure 12.2).

10. Karl Marx and Friedrich Engels, *The German Ideology* (New York: International Publishers, 1960), p. 39.
11. Karl Marx, "Preface to *A Contribution to the Critique of Political Economy,*" in *Selected Works* (Moscow: Foreign Languages Publishing House, 1958), 1:363.

Figure 12.2.   Marx's View of World History

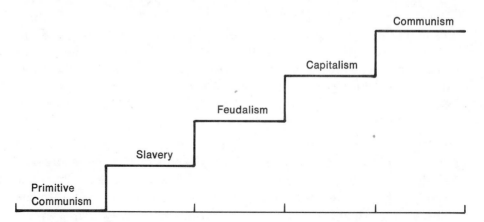

The first "epoch" of history, primitive communism, was characterized by common ownership rather than private property. For this reason it was a "classless" society. The second epoch, slavery, coincided with the rise of civilization and lasted until the downfall of the Roman Empire. In the Middle Ages, a third epoch, feudalism, emerged with land as the means of production and the land-owning aristocracy as the ruling class. The serfs were the bulk of the exploited majority.

However, even during the zenith of feudalism the urban dwellers or "bourgeoisie" were developing the foundations of the modern capitalist economy. In time the class struggle between the bourgeoisie and the old nobility intensified and was finally resolved by revolutions. The new economy was based on capital (i.e., financial power) rather than land ownership.

The fourth epoch, capitalism, is distinguished by production for profit and a legally "free" labor force. The bourgeois capitalists and the proletariat, the urban industrial working class, are the two main sides in the class struggle. In early capitalism the proletariat is too fragmented and unaware of its common situation to pose a threat to the system. However, in time capitalism also reaches its point of no return and becomes technologically dated. Symptom number one is the fall in the rate of profit.[12]

12. Marx calls this "surplus value" because it is taken away from the value given to the commodity by the worker. Marx considered human labor time as the source of value, so that when the capitalist took his profit, he by definition *exploited* the worker. The worker gets back less than he gave; the capitalist gets something for nothing. Even improved economic con-

In order to maintain their profits the capitalists are forced to squeeze the workers more and more. They can pull this off for a while, because there is an "industrial reserve army" of unemployed people willing to work for almost any wages. But this is a Pyrrhic victory for the capitalists, since it leads to the growing impoverishment, or "immiserization," of the proletariat and the "polarization" of wealth.

Put together, these latter two trends lead to a contracting group of superrich capitalists confronting a rapidly expanding mass of impoverished workers—in other words, the contradiction becomes more acute. This polarization occurs because the "buffer zone" of groups between workers and capitalists is forced down into the ranks of the workers. Spurred on by its very misery, the proletariat finally sees through the phoniness of "capitalist ideology" and reaches true class consciousness. This means that the proletariat on an international level spontaneously forms a political movement. At the proper moment this movement will seize power from the capitalists and set up a "dictatorship of the proletariat."

Although Marx was extremely vague about the nature of this "dictatorship," it was definitely seen as a brief transitional period. Soon to follow was the classless society of communism, which would also be propertyless and stateless. The first act of the new government would be abolition of private property in the means of production and exchange. This would destroy the foundation of classes, and thereby illustrate the unique character of the proletarian revolution as benefiting the majority instead of a minority.

Moreover, the state would become superfluous: "the government of persons is replaced by the administration of things, and by the conduct of processes of production. The state is not 'abolished.' *It dies out.*" [13] Likewise, the keynote of Communist economic organization is abolition of the mandatory division of labor. Previous economic systems had compelled different people to do specific jobs either by law and status (slavery, feudalism) or by the need to eat (capitalism). In communism Marx envisaged a purely voluntary division of labor, where people would shift from task to task according to their tastes and community needs.

---

ditions cannot eliminate this exploitative relationship. Moreover, by forcing the worker to give up his product and to do uncreative work, the system "alienates" his labor.

13. Friedrich Engels, "Socialism: Utopian and Scientific," in *Marx and Engels: Basic Writings on Politics and Philosophy*, ed. L. Feuer (Garden City, N.Y.: Anchor Books, 1959), p. 106.

Lenin

V. I. Lenin, the architect of Soviet communism, followed many of Marx's ideas. Two major factors, however, caused him to depart in important ways from the strictest Marxist orthodoxy. (1) Although Lenin came two generations after Marx, the spontaneous world revolution had not yet broken out. (2) Lenin came from Russia, a preponderantly peasant country, while Marx, a German, had projected his theories on advanced industrial societies such as Great Britain or the United States. Lenin's major contributions to Communist ideology on the party, the peasants, and imperialism derive largely from his attempt to deal with these two problems.

Lenin clearly rejected Marx's ideas about the spontaneity of the proletarian revolution. He argued that left to itself, the proletariat could generate only "trade-union consciousness." This meant exerting pressure for higher wages, better working conditions, and even government programs to aid workers. But these were demands *within* the capitalist system. Something more was necessary to bring the workers to revolutionary class consciousness and ultimately to the act of revolution. Lenin saw the missing ingredient in the role of the party.[14]

Rather than a mass party open to all workers, Lenin advocated an elite-party of professional revolutionaries. These full-time, fully-committed revolutionaries must spread the doctrine of revolution (propaganda and agitation) and mold the proletariat into a revolutionary striking force. The party would be, in Lenin's famous phrase, "the vanguard of the proletariat." To accomplish its mission the party would have to display "iron discipline." Lenin's formula for this was "democratic centralism": the first aspect of this concept involved the election of higher party organs by lower ones, coupled with the binding character of the higher organ's decisions upon the lower ones; the second aspect encouraged free and open debate at party congresses, with no open criticism of the "party line" once it has been set.

Marx did not think highly of peasants. He considered them petty bourgeois and hostile to revolution. Thus he spoke of the "idiocy of rural life," referring to the cultural isolation and backwardness of rural

14. See V. I. Lenin, *What Is to Be Done?* (New York: International Publishers, 1929).

life. Lenin, we saw in chapter 6, was willing to distinguish between rich, middle, and poor peasants and to ascribe revolutionary potential to the latter two groups.

Finally, Lenin's theory of imperialism pushed Communist ideology beyond where Marx left it. The theory also explained the tardiness of the revolution in the West. Quite simply, imperialism, or the development of colonial empires, had allowed the capitalists in "monopoly capitalist" countries to throw a few crumbs to the best-off workers. This situation had blunted the edge of the revolutionary movement.

Imperialism allowed the monopoly capitalists to capture a new source of their precious lifeblood, profits. By exploiting the peoples of colonial or semicolonial countries, capitalism got a stay of execution. Either through direct colonial possessions or through "spheres of influence," countries such as Great Britain, France, Germany, Belgium and others assured themselves of three important things. First, they obtained cheap labor from their colonial subjects. Second, they extracted cheap raw materials from their colonial possessions. Third, they created a "captive market" in their colonies.

Nevertheless, Lenin saw in imperialism something like a Trojan horse of capitalism. While it strengthened capitalism in the short run, it weakened capitalism in the long run. In the first place it would lead to "imperialist war," which would weaken capitalism. More importantly, it would provoke nationalism and anticolonialism in colonies or dominated regions. Even if these nationalists were non-Communist or even anti-Communist, their immediate goal coalesced with that of revolutionaries: destruction of Western imperialism. This meant that the class struggle was displaced from one within nations to one between nations.

Stalin

Stalin's ideological influence on modern communism is sometimes underestimated. Western revulsion, Soviet destalinization, and Stalin's own tendency to portray himself simply as a disciple of Lenin account for this. Yet in the areas of nationalism and the state, Stalin's ideological influence was and remains pervasive. While Marx's ideas on nationalism are more complex than sometimes thought, he clearly underestimated the force of nationalism. Lenin had to make concessions to nationalism because he operated in the multinational Russian Empire. But he too maintained an internationalist perspective. On the other hand, though Stalin never repudiated internationalism either in theory or practice, he became increasingly nationalistic, especially regarding the Great Russians.[15]

This shift came out clearly in 1931, when Stalin proclaimed that "in the past we had no fatherland, nor could we have one. But now that we have overthrown capitalism and power is in the hands of the working class, we have a fatherland, and we defend its independence."[16] This trend continued in the 1930s and 1940s with the "rehabilitation" of Russian national heroes and cultural figures, including some of the tsars previously condemned as "reactionary."

Regarding the theory of the state, Stalin began in an orthodox way by accepting Friedrich Engels' doctrine of the "withering away" of the state. Thus, in 1925 he defined socialism as the "transformation from a society with the dictatorship of the proletariat to a stateless society."[17] Over time, however, Stalin came to rely more and more on the active role of the state in "intensifying" the class struggle, defending the regime, and in building socialism and communism.

Thus in 1939 he took a further step and declared:

Will our state remain in the period of Communism also?

Yes, it will, unless the capitalist encirclement is liquidated, and unless the danger of foreign military attack has been eliminated, although naturally the forms of our state will again change in conformity with the change in the situation at home and abroad.[18]

That this deviation from Marxist orthodoxy was no momentary aberration due to a war scare is seen in Stalin's 1950 pronouncements on the "superstructure" including the state: "No sooner does it arise than it becomes an exceedingly active force, actively assisting its base to take

15. Some explain Stalin's fondness for the Great Russians by Stalin's non-Russian (i.e., Georgian) background. See Robert Tucker, *Stalin as a Revolutionary* (New York: W. W. Norton, 1974).

16. Joseph Stalin, *Selected Works* (New York: International Publishers, 1942), p. 200. This is in sharp and no doubt conscious contrast to Marx's rather rhetorical statement in the *Communist Manifesto* that the "workingmen have no country. We [the Communists] cannot take away from them what they have not got." In Feuer, *Marx and Engels*, p. 26.

17. Joseph Stalin, *Leninism* (New York: International Publishers, n.d.). This volume contains works first published in the mid-1920s.

18. Joseph Stalin, "Report to the 18th Party Congress of the CPSU (March 1939)," in *The Essential Stalin*, ed. Bruce Franklin (Garden City, N.Y.: Anchor Books, 1972), p. 387.

shape and consolidate itself, and doing everything it can to help the new system finish off and eliminate the old base and the old classes." [19]

Mao Tse-tung

Mao's contribution to Communist ideology is most visible in the areas of (1) voluntarism, (2) the peasants and "populism," and (3) nationalism. Lenin's stress on party leadership and Stalin's on the state represent a veering away from "economic determinism" toward voluntarism. Mao has continued this evolution of doctrine.[20] While the whole history and character of Chinese communism exhibit a faith in will power that runs counter to themes of developed Marxism, Mao has been careful not to burn his ideological bridges behind him. However, a late statement seems at least as "voluntaristic" as Stalin's ideas:

> When the superstructure (politics, culture, and so on) obstructs the development of the economic base, political and cultural changes become principal and decisive. Are we going against materialism when we say this? No. The reason is that while we recognize that in the general development of history the material determines the mental and social being determines social consciousness, we also—and indeed must—recognize the reaction of mental on material things.[21]

While Lenin made the peasants junior partners in the worker-peasant alliance, Mao once called the peasants the "driving force" of the Chinese Revolution. He has repeatedly hailed the sound common sense of the peasants, sometimes holding them up as a model for intellectuals and bureaucrats. This is related to his "populism." Mao has constantly deplored the separation between the cadres and the masses. This comes out clearly in his views on the role of the artist:

> no revolutionary artist or writer can produce any work of significance unless he has contact with the masses, gives expression to their thoughts and feelings, and becomes their loyal spokesman. . . . If he regards himself as

19. Joseph Stalin, "Marxism and Linguistics," in Franklin, *Stalin*, p. 408.
20. "Voluntarism" means that man does not have to be under the sway of impersonal forces. Instead, human will and effort can make a difference in the outcome of historical events. With Marx the pendulum was slanted toward determinism. Lenin moved more toward voluntarism, and Stalin did so still more. Mao has outdistanced all three with respect to voluntarism, but none ever totally abandoned deterministic elements.
21. Mao Tse-tung quoted in Frederick Wakeman, Jr., *History and Will* (Berkeley: University of California Press, 1973), p. 299.

the master of the masses or as an aristocrat who lords it over the "low people," then no matter how great his talent, he will not be needed by the people and his work will have no future.[22]

The "thought of Mao Tse-tung" illustrates what E. H. Carr has called the third phase of modern nationalism, which involves "the socialization of the nation" and the "nationalization of socialism." [23] In the Maoist doctrine this means the "sinification" of Marxism or the blending of principles of Marxism-Leninism with indigenous themes of Chinese culture. This is evident in an important essay of 1940, wherein Mao sounded definitely nationalistic notes:

> So-called "wholesale westernization" is a mistaken viewpoint. China has suffered a great deal in the past from the formalist absorption of things foreign. Likewise, in applying Marxism to China, Chinese Communists must fully and properly unite the universal truth of Marxism with the specific practice of the Chinese Revolution; . . . the truth of Marxism must be integrated with the characteristics of the nation and given definite national form. . . .[24]

The evolution of Communist ideology from Marx to Mao raises a serious question: how close are the links between a doctrine which is non- or anti-Western, extremely nationalistic, highly voluntaristic, and peasant-oriented—and the original theories of Karl Marx?

SOCIAL DEMOCRACY

Social democracy has some common ideological roots with communism. Many Social Democrats hearken back to Karl Marx and bitterly contest the Communist claim to him. Marx himself is partly responsible for this situation because at various times he spoke of the need for violent revolution *and* of the possibility of a peaceful transition to socialism. For this and other reasons, two main strains of thought regarding socialism (and many substrains) can be traced back to him: *revolutionary* socialism and *evolutionary* socialism. The first evolved into modern communism, while the latter contended that a peaceful growth into socialism, by ballots rather than bullets, was both possible and desirable.

22. Mao Tse-tung, "Talks at the Yenan Forum on Art and Literature," in *Mao Tse-tung: An Anthology of His Writings*, ed. Anne Freemantle (New York: Mentor Books, 1963), p. 257.
23. E. H. Carr, *Nationalism and After* (London: Macmillan, 1945), p. 19.
24. Mao Tse-tung, "On New Democracy," in *Selected Works* (New York: International Publishers, 1954), 3:154.

The evolutionary approach to socialism was originally known as "revisionism" because it ostensibly revised some basic tenets of Marxism. Revisionism is associated with German political theorist Eduard Bernstein (1850–1932). One of Bernstein's main targets was the "catastrophic" theory of revolution, whereby the "immiserization" of the working class would precipitate it into revolutionary action. To the contrary, Bernstein argued that the progress of socialism depended not on further misery, but on eliminating abuses. As conditions gradually improved, the workers would become more conscious, win power, and reach their goals peacefully. Unfortunately, "from the standpoint of the catastrophic theory a great part of this practical activity of the working class is an undoing of work that ought to be allowed to be done. It is not social democracy which is wrong in this respect. The fault lies in the doctrine which assumes that progress depends on the deterioration of social conditions." [25]

Moreover, Bernstein saw that social conditions were in fact improving and that further improvement was not unlikely. The improvements were not only economic; they were political as well. Universal suffrage meant that eventually the working class would contain the majority of voters. Thus socialism could be established by parliamentary procedures. Bernstein felt that socialism without democracy was undesirable. Accordingly, his vision of social democracy was a sort of "organizing liberalism."

Bernstein also attacked the idea of the "dictatorship of the proletariat." This he thought was atavistic, going backward. The true interests of the proletariat lay not in dictatorship, but in the perfection of democracy. In prophetic fashion, he claimed that "when the working classes do not possess very strong economic organizations of their own, and have not attained, by means of education on self-governing bodies, a high degree of mental independence, the dictatorship of the proletariat means the dictatorship of the club orators and writers." [26]

Bernstein's revisionism contains the germ of the whole tradition of evolutionary socialism or social democracy: (1) the catastrophic theory is wrong both as a description of history and a political strategy; (2) reformism can attain the goals of socialism; and (3) the rise of mass democracy makes talk of the dictatorship of the proletariat meaningless.

Social democracy for the first half of this century maintained the ideas of Bernstein and others that democracy and socialism were insepar-

25. Eduard Bernstein, *Evolutionary Socialism* (New York: Schocken Books, 1961), p. 213. This work was first published in English in 1900.
26. Ibid., p. 219.

able and that democracy itself would eventually bring about socialism. But socialism was still viewed as involving the "public ownership of the means of production and exchange." Social Democrats argued that full social justice could be served only in an economy where the government had "nationalized" at least the "commanding heights" of the economy.

Since the close of World War II, however, many Social Democrats have come to question the need for a totally, or even largely, national-ized economy. A leading British spokesman for this viewpoint, C. A. R. Crosland, has asserted that the traditional dichotomy of capitalism-private ownership/socialism-public ownership is increasingly irrelevant to social and economic realities. "Thus, ownership becomes of less and less importance for two separate reasons, both deriving fundamentally from the growth of scale: first, because the alienation of the workers is an inevitable fact whether ownership is 'capitalist' or collectivist, and secondly because even 'capitalist' ownership is increasingly divorced from effective control." [27]

It is thus wrong, in Crosland's view, to identify socialism with public ownership. This is to confuse means with ends and to transform the conventional Socialist wisdom of several generations ago into unalterable dogma. Instead Crosland suggests that the essence of socialism, what lies beneath the surface of contending schools of thought, is a set of "moral values." Table 12.2 represents the five principles involved: [28]

TABLE 12.2.   The Moral Principles of Socialism

1. A protest against the material poverty and physical squalor which capitalism produced.
2. A wider concern for "social welfare," for the interests of those in need, or oppressed, or unfortunate, from whatever cause.
3. A belief in equality and the "classless society," and especially a desire to give the worker his "just" rights and a responsible status at work.
4. A rejection of competitive antagonism, and an ideal of fraternity and cooperation.
5. A protest against the inefficiencies of capitalism, as an economic system, and notably its tendency to mass unemployment.

According to Crosland, such aspirations as these can be "incremen-tally" achieved in a society describable neither in terms of classic capi-talism nor classic socialism. In other words, progress is possible within

27. C. A. R. Crosland, *The Future of Socialism* (New York: Schocken Books, 1963), p. 37.
28. Based on ibid., p. 67.

the framework of the modern welfare state. It is thus that many Social Democrats conceive of socialism: *an agenda for the welfare state.*

However, there remains a Social Democratic "left," which persists in thinking that full realization of democracy and the other moral values of socialism demand a largely socialized economic system. G. D. H. Cole has pointed out that the welfare state is not socialism: "It is at most socialistic—if even that. For what we have been doing is not to put people on an equal footing, but only to lessen the extremes of inequality by redistributing grossly unequal incomes; and even this redistribution has quite largely taken the form of making the poor pay for one another's basic needs. . . ." [29]

While the welfare state has improved the conditions of the lower strata and reduced some of the more glaring inequalities and iniquities, it has failed to attack some of their root causes. The existence of a large "private" sector and the ability of the wealthy to pass on most of their wealth to heirs have been roadblocks to reaching the egalitarian society promised by socialism.

Ironically, by curbing some of the worst abuses of classic capitalism, the welfare state may "offer the prospect of even greater resistance to socialism than the society it has displaced." [30] Cole has even feared that the welfare state, rather than being a step toward the classless society, might be heading "towards a new stratification that is likely to persist and to become more marked." [31] He has thus asked those Social Democrats like Crosland, who considered themselves part of the Socialist tradition, whether their goal was the classless society or "only the so-called 'open society,' which is in fact still closed to the majority of the people?" [32]

CHRISTIAN DEMOCRACY

For a long time the social philosophy of the Roman Catholic church was essentially conservative.[33] This posture was reinforced by the influence of St. Thomas Aquinas (c. 1225–74) as semiofficial philosopher of the

29. G. D. H. Cole, "Socialism and the Welfare State," in *Essential Works of Socialism*, ed. I. Howe (New York: Bantam Books, 1971), p. 774.
30. Ibid., p. 777.
31. Ibid.
32. Ibid.
33. Though Protestants play a role in Christian Democratic parties, especially in Germany, the ideology of Christian democracy is basically a Roman Catholic enterprise.

church. Many of St. Thomas's ideas on politics and society resemble those of modern conservatives such as Edmund Burke (1729–97). From early modern times to recent times, the church has supported the union of "throne and altar" as well as the existing order. As a temporary casualty of the French Revolution, the church, its leaders and supporters, tended to reject all the ideas related to the Revolution.[34] This stance put it in conflict with many of the great social and ideological movements of the nineteenth century, such as liberalism, socialism, nationalism, and democracy.

An early and essentially negative response to these movements was provided by Pope Pius IX (1846–78), especially in his encyclical *A Syllabus of Errors* (1864), which attacked nearly all modern ideologies as rank heresy. Clearly a more positive response, one more willing to separate the good from the bad ideas in these ideologies, was necessary. Pope Leo XIII (1878–1903) was far more flexible in reinterpreting and revamping traditional views to provide distinctively Christian ideas for meeting the social problems of modern society. In this effort he was seconded by many laymen, who saw the extreme left as the main beneficiary of the church's losses among the lower strata of Western societies. Thus, in political Catholicism, Christian democracy represents a move to the left. The hope was to make the church's message relevant to the concerns of people in the middle and lower classes of society.

The fountainhead of Christian Democratic doctrines is the notion of Natural Law. This is the law that God has prescribed to govern the relationships among his rational creatures. It is a universal moral code known to us through right reason. While providing general moral rules, the Natural Law ordains no particular type of political regime, though some regimes and movements would obviously be ruled out. This flexibility on details allows the church to adapt its policies to a more democratic political order and a more egalitarian social order.

The doctrine of Natural Law means that neither the state nor the numerical majority is the true source of morality and justice. Accordingly, Pope Leo taught that

> it is not of itself wrong to prefer a democratic form of government, if only the Catholic doctrine be maintained as to the origin and exercise of power. Of the various forms of government, the Church does not reject any that

34. See Bela Menczer, *Catholic Political Thought 1789–1848* (South Bend, Ind.: University of Notre Dame Press, 1962), for a good selection of Catholic writers for this period.

are fitted to procure the welfare of the subject; she wishes only—and this nature itself requires—that they should be constituted without involving wrong to any one, and especially without violating the rights of the Church. . . .[35]

Thus, the democracy of Christian democracy is a limited democracy, which wishes to defend both moral principles and the human personality from the possible "tyranny" of mass democracy. Favoring equality before the law, Christian democracy at the same time warns against extreme social leveling.

Christian democracy's solicitude for human personality does not mean that it favors the "atomistic individualism" of nineteenth-century liberalism. The latter it considers a license for selfishness and a violation of man's natural sociability. Wishing to avoid both "statism" and unbridled individualism, Christian democracy naturally embraces a variety of pluralism. This pluralism, however, differs significantly from the Anglo-American variety discussed in chapter 6. The latter stresses voluntary associations or groups that one joins, whereas Christian Democrats look to primary or "natural" groups, such as the family, the church, and the local community. The concern for natural groups is reflected in the advocacy of special family allowances, aid to parochial schools, and related policies.

Christian democracy is a middle-of-the-road doctrine. It wants a happy medium between laissez-faire capitalism and the total planning of socialism. This suggests a moderate welfare state, though some Christian Democrats veer toward socialism and others toward "free enterprise."

LIBERALISM

The great liberal tradition has so many currents that any attempt to simplify it involves some distortion. Despite the divergent philosophical background of various liberal doctrines, five major principles are outstanding: (1) individualism, (2) parliamentarism, (3) equality of opportunity, (4) reformism, and (5) anticlericalism.

Individualism

If there is one idea that reveals the core of liberalism better than any other it is individualism. Of course, as we saw with anarchism, liberal-

35. Pope Leo XIII, "On Human Liberty," in *The Great Political Theories*, ed. M. Curtis (New York: Avon Books, 1963), 2:351–52.

ism has no monopoly on individualism. Moreover, modern liberalism has qualified its individualism in important respects.

Early liberalism was forthrightly individualistic. John Locke (1632–1704), for example, saw the very substance of government in the protection of individual rights.[36] Like many theorists of the seventeenth and eighteenth centuries, he spoke of a hypothetical "state of nature," which antedated the foundation of "civil society" or the state. In this individualist paradise, the God-given Natural Law regulated relations between men. Each individual not only possessed the rights of "life, liberty, and estate" (private property), but he was also the judge and executioner of the Natural Law.

The monkey wrench in the works of the state of nature was that since everyone was his own policeman and court, some people abused this right. The resulting conflict moved men to sign a *social contract* founding the state. The rationale of the state is to protect the rights of life, liberty, and estate. This orientation naturally led Locke and the whole liberal tradition to advocate limited government.

As "fiduciary" or agent of the people, government has no special sanction beyond the original purposes of the social contract. If the government acts arbitrarily (i.e., violates the rights of citizens), it can legitimately be overthrown. Examples of arbitrary rule are such things as (1) favoritism that violates equality before the law, (2) laws that are not directed toward the public good, (3) taxation without representation, and (4) delegation of legislative power without popular approval. While Locke's ideas are more complex than here suggested, there is some warrant in calling him "the prince of individualists."

Modern liberalism places the individual more firmly in a social context. In fact, John Dewey (1859–1952) complained that the ideas of classic liberalism, especially its doctrine of individuality, had become barriers to social progress. It had conceived "individuality as something ready-made, already possessed, and needing only the removal of certain legal restrictions to come into full play. It was not conceived as a moving thing, something that is attained only by continuous growth." [37] The earlier liberalism, Dewey charged, had ignored the social requisites of individual development. A true individualism for the masses as well

36. See John Locke, *Two Treatises of Government* (New York: Hafner Publishing, 1969). First published in 1689.
37. John Dewey, *Liberalism and Social Action* (New York: Capricorn Books, 1963), p. 39. First published in 1935.

as the social elite may require collective (i.e., governmental) action against poverty and ignorance.

While the classic liberal notion of freedom tended to be negative, modern liberalism leans to a more positive theory. Freedom is seen as self-realization and more emphasis is put on the individual's participation in the group. Hence modern liberalism represents a more pluralistic approach, as with John Dewey: "Liberty is that secure release and fulfillment of personal potentialities which take place only in wide and manifold association with others: the power to be an individualized self making a distinctive contribution and enjoying in its own way the fruits of association." [38]

Applied to public policy, the modern liberal doctrines reject some of the classic liberal catchwords about "the night watchman state" or that "government is best which governs least." Modern liberalism welcomes the coming of the welfare state, and it is very difficult to distinguish the modern liberal who has moved to the left from the social democrat who has moved to the right.

Parliamentarism

Liberalism has always advocated parliamentary government in the broad sense—a system in which an elective chamber exercises a check on the executive power. What liberals have not always favored is democratic government. This may sound strange, since nowadays most people assume virtual identity of democracy and liberalism. Nevertheless, the convergence of the two ideas is a historical development, not a logical necessity. We can grasp this better if we consider democracy and liberalism as concerned with two distinct, though interrelated, problems. As we saw in chapter 11 (political) democracy addresses itself to the question of "who rules?": the people, the majority, or an elite chosen by the people? Liberalism, on the other hand, addresses itself to "what government does": that is, what are the powers of government and the rights of citizens?

This distinction helps us appreciate why many early nineteenth-century liberals were fearful of democracy. They felt that if power were given to the ignorant and propertyless masses, they would inevita-

38. John Dewey, *The Public and Its Problems* (Denver: Allan Swallow, 1954), p. 150. First published in 1927.

bly abuse it. As George Grote, a prominent English liberal, put it in 1867: "I have outlived my faith in the efficacy of republican government regarded as a check upon the vulgar passions of a majority in a nation, and I recognize the fact that supreme power lodged in their hands *may* be exercised quite as mischievously as by a despotic ruler. . . ." [39]

Modern liberalism has made its peace with democracy, as the expression "liberal democracy" indicates. Indeed, its frequent charge is that the organization of the state is not democratic enough.

Equality of Opportunity

The classic liberal doctrine of equality of opportunity meant that status considerations should be irrelevant and wealth considerations should be minimal in determining how high one could rise. Achievement criteria such as talent, industry, and creativity, rather than ascriptive criteria such as birth, should mainly determine one's social position. While this doctrine required equality before the law, it did not in the classic liberal view require *equality of condition*. To level economic inequalities was to attack private property and to cause the state to interfere where it should not.

Modern liberalism is more egalitarian than its forerunners since it acknowledges that formal legal equality does not eliminate the vastly different life chances of the offspring of millionaires and paupers. Modern liberalism does not aim to erase such differences, but to offset them somewhat and raise up the lower grouping in the comparison. As L. T. Hobhouse wrote in 1911, "Every citizen should have the full means of earning by socially useful labour so much material support as experience proves to be the necessary basis of a healthy, civilized existence." [40] Hobhouse further specified that if the economic system did not so provide the citizen, he still has a "claim not as of charity but as of right on the national resources to make good the deficiency." [41]

Reformism

Liberalism has historically tried to steer a middle course between the revolution of the far left and the reaction of the far right. However,

39. Quoted in M. Ostrogorski, *Democracy and the Organization of Political Parties* (Garden City, N.Y.: Anchor Books, 1964), 1:56–57.
40. L. T. Hobhouse, *Liberalism* (New York: Oxford University Press, 1964), pp. 96–97.
41. Ibid.

depending on where and when, liberalism can assume either a revolutionary posture or a conservative one.[42] Nevertheless, liberalism is more true to itself, more comfortable, when it plays a reformist role. Liberalism believes that men are rational and responsible enough to reorder social and political institutions. But the reform should be deliberate and duly conscious: slogans like "trial and error" and "experimental approach" occur frequently in the liberal lexicon.

The liberal faith in reform is connected with its belief in historical progress. However, classic and modern liberalism have dealt with the notion of progress somewhat differently. Herbert Spencer (1820–1903) represents the older view that progress will flow almost automatically so long as state action does not interfere with laissez-faire and individual freedom. In one of his most optimistic moments Spencer declared that "progress is not an accident, but a necessity. Instead of civilization being artificial, it is a part of nature; all of a piece with the development of an embryo or the unfolding of a flower." [43]

John Dewey once again illustrates the modern liberal position by suggesting that progress is more problematic than just sitting back and watching it roll on. The earlier liberalism (for understandable reasons) confused mere change with genuine progress. To this Dewey objected, "We have confused the breaking down of the barriers by which advance is made possible with advance itself." [44] What is important in assuring progress is not the bare fact of social change, but "the direction which human beings deliberately give that change." [45] Progress thus needs active promotion of reform, not just passive acceptance of it.

Anticlericalism

Anticlericalism means opposition to allegedly excessive church interference in politics and social life. It does not necessarily involve atheism or irreligion; indeed many anticlericals have had strong religious convictions. Liberal anticlericalism is really an offshoot of its individualism,

---

42. In fact, contemporary American "conservatives" such as William F. Buckley, Ronald Reagan, and Barry Goldwater are actually nineteenth-century liberals. On the other hand, the ideology of many French revolutionaries in the 1790s was, abstractly taken, a moderate version of liberalism.
43. Herbert Spencer, *Social Statics*, quoted in Jay Rumney, *Herbert Spencer's Sociology* (New York: Atherton Press, 1966), p. 269.
44. John Dewey, "Progress," in *Characters and Events* (New York: Henry Holt, 1929), 2:821.
45. Ibid., p. 822.

which demands freedom of "conscience," as well as of the press, speech, assembly, and so on. However, the historical importance of this issue requires special mention of it.

The conflict with the churches originally arose because liberalism wanted to make religion a "private" or personal affair. This desire runs against the conviction of many established churches that it is fitting and proper that the official church should get public financial support and that nonmembers should suffer certain legal disabilities. Moreover, in the past churches have pressed for censorship of certain antireligious or "immoral" writings. It is thus no surprise that liberalism, especially in the nineteenth century, fought a cold war with the Roman Catholic church and the more conservative Protestant churches.

Liberalism advocates separation of church and state and freedom of conscience. As the church has retreated on these issues and general secularization has proceeded, both sides have mellowed. Nonetheless, certain issues in countries like France or Italy show that liberal anticlericalism is far from dead.

CONSERVATISM

Webster's New Collegiate Dictionary (Eighth) defines conservatism as "a disposition in politics to preserve what is established . . . a political philosophy based on tradition and social stability, stressing established institutions, and preferring gradual development to abrupt change." The first part of the definition suggests a widespread attitude, the disposition to preserve the status quo. This, however, is an attitude, not an ideology or political philosophy. The problem is that "what is established" can be a patrimonial kingdom, a modern constitutional regime, or a Communist dictatorship. There is no *doctrine* or *ism* common to these polities.[46]

The second part of *Webster's* definition, however, advances us because it involves a "political philosophy," based on tradition, stability, established institutions, and gradualism. It thus implies that conservatism is a *substantive political doctrine*, and not just an attitude toward change. As with most dictionary definitions of political terms, however, *Webster's* does not go far enough. The link with established institutions

46. For a contrary approach which tries to show that the meaning of conservatism is exhausted in its concern with defense of the status quo, see Samuel P. Huntington, "Conservatism as an Ideology," in *Political Thought Since World War II*, ed. W. Stankiewicz (New York: Free Press, 1964), pp. 356–76.

gives the impression that the conservative argument is: "The established institutions are good because they are old."

However satisfying such nostalgic sentiments may be, they are not a rational defense of the status quo. The conservative argument should run: "The established institutions are old *because* they are good." In other words the conservative position is not that mere age legitimizes institutions, but that established institutions have stood the test of time. Their longevity is proof of their answering the deepest needs of the people involved.

But this sort of conservatism is "adjusted conservatism," espoused by someone who sees a close symmetry between the existing order and the principles of his ideology.[47] What happens if we change the scenario and imagine someone with the same principles in a drastically different social and political setting? His conservatism will then be critical and alienated: he will attack, not defend, the status quo. He will want change, not more of the same.

What then are the principles common to both adjusted and alienated conservatives? The following six seem characteristic: (1) organicism, or the "organic" theory of society and the state; (2) aristocracy; (3) traditionalism; (4) authority; (5) social pessimism; and (6) union of church and state.

Organicism

The organic theory of the state and society is an old idea that sometimes takes bizarre forms. What is involved is a comparison—a simile or a metaphor—between society or the state, and a living organism. This analogy tries to show that society is a *unity of interdependent parts*. Moreover, just as the life of the whole organism takes precedence over its component parts (organs), the community welfare takes precedence over society's components, such as social strata, interest groups, and individuals.

That society and the state are real moral entities is expressed by the somewhat cryptic idea that "the whole is greater than the sum of its parts." In the conservative version of this idea, the social organism is structured hierarchically, with some parts playing a more important role than others. Edmund Burke expressed this idea in 1790 by giving the liberal idea of social contract a more organic meaning:

47. See Clinton Rossiter, *Conservatism in America* (New York: Vintage Books, 1962), chap. 1.

Society is, indeed, a contract. Subordinate contracts for objects of mere occasional interest may be dissolved at pleasure; but the state ought not to be considered as nothing better than a partnership agreement in a trade. . . . It is to be looked on with other reverence; because it is not a partnership in things subservient only to the gross animal existence. . . . It is a partnership in all science, a partnership in all art, a partnership in every virtue and in all perfection.[48]

Aristocracy

Conservatism believes in the natural inequality of men. There are serious disparities in the talent, intelligence, and character among different people and groups of people. In contrast to democratic theories, which also admit the fact of inequality, conservatism wants these inequalities to be reflected in a fairly rigid system of social stratification. Both privileges and duties are to be spread unequally among the different ranks of people.

The aristocratic principle is political as well as social. On its negative side this principle is antidemocratic: conservatism stresses the political incompetence of the common person. As Burke put it: "The occupation of a hairdresser or of a working tallow-chandler cannot be a matter of honor to any person—to say nothing of a number of other more servile employments. Such descriptions of men ought not to suffer oppression from the state; but the state suffers oppression, if such as they, either individually or collectively, are permitted to rule." [49]

The positive side of the aristocratic principle recommends that a small elite of qualified people should rule the state in behalf of the whole community. Burke spoke of a "natural aristocracy" distinct from the hereditary titled aristocracy as the backbone of the nation. More recently, the great poet T. S. Eliot expressed the aristocratic principle when he advocated "a form of society in which an aristocracy should have peculiar and essential function. . . . What is important is a structure of society in which there will be, from 'top' to 'bottom,' a continuous gradation of cultural levels. . . . A democracy in which everybody had an equal responsibility would be oppressive for the conscientious and licentious for the rest." [50]

48. Edmund Burke, *Reflections on the Revolution in France* (New York: Liberal Arts Press, 1955), p. 110.
49. Ibid., p. 56.
50. T. S. Eliot, "Notes Towards the Definition of Culture," in *Christianity and Culture* (New York: Harcourt, Brace, 1949), p. 121.

Traditionalism

Though attempts to equate conservatism with traditionalism are crudely simplistic, adjusted conservatives commonly defend tradition or call for a return to it. Tradition for conservatives is experimental politics, and the institutional results of the experiment should be given the benefit of the doubt. Like Burke, they are sceptical of utopian blueprints or even grandiose reform projects. Burke was critical of the abstract rationalism of the Enlightenment, which invested the individual reason with greater wisdom than it possessed, in his view.

However, Burke trusted in a concrete and historical reason that was embodied in tradition. Thus he spoke of "prejudices," not in the modern sense of bigotry, but as assumptions and preferences in favor of the established order. He contrasted the traditionalism of English thinkers with the rationalistic repudiation of the past by the French. The English, instead of "exploding general prejudices," used their wits to discover their "latent wisdom." After seeing this wisdom, "they think it more wise to continue the prejudice, with the reason involved, than to cast away the coat of prejudice and to leave nothing but the naked reason. . . ." [51]

Authority

Conservatism has great respect for constituted authority. Theologically inclined conservatives often preach that the powers that be are ordained by God. French philosopher Joseph de Maistre (1753–1821), who considered the French Revolution a divine chastisement for the sinfulness of the French, focused on the notion of sovereignty: "If sovereignty is not anterior to the *people*, at least these two ideas are collateral, since a sovereign is necessary to make a *people*. It is as impossible to imagine a human society, a people, without a sovereign as a hive and bees without a queen. . . ." [52] While not all conservatives will follow de Maistre in his conclusion that "every species of sovereignty is absolute of its nature," they believe that government should be strong and that the citizen should obey.

51. Burke, *Reflections*, p. 99.
52. Joseph de Maistre, *The Works of Joseph de Maistre* (New York: Macmillan, 1965), p. 98.

Social Pessimism

Conservatives are social pessimists: they believe that the traits of selfishness, irrationality, and aggressiveness are innate in "human nature."
Thus, the conservative rejects utopias based on altruism, rationality,
and pure benevolence. While narrow-gauge reforms are possible, defective social institutions are the product of defective men. To change
institutions without altering the men is to deal with the surface of social problems. Moreover, the attempted cure for social ills may be
worse than the disease.

Social pessimism also explains conservative aversion for the idea of
historical progress. Conservatives are more drawn than liberals to "cyclical" theories of the rise and fall of civilization.[53] For de Maistre the
weakness of human nature stems from the "original sin" of Adam's
disobedience in the Garden of Eden. There is thus a split or dualism in
human nature: on the one hand, man is elevated, noble, and happy;
on the other, he is degraded, ignoble, and miserable. Because he is
endowed with full self-consciousness, man "must continually contem-
plate himself, and this he cannot do without shame; even his grandeur
humiliates him, since the understanding that raises him to the angels
serves only to show him the abominable tendencies in himself that
degrade him to the brutes. . . ." [54]

Union of Church and State

Conservatism usually involves clericalism: interpenetration of church
and state. Because of the conservative's organic conception of society,
conservatism sees an intimate relationship between politics and morality,
and between morality and religion. The result is a sort of triangular
relationship between politics, morality, and religion. From this viewpoint, while church and state should have separate institutional identities, this does not require strict separation.

Thus, Edmund Burke approved wholeheartedly of the sentiment he
attributed to the "majority of the people of England," which considers

53. Another reason why conservatives attach themselves to cyclical theories
    and liberals do not is a difference in values, which causes liberals and
    democrats to view some events and trends as good, while conservatives
    and aristocrats see them as evil—symptoms of decay.
54. de Maistre, *Works*, p. 199.

the established Anglican Church "as the foundation of the whole constitution, with which, and with every part of which, it holds an indissoluble
union. Church and State are ideas inseparable in their minds. . . ."[55]

POUJADISM

Here we use the term "poujadism" somewhat more broadly than in our
earlier discussion of Pierre Poujade's movement of petty bourgeois protest in the closing years of the Fourth French Republic (chapter 7).
The broader "poujadism" refers to an ideology that has emerged in
various countries. Though on the right of the ideological spectrum, it
is neither conservatism nor true fascism.[56] The main points of poujadism are (1) anti-bigness; (2) attack on politicians; (3) defense of the
periphery against the center; (4) xenophobia; and (5) monetary or
tax reform.

Anti-Bigness

Poujadism idealizes the "small man"—the person who owns and operates
his or her own store, shop, or farm. It hails such "forgotten people" as
the backbone of the nation. It deplores the fact that the status, economic position, and self-esteem of these folk is menaced by the growth
of massive government organization, big business, and the trade unions.
The government overtaxes and overregulates these people; big business sells them its goods and services at a high price and, worse still,
drives them out of business when they cannot compete; and big labor
forces them to pay their employees wages higher than they can afford.

Poujadism bemoans these things and the social and economic trends
that give rise to them. It favors a rollback in the growth of the three
"bigs." Government spending and regulation should be reduced, especially where they affect the small person's activity or pocketbook. Big
business should be curtailed and decentralized and measures should be
taken to strengthen small business (tax relief, subsidies, etc.). The
unions should be "put in their place" and "cleaned up."

55. Burke, *Reflections*, p. 113.
56. "Populism" is just a little too broad for what we have in mind here.
    Poujadist ideological themes have been articulated by such parties and
    movements as Social Credit in Canada, the Farmer's party in the Nether-
    lands, McCarthyism in the United States in the early 1950s, and splinter
    parties in Europe and elsewhere.

Attack on Politicians

The poujadist tends to see his troubles as due to the machinations of discernible "bad men" rather than as due to inevitable sources of social change. Primarily responsible are the politicians—the insiders who prey upon the outsiders, the small people. Politicians are viewed as grasping, venal, and cowardly. All politicians are "crooks"; if they do not start out that way, they end up that way. With the politicians in control, it is no surprise that public policy is designed to crush the honest and hard-working part of the population.

Defense of the Periphery

What Philip Williams has written about French poujadism more or less describes other strains: "Provincial suspicion and dislike of the capital were as important Poujadist themes as the popular suspicion and dislike of the well-off, the well-educated and the well-placed. . . . Poujadism —like American populism—was a protest against metropolitan sophistication, wealth and success. . . ." [57] Poujadism is strong in small towns, where a sort of cultural inferiority complex is directed against the big city and its denizens.

Xenophobia

Xenophobia is hatred for things foreign and is manifested in two ways in poujadism. First, extreme nationalism demands a "go-it-alone" foreign policy free of international commitments and foreign "entanglements." In America this means "isolationism," the rejection of alliances and association with "immoral" or "decadent" Europe. Membership in international organizations such as the United Nations appears as an intolerable abridgement of national sovereignty. European poujadists would be hostile to such things as NATO or the European Common Market.

The domestic side of poujadist xenophobia comes out in attacks on "foreign" minorities. The Jews are sometimes singled out for special resentment, as in France and in the populist tradition in the United States. The poujadist preaches a return to the "true" traditions of the

57. Philip Williams, *Crisis and Compromise* (New York: Anchor Books, 1966), pp. 179–80.

nation, before alien forces distorted them. This tendency is seen in certain groups of the American "radical right," for whom "Americanism" is a "compulsive ideology rather than simply a nationalist term." [58]

Monetary or Tax Reform

Poujadism complains of an iniquitous system of taxation and erroneous financial policies. These are held to be destroying the sound middle classes. The "loopholes" for the rich and the "giveaway" programs for the poor conspire to swindle the small people out of their just rewards. The most ambitious poujadist economic program to date was exhibited by the Social Credit movement in Canada and elsewhere. During the Great Depression, Canadian "Socreds," strong in the province of Alberta, though they attacked the "Grain Exchange and eastern financiers, did not propose a fundamental change in the going capitalist system. [They] hoped to make capitalism work by nationalizing the banks and pumping new currency into circulation whenever prices fell." [59]

FASCISM

Our discussion of Fascist ideology relates exclusively to Fascist Italy. Even this simplification leaves certain difficulties. The ideology is less coherent than some others, and there definitely was no "Karl Marx of Fascism." Mussolini, though he had respectable intellectual credentials, was too much the man of action to produce a lengthy and definitive statement of Fascist doctrine.

Nonetheless, during the 1920s and 1930s a distinctive and fairly coherent set of Fascist principles emerged. They include (1) statism, (2) charismatic leadership, (3) elitism, (4) hypernationalism, (5) voluntarism, (6) antiparliamentarism, (7) anti-Marxism.

Statism

We have already seen that Italian fascism directed its notion of the "totalitarian state" against liberal individualism. As Mussolini put it:

58. Seymour M. Lipset, "The Sources of the 'Radical Right' (1955)," in *The Radical Right*, ed. D. Bell (Garden City, N.Y.: Anchor Books, 1964), p. 320.
59. Seymour M. Lipset, *Agrarian Socialism* (Garden City, N.Y.: Anchor Books, 1968), p. 135.

"For Fascism the State is absolute, individuals and groups relative. Individuals and groups are admissible in so far as they come within the State." [60] The Fascist view of the state is organic to the nth degree. The state endures, while individuals come and go.

Along with the notion that the state is somehow more "real" than the individuals and groups within it, goes the claim for its utter moral superiority. So thought Alfredo Rocco, Fascist minister of justice, when he argued that the state is "an organism distinct from the citizens who at any given time form part of it; it has its own life and its own superior ends, to which the ends of the individual must be subordinated.' [61] To achieve its intrinsic ends the state must have appropriate (i.e., forceful) means: "The State must be absolutely sovereign and must dominate all existing forces in the country, coordinate them, solidify them, and direct them towards the higher ends of national life." [62]

Charismatic Leadership

Max Weber considered charismatic leadership to be essentially nonrational. This raises no problem if we consider fascism as a movement flourishing on the "irrationalism" of its devotees. But an ideology must preserve the forms, if not always the substance, of rationality. In both theory and practice there was a tension between the Fascist "cult of personality" around Mussolini and statism.[63]

Fascists theorists were thus in a dilemma. To elevate Mussolini too high would be to lower the party, state, nation, and movement. To reduce his role too much would be insulting to the Duce and corrosive to the regime's legitimacy. In 1936 a Fascist theorist, Mario Palmieri, described the historical role of the Duce as follows:

> The man was simply the mouthpiece chosen by destiny to utter what needed to be uttered at a crucial time of human history; what he said all people were trying to say; what he did many people, perhaps, were trying

60. Benito Mussolini, "Political and Social Doctrine," in *Fascism: Doctrine and Institutions* (New York: Howard Fertig, 1968), p. 27.
61. Alfredo Rocco, "The Transformation of the State," in *What Is Fascism and Why?*, ed. T. Sillani (New York: Macmillan, 1931), p. 18.
62. Ibid.
63. This is also a problem for Communist movements, in which the doctrines, if not the practice, of Marx and Lenin have little place for charismatic or even very strong leadership.

to do. . . . Alone, he could achieve nothing. As a leader he could change, and is changing the aspect of the world.[64]

Fascism extolls the leader because of his unique capacity for discerning the "true" will of the people. Since state and nation are a unity, they have one goal, one will. The problem, similar to the one that confronted Rousseau in eighteenth-century France, is how to give vent to that national will. Fascism maintains that one man with extraordinary gifts has the "intuitive" power to do this. To give this "personalism" further justification, some Italian Fascists even paraded out medieval defenses of monarchy as the best form of government in terms of unifying the state.

Elitism

As fascism, despite some rumblings about being an "organic democracy," frankly stresses the leadership role of select minorities, some have seen the classic elitists Mosca, Michels, and Pareto as formative influences in Fascist ideology.[65] Fascism does accept the elitist first principle that the masses cannot rule in the sense of classic democratic theory. There are always "natural leaders" with the courage and force of will that will push them to the forefront of the political order. They should be allowed to rule as the collaborators of the charismatic leader.

However, this elite is not to rule for its own selfish interest—this is how elites operate in liberal regimes, under the cover of "individualism." The Fascist elite, in contrast, rules for the people and is recruited from the most vital and talented elements among them.

Hypernationalism

Fascist ideology embraces an extreme form of nationalism. As with many nationalistic movements, this ideology hopes to resurrect past greatness. With Italian fascism the obvious model was ancient Rome. As Mario

64. Mario Palmieri, "The Philosophy of Fascism," in *Communism, Fascism and Democracy*, ed. C. Cohen (New York: Random House, 1966), pp. 389–90.
65. A. James Gregor, *The Ideology of Fascism* (New York: Free Press, 1969). Gregor probably exaggerates this relationship, which appears rather indirect and concerns only one or two aspects of Fascist ideology. Mosca and Pareto remained within the liberal tradition.

Palmieri put it: "The historical continuity of political forms, social organization, religious expression and spiritual aspirations, in the life of the Italian people, which had lasted two thousand years . . . has been at last restored by Fascism, which is the direct heir of Roman traditions and of Roman ideals." [66]

Indeed this preoccupation with Rome resulted in an imperialist policy, exemplified by the Italian conquest of Ethiopia in 1935. Given the dynamism of any Fascist movement, it is likely that its nationalism will develop into an irredentist or pan-movement.

Voluntarism

Fascism puts great emphasis on will power and activism (see note 20). In some of its more extreme formulations it seems to accept the notion that reason and logic are as often encumbrances to action as they are aids to it. This aspect of fascism is influenced by romanticist and pragmatist doctrines to the effect that truth is no longer seen as an abstract correspondence between an idea and its object. Truth is instead seen as an active and dynamic process, and our ideas must therefore be constantly put to the acid test of practice.

This is why Alfredo Rocco declared that "Fascism is, above all, action and sentiment and . . . such it must continue to be. Were it otherwise, it could not keep up that immense driving force, that renovating power which it now possesses and would merely be the solitary meditation of a chosen few." [67] Likewise, Giovanni Gentile approved of fascism's "repugnance for 'intellectualism'" and its refusal to "waste time constructing abstract theories about itself." However, both he and Rocco drew back from the extreme irrationalism that the stress on will pointed toward. Gentile warned against viewing fascism as a "blind praxis or a purely instinctive method." [68] Both theorists assure us (and themselves?) that there is "thought," "system," "theory," and even "philosophy" in fascism.

66. Palmieri, "Philosophy," p. 384.
67. Alfredo Rocco, "The Political Doctrine of Fascism," in Cohen, *Communism, Fascism and Democracy*, p. 335. This tendency comes out even more forcefully in a speech of Mussolini's: "Our programme is quite simple; we wish to rule over Italy. People are always asking us about our programme. There are too many already. Italy's salvation does not depend on programmes but on men and strong wills." Quoted in Karl Mannheim, *Ideology and Utopia* (New York: Harcourt, Brace, n.d.), p. 134.
68. Giovanni Gentile, "The Philosophical Basis of Fascism," in Cohen, *Communism, Fascism and Democracy*, p. 366.

Antiparliamentarism

In chapter 4 we saw some of the phases of the destruction of Italian parliamentarism. Now we glimpse the ideological basis for it. Quite simply, fascism denies that parliaments elected by universal suffrage can represent the "true" will of the people. Parties, factions, and interest groups, which flourish under parliamentarism, fracture and fragment that unity so dear to the Fascist mentality. Such groups are so many barriers between the people and the state—barriers which fascism proposes to break down.

"One man, one vote" and "majority rule" falsify the true national will. Transitory majorities produced by slippery politicians make democratic parliaments a mockery of true representation. The Fascist remedy is to transform the executive into a virtual dictatorship and the legislative into a consultative body dominated by the ruling party.

Anti-Marxism

Mussolini once declared that fascism was "the resolute negation of the doctrine underlying so-called scientific and Marxian socialism, the doctrine of historical materialism which would explain the history of mankind in terms of the class struggle and by changes in the processes and instruments of production, to the exclusion of all else." [69] The determinism of classic Marxism conflicted with the voluntarism of fascism. Moreover, Marxism's early internationalism, and especially the doctrine of class struggle, ran directly counter to fascism's near obsession with national unity.

For Italian fascism the class struggle was no necessary feature of modern society. It emerged because the negative liberal state had shunted the working classes to the sidelines. The totalitarian state was specifically designed to bring all the people within the orbit of the state. In addition, Fascist corporativism was advanced as an alternative to both liberal capitalism and communism. This alternative would allow industry to remain in private hands, thus avoiding the growth of a massive state bureaucracy; and yet, the strong position of party and government in the corporative organization would ensure that public purposes were realized in economic life, as in all other aspects of social life.

69. Mussolini, "Doctrine," p. 20.

RACISM

The term "racism" is bandied about with nearly reckless abandon nowadays. It threatens to replace "bigotry," "bias," and "prejudice" in intergroup relations. However, our usage of "racism" here is narrower and may have little to do with the phenomena designated by the other usages. "Racism" in this narrow sense refers to *a philosophy of history that explains the cultural differences between peoples as resulting from biological differences*. Racism speaks of definitely "superior" and "inferior" races and holds that this inequality is the product of biological (today called "genetic") differences. We will briefly trace the development of racist doctrines from the stage of a grandiose philosophical system as represented by Count Gobineau to that of an ideology associated with Adolf Hitler.

Joseph Arthur de Gobineau (1816–82)

Count Gobineau, a French aristocrat, in the 1850s published his *Essay on the Inequality of the Human Races*, which has supplied much of the basis of later racist doctrines and ideologies. Though Michael Biddiss calls him the "father of racist ideology," [70] Gobineau was so pessimistic about the future of society that he had no program. His conviction that nothing could be done to prevent the degeneration of civilization deprives his views of the activism of a true ideology.

Gobineau's concern, a rather fitting one for a social pessimist, was to discredit the idea of progress and explain why so many great civilizations had traversed the familiar cycle of rise, decline, and fall. He rejected the usual cyclical theories that pointed to moral degeneracy or political corruption or loss of religion as the prime culprit in the decline and extinction of great civilizations. These explanations were wrong, he felt, either because they mistake symptoms for real causes or because they encounter too many exceptions to the rule. The moralistic theory, for example, flounders in the face of the high morality of certain civilizations on the verge of collapse.

Gobineau thought he spied a more profound explanation in the gradual change of racial composition among the people of great civilizations. Each civilization was founded by a certain racial stock, but over time

70. Michael D. Biddiss, *Father of Racist Ideology: The Social and Political Thought of Count Gobineau* (New York: Weybright & Talley, 1970).

peoples of differing races were brought in through attractive power or imperial expansion. This led to intermarriage and thus to a dilution of the quality of the original founding group. Thus commenced an inevitable process of racial degeneration accompanied by the decline of the civilization involved. In the end the original racial stock would have virtually disappeared and the civilization would fall into ruins.

In contrast to later racism, Gobineau preached the original unity of mankind. Far back in the mists of history there existed a primary race embracing the whole of mankind. Soon, however, three great "secondary" races—the white, the yellow, and the black—emerged. Since then, racial mixtures and remixtures have occurred, giving rise to complex "tertiary" and "quaternary" races. Strictly speaking, therefore, *pure* races disappeared long ago from this planet. Nevertheless, while some racial mixtures are positive in that the new group has better qualities than the two previous groups, others are negative and lower the general level.

Gobineau made a definite hierarchy of the three secondary races. At the bottom is the black race. The intellect of members of the black race "will always move within a very narrow circle." [71] However, this race has well-developed senses, desires, and passions. Though the black race can never be the basis of a higher civilization, the artistic or aesthetic dimension of certain civilizations is due to some influx of black "blood."

The yellow race ranks higher in Gobineau's racial scale. "Every founder of civilization would wish the backbone of his society, his middle class, to consist of them. But no civilized society could be created by them; they could not supply its moral force or set in motion the springs of beauty and action." [72]

At the summit of humanity is the white race, to whom Gobineau attributed a litany of positive virtues: "energetic intelligence," a "feeling for utility," "perseverance," a "greater physical power," an "extraordinary instinct for order," a "remarkable, and even extreme, love of liberty," etc.[73] No one should be surprised, then, that, according to Gobineau, most of the ten great human civilizations have "been produced upon the initiative of the white race." [74]

The ten civilizations are the Indian, the Egyptian, the Assyrian, the

71. *Gobineau: Selected Political Writings,* ed. M. D. Biddiss (New York: Harper & Row, 1970), p. 135.
72. Ibid., p. 136.
73. Ibid., pp. 136–37.
74. Ibid., p. 142.

Greek, the Chinese, the Italo-Roman, the Germanic-Western, and the three American (Alleghanian, Mexican, and Peruvian). Moreover, of the seven Old World civilizations, we find that one branch of the white race, the Aryans, was the prime mover of all of them. How far Gobineau would go in defending his claim for Aryan creativity is seen by his statement that "an Aryan colony from India brought the light of civilization to China also." [75]

Because of the dissolution of the Aryan element, the truly creative element in history has been dissipated. Gobineau viewed this as a *linear trend* (i.e., inevitable and irreversible). Eventually an "age of unity" will emerge, which "far from being the result of the direct union of the three main racial types in their pure state, will be only the useless residue of an infinite series of mixtures. . . . This will lead eventually to mediocrity in all fields: mediocrity of physical strength, mediocrity of beauty, mediocrity of intellectual capacities—we could almost say, to nothingness." [76] Gobineau's thought is a good example of how otherwise sensible and intelligent men can allow their mental processes to become overwhelmed by a single, bizarre vision.

Houston Stewart Chamberlain (1855–1927)

Chamberlain, an Englishman who emigrated to Germany, is a sort of link between Gobineau and Nazi racism. His massive *Foundations of the Nineteenth Century,* published in Germany in 1899, contained many ideas that resembled Gobineau's. However, Chamberlain was more prone to buttress his ideas with scientific-sounding theories of the post-Darwinian era, while Gobineau engaged in vague theological speculations.

Chamberlain also saw the main protagonists of history somewhat differently. He was particularly concerned with the "heirs of antiquity," the peoples who emerged after the collapse of the Roman Empire. According to Chamberlain, the empire had fallen because its vast territorial expanse had allowed all sorts of different groups to interbreed. The result was a "chaos of peoples," a hodgepodge of groups without a distinctive racial character. They were racially incapable of manifesting a high culture.

The Teutonic peoples descend from those tribes whose invasion sup-

75. Ibid., p. 143.
76. Ibid., pp. 172–73.

plied the coup de grace to the tottering, hopelessly decadent Roman Empire. Composed of the Celts and Slavs as well as the Germanics, this
group was characterized by Chamberlain as possessing "mystical tendencies," "thirst for knowledge," "force of faith," "impulse to create,"
"high organizing ability," "noble ambition," "need of ideals." [77] Equally
significant in the light of later developments is the prominent place
Chamberlain assigned to the Jews. His anti-Semitism did not consider the
Jews precisely as inferior, merely as alien. "The entry of the Jews into the
history of the West signifies therefore beyond doubt the entrance of a
definite element, quite different from and in a way opposed to all European races, an element which remained essentially the same, while the
nations of Europe went through the most various phases." [78]

Adolf Hitler (1889–1945)

In Hitler's *Mein Kampf* racism becomes a full-fledged, if erratic, ideology. Moreover, in it the cultural anti-Semitism of Chamberlain becomes fully politicized. In contrast to Gobineau's resignation and pessimism, the Nazi leader's views are wildly optimistic. The Aryan decay
through racial mixture can be stopped and reversed—a kind of repurifi-
cation. Likewise, the "threat" posed by the Jews to the Aryan culture can
be eradicated. Political action can set out on a road that will lead to a
racially pure Aryan "folk community."

Hitler, in developing Chamberlain's ideas, sees three different roles
for the various races: (1) culture creators, (2) culture bearers, and (3)
culture destroyers. Public policy should be designed to neutralize or
"phase out" the third group, lest they sully and tear down the noble high
culture created by the first. Thus, "it is the function above all of the Germanic states first and foremost to call a fundamental halt to any further
bastardization." [79] Moreover, "a folkish state must therefore begin by
raising marriage from the level of a continuous defilement of the race,
and give it the consecration of an institution which is called upon to
produce images of the Lord and not monstrosities halfway between man

77. Houston Stewart Chamberlain, *Foundations of the Nineteenth Century*
   (London: John Lane, the Bodley Head, 1913), 1:558.
78. Ibid., p. 335. Chamberlain's racial anti-Semitism must be distinguished
   from mere cultural and religious anti-Semitism. Aspects of all three flowed
   into political anti-Semitism which influenced the young Hitler.
79. Adolf Hitler, *Mein Kampf* (Boston: Houghton Mifflin, 1943), p. 402.
   Hitler, in contrast to Chamberlain, considered the Slavs as inferior
   non-Aryans.

Figure 12.3. Party and Ideological Spectrums in Italy

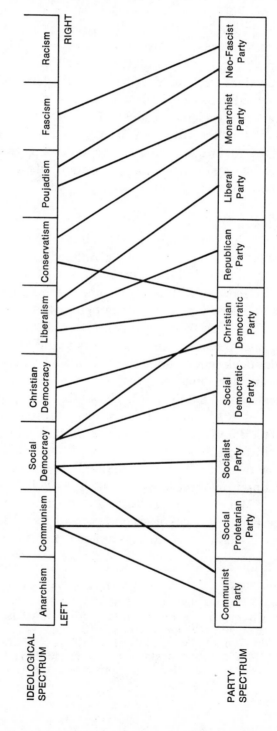

and ape." [80] One cannot accuse Hitler of pussyfooting or understatement!

An interesting difference between Hitler's racism and Mussolini's fascism concerns the theory of the state. Hitler's views cause him to lay far less stress on the state than his fellow dictator. He maintains that "the state represents no end, but a means. It is, to be sure, the premise for the formation of a higher human culture, but not its cause, which lies exclusively in the existence of a race capable of culture." [81] Even after the Nazi takeover, theorists whose views on the state would have pleased Mussolini were quickly muzzled.

PROBLEMS OF THE LEFT-RIGHT SPECTRUM

One problem with the left-right ideological spectrum is its failure to match the party (or movement) spectrum. We have identified and discussed nine main ideological tendencies. Perhaps in a perfectly rational universe we would find an eight-party system in competitive regimes— leaving the anarchists out because of their aversion to parties. If this were too demanding, we might have a four-party system with each party made up of two contiguous ideological factions. For example,

> Party A: Communists and social democrats
> Party B: Christian Democrats and liberals
> Party C: Conservatives and poujadists
> Party D: Fascists and racists

But even this degree of symmetry between ideologies and parties is denied us by the real world of politics. Several examples will help to make this clearer. Let us look at the membership of the Nazi party before 1933, a party dedicated to a racist ideology. Were all Nazi party members in 1932 really racist ideologues? No. In addition to the genuine racists, the Nazis also appealed to people of conservative, poujadist, and Fascist ideological persuasions. That these were deluded in pinning their hopes on the Nazis changes nothing. Nazi support was diverse, and Hitler's speeches in the first few years after 1933 still sounded some conservative, poujadist, and Fascist notes. Only later did the fundamental racism dominate the ideological scene.

Another example of ideological decentralization occurs with the Italian Christian Democratic party. While the solid core of the party adheres

80. Ibid.
81. Ibid., p. 391.

Figure 12.4.   The Internal Spectrum of Italian Parties

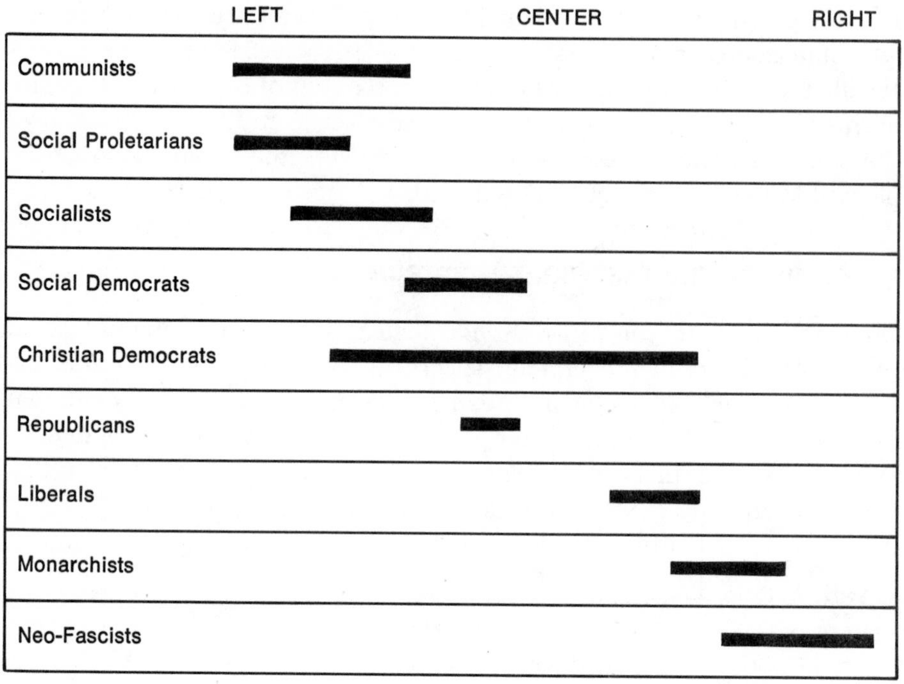

	LEFT	CENTER	RIGHT
Communists	▬▬▬▬▬		
Social Proletarians	▬▬▬		
Socialists	▬▬▬▬		
Social Democrats	▬▬▬▬		
Christian Democrats	▬▬▬▬▬▬▬▬▬▬		
Republicans	▬▬		
Liberals		▬▬▬	
Monarchists		▬▬▬	
Neo-Fascists			▬▬▬▬

Figure 12.5.   Modern Ideologies on a Anarchy-Statism Spectrum

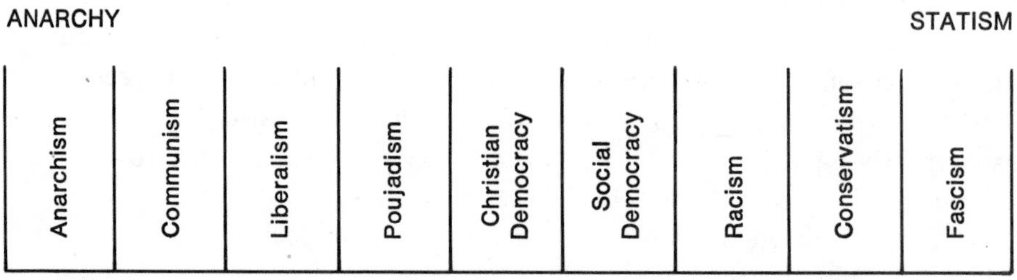

ANARCHY   STATISM

Anarchism	Communism	Liberalism	Poujadism	Christian Democracy	Social Democracy	Racism	Conservatism	Fascism

to the principles of Christian democracy discussed above, some members can be described as "left" social democrats, social democrats, liberals, and conservatives. Even the Italian Communist party today displays some ideological decentralization, with some members sticking to the Leninist-Stalinist line, others figuring as "left" social democrats, and still others as Bernsteinian revisionists. This is one reason why it is so hard to predict the long-run policy of the Communists, should they secure control over the Italian government.

Let us go further in our analysis and give a rough comparison of the party and ideological spectrums in Italy in the 1960s and 1970s. Italy is a good test case because ideology is more prominent in its political cul-

Figure 12.6.   Modern Ideologies on Equality-Inequality Spectrums

ECONOMIC EQUALITY   ECONOMIC INEQUALITY

| Anarchism | Communism | Social Democracy | Christian Democracy | Poujadism | Liberalism | Racism | Fascism | Conservatism |

POLITICAL EQUALITY   POLITICAL INEQUALITY

| Anarchism | Communism | Social Democracy | Liberalism | Christian Democracy | Poujadism | Racism | Conservatism | Fascism |

STATUS EQUALITY   STATUS INEQUALITY

| Anarchism | Communism | Social Democracy | Liberalism | Christian Democracy | Racism | Poujadism | Fascism | Conservatism |

ture and party system than in almost any other country. Figure 12.3 shows how the different parties draw some support from people adhering to different ideological strains. As the many crisscrossing lines suggest, members of one party may stand ideologically to the right or left of some members of other parties whose ideologies are supposedly more to the right or the left.

This point comes out more clearly if we situate each party on its own plane and place it in relation to the overall ideological spectrum. Figure 12.4 thus depicts each party's internal ideological spectrum and shows how much it "overlaps" with those of other parties.

As a second problem, let us recall that the idea of a spectrum is a spatial model that implies the continuous increase or decrease of something—as with wave frequencies on the light spectrum. If there were some core variable that increases across the ideological spectrum, there would be no problem with the left-to-right model.

Let us see how this might work by forgetting about parties and by taking, for example, anarchy and statism as the two extreme poles of a spectrum of continuum. Anarchy would be at the extreme left and statism would be on the extreme right. Anarchist ideology would have to fall on the left end of the spectrum, which would to a degree resemble the order in which we discussed the ideologies in this chapter. However, certain adjustments would have to be made, as figure 12.5 shows.

If we perform the same mental experiment for an equality-inequality spectrum, we get the results depicted in figure 12.6. This breaks down into the three dimensions of economic, political, and status inequality discussed in chapter 6.

If we turn to a religious issue and have our spectrum run from anti-religion through anticlericalism up to clericalism, we get something similar to figure 12.7.

Finally, if we look at the question of economic organization and run our spectrum from complete collectivism (public ownership) to complete individualism (private ownership), we get the picture of figure 12.8.

More such mental experiments would have similar results. Since ideologies address themselves to a number of important issues, no spatial model can do full justice to all the differences involved. The terms "left," "center," and "right" must therefore be used with utmost caution. Too much has happened in the last century and a half to consider them more than vague signposts.

Rather than summarize the nine ideological systems surveyed in this

Figure 12.7.   Modern Ideologies on a Religious Spectrum

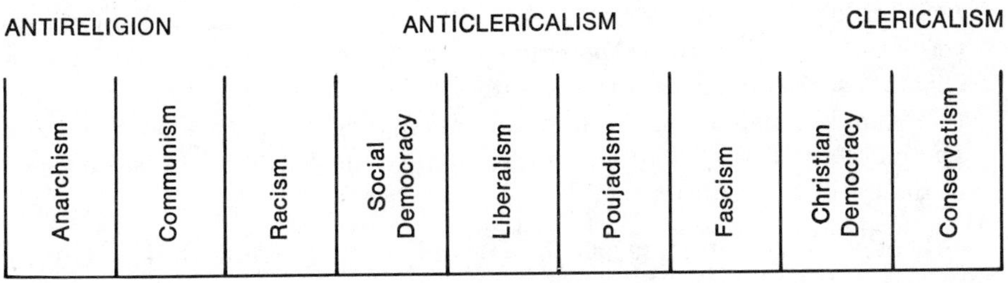

ANTIRELIGION			ANTICLERICALISM				CLERICALISM	
Anarchism	Communism	Racism	Social Democracy	Liberalism	Poujadism	Fascism	Christian Democracy	Conservatism

Figure 12.8.   Modern Ideologies on an Economic Organization Spectrum

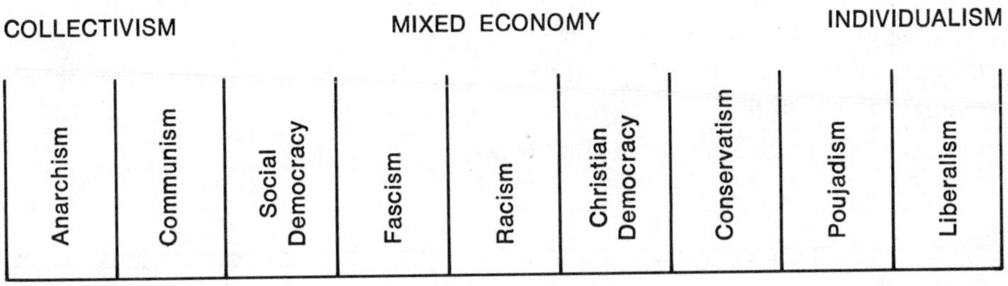

COLLECTIVISM			MIXED ECONOMY				INDIVIDUALISM	
Anarchism	Communism	Social Democracy	Fascism	Racism	Christian Democracy	Conservatism	Poujadism	Liberalism

chapter, let us stress two key points. First, no party, movement, or regime perfectly embodies anarchism, communism, or any of the other ideologies. Political organizations may espouse more than one ideological position, and the same ideological position may crop up in distinct political organizations. Such overlaps naturally give rise to bitter disputes as to which group represents the authentic version of the ideology in question.

A second major finding of our survey of ideologies is the difficulty in applying the left-right ideological spectrum. It is hard to focus on one issue (e.g., the state, freedom, economic organization, or equality) that increases or decreases uniformly as we traverse the ideological spectrum. Indeed, on certain issues the extremes of the ideological spectrum seem to have converged dramatically in this century. As A. James Gregor points out:

> The Fascist emphasis on economic and political independence, on the high emotional salience in which all these efforts were to be effected, on the quasi-military organization of society through the inculcation of "moral incentives," on the "primacy of politics," on a "collectivistic" rather than a "liberal" social order, on the necessity of "revolutionary" war . . . on nationalism as a mobilizing strategy, all are emphases that have become more and more characteristic of *all* radical political ideologies in the second half of the twentieth century.[82]

Gregor's conclusion suggests the confusion over "isms" that originally provided the organizing theme for our comparative introduction to political science. We have now examined the basic features of those regimes, movements, and ideologies that characterize contemporary political life throughout the globe. We can only hope that our approach has laid the foundations for understanding both modern politics and modern political science. Our trilogy approach to the three main organizing themes has allowed us to pick and choose those theories and concepts that were most useful to the subject at hand, instead of elaborating a single theoretical position. Some readers may eventually move beyond our eclectic approach, but hopefully exposure to this book will provide all readers with some alternative perspectives as well as substantial knowledge of basic politics and political science.

STUDY QUESTIONS

1. Contrast the meanings of the term "democracy" as used in the ideologies of communism, social democracy, Christian democracy, and liberalism.

2. Do the terms "left" and "right" mean anything any longer? Why or why not?

3. Discuss the chief similarities and differences of anarchism and communism.

4. Select three ideological systems and examine how each handles the problem of social and political equality.

5. Liberalism has been under fire in recent years. Show how a conservative, a social democrat, and an anarchist would criticize liberalism.

82. A. James Gregor, *The Fascist Persuasion in Radical Politics* (Princeton: Princeton University Press, 1974), p. 16.

6. Is racism merely an exaggerated form of nationalism? Why or why not?

7. Are Lenin and Mao truly disciples of Karl Marx?

SUGGESTIONS FOR FURTHER READING

(The suggestions here are restricted to secondary sources and representative anthologies; for primary sources the reader is referred to the text notes.)

AUERBACH, M. M. *The Conservative Illusion.* New York: Columbia University Press, 1963.

BIDDISS, MICHAEL D. *Father of Racist Ideology: The Social and Political Thought of Count Gobineau.* New York: Weybright & Talley, 1970.

DE RUGGIERO, GUIDO. *The History of European Liberalism.* Boston: Beacon Press, 1959.

GELLNER, ERNEST, and IONESCU, GHITA, eds. *Populism.* London: Macmillan, 1969.

GREGOR, A. JAMES. *The Ideology of Fascism.* New York: Free Press, 1969.

HOWE, IRVING, ed. *Essential Works of Socialism.* New York: Bantam Books, 1970.

HSIUNG, JAMES C. *Ideology and Practice: The Evolution of Chinese Communism.* New York: Praeger Publishers, 1970.

HUNT, R. N. C. *The Theory and Practice of Communism.* Baltimore: Penguin Books, 1963.

MANNING, D. J. *Liberalism.* New York: St. Martin's, 1976.

MARCUSE, HERBERT. *Soviet Marxism.* New York: Vintage Books, 1961.

MEYER, ALFRED G. *Leninism.* New York: Praeger Publishers, 1962.

O'SULLIVAN, N. K. *Conservatism.* New York: St. Martin's, 1976.

ROSSITER, CLINTON. *Conservatism in America.* New York: Vintage Books, 1962.

SCHEUTTINGER, ROBERT, ed. *The Conservative Tradition in European Thought.* New York: Capricorn Books, 1971.

STANKIEWICZ, W., ed. *Political Thought Since World War II.* New York: Free Press, 1964.

WOODCOCK, GEORGE. *Anarchism.* New York: Meridian Books, 1962.

Name Index

Subject Index

Administration
  committees and, 116–23
  decision-making and, 112–15
  legislative oversight of, 76–78
  modern, 109–23
  in Nazi Germany, 199–201
  patrimonial, 20
  politics and, 115–16
  policy and, 110–12
Anarchism, 451–54
Anarcho-syndicalism
  as socialism, 439
  as anarchism, 453–54
Arab Socialist Union (ASU), 164
Armies. *See* Military
Authoritarianism. *See* Dictatorship
Authority
  conservative view of, 477
  Weber's typology of, 10–12

Bureaucracy
  corruption and, 27–29
  modern state and, 22–24
  premodern, 22
  Weberian model of, 24–27

Cabinets
  in dictatorships, 149, 163, 190, 196–97, 210–11
  in parliamentary regimes, 59–60, 63–64
  in presidential regimes, 98–100, 101, 104

Capitalism
  neo-Marxist view of, 234–38
  welfare state and, 440
Catholic Action (Italy), 359–61
Charisma
  in fascism, 482–83
  Weber's notion of, 11–12
Chinese Communist party (CCP), 206–9, 212–14
Church
  conservative view of, 478–79
  in feudalism, 19
  liberal view of, 473–74
Citizenship, 39
City-state, 15–17
Classes, 242–44
Collective behavior, 260–62
Collegial executive, 106–9
Committees
  administrative, 116–23
  consultative, 118–20
  parliamentary, 70–71, 78
Communism
  Leninist version, 460–61
  Maoist version, 463–64
  Marxist version, 454–59
  Stalinist version, 461–63
  See also USSR, People's Republic of China
Communist Party of the Soviet Union (CPSU)
  since Stalin, 190–94
  under Lenin, 183–84